A Force for Change

A Force for Change

BEATRICE MORROW CANNADY
& THE STRUGGLE FOR CIVIL RIGHTS IN OREGON, 1912–1936

Kimberley Mangun

Oregon State University Press
Corvallis

Publication of this book was made possible in part by a generous gift from the Department of Black Studies at Portland State University, in memory of Berta Delman. Oregon State University Press is grateful for this support.

∞ This paper meets the requirements of ANSI/NISO Z39.48-1992 (Permanence of Paper).

Library of Congress Cataloging-in-Publication Data
Mangun, Kimberley Ann
A force for change : Beatrice Morrow Cannady and the struggle for civil rights in Oregon, 1912-1936 / Kimberley Mangun.
p. cm.
Includes bibliographical references and index.
ISBN 978-0-87071-580-8 (alk. paper)
1. Cannady, Beatrice. 2. African American civil rights workers—Oregon—Biography. 3. Civil rights workers—Oregon—Biography. 4. African Americans—Civil rights—Oregon—History—20th century. 5. Civil rights movement—Oregon—History—20th century. 6. Oregon—Race relations. I. Title.
F881.C36 M364 2010
323.09—dc22
[B]

2009052057

First published in 2010 by Oregon State University Press
Second printing 2026
Printed in the United States of America

Oregon State University Press
121 The Valley Library
Corvallis OR 97331
541-737-3166 • fax 541-737-3170
www.osupress.oregonstate.edu

To James and Shawn, for everything,

and more.

To Beatrice Morrow Cannady,

who refused to live her life behind the veil.

And in memory of my parents, Ruth and Jim,

who opened the door to history.

Contents

Introduction 1

One: From Texas to Oregon 5

Two: The *Advocate*: It Is Your Mouthpiece 39

Three: The Best Talent 62

Four: Building a Community 76

Five: We Must Cultivate One Another 93

Six: Spreading the Word 109

Seven: *The Birth of a Nation* 121

Eight: Oregon Was a Klan State 138

Nine: Standing Firm 148

Ten: In the Interest of the Race 169

Conclusion: Public Citizen 191

Acknowledgments 195

Credits 196

Notes 197

Bibliography 291

Index 314

Introduction

Beatrice Morrow Cannady was one of Oregon's most dynamic civil rights activists. Between 1912 and 1936, she gave hundreds of lectures to high school and college students about the importance of better race relations. She used the new medium of radio to share her message of interracial goodwill with listeners in the Pacific Northwest. She was assistant editor, and later publisher, of the *Advocate*, a weekly newspaper for Negroes founded by her first husband, Edward Cannady, in 1903. Cannady was the first black woman to graduate from law school in Oregon, and the first to run for state representative. She held interracial teas in her Irvington-neighborhood home in northeastern Portland. She met with Portland Mayor George L. Baker to protest repeated showings of the racist film *The Birth of a Nation*. And when the Ku Klux Klan swept into Oregon from California, she urged Governor Ben W. Olcott to act quickly to protect black Oregonians' right to live and work without fear. Despite these accomplishments—and many more during her twenty-five-year career—Beatrice Cannady fell into obscurity when she left Oregon in about 1938. She spent the next four decades in the Los Angeles area, still pursuing the issues she was passionate about, but in a far less public way. She wrote for the *Precinct Reporter*, one of several newspapers that served the black community in Southern California, and she resumed her interracial gatherings—renamed "fireside meetings"—at the Perris ranch she shared with her third husband, Reuben Taylor, whom she considered the love of her life.[1]

I "discovered" Cannady purely by chance during the summer of 2002 while doing research on the Oregon Historical Society Web site. A striking photograph, taken ninety years earlier when Cannady was twenty-three, captured her doing something she loved: reading a book. We will never know what volume she was holding with such care—perhaps a book of poetry by Paul Laurence Dunbar, one of her favorite writers. Nevertheless, the photo offers an important glimpse into her career: among other things, Cannady became known for her extensive library of "volumes of literature by and about the Negro," black newspapers, and collections of journals, which she made available to anyone who wanted to learn more about Negro history, culture, and art.[2] That photograph captivated me; I wanted to know more about Cannady and the *Advocate*, which came out nearly every Saturday for thirty-three years. I found brief information about her or the newspaper in a few publications, but no one had explored her noteworthy career in a documented biography.[3]

Marilyn Richardson, who edited a collection of essays and speeches by the nineteenth-century political writer Maria W. Stewart, observed that "readers searching for information on black women of outstanding prominence in their eras will quickly discover the gaping spaces of lost or thinly documented years in their recorded lives."[4] Many women, Cannady among them, left few personal documents like journals or diaries that might offer insight into their struggles and achievements. Brooke Kroeger calls this "poor planning for posterity."[5] While researching the white journalist Nellie Bly, she realized that "guaranteeing [oneself] a place in history ... takes more than living a phenomenal life. In most cases, it takes careful attention to creating a documented record of that life that isn't too hard to retrieve."[6] Women, whatever their race, often are marginalized in other ways, too. One source calls Cannady "fiery," a description seldom applied to men.[7] A striking photo published in the *New York Amsterdam News* was misidentified as "Atty. E. D. Cannady"—her husband's initials.[8] And throughout most of her career, she was known simply as Mrs. E. D. Cannady, in keeping with the conventions of the era.

The scarcity of primary documents does not mean women's lives cannot be studied; rather, scholars need to be more creative with their research, following hunches, cross-referencing leads, and reviewing endless reels of microfilmed text. So I slipped a reel of film onto the spindle of the massive machine, brought the *Advocate* into focus, and encountered the first of many dead ends: copies from September 1903 until May 1923, and from 1934 to 1936, were missing, a result of a library cataloging error and a lost opportunity to preserve holdings belonging to Cannady's son, Ivan.[9] Despite an exhaustive search and e-mails to discussion lists, reference librarians across the country, longtime Portlanders, and Cannady's great-niece, these issues of the *Advocate* appear to be lost to historians.

Still, more than five hundred issues of the weekly newspaper remain, a remarkable number considering that periodicals like the *Advocate* were, by their very nature, ephemeral. They were read, shared, clipped, sometimes even used in lieu of insulation; in 2007, a few copies of the *Advocate* were found stuffed inside a wood elevator hidden behind a wall in Cannady's Portland home.[10] Taken as a whole, the *Advocate* brings to life a tumultuous period in the state and nation and "shows us a world beyond the narrow limitations of traditional history"—a history that has emphasized Oregon's white male pioneers.[11] Seemingly unimportant details buried in the paper's seven dense columns reveal a striking amount about migration, employment patterns, social and religious life, entertainment, Jim Crow restrictions, and black-owned businesses. These topics have been the focus of articles and books about the black experience in the West from the 1500s through the 1800s; far less is known, however, about these issues in Portland during the first decades of the twentieth century. Scholars also have overlooked how terrifying events such as the arrival of the Ku Klux Klan in the spring of 1921, or repeated showings of *The Birth of a Nation*, the film that glorified the Klan's formation, might have affected Negroes who were trying to live, work, and rear children in Oregon. This book offers new information about the black experience that helps to dispel the myth that black women and men played a minuscule role in the state's history during the early twentieth century.

First and foremost, though, the *Advocate* is the story of Beatrice Morrow Cannady herself and her ongoing campaign for better race relations in Oregon during this period. Editorials delineate her stand on segregation and discrimination, while news items supply details about her extensive outreach to high school and college students, lectures to civic and religious groups, efforts to share black culture with white audiences, and the radio broadcasts she gave during Negro History Week, the forerunner of Black History Month. (This book retains the word "Negro" because it was the preferred racial description during this period.) Articles in the newspaper also make clear that her advocacy was not done in a vacuum: Cannady interacted with the period's leading black artists, editors, politicians, and intellectuals, including W. E. B. Du Bois, Langston Hughes, A. Philip Randolph, Oscar De Priest, Roland Hayes, and James Weldon Johnson.

To help reconstruct events that occurred between 1912, when Cannady apparently arrived in Portland, and 1923, the first year for which copies of the *Advocate* are available, a number of other primary sources were located and consulted. Among the most helpful were Cannady's scrapbook; records from the National Association for the Advancement of Colored People (NAACP); Harmon Foundation records at the Library of Congress; articles in other newspapers for black Americans; oral histories from longtime Oregonians; Governor Ben W. Olcott's scrapbook and papers; Ku Klux Klan records; City of Portland files; documents at the National

Bahá'í Archives and Austin History Center; and articles, editorials, and advertisements in Portland's white press. Combined, these resources illustrate the scope of Cannady's civil rights work on behalf of black Oregonians.

Her story is far more complete than I dreamed it would be at the outset, but I have been unable to answer some perplexing questions. When and where did she meet Edward Cannady, her first husband? Was their courtship truly conducted through a purely platonic exchange of letters, as Beatrice indicated in one interview? What caused their marriage to end in 1930? Was there a defining moment in the mid-1930s that prompted her to apparently abandon the *Advocate* and move to Southern California?[12] How did black Oregonians and subscribers react to the loss of the *Advocate*, their mouthpiece and defender? These and other mysteries may never be solved.

I keep a photo of Beatrice, Edward, and their young son George in my office, and the stunning black-and-white image of Beatrice draped in her handmade Spanish shawl is framed on my desk at home. These images remind me that the fight for equal rights and liberties has not yet been won, and that individual efforts *can* make a difference.

CHAPTER ONE

From Texas to Oregon

Get wisdom, get understanding, get health, get wealth and don't forget the teachings of the lowly Christ: practice the Golden Rule and all will be well.

— the *Advocate*, May 2, 1925, 4

In 1883, a former slave named Jackson Morrow donated a parcel of land he had been given by his owner, Christopher Hamilton McGinnis, for a new town.[1] But it was not named in his honor; instead, the site eighteen miles northeast of Austin, Texas, was called Littig, for a former employee of the Houston and Central Texas Railway who surveyed the area.[2] The Morrow clan—including Jackson, who had been born in Tennessee in about 1828, and his wife, Lucy—owned homes there, tilled the soil, reared children, and buried loved ones.[3] "It could just as well have been called Morrowtown for it was made up principally of our family and relatives," recalled Beatrice, whose father, George, was one of Jackson and Lucy's sons.[4] A map of Littig from 1896 reflects their influence in the area: Morrow Street was the main east-west thoroughfare; Jackson, Wesley, Edward, and Albert streets divided the blocks of homes into neat grids.[5]

George married a local girl named Mary Francis Carter in 1875; he was twenty, she was sixteen.[6] Beatrice described her father as a "pillar in St. Paul Methodist church" and a "successful" farmer who was "highly respected and beloved by both colored and white."[7] The couple had fourteen children, twelve of whom survived.[8] Census records for 1910 reflect an overflowing house: son Leroy (thirteen), and daughters Cora (twenty-five), Georgie (twenty), Beatrice (eighteen), Ella (seventeen), Carrie (fifteen), Bula (eleven), Mabel (nine), and Winnifred (seven).[9] All but Beatrice and the two youngest girls were described as laborers who helped on the home farm.[10] But their parents also stressed the need for schooling. "My father was a very well-educated man," Beatrice told a friend, who "made every effort possible to give his children a good education."[11] Most, if not all, of the siblings eventually earned a college degree and enjoyed successful careers. Beatrice's brother John, who was born in 1876, became a physician and worked in Jennings, Louisiana, midway between Houston and New Orleans.[12] Lucy graduated from Tillotson College, a historically black institution in Austin, and taught there for many years.[13] Bula earned a bachelor of arts degree from Sam Houston State Teachers College and was

Beatrice Morrow Cannady's mother, Mary Francis Carter, and father, George Morrow.

working on her master's thesis when she visited Cannady in 1932.[14] And Almus graduated from Northwestern College of Law in Portland, Oregon, before settling in Berkeley, California, where he worked in real estate and reared a family with his wife, Lillian.[15] But it was Beatrice who went on to earn national recognition for her career as an editor, educator, and a civil rights activist.

Beatrice Hulon Morrow was born at home on Wednesday, January 9, 1889—a year that proved to be remarkable.[16] In the United States, Jane Addams finalized plans to open Hull House in Chicago, and consumers discovered conveniences such as George Eastman's Kodak cameras.[17] A. Philip Randolph, who would become a leading civil rights activist, was born.[18] The bare-knuckle pugilist John L. Sullivan, who steadfastly refused to fight Negro challenger Jack Johnson, survived a seventy-five-round bout versus Jake Kilrain to retain the title of Heavyweight Champion of the World.[19] Stunt journalist Nellie Bly began her record-breaking trip around the world, and Confederate President Jefferson Davis died.[20] "Aunt Jemima" was introduced to market a new pancake mix.[21] And thousands of homesteaders—white as well as black—raced to Oklahoma to stake their claim.[22] Little is known about Morrow's childhood in Littig, other than her expressed love of music. "I was always singing," she told a friend in 1929.[23] She recalled being "stood up on the platform" and singing *Hello Central, Give Me Heaven*, a piece for piano and voice composed in 1901 by Charles Kassell Harris. The lyrics, which acknowledged the growing spread of the telephone, told the story of a "tearful little child" trying to call her "mama" in heaven.[24] "I would promptly begin to cry, as I could not bear the thought of my precious mother being so far away," Morrow said. "I was a tiny thing and it seemed to afford a lot of amusement for the audience, but to me, I lived through what I sang."[25] Even though she was not as young as she recalled—she was eleven when the song was published—music remained an important interest for the rest of her life.

The Morrow family may have subscribed to one or more of the weekly black newspapers published in the 1890s, including the *Texas Freeman*, the *Langston* (Oklahoma) *Herald*, or the venerable *New York Age*, edited by T. Thomas Fortune, one of the most powerful black journalists of the late nineteenth century.[26] Articles about politics, religion, education, and more may have been discussed when the family gathered for meals. Morrow's formative years undoubtedly were influenced by the U.S. Supreme Court's ruling in *Plessy v. Ferguson*, the landmark case that in 1896 formalized Jim Crow segregation, and by journalists such as the anti-lynching crusader Ida Wells-Barnett, who wrote for the *New York Age* after her own Memphis newspaper office was destroyed by a white mob in 1892. By the end of their careers, the two women had much in common—including unsuccessful bids for elected office and difficulties with the NAACP—and both were compared to Joan of Arc.[27] Equally important to Morrow's early life was the passing of a leader: Frederick Douglass died in 1895, just a month after Morrow turned six. Years later, as the idea of Negro History Week took hold, she would write fondly about the orator, publisher, and former slave.[28] Her public talks and editorials also reflected ideas drawn from Carter G. Woodson, the Harvard-educated scholar who has been called the "Father of Black History"; Booker T. Washington, president of Tuskegee Institute from 1881 until 1915; and W. E. B. Du Bois, the influential sociologist who co-founded the NAACP and edited its journal, the *Crisis*, for twenty-four years.[29] From Washington, Morrow borrowed the concepts of self-help, hard work, thrift, and racial solidarity, while Du Bois shaped her civil rights agenda and political activism. She also identified with Du Bois' concept of a black intelligentsia or "Talented

Tenth"—"exceptional" educated men (and women) who were expected to "guide the Mass away from the contamination and death of the Worst, in their own and other races."[30] And Woodson, who initiated Negro History Week in 1926, influenced her dual commitment to teaching black people about their past in order to "instill race pride," and educating white people about history and culture in order "to break down the opinion ... that the Negro never has and never will count for much in the building and developing of civilizations."[31]

Morrow attended schools in Littig, Houston, and New Orleans before reportedly graduating in 1908 from Wiley University, "the first Black college west of the Mississippi River."[32] However, there is no record of her attending, or graduating from, the institution.[33] The school, founded in Marshall, Texas, in 1873 by the Freedman's Aid Society of the Methodist Episcopal Church, was later made famous by its award-winning debate team.[34] Morrow noted that she "took a teacher's course" there, which probably meant that she completed the Teachers Normal Course.[35] She undoubtedly spent a great deal of time in the new Carnegie Library, a two-story brick and stone building funded by philanthropist Andrew Carnegie.[36] And one of her last class projects may have entailed reading the influential new book, *Following the Color Line: An Account of Negro Citizenship in the American Democracy*, by the muckraking journalist Ray Stannard Baker.[37] Two years after she graduated from Wiley, "Following the Color Line" became the standing headline for a column that was "eagerly read" in the NAACP's new monthly magazine, the *Crisis*.[38]

Her alma mater seemed to affect her deeply.[39] She later told an interviewer: "You know, perhaps, that Wiley College is one of the best in the United States for colored students."[40] President Matthew W. Dogan sent a typewritten note in 1917 to thank her for "the splendid write-up" she had given the school "in a recent edition" of the *Advocate*.[41] "I referred to the article in one of my chapel talks," he wrote, "at which time I told the students all about you. You have greatly helped our institution by your splendid sayings."[42] A few months later, he again acknowledged her promotional efforts. "I forgot to tell you how much I enjoyed reading your article on Wiley in one of the *Advocates* during the winter. After reading it, we put the copy where teachers and students could get hold of it."[43] Other letters thanked Morrow for her generosity to the college. Toward the end of 1919, she sent Dogan $44—worth about $550 today—to help offset "current bills ... at the institution."[44]

Morrow also contributed regularly to a fund to build a gym for the female students. "You cannot know, Miss Beatrice, how much I appreciate your efforts in trying to get a gymnasium here for our girls," wrote Dogan on Christmas Eve 1912.[45] "We have too long neglected this very important feature of every first-class college, so we must make amends in the future."[46] He calculated that it would cost $4,000—about $90,000 today—to erect "a nice frame building" and "fit it up," and noted that he was counting on her help to see the project to completion.[47]

She solicited donations from some of Portland's leading white businessmen. In December 1912, she called on William M. Ladd, president of Ladd & Tilton Bank. His father, William S. Ladd, who had co-founded the bank in 1859, the same year Oregon was granted statehood, was "involved in civic and business affairs throughout his lifetime."[48] Knowledge of Ladd's philanthropy may have prompted Morrow to ask his son for a donation to the fund. He was interested, but decided to check with the State Bank of Marshall to determine whether the "school for colored youth" was being "properly conducted and doing good to the freedmen."[49] The bank's cashier assured Ladd that everyone in the region felt "very proud" of the institution. "It is doing a great work for the general uplift of the colored race," he added, and stressed that the college was "well deserving of the moral and financial support" of people across the country.[50] Apparently that was all Ladd needed to hear, because he sent a donation to Dogan.[51] Once again, Dogan thanked Morrow for her efforts, and sent her some "printed matter" to use while canvassing people for contributions.[52]

Morrow told a friend that she began her brief teaching career soon after commencement in 1908.[53] First, she worked in the "literary and domestic departments" of Gilbert Academy and Agricultural College, a school for black children founded in Baldwin, Louisiana, in 1884.[54] Then she taught for a time at Logan County High School in Guthrie, Oklahoma, a land-rush city established the year she was born.[55] But Morrow's true passion was music. She later recalled, "I had great ambitions in those days and dreamed of an operatic career."[56] She was proud of the fact that she had spent two summers in Chicago studying "voice culture" with David Alva Clippinger, a conductor and teacher who boasted he had trained "a large number of conscientious young men and women" who had "gone out ... into the world to engage in the responsible work of voice teaching."[57] Although Morrow never realized her dream, she incorporated music into her interracial teas and used the *Advocate* to promote the careers of many individuals, including Roland Hayes, the first black "classical singer to have an international career on the concert and operatic stage."[58]

In between her studies with Clippinger, Morrow took "Special Courses in Domestic Science and Art and special physical training" at the University of Chicago.[59] She also found time "to exchange letters purely platonic" with Edward Daniel Cannady, with whom she had been "intrigued" by friends to "exchange letters." Cannady was the "hat-check man" at the luxurious Portland Hotel in Oregon and a co-founder of the *Advocate*, a newspaper for Negroes established on September 5, 1903.[60] Little more is known about Cannady, and published details are contradictory. According to a brief biographical sketch in *Who's Who of the Colored Race*, he was born in Jefferson City, Missouri, on November 27, 1877, to George Cannady and Caroline Wilkins, and attended public schools in Jefferson City and high school in St. Louis.[61] But the family does not appear in Missouri census records.[62] An article in the *Advocate* notes that Cannady worked at the Ryan Hotel in St. Paul, Minnesota, and also for the *Appeal: A National Afro-American Newspaper* in that city.[63] According to the masthead, the weekly was edited and published by J. Q. Adams and his brother, Cyrus; Cannady was not listed, but he reportedly assisted Cyrus with the newspaper.[64] If so, he may have had some interaction with McCants Stewart, who worked as business manager of two black newspapers in St. Paul before moving first to the Dakotas and then to Portland, where he would help launch the *Advocate* the year after his arrival.[65]

It is unclear exactly when Cannady moved to the Pacific Northwest, but by 1902 he was working at the Portland Hotel and establishing his reputation as a man with "a great memory for heads."[66] Three decades

Edward Cannady, left, and an unidentified man at the Cannadys' home.

later, an article in the *Morning Oregonian* noted that he was "known all over the world" for taking and giving "back tens of thousands of hats, overcoats and rubbers, but chiefly hats." The newspaper added that "many of America's greatest men [had] had their hats returned to them by this expert," including Presidents Theodore Roosevelt, William Howard Taft, and Woodrow Wilson.[67]

Cannady and Morrow continued their long-distance relationship until sometime early in 1912. Finally, she told a reporter for the *New York Amsterdam News*, she decided to purchase "a round trip ticket to visit points in the West"—and meet Edward.[68] As the train began its final leg into Portland's Union Depot, Morrow may have got her first glimpse of the Willamette, the river that ends its northerly course when it meets the Columbia. She also may have caught a reflection of herself in the glass, an image unlike that of the other passengers milling about the station. But any lingering doubts she may have had about settling in the city apparently vanished that June when the couple wed; she was twenty-three, he was almost thirty-five.[69] The account of their relationship prompted the *Amsterdam*'s reporter to observe, "There is romantic glamour that adorns this union."[70] Beatrice Morrow Cannady cashed in her return train ticket and began her new life in Portland, a city with just one thousand Negroes.[71]

Although she may have missed being part of a larger and more vibrant black community, Portland offered its own unique mix of progress and paradox for Cannady as well as for the other black women and men living in Oregon's largest city. After a forty-two-year struggle for (white) women's rights, Governor Oswald West had signed the Oregon Woman Suffrage Proclamation in November 1912, shortly after her arrival.[72] The opulent New Oregon Hotel—soon renamed the Benson—opened the following year, joining the Portland (1890) and Multnomah hotels (1912) as imposing landmarks and destinations for well-to-do travelers and a long list of presidents.[73] Black guests, however, were not welcome to stay at these establishments. Reed College held its first classes in 1911 and the following year Lincoln High School—the city's oldest—moved into its new building on Southwest Park Avenue.[74] Cannady was a frequent guest of both venues, where she discussed topics such as interracial relations, Negro history, and "The Negro's Contribution to Civilization."[75] She valued these opportunities to share information with white people in order to dispel race prejudice, which she believed was "the inevitable outcome of thorough instruction to the effect that the Negro has never contributed anything to the progress of mankind."[76] This outreach was important for the small black student body, too, because the facts Cannady shared helped validate the students' existence in an overwhelmingly white environment.[77]

Soon after her marriage, Cannady joined the *Advocate* as associate editor and manager and apparently assumed most of the responsibility for running the weekly newspaper.[78] The timing could not have been better: Edward, who worked long hours at the hotel, had grown weary of the time-consuming demands of publishing. Co-founders McCants Stewart, hotel waiter John C. Logan, barber Edward Rutherford, William H. Bolds, A. Ballard, and Reverend Carey F. B. Moore had "deserted before the paper was two months old," leaving Edward Cannady, Edward Ward, Howard Sproull, and Bob Perry to get the paper out each Friday.[79] The three remaining men gave "loyal and faithful service" to "the paper for a number of years," but may have moved on by 1912.[80] A decade later, Edward wrote in the *Advocate*:

> Right here we wish to state [that] when we were almost tempted to give up the struggle and let the paper die as a number of others have done, we led to the altar a woman whose equal is hard to find in any race; who, although inexperienced in newspaper work at the time, was possessed of a splendid education and unbreakable courage; she was a strong believer in "what others have done, I can do" principle, who came into the office and the community and with her wonderful assistance The Advocate lives on.[81]

Her efforts were recognized again in a front-page story celebrating the *Advocate*'s twenty-sixth anniversary: "Much credit for the continued success of the paper for the past 15 years is due to the untiring efforts and faithful service rendered by Mrs. Cannady, manager and Associate Editor."[82] After the couple divorced in 1930, she took over as publisher of the weekly newspaper, an enterprise to which she gave "the very best of time and ability."[83]

One scholar has observed that "individuals working in the African-American press have been some of the most important leaders of African-American history."[84] Frederick Douglass, T. Thomas Fortune, Ida Wells-Barnett, W. E. B. Du Bois, and Charlotta Spears Bass—to name only a few—had long careers as writers and publishers. Some, like Wells-Barnett, were recognized early in their careers; she was among the ten black women whose literary and journalistic accomplishments were lauded in the "Woman's Number" of the *Journalist*, a special issue of the trade publication that came out on January 26, 1889, two weeks after Cannady was born.[85] Others, including Cannady, were recognized by their peers but have been overlooked by scholars.

While there is no documentary evidence that Cannady ever met Wells-Barnett in Chicago, the Portland editor did have "a delightful chat" with

Defender publisher Robert S. Abbott at his "great plant" during a cross-country trip she made in 1927.[86] Her description provides insight into the operations of both newspapers: "The noise of the dozen or more linotype machines and the hum of the giant printing press, installed at a cost of $25,000, made us 'homesick' for the moment for our own little plant."[87] Cannady also stopped by the offices of the *Chicago Bee*, where the "pretty managing editor insisted that [Cannady] 'pose' for a special photograph for the *Bee*'s pictorial page."[88] During a trip to California in 1926 to speak at a national Bahá'í convention, Cannady visited with the "pioneering black reporter and historian" Delilah L. Beasley.[89] The gist of their conversation has been lost, but the women undoubtedly talked about their journalism and efforts to promote civil rights.[90] Cannady also would have been interested in discussing Beasley's book, *The Negro Trail Blazers of California*, the first history of the state's black population.[91] Following their meeting, Beasley sent a typed letter to Cannady that described more of her activities in the Bay Area. "I have been working [for the white *Oakland Tribune*] three years in an effort to break down some of the wall of prejudice in this part of California," she wrote.[92] This advocacy was true of Cannady, too. As she noted in 1931, shortly after the *Advocate* observed its twenty-eighth anniversary:

> We have been vigilant in our efforts to protect the rights of the Negro masses, we have fought segregation and social discrimination with all our strength and on the other hand have worked for equal rights and better interracial conditions; we have supported every worthwhile movement for the general welfare; we have urged our group to take part in civil, political, religious community activity, and among many other things, we have urged our young people to go to school and acquire education.[93]

This agenda guided Cannady's work in Portland for twenty-five years.

A number of influential journalists also passed through Portland.[94] In June 1923, for example, Joseph Bass, editor of the *California Eagle*, "one of the finest and best newspapers printed on the Pacific coast, was a pleasant visitor in Portland."[95] While in town, he spoke at Bethel African Methodist Episcopal (AME) Church, which boasted "the largest membership and congregation of any colored church in Portland," and visited the *Advocate* office.[96] And Cannady met Clara Belle Franklin in 1931, shortly after her retirement at the age of seventy from the *Kansas City Call*, a newspaper founded by her son, Chester, a decade earlier.[97] Cannady wrote that visiting with a colleague who had devoted her life to "the newspaper game" was "one of the most delightful experiences" she could recall.[98]

Cannady had some interaction, too, with John H. Ryan, who published the *Forum* with his wife, Ella.[99] The Ryans moved to Spokane in 1889, the year Washington was admitted to the Union—and the year of Cannady's birth.[100] After brief stays there and in Seattle, the couple settled in Tacoma, launched their newspaper in 1903, and helped found their local branch of the NAACP. But John Ryan was best known for his politics. In 1921, as the sole black member of the Washington State Legislature, he helped defeat a bill prohibiting interracial marriage.[101] Ryan, an *Advocate* subscriber, was on his way home from a vacation in Oregon in August 1923 when he stopped by the *Advocate* office to say hello to his colleague.[102] The "brilliant editor" told Cannady that "everything [was] 'tip-top' in his business" and he remained "optimistic over the political situation" in his state.[103]

Cannady also entertained Cecil E. Newman, the "youthful" publisher of the *Twin City Herald*, when he visited Portland for a few days in May 1928.[104] She wrote that she "experienced real joy in meeting this forward looking, upstanding, purposeful young man" and predicted he would enjoy a "useful and successful future."[105] He went on to found several publications, including the *Minnesota Spokesman-Recorder*, which continues to be an important source of news and information for readers.[106] Newman toured the Northwest again three years later, shortly after launching *Timely Digest*, a general-interest magazine for Negroes modeled after *Time*. Cannady was pleased to receive the first issue, which she described as "pregnant with timely information."[107] She also was happy to see Paul Robeson featured on the cover; the singer and actor had just become an *Advocate* subscriber.[108] Cannady hosted a small party for Newman at her home, and took him to visit Dr. DeNorval Unthank's medical offices and to meet the editor of the *Oregon Daily Journal*.[109] Upon his return to Minneapolis, Newman wrote in the *Digest* that he had "spent five hours in the most complete public library this side of Chicago," a nod to Cannady's extensive collection of books by and about Negroes.[110]

Newman was not the only visitor to browse Cannady's library; other houseguests enjoyed it, too.[111] Cannady also invited white students to come to her home at 2516 Northeast 26th Avenue to read periodicals, peruse newspapers such as the *California Eagle*, or borrow from her collection of several hundred books.[112] Among the titles she owned were *The Negro* by W. E. B. Du Bois, *My Bondage and My Freedom* by Frederick Douglass, Harriet Beecher Stowe's *Uncle Tom's Cabin*, and *William Lloyd Garrison on Non-Resistance* by Oswald Garrison Villard, grandson of the *Liberator*'s famous publisher and an influential editor in his own right.[113] Villard also was a co-founder of the NAACP and the son of Henry Villard, the initial developer of the Portland Hotel and a benefactor of the University of Oregon.[114]

New acquisitions were discussed often in the *Advocate*. In 1927, she received the fourth edition of *The Negro In Our History* by Carter G. Woodson, founder of the Association for the Study of Negro Life and History.[115] The book has "remolded the attitude of the popular mind, especially among Negroes, as to the place and importance of the Negro in American history," wrote Alain Locke, a professor at Howard University who reviewed the newest edition for the *Journal of Negro History*. Although Locke felt that "a more interpretative text" was needed for college students, he noted correctly that the "first phase" of revisionist history always entails filling in the gaps. In this case, Woodson's goal "was to supply the omissions of the current school histories and to stimulate race pride directly in terms of a knowledge of the salient facts about the Negro's historical past."[116] Cannady wrote that the "book as well as the *Journal* should be in every colored home."[117] Annual subscriptions to the *Journal* cost just $3.50, she reminded readers, for which they would receive "four large journals brimful of authentic information."[118] If people still were not convinced to part with the twenty-first century equivalent of $44, Cannady pointed out that the quarterly contained "important information bearing on every phase of the life and history of [the] race."[119]

Early in 1929, she announced that she had "added 44 volumes" to her library, bringing the total to "nearly 300 volumes of Negro literature."[120] In spring of the same year, she told readers she had added three more books to her collection, including *From Negro to Caucasian* by Louis Fremont Baldwin, reportedly a former Portland resident.[121] Cannady also browsed used-book stores during trips. On the way to New York City in 1927, she found two books "of interest" at a shop in Vancouver, British Columbia.[122] People she visited presented her with gifts, too. Longtime subscriber Warner Webb, who worked for the Dennison Paper Company in Chicago, gave Cannady "three rare Negro books" for her library.[123] She called him "one of the biggest boosters of the *Advocate*," and thanked him for keeping her "well supplied with leading white dailies of Chicago."[124]

For a time, Clifford C. Mitchell, whose columns "Timely Digest" and "Digesting the News" were carried in the *Advocate* and dozens of other black papers, reviewed books for Cannady's newspaper. In 1931, he discussed *From Captivity to Fame*, a new biography of botanist George Washington Carver, and *School Acres*, a nonfiction account of a school established in the midst of the Civil War on St. Helena Island off the coast of South Carolina.[125] Following one of Mitchell's articles, Cannady made a point of noting, "The editor of the *Advocate* wishes to announce that every book reviewed in these columns is to be found in her collection of books."[126] It went without saying that people were welcome to borrow any of the titles they found interesting.

Cannady occasionally donated books to the local library—probably Central Library in downtown Portland. Her gift of *Scott's Official History of the American Negro in the World War* was acknowledged by a representative of the Library Association of Portland who noted, "I can assure you it will be much appreciated."[127] The "profusely illustrated" tome by Wiley alumnus Emmett J. Scott offered "a complete and authentic narration ... of the participation of American soldiers of the Negro race in the world war for democracy."[128] Cannady also never hesitated to suggest titles she felt Portland's libraries should purchase for its patrons, black as well as white. In October 1925, she told readers she had sent the librarian "a long list of books about the Race" that included *Up From Slavery* by Booker T. Washington, Frederick Douglass' autobiography, *The Complete Poems of Paul Laurence Dunbar*, and *The Emperor Jones*, Eugene O'Neill's Pulitzer Prize-winning play that featured black actor Charles Gilpin in the lead role when it was first staged in November 1920.[129] In all, twenty-five works were added to the public library at Cannady's suggestion.[130] Titles and call numbers were published in the *Advocate* and the editor encouraged readers "to cut out [the] list and place it conveniently for quick reference."[131] Cannady's efforts to promote racial uplift did not go unnoticed. The Reverend Lewis B. Stewart, who served in Portland for a time before assuming leadership of the AME Church in Anaconda, Montana, named his church's reading room after her. In a handwritten letter to her in 1927, he noted that the designation was in recognition of her "untiring efforts to bring before the public the true history of the Negro race and her work to bring about a better relation between the two races."[132]

Cannady also encouraged families to start their own libraries, or add to existing collections. "Parents of Negro children who have no books about their own leaders and about their own history in general ... ought to realize what an injustice it is to their children to be deprived of this information and entertainment," she wrote shortly before Negro History Week in 1932.[133] Cannady suggested a new thirty-four-page booklet about Frederick Douglass that she promised "would enhance anyone's library on Negro life and history."[134]

Other meaningful gifts were acknowledged in the newspaper as well. The suffragette Alice Park sent Cannady several reproductions of an oil painting of Frederick Douglass by an artist in Pasadena.[135] The composer W. C. Handy mailed the *Advocate* "a complimentary copy of his latest composition, 'Way Down South Where The Blues Began,'" which Cannady predicted would "become as popular as his world-famous 'St. Louis Blues.'"[136] Maud Cuney Hare, a well-known music historian and pianist who wrote for the *Crisis* and other publications, promised to send Cannady a copy of one of her books "as a little mark of appreciation for [her] kindness and ... work in Portland."[137] Cannady received Nellie M. Fall's new book of poems after the author visited Portland in 1922.[138] Publishers in Buffalo, New York, sent Cannady a copy of the sheet music for *Sorrow Is Mine*, a "beautiful and appealing" song dedicated to her friend the clubwoman Mary B. Talbert, who died in 1923.[139] George E. Haynes, a co-founder of the National Urban League, mailed her an autographed copy of his book, *The Trend of the Races*, in 1927.[140] And Cannady was particularly delighted to receive in 1932 an autographed copy of *Scottsboro Limited; Four Poems and a Play in Verse*.[141] The powerful collection by Langston Hughes was a response to the ongoing legal battle being waged on behalf of nine young black men who had been wrongly convicted of raping two white women in Alabama. Cannady printed dozens of articles and editorials about the Scottsboro Boys in the *Advocate* between 1931 and 1933.[142]

But she also used the newspaper to build as well as defend the local black community. She promoted success stories—teens graduating from high school, men starting businesses, families buying homes—and she editorialized against discrimination in restaurants, jobs, and theaters in an effort to erase color lines, correct wrongs, and illustrate inequities. The *Advocate* was simultaneously a mouthpiece and historian, decrying and documenting instances of racism, and extant copies demonstrate that black Portlanders worked hard to put down roots despite racial antipathy.

Segregation in Oregon worsened during the 1920s, especially after the Ku Klux Klan swept into the state, but the color line had been drawn years earlier. In 1857, white male voters in the Oregon Territory approved their new, hand-written constitution and settled the question of whether Oregon should be a slave-holding state. Voters overwhelmingly rejected the idea, but even more opposed the admission of "free Negroes in Oregon."[143] The editor of the *Oregon Weekly Times* echoed what most settlers were thinking: "Oregon is a land for the white man, and refusing the toleration of negroes in our midst as slaves, we rightly and for yet a stronger reason, prohibit them from coming among us as free negro vagabonds."[144] Two sections were subsequently added to the state's Bill of Rights. The first outlawed slavery and involuntary servitude, except "as a punishment for crime"—and only after an individual had "been duly convicted."[145] The second passage was "aimed at putting black and mulatto residents in a state of complete subordination and even rightlessness":[146]

> No free negro, or mulatto, nor residing in this State at the time of the adoption of this Constitution, shall come, reside, or be within this State, or hold any real estate, or make any contracts, or maintain any suit therein; and the Legislative Assembly shall provide by penal laws, for the removal, by public officers, of all such negroes, and mulattoes, and for their effectual exclusion from the State, and for the punishment of persons who shall bring them into the State, or employ, or harbor them.[147]

Cannady and other black Oregonians considered this wording a "disgraceful blot" on the state and its constitution and worked for years to remove the language from the document.[148] Measures to repeal the "Negro and Mulatto Section" were voted on in 1916, 1926, and 1927, and failed each time.[149] Finally, in November 2002—ninety years after Cannady's arrival in Portland—Measure 14 amended the Constitution and removed the last of the "historical racial references" from its long-obsolete sections. Even so, the vote was 867,901 in favor—and 352,027 against the measure.[150]

One scholar maintains that the West, while not the proverbial "Promised Land," nevertheless offered Negroes "an opportunity to make a better life for themselves."[151] Another historian has described efforts by a handful of black settlers to make a living as farmers, cooks, or barbers in the fertile Willamette Valley, in Portland, or in Oregon City, the terminus of the Oregon Trail.[152] Still, the exclusionary provisions, commonly called the Black Laws, represented a physical and psychological barrier for Negroes who looked to the West for a new beginning. Black women and men were arriving in California, Washington, and British Columbia in increasing numbers, but less than two hundred individuals called Oregon home in 1860.[153] The small number, coupled with the fact that they were dispersed in fourteen of Oregon's nineteen counties, made it "difficult to characterize" the inhabitants "as a 'community' having a collective identity, shared goals or institutions." Yet it "would be equally misleading to ignore their residence in the region."[154] Between 1860 and 1900, Portland's black population increased from sixteen to 775, still small, but large enough to support two churches, a few businesses, and the *New Age*, a newspaper established in 1896.[155]

Edward Cannady arrived a few years later, as did McCants Stewart.[156] But Stewart quickly became disillusioned with Portland. His law practice was disappointing because white people "rarely hired black attorneys, and the prevalence of unskilled laborers and service workers among Oregon's small black population guaranteed" few clients.[157] He did have one high-profile case in 1905, though, involving a discrimination suit brought against the manager of the Star Theatre. An usher informed Oliver Taylor, a Pullman Car conductor, and some friends that house rules barred them from occupying box seats. The men refused to sit elsewhere in the theater and the group left. Taylor subsequently sued for $5,000 in damages—about $120,000 today—citing humiliation over the way he and his party were treated. But the court ruled that "a theater ticket was nothing more than a license" and thus revocable; patrons were entitled only to a refund of the cost of admission and transportation. The *Morning Oregonian* reported that the decision applied equally to white and black patrons, "and the mere fact that Taylor happened to be colored did not in any way affect the question." But the Oregon Supreme Court later awarded Taylor "a favorable judgment."[158]

Despite the *Oregonian*'s opinion, skin tone remained a criterion for admission and seating. Cannady and sons George, fifteen, and Ivan, thirteen, were discriminated against in 1928 when an usher at the Oriental Theatre tried to direct them to the balcony rather than the main floor, which was reserved for white patrons. She described the painful experience as a play in three acts with the following cast: "One usher and three guests. Usher of white race, guests of colored race; usher's profession, ushering; guest's profession, editor and lawyer." In the first act, the usher tries to seat the guests in the balcony. When the guests ask whether seats are available on the floor, the usher tells them, "Yes, but I'm sorry I can't seat your people downstairs." The second act involves confrontation and compromise. She tells the usher that "plenty of seats [are available] downstairs, and ... as I am a law-abiding citizen, presentable and have paid admission ..., I prefer to sit downstairs and shall do so." When the guests proceed to look for seats, the usher leads them to a side aisle. The denouement occurs in the third and final act: "Three lovely seats are vacated on center aisle. Guests move over and occupy them and nobody moves because of their presence. Guests see show but can't enjoy it because of the humiliation in obtaining seats." In the end, Cannady observed wryly that such treatment was a "regular occurrence" in Portland, "'the land of the free and the home of the brave.'"[159]

During the 1920s, discrimination was commonplace in public venues. Otto Rutherford, president of the NAACP Branch in the 1950s, recalled that whites-only signs were displayed prominently in most downtown eateries.[160] Some individuals went as far as affixing signs to their windows that featured the word "NO" in large letters along with pictures of a dog, "a black guy lookin' like Little Black Sambo," and a stereotypical Native

American. Even if individuals couldn't read, Rutherford said, they could see the images and know they were not welcome.[161] Offensive signs had been a topic of conversation in Portland since at least 1902, when City Councilman Fred T. Merrill reportedly ordered several signs to be removed from places of business on Burnside Street and other thoroughfares.[162] Edward Cannady and three other members of the Colored Taxpayers League pointed this out in a letter to Mayor Harry Lane in 1909.[163] They also asked him to deal with a sign displayed "in full view of pedestrians" at a downtown restaurant. It was "publicly insulting," they argued, as well as "undemocratic" because it created "a line of distinction based upon race and color" that was apt to intensify "race antagonism and conflict" in the city.[164] Police instructed George Henry, proprietor of the Owl, to take down the sign "No colored patrons wanted."[165] He was "quite angry," observed Police Chief Charles Gritzmacher.[166] Nevertheless, Gritzmacher reported in a handwritten note to the mayor that the sign had been removed—"at least it cannot be seen from the outside or sidewalk."[167] This sort of qualified victory was common, as Beatrice Cannady noted in the *Advocate*. In the summer of 1933 she convinced the new chief of police Burton K. Lawson to order the removal of "an obnoxious sign, 'We cater only to white trade,'" from a restaurant on the corner of Broadway and Glisan.[168] But the very next week, the *Advocate* carried a news brief about waiter Juneious Pugh, who had been arrested after tearing down another sign from the window of Heller's Café.[169]

Continual setbacks in the struggle for civil rights may have prompted the Cannadys to join with Dr. James A. Merriman, chef James Williams, tailor J. W. Miller, clerk Eugene Minor, waiter and aspiring photographer James S. Bell, and more than one hundred other women and men to found the Portland Branch of the NAACP in January 1914.[170] According to one report, Beatrice was elected to serve as the group's first secretary; branch letterhead, however, lists her as vice-president and Edward as chair of the executive committee.[171] The group wasted no time trying to effect reform. At the end of December, Edward sent a letter to Mayor H. Russell Albee, on behalf of the Branch's executive committee, regarding an incident at a downtown restaurant. Police officers passing by the establishment one Friday evening observed a white woman dining in the black-owned business. "In the midst of her meal," Edward wrote, "the officers on the beat ... entered—ordered her up from the table and out of [the] place, with disparaging remarks about all concerned." He asked the mayor whether officers had standing orders to "eject any white persons found patronizing a colored place of business"—a practice that clearly was "against all rules of fairness and justice." The letter concluded with an appeal to reason, just like so many other letters and petitions over the years: "We appeal to you in the name of all law abiding citizens of color and ask that you encourage, not discourage, our humble efforts whenever they are decently conducted; and lend us your support in eradicating an incident which may easily become a precedent by short sighted officers whose capacity for expediency is subservient to their conscience."[172] Branch records are incomplete, so it is impossible to say whether Mayor Albee replied to Cannady and the executive committee. Albee had his hands full in 1914: in February, just seven months after he took office as Portland's thirty-eighth mayor, disgruntled voters launched a drive to recall him over alleged violations of the city charter.[173]

During Beatrice Cannady's fourteen-year association with the NAACP, she promoted the national organization and the Portland Branch, as well as their activities, in the *Advocate*. In 1923, for instance, she posed a rhetorical question: "What has the National Association for the Advancement of Colored People done?" Then she outlined some of its recent accomplishments, including providing Congressman Leonidas C. Dyer with "data on lynching" to support "his arguments before the House [of Representatives] on his anti-lynching bill." Cannady wrote that she could "cite case after case where splendid results" had been "accomplished by" the organization, but she simply did not have the space for such a lengthy list. Instead, she urged her readers to peruse "the annual reports and read the colored newspapers."[174] Portlanders who did not support the organization—or papers for Negroes—were criticized in the *Advocate*. "It costs only a dollar to become a member for a whole year; why not do it? ... There is no need for us to spend more money to get this preachment printed telling you why you ought to [join], for you already know it is your duty to get in and help lift up yourself, and every one around you."[175]

Cannady also helped to establish NAACP branches in Vernonia, Oregon; Longview, Washington; and Elgin and Littig, Texas. She was particularly hopeful that the new Longview Branch, organized in September 1925, would be able to address some of the "urgent needs of the colored district" there, including schooling for the children. Cannady walked the two-block neighborhood and "called at every house." She found the residents to be "delightful people," despite the deplorable conditions: "There is no sanitary sewerage system in this section; no paved sidewalks, no paved streets, no street lights, no telephones!"[176] She "authorized" President William Gildon and the fifteen others who had joined to "begin work at once," even though there were not enough members yet to obtain their charter.[177] Robert Bagnall, the NAACP's director of branches, was convinced the branch would be one of the organization's "very live units," thanks to Cannady's "guidance and inspiration."[178]

The work she did in Longview and other cities was critical to the underfunded organization, which relied on "volunteer workers wherever possible to visit branches, address mass meetings, organize new branches, and to instruct in methods of work."[179] By July 1925, national officials were so pleased with her efforts that Bagnall told Cannady he was adding her to the organization's speakers bureau.[180] She considered it "an honor ... to be included" and assured him she would do her "best" to promote the NAACP.[181] Soon after their correspondence, Bagnall wrote Portland Branch President Jesse A. Ewing: "You have no doubt noticed that your branch has been complimented in the appointment [of Cannady] as Branch Organizer for the Northern Pacific Coast."[182] Some local members, however, viewed her selection for this volunteer position as an affront, especially when the title "Northwest Supervisor of Branches" appeared on her letterhead.[183] Her role in local as well as national operations quickly became the subject of a heated debate that lasted more than two years—from June 1926 through July 1928—and flared up again in 1932 when she ran for state representative.

Lee C. Anderson, secretary—and later president—of the Portland Branch, appeared to spearhead the efforts to strip Cannady of her title. He read a two-page, typed, single-spaced report at the annual fall meeting in November 1926 that criticized her for being "selfish," monopolizing Robert Bagnall's time during a recent visit to Portland, and failing to cooperate with "local officers" to ensure that William Pickens, the NAACP's field secretary, had a "pleasant" time during a trip through the city that May. Anderson also used the report, which was sent to NAACP headquarters in New York City, to publicly question Bagnall's judgment: "How does he expect our people to support the branch, when he stands behind the selfish motives of his appointee?"[184]

Two women in the crowd of at least seventy black and white members felt Anderson had "turned the meeting into a demonical destroying mob" bent on insulting Cannady "with their leering glances, murderous looks, and poisonous words." They also implicated "Portland's most intelligent club women," local members of the National Association of Colored Women's Clubs, whose attacks were motivated by "personal feeling, and jealousy."[185] Although the NACWC's objectives mirrored Cannady's, documentary evidence suggests that she was minimally involved by 1926. She had attended the eleventh biennial meeting in Denver in 1918, when "some resolutions" she had prepared pledging the women's "whole-hearted co-operation and support to the United States" and to its wartime allies were reportedly sent to President Wilson.[186] She also corresponded with Mary Talbert, president of the NACWC from 1916 to 1920, and was in "charge" of her "Portland engagement" in March 1920.[187] And Cannady interacted frequently with Nettie J. Asberry, president of the Washington State Federation of Colored Women's Clubs and a founder of the Tacoma NAACP Branch.[188] But Cannady may have dropped her membership in the NACWC when she grew busier with her own civil rights work. Or she may have preferred to promote racial uplift using her own strategies. Either way, she may have been criticized for not taking part in the organization on the regional or national level.

Also worth noting in the context of the criticism of Cannady at the 1926 NAACP fall meeting is her troubled history with James Merriman, a charter member of the Portland Branch who held several positions in the organization, including a stint as its first president.[189] Merriman, a physician and surgeon born in Alabama, published a competing newspaper for black Portlanders from 1918 until 1923.[190] Cannady apparently made comments about him to Wiley President Dogan in the fall of 1919. He replied: "Am sorry your physician has not measured up to expectations. As soon as I can locate the right man I will be glad to write you."[191] Three months later, both the *Morning Oregonian* and *Portland Telegram* reported the out-of-court settlement of a libel suit brought against Merriman by Cannady. She had charged that an editorial in Merriman's *Portland Times*, headlined "Two Vampires," questioned her "reputation and character." Merriman agreed to retract his statements and publish a two-paragraph apology, which also appeared in both white papers. He noted, in part, "We find, after careful investigation, that the statements ... concerning Mrs. Beatrice Cannady are unfounded and we herewith [retract them] with apologies to Mrs. Cannady."[192] Still, Merriman may have harbored a grudge toward his rival that ultimately played out in Branch politics several years later.

By the end of the Portland Branch's 1926 fall meeting, the factions appear to have solidified into two camps: those who supported Cannady and her work, and those who continued to call for her resignation. That latter effort intensified when Lee Anderson retained the position of secretary, edging out his competitor—Cannady—by just three votes.[193] Anderson continued to send correspondence to the NAACP, ultimately involving Executive Secretary James Weldon Johnson in the acrimonious discussion. A letter signed by all twelve members of the newly elected executive committee urged Johnson to use his "influence" to abolish "the office of Northern Pacific Organizer and Supervisor."[194] He refused to do so, but he did clarify "an apparent misimpression" regarding the position and its "relation to the branch." Johnson told the committee the officeholder had no "authority over any organized branch," but groups had "the right to invite her aid in stimulating and strengthening [their] work," something she was "ready" and willing to do.[195]

Although Johnson urged the Portland Branch to "smooth out its differences" so "its officers and members" could "work in harmony" in 1927, local officials continued their efforts to remove Cannady from office.[196] Johnson, who had worked as a lawyer and diplomat before joining the NAACP, was accused of being "blind to subterfuge" and uninterested in the branch's "welfare."[197] Johnson observed in his brief reply in mid-January that the accusations were "both unfair and unworthy of the Portland Branch."[198] The historical record does not resume until the summer of 1928, when an entire board meeting was devoted "to a discussion of their situation in relation to Mrs. Cannady." She was accused, in absentia, of a laundry list of sins that included giving "the National Office the impression that she alone [was able to] make contacts with the whites."[199] The Portland Branch, one of the oldest on the West Coast, was in shambles and the national office—in the form of Mary White Ovington—decided to intervene.[200]

Ovington's views about class and race were influenced by her abolitionist grandmother, stories she read as a child about fugitive slaves, and the opportunity to hear Frederick Douglass speak in a Brooklyn, New York, church in 1890.[201] But it was a meeting with Booker T. Washington in 1903 that changed the direction of her life.[202] By the time Ovington toured the Pacific Northwest in July 1928, she had written five books and served the NAACP in numerous capacities, including chairman of the board, and was respected by white and black people alike.[203] Given that Portland Branch members were upset with Bagnall, Pickens, and Johnson, her fact-finding visit may have been viewed as a conciliatory gesture on the part of the organization.

Ovington filed a detailed report following her busy weeklong stay in Portland, which included interviews with reporters from the *Morning Oregonian* and *Oregon Daily Journal*, speaking engagements to the City Club and other white groups, meetings with ministers, and and diversions such as dinner at Chin's China Tea Garden and a picnic luncheon at a fish hatchery by the Columbia River. Throughout the week, Ovington visited with white people who knew Cannady and were acquainted with her work. The feedback was mixed. George Orr Latimer, a Portland Branch member and a well-known teacher of the Bahá'í Faith in the U.S. and Canada, told her Cannady "could at one time have had the leadership of the branch had she been equal to it, but she did not cooperate as she should have."[204] Alice Handsaker, whom Cannady considered "an outstanding contender for the rights of Colored people," was "very sympathetic with" Cannady.[205] But another woman, who admitted she was not a friend, told Ovington that Cannady thought "first of herself and only quite secondarily of her cause."[206] Missing from the report are the opinions of black Portlanders, as well as comments from Ewing, Anderson, or the aggrieved board members who had called for the editor's dismissal. Also absent is Cannady's voice. The two women took a long Saturday-afternoon drive, but "talked about everything but the branch."[207]

However, after reading minutes from Branch meetings spanning seven years, Ovington acknowledged problems with the local organization and its inability to do much—particularly under Ewing's direction.[208] Two years earlier, during the contentious annual meeting, Cannady had supported dentist Elbert Booker for Branch leadership. She lamented Ewing's lack of "executive ability" and felt that he was "not in a position to represent the cultural forward-looking group of [the] race" because he worked as a janitor in a meat market.[209] It is difficult to disentangle the class bias in Cannady's comment, yet her reasoning was consistent with that of other members of the black intelligentsia who "took for granted that black elites, as 'representative Negroes,'" should speak for "the black majority."[210] Ovington, too, felt that Booker "was unquestionably the better man," but he was defeated by a vote of thirty-two to twenty-four.[211] In the ensuing two years, she observed that the board had "done little" in Portland.[212] Still, she felt that the Branch could "work out things" if NAACP officials refrained from making "any visits for a while," and also stopped giving "the impression that Mrs. C. is superior to the branch."[213] Finally, Ovington recommended abolishing the "office of organizer."[214] That became a moot point. The controversy had deeply wounded Cannady, and she apparently left the branch she had helped found. Robert Bagnall checked in with her in 1930: "I have not heard from you for a long time and I have wondered whether you have found time or opportunity to do any work for the Association." In fact, he hoped she would be able "to revive the branches in Vernonia and Longview" she had organized five years earlier.[215] There is no evidence that she responded to his query.

Three months after Ovington's visit, Branch President Lee C. Anderson felt compelled to clarify his relationship to Cannady. "It seems that you have been informed that I am hostile and … fighting Mrs. E. D. Cannady …," he wrote to Ovington. "I wish to say that … I always have and always will hold the highest esteem for [her], and feel that she is the greatest woman in our community."[216] However, Anderson made it very clear that he was more qualified than she: "I know my people in Portland as well or better than any one here as I have worked among them and for them ever since 1910. I have studied their needs and know how to get the best results from them."[217] This oblique reference to the charge that Cannady was self-centered illustrates the gendered nature of civil rights work in the late 1800s and early 1900s.

The historian Kevin K. Gaines points out that black women intellectuals often were "relegated to the sidelines" due to the "middle-class ideology of racial uplift that measured race progress in terms of civilization, manhood, and patriarchal authority."[218] Even when they claimed center stage, such as when Cannady spoke at the NAACP's nineteenth annual conference, many black women found themselves caught between the domestic sphere and the need or desire to advocate for reform in the public sphere. Cannady told attendees that women needed to finish the work started by their foremothers who had done so "much for the race and country." Yet she also reminded listeners that "Negro women [could] do their finest piece of work for the race and nation" by caring for their husbands and ensuring their children grew up with race pride.[219]

Cannady may have been conflicted about the best way to navigate the intersecting public and private spheres, but much of her career involved making a stand—against *The Birth of a Nation*, against the Klan, against Jim Crow. In September 1916, the *Morning Oregonian* reported that she had "filed an action in the Circuit Court ... to restrain the School Board from denying her" the pleasure of swimming during the hours "open to [white] citizens and taxpayers." She "demand[ed] to be placed on an equal basis with other women ... and to be allowed" to use the pool at Couch School in downtown Portland on Tuesday and Friday nights, and not solely on Saturday nights.[220] Cannady's attorney was a white man named Arthur Moulton, a Portland Branch member whom she described as someone who "stood for justice to all alike."[221] But the judge did not share this conviction. Two months later, Henry McGinn ruled that the "School Board was clearly within its constitutional rights in segregating white and colored races in the use of the public bathing pools" at Couch as well as Shattuck Elementary School, where Negro men had faced similar segregation. Noting that the "proportion of the colored to the white population is such that one night a week is far in excess of their share of the time, if time was allotted on a tax or population basis," McGinn dismissed the case.[222]

Cannady might have abandoned her burgeoning civil rights career then and there. She was busy with the *Advocate*—writing, editing, collecting accounts and sending out renewal notices, typesetting, and doing all the other time-consuming tasks associated with publishing a weekly newspaper. And the twenty-seven-year-old had two young sons to care for: George was born May 1, 1913, and Ivan had turned one in the middle of his mother's court battle. But she may have been inspired to continue working for equal rights and liberties with an eye toward improving life for her boys. Still, the definitive crack of the judge's gavel must have left her wondering how to advocate for reform in a city where "separate but equal" was accepted without question.

Copies of the *Advocate* are missing during these years, and Cannady did not leave a diary, so one can only imagine how she began to position herself as an activist. But by 1920, many people were taking note of her efforts to promote racial uplift and secure equal rights for black Oregonians. Maud Cuney Hare, for example, told Cannady: "You quite deserve your reputation ... as the person who *does things* in Portland."[223] People talked about her at gatherings, during chance encounters with friends, and at religious meetings. One Brooklyn friend told Cannady that Bahá'í leader Louis Gregory had spoken "feelingly" about her and her work and noted how "busy" she was in her "calling."[224] And Lewis B. Stewart, the pastor in Anaconda, "discussed" Cannady with a woman from Washington when both happened to be in Boise, Idaho. "We agreed that you are incomparable," he wrote.[225] Cannady became Portland's most visible and outspoken Negro, and was often referred to as the city's unofficial "ambassador of good will."[226] Her standing in the white community was particularly apparent when officials sought her opinion on matters "affecting the harmony of relations between the races," such as when theater owners requested permits to show D. W. Griffith's controversial film, *The Birth of a Nation*.[227]

Cannady consistently wrote about her lectures, teas, radio broadcasts, and other modes of outreach in the *Advocate*, which fueled charges by some Branch members that the editor was vainglorious and using "the columns of her newspaper to boost herself."[228] She unabashedly used the *Advocate* to promote her speaking engagements and included countless articles that described her outreach to high school and college students as well as their reactions to her talks. But this was not uncommon in the black press.[229] Cannady also reprinted letters from people who were grateful to receive books she had loaned them about Negro history, or from students who thanked her for helping with a research project. Many times, these items appeared on the dense front page of the *Advocate*, sandwiched between national news stories, advertisements, and society news about black Portlanders. The placement and frequency of the articles makes it easy to dismiss her work, as Branch board members did when they observed in 1928 that Cannady used the *Advocate* "for her own exploitation."[230]

But this meticulous documentation of her advocacy must be viewed as an integral, if complex, component of Cannady's efforts to promote racial uplift, an ideology that emphasized "self-help, racial solidarity, temperance, thrift, chastity, social purity, ... and the accumulation of wealth."[231] Like the journalist and civil rights advocate Josephine St. Pierre Ruffin, who launched the black women's club movement in 1895, Cannady believed that Negro women had an obligation to "present a positive image of the race to the world."[232] Her status as an ambassador of goodwill fit squarely with this mandate, as did the subsequent publicity of her outreach in the *Advocate*. Cannady took her role seriously, noting that the "interpretation of [her] race to others" was at the forefront of her work "on the public platform and in pulpits."[233] Saidie Orr Dunbar, a prominent white woman in Portland and friend of Cannady's, observed: "I can only say that more than any other one person in the great Northwest, Mrs. Cannady has interpreted the problems of her race, has consistently worked for justice and has maintained and upheld before her own people and others all the standards of relationships between the races."[234] Robert Bagnall also acknowledged that Cannady had "acted as arbiter in differences between the races."[235] Further, printed descriptions of the warm response white audiences accorded her and her message signaled that Cannady was in step with other "elite blacks [who] believed they were replacing the racist notion of fixed biological racial differences with an evolutionary view of cultural assimilation."[236]

Gaines notes that many of these leaders "sought status, moral authority, and recognition of their humanity by distinguishing themselves, as bourgeois agents of civilization, from the presumably undeveloped black majority."[237] Articles about Wiley University can be seen as an example of this class distinction; Cannady was one of the few individuals, female or male, to earn a college degree in the early 1900s. One source notes that "at the time of the Harlem Renaissance in the 1920s, at best 10,000 American blacks—one in 1,000—were college educated."[238] References to her alma mater reinforced the idea of elitism and added to the status and moral authority she needed to represent her community to white audiences. She willingly took on the role of spokeswoman, and the publicity she garnered in the white press enhanced her credibility and led to additional speaking engagements. But, as her reputation grew, so did the backlash from members of her own community who were jealous and resentful of the attention she was receiving from white Portlanders, black editors, and NAACP officials.

The chasm between Cannady and the black majority grew wider when she decided to challenge racial and gender norms and become a lawyer. Wiley President Matthew Dogan was not surprised by her announcement, however. "So you are going to practice law? Well, that is just like you," he wrote. "You are indeed a hustling young woman. I have been pleased to note from time to time just how you have done things out there in the West."[239] Maud Cuney Hare also sent encouragement: "I hope you will be successful in your present ambition and be able before many years to put out a new sign of Attorney-at-Law!"[240] Cannady made history in 1922 when she became the first black woman to graduate from Northwestern College of Law, which subsequently merged with Lewis & Clark College.[241] But her achievement was bittersweet. On Wednesday evening, May 24th, the college held its graduation ceremony just blocks away in the stately Multnomah Hotel. Candidates and their families, dressed in their finest, gathered in the hotel's "ballroom of palatial grandeur" for the awarding of degrees.[242] Among the proud class of twenty-two were Cannady and her brother, Almus.[243] She had another reason to be happy that night: She was on the program to sing two solos, including *By the Waters of Minnetonka*, a composition "inspired by a Sioux Love Song" and published in about 1913.[244] But when she was finished, the dean, John Hunt Hendrickson, "publicly insulted and humiliated" Cannady and her brother "by asking them and their invited guests" to leave."[245] She later recalled in an interview, "Of course, I do not forget such experiences, and no one can fully appreciate the distress, unless he has suffered in the same way."[246] This sort of discrimination may have inspired her to attend night school to earn her law degree; perhaps she thought she could effect reform and promote racial uplift by filing additional civil rights suits such as the one against the Portland Board of Education in 1916. She also may have felt she could fill the void created when attorney McCants Stewart left Portland for San Francisco in 1917. Or, maybe she was inspired by George W. Carry, a lawyer she met in Guthrie, Oklahoma, who helped clear a black man who had been denied his constitutional rights.[247] Carry wrote her: "You have done exceedingly well in completing the course in law and I am sure you will enjoy the work. There is nothing, in my mind, so fascinating as the study of law, and when you get into the practice the real fascination begins."[248]

Cannady occasionally discussed her work with the NAACP's Robert Bagnall. "Had three cases ... this week," she wrote in 1926. "Tried two yesterday, winning both. One a very interesting case which I would like to detail to you when I have more time to write, other one I had postponed until next week."[249] Articles also appeared in the *Advocate* from time to time. Cannady apologized to her readers at the end of 1927 for omitting some "church notes and other important news," but she had been unable to get everything typeset before heading south to Corvallis, where she had spent two days in court as associate defense counsel for Herman Trimble.[250] Her "impassioned plea for the defendant" reportedly "had the whole jury" and much of the "packed" courtroom "in tears." The jury of eleven men and one woman deliberated all night, according to Cannady, but failed to reach a verdict; the judge dismissed them the next morning and scheduled a new trial the following week.[251] Cannady again served as co-defense for Trimble, who stood charged with assault and battery. But this time, she announced that he had been found innocent. The article noted that she "was warmly congratulated by lawyers and laymen alike for the fine way in which she analyzed the evidence and presented her argument."[252]

For a time, Cannady enjoyed her reputation as the first black female lawyer in Oregon. The *Oregon Daily Journal* printed a photograph of her in cap and gown along with a brief story headlined, "First Colored Woman Lawyer in Northwest."[253] And Lawrence Dinneen, editor of the *Mt. Scott Herald*—which soon would be acquired by the *Advocate*—sent a telegram congratulating her on the "unique distinction of becoming the first lawyer of [her] race in the northwest."[254] But Oregon State Bar records indicate that she failed the bar examination on five occasions between 1922 and 1930.[255] She continued to practice, however, eventually prompting the OSB's Board of Governors to discuss the fact that she had been "representing herself as an attorney at law" in criminal and probate proceedings. President Robert Maguire told the board he had written her late in 1935 "inquiring as to her rights to practice," but had not received an answer. So the board voted to have Maguire send another letter informing her that until she was "regularly and properly admitted to the Bar of the State of Oregon, she must desist in further attempts to practice law" or face "criminal proceedings."[256] Cannady continues to be recognized as the first black woman to practice law in the state, in part because the label fits so well with her civil rights work. The honor, however, rightfully belongs to Mercedes Deiz, a New Yorker who was admitted to the bar in 1960.[257]

Cannady's legal career did not go as she had hoped or planned, nor did her marriage to Edward. In 1930, two weeks shy of their eighteenth wedding anniversary, the couple divorced. The painful personal event was made public when Bonnie Bogle, editor-manager of the Seattle *Enterprise*'s "Portland News Section," revealed details of the couple's "family troubles."[258]

Cannady wrote, "In view of the fact that Mrs. Bonnie Bogle ... seems to be taking unusual interest in MR. CANNADY'S private affairs, which he has indicated to me over a period of years, and which had much to do with the course I pursued by resorting to the courts, I [am] publishing the decree ... so that she may know just what disposition has been made of our business." The lengthy document mandated monthly child support payments for George, seventeen, and Ivan, fourteen, and an additional sum toward the mortgage on the house in northeastern Portland. Decree No. N-9539 also ordered Edward to transfer ownership of several parcels of land to Beatrice, including a lot in Bayocean, a project in Tillamook County that once was touted as "queen of the Oregon resorts." And the document spelled out the disposition of the "office furniture, together with the printing outfit and utensils" associated with publishing the *Advocate*: All items became Beatrice's, as long as she continued to publish the newspaper. In the event that she discontinued it, Edward was granted "the right and option ... to take over said office fixtures and furniture and said printing establishment at one-half of the inventory price of the same" as agreed upon by the estranged couple. Finally, she was listed as the "sole owner" of two automobiles, a 1927 Buick sedan and a Star roadster.[259] Cannady may have regretted later the rash decision to print the particulars; certainly it was uncharacteristic of the editor, who family say was very guarded about her private life.[260] Yet the document provides insight into the lives of an upper-middle-class couple and illustrates that they were doing well financially, even if the *Advocate* was struggling to make ends meet.

One year later, Bogle contacted the Associated Negro Press with the news that Cannady had quietly married the *Advocate*'s linotype operator, Yancy Jerome Franklin, on July 18, 1931.[261] Cannady issued a reserved statement: "The couple are indebted to Mrs. Bonnie Bogle who so kindly sent the marriage announcement to the [ANP], although it was a little earlier than Mr. and Mrs. Franklin intended .... Formal announcements have just been issued."[262] Cannady noted that she and her new husband had received "numerous letters and telegrams of congratulations and best wishes from friends and acquaintances in various parts of the country" as a result of ANP's release.[263] Still, she may have been concerned about impropriety: she had not been divorced very long, and Franklin was an employee.[264] Beatrice also was nearly twenty years older than Yancy, who was barely five years older than his new stepson, George.

Franklin, who went by Yancy as well as Jerome, was born February 6, 1908, to Cora Yancy and Alfred Franklin, Jr., a soldier in the Spanish-American War.[265] By 1920, the large family had moved from Washington to Portland; they purchased a home on East Davis Street and Alfred ran a

George Cannady, top left, earned degrees from Willamette University and Howard University and practiced law in Los Angeles. He also played football in high school and college, and was known for his achievements on the field as well as in the classroom. Ivan Cannady, top right, earned a law degree from Lincoln University and had a successful real estate career in Los Angeles.

cigar shop.[266] Yancy began working for the *Advocate* as a linotype operator and office assistant in February 1928. The following year, the Reverend Daniel Hill wrote an article about printing, which he felt was a fine vocation for people seeking employment. He praised Franklin for "the meticulous care and healthy enthusiasm with which" he did his work.[267] "His jobs show neatness, originality, artistic appreciation and pride of the native artisan," he wrote.[268] After their marriage, Franklin was listed as assistant manager and compositor.[269] He also apparently flirted with the idea of a legal career: the *Advocate* reported he had enrolled in the school of law at La Salle Extension University in Chicago.[270] Other notices in the *Advocate* describe the various social activities the couple engaged in, including dinner parties with friends and family, but their relationship was difficult due to societal norms regarding their age difference. The couple apparently divorced by 1936.[271]

Edward Cannady died in Portland five years later, at the age of sixty-three.[272]

Beatrice's son George remained a constant in her life, as well as a source of great pride, and the *Advocate* is filled with news of his accomplishments and activities. In June 1923, the ten-year-old won his fifth blue ribbon in as many years for the "most beautifully decorated bicycle" in the Grand Floral Parade, a much-anticipated aspect of the seventeenth annual Rose Festival. He competed against "eight other lads, all older and all of the opposite race," but judges were impressed with the "flowing and fragile appearance of the slender cornucopia of mass roses [that was] attached to the back of the bicycle," as well as the wheels, which "were rolling circles of red and pink roses, arranged in blending tone colors." George told the *Morning Oregonian* that his mother deserved all the credit for the "masterpiece of floral decoration."[273] She reprinted the *Oregonian* article on the *Advocate*'s front page, along with a photograph that appeared in the *Oregon Daily Journal* and his invitation to attend an awards luncheon given by the Chamber of Commerce.[274] His prize was a check for $50—about $625 today.[275]

George and Ivan spent many summers at Spirit Lake YMCA Camp, one of four popular lakefront sites demolished when Mount St. Helens erupted in 1980.[276] They were the "only colored boys in the camp" for several years, yet Cannady often noted that "the spirit of goodwill and brotherly fellowship existing between [her sons] and the other eighty boys at camp [was] beautiful to behold."[277] Articles in the *Advocate* describe the fun and games Ivan and George enjoyed, from track meets to swimming contests to participating in the camp choir. But Cannady clearly took pride in the older boy's accomplishments and listed them in the newspaper: George received the "camp award for general all-around excellency"; he set records in the one-hundred-yard dash and won a three-mile race; he was elected governor of the camp and prosecuting attorney for the "kangaroo court"—an incident that foreshadowed his future legal career.[278] Cannady also printed a number of the letters he wrote her during his absence; they reveal the pitfalls of camp life—"the mosquitoes were BAD!"—as well as the pleasures: "Great trees of all kinds stood with their heads high in the air—thick moss covered the ground—small creeks crossed and recrossed the trail now and then—the birds were singing all the time—it was certainly awe-inspiring!"[279] The correspondence also provides insight into their relationship. "Thanks for the box," he wrote, "it sure was timed right. ... With loads of love, George."[280]

In 1930, George's essay on the "Renunciation of Wars as an Instrument of National Policy" tied for fourth place in a contest sponsored by the American Friends Inter-Racial Peace Committee, an organization established by the Quakers whose executive secretary was Alice Dunbar-Nelson.[281] George, a senior at Grant High School, shared his prize with Ethel Payne, a freshman at Crane Junior College in Chicago.[282] He was in good company: Payne went on to have a very successful career in journalism as a political correspondent for the *Chicago Defender* and commentator on CBS radio in the 1970s, and was widely regarded "as the nation's pre-eminent black female journalist."[283] First prize went to William Edward Harrison, a sophomore at Harvard University who became one of the editors of the *Boston Chronicle*, a black paper that vied with William Monroe Trotter's *Boston Guardian*.[284]

George amassed other honors before graduating in June 1931.[285] He was elected treasurer of his senior class and was an award-winning football player and hurdler.[286] In 1930, the *Portland News* reported that the "Negro halfback" had been awarded a "cup" by his coach for "maintaining the highest scholastic average."[287] George also was one of only fifteen players to receive a varsity letter at the end of the season.[288] He was an accomplished speaker, too, who gave many talks during the late 1920s and early 1930s. Cannady wrote that she used her sons as "'missionaries' to aid in bettering race relations" because they knew "more of the past and present history of the Negro than many leading Negro adults."[289] In February 1929, the fifteen-year-old discussed "Some Famous Negro Characters" and "Abraham Lincoln and the Negro" at two white churches, probably in conjunction with the local celebration of Negro History Week.[290] He talked about "Youth and Interracial Amity" at a dinner for two hundred people sponsored by the Portland Bahá'í Assembly in November 1930. George told attendees that youth left to think for themselves "without contamination from outside influences" were "without race prejudice."[291] The following fall, he talked about "the American Negro's achievement in music, literature, art and science" with some white clubwomen near Salem.[292] And in 1933, he went to Corvallis to tell three hundred people about "achievements of the Negro race."[293]

George enjoyed a stellar collegiate career at Willamette University in Salem, Oregon. Among other things, he was inducted into Pi Gamma Mu—an international honor society in social sciences whose members included Jane Addams and William T. Coleman, Jr., "author of the winning legal brief" in *Brown v. Board of Education*—and Blue Key National Honor Fraternity, which values "all-around leadership in student life, high scholastic achievement, service to others, citizenship, and an adherence to principles of faith."[294] He was president of the International Club for two years, treasurer of his class, and he lettered in football.[295] One article in the *Willamette Collegian*, the school newspaper, noted that George was "the fastest man on the squad—in fact so fast that he has difficulty keeping behind his interference."[296] Cannady threw a "pretty seasonal party" for George and his teammates in 1932 after a game at Multnomah Civic Stadium between Willamette and Pacific University. Some of his Portland friends were invited; Ivan was there; George's roommate, Wallace Turner, spent the weekend with the Cannadys; and a few people drove down from Seattle for the game. George may have been a bit embarrassed by the attention: the buffet table was decorated with trophies won by "the guest of honor" in high school and college and "brown paper football helmets were presented to each guest."[297]

Two months after his graduation in June 1935 with a degree in political science, the *Oregonian* announced that George had been awarded a scholarship to pursue a law degree at Howard University, a historically black college founded in Washington, D.C., in 1867.[298] He eventually ended up in Southern California, where he worked as an attorney.[299] Not long after he celebrated his fifty-fifth birthday in 1968, he was murdered in his home; the crime remains unsolved.[300] A Bahá'í and Christian memorial service was held for George Edward Cannady on Saturday, July 27th, at the Chapel of Remembrance in Los Angeles; he was interred at Valhalla Cemetery in North Hollywood.[301]

Far less is known about his brother, Ivan Caldwell Cannady, who was born October 7, 1915. He was named after his godfather, Ivan Harold Browning, a tenor who sang with the Harmony Kings, recorded with Eubie Blake, and performed on Broadway in *Shuffle Along*.[302]

Ivan graduated from Fernwood Grammar School in June 1928—the same school that made news when his brother was denied admission to a graduation party at a skating rink.[303] Four years later, Ivan was one of 329 students to graduate from Grant High School.[304] He and some friends were "entertained at an informal party" at home, where "dancing and games were the diversions."[305]

Most articles in the *Advocate* were about Ivan accompanying his mother and brother on excursions: to Tacoma, Washington, so Cannady could address the Washington State Federation of Colored Women's Clubs; to Salem, where his mother met with Governor Walter M. Pierce about "a very important matter."[306] But on one occasion, mother and son enjoyed a special evening together at the Municipal Auditorium, where Jascha Heifetz "charmed a capacity house" with a "delightful program" played on his new Guernerius violin.[307]

Like his brother, Ivan did some public speaking. When he was twelve, he accompanied Dr. Elbert Booker to First Christian Church. Booker discussed "the race question" and Ivan "exhibited large photographs of twelve internationally known Negroes and gave a brief biography of each."[308]

Ivan went to the YMCA Camp on his own once George had "outgrown" it.[309] *Advocate* notices rarely elaborated on his summer experiences, but in 1931 it was reported that Ivan had been elected the camp's lieutenant governor.[310]

He planned to attend Willamette University, but returned to Portland when he could not register for the journalism and commercial art courses he was interested in.[311] Instead, he wrote a few articles for the *Advocate*, including a profile of Lee Roy Kinard, the new pastor of First AME Zion Church.[312]

Ivan apparently returned to Willamette for his bachelor's degree, and earned a law degree from Lincoln University in Oakland, California. He served in the U.S. Marine Corps from 1943 to 1946, and then settled in Los Angeles, where he established a successful real estate career. He belonged to the Urban League and NAACP, and served on the Board of Directors of the California Association of Real Estate Brokers.[313]

In 1982, Ivan returned to Portland to attend a dinner honoring twenty-one women—including his mother—who had been selected for inclusion in the booklet, *Notable Women in the History of Oregon*.[314] Cannady continued to generate publicity, even after her death in 1974: the event was covered in the *Los Angeles Sentinel* as well as the *Oregonian*.[315]

Five years later, on December 14, 1987, Ivan Cannady died after an extended battle with cancer.[316] He was seventy-two.

In 1929, the Portland Council of Churches nominated Beatrice Cannady for the William E. Harmon Award for Distinguished Achievement Among Negroes in the field of race relations.[317] Among other things, the Harmon Foundation provided awards for "constructive achievements among Negroes" during the Harlem Renaissance of the 1920s.[318] Work in nine fields was recognized, including education, literature, music, and race relations. Cannady's "splendid grasp of affairs in a wide range of fields, cultural and social, civic and racial, legal and religious, has been impressive," wrote Executive Secretary E. C. Farnham in the nominating letter. "In addition, her activity as editor, public speaker and leader in civic and social affairs has been very definite and a direct contribution to racial understanding."[319] But she faced stiff competition for the gold medal and $1,000 honorarium: Dr. Robert R. Moton, president of Tuskegee Institute, NAACP co-founder Mary White Ovington, and journalist Delilah Beasley were among the twenty nominees.[320]

Cannady's supporters included an eclectic group of individuals, white and black: professors, local ministers, Portland's mayor, friends, and the president of the Oregon Prison Association. Some of the letters, handwritten and pages long, described the work she had done in the Northwest; others were typed and just a few paragraphs in length. All of them conveyed respect for Cannady's tireless commitment to improving race relations locally and nationally. For example, Levi T. Pennington, president of Pacific College, wrote: "Mrs. Cannady is an outstanding citizen and leader of Portland, of Oregon, and in a still wider circle. In movements for civic, religious, social, industrial, or international betterment, she is a figure of consequence. To have a cultured, refined, highly educated, and thoroughly efficient woman of her race serving her city, state, and nation, and helping to build up better world relationships is in itself a thing that adds in the promotion of right feeling between the whites and the Negroes."[321]

Franklin T. Griffith, president of the Portland Railway, Light & Power Co., noted: "Mrs. Cannady is an able and sincere woman and a leader among the people of her race. If anyone in Portland is entitled to the Harmon Award, I think Mrs. Cannady is that person."[322] The pastor of Ellis Avenue Community Methodist Church observed, "In leading pulpits, on platform, in state and national conventions, this modest, unassuming, gifted lady is doing a constructive, outstanding service in race relations."[323] Mayor George L. Baker wrote, "I am glad of the opportunity to endorse the nomination of Mrs. Cannady. I am acquainted with her work over a period of years and keenly appreciate the fine spirit of fellowship and good-will existing between the negro and white races here, which I feel certain, to a large degree, is due to her personal efforts."[324] And the pastor of the First AME Zion Church noted: "As I think of the people who have labored for better race relations in America, I can think of none who have wrought more nobly than Mrs. Cannady. While she has lived in Portland, and therefore her labors have been chiefly in the Pacific Northwest, yet she has made contacts and has influenced RACE RELATIONS in many sections of the United States."[325]

Despite these letters of support, and a scrapbook of some two hundred pages filled with supporting evidence of Cannady's work as an ambassador of race relations, Dr. Moton was awarded the medal and cash prize, worth about $12,500 today.[326] Cannady was undoubtedly disappointed; the honorarium would have helped considerably during the Depression. She also would have appreciated the national recognition of her eighteen-year career advocating equal rights and liberties. But she could not dwell on her disappointment for long. Five days after the *New York Times* reported Moton's selection, the January 11, 1930, issue of the *Advocate* hit the streets with the news that several janitors at the American Bank Building on Southwest Morrison Street were being replaced by white workers.[327] The little security that black Portlanders had quickly disappeared during the Great Depression, but Beatrice Morrow Cannady and the *Advocate* documented this fight—and many more—between 1912 and 1936.

CHAPTER TWO

The *Advocate*: It Is Your Mouthpiece

There are many reliable subscribers who do all they can to support us both morally and financially, for they realize what a terrible calamity it would be for the colored people not to have a mouthpiece in the community.

— "Is It Fair?" the *Advocate*, September 12, 1931, 2

Enclosed herewith you will find [a] money order for $2.50 for one year's subscription to The Advocate .... I am making this subscription because I do not feel that I can any longer do without the intelligence of the valuable columns of this enterprising Paper. With every best wish for your continued success in this field, and otherwise, I am, yours respectfully, Phil Reynolds.

— "We Thank You," the *Advocate*, March 19, 1927, 1[1]

Portland resident Phil Reynolds and his wife, Elise, weren't the only ones who felt they could no longer do without the *Advocate* in 1927.[2] That year, Lincoln High School took out a one-year subscription for its library and the Baldwin restaurant began offering the paper to its customers.[3] James Botts, who had relocated to Chicago with his wife, Martha, to work as comptroller of the Pullman Porters Benefit Association of America, asked to have the *Advocate* sent to him there.[4] And George B. Durham of Brooklyn, New York, began subscribing after seeing an *Advocate* editorial in the *New York Age*, which he read while in Boston.[5] "So on my return home I decided to have you send me the paper—The Defender of our race in the West," he wrote in a note to Beatrice Cannady. "I congratulate you on your success which I hope you will continue to have."[6]

The *Advocate* fostered an extended, imagined community that was critical for individuals who continued to be excluded from society.[7] Cannady also used the newspaper to create a *real* community for Oregonians who were socially or physically isolated. Only 2,144 Negroes lived in the entire state in 1920.[8] In Portland, Negroes constituted approximately 0.6 percent of the total population of 258,288.[9] A longtime resident recalled being able to walk around for hours without ever encountering another black person. Desperate to see someone who looked like her, she would go to Union Depot and sit, just watching the "colored waiters."[10] The small population made it difficult to effect reform, recalled Portland native Otto Rutherford:

"It wasn't that we lacked unity, it was just that we lacked numbers."[11] It also was a factor in the pervasive discrimination of black Oregonians, because the lack of contact between races contributed to the stereotypes and biases many white people held. Lee C. Anderson observed in 1925, "We are surrounded by a prejudice which you do not find in our neighboring states. There is no colored district in Portland. Our people are scattered throughout the city." However, he admitted that might have its advantages: "This scattered population gives a better chance for first-hand acquaintance between the races, for prejudice is the off-spring of ignorance. Removal of racial obsessions will in time make a better citizen of black and white."[12]

The isolation that many black people felt, whether in Portland or elsewhere, became blurred upon receipt of one or more favorite weekly papers. As Mr. Ballard, a co-founder of the *Advocate* who moved to Norfolk, Virginia, observed: "When I receive *The Advocate* every week I feel as if I am having a talk with my old friends in Portland."[13] For an hour or two, readers could peruse hometown news, learn about race relations across the country, participate in a lively editorial debate about civil rights and liberties, and, as George Durham did, engage in a long-distance exchange with new friends. Cannady encouraged these conversations by publishing letters regularly in the *Advocate*, nicknamed "old reliable."[14] In the process, she created a strong community and left clues that yield a striking amount of information about culture, migration, employment opportunities, social networks, and civil rights leaders who interacted with Cannady.

Texans Nat Q. Henderson and his wife, Mamie, took out a two-year subscription to the paper in 1930 after spending "a glorious summer on the Pacific Coast" as well as a long weekend with "time honored" friend Beatrice Cannady. She told readers they wanted to stay in touch with "friends and acquaintances in Portland," and called their attention to the fact that Henderson was principal of one of Houston's public schools.[15] In fact, he was principal of Bruce Elementary School from 1909 until 1942, mayor of the Fifth Ward—a neighborhood settled by freedmen after the Civil War—founder of Houston's first public library for people of color, and much more.[16]

The Reverend J. Milton Waldron and his wife, Martha, were *Advocate* subscribers, too. Waldron, founder of the Afro-American Benefit Association, had a long history as an activist.[17] He traveled to Harper's Ferry, West Virginia, in 1906 to attend the Second Annual Meeting of the Niagara Movement.[18] Three years later, Waldron, along with Ida Wells-Barnett, Jane Addams, Mary White Ovington, W. E. B. Du Bois, and forty-eight other individuals, signed "The Call," a statement written by Oswald Garrison Villard that called for a "national conference [to be held in New York City] on the Negro question."[19] That meeting was the genesis of the NAACP, which would have a branch in Portland by 1914.

The Waldrons spent a week in the city in September 1926 as part of a West Coast vacation arranged by members of his church.[20] Cannady may have coordinated a speaking engagement for him at Lincoln High School; she introduced him to the "packed audience" on Tuesday morning, September 14th, and reported that he was "well received." Afterward, she hosted a luncheon for the couple, and then took them for a drive on the scenic Columbia River Highway to Multnomah Falls.[21] Cannady reported that he was "greatly pleased with the 'Far West,'" and particularly taken with Portland: "Nowhere on his journey were he and his good wife treated more splendidly than in Portland," she observed with pride.[22] During a long interview with the *Advocate*, Waldron "expressed deep regret at the injustice done the Japanese and Chinese" as a result of immigration laws in the United States. But that provided an opening for Negroes to step in to "help to develop the West, and reap the golden harvest that awaits their presence and their labor." Despite the promise of opportunity, though, Waldron said he believed that "injustice" was "beginning to make itself felt" in the region. "We must, as a people, come here and settle down and see to it that Race-hatred and color-prejudice advance no further," he said. To that end, he reportedly called on people to support the *Advocate*: "We have larger papers," he observed, "but none that ring more true to the vital things of the Race than *The Advocate*; its editorials, especially, are worth-while—they are sane, practical, ... and statesmanlike; the people of Portland ... owe it to themselves and our country to stand by *The Advocate*."[23] He practiced what he preached: Two months later, he wrote from Washington, D.C., that he and Martha "look[ed] forward, each week, with real pleasure" to receiving the *Advocate*. "You are getting out a paper, worthwhile. It strikes from the shoulder and strikes in the right direction. Keep up the good work."[24]

Another influential reader was Walter L. Cohen, who renewed his subscription for two more years in October 1929.[25] Cannady described him as "perhaps the most outstanding Negro politician in the South," and noted that he had been a "regular subscriber to *The Advocate*" for some time.[26] Cohen was appointed to "the powerful position of secretary of the Republican State Central Committee," a post he held until the late 1920s.[27] He was selected for a number of other important positions during his lifetime, too, including "Controller of Customs" in New Orleans, a job with an annual salary of $5,000, about $64,000 today.[28] When he died on December 29, 1930, Cannady observed that "*The Advocate*, along with

America's twelve million Negroes, mourn[ed] the passing of this colorful character." She called Cohen "a fighter who knew no defeat," and wrote that "efforts ... to discredit him by his white opponents and to wreck him politically were always overcome by this indomitable figure."[29]

Also living in New Orleans was the Reverend James Gordon McPherson, better known as "Black Billy Sunday"—a "large, loud, demanding, and sensual" preacher who "spoke the language of the New Testament" in true fire and brimstone fashion.[30] "I am sure this will come as a surprise ... since it has been such a long time since I have seen you in person," he wrote Cannady in 1931. "But I have a delightful visit with you each week through the dear old *Advocate*, which has become an expected visitor to our Southern home here in the Old Pelican State."[31] McPherson's charismatic sermons at Greater Providence Baptist Church in Algiers, a community across the Mississippi River from New Orleans, inspired the character "De Lawd" in the Pulitzer Prize-winning play, *The Green Pastures*.[32] Cannady was thrilled when the play came to Portland for a five-day run in 1932, and promoted it heavily in the *Advocate*.

The *Advocate* had many well-known subscribers on its books, but most readers were hard-working individuals scattered throughout Oregon and at least eighteen other states, as well as Washington, D.C., London, Germany, and Bermuda. The newspaper was a lifeline to Portland and its residents for people like Etta Graham, whose husband, David, was president of a college in Liberia created by the American Colonization Society in 1822 for freed slaves.[33] She asked the *Advocate* to tell her friends that she thought about them "constantly" and loved "them in the same old way even though" she did not "have time to write."[34] She also undoubtedly missed her daughter, Shirley Graham McCanns, who was establishing a considerable reputation in Portland as a composer, singer, and conductor, and later would become W. E. B. Du Bois' second wife.

John L. Jones, a former Portland Hotel waiter who relocated to Pasadena, California, sent $5—more than $80 today—for a two-year subscription along with a note asking Cannady to convey his "best wishes to Portland friends."[35] R. L. Hall wrote from Detroit: "I enjoy reading *The Advocate* each week. Through it I learn of Portland so much .... I wish you continued success."[36] London M. McGhee mailed a letter from Memphis "telling how glad he [was] to welcome *The Advocate* each week."[37] And Alaska resident Dora Gulliford asked Cannady to tell her Portland friends that she made it "back home to Dawson" safely and anticipated "returning to the States in the early fall"—a reminder that Alaska still was not part of the Union in 1923. Cannady added, "In order that she may keep in touch with the activities of her friends here she sent in her subscription to *The Advocate*."[38]

Even residents who expected to be away from Portland for a few weeks or months arranged to have the *Advocate* sent to them.[39] In January 1926, Cannady informed readers that James H. Williams had returned from Chicago, where he had spent the holidays with his family. "He says he kept in touch with Portland through *The Advocate* at his Chicago address."[40] And Pollyann Reed, the *Advocate*'s former society editor, had the newspaper forwarded to her during a long trip to Oklahoma in the summer of 1931. At the end of August she wrote, "Have received each *Advocate*. Thanks. Shall start toward home soon."[41]

The ongoing, and often heartfelt, correspondence from these subscribers and countless more demonstrates the bond they felt with the *Advocate* and illuminates Cannady's ability to sustain a vibrant, imagined community of readers. Letters sharing good news or bad, changes of address or fortune, were sent to the editor, who printed the updates in the *Advocate*. One subscriber captured the importance of this network when he declared: the *Advocate* "has kept the entire country apprised of the activities of the people of the State of Oregon and the City of Portland."[42] During the early 1900s, when automobiles still were a luxury item and cross-country travel was time-consuming and difficult due to Jim Crow laws, the newspaper was a tangible connection to others. Even in Oregon, where advertisements for the Pacific Telephone and Telegraph Company promoted phones as a way to keep "friendships alive ... without regard to distance," most people did not have phone service in their homes until the 1930s.[43]

Readers counted on the newspaper for "information, education, ... inspiration."[44] A study of Portland's black population deemed its press "one of the most important ... institutions" due to its "ability to counterbalance the neglect and distortions African American news and individuals suffered in the hands of the dominant [white] press."[45] Positive news about black people, whether in the Northwest or the nation, was left out, relegated to the back of a section, or condensed into a paragraph or two. More typical was news of crimes allegedly committed by "negroes"—always with a lower-case "n." These omissions rendered black people invisible at the group level and nameless and faceless on an individual level. But in the *Advocate* and other black newspapers, people could read about their family, friends, and neighbors, and share in their joy and sorrow. Week in and week out, Cannady sought to promote racial uplift and raise self-esteem by presenting positive images of people succeeding in business, education, culture, and life.[46] She also featured the sort of news that is critical to a community's identity. As Edward Cannady and his colleagues noted in the first issue in 1903, news of "our weddings and births, our arrivals and departures, the lucks and accidents produced among us, does much to ... establish pride."[47]

People were quick to express their dismay when the *Advocate* did not arrive as expected. "During the week we received numerous calls about [the paper] being late," Beatrice Cannady wrote in 1931. "This we appreciate very much because it indicates that *The Advocate* is a popularly read newspaper and when it does not arrive on time, the subscribers miss it."[48] That was particularly true for longtime subscribers like Charity Binford, who "says if the post man doesn't bring it on time every Saturday she gets after him for Mrs. Binford must have her paper."[49] Similarly, James Wilson wrote from Radford, Virginia, that he was "sorry" he had "missed a copy of *The Advocate*" after it apparently was lost in the mail. For Wilson, who attended a Legionnaires' convention in Portland in 1932, the newspaper was a link to happy memories: "I must say that my visit to your city of Roses was a royal one. I shall remember you and the people of Portland and how pleasant they were to me in making me welcome. Remember me to all who know me."[50]

Although Cannady frequently mentioned new and renewing subscribers by name, circulation figures never were published.[51] Some years later, she told a contemporary that circulation was "approximately three thousand"; actual readership may have been higher, since people tended to share copies with family and friends.[52] Regardless of the exact figure, Cannady used the *Advocate* to call attention to the fact that the Negro population in Portland was sizeable enough to support a newspaper, long considered to be an institution that represents permanence in an area. As she told a reporter for the *New York Amsterdam News*, a black paper founded in 1909, "We have one large hotel"—the Golden West—"a newspaper, three modern barber shops, a confectionery, beauty parlor for the wealthy people, a branch Y.W.C.A., three churches and two missions."[53]

Most subscribers were Negroes, but a number of influential white individuals took the paper as well. In 1930, for example, she reported that attorney John W. Kaste was "among *The Advocate*'s regular readers." When "an *Advocate* representative called on him to collect another year's subscription ..., he voluntarily paid for two. He pointed to the *Advocate* lying on a table near-by, stating that he read it every week."[54] More prominent white subscribers who were in a position to assist Cannady's fight for equal rights included Congressman Maurice E. Crumpacker; Edward Boyce, one of the owners of the Portland Hotel; Oregon Supreme Court Justice

John M. Rand; Congressman Franklin F. Korell, who wrote, "I receive *The Advocate* each week and enjoy reading it"; Governor Albin W. Norblad, who used the paper "to keep in touch with the Colored people of the state"; and Franklin T. Griffith, a lawyer and president of Portland General Electric Company and a "supporter and reader of *The Advocate*!"[55]

Other white subscribers valued the newspaper, too. J. L. Stewart, a longtime reader in eastern Oregon, inadvertently set off a "friendly rivalry" with a subscriber in Maxville when he renewed promptly in 1928.[56] F. D. Cooper then paid through 1929 because he felt "Brother J. L. Stewart of La Grande ... [was] a fine pattern to work by."[57] And Eva Pillsbury, who worked as a probation officer at the Multnomah County Courthouse and was active in the Woman's Christian Temperance Union, wrote: "I find your paper 'The Advocate' so interesting, and so full of informative material that I do not want to be without the help that it gives me; therefore am sending check to cover six months' subscription and will renew when that time expires."[58]

Cannady envisioned the *Advocate* as "a mediator ... between the white and Negro races in the state." In fact, she wrote in 1933 that its "sole reason for existing" was to promote "more friendly relations between the races by disseminating [helpful and necessary] information" about "the Negro, what he is doing, how he is faring and what he is thinking." Black Portlanders could keep up "fairly well ... with the white world" by reading the local newspapers. But white papers contained "very little constructive news pertaining to the Negro," so Cannady believed that "intelligent" white people "should make it a rule to buy at least one good Negro newspaper"—preferably the *Advocate*. "How else can one become fully developed if he leaves out of his education such an important study as the American Negro?" she asked.[59] Clarence Yeager, a motion picture attorney in Portland, may have decided to subscribe to the *Advocate* for these reasons. Later that year, he congratulated Cannady on the newspaper's thirtieth anniversary and noted: "It is a newsy periodical, and I believe correctly advocates its aim" of serving as a "bridge between the Negro and the white races in Oregon."[60]

For a few months in 1933, Cannady's motto was "*The Advocate* in Every White Home in Oregon."[61] Current readers were urged to "take the responsibility of sending in at least one white subscriber. This can be easily done," she told them, "by asking your grocer, butcher, tailor or whoever you spend your money with, for a subscription."[62] The campaign generated at least a few new subscribers, as evidenced by the list of attorneys, nurses, businessmen, and students published in the *Advocate*.[63] It also garnered national attention when correspondent Clifford C. Mitchell wrote about the subscription drive in his widely circulated column, "Digesting the

News."[64] Cannady reported that she was "quite satisfied and encouraged with the results to date," but she also observed that "subscriptions could come in more promptly and in larger numbers. We hope every reader of *The Advocate* will do his and her utmost to get new subscribers to the paper."[65]

Cannady stressed this theme frequently.[66] One booster, as she called individuals who did their duty to the newspaper, was Portland resident Sherman Pickett.[67] Not only did the paper go to his home, he also took out a subscription for his nephew in Alabama.[68] Sometimes all it took was a single issue of the *Advocate* for an individual to become an avid reader. D. H. Kimbrough, who operated a shoe repair shop in Ilwaco, Washington, wrote in 1931: "A friend of mine sent me one of your papers the other day. I like it very much and am enclosing my check for subscription to same."[69] Gift subscriptions added to the newspaper's bottom line; they also helped Cannady promote Portland as a livable and welcoming place. "Your paper is a very inexpensive way of advertising your city and its people; it is one of the surest ways of giving the stranger a quick and comprehensive view of its resources and possibilities," she wrote. "Therefore, if you have relatives, friends, or acquaintances, and want them to know about your city and state, send them *The Advocate*."[70]

Holidays and anniversaries were good opportunities to give the *Advocate*. "Send a year's subscription for *The Advocate* as a Christmas present to your friends," she wrote in December 1927. "Nothing would be more highly appreciated by those who desire to keep in touch with the progress of the Race. Only $2.50 per year, sent anywhere."[71] The following year, Cannady tied the idea of one's duty to the newspaper with its twenty-fifth anniversary: "We have done our best to give a good paper to our patrons. We greatly appreciate the support they have given us all along. For a birthday present to 'The Advocate,' send a year's subscription to your friend back home—pay up what you owe on your own, and say a good word to your friends about the 'Old Reliable.'"[72] It is impossible to say whether this appeal brought in capital; Cannady made no mention of new subscriptions, nor did she thank any readers for bringing their account current. But she did print the names of individuals who had subscribed to the *Advocate* since its first issue in 1903, including Daniel Parker, Dora and Virgil Keene, Anna Peek, who "rendered yeoman service" as the *Advocate*'s first society editor, and Charity Binford, who "says she has read one thousand and three hundred *Advocate*s which represent its whole life of twenty-five years."[73]

Other individuals who were acknowledged in the newspaper included those who renewed promptly, especially for several years at a time.[74] "It is a great help to us if we do not have to send out so many notices," Cannady wrote during the Depression. "Those 3-cent stamps on each notice amount up in a little while."[75] Lywood Kyles, bishop of the AME Zion Church in St. Louis, Missouri, sent his check for $2.50 after receiving notice that his subscription was expiring. "Accept my thanks for the very excellent paper which The Advocate Publishing Co. is issuing and for the promptness with which it has come to my office," he wrote.[76] Ella and Jack Ryan, a prominent Houston couple who had taken the *Advocate* since 1913, renewed for two years at a time.[77] William H. Willis, the *Advocate*'s former advertising solicitor who was working as a printer in New York City, sent his check for $7.50 along with congratulations on the paper's twentieth anniversary in 1923, and then renewed for two more years when the *Advocate* turned twenty-five.[78] Cannady thanked Payton D. Young, too, whom she described as "one of the most prominent bakers in the whole South." Her "old friend and good booster" in Dallas renewed for another year, "saying, 'I must have it.'"[79] But new subscribers also were recognized. A reader in Calgary, Alberta, sent "a New Year's gift in the form of a ten-dollar subscription"—more than $140 today.[80] And Cannady was "glad to welcome" Emogene Clarkston to Portland in 1923, especially since "one of her first purchases upon arriving [from Washington, D.C.] was a subscription to *The Advocate*."[81]

Many subscribers—including Phil and Elise Reynolds, the Waldrons, George Durham, and Walter Cohen—took on their obligation willingly. In fact, two years after first discovering the *Advocate* in Boston, Durham wrote, "I am still reading *The Advocate*, the great defender of our race in the Northwest, with a deal of pleasure and pride."[82] But others had to be convinced to part with their hard-earned money. So Cannady, like her colleagues and their predecessors, emphasized an individual's duty—to the race, to their newspaper and its editor, and to citizenship. As she observed in 1925, "If you chance to know a colored man who is not subscribing for some newspaper published by his own racial group, you may mark it down that such an [individual] is not doing his full duty as a good citizen."[83]

Cannady decided to launch an elaborate circulation contest—"unlike anything ever before attempted here"—in 1931.[84] The campaign may have been a desperate attempt to bring in subscribers during the Depression, though she acknowledged she had "made a lot of friends" recently and increased circulation "in spite of the adverse circumstances."[85] But she also wrote that the Depression had "hit the small weekly publication harder than many other business enterprises."[86] Newspapers could be dispensed with when disposable income was tight, she noted, and some subscribers had "found it necessary to discontinue their newspaper" so they could pay other bills.[87] Even Portland's daily press was not immune. The *Portland Telegram* announced its merger with the *Portland News* in May 1931 because "developments of the past few years [had] shown conclusively that three afternoon newspapers overcrowded the Portland field."[88] Cannady was forced to scale back operations considerably in 1931. She closed one of her two downtown Portland offices on Washington Street in June "to cut down overhead expenses during the dull summer period."[89] Two months later she reported the *Advocate* would be published just twice a month to "cut down on the great expense involved in" putting out the newspaper, and added that she was compelled to "make this retrenchment" because she was "in great need of some rest"; publishing a weekly newspaper with little help had taken its toll.[90]

Whatever the reasons behind the contest, Cannady told readers the *Advocate* hoped "to secure more subscribers [and] renewals and ... make it easy" for delinquent subscribers "to pay up." The editor pointed out other advantages, too. "Subscriptions give a newspaper prestige, power and enhance the value of its advertising columns," she wrote. The contest would more than pay for itself if she could increase circulation to the point where she could charge advertisers more "to reach a greater number of people."[91] She also pledged to "add new features [to the *Advocate*] and make every warranted improvement."[92] Cannady did invite a number of people to begin contributing to the *Advocate* that spring.[93] For example, "Helpful Hints," by Nancy Lee, was "devoted to advice on friendship, love, and all matters pertaining to the home."[94] And "Keeping Fit," by Dr. DeNorval Unthank, addressed issues ranging from "superstitions and fads" to curing the common cold.[95]

Contestants were awarded scores ranging from three thousand to three hundred and sixty thousand points for each subscription they secured during the ten-week period.[96] People were encouraged to aim for "clubs" worth at least $12—about $170 today—and consisting of five one-year subscriptions, one six-year order, or any combination thereof.[97] The grand prize was a "handsome, speedy" Hudson automobile on display at a local dealership; runners-up received between $40 and $100 in gold.[98] Cannady devoted hundreds of column inches to the contest. Advertisements, notices about the rules and regulations, extra "opportunity coupons," and front-page articles ran week after week.[99] She hoped to "add hundreds of new subscribers" to her books, but her optimism waned when results did not materialize.[100] She lamented the lack of participation, especially since so many people were jobless due to the Depression, and observed: "In truth, the present status of this [contest] would not justify *The Advocate* in putting up more than a cheap diamond ring—a flashy watch, or a music box!"[101] Nevertheless, Cannady continued to encourage people to take part by hyping the campaign.[102] Days before the vote tabulation she reported the race had become "mighty spirited" and that "rivalry of the keenest sort [was being] manifest on every side."[103]

When the campaign concluded at the end of June 1931, Cannady announced the addition of a "host of new paid-in-advance subscribers" and she thanked all of the participants for their part in "making the campaign [such a] rousing success."[104] Noticeably absent, though, are the actual figures. She never revealed how many new subscribers or renewals resulted from the competition. The car itself was valued at $1,155—more than $16,000 today; if she paid full price for it, she would have needed 462 one-year subscriptions just to break even.[105]

Several factors may have affected the drive for new subscribers. Certainly, the Depression and worse-than-usual job prospects for Portland's black residents did not bode well for the contest. She admitted that times were tough, but argued that individuals should be working that much harder to earn a dollar.[106] However, people had more to worry about in the spring of 1931 than canvassing for subscribers. The *Advocate* reported during the contest that vandals had targeted the Unthank home on Knapp Street, smashing nearly twenty windows in an attempt to prevent the family from

Edward Cannady founded the Advocate *in 1903 with nine other men. He continued working for the Portland Hotel as its "hat-check man," and earned a reputation for his "great memory for heads."*

moving into a white neighborhood.[107] One week earlier, the *Advocate* had printed the shocking news that the Portland Hotel, a longtime employer of Negroes, had abruptly discharged eleven men—including Edward Cannady, who had worked there more than thirty years—and replaced them with white waitresses. An editorial pointed out that some felt the wholesale firings were due to "race prejudice," but Beatrice Cannady wrote that the "change" probably was "an outgrowth of the present, almost universal, economic depression and an effort on the part of the business to adjust itself to the condition."[108] Given the tense situation in Portland, a contest to boost the *Advocate* could not have come at a better time: as the Depression deepened, the newspaper played an increasingly important role in helping Portland's Negro community through the crisis. It resumed its weekly schedule in October, when a new typesetting machine was installed in Cannady's remaining office in the Macleay Building. But by 1933, the weary editor commented:

> We have done our best to give a good paper—a paper that all can feel proud of; we have complained less than most papers that come to our exchange desk about the depression; we have sacrificed so that you can have your papers each week; we have stayed up nights working while you slept and rested so that you could have your paper each week, but there is a limit to everything. We are only human and we cannot exercise superhuman powers in order to raise money to pay for equipment, stock, etc., so that you can have your paper.[109]

Publishing a weekly newspaper was an expensive and exhausting venture, one that required a profound commitment to advocacy and selfless dedication to racial uplift. As one editorial observed, most publishers did "not have money making" as their primary objective; if they did, they "would find other occupations" that yielded "better returns."[110]

Cannady's efforts to increase circulation during the 1930s dovetailed with the week-in, week-out work she did to collect past-due accounts. Although subscriptions were always "payable in advance," few publications were able to enforce that requirement.[111] Collecting delinquent accounts often became a full-time—and thankless—job, and Cannady spent hours crafting notices to encourage people to subscribe, pay for their ads or printing, and bring current their overdue accounts.[112] Revenue was necessary for paper, postage, ink, and the sundry other things she needed for publishing the newspaper. But it also allowed her to focus on her calling: "*The Advocate*'s mission is to give to the people the news, fight segregation, jim crow practice and race prejudice between the races, whether they are black, brown, white, or yellow," she wrote in 1926. "If we have the support and cooperation of our own group, we believe that we can convert many of all races to a saner consideration of interracial relations."[113]

Many notices were crafted to appeal to her readers' practical side. In May 1923, a single sentence appeared on page four: "Come in and pay your subscription to the *Advocate*, also your other obligations, so Mr. Pacific Telephone and Telegraph Company will not tell you 'Temporarily disconnected.'"[114] Other pleas for payment were more creative: "If you have severe headaches, dizziness and fainting spells, accompanied by rheumatism, cramps, lumbago and fits, it's a pretty good sign you are not well, and are liable to 'croak' at any time. So pay your subscription to *The Advocate* so you can meet old St. Peter with a clear conscience."[115] Many notices emphasized the idea that readers were morally obligated to the newspaper and its success. In 1928 Cannady asked people point blank, "What is *The Advocate* worth to you?":

> The cost of publishing a weekly newspaper such as *The Advocate* is tremendous, and we believe that all the friends of free speech ought to show their appreciation of such a paper by at least paying a year's subscription to same. We cannot publish a newspaper and increase its circulation and its power for good in the community by a few folk dropping in occasionally and buying a few copies containing some special article which has attracted the individual or individuals.
>
> If you like *The Advocate* and wish it to grow and become a power for good in the community and nation, just sit right down and mail us a check for at least $2.50.[116]

When all else failed, including threats to discontinue subscriptions, she warned of eternal damnation: "To our delinquent subscribers. If you believe in heaven or hell, come in, call or send in your subscription money."[117]

Cannady invested considerable time, energy, and money into running the business and ensuring that the *Advocate* was mailed each Friday.[118] This consistency was critical, as she succinctly observed one January: the newspaper "must come out with regularity if it is to be of any influence."[119] Attending to overdue accounts and delinquent subscribers were aspects of her job that took time—time Cannady felt would have been better spent fighting for equal rights and liberties for black Oregonians. "We cannot give our best thought to our work when we have to spend most of our time chasing the dollar," she wrote during the Depression.[120] She struggled with this conflict, even sharing her thoughts with the NAACP's Walter White in the middle of 1926: "If I were able to be relieved of some of the mechanical part of my own business so that I could devote more time to the cause of the N.A.A.C.P. throughout this western territory, I am sure great things could be accomplished."[121] Had she *not* focused so much attention on the *Advocate*'s success, though, it might well have ended up in the "journalistic grave" like James Merriman's *Portland Times* and so many other black papers in the nineteenth and early twentieth centuries.[122]

Subscription revenue was important, but so was advertising income. Scattered across the *Advocate*'s front page and throughout the newspaper were advertisements for a variety of products including Mrs. Winslow's Syrup, a laxative "for all stomach and intestinal troubles and disturbances due to teething"; Murine eye drops; Listerine mouthwash and toothpaste; Camay, "The Soap of Beautiful Women"; Feen-a-mint, "The Laxative You Chew Like Gum," available at druggists for 15 cents and 25 cents; Flit bug spray, which became even more popular after Theodore Geisel—better known as Dr. Seuss—was hired to illustrate the ads; KC Baking Powder; C. Gee Wo's "Medicinal Herbs and Roots," which could "prevent operations for Diabetes, Catarrh, Lung, Throat, ... and all female disorders" if taken in time; and East India Hair Grower, a remedy containing "medical properties" that promised to promote hair growth and restore its strength, vitality, and beauty.[123]

Other products were more controversial. Ads for a skin-whitening product featured a photograph of a woman looking over her bare left shoulder with the caption: "BEWITCHING because she has light, smooth, soft skin. This young lady has found the secret of bewitching beauty. ... Regular use of this preparation along with the other Dr. Fred Palmer Skin Whitener Preparations keeps your skin light and soft and makes you look bewitching."[124] Some felt the advertisements for Ko-Verra, a cream "guaranteed to lighten the skin without bleaching or injuring it in any way!" also were offensive. Elnora Gresham, president of the Iowa Federation of Colored Women's Clubs, was quoted as saying, "Since I have been using Ko-Verra many of the white ladies who come to my beauty shop say they would hardly know I am a Colored lady."[125] Cannady may have felt conflicted about accepting advertisements for these sorts of products. The money helped the newspaper's bottom line and enabled her to publish the paper regularly, but editorials made clear how she felt about "passing": "We still have amongst us that class of individuals who live in fear of detection, night and day, as they paint and powder up and pass for white. It is too bad that our people as a whole do not recognize how wonderful and how beautiful the Race is. It is like unto a flower garden with its red and black and white tulips." She argued for collective action and racial uplift: "Let us get together, stand together and pull together so that everyone, both in and outside of our Race, will recognize and respect us, and take pride in being identified with the Race."[126]

Overall, advertising revenue was difficult to come by. Until the late 1920s, when local retail advertising became more prevalent, newspapers such as the *Advocate* were dependent on black-owned businesses, most of which were located in their own community, and the few white-owned companies that were interested in targeting black consumers.[127] Those merchants were praised, often effusively so, in the *Advocate*.[128] For example, when the owner of the Bradford Clothes Shop on the corner of Washington and 4th "greatly enlarged and beautifully decorated" his store in 1930, Cannady observed that the shop was "one of the smartest in the city and show[ed] its appreciation for colored patronage by advertising in the columns of *The Advocate*."[129] The shop "Where Young Men Buy" consistently ran a small one-column ad, yet its wares probably were beyond the reach of most Negro men in the city: items for sale ranged from $25 to $45, the equivalent of $400 to $700 today.[130]

Another regular advertiser was the Eastern Outfitting Company, originally located at Washington Street and 10th Avenue in downtown Portland. Again, though, the merchandise may have been beyond the means of many readers. One three-column ad promoted "ultra coats for women and misses" with "gay, jaunty side tie effects" and fur trim for $59.50—about $1,000 today.[131] Nevertheless, Cannady thanked owner Joseph Shemansky for using the newspaper's "columns to let the colored people know ... their patronage" was "appreciated." In return, she observed that people had "spent many dollars with the Eastern."[132]

The Meier & Frank Co. also advertised consistently. The department store was founded on Front Street in 1857 by German Aaron Meier. He was joined in 1873 by Emil Frank and as their business grew, so did the size of their store; Meier & Frank eventually settled into a new fifteen story building across the street from the Portland Hotel in 1932.[133] Cannady wrote in the *Advocate* about the Meier family. Aaron's son, Julius, a contemporary of hers, was elected Oregon's twentieth governor—and the state's first Jewish leader—in 1931.[134] And she wrote fondly about Abraham, Julius' older brother: "Mr. Meier is well known and liked by all the patrons, most of whom he addresses by name as they enter the store."[135] In 1930, she reported his death and noted that "he had many friends young and old—black and white—recipients of his loving generosity who will sadly miss him."[136] Meier & Frank's slogan, "The Store For Everybody," appeared to hold true for black patrons as well as white while she lived in Portland.[137] Nevertheless, Negro women were employed as "comfort maids" in the store's restrooms, not as salesclerks.[138]

Bigger accounts were few and far between, so when a paper such as the *Advocate* landed a display ad for the J. C. Penney Co., which promised to "serve well" and pack "Service with each purchase"; for the 1928 Buick, available at Howard Automobile Co. at 13th and Burnside; or for Shell Oil Company, it warranted comment on the editorial page.[139] In 1929, Cannady welcomed back the department store, "our old friend," after a few years' absence. "The new manager believes *The Advocate* a good medium through which to announce the store's good merchandise," she wrote.[140] Cannady also called readers' attention to the new ads for Shell, which had emerged as "the world's leading oil company" by the end of the 1920s.[141] "The Shell Oil Company of California has placed its advertisement in *The Advocate*, your paper, which is proof positive that the Company wants your patronage," Cannady pointed out.[142] She hoped that all *Advocate* readers would "take notice and patronize" Shell stations and thus help the newspaper "to live and fill its mission in the community."[143]

Of course, Cannady urged people to support black-owned businesses, too. In June 1924, she announced that Eurastus Richardson had "opened one of the best looking ice cream parlors in the city in the Golden West Hotel" at the corner of Broadway and Everett. "All kinds of confections, candies and cigars, newspapers and periodicals can be had there," she wrote, including the *Advocate*. "It is to be hoped that the people will give Mr. Richardson their hearty support and patronage in this badly needed business enterprise."[144] By 1929, Richardson was advertising his confectionery "and fountain lunch," featuring "beef and pork barbecued by 'Fat Boy Maxwell' of Salem, Oregon."[145] Charles Maxwell's cooking had garnered quite a following by then; Cannady wrote about making the trek to Salem for his "famous ... sandwiches."[146]

A couple of years later, she acknowledged the "business sagacity of an enterprising local colored man" who had just opened his own fully equipped garage in a large brick building on Ross Street.[147] Demand existed for something like the U.S.A. Garage; even though the black population in Portland was small, people owned quite a few automobiles. Cannady urged "Colored people ... and as many whites as can be influenced to do so," to patronize the new establishment.[148] She did her part over the years to support black-owned businesses. In 1931, she took her son, George, and eleven of his friends to a club owned by a former Portland Hotel waiter for a "delicious chicken dinner" to celebrate his graduation from Grant High School. The party cost her about $15—approximately $200 today—but another article in the *Advocate* reminded readers that Charlie Redd's Cotton Club was "a fine place to entertain the graduates" and, at $1.15 a dinner, less expensive than throwing a party at home.[149]

Testimonials helped emphasize the *Advocate*'s effectiveness as an advertising medium and reinforced the idea that people had a duty to support the local newspaper. Reverend Edward Magruder, pastor of the First AME Zion Church on Williams Avenue, believed in "setting a certain amount aside each month for publication" in order to keep the church's "weekly doings before the people." He told Cannady how much he appreciated the *Advocate*'s help with this and noted, "I feel that through the columns of your paper my church has been greatly benefited." The reverend promised his continued financial support, which no doubt pleased the editor: "In the future I hope to have more publicity, and I assure you that you also will receive more than a mere 'God bless you.'"[150]

Cannady also related an interesting story about the Up-To-Date Cleaners and Tailors on Union Avenue—and a loyal reader in Bermuda—in an article headlined, "Advertising Pays in *The Advocate*." The firm's owners, the Ingersolls, had received a Panama hat to be cleaned and blocked from a reader in "the Bermudas" who had seen their advertisement in the newspaper.[151] It is possible the individual was the Reverend Joseph Miller, whose subscription followed his move from Portland to the islands.[152] But whether Miller or someone else, the reader represented the best of all possible worlds: he subscribed to the newspaper and thus stayed connected to Portland via the imagined community, and he patronized a black-owned business that advertised its services in the *Advocate*. This continuous circle of support was proof positive, in Cannady's eyes, of the *Advocate*'s many vital roles.

Despite support from white-owned firms such as Meier & Frank and the Eastern Outfitting Company, others steadfastly refused to consider advertising in the *Advocate*, or pulled out under pressure. That may have been the case when the Powers Furniture Company, a long-standing Portland business, cancelled its ads in the *Advocate* and Dr. Merriman's *Portland Times* in 1923. By then, the Ku Klux Klan wielded considerable power in the city, which included exerting pressure on businesses to conform to its standards of "pure Americanism."[153] If Cannady had her suspicions, she did not discuss them in the *Advocate*. She did, however, write a front-page article condemning the company. She also wrote "several personal letters to Mr. Powers" to try to discover "just what was the trouble." The letters were turned over to a representative of the furniture store at 3rd Avenue and Yamhill Street. Cannady met with Mr. Gaylor, fully "expecting to be told that weeklies would not be used for the present or some such explanation." She was not prepared to hear that "colored trade" was no longer wanted. "Imagine our surprise, dear reader, when we were told that 'Mr. [Ira] Powers does not care to have the colored trade; is not seeking or soliciting it and does not want it.' When asked the reason,—'COLORED PEOPLE DON'T PAY THEIR BILLS.'"[154]

Cannady wrote that she tried to "conceal" her emotions and "keep [her] composure" in light of this news, yet the article reveals the extent of her disappointment with Powers Furniture, established in 1865 by Ira Powers, Sr., who was known for his "spirit of helpfulness that was [repeatedly] manifest in his relations with individuals and also in association with organized charities and benevolences." Cannady observed that "if Mr. Gaylor had told us that we did not pay our bills (for often we cannot), or some other colored people didn't pay their bills, we might have understood him, but to brand a whole race of people in a given community as undesirable, we believe is not only an insult to the race but is an insult that should be resented." She added that Gaylor had told her the store was doing so well it did not have to bother with "'this class' of trade." However, she pointed out that the store's success had been built, in part, on exactly that clientele: the "poor colored and whites" who had paid "so much down and so much a month" for their furniture.[155]

Cannady gave up on Powers Furniture, but she did not stop writing about the relationship between advertising and "colored patronage." An editorial directed specifically to white advertisers asked: "We wonder how many of you have ever stopped to consider the amount of money colored people spend in your stores, and if you are giving their newspaper its proportion of your advertising?" Then, she observed: "We know business places in the city getting at least 50 per cent of the colored patronage in their line of business, and yet they are too 'stingy' to patronize the colored newspaper, or they simply feel they have a cinch on the business of the race and do not have to consider their organ—the newspaper."[156]

Even though finances were a constant worry, Cannady felt it necessary to upgrade her equipment periodically. In the summer of 1925, she interrupted her vacation in Seaview, Washington, to supervise the installation of a new linotype machine in her office.[157] She was "pleased to announce" that it was in place, and told readers the machine would enable her to provide a more informative newspaper, in part because the ninety-character keyboard made typesetting faster and easier.[158] Cannady was so excited about the improvement, which coincided with the *Advocate*'s twenty-second anniversary, that she invited people to stop by to see it for themselves.[159] One week later, she reminded people: "We have made a large investment in a typesetting machine which will enable us to give our readers a better and more newsy paper, and we need money, and lots of it, to make it go. If you owe *The Advocate* kindly pay, no matter how small the amount."[160] The *Advocate*'s anniversary provided one more opportunity to drive home the importance of financial support. According to the front-page article, "several thousand dollars" had been invested with the goal of making "the paper bigger and better."[161] The Advocate Printing Company had done its part; now it was up to individuals to subscribe, bring their accounts current, and order job printing—programs, letterhead, and the like—to keep the presses running.

The next upgrade also happened to coincide with an anniversary: the *Advocate*'s twenty-eighth in 1931. As before, a front-page article announced the purchase of an Intertype typesetting machine and other equipment for producing a superior newspaper. "We know our readers and supporters will be [as] happy as we are for our success in being able to purchase this equipment in order that we may be better enabled to serve our patrons and to give the public a better newspaper," she wrote.[162] Advertisements in subsequent issues bragged about the newspaper's progress: "Read THE ADVOCATE only Negro newspaper published in the State of Oregon and the only one owning its own plant North of Frisco."[163] She reported receiving "many compliments on [the *Advocate*'s] appearance," most notably from the Reverend J. Gordon McPherson, who praised Cannady for the "wonderful improvement … made on the old journal both mechanically and the general display of news matter."[164] And W. J. Wheaton, who wrote for the *San Francisco Spokesman*, the *California Eagle*, and occasionally the *Advocate*, noted, "Congratulations on the improvement, in the mechanical appearance, of *The Advocate*. Glad to see that it is keeping up the literary standard and the NEWS of racial interest."[165] But upgrades were not limited to the newspaper's appearance. Cannady also spruced up the office with "newly decorated walls in 'jazz' finish, new linoleum," and "harmonizing draperies in the paisley pattern."[166]

Cannady had high hopes that she would recoup the money she had spent on improvements by taking on additional job printing, which included event tickets, business cards, and fliers.[167] Not only was the extra work an important source of income, but it also represented an opportunity for individuals, churches, and clubs to support a black-owned business. And, as Cannady pointed out frequently, individuals who used her company for their printing needs were helping to ensure their journal's longevity in the community. She reminded readers how important this was: "The Negro press is the only dependable champion of the Negro's rights—if the Negro paper stops, the very backbone of the race is threatened. … Pay up your subscriptions! Give the press your job printing—bring in some advertising—and support your paper as it supports you!"[168]

It is unclear whether the Cannadys had their own press prior to 1924. But that year, an article acknowledged the many individuals and businesses to give the company job printing since the installation of its equipment that March. Eighty individuals—some from as far away as Seattle and Berkeley, California—as well as businesses, churches, and fraternal organizations were listed as having ordered printing during the previous six weeks.[169] Advertisements continually reminded subscribers that The Advocate Printing Company was able to do a wide variety of "artistic job printing" on its own press, especially for holidays and special occasions.[170] People could order "beautiful personal Mother's Day cards for 25¢ and 50¢ each," for example, or "individual, distinctive Christmas Cards."[171]

Cannady printed numerous testimonials for this work in the *Advocate*, including one from her "good friend Overton," owner of the Overton Transfer Company. When he called for his work one day, he reportedly said, "'I believe this is a better job than I had before; I am more than pleased with the work and the price, and I shall tell everyone I see that when they want good job printing to go to The Advocate Printing Company.'"[172] Cannady acknowledged other loyal customers, too, such as James H. Reed, owner of Bird Legs Poultry Farm, who placed a "fine order of printing" and renewed his two-year subscription—"which he says he cannot do without"—at the same time.[173] William and Edna Gildon, who moved across the border to Kelso, Washington, were thanked for their business, too.[174] The former Oregonians may have ordered stationery for the Longview NAACP Branch that Cannady helped to organize in September 1925.[175]

She could not overlook the value of white support, however. "We wish to take this method of thanking our friends—both white and colored—for the large amount of job printing brought to our shop recently." She boasted in 1929 that "thousands of runs for large white business concerns and several large runs for colored organizations" were listed in her books, and added, "We certainly do appreciate your patronage and we will do our best to give your orders prompt attention, and our best effort."[176] All job printing—whether small or large orders—helped the bottom line, as long as the debt could be collected. As with subscriptions and advertising, payment was not always forthcoming and Cannady was forced to turn to notices in the *Advocate* to convince clients to pay promptly: "We are not complaining—we're explaining and we know you will appreciate same. We ... want to do all we can to please. So let's cooperate."[177]

Cooperation often was framed in terms of "fair play" or "reciprocity," concepts that underscored Cannady's frustration with delinquent subscribers and printing customers, as well as her impatience with people whom she called "parasites"—individuals who borrowed the *Advocate* instead of purchasing it for a nickel at a local distribution point or expected Cannady to publish "their social doings" but did not subscribe.[178] She reminded readers the *Advocate* was there "to serve the public; it is the only colored newspaper in the state; it is an independent newspaper devoted to the interest of the people."[179] In turn, though, the editor expected readers to support the *Advocate*:

> We just wonder if it would not be fair for those organizations who wish us to give publicity to their efforts through the columns of The Advocate to give us their job printing? We know of some ... organizations and clubs who use our columns for gratis publicity, yet when they have a window card, a ticket or letter heads and the like, for which they have to pay out money, they take that to the white job printer who will not patronize his affair, and who will certainly not give it any publicity through the newspaper press. Think on this matter, readers, and see if you are guilty of this practice. Is it fair?[180]

Choosing a white-owned business over The Advocate Printing Company was an affront to the race. The decision also affected the *Advocate*'s bottom line and jeopardized its weekly appearance, which became even more critical once the Ku Klux Klan moved into the state and black Oregonians needed a voice to "champion [their] cause" and call attention to escalating mob violence and segregation.[181]

Despite complicated rules for second-class mailings and postage rates ranging from one to ten cents, many editors made it a practice to exchange papers with their colleagues to stay informed about the Klan's activities and other issues affecting black Americans.[182] Cannady sent copies of the *Advocate* to Charlotta and Joseph Bass, publishers of the *California Eagle*; John Lincoln Derrick, publisher of the *Western Outlook*; Robert Vann, the influential publisher of the *Pittsburgh Courier*; and reportedly two hundred and fifty other editors across the country.[183] The journalists frequently carried on lively conversations with one another through their publications, commenting on editorials, noting which newspapers had folded, and recognizing new additions to the informal exchange network.[184]

In 1923, Cannady extended "a hand of welcome and congratulations to the *Arkansas Survey*," a weekly published in Little Rock that was "very interesting and creditable ... to the race."[185] Two years later, she told readers that the first issue of *Reflexus*, a new magazine with the motto, "Of colored people, by colored people and for colored people," had arrived. Like the *Advocate*, annual subscriptions were $2.50; she felt the publication was "worth every bit of it."[186] The *Chicago Bee* was the next paper to cross her desk. "It is a twelve-page journal, well edited and brimful of newsy news. *The Advocate* is glad to place it on the exchange list."[187] Other editors made sure they continued to receive the *Advocate*. The Reverend W. W. Matthews, the Philadelphia editor of the *Missionary Seer*, wrote, "We regard *The Advocate* as one among the exchanges that we prize very highly, and trust you will continue it on our list."[188] This was quite a compliment, because the *Seer* was "issued by" the AME Zion Publication House.[189] Matthews subsequently wrote: "I have been making a study of your methods in secular journalism, especially as it relates to racial issues, ... and I have noted that not only are you progressive as to your methods of approach, but that you are also intensely aggressive. ... I have decided to keep a closer observance hereafter on the editorial columns of *The Advocate*."[190]

The average lifespan of a black newspaper was only nine years, so editors who beat the odds were justifiably proud.[191] Anniversary issues provided opportunities for editors to celebrate milestones and recognize service to the race. Cannady congratulated the *Western Outlook* for "fighting for the right and condemning the wrong" for thirty years. She observed that the *Outlook*, like most of the journals published by Negroes, had "had a mighty hard struggle to weather the storm of oppression, of opposition and adversity, from within the ranks of the race as well as without."[192] In 1924, Cannady commended the *Philadelphia Tribune* and its special fortieth-anniversary edition, which she called "unequaled in Race journalism for illustrations, up-to-date news, size, and general makeup."[193] Another paper celebrating its fortieth anniversary was the Cleveland, Ohio, *Gazette*, whose editor, Harry Smith, was an outspoken critic of the film *The Birth of a Nation*. "We extend our most hearty congratulations ...," wrote Cannady, "knowing as we do that the average race newspaper's life is of a few years' duration and full of hardships, trials and tribulations."[194]

Meanwhile, editors across the country were commenting on the *Advocate*'s success.[195] Derrick told *Outlook* readers that the newspaper, which turned twelve in 1915, should be congratulated for its "past success" and service "to Portland and the race."[196] On the *Advocate*'s twentieth anniversary, Derrick wrote that the paper deserved praise for navigating the "rocks and shoals in the journalistic sea" for two decades.[197] Another editor praised the "whopping" ten-page issue that was published to commemorate that anniversary, and Harry Smith called it "a special and well illustrated edition" that was both "interesting" and "very creditable."[198] Five years later, the *Broad Ax* commended the *Advocate* for its faithful service to "the reading public of Portland and other nearby cities."[199]

From 1903 until 1936, thousands of people relied on the weekly newspaper for articles and editorials about segregation, lynching, employment opportunities, the NAACP, and other issues. "The paper was very instrumental in keeping the black community informed, indeed so," Otto Rutherford recalled nearly four decades after the final issue hit the streets.[200] People also read the *Advocate*'s seven packed columns for birth and death announcements, society and church news, information about the people who worked at the Portland Hotel, and general "good news about 'the race.'"[201] One June, for example, Cannady reported that Louise Russell Lewis, William Duncan Allen, Jr., whose father founded the Golden West Hotel in about 1903, and Rutherford's cousin, Octavia Rutherford, were "the only colored members" of the graduating class of two hundred and fifty at Portland's Jefferson High School. This news was important, but Cannady also reported that Rutherford wrote the words to the class song, "which was said to be the prettiest the class has ever had," and Allen composed and performed the music.[202] Years later, after a "full career as a musician, a concert pianist, and one of the most renowned accompanists" of the twentieth century, he recalled how thrilling it was to play the pipe organ while members of the predominantly white graduating class sang his original composition.[203] By capturing events that are so central to the fabric of life, the *Advocate* promoted racial uplift and fostered a *real* community based on common interests, needs, desires, and culture.

CHAPTER THREE

The Best Talent

The pulse of the Negro Race in Portland beats in harmony with The Advocate, *and its program.*

— "Representative," the *Advocate*, April 12, 1930, 2

A few weeks before the noted tenor Roland Hayes performed in Portland in 1919, the *Telegram* noted: "With the firm purpose of establishing generally a bigger demand by her own people for classical works and to create a better relation between the two races, Mrs. E. D. Cannady has been untiring ... in her efforts to present to Portland audiences the best talent of the colored race."[1] In particular, she "believed that it was necessary to present" gifted singers, poets, musicians, politicians, and speakers to Portlanders in order "to offset the unjust propaganda disseminated ... by the newspaper press of the country" and counteract "front-page stories of Negro crime."[2]

Cannady "was one of the very first to call attention to the talent of" Roland Hayes—typically described by the white press as "the negro tenor"—who enjoyed a successful career in Europe as well as the United States. But she recalled that she had to persuade Mayor George Baker, former Senator Robert M. Stanfield, and others to attend his first concert in 1918. "I had the dickens of a time trying to convince people ... that [he] was a great singer," she told a *Journal* reporter. She ended up closing her office so she could go "from individual to individual" to tell them about the "great discovery" she had made. About a thousand "white and colored people" ultimately attended the concert at the Masonic Temple and Auditorium on Yamhill Street.[3] After all of the bills were paid, Cannady cleared $150—about $2,200 today—just enough to pay Hayes, his accompanist, and their expenses. "I thought then, what a shame that such a beautiful voice couldn't command a larger fee," she said.[4] But after he performed for King George at Buckingham Palace in 1923, "then Portland believed" the tenor was "great."[5]

Hayes was scheduled to return to Portland in March 1925 as part of the Elwyn Artist Series, which featured the "most talked-of artists of the day." Cannady began advertising the concert months in advance; she assured people that ticket prices were "popular and well within reach of the most modest purse," but urged them not to delay because the

Beatrice Cannady, second from right, dreamed of being an opera singer when she was young. Music remained an important part of her life and she incorporated performances into her interracial teas.

event was sure to sell out.[6] Three days before his concert, the *Advocate* featured a front-page story about the tenor and a striking two-column photograph of Hayes. Cannady wrote that the "secret" to his success was his "wonderful spirituality." He had managed to keep "his hand in the hand of the Great Conductor of the Universe" and still remember his Georgian roots, despite fame and wealth. She also praised his ability to sing away "the prejudices of a lifetime against his race" and instill "a practical interpretation of the Brotherhood of Man" in his audiences.[7]

She had another opportunity to promote Hayes in 1931, when he began the "season's tour in the Northwest" rather than in the East, as she had previously reported.[8] As the October date drew nearer, she observed that many "in music circles" were looking forward to the concert by the "world renowned tenor."[9] She published a short editorial as well as a brief review following the Saturday-night event. "I thought Mr. Hayes' concert the loveliest he has ever given here with the possible exception of the two or three times which I had the pleasure of presenting him before he became renowned," she wrote in her review. "At the close of the program the audience lingered for a good many minutes in an effort to induce the singer to sing just one more number."[10] She praised his performance in her editorial, too, and then noted that he continued "to be the same fine, unspoiled, lovable personage he was before he ever crossed the ocean."[11] Hayes spent the following day with Cannady and was her special guest at a dinner party for seventeen at her home; her sons were there, as were George Orr Latimer; her sister and brother-in-law Cora and Elbert Jamison; her sister-in-law Catherine Franklin; and Levi McGruder, a "prominent musician of Seattle" who considered it a "rare privilege" to meet the singer.[12] Afterward, Cannady hosted an informal reception for fifty additional guests, "both colored and white, to meet the distinguished visitor" before he left for engagements in San Francisco.[13]

Cannady probably discussed the singer's accomplishments with Reed College students during a noontime musical program in March 1924. She talked about "The Composers of the Race," then introduced "noted London baritone" John Payne and his accompanist, Lawrence Brown, who typically toured with Hayes. The men performed a number of pieces by some of the people she had just discussed. "It was evident that the program was highly enjoyed," Cannady wrote, "for the audience as one person applauded vociferously and long (it is not customary for the students to applaud in Chapel service) and encores were responded to." The program continued in the college's dining room, where students asked Payne to sing three more songs. Later that night, twenty-five Reed students, at Cannady's request, attended the performers' concert at Bethel AME Church.[14]

Another notable individual was J. Rosamond Johnson, who performed numerous times in Portland.[15] Following a three-day engagement at the Heilig Theatre in 1923, Cannady wrote that he was doing his "share in lifting the race's status," and lauded him for introducing a "woman into his act who" was neither "the black mammy, nor the pickaninny type, but a real clever little singer and dancer who wears bobbed hair and pretty gowns." Cannady predicted this would make it "easier for other colored girls to get into high-class vaudeville." During his visit, she hosted "a delightful party" for him and about thirty other guests at her Irvington-neighborhood home. Johnson sang "a group of his own compositions" and played the piano while she sang *Three Questions*, a ballad co-written by Johnson and his brother, James Weldon Johnson. Apparently there were no formal remarks at the gathering; Cannady described her houseguest as "active and buoyant," yet just as reluctant "to talk of himself and his work as ever."[16]

Johnson returned to Portland in April 1927 for a "Program of Negro Spirituals" presented by Cannady. A three-column advertisement in the *Advocate* featured a photograph of the composer seated at a piano; leaning on it was his accompanist, Taylor Gordon, whose voice—according to *Time*—was "like molasses and a clear bell."[17] Proceeds from the Monday-night concert went to Cannady to help defray expenses associated with her upcoming trip to the East Coast for the Fourth Pan-African Congress.[18] She also hosted a "most delightful" interracial afternoon tea for the performers and about one hundred other guests at her home.[19]

Cannady was able to share the Johnson brothers' talents with white clubwomen in central Oregon, too. Aileen Davidson had heard Cannady sing "a very beautiful solo" some years earlier at a "music week" concert, so that may be why she turned to Cannady for help with an upcoming program. Davidson had tried to check out Alain Locke's newest book, *The New Negro*, from her library in Prineville, but it had no copies. A search of other collections, including the Oregon State Library in Salem, was equally disappointing. "The library sent me a lot of stuff that is old," Davidson wrote; "We want something up to date in regard to the subject." So she asked Cannady if she could borrow a copy. Failing that, Davidson asked about a number of other possibilities, including books by the poet Countee Cullen, current copies of *Opportunity* with prize-winning "stories written by Negroes," or spirituals "by colored composers" that "could be used for solo soprano voice."[20]

Cannady was "very happy to know that women of broad vision [were] seriously seeking the truth regarding" Negroes. She sent everything Davidson requested, and much more:

> I am mailing under separate cover several copies of 'Opportunity,' a magazine of Negro life; several copies of 'The Crisis,' the most widely read Negro magazine; 'The Weary Blues,' by Langston Hughes; [*The Book of American Negro Poetry*] by James Weldon Johnson; and 'The New Negro,' by Alain Locke, together with a collection of Negro Spirituelles in solo arrangement for soprano—all arranged by Negroes. There is also a copy of a collection of Negro Spirituelles in book form, by two brothers, James W. and J. Rosamond Johnson.[21]

James Weldon Johnson, her colleague at the NAACP, composed *Lift Every Voice and Sing*—the Negro National Anthem—with his brother.[22] They also collaborated in 1925 on *The Book of American Negro Spirituals*. The *New York Times* observed that the collection offered "a deeper insight into the psychology of a race which has remained essentially alien, even to the Southerners who have known it best."[23] Cannady shared this book—or perhaps the second volume published in 1926—with Davidson, but asked her to return everything once it had "served the purpose" because she had "numerous [requests] similar to the one from" Davidson.[24] A couple of months later, Davidson carefully packed everything except *The New Negro*, which the club planned to study more extensively, and returned the materials with a note expressing her deepest appreciation.[25] Cannady was happy to have the "opportunity of service," and told Davidson she would be "delighted" to help again.[26] The clubwoman took her up on her offer in 1930. This time, she was seeking a list of spirituals sung in *The Green Pastures* because a member was planning to "give a review" of the Pulitzer Prize-winning play.[27] Cannady may have sent Davidson the following titles: *When the Saints Come Marching In*; *Hallelujah*; *A City Called Heaven*; and *Go Down Moses*.

The Green Pastures, suggested by Roark H. Bradford's book, *Ol' Man Adam an' His Chillun*, opened at New York City's Mansfield Theatre in February 1930.[28] Black actors reenacted stories of the Old Testament, including Adam and Eve and Noah and the flood, but with a twist: "De Lawd," played by Richard B. Harrison, wore a white suit and tie, smoked cigars and hosted fish frys, and ran Heaven with Gabriel's help; Adam wore farmer's clothes and Eve was dressed in gingham; and Babylon was depicted as a New Orleans jazz club.[29] The play was a hit among white theatergoers and reviewers alike.[30] Finally, after eighteen months and six hundred and forty performances, *The Green Pastures* closed in New York City and the cast and crew prepared for another opening night, this time at the Illinois Theatre in Chicago.[31] It would be another seven months before the "Green Pastures Special train" pulled into Portland's Union Depot.[32]

Cannady observed that the five-day run "created an unusual opportunity ... to extend a fine courtesy to the distinguished visiting members of the Company."[33] Because Portland's white-owned hotels refused to rent rooms to black guests—and the black-owned Medley Hotel could not accommodate everyone—it was imperative that people open their homes to visitors. Readers were encouraged to contact the general stage manager in Seattle and advise him of the number of available rooms, their "character," rate, and distance from downtown. Or, if people preferred, they could write or call the *Advocate* office to list their rooms: "DO IT NOW! GARFIELD 7523."[34]

The following week, Cannady wrote that Portland citizens seldom had the opportunity to entertain "such a distinguished group of stage people"; she hoped they would be as happy to be in the city as Portlanders were to have them visit. To quell any fears people might have had about hosting show people, she observed, "They are fine, intelligent, deeply religious people who go about their work in a serious manner." To illustrate her point, she told readers the thirty-six-voice "Heavenly Choir" had left the KGW studio so quietly after its half-hour performance, it was difficult to believe the singers "were ordinary flesh and blood."[35] Portlanders must have been convinced: Cannady reported she had "received many calls from readers" interested in listing their rooms.[36]

A large advertisement in the *Advocate* called *The Green Pastures* "The Show of Shows!" Matinee tickets ranged from $1 for balcony seats to $2.50 for seats on the floor of Civic Auditorium; evening shows were more expensive, with the best seats costing $3—about $50 today.[37] Cannady treated her sister-in-law, Catherine Franklin, and Rosalie Bird-Holmes, the paper's society editor, to a Tuesday-night performance.[38] She also hosted a dinner for Richard Harrison, who had been awarded the NAACP's prestigious Spingarn Medal on stage in New York in March 1931, George Randol, who played "King Pharaoh," and Nell Hunter, the Heavenly Choir's "leading soprano," at her home on closing night. Afterward, twenty-five guests joined the "distinguished group" for "an informal interracial reception." Hunter "favored the guests with a song" and Harrison "gave a brief farewell talk in which he thanked all the citizens of Portland on their hospitality." Before leaving for Union Depot with the Unthanks, Harrison gave Cannady an autographed photograph.[39]

The five-day run of *The Green Pastures* had just closed when Cannady boasted in the *Advocate*: "Portland colored citizens have just reason to feel exceptionally proud of the fact that in recent months many notables of the race have visited our city." She reviewed the visits by Harrison and Bill Robinson, the "internationally known comedian and king of tap-dancing," and looked forward to the arrival of Langston Hughes, the "famous young Negro poet, author and lecturer."[40] A two-column advertisement on another page promoted his event at Bethel AME Church, where admission was fifty cents for adults and thirty-five cents for students like George Cannady, who drove up from Salem for the special evening.[41]

Immediately following the reading, Cannady penned a hasty review for the next day's issue of the *Advocate*.[42] "For a long time, I have cherished the poems of Langston Hughes, the versatile, brave and daring young writer," she wrote in the lead paragraph. "In church, school, college and over the radio I have read from" *The Weary Blues*, his first collection of poetry and "one of the most valuable books" in her library. As a result, she told readers, she had received letters from people "all along the [Pacific] coast" asking about the poems and their author. Cannady was thrilled to finally meet the "young, good-looking, vivacious" man, and observed that her "admiration for him and his work was not marred in the least but greatly enhanced" as a result of hearing the "interesting and entertaining ... speaker."[43] During the evening, Hughes mixed stories of his travels around the world with personal anecdotes. He had lived in Paris and Toluca, Mexico; sailed on a freighter to Africa and visited Senegal, the Congo, Nigeria, the Gold Coast, and other countries; traveled to Haiti; toured the southern United States under the auspices of the Rosenwald Foundation; and talked with some of the nine Scottsboro Boys who were on death row in Kilby Prison in Montgomery, Alabama.[44] Each encounter, in its own way, informed his body of work. But Hughes told the audience that he considered his sojourn in Africa in 1923 to be "the dream trip" of his life, in part because it caused him to identify and embrace his identity as an "American Negro." Cannady called the lecture "an autobiographical word-picture of his life [that] was punctuated with poems illustrative of how his experiences reflected in his poetry."[45]

Hughes read one of Cannady's favorites, "The Negro Speaks of Rivers," a powerful piece first published in the *Crisis* in 1921 that begins:

> I've known rivers:
> I've known rivers ancient as the world and older than the
>   flow of human blood in human veins.

Hughes also recited "I, Too," a poem that gave Cannady the strength to endure discrimination while traveling on a train through the South in 1927. She concluded her review with the following observation: "His nomadic nature; his unafraid attitude towards life; his willingness to work; his desire to investigate and experience for himself; his disregard for conventions in writing; his sense of values and his keen intellect and personality are rich possessions which will indeed carry him to unscaled heights in the realm of modern poetry."[46]

A number of politicians and activists passed through Portland in the early 1900s, too. Illinois Congressman Oscar De Priest visited in 1929. A front-page article in the *Advocate* announced his lecture on Monday, September 23rd, at Lincoln High School—an event that Cannady promised would "be of unusual interest to white and colored alike."[47] The *Morning Oregonian* reported that "800 negroes" turned out to hear his ninety-minute discussion of "race prejudice, discriminatory measures adopted in some southern states against the negro, ... and failure of the country to enforce the 14th amendment."[48] Cannady wrote a long article about his talk, too, which she said "held the undivided interest of his audience to the last." One point that resonated with her was his criticism of the federal government. "The government is spending millions to enforce the 18th amendment," De Priest told the packed auditorium. "Isn't it right to spend a few millions to enforce the Fourteenth? One says a man shall not drink and the other says he shall vote. I would rather spend a million to enforce the Fourteenth Amendment than 14 to enforce the Eighteenth!"[49] Cannady also frequently called attention to the absence of equal rights and urged the government to take action to stop atrocities committed against its black citizens in order to preserve peace in the country. She censured President Herbert Hoover, for example, for spending "millions of dollars for the suppression of the liquor traffic, but hardly a cent to enforce the law granting civil and political rights to 15,000,000 of her people."[50] De Priest told the audience that "the ballot is the only weapon the black man has," so enforcement of the amendments was crucial to equality.[51] Cannady called him "a conservative, plain speaking, well-informed gentleman" who demanded the "rights guaranteed him under the Constitution of the United States."[52] The congressman was so pleased with the "very graphic report" she wrote for the *Advocate*, as well as her editorial, that his secretary asked her to send six more copies of the issue to his Washington, D.C., office.[53]

Portlanders had another opportunity to hear Congressman De Priest on October 1, 1932; he was in the city to stump for President Herbert Hoover, who was running against challenger Franklin D. Roosevelt.[54] De Priest had his work cut out for him: Cannady observed that "Negroes all over the country [were] dissatisfied with the present administration" and its handling of the worsening Depression.[55] Roosevelt himself had just "won many over to his ranks" when he spoke at City Auditorium at the end of September.[56] Cannady urged readers to think carefully about the candidates before voting on November 8th. "The political party that should command the support of the colored voters is the party that is willing to meet the Negro question squarely, boldly and courageously" and advocate "sane treatment of our problems—equal political, economic and social rights," she wrote shortly before the election.[57] People apparently were ready for change—in Portland and across the United States—because Roosevelt defeated Hoover by seven million votes.[58] Cannady wrote, "The American people have shown by their vote that they want a new deal in politics," referring to FDR's ambitious plan to stimulate the economy and "provide relief, recovery, and reform."[59]

Labor organizer and editor A. Philip Randolph visited Portland in July 1932 as part of a cross-country trip that included stops in Missouri, Colorado, Utah, Washington, and California.[60] Cannady was one of the individuals on the program to welcome "the distinguished guest" to Mount Olivet Baptist Church, where he delivered "a masterful address" on "The Negro in the Economic Crisis." He discussed the Depression—"its scope, causes and remedy"—and reiterated the need for black men to "organize and pool [their] power." He also described some of the strategies the Pullman Palace Car Company used to keep its railroad employees "in a happy-go-lucky frame of mind" in an effort to divert their attention from the "real issues": low wages, long hours, little time off. Randolph "elicited laughter" when he said "the Pullman porter [was] three years behind in his sleep," but the men responsible for ensuring that passengers had a comfortable trip knew it was no joke.[61] Employees, who numbered more than twenty thousand by the 1920s, "were required to work 400 hours per month or 11,000 miles—whichever occurred first, to receive full pay."[62] Inequities such as these had prompted men to fight for recognition of the Brotherhood of Sleeping Car Porters and make "the utmost sacrifices for the cause," he told the "large and appreciative audience."[63] An *Advocate* editorial added a postscript to the activist's visit: "He is intelligent, learned, self-sacrificing, fearless and courageous and under such a leadership, the cause he represents cannot fail. The race needs more men like Randolph with guts and back-bone to represent it before the eyes of the world."[64]

Field Secretary William Pickens and other NAACP officials stopped in Portland, too. Pickens was in the middle of a western tour in 1926 when he received the Branch's itinerary for his six-day Oregon stay, which included sixteen talks.[65] Already tired from his trip, Pickens asked President Lee C. Anderson to eliminate six of the scheduled talks.[66] Nevertheless, Cannady wrote Pickens to see if he could "give more time to Portland" than he planned because she had "had more than a dozen requests from various groups and organizations" desiring to meet with him.[67] She ensured that his visit was well publicized: she covered several of his engagements, which included talks to the Portland Branch and to students at Willamette University and Reed College. Cannady noted that he "was in excellent form" at the Branch meeting, "his speech abounding in wit, humor and eloquent periods which by turns entertained and thrilled his audience."[68] The following week, Cannady alluded to Pickens' visit when she observed that Portland had "been wonderfully blest ... by the presence of a number of notable educators [and] lecturers" who had "made a marvelous and lasting impression for good upon the people who had the pleasure of contacting them."[69]

Pickens visited the Northwest again in the spring of 1928, shortly before heading to Los Angeles, where he and Cannady were scheduled to attend the NAACP's annual conference. She reported that he addressed Lincoln High School students in the morning and spoke at a Branch meeting in the evening; in between, Pickens spoke to the City Club in the Benson Hotel's Crystal Room. Cannady, Reverend John F. Moreland, Dr. Elbert Booker, and Lee Anderson accompanied Pickens there. The club's secretary invited Cannady—billing herself as the NAACP's Northwest organizer—to introduce Pickens, who discussed "the Negro problem."[70]

Two years later, an *Advocate* headline proclaimed: "Pickens Triumphs! Crowds Pack Bethel to Hear Famous Orator."[71] Cannady reported that more than seven hundred people had squeezed into Bethel AME Church to hear the "educator, author, [and] philosopher" speak.[72] She described the event as "an interesting picture—the myriad of white and black faces intermingled in one congenial body to listen to the noted orator deliver his famous address, 'Abraham Lincoln, Man and Statesman.'" In the "cosmopolitan audience" were "professional men and women of both races" as well as students and faculty from Portland-area schools, Reed College, the University of Oregon, and Pacific College. Pickens "held his audience spell-bound" for nearly ninety minutes "by his masterful delivery and eloquent utterances." As usual, this event was just one of many scheduled during his Portland visit. Cannady listed two engagements at Reed College, the second "in response to a special petition circulated and presented by the student body," as well as an address at Pacific College—now known as George Fox University—and one before the City Club "on the subject 'Can the Race Problem be Solved?'"[73]

His social calendar was filled as well. He dined with Cannady's sister and brother-in-law, Elbert and Cora Jamison, at their home on Garfield Avenue.[74] Dr. Booker and his wife, Maude, invited Pickens to their home on Williams Court for dinner the following night. Afterward, they took him for a drive to see some of Portland's sights, including the "famous Grotto," a Catholic shrine and botanical garden in northeastern Portland.[75] Pickens had dinner at Chin's China Tea Garden with Cannady and other members of the Esperanto club on Saturday. He and Cannady then spent a "delightful evening" at a party with two Chinese students who were attending Reed College, the Reverend Daniel G. Hill, Jr., and his wife, and the Reverend Walter Lovell and his wife.[76] Festivities may have included a toast to Hill, who had earned a bachelor's degree from the University of Oregon School of Applied Social Science.[77]

Cannady promoted a unique cultural event in May 1929. She announced in the *Advocate* that she was selling seats for a "special midnight matinee performance of the sensational all-talking, singing and dancing motion picture production" *Hearts in Dixie*. But that was not all: a "seven-act stage show" was planned for the evening at the Rivoli, too. Local performers included Gwendolyn Hooker, who was scheduled to do "dialect readings," and Maudie Booker, Dr. Booker's ten-year-old daughter, who was going to do a dance routine with a group of "sensational child steppers."[78] Cannady described *Hearts in Dixie* as "the first authentic story of the real Negro that has come to the stage or screen."[79] One scholar notes that the film, which launched Stepin Fetchit's career, "is seldom mentioned today, save by those who know only of its cloying title and of the notorious presence of" the Hollywood star.[80] Cannady overlooked Fetchit's performance; instead, she focused on the fact that the entire cast was black, with the exception of the "comparatively minor role of a white doctor" played by Richard Carlyle. Given that "the most prominent black figures viewed by whites" heretofore had been "servants and entertainers and the unctuous shoeshine boys and hustlers," *Hearts in Dixie* was considered by many—including Cannady—as a positive move by the motion picture industry.[81] Her endorsement of the movie also may have been influenced by the fact that music was such an important part of her life as well as an integral component of her interracial teas. She described the musical numbers, which ranged from "songs of the Old South" to "immortal spirituals," and noted the appearance of A. C. Bilbrew's choir, the first black "chorus used in Hollywood in talking pictures."[82] Some of those singers had been trained by Portlander Freita Shaw, "the first woman to lead an otherwise all-male group on the steamship *H. F. Alexander*, a Pacific Coast cruise liner" that Ivan Cannady worked on as a busboy in 1933.[83]

Many individuals passed through Portland once they had achieved some measure of success. Others, like Shirley Graham McCanns, got their start in Portland.[84] She and Cannady apparently hit it off, perhaps because they had a mutual love of music and books, shared an interest in activism, and had been turned away from a swimming pool because of their skin color.[85] In October 1926, the women held a program at the First Congregational Church; Cannady gave an illustrated talk on the "progress of the colored race since emancipation" and McCanns sang Negro spirituals.[86] Three months later, they drove south to Salem to attend legislative sessions. They interviewed "several members of both houses" about "proposed legislation," called on Secretary of State Sam Kozer, and interviewed the new governor, Isaac Patterson, about the possibility of jobs for black Oregonians. Cannady reported that Patterson told them: "'I believe that the people of Oregon think that the only function of this office is to distribute patronage,' and added 'I wish I had nothing to give or something for every one.'" She may have pressed him on this issue, but wrote, diplomatically: "The Governor is a very busy man with many people from all parts of the state awaiting a turn to see him; with numerous committee meetings demanding his presence and with a thousand other duties incidental to his high office."[87]

McCanns, director of the choir at Mount Olivet Baptist Church, spoke at the YWCA in April 1927 about "the important role [of] Negro music ... in the development of mankind"—a theme much like the one Cannady had discussed with Reed College students. McCanns "interspersed her graphic talk with several Negro songs," noted the *Advocate*, including J. Rosamond Johnson's *Since You Went Away*. Maude Booker accompanied her on the piano; both women were presented with flowers at the end of the program for their "splendid contributions to the success" of the musical club's meeting.[88]

McCanns ultimately had a long and successful career, beginning with the opera *Tom-Tom*, "the first Negro opera ever staged and performed by an all-Negro cast" and the first opera by a black woman to be produced.[89] After its debut in Cleveland in July 1932, Cannady wrote, "Shirley has accomplished her life's big dream. She could not fail for she is made of the stuff that spells success." The editor was "proud of the fact that she" had given McCanns a "lift" and "encouraged her when she needed it," and hoped to be able to see *Tom-Tom* and "personally congratulate" her friend.[90]

Headlines in the *Advocate* during the previous summer had been much more grim. The August 15, 1931, issue, for example, reflected the escalating violence across the United States: "Negro Worker Lynched"; "Cops Murder Victims of Unemployed"; "Sixteen Yr. Older Lynched."[91] *Time* reported that "black and white blood was plentifully spilled" across the country that week.[92] In fact, brutality had increased so much by the middle of 1930 that the Commission on Interracial Cooperation, founded in Atlanta a decade earlier, launched "a thorough study of the lynching phenomenon." Overall, the numbers were staggering: at least 3,724 people had been lynched between 1889—the year Cannady was born—and the end of 1930.[93]

Cannady kept readers updated on the Commission and its findings, and continued to run stories about lynching, unemployment, the Scottsboro

Boys, and other issues affecting Negroes locally and nationally.[94] But she needed to offer local subscribers some respite, too, from the challenges facing them on a daily basis. So on August 15, 1931, Cannady also reported that Elmer C. Bartlett, the organist for the First AME Church in Los Angeles, was in Portland to organize a concert featuring "music of the Negro race." The Reverend Daniel Hill had been corresponding with Bartlett "for more than a year with the view of forming such a chorus," so it was exciting to have the musician in town for the summer.[95] It was an honor as well: the journalist Delilah L. Beasley, who included a brief sketch about Bartlett in her book, *The Negro Trail Blazers of California*, called him "the best pipe organist of the Negro race."[96] Cannady wrote that fifty people already had begun rehearsing for the September 14th event; Bartlett hoped for even more "voices to sing the story of Negro music."[97]

Two days before the concert, which had swelled to two hundred participants, the *Advocate* published Bartlett's photograph and an advertisement promoting the event at Civic Auditorium—now known as Keller Auditorium—at Clay and 3rd.[98] The *Oregonian*'s music columnist wrote that "Portland's newest singing asset ... gave pleasure to a highly appreciative audience" that asked for numerous encores. The chorus had "a swing, a deep, strong sense of rhythm, a spontaneity and a deep choral volume."[99]

Bartlett apparently was so taken with Portland that he decided to remain. He began advertising instruction in piano, harmony, voice, and pipe organ for students of all levels at his place of business at 874 Union Avenue North.[100] By July 1932, his students were ready to give a recital at Bethel AME Church; a front-page article in the *Advocate* noted that the program promised "to be a most interesting one," in part because many original compositions by "members of the Negro race" were going to be performed for the first time in Portland.[101] A large audience turned out—and probably many proud parents—and "greeted each participant" with "liberal applause."[102]

Bartlett also directed the Bethel choir at a number of events, including a fall concert in Newberg, Oregon.[103] In addition, the group performed "Negro Spirituals" during KWJJ's Jubilee Hour one Sunday night in 1932. Cannady wrote that the "music was beautiful and ... well nigh perfectly rendered," and noted that Bartlett was "due loads of praise for he [had] worked wonders with this aggregation of musicians."[104] That summer he directed the Portland Negro Chorus, composed of the Bethel choir and other singers, in a series of concerts dubbed "Spirituals Under the Stars." Many "prominent colored and white people were noted in the large audience" at the first concert at Multnomah Civic Stadium—now called

PGE Park—and Bartlett and Reverend Hill were hopeful that the event would become an annual offering.[105]

Mayor George L. Baker wrote in 1929: "On numerous occasions [Mrs. Cannady] has invited me to welcome to our city distinguished men and women of color whom she has presented to the public in our city and I have always appreciated the honor it afforded me. Her audiences are usually composed of both white and colored people."[106] Portland's black population may have been small, but that did not deter luminaries like Langston Hughes, Oscar De Priest, or Roland Hayes from visiting in the 1920s and 1930s. Many of the events were covered in the white press; the complimentary articles reinforced Cannady's efforts to dispel negative portrayals of black people. The concerts, poetry readings, lectures, and other affairs were critical, too, for race pride, and enabled Cannady to boost Portland as a progressive place to live during the early 1900s.

CHAPTER FOUR

Building a Community

If at any time you are inclined to be the least skeptical about this city's continued growth, hop right into an automobile and drive around the town. You will be agreeably surprised to find that Portland is growing steadily and rapidly. … Keep an eye on Portland and watch it continue to grow.

— "Portland Is Growing," the *Advocate*, August 27, 1932, 2[1]

Cannady was adamant about the need to promote Portland as a vibrant, livable place, so she continually reminded people of their duty to their city and its black citizens. "When a fellow boosts his own town he does not stop there; he is performing an act that improves his own condition," Cannady proclaimed in 1929. "Think it over and then join the Boosters Club."[2] She had no patience for individuals at the other extreme, those who seemed to "have a grudge against the city" where they lived and worked. She called them "laggards," "knockers," and "hammer throwers," and likened knocking to "a disease to be dreaded" because it infected citizens and spread throughout the city, hindering progress and discouraging newcomers.[3] It also affected racial unity and individual and group uplift, themes that she and other black leaders wrote about frequently.[4] Unity was particularly important in cities with small black populations. "Portland has … as fine a people as God ever made, and great opportunities [are] in our reach if we will only unite our forces and work together for the interest of all," she told readers in 1928.[5] Consensus was necessary to achieve equal rights and liberties, particularly when black Oregonians' very existence was threatened by external forces such as the Ku Klux Klan. Absent a unified front, she feared that conditions would grow even worse and that Jim Crow laws would become immutable.

However, Cannady did not always live up to her own mandate. She could be blunt about race relations in Portland, and stated unequivocally in 1925 that "colored people are not treated on equality with other racial groups in Oregon."[6] But even the darkest of editorials could offer hope for a better future. And articles in the *Advocate* frequently illustrated the ways in which people used creative resistance to overcome Jim Crow, in the process creating tight-knit communities and a burgeoning civil rights movement.

Cannady enjoyed the visits by Langston Hughes, Roland Hayes, J. Rosamond Johnson, and other distinguished individuals. But Hughes stayed with the Graysons while he was in Portland, and Cannady hosted Hayes when he toured in 1925.[7] Jim Crow laws made it difficult for people to travel, but legal—or extralegal—segregation of accommodations, places of amusement, public transportation, and restaurants did not prevent people from pursuing a career or families from taking trips. Instead, "lives [became] interwoven with people in other cities." Kathryn Bogle recalled that it was common practice to call friends to see if they knew anyone living in cities where she and her family planned to travel. If they did, a letter would be sent to introduce the family and inquire whether it would be possible to stay a few days. She said lodging "operated that way" in Portland, Seattle, San Francisco, Los Angeles, and other cities and towns across the country.[8]

Cannady alluded to the importance of these cross-country connections by reporting the details of readers' journeys. Lena Bowers, for example, returned safely to Portland in the fall of 1926 after "a month's visit to Chicago, Cincinnati, Nashville and other cities of interest."[9] She "was royally entertained" in Nashville by Bula Morrow Oliver, a connection probably arranged by Bula's sister Beatrice some two thousand miles to the west.[10] The Cannadys opened their Irvington-neighborhood home to visitors, too. Longtime subscriber Daniel Parker and his friend, Fred U. Harris, secretary of the Tacoma, Washington, NAACP Branch, stayed with the family during a visit to Portland in October 1923.[11] The following summer, the Cannadys welcomed Richard H. Cole for three nights. The principal of Edward J. Simmons School in St. Louis, Missouri, was described as "a wide-awake, broad-minded and far-seeing man" who participated in his city's religious, social, and civic life.[12]

Hosting guests also was an opportunity to roll out the welcome mat. Society notices in the *Advocate* reveal how Portlanders enjoyed themselves despite Jim Crow restrictions on theaters and restaurants, places one might normally take a visitor. Black-owned cafés were one option, though Bogle said it "was no big thrill" to patronize them because they usually were furnished simply "with a counter and stools."[13] People also were welcome at Chinese restaurants, or "noodle joints," recalled Otto Rutherford.[14] Cannady entertained special guests at Stanley and Lillian Chin's China Tea Garden at the corner of 3rd and Stark in Portland's Chinatown, second only to San Francisco's district between 1880 and 1910.[15] In April 1927, for example, the Cannadys enjoyed a "Chinese supper honoring" J. Rosamond Johnson.[16] Another visitor, social-welfare worker Addie W. Hunton, was treated to an "after-church supper" there during a 1926 trip through Portland.[17]

Many people also entertained visitors with buffet luncheons, radio and dancing parties, card games, and elaborate multi-course dinners, and these were often reported in the *Advocate*. Mr. and Mrs. William Taylor, for example, had fourteen friends over for a "delicious buffet supper" followed by "cards and dancing."[18] In November 1923, Cannady began planning a "unique party" featuring mahjong, the Chinese game of decorated tiles; friends were "already designing ... costumes" to wear at the gathering.[19] Mr. and Mrs. Lay hosted a card and dancing party in 1932 for cast members of *The Green Pastures*.[20] And Lizzie Weeks held a lavish affair for Mrs. Cranshaw one fall afternoon. "Fifteen attractive matrons" attended the "five-course luncheon" for the visitor from Los Angeles; "Kodak pictures of numerous poses of the guests ... were made" by co-host Cinderella Wisdom.[21]

It was not unusual for guests to stay for a week or two, or even a few months, with friends or family members. So articles in the *Advocate* such as the one about Cranshaw's luncheon helped to introduce visitors to the Portland community and make guests feel at home. They also may have mailed clippings to friends or relatives along with news about their stay in the city. These reports would have reassured family concerned for the travelers' well-being, provided other visitors with travel and recreation information, and perhaps encouraged people to relocate to Oregon. Visitors certainly talked about the beauty of the Pacific Northwest, which was unlike the landscape most were familiar with. They were often treated to "auto trips" on the narrow, twisting Columbia River Highway, which became the nation's first scenic highway when it opened in July 1915.[22] Multnomah Falls, the "second-tallest year-round waterfall in the nation" at six hundred and twenty feet, was a highlight of the drive.[23] Other popular destinations included Terwilliger Boulevard, with its panoramic views of Portland and the Willamette River, and Oswego Lake, about ten miles south.[24] Visitors expressed their "keen delight" with Portland and were described as enjoying "themselves immensely."[25] Daniel Parker and Fred Harris, for example, "were loud in their praise of the highway scenery" after a ride in Charlie Redd's new Nash.[26]

The *Advocate* office on Washington Street between 2nd and 3rd avenues was frequently included in tours of the city and environs.[27] The newspaper was a sign of progress in the city, and, as the oldest black-owned business in town, a source of pride to residents and visitors alike. Mary Wilson, a guest from Oakland, California, was taken on "a tour of the business district" by her Portland friends. The trio then "dropped in to meet *The Advocate* staff" before going to John and Clara Logans' home for an early dinner and a "drive over the Columbia River Highway."[28] In 1930, Cannady reported that Duke and Estella Diggs, "prominent citizens" of Jefferson City, Missouri, were among the "pleasant callers at *The Advocate* office."[29] And on one fall day in 1923, seven women called at the office—two from Austin, Texas, one from Pocatello, Idaho, one from Los Angeles, and three Portlanders—all of whom "expressed keen appreciation of [the] office and its location."[30] Other visitors, such as Emma Clemens, made the *Advocate* office their final stop before heading home—and subscribed to the newspaper to keep in touch with new and old friends alike.[31]

Visitors who dropped by the office usually were described as prominent or distinguished members of their community, thus emphasizing racial uplift and pride in citizens' accomplishments. One important tourist was Dr. John Walter Fridia of Waco, Texas. Cannady told readers that Fridia, an "eye, ear, nose and throat specialist with offices in his own ... building," was "one of the wealthiest colored men in the state."[32] In fact, Fridia, who practiced medicine for thirty-five years, "owned a three-story building bearing his name" in downtown Waco. He opened the Mecca Drug Store on the first floor, which he later sold to a pharmacist; the Mecca Clinic, on the second floor, was staffed by a number of physicians over the years.[33] Cannady noted in the *Advocate* that he was "prominent in church and fraternal circles," and had a reputation as a poet whose work was published in the *Houston Informer*.[34] Fridia may have read that paper, and perhaps the *Waco Messenger*; by 1930, he also was subscribing to the *Advocate*.[35]

Another "pleasant visitor" was Ed Lane, reportedly a "well known jockey." According to the *Advocate*, he had accompanied "several horses" from the "Spreckels stables in California" and was scheduled to ride in the sixty-ninth Oregon State Fair, which opened in Salem on September 21, 1930.[36] Lane may have worked for sugar tycoon Adolph B. Spreckels, Jr., whose father, "a racer and a breeder of thoroughbred horses, ... raised some of the greatest performers in the history of the sport on" the West Coast.[37] During some free time before the fair began, Lane invited Charles Maxwell's son Merriman to take a drive with him to Portland in his "pretty new" roadster. They called on Cannady while in the city and Lane "subscribed to the 'old reliable' for a year."[38]

The Reverend J. H. Wilson visited the office, too, while in Portland in 1923 to deliver a sermon at Bethel AME Church.[39] Wilson had an interesting history: he was presiding elder of the oldest black church in San Francisco when three hundred miles of the San Andreas Fault ruptured on the morning of April 18, 1906.[40] The building on Powell Street survived the earthquake, only to be destroyed the following afternoon by the subsequent fires that obliterated more than five hundred blocks in the city center.[41] Six years later, Pastor Wilson was asked to oversee construction of the new church.[42] Cannady described him as "a splendid example of leadership of the race" who stood "very high in the church and fraternal circles." She also told readers he had renewed his subscription to the *Advocate*—"which he says he enjoys very much"—for another three years.[43]

Cannady sought to create an inclusive environment, in the pages of the *Advocate* if not the city itself, and was determined to show off her adopted home. After the Oregon Federation of Colored Women's Clubs and a number of other organizations held meetings in Portland during the summer of 1930, she wrote, "Judging by the large number of conventions here this summer, the Colored population is adding to the popularity of Portland as a center for the meeting of the elite in the various pursuits of life." The gatherings were important for promoting the groups' goals; they also were "a good medium for advertising [the] great Pacific Northwest."[44] Cannady hoped visitors would "be so favorably impressed" with the city and its people they would "wish to come again"—and perhaps stay for good.[45]

Portlanders had the perfect opportunity to promote their city in 1932, when thousands of men were expected to arrive in September for the Fourteenth Annual National Convention of the American Legion. "Among the throng will be many Negro ex-service men," Cannady observed. "We are sure that no group can or will be more hospitable than our colored citizens. They will open their homes and their hearts to welcome the defenders of 'Old Glory.' They will register their cars at the Legion convention headquarters to assist in showing off our city and environs to our guests."[46] One month later, she noted how people had pitched in to help make the event a resounding success. "A newly decorated bed-room, the old chair received a new coat of paint, the kitchen walls underwent a vigorous scrubbing and in a hundred other ways, the preparation has been going cheerfully on," she wrote.[47] Cannady did express concern, however, about discrimination. An article asked city officials do everything "within their power" to ensure that no "insulting" signs were posted "in restaurants and other places of accommodation and amusement," and insisted "that all citizens and visitors ... be treated with the utmost courtesy and love."[48]

The *Advocate* was forced to expand to six pages from its usual four pages to accommodate the number of advertisements welcoming the influx of guests. Arrow Cleaners on Union Avenue North greeted the "Colored American Legionnaires" and offered same-day service on cleaning, pressing, and repairing items. Black visitors were invited to shop at

Broadwill Drug Store on the corner of Broadway and Williams Avenue. Dr. Unthank extended "greetings to The American Legionnaires." Iver Elde, a white man who worked as a chauffeur and also operated Elde's Packard Towing Car Service out of the Portland Hotel, informed visitors that their trip to the Northwest would not be "complete" without a tour of Portland and its "gorgeous scenic highways." He invited people to give him "the pleasure of showing them" the sites. And the United States National Bank on Broadway hoped visitors would be so enthralled with the area that they would want to remain in Portland, a city that offered "just the proportions of business opportunities and personal enjoyment one could desire."[49]

Several special events were held "in honor of the visiting colored legionnaires," including a "spectacular dance" at Ringler's Cotillion Hall—now the Crystal Ballroom. The highlight of the evening, for visitors and locals alike, was dancing on the "floating" floor: the wooden floor was laid atop ball bearings, giving the surface a "spring" that some equated to "dancing on clouds." Cannady noted that the visiting legionnaires, who hailed from California, Arizona, Oklahoma, and other states, "expressed appreciation for the excellent social entertainment arranged for their pleasure and in their honor."[50]

But at least one black Legionnaire was angry over what he perceived to be separate headquarters for white and black attendees. Isaac L. Moore, past commander of a post in Minneapolis, was shocked to see a notice on page forty-four of the official program that advised attendees to go to the Williams Avenue YWCA.[51] He roundly criticized organizers in a letter that was published in the *Advocate*: "My idea of the Legion is there are no Colored Legionnaires. We are all just Legionnaires everywhere I have ever been. ... When some self-appointed leaders of our group either thro' ignorance or for some reason which we can't understand allow themselves to be used as a tool ... to embarrass a race of people, I most feelingly condemn the action."[52] Cannady was quick to point out that there had been a misunderstanding; the notice was not a result of Jim Crow, but rather an effort on the part of the committee to ensure that guests were met at their train, helped with registration, and had suitable accommodations at the Medley Hotel or in a private home. Cannady, in fact, was one of the women on the reception committee charged with taking a shift at Union Depot; she and Thelma Unthank waited at the station for five hours to greet the "colored legionnaires" and direct them to their destination.[53] Cannady admitted that publishing the notice in the "official program" was misleading and certainly could have prompted other attendees to "arrive at the same conclusion." But she observed that nothing in Moore's letter hinted of "any segregation at official gatherings, sight-seeing trips, meetings," or other events, which was a step forward in interracial relations in Portland.[54] Nevertheless, she chose to overlook the fact that the black visitors could not stay in white-owned hotels like their counterparts.

When people moved to Portland "for good," it was cause for celebration, and a bit more boosting, in the pages of the *Advocate*.[55] Cannady reported that R. T. Robinson and his wife, who had relocated from Flint, Michigan, were very "impressed with the business outlook in Portland." Mrs. Robinson opened a beauty parlor on Williams Avenue, which she advertised in the *Advocate*, and her husband was "thinking seriously of going into the restaurant business on the East Side."[56] On another occasion, Cannady informed readers that Mr. and Mrs. Charles Miller, "well known and prosperous citizens" of El Paso, Texas, were so "favorably impressed" with their visit to the Rose City they planned to make Portland "their home." The underlying message was that *Advocate* subscribers Mr. and Mrs. Henry Myles, who had hosted the Millers during their stay, had boosted the city and environs—just as Cannady continually urged people to do.[57]

However, newcomers and current residents alike had a difficult quest for affordable housing due to legal and extralegal restrictions on renting or purchasing property. Realtors generally were uninterested in helping Negroes locate homes in "colored" areas—near Union Depot or east of the Willamette River, for example—and typically refused to sell them homes in white neighborhoods, citing a "depreciation in property values" following "an influx of colored or oriental population" in a specific area.[58] White people who challenged the status quo were featured in the *Advocate*. In March 1930, for example, Cannady told readers about William Hoesley, a deputy district attorney for Multnomah County who planned to sell his home at 318 Sacramento Street to the Ingersolls, the black couple who operated Up-To-Date Cleaners and Tailors. Hoesley canvassed the Albina neighborhood in northeastern Portland and secured enough signatures "to meet the requirements of a city ordinance" regulating the operation of a home business. But soon after, all but two people asked to have their names removed from the petition, thereby preventing the Ingersolls from running their business from the house. Hoesley said he had "no patience with that sort of prejudice" and would "have colored tenants [even] if he [had] to give them the rent and pay them to stay there." He hung a large sign on his house that read: "This place will be ready for occupation about May 1—Colored Tenants Desired."[59] It is unclear, though, whether the Ingersolls moved ; an advertisement in the May 24th *Advocate* still listed their business at 496 Union Avenue North.[60]

Homeownership was so important that Cannady linked it to boosterism. Shortly before Christmas 1928, she cautioned readers not to engage in gossip with visitors. "No well thinking, worthwhile visitor to one's city is interested in the petty jealousies and misunderstandings that usually arise among the people of any city," she wrote. "What they want to know [about is] our progress. How many homes we own, how we live, what we are worth to the community socially, economically and spiritually."[61] This became clear when editor Cecil Newman visited Portland that year and commented on the number of black Portlanders who owned or were buying their homes.[62] Cannady urged people to "turn over a new leaf" and become "boosters and not knockers."[63]

Despite discrimination and segregation, black people living in Portland during the early 1900s continued to try to put down roots and become permanent members of their neighborhood and community. "In those days," recalled Otto Rutherford, "a man's worth was his property."[64] The *Advocate* echoed that sentiment: "Honesty, civic pride and home buying are three things that will command the respect and consideration of people in all walks of life."[65] Because black homeownership was a good indication of a city's race relations, an overall "barometer of good times," and a tenet of racial uplift, Cannady published many notices about successful sales.[66] In 1923, for example, she reported that Willis Garnet and her husband, Roy, a Portland Hotel waiter, had become "the proud owners of a modern seven-room bungalow" in northeastern Portland.[67]

Cannady's brother, Almus Morrow, worked as a compositor for the newspaper and also operated a real estate business for a time in the 1920s.[68] He promised to put people into "just the kind of home [they had] always wanted" with only "a small down payment."[69] Morrow brokered a deal for a "five-room completely furnished house" for Ida Schweich, formerly of Columbia, Missouri, just in time for Thanksgiving.[70] He also may have helped the Agees buy their six-room "modern home" at 718 Union Avenue North in 1924.[71] Cannady described Agee as a "prominent businessman of the city" and "proprietor of the Elks Sanitary Barber Shop," which he had "conducted in an ... excellent manner for a number of years."[72] Agee was proud to carry a variety of "Hair and Beauty Preparations," including products created by businesswoman C. J. Walker.[73] The Agees likely were regular readers as well, since the barbershop on 6th Avenue was one location where the *Advocate* could be purchased for a nickel each Saturday.[74]

Readers may have been surprised by the front-page news item about the formation of the Cannady Real Estate Co. in the fall of 1929. Edward wrote that because so many people had had "great difficulty" with "buying and renting homes and arranging mortgages," he had "decided to enter the real estate business."[75] However, it could be argued that the Cannadys had an economic interest in the city's success and that, by boosting Portland to new residents, they stood to profit personally and professionally. There is no evidence that Edward ever completed any real estate transactions, though. And his timing could not have been worse: the announcement was made just weeks before the stock market crash.

Because Beatrice Cannady devoted so much time and energy to building a strong black community in Portland, it was discouraging to her when businesses closed and entrepreneurs like photographer James S. Bell moved on. He had originally settled in Los Angeles "to make his fortune," but by 1914 he had relocated to Portland, where he took a job as an "extra waiter" at the Portland Hotel.[76] Bell later established a photography business in the Goodnough Building at 5th and Yamhill.[77] Cannady published his photograph in the twentieth-anniversary issue of the *Advocate*, and observed that he had developed "a lucrative patronage among both races."[78] But she may have been trying to boost his business. A few months later he told her that support had been so poor he might be forced "to seek a city more thickly populated with colored people who [had] more race pride ... than they show[ed] in Portland."[79]

Nearly a year to the day that he was featured in the newspaper, the *Advocate* informed readers that Bell had sold his studio. "The going of Mr. Bell leaves Portland without a colored photographer," she added.[80] His decision to quit the business also meant the loss of a regular advertiser.[81] It is unclear whether he did leave the city; if so, the black community would have lost more than just a businessman. He was one of the founders of the Portland Branch, he signed the petition to ban *The Birth of a Nation*, and, as the "pilot" of the Portland Bees, had been trying to "gain recognition for the [city's] colored ball players."[82] Setbacks such as these prompted Cannady to observe on more than one occasion, "If every citizen would constitute himself a booster for Portland and its legitimate business enterprises, the results collectively would be many times greater opportunities for self improvement as well as greater improvement for our city."[83]

Overall, the special ten-page issue celebrating the *Advocate*'s twentieth anniversary was bittersweet. Numerous advertisements acknowledged the milestone. J. K. Gill & Co., a publisher and stationer founded in 1866 and located at 5th and Stark, observed: "We most heartily congratulate the *Advocate* .... Twenty years in the business of publishing a newspaper continuously is a long time. We other pioneers in different fields have a measure of understanding of what this means. We rejoice with you."[84] An advertisement for the Portland Railway, Light & Power Co. noted simply: "In Appreciation of Your Twenty Years Service in the Community." And a half-page ad for the department store Lipman Wolfe & Co. stated, "Wishing You Success and Continued Prosperity with Your Publication."[85] The anniversary issue also lauded people such as Bell; Isa Vessell, a "fashionable modiste" and one of the most "industrious, ambitious and progressive matrons in the city"; and attorney Eugene J. Minor, who enjoyed "a lucrative practice, not alone among his own people but the other race as well."[86] But the *Advocate*'s anniversary also offered an opportunity to reflect on Portlanders' progress—or lack thereof. Cannady observed that a lot had changed in two decades: Few "finely equipped beauty and dressmaking parlors" were as "prominently situated" in the downtown as before, and businessmen had "become contented and happy and ... fallen in the habit of waiting for business to come" to them, rather than "hustle" for it like "the businessmen of other races." People had not "kept up with the rapid advancement of this day and this city," but Cannady still found reason to be optimistic about the future and boost entrepreneurship. "*The Advocate* ... hopes that in the next twenty years there will be wonderful improvement amongst the race in the business as well as other circles."[87]

The grand opening of the New Golden West Hotel late in 1933 represented exactly the mix of personal and public development she had in mind. Originally established in 1906 by William Duncan Allen, the hotel at Broadway and Everett rented rooms to travelers and railroad employees, and featured a barbershop, restaurant, and confectionery shop.[88] Allen closed the hotel in 1931 and it remained shuttered for two years, leaving the city again with just one hotel that would rent rooms to black guests.[89] The news that Catherine Byrd had leased the building and planned an extensive renovation of the property in the middle of the Depression caused considerable excitement in a community that had been struggling mightily to make ends meet. Twenty-five Pullman porters had been laid off in February 1933; Cannady observed that twenty-five families depended on the men for "maintenance and support."[90] In general, the "extent to which colored men in the City of Portland have been retired from their jobs has reached the point of alarm," she noted, particularly with winter looming.[91] So she sincerely appreciated Byrd's "courage and optimism and faith in the return of normal business conditions."[92]

While Byrd was shopping for rugs, furniture, linens, and drapes, the *Advocate* reported that "colored men [and] women of all sizes and ages ...

swarmed in and out [of the hotel] like bees around a hive trying to get a job of some kind or another." It is debatable whether the New Golden West Hotel made much of a dent in the unemployment situation, however; two of Byrd's six children had jobs at the hotel and the *Advocate* did not list the Portlanders who landed a position there.[93] Nevertheless, the hotel was an important symbol of hope for black Oregonians, and its Phoenix-like rebirth was celebrated. As Cannady wrote in one editorial, "*The Advocate* stands ready to cooperate with Mrs. Byrd and her coworkers in putting over her program of service in our community where she has chosen to cast her lot."[94]

After calling on Portlanders repeatedly over the years to boost business enterprises, Cannady was pleased to see a large turnout for the grand opening on November 12th. "Without a doubt," she wrote, "the biggest social event in the life of the colored citizens of Portland, for 'many a moon,' took place ... Sunday afternoon when between two and three hundred guests called to inspect the New Golden West Hotel and congratulate its lady proprietor." Cannady served as one of the hostesses and also announced the program, which featured a poetry reading by young Eunice Mott; several singers, including Ivan Cannady; speeches by Byrd and others; and the reading of "congratulatory letters and telegrams." Attendees were taken on tours of the five-story hotel and shown some of its ninety-six rooms.[95] Cannady described in detail the hostesses' outfits, baskets of fall flowers, hanging ferns, and mahogany serving table with its centerpiece of candles and flowers, allowing the extended community of readers to share in the grand opening.

Her vivid descriptions also may have quelled doubts about the hotel's longevity. "Some have been very liberal in giving her six months before her doors will close—others not quite so optimistic say three or four months at the most," Cannady wrote. But she pointed out that Byrd had prior experience with hotel management in Denver and "other cities and [had] a record of success."[96] As an extra precaution, though, Cannady continued to boost the hotel and its role in helping to rebuild Portland's black community. "Let us hope that [the colored business people of Portland] will ... give her their full cooperation and make her business something to be proud of and pointed out to visitors in our city," she wrote.[97] Residents may have included the hotel in sightseeing trips; it was just a few blocks away from the *Advocate* office. It is also possible they sent clippings of Cannady's articles to family and friends in other states, thus showing off their city's progress in spite of the Depression. And editors across the country would have read in the *Advocate* about the grand opening, and likely commented on the fact that a Negro woman was succeeding in business. Cannady would have been pleased if the grand opening of the New Golden West Hotel had generated even a few additional comments, but she was equally happy to boost a new business at a time when her community desperately needed it.[98]

Three years into the Depression, Cannady succinctly observed that the "economic status of the Negro, which has never been any too high, is at a low ebb and if we are not to be totally wiped off the economic map, what businesses we have must receive our support in this time of crisis." She listed the same establishments she had so proudly named in an article for the *Oregon Daily Journal* more than a decade earlier: "restaurants, barbershops, hotels, newspapers."[99] But it was more critical than ever to support them "and other places where colored people" were employed, she argued, since individuals could not count on help from "the white man."[100] They also could not count on the white press to cover issues such as mass unemployment and poverty in the black community. As white newspapers increasingly focused on the plight of their white readers, black Oregonians became further marginalized and forgotten in the daily press. The *Advocate* was an important corrective to this erasure. Cannady also used her newspaper to help improve morale, keep people informed, secure work for people, and coordinate food efforts.

She printed numerous observations from subscribers in other parts of the state and across the country to help lift "the weight of pessimism from [those who felt] that the depression [had] been the worst in history." For example, Ella and Ernest Allen, longtime residents of Pendleton, wrote: "We are about the busiest people in town. ... In fact, I believe the depression hasn't bothered us at all. Our rents are just the same and we have never been cut on a job; our salary has been raised."[101] Cannady visited their home in northeastern Oregon in 1931 and was impressed by what she saw. "For 27 years they have ... saved and invested their money so that today they are the proud owners of a beautiful home, several pieces of choice residential property which they rent to prominent members of the other race, and a beautiful new Cadillac sedan," she wrote.[102] She also reported that Ella Allen, who renewed the family's subscription regularly, had agreed to "serve as [the *Advocate*'s] representative in Pendleton."[103]

Subscriber J. T. Johnson updated Cannady—and *Advocate* readers—on conditions in Baltimore, Maryland. Wages were lower there than in Portland, he noted, but so were living expenses. Even better, he reported "a diversity of work for colored people" in case someone needed to relocate for job opportunities.[104] Dr. Unthank wrote the *Advocate* from Kansas City,

Missouri, where he was visiting his sick uncle: "The depression can be seen on every hand—worse than we have felt it in Oregon."[105] A Portland man who went on a business trip to Oakland, California, also weighed in: "The economic condition of the Negro in that state is no better and perhaps worse than in Portland."[106] And Dan Byrd, a former Oregonian living in Seattle, confirmed that the "unemployment condition" was worse there than in Portland.[107]

The *Advocate* was important, too, for keeping readers informed about success stories. Even if they were few and far between, they helped lift spirits during a trying decade for black Oregonians. Cannady told readers about Alex Coffey, "the barbecue man," who was "battling 'old man' Depression" by working for the city during the day and at his stand on Williams Avenue at night. Cannady called him "quite industrious as well as thoughtful."[108] And in January 1931, Cannady reported that a special committee comprising Portland Branch members had acted quickly on the news that Olds, Wortman & King had "decided ... to discontinue the use of Negro help" at the department store. Three employees, a doorman and two maids, were let go just after the new year. Branch President Clarence Ivey investigated the situation and met with management, who agreed to reinstate one individual. Ivey also obtained a pledge that the store would work with the Branch to help place other unemployed workers.[109] In March, the Branch reported it had found work for Alice Wilson and University of Oregon football player Chuck Williams at a local department store, and Effie Lee was hired as a "special maid."[110]

Many other articles, though, reflected the vagaries of the local economy by documenting the ebb and flow of people's fortunes as well as their "uncertainty and hope."[111] Toby Johnson, "the shine artist," decided to store his Essex coupe because "'Old Man Depression'" had caught up with him.[112] J. W. Simms, who had gone to Seaside, Oregon, to work as a cook, returned to Portland when his employer failed to pay him.[113] And Roy Garnet, who had been so happy to buy a home for his growing family in 1923, was forced to seek employment in Seattle after he lost his job at the Portland Hotel.[114] Willis Garnet finally resigned her job as a maid in Lipman Wolfe & Co.'s beauty parlor months later and joined her husband in Washington; he was working as manager of the Angelus Mortuary and she was able to land a position there as a "lady attendant."[115] An *Advocate* article also reported on changes that affected black employees of the Oregon-Washington Railroad and Navigation Company, including Sherman Pickett, the subscriber who sent his nephew in Alabama a gift subscription. Pickett reported that rather than discharge any of the men, the company had instituted a five-day week instead of the six- or seven-day schedule workers were used to.[116]

Implementation of a standard workweek seems like a positive change, and certainly was better than letting the men go. For families reliant upon the income generated by working more hours, however, the reduction represented additional hardship during an already trying time.

The *Advocate* also was filled with sentence-long descriptions of the city's transient community: desperate men who traveled back and forth from California to Washington, always hopeful they would find a job in Portland, Seattle, or Los Angeles.[117] But reports were not promising. George Williams, "a very likable young man" who left Oakland, California, "on account of the depression," found Portland to be no better. Jim Bland decided to take his chances in California anyway, "after trying for months" to find a job in Portland.[118] Others, like George Sanders, returned to Portland after discovering that Los Angeles was "running over with unemployed men and women of all races."[119] Men traveled west, too. George Sampson, "like many another" individual, was "looking for a job" in Portland after making the long trip from Jackson, Mississippi.[120] Sam Johnson, who moved to the city from Texas, had better luck than most: he relocated again to the central Oregon town of Bend "to become a porter in a barbershop."[121]

In 1930, Cannady reflected on the drastic economic picture. "A few years ago," she wrote, "there were certain jobs that were taken for granted to be for colored people. We could go anywhere and apply for the job of a porter, elevator operator, bellhop, waiter, cook, with good prospects of getting the job." But now those "personal service jobs" were being filled by unemployed white men and women.[122] Cannady suggested two possible options for resistance: entrepreneurship and economic boycotts—the latter had proved successful in Chicago in 1929 and in Memphis in 1892.[123] People in a number of cities had "adopted the slogan ... 'Don't Spend Your Money Where You Can't Work' as one means of opening up new avenues of employment to the colored youth," she wrote. There was no reason why such a strategy could not be tried in Portland, since residents spent thousands of dollars each month on "food, clothing, rent" and other necessities.[124] Cannady also believed the campaign could be an effective strategy for protesting segregation. In 1930, the *Advocate* reported that a restaurant on Alder Street had refused to serve Pearl Stewart, a "prominent" local clubwoman. Cannady called readers' attention to this incident and observed that it "might be advisable for ... people who have been patronizing" the restaurant to avoid it until its policy changed. "Colored people must learn not ... to spend their money where they cannot work [and] also not to spend their money where they cannot eat," she asserted.[125] During the next two years, Cannady regularly printed the slogan in the *Advocate* to remind readers of the importance of this campaign.[126]

The *Advocate* also began assisting with job placement in an effort to keep people in Portland and shore up the sagging community. In January 1931, Cannady reported that through her "efforts," John Minor and the Reverend Walter Lovell had worked the "holiday rush" at the post office.[127] Two months later, she wrote that the *Advocate* had "secured work for several of its subscribers—chauffeur, general house maid and cook. A large number of unemployed [have] registered with us during the past several weeks."[128] She announced the following week that she had "succeeded in placing three persons" in jobs involving "general housework" and cooking.[129] But Cannady was less optimistic by June. "Unless something is done or some means found for employment, the outlook for many Negroes in Portland this winter is anything but encouraging. With many let out of the [railroad] and hotel service, few are left with paying jobs. If it were not for the domestic service rendered by our women, it would be a tragic situation."[130]

These updates shed some light on the Depression and how it affected black women in Portland, something that had been missing in the newspaper to that point.[131] But that changed in 1932, when several notices appeared in the *Advocate*. Louise Randolph lost her job with S. H. Kress & Co., a chain of five-, ten-, and twenty-five-cent stores, as a result of its "economy program."[132] Cannady had helped Randolph get her job there nearly five years earlier when she graduated from high school. Kate Lewis, a "comfort station" attendant, fared somewhat better when the City of Portland implemented its own "economy program" that spring. Her hours staffing public toilets were "cut in half"; Josephine Duke was let go, however, perhaps because she had just taken time off to have her daughter.[133] Prospects for women continued to worsen until there was little left to say except the "women, some of whom helped with the family upkeep by rendering domestic service, have been laid off."[134]

Responding to the grim situation, Cannady made an important announcement in January 1933. "In keeping with its program of service to the community, *The Advocate* is establishing a small relief depot to help those out of employment and who are in need," she wrote. The goal was to supplement work being done by other agencies, which often had considerable "red tape" one had to deal with before receiving assistance. Cannady told readers that the Reverend Lee Roy Kinard and First AME Zion Church were accepting "donations of food, clothing, fuel, money and other supplies" and planned to distribute them to anyone in need regardless of "race, color or creed." She also tried to rally people and keep up their hopes: "These are times when we must help one another. The greatest exponent of social welfare work said that he [who] is the greatest among you must be the servant of all. Another has said that the servants of humanity are the greatest men of whatever race, nation or creed. We find plenty of time for recreation and play, let us devote a little in service."[135]

Toward the end of February, Cannady reported that the women of the church's Home Missionary Society had taken "charge of the relief work" and were helping the *Advocate* put "over the program which was started several weeks ago." She was "proud of the work" the churchwomen were doing, which included altering donated "undergarments, dresses, [and] coats ... to meet the needs" of the destitute.[136] Davidson's Bakery Company was supplying "at least fifty loaves of good, wholesome, fresh bread" twice a week, and Safeway Stores, Inc., had donated a one-hundred-pound sack of lima beans.[137] "We give the source of this gift in order that our people may be guided in their purchases to patronize those stores that appreciate and help our race," she wrote.[138]

The final issue of the *Crisis* for 1933 featured a two-page article headlined, "What Price National Recovery?" For more than four years, "citizens of the United States [had] felt the effects of an economic condition [that had] steadily grown worse." Unemployment had increased, banks were failing, and "the normal agencies for charity and relief were unable to cope with the need of millions of jobless men and women." In the midst of this bleak picture was the Negro, who had "suffered most" as a result of the depression:

> A marginal worker, he was the first to lose his job. A low paid worker, he had less reserve on which to live during unemployment. Often discrimination on the ground of color prevented him from securing his full share of the private and public charity furnished to unemployed workers generally. The so-called 'Negro jobs' were invaded by white workers who had been displaced from better jobs.[139]

The outlook was grim for Negroes from coast to coast. But there were things to look forward to, as Mary White Ovington pointed out.

On February 12, 1934—Lincoln's birthday—the NAACP planned to observe its twenty-fifth anniversary. The organization was still growing; Ovington reported 378 branches with "smaller cities ... starting new branches every month"—and its "news stories" had "millions of readers." The organization also had a new "Marching Song" set to the tune of *Marching Through Georgia* to commemorate the anniversary and rally the "hard-working men and women" across the country to continue the "struggle for civil and political liberty":[140]

> Twenty-five full years ago we started on our way,
> Bound to give the colored man his place before the day—
> Everybody knows that we are here and here to stay
> As we go marching together.
> Hurrah! Hurrah! We'll shout the Jubilee!
> Hurrah! Hurrah! For the N.A.A.C.P.!
> East and West and North and South unite for victory
> As we go marching together.[141]

The *Crisis*, too, sounded a positive note that likely resonated with Beatrice Cannady: "We are going to take for granted that in 1934 the slow beginnings of economic recovery will be far enough along to enable THE CRISIS to think more of literature and art, to bring back significant episodes and persons in the history of the Negro race, and to encourage fiction and poetry."[142] After a long, difficult year in Portland, she was undoubtedly also looking forward to returning to promoting her community, welcoming visitors and newcomers to the city, and hosting interracial teas to celebrate culture and the accomplishments of men and women of the "Negro race."

CHAPTER FIVE

We Must Cultivate One Another

It is a picture never to be forgotten for its great beauty and the joy it affords to witness one of these gatherings where white and black, rich and poor, Christian and Jew mingle freely and discuss their common interests while sipping together a cup of tea!

— "Interracial Teas," Cannady Scrapbook

In February 1928, in the midst of a rainy Portland winter, Beatrice Cannady received a brief, typewritten note from NAACP Secretary James Weldon Johnson: "I am writing you as a representative woman of the race to extend to you a cordial invitation to be one of our speakers at the 19th Annual Conference of the Association to be held in Los Angeles."[1] Other luminaries scheduled to attend included W. E. B. Du Bois, William Pickens, and Mary White Ovington. Cannady was happy to accept the request and looked forward to the event that summer, especially since a protracted illness had caused her to cancel her address at the meeting held two years earlier in Chicago.[2] She also apparently engaged in some self-promotion: "I am advised by Mrs. E. D. Cannady that she is to represent negro womanhood of America on the program of the Annual Conference of the [NAACP]," Governor Isaac Patterson wrote Johnson. "I am very happy that this honor has been accorded to an Oregon woman, and particularly to one so well qualified as Mrs. Cannady."[3] Brief notices also appeared in the *Oregon Daily Journal* and *Sunday Journal*; they may have originated with the NAACP or Cannady herself.[4]

With just four months to prepare for the trip and write her speech, Cannady felt "compelled to decline" a number of speaking engagements during March and April.[5] But she still found time to visit two churches to talk about "The Negro Problem and Interracial Relationships," and she shared information about the NAACP with another congregation.[6] She discussed "Labor and the American Negro" at a Portland Labor College forum, and also entertained Cecil E. Newman, the *Twin City Herald* editor who visited Portland for a few days in May.[7] Finally, when sons George and Ivan were in bed, the accomplished seamstress may have sewed some new clothes to take with her so that she looked her best while in Los Angeles.[8]

Cannady departed from Union Depot on Wednesday, June 20th, for the journey south.[9] The long train trip down Oregon and California gave her a chance to make a few more revisions to her remarks, which filled thirteen pages in a notebook small enough to tuck into her purse.[10] She penned notes in the margins, underlined key words, added carets and a few words here and there, and scratched out phrases that no longer conveyed her ideas. By the time she arrived in Los Angeles, she would have been prepared for her address.

Delegates, attendees, and NAACP officials were welcomed with enthusiasm. "The streets all through the colored business section and downtown in the white business section in the immediate vicinity of Philharmonic Hall and Shrine Auditorium were gayly decorated with bunting, flags, and N.A.A.C.P. posters," reported the *Advocate*.[11] The *Los Angeles Times* and *California Eagle* also covered the conference, which began at 8 p.m. Wednesday, June 27th, with addresses by the mayor of Los Angeles, the president of the Los Angeles NAACP Branch—her good friend and fellow Wiley University alumnus H. Claude Hudson—and Du Bois, who spoke about "The Presidential Election, Black Votes and Democracy in the United States."[12] More than three thousand people packed the Philharmonic Auditorium at 5th and Olive; another four thousand reportedly were turned away.[13]

Twenty-four hours later, Cannady discussed "Negro Womanhood as a Power in the Development of the Race and the Nation" from the pulpit of Second Baptist Church on Griffith Avenue.[14] During her talk, she peeled back the multiple layers of oppression that kept black women at society's margins, revealing the intersecting realities of race, gender, patriarchy, and power in 1920s America.

> That she may serve well, the Negro woman must first learn to believe in herself and her race—ridding herself always of any false notions of racial or self-inferiority. We must admit that this is often hard to do, hampered as she is by her sex in what we sometimes term a man's world and by her race in a white man's world. But it can be done. ... The time demands real women.

Her talk became an opportunity to emphasize unity and diversity while calling attention to the need for action. In particular, she used the occasion to urge women to become more involved in the organization. "This is a big program in which the Negro womanhood of America will find abundant opportunity for service ... not alone to the Negro race but to the white race as well," she told the crowd. "Paradoxical as it may seem, the Negro women of America must become the teachers of the white race."[15]

Cannady had been trying to educate white audiences for years. She hosted interracial teas to educate white individuals about Negro culture and history. She also spoke to countless white groups about subjects ranging from the work of the NAACP to "The Negro Woman in Business."[16] These forms of outreach were so important to her, in fact, that she filled the rest of her time in Los Angeles with a variety of speaking engagements. Cannady recounted her busy schedule in the *Advocate* following her return home. Among other things, she gave two brief addresses to youth at the Methodist Episcopal Church in Pasadena; spoke for an hour about the NAACP to a white congregation in Hollywood; delivered another hour-long talk to the white members of the Free Catholic Church, also in Hollywood; addressed a gathering of Bahá'ís; and spoke to a white group at Long Beach City Hall. Cannady noted that she had so many demands on her time, she "was compelled to forego" several more requests and cancel a couple.[17]

Cannady kept up this rigorous schedule throughout the 1920s. She was a popular speaker who believed passionately in her cause; she also hated to turn down any engagements that were in keeping with her work to improve race relations. But this drive and determination—or what Robert Bagnall called her "unbounded enthusiasm"—took a toll on her health. He commented on this to her white friend Alice Handsaker: "I feared when I was in Portland that her many activities would overtax her strength because I could not see how one little person could ... continue to do so many things—important as they all are."[18] Indeed, even while on "her sick bed," Handsaker told him, Cannady thought about ways to "promote the cause so near her heart."[19]

One strategy involved talking with high school and college students to counter the "prejudice and race hatred" taught to them by others.[20] Lincoln, the city's oldest high school, kept her especially busy during the 1920s. In March 1925, she spoke to two hundred and fifty students about "The Political Status of the Negro During Reconstruction."[21] She revisited the school two months later to talk to "a graduating class in history ... on inter-racial matters."[22] The *Advocate* reported that "several young men and women remained" after class to talk with Cannady, who "was heartily thanked by the teacher and the students" for visiting numerous times during the term.[23] Hilma Anderson later told Cannady that the interaction with her students had been invaluable for "opening [their] eyes to the brotherhood of man":

> I might talk to them on the Negro "problem" for many days and not accomplish what you can do in one hour. Unfortunately we have a large number of students who are either ignorant of the difficulties of the

> colored people or who are prejudiced against them. Much of this feeling is due to improper contacts with people of color. You come to us without bitterness and simply and frankly put the problem before us. Scarcely a student goes away without feeling that beneath the color all people are alike in thoughts, hopes and aspirations. By touching, as you have here, between one hundred fifty and two hundred students per year you are doing a *great work* towards promoting good will and happy group relations in Portland.[24]

Anderson identified a key aspect of Cannady's civil rights work: contact. Too often, contact between the races had been "largely the wrong kind and on the wrong plane," which led to segregation and ill will.[25] The talks Cannady gave to students and community members were an important countermeasure. As she wrote in the *Advocate*, "We cannot have this good-will ... by simply talking about it; we must cultivate one another and by frequent helpful contacts, come to a sympathetic understanding of one another."[26] This idea was put to the test during another visit to Lincoln High School in the spring of 1926.

A brief notice on the *Advocate*'s front page informed readers she had twice discussed the "so-called race problem" with students in Ernest E. Schwarztrauber's history classes.[27] The talks apparently culminated a unit focusing on the "study of the Negro," which included reading *The Souls of Black Folk* by Du Bois.[28] Students then were asked to write essays describing their reaction to the information she presented.[29] Cannady felt the compositions were "so interesting ... from so many angles," she asked the teacher's permission to publish all thirty-nine in the *Advocate*.[30] What ensued was an illuminating seven-week-long conversation about race relations.[31] Many students admitted their naiveté: "The study of the Negro problem has opened my eyes to many of the handicaps a Negro passes through in trying to make a living. It also brought before me the achievements of the Negroes and showed clearly that they want to become educated."[32] Another wrote: "This subject has brought to my knowledge so many new facts that as yet I have no decided opinions. Before studying the problem I had never given it a thought one way or the other. I merely accepted the negro as he was and did not think of what he might deserve to become."[33] A third student admitted, with no small amount of foresight: "Although I did not especially like the subject I really learned some things about the Negroes that I had never known before. I think that it is a good thing that this subject is taught in the schools for since the Negro problem is one of the greatest before this country today and will increase in importance with time it is ... essential that we all understand both sides of the question."[34]

Other students openly acknowledged their prejudices: "From this study I agree that the Negro ought to be educated and helped but I would not want to associate very much with them. I guess there are Negroes better than I even, but to me a Negro is a Negro."[35] A number of pupils recognized the reasons why black people were not on par with white individuals: "The study of the Negro problem … brought home to me the fact that the Negro is held down and willfully subjugated by the whites regardless of the Fourteenth Amendment. He is frightened into obeisance to whites by fear of mob lynchings."[36] Another student realized that white people had caused much of the "problem" by enacting "political, industrial and educational limitations," and participating in "the national disgrace, lynching."[37] Still others acknowledged the injustice inherent in Jim Crow laws: "As to his being excluded from eating in restaurants, from riding in the same street car as the white people, and going into various other places I think that he should be given this right as well as the white man, because he is a citizen as well as we are."[38]

And a few students reiterated Cannady's belief that families impart their own biases and stereotypes to their children. One wrote, "Before studying the Negro question, I was prejudiced against the Negro. From all that I heard the Negroes did more harm than good. But after studying it, I can now see the Negroes' side of the question; also I found that I was prejudiced just from what the people around me thought."[39]

Cannady "commended" Schwarztrauber for allotting so much time to "the study of 'The Negro.'"[40] She also appreciated his "sympathetic and serious consideration" of the subject and his efforts to teach his students "the true and correct information about this noble race of black people."[41] And she called on other history teachers in Portland's public schools to follow his lead and incorporate meaningful conversations about race into their curriculum.[42] Overall, the essays confirmed Cannady's belief that interaction between white and black people was an important step toward eliminating race antipathy. As she told a white acquaintance and subscriber in eastern Oregon, "Remember that segregation is the root of all evils, for when people do not know one another they are suspicious and distrustful of one another. Only by contact of the races will … an understanding be reached."[43] The students' responses underscored her belief that educating white people was crucial for better race relations, and reaffirmed her conviction that she was the one to "teach the true history of her race."[44] That "true history" was shared again with Lincoln students in January 1927, when Cannady also offered ideas to "help solve the race problems."[45]

Her outreach did not go unnoticed by the white press, though it is possible that she notified the papers of her activities. In June 1930, the *Oregon Daily Journal* reported that two recent lectures on "The Negro's

Contribution to Civilization" to history classes at Lincoln High School were part of a program she had done there "for five years."[46] A profile in the *Sunday Oregonian* concluded with a description—albeit exaggerated—of Cannady's community service, which included lecturing "to students of almost every high school and college in the state."[47] Other articles, such as the *Journal* story about Cannady's invitation to address the NAACP conference, noted that she had "made about 100 addresses during" the previous year, "most of them being to church groups, women's clubs, colleges, and schools."[48] A few days later, a similar notice in the *Daily Journal* stated, "She is widely sought as a speaker before women's clubs, church groups, colleges and schools."[49] Even if Cannady *did* engage in self-promotion, Portland editors could have chosen not to publish stories about her activities. That they deemed her interracial work sufficiently newsworthy to include in their newspapers speaks volumes about her standing in the community.

Cannady could reach several hundred pupils during just one trip to a high school. But she also welcomed interactions with individual students. A Washington High School senior met with Cannady at the *Advocate* office to learn more about Tuskegee Institute; another white Washington pupil sought help with "her term project on 'The Negro.'"[50] Toward the end of the 1926 academic year, Cannady received a letter from the white minister at Rose City Park Methodist Episcopal Church. A Lincoln High School senior staying with his family had been assigned a paper on "The Problem Facing the Negro." He told the girl that the "chance to talk to" Cannady "about the subject" would be much better than reading about it.[51] Students, like others interested in the topic, also were welcome to come to Cannady's home to browse her collections of the *Crisis*, *Opportunity*, and the *Messenger*; read exchange newspapers; and borrow from her extensive personal library. Cannady was delighted to help whenever possible and believed she had "interested" many people "in the study of the Negro" with an eye toward improving "the relations between the races."[52]

But her assistance was not limited to Portland-area youth. Richard Brink, a Bend High School student, wrote Cannady on behalf of his sociology class, which was "studying the colored race." He and his peers hoped she could supply information they had been unable to find in textbooks, such as the number of black Oregonians, "their occupations, activities and organizations," and "how the colored race [fared] in relation to the other races in Portland." Finally, he asked Cannady whether "anything special [was] being done for the betterment of the race."[53] She probably typed a long response to his queries; she also sent a copy or two of the *Advocate* as he had requested.

Cannady fielded inquiries from people across the country, too. One noteworthy request came in 1932 from Harold F. Gosnell, who told her he was examining race relations in Chicago's politics.[54] He asked for a copy of the September 28, 1929, *Advocate*, which featured Cannady's long article about Congressman Oscar De Priest's Portland visit. In fact, Gosnell was an associate professor of political science at the University of Chicago whose "greatest and most enduring work," *Negro Politicians: The Rise of Negro Politics in Chicago*, was published in 1935. The book was "an expansive study of the place of African Americans in the politics of Chicago" and featured a profile of the congressman.[55]

Cannady was proud to be able to fulfill each and every request over the years, and considered her interactions with inquisitive white people to be an invaluable step toward equal rights and liberties. As she wrote in one editorial, "It is clear that a new light is dawning in race relations. ... Wise men realize that each group has a contribution to make to the world's civilization, and the sooner all groups can be brought to efficiency, the sooner will the world be blessed with all these contributions."[56]

This awareness was particularly evident among students at Willamette University, in the state capital of Salem, who invited Cannady to speak numerous times on a variety of topics. In March 1926, for example, she discussed the history of the NAACP with about three hundred and fifty students at the mid-morning chapel service. The *Collegian*, the student newspaper, observed: "Mrs. Cannady offers one of the first practical programs for the elimination of racial differences that has ever been presented to students at Willamette."[57] After the service, she accompanied senior Ann Silver to her sorority house for lunch and "a pleasant visit" with other house residents.[58] Silver was so interested in the work of the NAACP that Cannady promised to ask Robert Bagnall, director of branches, to send her everything she needed to organize a chapter on campus. Cannady subsequently told him, "I do not know of anything which would please me more than to have a Branch entirely composed of white Students."[59]

Her meeting with a fraternity later that afternoon also was productive. A committee was selected to work with Cannady to "draw up resolutions condemning lynching and sundry other injustices to colored American citizens and to draft telegrams [urging Oregon senators] to work for passage of the Dyer-McKinley anti-lynching bill," first introduced eight years earlier in the House of Representatives by Missouri Congressman Leonidas Dyer. Finally, she attended a dinner meeting at the home of some "prominent citizens of Salem."[60] She reported that about forty people, including Willamette University professors and students and public-school principals, listened to her hour-long talk "on the N.A.A.C.P. and the Race Problem."[61]

Cannady's messages continued to resonate with Willamette students. A week after her visit, the *Collegian* reported that the student body had adopted—and acted on—the resolutions that she and the committee had drafted.[62] She sent the *Collegian* articles about her visit, with the relevant portions marked, and a note to the NAACP's publicity department: "If you think it is worthwhile, perhaps the *Crisis* would like to make a brief item of the Willamette University news."[63]

Cannady returned to Willamette University several times during the 1920s to address a wide variety of groups.[64] But she also enjoyed intimate interactions with students at Reed College, a liberal-arts school in southeastern Portland known for its commitment to "intellectual excellence."[65] One Valentine's Day, she hosted a celebration at her home to honor the memory—and birthday—of abolitionist Frederick Douglass. An "international group" that included about twenty Reed students attended the party and listened to Sam Gill, who had "heard Douglass deliver a speech," share recollections of the orator.[66] Following the Sunday-evening event, a white high school teacher wrote that images of the interracial party lingered in her mind. "It was a unique experience," observed Blanche Thurston, who was moved by "the mingling of white faces and dark; the friendliness that pervaded the atmosphere, ... the gathering of races around the piano, and the joining of their voices in song—the assemblage of these things forms a memory touching and deep." Cannady also carefully crafted her image at these events. Thurston noticed this and told her hostess she was "quaint and dainty enough to have stepped out of the Valentine decorations." Dressed in "black and white and scarlet organdy," Cannady "matched the red hearts and candles, and candies and streamers." If her goal was to stand out as a charming and refined hostess, then Cannady succeeded. But she may also have tried to create an image that blended in with the event, to the point of matching the ornamentation. In this way she allowed the speakers and guests to take center stage and fostered a creative, dynamic, safe environment that encouraged people to mingle and become acquainted. As Thurston observed: "Such affairs must dim the interracial lines and make folks realize the brotherhood of man. It was a privilege to be there."[67]

Cannady continued to impact Reed College as well as its students and professors—so much so that a teacher of political science supported her 1929 nomination for the Harmon Foundation's award for race relations. "For some years I have been familiar with Mrs. Cannady's untiring work in this community in behalf of better race relationships," wrote George Bernard Noble, a Rhodes Scholar who joined Reed's faculty in 1922. She had visited the college "repeatedly," each time "bringing helpful information and stimulating suggestions on the whites and the negroes." Cannady also facilitated campus visits by William Pickens and other "leaders of her people who [had] contributed materially in promoting understanding and better feelings between the races."[68]

Two years after writing this letter of endorsement, Noble invited Cannady to his home to address the college's Social Science Club. Students listened for more than an hour as "Oregon's outstanding crusader for negro rights" discussed her "program" for "changing racial attitudes" with the goal of improving the "behavior of individuals toward each other."[69] Cannady shared some of the essays written by the Lincoln High School students to "prove beyond a doubt" that people can reevaluate their beliefs if they have sufficient knowledge to make informed decisions. She also commended "white youths in Oregon colleges" for becoming more open-minded about interracial relations. Following the program, Cannady reported that several students "made appointments for personal interviews and for help in assembling information for their theses."[70]

Although Cannady valued the opportunity to interact with small and large audiences and answer questions, interracial teas such as the gathering honoring Frederick Douglass allowed her to promote race relations through "productive" contact with others.[71] The idea for the teas grew out of a "front porch recital" Cannady hosted at her home one summer night in 1922. Motorists were invited to park near her residence and enjoy a "fried chicken dinner," recitations of Paul Laurence Dunbar's poems, and a "program of negro spirituals and old fashioned plantation melodies" featuring soloist Marie Maxwell.[72] Cannady recalled that "white people in automobiles [filled] the streets for blocks" and inspired the "new work of bringing whites and blacks closer together."[73]

Soon, she began working with her white friends Millie Trumbull, executive secretary of the Oregon Industrial Welfare Commission, and Alice Handsaker, a Portland Branch member and self-described "clergywoman" who was "of the same mind" that something needed to be done to "iron out ... misunderstandings between the races."[74] Cannady told a reporter for the *New York Amsterdam News* that the women called themselves the "Three Musketeers, fighting with the sword of love, which is invincible."[75] Small meetings, held in public places, featured informative programs "using largely Negro music and literature since both races knew already much more about the works of white artists."[76] By sharing spirituals or the moving poetry of Langston Hughes, Cannady hoped to instill cultural pride in black people and "stimulate the interest of white people in the Negro."[77] The teas initially attracted white people from the "professional and business class," according to Cannady: college presidents and professors and their wives, high school teachers, doctors, lawyers, public servants, and ministers and their wives. Eventually, however, attendees also included "the plain, everyday people who needed most of all the contacts."[78]

As the teas grew in popularity and attendance increased from a handful of guests to several hundred, Cannady realized the meetings needed to move from the porch to a more intimate setting: the living room. "Even the bitterest of enemies would sit in a public meeting place together," she wrote, but the real test would be getting these individuals to gather in a home—particularly when it meant crossing socially constructed boundaries of race and class.[79] Many white people were averse to entering a black person's home, recalled one longtime Portlander: "They expected it to be full of rats and dirty, so you didn't bother with explaining it wasn't."[80] But Cannady successfully challenged these stereotypes. "White people who have never been in a colored home have an opportunity for the first time to see something of the home life of colored people," she wrote. "Here many see for the first time books written, pictures painted, music composed by Negroes," all of which gave visitors insight into "culture, refinement and accomplishments."[81] Cannady saw her large home as a sanctuary, a "civilizing" refuge, where "racial barriers" could be destroyed by encouraging people to "mingle freely" and gain a "'close-up' view of one another."[82] She ensured this mixing by not allowing guests who already knew each other to "corner off."[83] Instead, individuals were expected to "chat" with someone they had just met and "get acquainted." She reported that this practice had helped to lift the "veil of mystery surrounding each race ... as nothing else has done." Cannady offered the following anecdote to illustrate her claim: "A professional man who regularly attends our interracial gatherings (a white man) once stated ... in this rather inelegant phraseology, 'You don't learn much by running with your own crowd all the time.'"[84]

Descriptions of the teas frequently were published in the *Advocate*. But the short articles often underplayed the importance of Cannady's guests and minimized the dynamic intellectual environment she was part of during the early 1900s, even in a place as seemingly remote from intellectual centers as Portland. In 1931, for example, she invited fifty guests, including Pacific College students, to her home to meet Martha Root, a "traveler, lecturer, journalist" and "world-famed religious teacher."[85] *Advocate* readers scanning the brief biographical sketch would have been unaware that Root grew up in Cambridge Springs, Pennsylvania, just ten miles from the former home of the abolitionist John Brown. Nor would they have known that she worked for the *Pittsburg Dispatch*, the same paper that launched Nellie Bly's journalistic career. Root also had converted to Bahá'ísm after meeting New Yorker Roy C. Wilhelm, who later befriended Cannady, while on an assignment in 1908. By the time Root visited Portland in 1931, she had traveled to Spain, Greece, Egypt, Syria, India, China, Japan, Australia, South America, and many other countries to spread the word about the Bahá'í Faith, sometimes giving those talks in Esperanto.[86] She drew on her world travels to give a lengthy discourse on Japan and China at the interracial gathering at Cannady's home.[87]

Cannady wrote that the lecturer had "been kept busy filling ... engagements" since arriving in Portland on February 23rd.[88] Root broadcast over KGW and KOIN; talked to more than two thousand students at Jefferson High and Grant High, George Cannady's school; spoke at the Bahá'í Assembly; gave several talks to large crowds at the Portland Metaphysical Library on Yamhill and 10th; and spoke with students at Reed College, a program likely facilitated by Cannady. Root also addressed Cannady's Esperanto club, which met at President Elise Reynolds' home.[89] Cannady praised Root for being able to reach out to people of diverse beliefs and backgrounds in order "to promote fellowship and friendships between the members of God's household on earth."[90]

Cannady hosted another "program of rare beauty" in July 1924. Although the tea was described in detail in the *Advocate*, articles about the gathering included little biographical information about her guests, Nellie Mapps, "honorary president" of the Washington State Federation of Colored Women's Clubs, and Alice Park, a white "activist" from Palo Alto, California, who "wrote and spoke tirelessly for decades on the issue of suffrage."[91] Because Park was "internationally famous ... for her world peace efforts and humane work," Cannady invited people "representing different races and varied interests" to "give the evening a sort of international aspect." A "Chinese children's quintette" that included Lillian Chin's children Madeline and Maxine opened the program with several songs.[92] Then a number of Portlanders spoke. Millie Trumbull was invited to "tell something of the Child Welfare Work"; the Reverend John Handsaker discussed the needs of orphans in the "Near East"; George Orr Latimer, a local Bahá'í leader, gave an "impressive talk" about the "oneness of the world of humanity"; and Saidie Orr Dunbar reported on the recent meeting of the General Federation of Women's Clubs. Mapps spoke next. "We have had almost all races represented here tonight," she said, "and the friendly spirit shown convinces me that it is only a question of time before all the misunderstandings will have been put away and we will know that it is worth that counts, regardless of race and religions." Park kept her comments brief, perhaps because it was nearing midnight, but told guests she was "a great believer in organization" and suggested that people needed to work together "far better" than they currently were "in order to attain peace."[93]

New Yorker Addie W. Hunton was honored at a tea at Cannady's home, too. The *Advocate* reported few details about her experiences and achievements, but perhaps her reputation preceded her. By 1926, Hunton was known as an outspoken proponent of world peace and racial justice whose "political sensibilities" had been informed by a thirteen-month stint in France with the American Expeditionary Forces during World War I.[94] She also had written a memoir with fellow volunteer Kathryn Johnson that today is considered to be "the most detailed and complex account there is of the African American experience in World War I."[95] Hunton was a founder of the Circle for Peace and Foreign Relations, a field secretary for the NAACP, president of the Empire State Federation of Women's Clubs, and more.[96] When she visited Portland in September 1926, she was wrapping up a speaking tour of the Pacific Coast to discuss a recent "interracial investigative and friendship mission" to Haiti under the auspices of the Women's International League for Peace and Freedom.[97] During the afternoon tea, Hunton spoke about the need for "international and interracial understanding and harmony as the essence of world peace and advancement." Other guests representing a variety of clubs, churches, and governmental agencies also spoke during the three-hour gathering, including Dunbar and Trumbull, and Frank E. Carlson, pastor of Waverly Heights Congregational Church. "The party was not entirely made up of speeches," though; guests were "treated to a number of musical selections" as well as some "Negro spirituals."[98]

This mix of music and speeches also was evident at two interracial teas held in May 1926. The first event celebrated International Good-Will Day, a day designated by the World Conference on Education to promote "the spirit of international good will ... in the schools of the world."[99] Cannady invited fifty people of different races, ethnicities, and religions—white, Negro, Japanese, Chinese, Bahá'í, Jewish, Catholic—to her home to honor Elizabeth Greenleaf.[100] The Chicagoan had been instrumental in "the formation of new Bahá'í communities" across the country and had just attended the annual convention of the Bahá'ís of the United States and Canada, held in San Francisco.[101] Her "radiant spirit, staunch loyalty, noble character, [and] effective teaching method were distinguishing features of her consecrated life"; these characteristics may have prompted Cannady, who spoke at the convention, to invite Greenleaf to come to Portland for this special Sunday-afternoon tea.[102] Following talks by Greenleaf, George Orr Latimer, John Handsaker, and others, Cannady sang some "piano numbers."[103]

She barely had time to clean before the next tea, an event for two hundred people honoring special guests William Pickens and Louis Gregory, a Howard University alumnus and lawyer who had been introduced to Bahá'ísm by a white coworker at the U.S. Treasury Department. Gregory had an opportunity to visit 'Abdú'l-Bahá, leader of the Faith, in Egypt in 1911. When he returned to the United States, he made a commitment to try "to unify the white and colored peoples of the world and to aid in establishing the oneness of humanity."[104] Pickens and Gregory addressed the large crowd packed into Cannady's home, then other attendees spoke briefly, including: Branch President Jesse Ewing; Harry B. Sell, who had just joined Reed College as a professor of sociology; George Orr Latimer; Portland Board of Education member George P. Eisman; Alice Handsaker; and Albert R. Vail, a graduate of the Harvard Divinity School who had converted to Bahái'ísm in about 1918. The *Oregon Daily Journal* reported that the tea was just one of "a series ... given frequently on Sunday afternoons at the Cannady residence ... to bring about a better understanding between races and religious elements as a part of the general movement to establish world peace." That gathering was particularly successful in drawing a diverse group of guests; Negroes, Japanese, Chinese, Koreans, Germans, Swiss, French, Spaniards, Armenians, and Greeks were in attendance.[105]

Cannady held several teas for Ida Finch of Seattle, who had helped Martha Root promote Bahá'ísm in Japan and happened to be in Tokyo when a massive earthquake struck in 1923.[106] Among the forty guests assembled in August 1930 was Alexander Goldenweiser, a preeminent anthropologist originally from Kiev, Ukraine.[107] The scholar was visiting from New York City, where he was a lecturer at the Rand School of Social Science, but he soon would become a member of the faculties of the University of Oregon and Reed College. Goldenweiser was described as "a popular speaker" who "easily established rapport with his audience"; people who knew him "found him stimulating, entertaining, and a genial companion."[108] Another distinguished guest at the summer tea was John Lovell, Jr. He had just joined the faculty of Howard University as a professor of English; he would enjoy a productive career as an "outstanding scholar" and "an active and influential member of the Howard University community for forty-four years."[109] Lovell, Goldenweiser, Finch, and two other guests "gave brief, interesting accounts of their respective activities" before enjoying music and refreshments.[110]

The teas continued to grow in popularity and soon a few white women were hosting them, too. "Interracial teas are becoming quite the order of the day," Cannady observed in the *Advocate*. "No better way can be devised for promoting interracial good will. We hope that the good work will keep up."[111] She may have been referring to a "happy gathering" held at Alice Handsaker's home on East 31st Avenue.[112] One hundred "white and colored guests" were invited to attend the Negro History Week event honoring the late Paul Laurence Dunbar. Carrie Adams played "a number of negro songs," including an original composition featuring the words to his poem *The Old Front Gate*.[113] Marie Maxwell "beautifully sang 'The Birth of Morn,'" another Dunbar poem "set to music," and Shirley McCanns, who was then directing a group calling themselves the Roland Hayes Quartet, sang *Who Knows*? Cannady termed the interracial gathering "a brilliant affair."[114] Other teas were not linked to any particular event; they simply were opportunities to visit and enjoy music, and spend time with interesting people who were making a difference locally and nationally. One afternoon in August 1931, for example, Myrtle Campbell, a white woman who wrote occasionally for the *Advocate*, hosted a tea "in her beautiful flower garden." Ida Finch and Nettie Asberry were among the out-of-town guests; Portlanders who attended included Cannady; Jessie Coles-Grayson, who worked as a hat checker at the Portland Hotel; beautician Elise Reynolds; and Cannady's sister, Cora Jamison.[115]

Cannady believed so strongly in the teas as a way to foster "understanding and appreciation" for others that she discussed the idea whenever she traveled.[116] She told Clifford Miller, a reporter for the *New York Amsterdam News*, that the social occasions were used to "get across [the] propaganda, 'You don't know what you're missing if you don't know the Negro at his best.'" Mindful that she had an opportunity to promote her civil rights work—and Oregon as a progressive state—she informed Miller that the "message of love between white and black" had swept through the "state like a forest fire until" it had become "popular ... for one to be conversant on interracial issues and problems."[117] During the same East Coast trip, she told the *Chicago Defender*: "The good that is resulting from these teas can hardly be estimated."[118] And at the NAACP conference held in Los Angeles in the summer of 1928, she told attendees the idea for the interracial teas "was fostered by a few advanced thinkers who oppose[d] racial barriers and distinctions." The plan had been "an overwhelming success," according to Cannady, because it had promoted contact as a way to foster understanding.[119]

Following the NAACP conference, W. J. Wheaton, a fellow journalist at the *San Francisco Spokesman*, wrote an effusive tribute to Cannady and her civil rights work. Portland used to be "a hot bed of racial prejudice," he wrote. But Cannady "saw the situation, studied the conditions, and mapped out a program" that included assembling "the brightest minds of the varied races" to assist her with her ambitious plans. She used "her musical afternoons [as] the basis of her endeavors. Gradually the effects of contact began to tell and today the city of 'Roses' is among the most tolerant." Wheaton cited her tact, diplomacy, and courage, and observed that she was in the forefront of "America's brainiest and most useful [race] women."[120] Despite this praise, Wheaton may inadvertently have identified a reason why Cannady's civil rights work has largely been forgotten. Schools and homes are two venues that have long been associated with "women's work," making it easy to dismiss visits with students, and the interracial teas and other gatherings she hosted, as feminized forms of labor. Unpaid, behind-the-scenes reform seldom makes it into history books. Yet her efforts to promote interracial relations were grounded solidly in black history, politics, culture, and religion—subjects that revealed the depth of her knowledge and her belief in the importance of education as one way to eliminate race antipathy. And while a Sunday tea party may seem trivial—especially considering the external forces that challenged black Oregonians' existence during the 1920s—they allowed her to build and defend her community in ways that were seen as non-threatening by her white guests.

Millie Trumbull, one of Portland's prominent white women, commented on this milieu in the fall of 1925 after attending a tea at Cannady's home to honor royalty from East Africa. "In the Cannady home one finds … the beauty of a wide tolerance, a deep warm coloring of sympathy and the gentle perfume of hospitality that make of such occasions a rare treat."[121] Cannady celebrated diversity, something first-time guests surely sensed the moment they crossed the threshold and entered her home. As they scanned the room they would have seen people who looked like them—or not—and taken in the festive atmosphere that belied the serious focus of these gatherings. Cannady's residence was an oasis for many, if only for a few hours on a Sunday afternoon.

CHAPTER SIX

Spreading the Word

Each year The Advocate ... *sponsors a program of radio talks, school and college lectures and Negro literature public exhibits.*

— "Negro History Week," the *Advocate*, January 23, 1932, 2

We shall continue our program in an effort to harmonize relations between the Negro and white races. To that end, we favor interracial contacts through churches, conferences, parlor-groups et al.

— "A New Year," the *Advocate*, January 2, 1932, 2

Radio was an increasingly popular form of entertainment and information in Oregon, and across the United States, in the 1920s. Governmental restrictions on the use of radio waves during World War I had been lifted, and David Sarnoff's dream of a "Radio Music Box" in every home seemed destined to become reality—especially after he was promoted to general manager of RCA in 1921.[1] That summer, he "made the burgeoning radio business a national institution overnight" when the company donated a "radiophone transmitter" to broadcast the Jack Dempsey-Georges Carpentier fight from New Jersey. (Dempsey won the fight. One week later, he announced that he "was unwilling to fight Jack Johnson, 'or any other negro fighter.'")[2] More than half a million people were projected to listen to the July 2nd boxing match; that did not include the huge crowd expected to jam Times Square in New York City, where three large horns had been mounted so people could hear updates relayed from ringside.[3] One year later, Westinghouse could not keep up with demand for its radio sets—the company was churning out twenty-five thousand per month in 1922—prompting the *New York Times* to observe that in just "twelve months," radio had "become the most popular amusement in America" due to the variety of "programs suited to all ages and tastes."[4]

For Negroes, the radio opened up a world of entertainment that often was denied them due to Jim Crow restrictions at clubs, theaters, and dance halls. Black Portlanders invited friends and visitors over for elaborate dinner-dancing parties that lasted well into the night and featured musical broadcasts.[5] When the cast of *The Green Pastures* was in Portland, for example, Cannady let Thelma and DeNorval Unthank use her home to host "an informal reception and dancing party" for about sixty people. The "delightful affair" began at 11 p.m and lasted until 3:30 a.m. and included music from the radio and an "impromptu program" of songs by cast members.[6]

Once local radio stations became affiliated with networks like the National Broadcasting Company, founded in September 1926, black families in Portland and around the nation were able to participate in milestones such as the fiftieth-anniversary celebration of Tuskegee Institute, or the first broadcast by a sitting U.S. president.[7] And when the Mills Brothers made it big in the early 1930s with hits including *St. Louis Blues*, Cannady commented on radio's ability to break down color barriers: "Weekly, millions of people welcome Negro artists into their homes via ... the radio."[8] People could listen to the deep voice of Paul Robeson or dance to the music of Louis Armstrong, Duke Ellington, and other jazz artists—though the musicians, and the genre, remained controversial through the 1920s.[9]

Listeners in the Pacific Northwest welcomed the Mount Olivet Baptist Church choir, directed by Shirley McCanns, into their homes, too. One Sunday evening in 1927, a remote feed from the church sent "Negro Folk Songs" out to listeners around the state.[10] Aileen Davidson, the white clubwoman in central Oregon who had sought Cannady's help, told Cannady how much she and some friends had enjoyed the broadcast.[11] This feedback—coupled with the number of letters sent to Mount Olivet's pastor—prompted Cannady to observe: "The program was greeted by a large and enthusiastic visible audience and a still larger invisible audience. Even before the program was well under way, telephone messages of congratulations were pouring into the KGW radio station. ... Keep it up, Mt. Olivet—" she added, "it is just another means of helping to solve the race problem."[12]

Cannady also was a frequent guest of KGW, which offered a variety of programs to help fill its round-the-clock format.[13] She parlayed a focus on public health into a number of broadcasts during the annual observance of National Negro Health Week, established in 1915 by Tuskegee Institute President Booker T. Washington to encourage the "federal government to pay increased attention to Black health problems and issues."[14] Her versatility was particularly apparent in April 1932, when she managed to combine her civil rights work and passion for music with talks on health. She opened the week with a discussion of "The History and Need of Negro Health Week" on KGW, and concluded it with a Saturday broadcast on KXL about "The Influence of Music on Negro Health."[15] In between, Dr.

Yancy Jerome Franklin, Cannady's second husband.

Unthank and the Reverend Walter R. Lovell gave "radio talks" over KWJJ and KTBR, and Cannady's second husband, Yancy Jerome Franklin, discussed "The Influence of Play on Negro Health" on KXL.[16]

Even more important than this yearly event, however, was Negro History Week, observed during the second week in February to coincide with the birthdays of Abraham Lincoln and Frederick Douglass. Cannady was invited to speak on the stations owned by Portland's daily newspapers, the *Oregonian*, the *Telegram*, and the *Oregon Daily Journal*. The invitations may have represented an effort by station owners to be socially responsible to the communities they served. In 1927, for example, the Federal Radio Commission praised KGW "for its service, popularity, and charitable contributions."[17] But the invitations also are a good measure of Cannady's reputation in the white community and her standing as the city's unofficial ambassador of race relations.

Little documentary evidence remains of these programs, but brief articles in the *Advocate* help to reconstruct the details of some of her radio addresses and audience reaction to them. One February night in 1928, for instance, Cannady was allotted half an hour on KEX, the *Telegram*'s station, to discuss "The Economic, Social and Spiritual Contribution of the Negro to American Life." She encouraged her "friends to listen in and offer constructive criticism."[18] She was on KEX again two months later; this time, she was invited by U.S. Marshal Clarence R. Hotchkiss to discuss "The Negro's Contribution to American Citizenship" as part of a series of radio programs he was organizing about the duties and responsibilities associated with being a community member.[19]

A brief article in February 1931 mentioned how "grateful" Cannady was "for the many calls, letters and other expressions of appreciation" she had received following a Saturday-afternoon address on Negro history over KGW.[20] Later that year, she used that station to call for an end to race antipathy, invoking Du Bois' metaphor of living behind the veil of segregation when she told listeners:

> A moratorium on race prejudice would mean that 13 millions of colored people in America would become politically free from disenfranchisement; physically free from lynching; mentally free from ignorance and socially free from insult. It would mean that the veil, however superficial or real, however right or wrong, would be rent and the two races would, for the first time in America, be enabled to look each other squarely in the face from a common footing, without fear of private or public censor or censure.[21]

And in 1932, the *Advocate* "officially opened the local observance of the seventh annual Negro History Week" with a fifteen-minute broadcast from the *Oregonian*'s studio on the eleventh floor of its downtown Portland building. Cannady used her time on KGW to discuss reasons why the celebration was important and to promote upcoming events during the week. The following day, the editor had two engagements. She went to KOIN's studio in the Heathman Hotel to talk about "successful local efforts in teaching Negro History in the public schools." Cannady read an excerpt from an essay by a white Lincoln High School student to illustrate one pupil's reaction to the subject. At 9:30 p.m., she went to the Multnomah Hotel—the site of her graduation ceremony—to share information about "Negro Poetry" with those listening to KXL. Two more broadcasts over the weekend rounded out her full week: Saturday's topic was "The Negro Brings His Gifts" while Sunday's talk on KTBR was devoted to "Negro History and Race Relations."[22]

Cannady's activities in 1929 exemplify the scope of her work to promote racial uplift and interracial relations. A detailed *Advocate* article informed readers of her busy broadcast schedule: programs on the *Daily Journal*'s KOIN on February 4th and 6th; fifteen minutes on KGW on the

7th; a show on KEX from 11 to 11:15 a.m. on February 8th. But that was not all. Cannady spent the fourth-annual observance of Negro History Week talking to church groups about "The Influence of Christianity on Race Relations," and she made the trip south to Salem once again to address Willamette University's student body, teach "a special class in race relations," and meet with a missionary society.[23] Cannady also submitted long articles to each of the city's leading newspapers, a strategy that places her among other "cause" journalists—including suffragettes and abolitionists—who relied on favorable coverage in the press to try to reach people who were undecided about issues or unaware of them altogether.[24] Her work meshes, too, with that of other leaders of her day, including W. E. B. Du Bois, whose article, "Fifty Years Among Black Folks," was published in the *New York Times* in 1909.[25] Combining multiple forms of media—in this case teaching, public speaking, writing for her own newspaper and the white press, and broadcasting—was a shrewd way to disseminate her message to an even wider audience that year.

Overall, she felt that Negro History Week had been "fittingly" celebrated by Portlanders in 1929. J. K. Gill & Co. had displayed a number of books by Negro authors; photographs of black leaders from Cannady's collection enhanced the "artistic exhibit" at the store. Central Library "had its usual large collection" displayed; some of the city's women's clubs held programs featuring "Negro History"; the Bahá'í Assembly devoted an entire service "to the discussion of [the] Negro in American history"; and Meier & Frank's book department "arranged a nice display with a card announcing Negro History Week."[26]

Cannady was passionate about her subject, but perhaps no more so than in 1927. That year, her broadcast for Negro History Week occurred in the midst of a trying personal event that had ramifications for all of Oregon's black citizens. Cannady's thirteen-year-old son, George, celebrating his graduation from Fernwood Grammar School, had been refused admission to a local skating rink while white students attending the graduation party were welcome at the establishment. Given Cannady's status in Portland, the city's leading dailies might have devoted a brief paragraph to the story. But it became front-page news when the forty-one white students in the class decided to give up the "fun and festivities" and leave the rink. Principal Hugh B. Dorman told the *Oregonian* that the party would have been held elsewhere, "had it been known that the rules of the Imperial rink would bar one of the students." Charles A. Rice, superintendent of public schools, and George P. Eisman, a board of education member who had attended one of Cannady's teas, agreed with Dorman, "declaring that the schools were open to children of all races and religion." Cannady thanked the students for their stand "and expressed the hope that it might prove helpful in saving other colored students in the public school system from similar embarrassment."[27] She chose not to write immediately about the incident. Instead, she reprinted articles published in the *Oregonian* and *Oregon Daily Journal*, as well as a letter from board of education member Frank L. Shull to Principal Dorman. "I think that these young people ought to know that their action is approved and appreciated by all good citizens," Shull wrote. He also asked Dorman to acknowledge the teachers' role in the protest, since the students' action was "a reflection of the attitude of those who are over them in an advisory capacity."[28]

Two weeks after the incident, Cannady editorialized about children being "taught prejudice and race hatred by grown-ups." She wrote, "They know nothing about race prejudice and care nothing of racial differences, and would grow to manhood and womanhood admiring the worthy" if only they were allowed "to play together, ... go to school together, eat and sleep together." In fact, she argued, "If left alone, the children would solve our race problem."[29] The same day her editorial was published, the *Philadelphia Tribune*, a black newspaper, weighed in on the controversy in Portland. The column emphasized the important role of "mixed schools" in eliminating prejudice and fostering appreciation of others, and pointed out: "The parents of that city have learned a lesson in fair play and as in ages gone by—a little child shall lead them."[30]

The *Tribune* also printed a front-page story about Cannady's subsequent broadcast on KGW.[31] The *Southwest Review* in Albuquerque, New Mexico, picked up the story; other black newspapers across the country probably published it, too.[32] Cannady used her son's humiliating experience to call attention to the insidious nature of prejudice, and she issued a challenge to those listening to her that February: "May I urge you, every one of you, to read some of the literature of the Negro race, written by the Negro himself, during this week and the other 51 weeks of the year." If people had nothing in their personal libraries "concerning the history of the Negro race," she offered to loan items from her own extensive collection.[33] One white listener responded immediately: "Your lecture ... was splendid! Now would you please call up ... as I should like very much to ask you about some literature on the Negro question."[34] A woman in Washington contacted the *Oregonian* to inquire where she could obtain a copy of Langston Hughes' poem, "The Negro Speaks of Rivers."[35] And the white president of the Missionary Society of Unity Presbyterian Church asked Cannady to share "a message along the lines of [her] radio address" at an upcoming meeting about "The

Negro in America."[36] Cannady accepted the invitation and discussed the NAACP with about fifty women who reportedly "were greatly pleased with her message and invited her to return."[37] It is possible that she also solicited donations. At the peak of her outreach for the NAACP she informed Robert Bagnall, director of branches, that she was "planning to speak at several local large white churches for the sole purpose of raising funds for the National office."[38] James Weldon Johnson appreciated her efforts and noted, "We can always count upon you not to let an opportunity pass for bringing to the attention of the public the cause of the Association."[39]

Cannady spoke at many churches over the years, and frequently used two broad themes to frame her message of interracial goodwill: contact and cooperation, or Negro progress, history, and accomplishments. She emphasized the former during an address at St. Johns Community Church, where a two-day conference for church delegates from four states was held in 1925. According to the *Advocate*, she "discussed problems confronting the races ... and urged for closer contact, sympathetic understanding and more goodwill."[40] Cannady drew on the other topics for several talks she gave in churches in 1929. In January, for example, she visited Shiloh Baptist Church to discuss "Some Things That Retard Race Progress"; in April she traveled to a Methodist church in McMinnville, forty miles southwest of Portland, to talk about "Africa's Contribution to American Civilization."[41] Cannady also was invited to deliver a sermon in observance of "Inter-racial Day" to white parishioners at Portland's Centenary-Wilbur Methodist Episcopal Church. She discussed "the progress" of black Americans since Reconstruction—"although handicapped"—and described some of "the prejudices against" black Portlanders. She concluded with a plea "for a better relationship between the races."[42]

These gatherings were important to her civil rights work, but she also hoped to make a difference by meeting with small groups of young white church members, many of whom had had little or no contact with Negroes. Cannady believed that interaction was vital; she felt she could affect young people—as well as influence them—by sharing ideas and information in non-threatening settings. In addition, these meetings allowed her to link Christianity and race relations. Cannady gave meaningful talks to three groups of students at the Daily Vacation Bible School in Newberg in 1924. She told them about "the wonderful advancement of her race and argued that a race" that "was capable of producing" men such as Booker T. Washington, George Washington Carver, and others, "was deserving of respect, honor and love." Then she drew on one of her favorite analogies. "God created a garden of beautiful flowers of all colors," she told the pupils. If "flowers, representing many colors and perfumes, could get along so beautifully and harmoniously," then it was even "more essential" for "God's children, who were of a higher creation, [to] live side by side in peace and harmony." She urged the young people to look beyond markers such as "color, creed and circumstances of birth," and work toward "more friendly" relations among groups. That was a foreign concept to students who had never had contact with black people. Census records for 1920 reflect just eight Negroes in Yamhill County; none apparently lived in town, because Cannady told the students that even though they "had no colored neighbors" yet, Newberg was "likely to get her share" as more Negroes settled in the state. When that happened, she hoped the children would "extend a helping hand ... to their colored brothers and sisters" instead of viewing them with "hatred, suspicion and fear."[43]

Cannady traveled frequently to talk to youth groups, congregations, missionary societies—anyone who would listen to her message about race relations. Occasionally, though, she invited people to come to *her*. A large, front-page ad in the *Advocate* in October 1926 encouraged readers to come to the First Congregational Church in downtown Portland for an "illustrated lecture depicting the progress of the colored people in the United States since their emancipation from chattel slavery." In case readers missed this two-column notice, a brief announcement on the back page called attention to the opportunity to learn more about history, art, poetry, and music.[44] She wanted all of her friends, "both white and colored," to attend, but felt the program would particularly help students "in their school work."[45] The *Portland Telegram* publicized the event, too, by printing Cannady's photo and a description of the program featuring "negro spirituals" by Shirley McCanns.[46]

In December 1925, Cannady "gave an illustrated talk ... to a full house" at Woodstock Methodist Episcopal Church.[47] She was especially pleased to see several Reed College teachers and students in the audience. And late in 1928, the *Advocate* reported that about a hundred "colored and white friends" had attended her "impressive address" on "The Negro's Contribution to American Life" at Bethel AME Church. Cannady used a stereopticon—a type of projector with two lenses—to show slides "depicting the progress of the American Negro."[48] Images were critical because they introduced white audiences to prominent individuals, both living and deceased. The slides also helped to dispel the stereotypes that were perpetuated in history books and many white newspapers. And Cannady was able to instill race pride in her black audiences. "The Negro knows practically nothing of his own history, ancient or modern, and the masses of the white race know less," she wrote in one editorial. "Writers have surfeited us with that sort of history which is little more than a register of the crimes and misfortunes of mankind, instead of emphasizing the virtues of the heroes and the heroines who ... have suffered and died for ideals."[49] Holding the illustrated talks in churches may have enhanced her message, too: seated in a church with the lights dimmed, watching larger-than-life images and listening to her "logical conclusions," it would have been difficult to ignore her efforts to secure equal rights for black Oregonians.[50]

Homes offered another intimate setting for her talks about interracial relations. As Cannady discovered with the teas, ideas could be discussed more openly in the private sphere, where the informal environment encouraged people to "get near each other" and confront their stereotypes and misconceptions.[51] In this case, though, Cannady was the one who crossed the color line when she was invited to bring her message of interracial goodwill into white homes. These gatherings usually were hosted by women who belonged to missionary societies affiliated with Portland-area churches. Cannady shared their devotion to religion and belief in the uplift of humanity; this commonality helped equalize the obvious differences in skin tone as the women looked into their souls for answers to problems facing Portland and the nation in the early 1900s.

Articles in the *Advocate* about Cannady's talks to these religious groups read more like calendar entries; there are plenty of facts, but few substantive details. Nevertheless, information about the groups she met with and topics she discussed help to bring the overall picture of Cannady's advocacy into sharper focus. On a Wednesday afternoon in 1928, for example, she was invited to Reverend Lemon's home to speak to the missionary society about the "great contributions to art, science, music and literature ... made by Negroes."[52] One spring, fifty women from Laurelwood Methodist Episcopal Church gathered at Stella Bellingham's home on 101 Street to hear Cannady talk. She blended several themes that day when she discussed "the handicaps, the accomplishments and the hopes of her race." Then she urged the white women "to contact the colored race" and work toward "a better understanding ... and ultimate peace."[53] And on a fall Friday afternoon, Cannady was invited to Leona Beeson's home on Glenn Avenue in northeastern Portland. More than fifty women of the Home and Foreign Missionary Society of Unity Presbyterian Church listened to her ideas for solving "the race problem."[54]

Religion always had been a central part of Cannady's life. She attended services at St. Paul Methodist Church in Littig during her formative years;

as an adult she considered the First AME Zion Church "her church home."[55] But she also found herself drawn to the century-old Bahá'í Faith and its focus on brotherhood, unity, and human rights.

James and Harriet Latimer may have "aroused" her interest in the religion, which she said was "attracting the attention of thinking people all over the world"—including the philosopher Alain Locke, who became a convert in 1918.[56] The Latimers' son, George, had spent two weeks in Haifa, Palestine, shortly after World War I ended. A highlight of his twelve-day trip was spending time with 'Abdú'l-Bahá, the oldest son of, and successor to, Bahá'u'lláh, whose teachings formed the basis of the Faith. Latimer chronicled his visit in *The Light of the World*, which he self-published in 1920.[57] He may have given Cannady a copy to read, or perhaps she attended a meeting of the Portland Bahá'í Assembly with the family one evening.[58] The story of her conversion has been lost, but records indicate that she was a "recognized believer" by 1928.[59] She embraced the Faith's tenets and made the religion part of her life and civil rights work for the next fifty years.[60]

Cannady traveled to San Francisco in April 1926 to speak at the eighteenth annual convention of the Bahá'ís of the United States and Canada. According to an *Advocate* article by Louis Gregory, who had attended an interracial tea at Cannady's home weeks earlier, she "presented the greeting of the [NAACP] and described some of the difficulties of life among colored Americans."[61] Cannady said she had never "witnessed such complete harmony and love existing between individuals" and hoped to "have the pleasure of attending such a convention again." Seven months later, she was "utterly surprised" to learn that she had been asked "to teach in the cause." She called it "a rare opportunity to serve humanity" but recognized that she needed "to seek sufficient understanding and knowledge of the Word of God" so she could "impart helpful information to those with whom" she came "in contact."[62] As always, Robert Bagnall was pleased to hear about her accomplishments: "Congratulations on the splendid work you are doing, and especially on your address before the Bahá'íst Conference in San Francisco. Good work!"[63]

In 1927, Cannady spoke at the Portland Bahá'í Assembly on Yamhill Street about her trip to the East Coast to attend the Fourth Pan-African Congress.[64] She surely would have highlighted some interesting aspects of her journey, including meeting stockbroker Roy Wilhelm, the man who inspired Martha Root to convert to the Faith.[65] And she would have shared details of an address about "Racial Understanding" that Wilhelm arranged for her to give in Teaneck, New Jersey. According to a local newspaper, she dwelled "at some length on the Bahá'í influence for racial amity." Forty people, "some coming a long distance in spite of the heavy downpour," listened "in rapt attention" to her "remarkable talk."[66] Cannady also would have told the Portland Assembly about her short stay at Green Acre Bahá'í School in Eliot, Maine; the former hotel recently had come "under the direct supervision of the National Spiritual Assembly of the Bahá'ís" of the United States.[67] Cannady noted that her "brief sojourn" at Green Acre "was a spiritual treat"; it was a working holiday, too. She delivered an evening address "to a large audience" that included a Dartmouth College professor about the "necessity for inter-racial co-operation in solving the Negro problem." After breakfast the following morning, she shared information with thirty people about the upcoming Pan-African Congress. Four people reportedly were inspired to attend the conference in Manhattan as a result of her remarks.[68]

In 1929, Cannady took her interest in Bahá'ísm to another level when she helped found the Esperanto Breakfast Club, or *La Esperanto Matenmango Klubo*.[69] The Esperanto communication system was created to "allow people who speak different native languages to communicate, yet at the same time retain their own languages and cultural identities."[70] Leader 'Abdú'l-Bahá encouraged followers to study Esperanto because it was seen as a way to spread "the message of world peace."[71] Cannady had taken a course in Esperanto the previous winter; she offered to give Elise Reynolds, her sister Cora Jamison, and the other members weekly lessons "and to outline a course in [the study of] Negro history."[72] Topics included "the Negro in politics," which coincided with an upcoming visit by Congressman Oscar De Priest, "The Negro Folk Sermon," Negro History Week, and poetry by James Weldon Johnson and Langston Hughes.[73] Cannady's language training was put to good use when she entertained Martha Root, an expert Esperantist, in 1931.

Pacific College President Levi T. Pennington wrote in 1929: "Mrs. Cannady's contributions toward better race relationships are so many and so varied that a mere catalog of them might be tedious."[74] But cataloging is a necessary first step toward restoring her civil rights work to its rightful place in history. Accounts in the *Advocate* and other black newspapers, in the white press, and in NAACP files help illustrate the scope of her outreach during the early 1900s. Cannady was constantly on the go, broadcasting during Negro History Week, talking to missionary societies and youth groups, even speaking from the pulpit on numerous occasions. That she was such a popular speaker makes clear that at least some white individuals were interested in promoting harmony between the races, one of the messages that Cannady preached.

A contemporaneous newspaper article described Cannady as a "woman of unusual ability, tact and perseverance" who offered audiences a "brilliant array of logical conclusions that ... caused them to think more seriously of the problems [confronting] the race."[75] While this description may be exuberant, it nevertheless gives some insight into how she presented information to her radio and religious audiences. Cannady may have drawn on rhetorical strategies learned in her law classes, or perhaps she modeled her delivery techniques after orators she admired, including the NAACP's James Weldon Johnson or William Pickens. Or she may have known intuitively how to analyze and evaluate her audiences, organize and deliver her thoughts, describe the need for reform using concrete details, provide vivid examples, and examine the cause and effect of race antipathy. A white lawyer commented on this in 1932 after hearing her speak. "As a former professor of public speaking at the University of Oregon, I want to go on record as saying that your speech was a little gem. It was crowded with meaning, and phrased in such clear, concise, effective English that it might well be a model for public speaking students to study," he wrote.[76] Depending on the group, Cannady also offered practical suggestions for action, such as when she urged people to join the NAACP or support the Dyer Anti-Lynching Bill. Although she acknowledged the power of the press—both for education and condemnation—she was deeply aware of the power of oratory to proselytize.[77]

By necessity, most of her engagements were in Oregon. Limited finances, family obligations, and editorial duties kept her close to Portland and the community she primarily served. But many people, including her good friend Alice Handsaker, recognized Cannady's concerted efforts to effect reform. "She is in constant demand as a speaker on race relations before churches, clubs, missionary societies, etc., always giving her time and strength freely," she wrote in 1929. "Her influence has reached out into the remote parts of the state and has become a mighty force in molding thought regarding inter-racial relations."[78] Cannady's civil rights work must be seen, finally, for what it was: an important contribution to the work other lecturers and editors were doing during the 1920s and 1930s. W. E. B. Du Bois, William Pickens, Robert Bagnall, Nettie J. Asberry, A. Philip Randolph, Charlotta Bass, and others also were pushing for reform during those decades. These individuals interacted on many levels, from interracial teas to national conventions, and each, in her or his own way, built on the vital work the others were doing.

CHAPTER SEVEN
The Birth of a Nation

Promoters of 'The Birth of a Nation' film petitioned the city council again on last Wednesday morning for a rehearing to show the film in Portland. The editor of The Advocate *was summoned and spoke against the film, pointing out that it was not only historically untrue but that it incited hatred between the races.*

— "'Birth of Nation' Film Again Unanimously Denied by City," the *Advocate*, April 11, 1931, 1

The nation's first full-length motion picture featured a cast of eighteen thousand people, including the rising star Lillian Gish, took eight months to complete, and by some accounts cost a reported $500,000 to make—a staggering sum for 1915.[1] Although some reviewers were critical of the film's conflation of "the negro with cruelty, superstition, insolence and lust," most were spellbound by the story as well as the cinematography, and applauded the silent picture that "at once became the most controversial and successful film in the history of cinema."[2] The story was based on novels and a play by Thomas Dixon, Jr., though director David Wark Griffith added many of his own touches to the script before shooting began in Southern California on July 4, 1914.[3] Griffith described the massive project as a "picturisation of history," but, as scholars have pointed out, the melodrama about the Civil War and its aftermath was told from the perspective of two Southerners still trying to come to terms with defeat and the abolition of slavery.[4]

The film follows two white families who have known each other for some time—the Stonemans in the North, and the Camerons, plantation owners in South Carolina—through the idyllic antebellum period and the ravages of the Civil War.[5] But according to the film, the war was nothing compared with Reconstruction; Griffith portrays the twelve-year period as a humiliating time for Southerners who were "forced to acknowledge blacks as equals." Ben Cameron, a wounded veteran, is particularly "tormented by the ruin he sees all around him." But he has an epiphany when he sees a group of children wearing white sheets and pretending to be ghosts. The costumes frighten some black children, and their terrified reactions give him "the inspiration" he needs to form the Ku Klux Klan.[6] The remainder of the film shows the Klan restoring law and order to the land. In the process, according to both Dixon and Griffith, a new nation is born, one in which white supremacy becomes the order of the day.

Negroes in Southern California were alarmed by the film's message as well as its celebration of the KKK.[7] Charlotta Bass, editor of the *California Eagle*, wrote in her memoir that she "knew ... the production of such a motion picture would be a major social, intellectual and artistic block in the path toward ... civil liberties for all." In addition, she feared the story "would have a devastating effect on better race relations in Los Angeles" as well as "in the state and nation," and urged that filming be halted at once.[8] But work continued, and by the time production concluded at the end of October, Griffith had amassed nearly one hundred and forty thousand feet of film and was forced to "condense, condense, condense." He finally managed to pare down the film to about thirteen thousand feet, or a running time of just under three hours.[9]

Patrons in Riverside, California, had an opportunity to preview *The Clansman* on January 1, 1915.[10] A "capacity audience" at the Loring Opera House enjoyed the film, as did a reporter for the *Daily Press* who believed it was "certain to win public favor in the east as well as in other parts of the country where it is shown."[11] Two months later, the renamed film opened to acclaim in New York City.[12] But the NAACP, headquartered there, had been marshaling members and materials to protest the film in New York and in other Eastern cities. The *Crisis*, edited by NAACP cofounder W. E. B. Du Bois, kept Cannady and other readers apprised of the organization's strategies and last-ditch efforts to convince the National Board of Censorship of Motion Pictures that *The Birth of a Nation* was harmful to race relations.[13]

Even as the NAACP fought to have *The Birth of a Nation* banned from New York, Boston, and other cities on the East Coast, it reached out to branches across the country to see how they were faring in their efforts to do the same. A two-page typed letter from National Secretary Mary Childs Nerney arrived in Portland in mid-April and posed three questions:

> Is the moving picture play, 'The Birth of a Nation' ... being played in your city? If not, is it advertised for production and on what date?
>
> Has your city or state a local censoring committee or board? If so, send us immediately their names and addresses.
>
> Has your city an ordinance regulating the production of moving pictures? What is it?

If the movie already was scheduled to be shown, Nerney advised branches to take immediate action and "interest the local clergy, colored and white, civic organizations, welfare societies, secret societies, women's clubs, etc., to unite ... in a protest." Next, she urged branch officers and representatives of the organizations she listed to send letters to the mayor, police chief, and other local officials to protest "against the play on the ground that it endangers public morals and may lead to a breach of the peace."[14] Nerney offered background information on the NAACP's fight in New York and Boston, quotes from social worker Jane Addams, who condemned the film in an *Evening Post* article, and comments from Francis Hackett's critical column in the *New Republic* in case branches needed supporting details for their letters.[15] Finally, she urged branches to act immediately and make every effort "to secure the cooperation of all elements of colored people and prominent white people."[16] Cannady replied to the query; she may have told Nerney about Portland's new Board of Motion Picture Censors and the ordinance that created it. One week later, Nerney wished her "success" protesting *The Birth of a Nation*, and promised to send details of the victorious fight to bar the film from Chicago in case they proved helpful to the battle in Oregon.[17]

That struggle appears to have started on June 21, 1915, when Cannady and other members of the Executive Committee of the Portland Branch wrote Mayor H. Russell Albee to protest the "very vicious play designed to create prejudice and race hatred against the colored people." The committee told him they believed him "to be a fair and impartial justice-loving Christian gentleman," and asked him to watch the film with members of the city's Board of Motion Picture Censors. They hoped he would see reason and "use [his] influence to prevent" *The Birth of a Nation* from showing in Portland theaters. But in case he still was not convinced, Cannady tucked in a few clippings—perhaps Jane Addams' *Post* article—for him to read to help "prove conclusively" why the film should be banned.[18] Yet two weeks later, on July 4, 1915, the *Morning Oregonian* announced: "Protests from the negroes are the result of reports that the photoplay 'The Birth of a Nation,' known also as 'The Clansman,' is to be shown in Portland soon."[19] The irony was not lost on Cannady: while the nation was celebrating Independence Day, Negroes found themselves on the defensive, protesting a film that exacerbated their second-class status in America.

Rather than report on the protest, both the *Oregonian* and *Oregon Journal* printed a long letter Cannady had sent to the editors that outlined the reasons why the film should not be shown. "I wish to make an appeal through your valuable paper to the civic organizations, churches and societies of Portland to protest against the showing of the vicious photoplay

... anywhere in this city," she wrote, drawing on Nerney's suggestions. Cannady then discussed the reasons why *The Birth of a Nation* should be banned, including its historical inaccuracies, scenes that aggravated "race rancor and prejudice," and approbation of the Ku Klux Klan.[20] She also referred to the "Gus chase," a long scene featuring Gus, "a lust-maddened Negro," who surreptitiously follows Flora Cameron, a white woman, from her home to a nearby spring.[21] He rushes from the bushes, grabs Flora's elbow, and announces via an intertitle that he wants to marry her.[22] Apparently aghast at the thought, she breaks free and runs headlong to the top of a hill. Griffith's unique cinematic techniques, coupled with the score and "Flora's zigzagging course," help convey her "desperation" and add to the suspense.[23] From the precipice, a wild-eyed Flora watches Gus—by now foaming at the mouth—scrambling toward her, leading audiences to believe he wants to rape her. "Stay away or I'll jump!" she screams silently as another intertitle flashes on the screen.[24] But he continues to advance, and Flora jumps to her death rather than face Gus. Justice is promptly served when the Klan—organized by her brother, Ben—pronounces Gus guilty and dumps his body, with a note bearing a skull and crossbones and the letters KKK, on the porch of a power-hungry mulatto politician. Although the National Board of Censorship had recommended "a substantial reduction in the details of the chase of the white girl ..., which in the original [was] said to have been the most dreadful portrayal of rape ever offered for public view," it still was a scene that provoked intense reactions from white theatergoers.[25] The *Evening Post*, for example, reported that it "called forth many excited whispered comments; and from then on to the end of the film there was ready applause for anything derogatory to negroes and for the activity of the Ku Klux Klan."[26]

Cannady, in her letters to Portland's leading newspapers, observed that the "Gus chase" and scenes glorifying the Klan helped "poison the minds of the young, those with whom our young must live and work out their destiny." More broadly, she wrote, "The whole play is a diabolical scheme of false impressions, wrought by a master hand bent on prejudicing the public mind against the colored American, and utterly destroying him." She called on all "well-thinking men and women" in Portland to come together to protest *The Birth of a Nation* for the sake of "peace and harmony": "I know that you will agree that the perpetuation of amity in community conditions depends entirely on respectful friendliness of one race or group for another."[27]

In asking for their assistance, she and other Branch members also may have hoped that the city's new seven-member Board of Motion Picture Censors would rise to the occasion and refuse to allow *The Birth of a Nation* to be shown in local theaters. Ordinance No. 30154 stipulated that no film could be exhibited, sold, rented, or loaned unless at least four members approved of it in writing, and provided for a fine of up to $500 (more than $10,000 today) or imprisonment for a period up to six months for anyone convicted of violating any of its provisions.[28] Board members were given the power to refuse films depicting violence, "obscene, indecent, or immoral" material, "cruelty to human beings or animals," or topics that might "disturb the public peace."[29] All films deemed appropriate for exhibition were given a "certificate of approval," but censors could make that contingent upon required "excisions or alterations."[30] Equally important, the board could "withdraw its approval of any film for cause" with a unanimous vote.[31]

With this public declaration of the Portland Branch's stance on *The Birth of a Nation*, Cannady entered a debate being waged by other black editors across the country: should their newspapers keep silent or editorialize against the racist film? A front-page article in the *California Eagle* observed that some "Caucasian Americans and Afro-Americans ... seem to think that the efforts made by members of the race to stop the showing of [*The Birth of a Nation*] ... was a mistake, and that [protests here] only stimulated a greater desire by a greater number to see the film." But Bass felt "that as long as the Afro-Americans of this country sit supinely by and raise no voice against the injustice heaped upon them, conditions for them in this country will gradually grow worse."[32] Harry C. Smith, publisher of the *Gazette* in Cleveland, Ohio, also felt activism was important. He devoted "more space to his campaign against the film than he gave to any other political topic" during 1915, printing letters to and from Ohio's governor, articles from other newspapers, editorials, and news items in an effort "to persuade state and city officials—especially Governor Frank Willis—to censor the film."[33] At the other end of the spectrum was W. Calvin Chase, editor of the *Bee* in Washington, D.C., who believed that "protest against the presentations of the 'Birth of a Nation'" only served "to advertise the photo-play."[34] Cannady acknowledged that her Branch's efforts to ban the film could "help to advertise the play further." Nevertheless, like Bass and Smith, she felt the issue was too important to keep silent. "I think we as citizens owe it to ourselves to enter a protest and let it be known that the types of colored people shown and the American sentiment expressed do not meet our approval," she wrote in her letter to Portland editors.[35]

Between July 4th, when the *Morning Oregonian* and *Oregon Journal* printed Cannady's letter, and August 29th, when the movie opened at the Heilig, Cannady and the Portland Branch did everything in their power to convince the Board of Motion Picture Censors to ban the film. Cannady contacted Governor James Withycombe and told him she feared the film "would be likely to inflame prejudice against the colored race, and add further to the difficulties of ... colored citizens." He, in turn, informed Mayor Harry Albee that "if the charges concerning this film are well-founded, it would seem to me most desirable that it be examined carefully; for certainly we owe protection and recognition to our colored citizens."[36] Albee thanked his colleague for "calling attention to the protests of the colored people over the exhibition of the film 'The Birth of a Nation.'" Then, sounding every bit the politician, he replied: "I ... feel just as you do in the matter—that the film should be examined most carefully before it is presented to the public .... Our Board of Censors here is composed of members whose judgment has been tested through several years of work along this line, and they are preparing to give the film a thorough viewing."[37]

On July 12th, a petition backed by Cannady and Branch President James Merriman, and signed by Ervin Flowers, Lillian Morrow, Wyatt Williams, James Bell, Charity Binford, and more than three hundred other people, was sent to Mayor Albee and the Board of Motion Picture Censors. The petition began: "The Portland branch of the National Association for the Advancement of Colored People, viewing with alarm the coming of ... 'The Birth of a Nation,' ... earnestly requests you to prohibit its exhibition any where in this city." The typed, single-spaced document then repeated Cannady's concerns about the film's effect on racial harmony and its derision of black Americans. Finally, if board members missed the subtle reminders that they were empowered to refuse any films affecting the public peace, the last paragraph aimed to convince them of the need to take action: "In the name of 'PEACE' which is uppermost in the minds of all loyal Americans ... [and] in all fairness and justice to the colored American who at this time is making such an uphill struggle, we earnestly pray you to grant our request."[38] Albee apparently continued to weigh the pros and cons of the film for the next six weeks. He sought information from the mayors of Oakland, California, Cleveland, and Tacoma, Washington, about how they had dealt with the controversy.[39] He also responded to a Portland man who was against the exhibition. "I believe much of the objection to the film comes from those who have not seen it; however, the matter is entirely in the hands of the Board of Censors," Albee wrote.[40]

Despite the outcry from black Portlanders and some white residents, *The Birth of a Nation* debuted in the city on Sunday, August 29, 1915. That morning, the *Oregonian* added to moviegoers' anticipation by publishing a review by Edith Knight Holmes, who felt "fortunate" to attend the "exhibition ... given before the Portland censors." Calling the movie a "superb achievement"

as well as "a triumph in film production," Holmes proclaimed every one of the film's twelve reels "a brilliant gem, a marvel to the beholder." She summarized many of the "tremendous, gripping, soul-stirring and tragic" scenes—all of which were "appropriately cast" and flawlessly interpreted—before noting how impressive it was to watch the "Ku Klux Klan dashing out to take the law into their own hands."[41] The combination of pageantry, new cinematic techniques, and rousing orchestral arrangement affected white audiences in Portland, as elsewhere, like no other movie to date. Individuals made plans to see the film with friends and family, which the daily press found to be newsworthy; the *Oregonian*, for example, reported that a "number of society matrons" had hosted parties in conjunction with viewing *The Birth of a Nation*.[42]

But Cannady still was not ready to give up the fight. "The colored people think that the picture should never have been passed by the censorship board on the ground that it is libelous to that race," said attorney A. Walter Wolf, representing Cannady and other black Portlanders. Wolf asked the judge "to issue a warrant for the arrest of the owners and managers of" the film; he refused, reportedly because "he did not feel like taking any action after the picture had been passed by the censorship board."[43] Bart Bertelson, the film's manager, said in a prepared statement: "I can see no reason for the colored citizens seeking to stop the exhibition of this film, which has been shown in almost every large city in the country." In fact, he believed their actions were "discriminatory and unfounded," and observed, "What reason they can find for objecting to a film which has been passed by a board that is known to be more painstaking than the average censor board, neither I nor anyone else can see."[44]

If there were further protests by Cannady and other Portlanders, they were drowned out by the applause of enthralled audiences who paid as much as $1 for a box seat—the equivalent of about $21 today.[45] John W. Kelly declared in the *Evening Telegram*: "'The Clansman' was a mediocre novel; dramatized it was a cheap play, but under the directing genius of D. W. Griffith it is expanded and transformed into a photoplay of such resplendent power that it can hold an audience for three solid hours."[46] The *Morning Oregonian* reported that audiences who saw the "marvelous" film "went wild with enthusiasm. They applauded, they cheered, they stood up in the intensity of their emotions as they saw the great army of mounted Ku Klux Klan sweeping down the road, fording streams, dashing to the rescue of either Northerner or Southerner in peril."[47] To help set the mood, the boxes and balconies in the theater were draped with U.S. flags, and a twelve-piece orchestra was hired to play "the incidental and descriptive music."[48]

Cannady and other black Portlanders probably were shocked to see the large, five-column advertisement for the film that appeared in the *Sunday Oregonian* on September 12th. "Your Last Chance to See THE BIRTH OF A NATION," proclaimed the ad. "LAST WEEK OF PORTLAND'S BIGGEST THRILL." More disturbing, though, was the border; an image of a Klansman dressed in regalia and sitting astride a horse was repeated to frame the text and call attention to the film's "Gripping, Appealing, Blood-Tingling, Soul-Stirring" scenes.[49] A week later, the Heilig made an "Announcement Extraordinary!": *The Birth of a Nation* would be shown twice daily for "An Extra Week!" "to accommodate the many hundreds who

wished to see Griffith's Half-Million Dollar Masterpiece." The extended engagement also featured reduced prices, which made it possible for those who still had not seen the "spectacular production" to partake of its "educational value."[50]

It was with sadness, then, that the *Sunday Oregonian* finally announced the film's final two "performances" on September 26, 1915. The four-week engagement set a "new record for a production in Portland" and "establishe[d] a precedent which has made theatrical and picture house managers sit up and take notice." The columnist summarized the "remarkable motion picture" and its realism that allowed patrons to feel as if they were "actually living in the Civil War period. For three hours the most thrilling historical incidents and happenings unfold themselves before [one's] eyes. ... It is no wonder that the audience goes wild with enthusiasm. ... It is all action and thrills and patriotism." In four short weeks, *The Birth of a Nation* had "become the talk of the town" and "struck a popular chord with Portland people."[51] But forgotten in the gushing description was Cannady's protest of the racist film and its effect on race relations in the city.

The Birth of a Nation returned to the city for a seven-day run at Sunset Theatre beginning on Palm Sunday 1918. Moviegoers could attend a weekday matinée of the silent spectacle for a quarter; for a dime more, patrons could spend a relaxing evening watching the drama of the Civil War and Reconstruction unfold.[52] But not everyone in Portland turned out for the re-release of the motion picture. Cannady led a "storm of protest" over the racist film, which reportedly resulted in the deletion of a number of objectionable scenes.[53] After viewing it again, however, she remained convinced that it should not be shown in Portland and renewed her objections during a meeting at the office of George L. Baker, who had been elected mayor five months earlier.

Baker found his hands tied. Although he agreed that the picture was "decidedly bitter" toward "the colored race"—interesting comments given his purported membership in the Portland Klan—he did not have the authority to halt "motion pictures or other entertainments of an undesirable nature" after they had been approved by the local Board of Motion Picture Censors.[54] To his credit, Baker instructed the city attorney to draft an emergency ordinance giving the mayor and two commissioners legal authority to "stop the picture because of the race hatred element involved." But a divided city council rejected the proposed law. Unwilling to pay between $750 and $2,000 to the Sunset's owner, who threatened to sue for lost revenue if the movie were banned, the council allowed the film to continue its run.[55] Cannady took the decision personally. "Soon after the action by the council," the *Morning Oregonian* reported, she "broke down and wept bitterly in the council chamber because she had failed after nearly a week's fight to get the picture stopped." Cannady told the reporter "she had gone for a week with little sleep and irregular meals and the strain was too great after her mission failed." The theater's manager, John A. Jennings, informed reporters he believed "an injustice [had] been done him in the criticisms of the production at his showhouse." He reminded critics he had "voluntarily" made all the "eliminations the colored people" requested, and maintained that the film depicted "nothing that should cause race hatred or should be distasteful in any way to the colored people."[56] Black Americans like Beatrice Cannady, however, saw *The Birth of a Nation* as "a rough and cruel racist slander upon Afro-Americans during Reconstruction" and vowed to continue to object to showings of the film.[57]

Despite this devastating setback in 1918, Cannady protested the movie again four years later. But by then, Oregon was a vastly different place for Negroes due to the Klan's arrival in the state in the spring of 1921. Burning crosses illuminated nighttime initiation ceremonies. Parades in the state capital and other Oregon towns were occasions for Klansman to don their peaked caps and white robes. And a near-lynching in Medford, an "eviction" in Roseburg, and recruiting films for the Klan added to the overall climate of terror in 1922.

Fearful that "what was depicted on the screen could easily be acted out against [Negroes] in reality," Cannady injected a palpable sense of urgency into her campaign to defend black Oregonians against the external threat posed by additional showings of the film.[58] At the end of March 1922, days before it was scheduled to begin a limited run at the Blue Mouse, Cannady sent a telegram to NAACP headquarters in New York. She requested details about which governors had banned *The Birth of a Nation*, and asked the organization to contact Governor Ben W. Olcott immediately. To underscore the urgency of her telegram, she added that more than five thousand Klansmen were in the city.[59] James Weldon Johnson acted immediately and wired the governor. "This film has caused serious race clashes in many places by stirring up race prejudice," he wrote. "In the interest of law and order we urge that you prohibit this exhibition."[60] Executive Secretary Walter White, responding directly to Cannady's request for information, told her the NAACP had considerable information about struggles to bar *The Birth of a Nation*, but noted that "it would be impossible" to get materials to her "in time to prevent the showing of the film in Portland." Instead, he urged her to contact E. Burton Ceruti, a founder of the Los Angeles NAACP Branch, who had engaged in the fight against the film there. Meanwhile, Cannady was encouraged to continue her efforts: "We are much interested in the fight and hope that you will advise us of its outcome."[61]

But again, the fight did not end as she had hoped. The film began a limited engagement at the Blue Mouse on April 1, 1922. Advertisements in the *Morning Oregonian* proclaimed the film the "8th WONDER OF THE WORLD" and noted that the Blue Mouse Orchestra would play the "famous original 'Birth of a Nation' musical score" five times daily.[62] An opening-day review informed readers that the manager had obtained "a brand new print of this picture" just in time for its "popular return here." With its "many memorable scenes," "important events in the history of the nation," and all-star cast, the columnist observed, "[T]here is little wonder that 'The Birth of a Nation' is still such a great production."[63] What the reporter failed to mention, however, was the movie's depiction of the birth of the Ku Klux Klan. But Cannady and other black Portlanders undoubtedly noticed the fine print in the advertisement for the film: "100% John Hamrick."[64] The manager's public declaration of his "100 percent pure Americanism," a requirement for Klan membership, certainly added to the growing sense of alienation and fear felt by Portland's black citizens.

The film returned to Portland in December 1923. This time, however, there apparently was no outcry from the black community. Beatrice Cannady, who had led the earlier protests, had been injured in a car accident and was confined at home under a doctor's care.[65] But that did not keep her from working on the newspaper. The final issue of the *Advocate* that year carried a short but pointed reference to the community's silence: "Recently the picture was shown in several motion picture houses in Portland, but not a word of protest was heard from the local branch."[66] Cannady frequently was at odds with the Branch for what she perceived to be indifference over race relations in Oregon, but it does seem unusual that no one picketed outside theaters as branch members in Los Angeles, New York, Boston, and other cities had done in previous years.[67] Yet the Portland Klan, which was very visible in the city by then, outnumbered Negroes by as much as ten to one. Fear of reprisal may very well have kept people at home; after all, a near-lynching involving a black man in nearby Oregon City was still fresh in people's minds.[68]

Cannady contrasted the overwhelming acceptance of the film in Oregon—and most of the United States—with the French government's reaction. In August 1923, a banner headline in the *Advocate* read: "French Stop Birth of a Nation Film." According to the front-page article, the French government had banned it because it disagreed with the film's portrayal of "relations between the white and black races." The article also noted that the French had been "aroused" by the way white American tourists were treating black Parisians, the majority of whom were French citizens "from her colonies" and thus entitled to the same "rights and privileges" as "every French citizen."[69] Cannady took advantage of these sentiments to criticize Americans for their behavior abroad. She also used the French government's actions to illustrate the deplorable conditions facing black Americans in the 1920s: "France shows her appreciation for the loyalty of her black subjects and soldiers by extending" equal rights to them, "while America (God save her) expresses her gratitude by lynching and burning at the stake her black subjects and soldiers."[70] The remark about lynching soldiers likely referred to the "martyrs" of Houston, Texas, where a hundred black soldiers who were fed up with Jim Crow restrictions and police brutality rioted on August 23, 1917. Thirteen men were tried and executed for their role in the riot; following subsequent trials, an additional sixteen soldiers were sentenced to hang and fifty-three were sentenced to life terms to be served at the United States Penitentiary at Leavenworth.[71] Those men, all members of the 24th Infantry—more commonly known as the Buffalo Soldiers—were in the news again in 1923 when the NAACP launched an aggressive campaign to obtain presidential pardons for them.[72]

All of this was surely on Cannady's mind when she editorialized against *The Birth of a Nation*. And, no doubt recalling the unsuccessful efforts to block Portland showings in 1915, 1918, 1922, and 1923, Cannady wrote: "The French government did not have to be implored, begged and threatened for her to know and do her duty towards her black subjects, while all the tears, prayers and petitions of twelve millions of black Americans and the same number of fair-minded white Americans combined, failed utterly to impress the American government that it was its plain duty to prevent that vicious photoplay, 'The Birth of a Nation,' from showing in this country."[73] Just two months later, Cannady observed that the film had been banned a second time in Paris until "all scenes containing Negroes or the Ku Klux Klan [were] eliminated."[74]

Meanwhile, Cannady monitored what other black journalists were writing about *The Birth of a Nation*. Nick Chiles, "heralded as one of the greatest agitators and fearless fighters for justice and equal rights," sparked a controversy in 1924 when he did an editorial about-face in his *Topeka Plaindealer*.[75] "As a race we are spending too much time and money in opposing such worthless things as *The Birth of a Nation*," Chiles observed.

"We wish to say now that after giving the matter full consideration we have changed our minds about [the film]. If the white people of Kansas can stand *The Birth of a Nation* to be displayed on the canvas, the colored people can stand it."[76] Cannady reprinted a portion of his comments along with an editorial by the *Pittsburgh Courier* that reflected her own position on the film and race hatred: "When a Negro says that he doesn't care if a thing of this nature is shown he admits that he is totally ignorant of the influence of such a scene in public opinion. It is certain that the film propaganda will arouse ill-feeling, even in Kansas, and it follows that Negroes could not prosper economically without the good will and assistance of their white neighbors." Ultimately, noted the *Courier*, "We feel more like pitying the man who thus expresses himself than censuring him."[77] Although Cannady did not comment on Chiles' controversial position, reprinting the editorials enabled *Advocate* readers in the imagined community to participate in the conversation between editors in Pittsburgh and Topeka and thus stay informed about an issue that affected Negroes across the country.

Cannady may have learned of the 1931 re-release of *The Birth of a Nation* through this interconnected network of black newspapers. Early in the new year, she found it necessary to editorialize once again about the "dangerous" film.[78]

> *The Birth of a Nation* film has been recast and comes out all dressed up as a talkie. It was vicious as a silent drama but now that it talks we are of the opinion that it is much more vicious. ... It might be advisable for the people of Portland, the local NAACP in particular, to get busy before it is too late. *The Advocate* and others waged a battle against it years ago when it came to Portland, succeeding in many eliminations and finally in running it off the local screen. With such pioneering already done, it wouldn't be hard to keep it out of the city entirely.[79]

As Cannady feared, renewed interest in the film spread quickly across the country.[80] One month after her prescient editorial, the Triangle Film Co. petitioned the city council to show *The Birth of a Nation* in Portland.[81] Hunter Glover, the company's vice-president, informed commissioners that "the picture had been shortened by two reels, thereby eliminating many features considered by some as objectionable."[82] Eleanor Colwell, secretary of the Board of Motion Picture Censors, and Cannady, "representing the Negro race, were extended the privilege of the floor."[83] Commissioner Ralph Clyde then seconded a motion to deny Glover's petition to show the film;

it "carried unanimously."[84] Cannady commended Clyde for his actions, and noted that he had "proven his friendship for colored people" by "protect[ing] them from movements to stir race prejudice."[85] The Branch's press committee contributed an article to the *Advocate* that summarized its "protest" and also shared its victory with the national office.[86] Robert Bagnall told the Branch he was "very pleased to hear" about "the successful work it did in having the 'Birth of a Nation' barred from Portland."[87] Equally relieved that a showing finally had been averted, Cannady used the *Advocate* to express "sincere thanks" on behalf of "the people it represents to the Mayor and City Commissioners for their manly stand in refusing to grant permission to the promoters of the 'Birth of a Nation' film for exhibition in Portland theaters."[88]

But Glover was not about to give up: he petitioned the city council in April "for a rehearing to show the film in Portland." Cannady "was summoned" to discuss the merits of *The Birth of a Nation*. Just as she had done sixteen years earlier, she pointed out that the film was not only "historically untrue," but that it also "incited hatred between the races." Colwell "presented records showing that the film had been barred a number of times previously." A motion was made, Commissioner Clyde again seconded it, and the petition to show *The Birth of a Nation* was unanimously denied once more.[89]

Or so people thought. On December 24, 1931, the Board of Motion Picture Censors approved a weeklong showing of the film at the Heilig.[90] The *Oregon Daily Journal* announced that Portlanders were in for a "holiday treat" when the "favorite of old" began on Christmas Day.[91] "Untold multitudes were thrilled by this great picture" when it was first released in 1915, and the "sound reissue is said to have lost none of its poignant appeal."[92] But Cannady reported that people were stunned by the decision, especially since the film had been barred earlier that year "on the ground[s] that it was inimical to the peace and happiness between the races in the community."[93] Even the *Oregon Daily Journal* seemed a bit surprised, noting that the city council had rejected the film numerous times due to "vigorous protests from Negro leaders and others."[94] Hunter Glover, who owned the rights to show the film in Oregon, assured the board as well as the city council that "all the objectionable features and scenes had been deleted, and with the [addition of] sound, the picture was the kind that any one would desire to see." Edits notwithstanding, two commissioners felt that "the colored people should be given an opportunity to view the picture and see what they thought of it since its 'revision.'"[95] So Secretary Colwell, an outspoken critic of the movie, contacted Cannady.[96]

Cannady immediately mobilized the black community and selected white supporters. She called DeNorval Unthank and other Portland

Branch executives, Reed College President Norman F. Coleman, attorney John Jamison, Alice Handsaker, Bahá'í leader George Orr Latimer, and many more to attend a private viewing of *The Birth of a Nation* at 8 p.m. on December 23rd. "It was the consensus of opinion" following the viewing, she reported in the *Advocate*, "that no material deletions had been made and that the picture was just as objectionable ... as ever before."[97] Cannady, who served as chair of the hastily assembled group, urged the representatives of the various clubs, churches, and other organizations present to attend the special meeting of the council scheduled for the following morning. She also encouraged them to try to reach even more supporters during the night and invite them to the meeting.

Cannady, meanwhile, spoke with Floyd Maxwell, the theater's general manager, to urge him to "abandon the idea" of showing the film because it was "a detriment ... to the peace and harmony between the white and colored races." She noted that he "was quite frank in his position, stating that he had not thought of the picture in that light and expressed his appreciation for the call and for the information regarding the play, its history and its detrimental effect."[98] Cannady often discussed her interracial work in terms of her ability to change public opinion following such informational conversations and appeals to logic. Whether Maxwell truly had a change of heart is impossible to say, but the *Advocate* reported that he promised her that he would contact members of the American Legion, which was to share in the ticket proceeds, and see what could be done. "Everyone was agreeably surprised" when Mayor Baker announced the next morning that Maxwell had decided to withdraw his application to show *The Birth of a Nation* over the holidays.[99] The mayor adjourned the special meeting shortly thereafter, prompting Cannady to observe that "for the fourth time the 'Birth of a Nation' was denied exhibition in the 'City of Roses' [through] the beautiful spirit of co-operation."[100]

President Clarence Ivey sent a clipping to Bagnall with the news that the Branch, "along with other interested parties," had managed to get the film banned from Portland.[101] The national office issued a press release celebrating the success, which was likely published in black newspapers across the country.[102] Cannady summarized the continual fight to ban *The Birth of a Nation* with a three-word headline: "That film again." "Just when it seemed inevitable that the Xmas Spirit in Portland would be marred by the exhibition of the obnoxious film," she wrote, "the City Fathers, Colored people, the Council of Churches" and other concerned individuals joined forces to bar it. Despite being tired of the sixteen-year struggle, Cannady focused her editorial on positive aspects of the most recent fight. She commended the cooperative effort of the various groups and individuals, and praised Maxwell for exhibiting "splendid sportsmanship" by withdrawing his application to show the film. She also observed that over the years some people had changed their opinion of the film and "decided that [it] was an enemy to interracial peace and harmony." This sign of progress, of goodwill between the races, led her to proclaim that "human rights, the greatest of all rights and human happiness, again triumphed" in Portland.[103]

But her joy was short-lived. Just two weeks into 1932, she reported that Glover had sued the city council for "interfering with his right to exhibit the picture."[104] Glover claimed the Board of Motion Picture Censors had granted him a permit to show the movie. The City, on the other hand, contended the board had overstepped its bounds when it issued the permit without consulting the city council.[105] Cannady quickly notified people of the circuit court date and she, along with many of the individuals who had been present at the private viewing of the film at the end of December, attended the afternoon hearing. Also in the courtroom "were a good many [white and] colored people who had expressed opposition to the picture on numerous occasions before," including Latimer, Ivey, the Reverend Daniel Hill, Virgil Keene, and Dr. E. C. Farnham representing the Portland Council of Churches. Judge Jacob Kanzler listened to arguments presented by both sides before dismissing the suit without comment. "The merit of the picture was not considered at the hearing," Cannady reported, even though "the colored people who were there [were] prepared to testify against the picture if necessary."[106]

Nearly two years later, a single paragraph in the *Advocate* reminded readers that the issue was by no means over: "A three-day performance of 'The Birth of a Nation' photoplay at a down-town theater this week did not disturb the slumber of the local branch," she wrote in November 1933.[107] Perhaps people were tired of the ongoing fight to ban the racist film. Others may have had more on their minds then, like trying to hold on to a job in the middle of the Depression. But *The Birth of a Nation* was back at a time when race relations already were strained due to competition for jobs and resources.[108]

Film scholar Ed Guerrero believes that the "intense organized protest against" D. W. Griffith's film can be seen "as a good index of the brutal climate that African Americans faced under the Wilson administration, a historical moment marked by frequent lynchings throughout the South, a resegregated federal government, and the rise of a reinvigorated and popular Ku Klux Klan."[109] Although the protests in New York, Boston, and Los Angeles took center stage, local campaigns also were being waged across the country. In Portland, Beatrice Cannady fought against the insidious film as only she knew how to do: with words and typewriter. She met with Mayor George Baker and other city officials to try to persuade them of the film's deleterious effect on race relations in the City of Roses.[110] She implored white citizens to take a stand against the racist film and thereby show respect for their Negro neighbors. And she editorialized against the historically inaccurate film and its power to "poison" peoples' minds. As Guerrero suggests, her advocacy must be viewed in terms of the deteriorating state of affairs, both locally and nationally, particularly once the Klan moved into Oregon.

The record offers conflicting evidence regarding the number of times the film was shown and how many times it was blocked. Specific details may be less important than the fact that there were so many attempts to show the racist picture in Portland between 1915 and 1933. *The Birth of a Nation* also played in Tillamook, where an estimated forty thousand people packed into the fairgrounds to witness the "famous picture," and probably other Oregon cities as well.[111] Announcement of the coming attraction in Salem, Medford, or Eugene must have been particularly frightening for Negroes in those towns, given that so few were living there. Although Cannady's protests may not have been as vocal as those in other cities, she spent eighteen years talking to politicians, the white press, and Portlanders in the hope that someone would hear her straightforward message about the film's harmful effect on the city's tenuous race relations. Cannady lost more battles than she won, but keeping the issue on the public agenda enabled her to continue to defend the black community's right to coexist peacefully with Portland's white citizens. This activism became even more crucial when the Klan arrived in Oregon.

CHAPTER EIGHT
Oregon Was a Klan State

At first I thought it a frightful menace but I am coming to believe that its influence is waning. I am saddened when I think of its unintelligent, un-American attitude. Its presence and its activities must be taken into account, but I feel no special bitterness towards its members as I have found the same spirit of intolerance amongst the white people who are outside of the Klan; the only difference is that the Klan is organized.

— Beatrice Morrow Cannady[1]

"Many speakers have come to Portland, made their impressions and gone on their journey," Cannady wrote in the *Advocate* in May 1923. But none, she observed, had "made a deeper and more lasting impression for good upon the minds and hearts of the people than" Missouri Congressman Leonidas C. Dyer, who had been motivated to author a bill making lynching a federal crime after a race riot in East St. Louis in 1917.[2] Members of the House of Representatives passed it early in 1922 by a vote of 230 to 119, a victory the NAACP called "one of the most significant steps ever taken in the history of America." But the organization warned against celebrating until the Senate had set its "stamp of disapproval on mob murder," and called on citizens "to do all in [their] power" to ensure the bill passed.[3] Thousands staged a "silent parade" in Washington, D.C., and a "delegation of negro women" met with President Harding to get him to "urge final Congressional action" on the measure.[4] At the end of 1922, however, the *New York Times* reported that the bill was "dead." Filibustering Democrats had managed to tie up the session for a week, and Republican senators finally "decided very reluctantly that it was [their] duty to set aside the Dyer bill and go on with the business of the session."[5]

Five months later, the congressman was in Portland—reportedly with the *Advocate*'s help—where he spoke "before a representative audience at Lincoln High School auditorium" on Sunday, May 13th, "delivered a very interesting address" at Mount Olivet Baptist Church later that evening, and attended a Portland Branch meeting on May 14th. Cannady "presided" over the gathering at Lincoln, where Dyer told the audience that "the ballot and its proper, intelligent exercise" was essential for "blotting out present-day mistreatment." Along those lines, he "took a fling" at the senators representing Oregon and urged his listeners to remember "their stand on this bill when they [ran] for re-election." Finally, he pledged to reintroduce his bill in the next session of Congress.[6]

Dyer's visit came in the midst of a "momentous crisis" in Oregon's history.[7] In the summer of 1921, the Ku Klux Klan "invaded" the small agricultural community of Hood River looking for "native born Americans" to join the secret organization and its fight to preserve "pure womanhood, constitutional freedoms, the common people, and public education."[8] An editorial in the *Glacier* suggested fighting back with "ridicule," the "most effective weapon that can be employed against such an organization as the Ku Klux Klan."[9] Some white residents, though, voiced the need for greater protection against what they called a "relic of the dark ages." One man, who noted that he had "never even had a popgun" in his home, told the paper that news about "such an instrument of violence" as the KKK made him feel as if he should purchase "the highest powered rifles."[10] Six weeks later, the Klan organizer who "dropped without previous announcement into the midst of Hood River" apparently left just as "mysteriously." Some speculated that the $10 initiation fee—about $120 today—was too much for prospective members who had not yet realized returns on the apple harvest, even if they were "at first tempted by the thrill of possible adventure."[11]

Hood River's brush with the Klan ended well, but many other Oregon communities were not so fortunate. In Roseburg, a "great cross" formed on a steep hillside "cast a red glare high into the heavens" as "a class of more than 100 candidates [was] received into the invisible empire" in July 1922. A reporter for the *Roseburg News-Review* was deeply affected by the "awe-inspiring" event that was "witnessed ... by more than a thousand klansmen [and] hundreds of spectators." He described the ceremony in ghostly terms: "Silhouetted in the bright glare the marching figures passed in an endless array like silent wraiths, bent upon some solemn mission: ever-silent, ever-moving, a dauntless power, an irresistible force, moving on and on, ever beneath the cross, ever yielding to its glory and magnified by its power."[12] In Portland, two "fiery crosses ... burned continuously" on Mount Scott, where a "picturesque ceremonial" was held in June 1923 to initiate two thousand new members.[13] And in Eugene, more than a hundred men were welcomed into the Klan as "the radiant light shed by a huge cross of fire" illuminated the open-air ceremony.[14]

One of the more memorable displays, however, may have occurred in the state's capital. While some fifteen hundred robed Klansmen participated in the "longest parade ever held in Salem," an airplane decorated with an illuminated cross and "the words 'Join the KKK'" circled the city. The parade ended at the fairgrounds, where an "immense illuminated red cross burned vividly ... near the grandstand." Thousands of chilled spectators huddled together in the bleachers and watched the proceedings. Finally, Grand Titan V. K. Allison, a pastor from Lebanon, Oregon, addressed the crowd at 11 p.m. Known for his powerful oratorical skills, wit and humor, and ability to hold his audience's attention for up to three hours, Allison told the audience that the Ku Klux Klan aimed "to teach the doctrine of pure Americanism." The "white race is supreme," he proclaimed, "and the Anglo-Saxons are ordained by God to be the leaders of the world and to assist inferior races."[15] From Medford to La Grande, Roseburg to Tillamook, "100 percent pure Americanism" became the watchword.[16] It is no wonder, then, that Beatrice Cannady grew alarmed when the Klan "broke out" in Portland.[17]

Toward the end of June 1921, she informed the NAACP's Robert Bagnall that the Branch had called a mass meeting "to appoint a committee to wait upon" Mayor Baker "to prevent the holding of a street parade."[18] Two months later, Cannady and the other members of the committee on legislation and legal redress drafted a petition to Governor Ben W. Olcott. It called his "attention to the ... rapidly spreading organization known as the Ku Klux Klan," which acted "under the pretense of promoters of law and order but aimed unquestionably at the persecution of individuals who may incur their disfavor." The petition stipulated that "all citizens" deserved "a sense of security in their homes at night, and peaceable protection in their places of business and employment during the day." To that end, Cannady and the other signers asked Olcott "to prevent ... any organization or public demonstration of the said notorious Ku Klux Klan under any pretext whatsoever."[19] Cannady, always careful to publicize issues and events related to Portland's black community, probably furnished the *Morning Oregonian* with a copy of the petition in an effort to generate support for the Branch's request; a short news item appeared in the paper on August 20th.[20] Governor Olcott addressed Cannady's concerns that day, too, but his reassuring words would come back to haunt him. "[You] need not be apprehensive about the Ku Klux Klan becoming any very serious menace to our government," he wrote her. "I have a great faith in the sound sense of the people of our commonwealth, and I think our laws and our form of government require no secret associations to assist them in properly functioning for the liberty and happiness of our people."[21]

The following month, Olcott received a telegram from the executive editor of the *New York World* asking for a "definite statement of [his] position" regarding the KKK.[22] The governor acknowledged that it had tried to "invade the state," but it had "made little or no progress" thanks to "wholesome conditions in Oregon, with little discontent and a satisfied people." For these reasons, Olcott wrote that he had "deemed action or any particular comment unnecessary."[23]

But the governor was not the only one who underestimated the scope and agenda of the KKK in Oregon.[24] An editorial in the Eugene *Morning Register* suggested that most "100 per cent Americans are likely to find a better use for their leisure hours than getting out at night in ghostly party clothes and scaring the daylights out of somebody." Those who did insist on "parading the streets attired like a cheap ghost in a home talent melodrama" could be ignored, since the costumes were "chiefly useful for concealing the lack of furnishings in the wearer's attic."[25] Readers in Albany were told the Klan would not be "of long life" in that community. "'White Trash' and the like may derive some thrill of pleasure from fancied prestige gained through the wearing of the cloak ...," observed the editors, but "its roll will lack the names of those who think and reason."[26] The state's leading daily, the *Morning Oregonian*, also dismissed the growing threat the Klan posed to civil liberties. Articles during the summer of 1921 lampooned the organization; among other things, the Klan was dubbed the "Order of Sheet and Pillowcase," the hood was referred to as a "duncecap," and Luther Powell, one of several men charged with organizing klaverns, or chapters, in the Pacific Northwest, was called the "king dodo of the comic opera Klan, Knights of the Nightshirt."[27]

Nevertheless, activities of the Invisible Empire had deeply divided Oregonians by the spring of 1922 and focused unwanted national attention on the state.[28] In particular, the abduction and near-lynching of three individuals in southern Oregon led to a grand jury investigation and an attempt to recall the Jackson County sheriff, events that dominated local and state news for months.[29] Ironically, though, it was not the violence that incensed most people, but the subsequent indictment of six "upstanding" white citizens for crimes committed against Arthur Burr, a "negro bootblack," Joseph F. Hale, a white piano salesman, and Henry Johnson, a young man initially described as black in press accounts.[30]

Another "negro bootblack" living in Roseburg barely escaped a similar "necktie party" one Saturday night in April 1922. According to the *Roseburg News-Review*, Klansmen were informed that Sam Jackson had "made several insulting remarks" to a young woman working at a confectionery. Between twenty-five and thirty Klansmen "in full regalia" spent hours searching the city, but Jackson managed to stay "carefully hidden" until the following morning. When he finally dared to reappear, he was told to leave town before nightfall or "he would be taken in hand by local Klansmen and escorted out of the city in no gentle manner." The *News-Review* reported that he must have "heeded the advice" because "he [had] not been seen since." Jackson was lucky: Klansmen and their guests had attended a talk earlier that night by one of the state's most popular lecturers, former Portland minister Reuben H. Sawyer, who "delivered a very forceful address."[31] Afterward, they watched the recruiting film, *The Face at Your Window*, which "made more vivid some of the startling statements ... he presented."[32]

With the grand jury investigation into the near-lynchings in southern Oregon dominating the news, Governor Olcott issued an official proclamation on May 13, 1922. "Dangerous forces are insidiously gaining a foothold in Oregon," he wrote. "In the guise of a secret society, parading under the name of the Ku Klux Klan, these forces are endeavoring to usurp the reins of government, are stirring up fanaticism, race hatred, religious prejudice and all of those evil influences which tend toward factional strife and civil terror." Olcott called on the state's officials to put an end to the "unlawful deeds" committed throughout the state and asked "all law enforcing arms of the government ... to insist that unlawfully disguised men be kept from the streets."[33] The official proclamation may have temporarily reassured the state's twenty-one hundred Negro citizens, but race hatred divided Oregon communities again the following year.

The *Morning Enterprise* reported that Perry Ellis, owner of an auto-washing business in Oregon City, was the victim of a "midnight lynching party" in June 1923. Ellis said he had received a late-night phone call from an individual who stated his wagon had broken down on the outskirts of town. When Ellis arrived on horseback, he was surrounded by armed men "dressed in white robes and hoods" who ordered him to dismount. According to the *Enterprise*, he was "blindfolded, threatened with being shot full of holes if he tried to get away, and driven ... 30 miles further out into the country." Then he was told he would be hung "if he did not tell the truth about certain escapades with white girls." He continued to protest his innocence, despite having a "noose about his neck and the free end of the rope slung over a convenient limb of a tree." The "hooded gang" removed his blindfold at that point, pointed at a nearby lake, and told Ellis that was where they threw "the bodies of their victims." His captors then debated whether to free him or carry out "a sterilization operation." The "latter plan, while commenced, was not carried out," and Ellis was told he would not be harmed if he left Oregon City. He was finally returned to the outskirts of the city at dawn.[34]

An article about the frightening experience was reprinted without comment on the front page of the *Advocate* on June 9th.[35] But two weeks later, Cannady made the following observations: "Regardless of the fact that many colored people have been run away from their homes and worldly possessions, beaten, lynched and murdered by the Ku Klux Klan," and despite the fact that "a colored man in Oregon City was recently beaten, strung up and when released run out of town," she wrote that "some colored 'nuts' are still heard to say that the 'k.k.k. ain't after us.'"[36] Meanwhile in Oregon City, a divided city council discussed the incident at a special afternoon session. The men narrowly passed a resolution condemning the actions of the "perpetrators" who had deprived Ellis of his Constitutional rights and forced him "to flee" the state. The "outrage" had "disgraced" Oregon City as well as the entire state; further, the community would remain disgraced "until the perpetrators" were "brought to Justice to answer for their crime." A copy of the resolution was sent to county law-enforcement officials as well as Governor Walter M. Pierce—Olcott's successor, a Democrat backed by the Klan—with a request to help "run down, discover and prosecute all the un-American cowards who took part before, at, or after the fact in the outrage, to the end that such acts shall cease forever in our midst."[37] Pierce responded, but his offer of assistance fell short of expectations. According to the *Morning Enterprise*, Pierce said his office was ready to "aid in enforcement of all Oregon laws," but added that it was neither his "purpose nor ... policy to tamper with local affairs" unless officers sought "aid from the state" or were suspected of negligence.[38]

One year later, however, Governor Pierce was forced to intervene when the mutilated body of a black man was discovered near the coastal town of Marshfield, now known as Coos Bay. "Those who committed this dastardly crime must be apprehended and properly tried," he wrote the sheriff and district attorney. "Do everything in your power to secure evidence against the guilty ones."[39] Even though it was never proven, members of the Portland Branch were convinced the Klan was involved in the attack on Timothy Pettis in the summer of 1924. In fact, they wrote James Weldon Johnson that "Marshfield is infested with the Ku Klux Klan and we are of the opinion, [as are] the colored people who live in Marshfield, that all efforts are being made to cover up the crime."[40] Some of the area's white residents may have had their suspicions, too. Eight months earlier, a public forum had been held in the neighboring community of North Bend to discuss whether the Ku Klux Klan was a "menace or a blessing." Most attendees felt the organization was a threat to society, but "the Klan had several exponents" in the audience, including a minister who spoke about the "negro problem."[41]

Although the investigation into the Marshfield murder started well, rumors soon replaced leads and the search for clues all but ended two weeks later. A coroner's jury was impaneled to consider evidence within hours of the discovery of the body. The *Coos Bay Times* reported that "eight or ten colored people attended the inquest and one, [Gaston] Campbell, took an active part toward the end of the hearing, bringing out several important points not before touched upon." Campbell asked the undertaker "point blank" whether Pettis had been mutilated. The undertaker stated unequivocally that Pettis had been "the victim of a heinous crime either before or at the time of his death."[42]

Beatrice Cannady, along with other members of the Portland Branch, closely monitored developments in the case. She reprinted the initial *Coos Bay Times* article about the murder to keep readers apprised of the realities of racism elsewhere in Oregon.[43] And she used the *Advocate* to applaud Campbell and his efforts to uncover the truth about the crime. "G. L. Campbell is standing upon his rights as an American citizen and is not fleeing from Marshfield, Oregon, where a cowardly mob of whites [has] brutally murdered a colored man. ... Campbell is one man in a thousand who would do what he is doing, and is deserving of great praise for his brave stand in the case, almost single-handed ... against the mob spirit which seems to dominate Marshfield."[44] Even as she praised Campbell, Cannady criticized the government for failing to protect its citizens: "Isn't it about time for the Federal government to speak or step out against the many brutal murders, whippings, intimidations and the branding of peaceful, law-abiding citizens by mobs, which are being done in many parts of the country?"[45] The reference to branding may have been an oblique reminder of the fall 1921 attack on Elise Reynolds, who operated a beauty parlor out of her Portland home.[46] According to the *Portland Telegram*, police were "trying to determine whether the attack" on the twenty-six-year-old "was due to robbery, an effort by residents of the district to drive out the negro family, or to the Ku Klux Klan." A large "K" reportedly was etched on her cheek with acid while she was unconscious, and a "threatening note signed 'KKK'" was left on the door by the two assailants. The Klan disavowed any knowledge of the attack and told the *Telegram*, "We do not countenance outrages. We will gladly co-operate with the authorities to run down the perpetrator of this crime."[47]

Governor Pierce demanded that Marshfield's law enforcement officers "bring to justice the murderers of Timothy Pettis."[48] However, the district attorney, sheriff, and deputy sheriff all were out of town during much of the brief investigation, prompting the newspaper to observe that the "sheriff's office has not been able to investigate much."[49] Area residents formulated their own ideas about the crime. Following the inquest, the *Coos Bay Times* reported that the "general theory, especially among the colored folk, is that Pettis was the victim of a gang."[50] The Portland Branch, frustrated with the pace of the investigation, sent a telegram to New York: "Colored war veteran mysteriously disappeared July sixth, recovered week later from Coos Bay; testicles missing; crime apparently being covered [up]; no clue found; outside assistance needed: send investigator."[51] James Weldon Johnson wired his reply the next day: "Case cited one which state legal machinery should handle. If state does not take prompt action, communicate with us giving full details."[52]

Branch members "called on" Governor Pierce and asked him to "offer a reward for the apprehension of the guilty parties" and place a "special investigator" on the case. But, observed the Branch's secretary, "We are of the opinion since nothing has been reported from [Pierce] that he has not done anything of the kind."[53] The *Coos Bay Times* reported that the county court had offered a $500 reward—about $6,500 today—to anyone with "information leading to the arrest and conviction of the person or persons alleged to have mutilated and murdered Timothy Pettis." In addition, the small black community in Marshfield managed to raise $100, which was added to the court's offer.[54] But the Portland Branch remained dissatisfied with efforts to solve the crime. Its status report noted that "outside sources" were required to move the case forward, and hinted that if a "white investigator" were to come "on the scene," he might be able to "solve the mystery."[55] The national office was unable to offer assistance, however. "At various times in the history of the Association we have employed detective agencies including the Burns, the Pinkerton, and others," replied Walter F. White, assistant secretary of the NAACP. "On every occasion we were forced to pay a considerable sum [but not once] did we receive anything like adequate or satisfactory returns."[56] Lacking the funds to hire its own detective, the Portland Branch apparently took a "wait and see" attitude. But by September, two months after the murder, the *Coos Bay Times* had stopped printing updates. In its annual report to the national office, the Branch stated it had investigated the "brutal murder [of Timothy Pettis] ... as far as physical power could act."[57] The homicide apparently never was solved.[58]

It is tempting to view the Roaring Twenties through rose-colored glasses. Larger-than-life images of Babe Ruth swatting a home run at Yankee

Stadium, or of "Lucky Lindy" flying the Spirit of St. Louis across the country on a three-month tour of ninety-two cities—including Portland in September 1927—crowd out ugly photographs of hooded men marching in cities throughout the United States.[59] But Negroes living in Oregon in the 1920s endured a decade of prejudice, segregation, and wanton acts of violence. As Cannady observed in January 1924, "The Ku Klux Klan are still scrapping here as well as elsewhere."[60] Otto Rutherford was more blunt: "Oregon was a Klan state."[61] By the end of 1923, *Oregon Voter* reported fifty-eight chartered klaverns in the state; seven more chapters had provisional charters.[62] As many as fifty thousand white men in Oregon may have taken the oath of allegiance during the decade.[63]

Cannady and her family appear to have fared surprisingly well, considering her outspoken fight for equal rights.[64] But the Klan did picket at least one of her talks. In 1923, Cannady was invited to speak to students at a summer Bible school in Newberg, Oregon, on the subject of race relations. Staff had "unanimously approved" her visit, "but one Judas in the group saw fit to report the invitation to the Ku Klux Klan, which at that time was very strong in the city," recalled Alice Handsaker. "As a result many of the pupils heard conversations in their homes criticising the action of the teachers ..., advocating rudeness and unresponsiveness to [Cannady's] message, and attempting to arouse in her hearers a spirit of hatred, prejudice and antagonism." Cannady arrived at the school and found the building surrounded by Klansmen who were distributing fliers to the students: "ATTENTION! WE ARE WATCHING YOU! ... Fellow citizens: If you believe that your children should associate and marry Hindus, Chinese and Negroes attend this lecture. If you attend your name will be read from the housetops." School staff worried about Cannady's safety, but the event apparently went as planned. Some years later Handsaker recalled, "I am sure that many Ku Klux Klan parents of that community had much 'explaining' to do that night for under Mrs. Cannady's persuasive eloquence their children had seen the light."[65] Cannady, for whatever reason, did not write about the incident in the *Advocate*.

The acts of violence committed against black Oregonians during the early 1900s illustrate the challenges they faced as a minority population in the state. In addition, Klan rhetoric emphasizing white supremacy would be considered hate speech by current standards and thus another form of violence directed at black Americans. Scholars describe the "mental or emotional distress" such language causes, as well as the fact that it denies individuals "a sense of dignity, resulting in loss of self-esteem, personal security, and sense of community membership."[66] Further, racial insults communicate "the message that distinctions of race are distinctions of merit, dignity, status, and personhood."[67] That was clearly the case in Oregon, where efforts to keep the state "pure" added to people's sense of isolation and alienation.

Racial stigmatization also can cause self-hatred, affect one's ability to relate to others, and lead to anti-social behavior.[68] Cannady related these issues to a tragic event that occurred in 1924 in order to make a point about the KKK and the urgent need for reform in the United States. On June 20th, William R. Ward was hung just before dawn at Arizona State Prison in Florence for killing a University of Arizona student-athlete.[69] The motive: race hatred. Ward, a Negro, had "witnessed the burning at the stake of six Negroes by a [white] mob in Paris, Texas," a gruesome scene that ultimately fueled his "hatred for Caucasians."[70] Cannady seemed particularly moved by Ward's account. "It is a wonder ... there are not more William Wards" trying "to get even with the white race for the many atrocities committed ... against the blacks in this country," she wrote. The time had come to stop the vicious cycle of hatred: "If a race teaches its members to hate another race, it is wrong and all these institutions founded upon hatred ... must surely die."[71]

CHAPTER NINE

Standing Firm

I think The Advocate *is one of the West's greatest Negro defenders. I must congratulate you on your fearless stand in defense of the race's cause and I hope that in all issues, in which the race is involved, that this great paper will continue to stand firm in the cause of the race as it has always done in the past.*

—J. A. G. Washington, "*The Advocate* Given Praise,"
the *Advocate*, January 1, 1927, 1, 4[1]

Discrimination because of color was the constant that tied together years of *Advocate* articles and editorials and illustrated an important reality of interracial relations in Oregon during the early 1900s. Even when Beatrice Cannady was not discussing overt racism, it is clear from her writing that skin tone dictated all aspects of an individual's life: from the church one attended to the jobs one held; from the restaurants one could enjoy to the neighborhood where one lived. In this respect, Oregon was not much different from Southern states. But Negroes living in Oregon also faced unique challenges due to the small size of their population and their subsequent isolation. Some towns had fewer than a dozen black residents; an encounter in 1930 with "three negroes in one block" prompted the editor of the *Roseburg News-Review* to reflect: "Oregon, which bears the negro no ill will and regrets the wrong that has been done him, is fortunate because it has only an infinitesimally small negro population. We are spared thus one of the problems which many other states have to solve."[2]

Even in Portland, where the majority of the state's black citizens lived, individuals were scattered widely. "There was no black community when I was a kid," Otto Rutherford said. "We lived all over the city." In addition, "the majority of the men were railroad men. They were out of town. The women who did work were doing menial jobs like housework or day work as they called it then, getting a dollar a day," he said. This made it difficult to try strategies such as economic boycotts to press for equal rights. Although Cannady promoted the *Chicago Whip*'s "Don't Buy Where You Can't Work" campaign, such sanctions "didn't amount to much" in Portland, Rutherford noted.[3]

Cannady may have been unable to promote a sweeping boycott of white-owned businesses, but she *was* able to defend her community against covert and overt racism by writing editorials, reporting acts of discrimination, and participating in the nationwide debate about civil rights and liberties. By the 1920s, long-standing racism, combined with the arrival of the Ku Klux Klan in Oregon and repeated showings of *The Birth of a Nation*, confirmed the importance of the *Advocate*'s role as a mouthpiece for the black community. Colleagues at other newspapers across the country commented on Cannady's activities, which enhanced her visibility and standing in the NAACP and among other black leaders. Support from peers also must have encouraged her to continue the difficult and often lonely fight for equal rights and liberties in Oregon.[4]

On September 1, 1928, the *Advocate* marked its twenty-fifth anniversary with its customary banner headline, testimonials, pleas for payment, congratulations from advertisers, and an editorial reflecting on the newspaper's rocky past and hope for the future. During the previous quarter-century, Cannady wrote, the *Advocate* had "persistently and consistently opposed and fought wrong—both in high and low places." But she recognized that this gloves-off policy had not always "pleased everybody." Cannady admitted to her readers, "We have made enemies during the 25 years of our existence—and they were made because their faults, sins and narrowness were ruthlessly attacked and hypocrisy laid bare by the uncompromising position of this paper against the evils and ills of our day and age."[5] That was the case, for instance, when Cannady took up the issue of a segregated YWCA.

The controversy began in 1921, when it was announced that an "extension branch of the Young Women's Christian Association for colored girls and women" would be built on the corner of Williams Avenue and Tillamook Street.[6] But white people in the area "objected," claiming that "acquisitions of property by colored persons" depreciated property values. The *Morning Oregonian* noted the unique nature of the complaint: "While protests have been made from time to time against the intrusion of negroes into a neighborhood settled by white persons, settlements of difficulties of this nature always have been effected outside of the council." City attorney Frank S. Grant invoked the Thirteenth and Fourteenth Amendments to argue that the city council had "no authority to enact an ordinance prohibiting colored people from constructing a building on a piece of ground owned by them solely [because] they are colored people."[7] Cannady sent Grant a letter thanking him for the "splendid manner in which [he] rendered service to [her] people." She particularly commended him for citing the amendments, which "caused much publicity through the daily press [and] naturally came to the notice of many people who thought that colored people are not yet 'free' in this country."[8]

The building was intended to be used as a "temporary headquarters" until sufficient funds could be raised to build a larger structure.[9] Plans for the permanent building finally moved forward in 1926 after it was announced that Mary Collins, a white woman, had donated $12,000 for construction—about $145,000 today. But Cannady apparently felt that her generous gift was intended to reinforce the notion of "separate but equal" institutions. "The colored people are divided in their opinion as to whether or not a segregated Christian organization is for the best good," Cannady wrote in the *Advocate*.[10] "Some say it is what they need; ... some are of the opinion that it is the stepping stone to separate public schools," since the "husband of one of the women prominently connected with the colored work operates a business College and will not admit colored students." Cannady was referring to YWCA board member Laura Walker, whose husband, Isaac, was president of the Behnke-Walker Business College.[11] Cannady had called him a hypocrite for refusing to admit a "young colored girl" to his school, even though he served as a deacon in one of the city's "biggest churches."[12] Mary White Ovington met with Walker and Collins when she visited Portland in 1928. They recalled that Cannady had "not only attacked the principle of the YW but the character of the white people helping it and made many enemies."[13]

Cannady continued to editorialize about the YWCA in articles and editorials. On February 6, 1926, a front-page story reported that the building "to house the colored work department of the Y.W.C.A. in Portland" was being erected. But the article noted that individuals who seemed to "lack ... enthusiasm" for the project were being accused of being "suspicious" of the donor's motives. Cannady, who was probably describing herself, felt this reaction was understandable, given that "the Negro has been segregated, jim-crowed, set apart like a leper; lynched and cooked alive, for so long in this ... country by people who claim to 'understand the Negro.'" Still, she hoped the "diverse opinions" about the project would lead to a better understanding of "all groups" as well as a "better understanding between the groups."[14]

But this optimism was absent from a long editorial in the same issue. Cannady addressed the politics of patriarchy and power, and again called attention to the hypocrisy of those who discriminated against people "in the name of Christ."

> Now let us suppose that there is a church, a Y.M.C.A. or a Y.W.C.A., a hospital, or other institution existing for the benefit of all, a community institution. Let us suppose that the heads of those institutions are white

> persons who decide that building No. 1 is to be reserved for white people, and building No. 2, for instance, for colored. Surely there can no longer be any question [that] that is segregation of the objectionable kind based on race and color; it brands the one not in control as inferior. That is segregation, jim-crowism and discrimination on the ground of race and color, all in one.
>
> And always remember that when white people set aside a separate place for a race of people to carry on similar activities, the power lies in the more powerful group.[15]

Collins may have been offended by these comments, especially if she felt her sizeable donation was being spurned. Ironically, Cannady announced in the same issue of the *Advocate* that she was "pleased" to welcome Collins as a new subscriber.[16] The YWCA opened its doors in June 1926 and William Pickens, who was in Portland on one of his speaking tours, was among "the large groups of persons inspecting the new building."[17] Cannady did not share her own impressions, though Ovington observed later, "Like [*Guardian* editor William] Monroe Trotter in Boston, for a time she refused [to] enter the colored Y.W. here because it [was] segregated." When the Portland NAACP decided to move its meetings from local churches to the YWCA, Cannady was forced to enter the building or forsake Branch meetings; Ovington noted, "Since it has become a community centre for all colored work [Cannady] has had to give up that platform."[18]

~

But Cannady did not stop editorializing about de facto segregation, which she argued was intricately linked to the concepts of community, citizenship, and race. In 1930, she warned readers that if they were not careful, they might find themselves encircled by a "'black belt,' just as the Colored people are in practically every Southern city of any size in the United States." She compared Portland's Williams Avenue, where the YWCA was located, to Central Avenue in Los Angeles and State Street in Chicago—arbitrary lines that divided neighborhoods and people. "We all know what residential segregation means," she wrote. "It means poor housing, bad streets, and if the streets are paved, poorly kept [with] deficient lighting. It also means separate schools and their attendant shortcomings. It invites race riots, because the stronger race will feel that the weaker has no rights outside of its restricted district, and any attempt on the part of the weaker to exercise its rights of liberty ... is met with opposition from the stronger."[19] But segregation was not limited to residential areas; two of Portland's black professionals were discriminated against when they tried to rent office space in the city.

Cannady related the difficulties Elbert Booker had faced when trying to establish his dental practice in Portland in 1927. After he had toiled "both night and day" to complete his studies at North Pacific Dental College—now part of Oregon Health & Science University—and support his wife and two daughters, Cannady reported how glad she was that he had decided to remain in the city.[20] She hoped that "all Portland" would give him "the hearty welcome he deserve[d]."[21] But Dr. Booker was repeatedly refused office space "solely on the ground of his color," she wrote, "and for a time it seemed that he would not be able to secure an office in any modern reputable office building." He finally was offered "a most desirable suite of rooms" in the Panama Building at 3rd and Alder, but only after he asked the *Morning Oregonian* to publicize the "difficulties he was facing." Cannady believed his story demonstrated that people should "be willing to contend strongly for [their] 'place in the sun,'" because by doing so, they were "helping others of the race."[22]

Three years later, Cannady used the *Advocate* to welcome DeNorval Unthank, the "brilliant young physician" who had come from Kansas City, Missouri, to "pioneer in the great Northwest with the rest of us."[23] She encouraged readers to give Unthank "their moral support" as well as "their dollars and cents by calling upon his services whenever in need of medical care."[24] However, she soon reported that Booker and Unthank, who had opened an office together, had been "notified by their landlord that they would have to move out" because other tenants had protested. Dr. Booker moved back into his former office on another floor and Dr. Unthank relocated to the Commonwealth Building a few blocks away.[25] He moved at least two more times during the next year before settling on the Arata Building on 6th Avenue in April 1931.[26] A few months later, Booker closed his office in the Panama Building and relocated to the Guardian Building, apparently working with a white doctor named R. W. Donohue.[27]

The *Advocate* also announced in April that the Unthanks had purchased a "beautiful, modern, 4-room bungalow" in the Westmoreland neighborhood and were preparing to move into it despite opposition from neighbors.[28] Some seventy-five residents had signed a petition "objecting to his moving in," which was presented to the Unthanks "by a delegation from the Better Homes group of that neighborhood." Cannady reported that Dr. Unthank "offered to move if they would pay him a bonus of $700 on his contract. The apparent leader of the group called this blackmail."[29] When the Unthanks and their young son arrived to take possession of the home at 750 Knapp Street, they discovered that vandals had broken eighteen windows.[30] The *Oregon Daily Journal* published a long article on the front page that went beyond a simple summary of the facts of the crime; it also reported that

Dr. Unthank had written to the chamber of commerce before relocating to ascertain whether the family would "be welcome to move to Portland. He was assured [they] would be." But, the reporter noted, he "had been forced to move his office four times" since arriving fourteen months earlier.[31]

Cannady called the attack the "latest outrage against a Negro member of the community."[32] She also observed that Portland shared "the ignorant characteristic of the south" because it continued "to try to force colored people to live in the most undesirable districts. In fact," she wrote, "we are of the opinion that they are not wanted anywhere."[33] Most Portlanders appear to have been unconcerned by the attack on the Unthanks' home. However, one individual, whose father and grandfather were Southern slaveowners, expressed his outrage in a letter to the *Oregon Daily Journal*: "An eminent Portland physician, whose work is to help and heal those in suffering and pain, had his house wrecked by vandals because the doctor's skin happened to be of a different color from that of his neighbors. ... One wonders ... how many preachers and churches will join The *Journal* in its protest against this outrage."[34]

Ongoing coverage in the *Advocate* kept readers apprised of new developments involving the Unthanks and "their recent experience in buying a home in Portland."[35] These articles served another important function, too. A local "correspondent" for the American Civil Liberties Union sent clippings from the *Advocate* and *Oregon Daily Journal* to ACLU headquarters in New York City. The director forwarded them to the NAACP with a note stating that they "may be of interest to you."[36] Robert Bagnall wrote the secretary of the Portland Branch soon after: "The attack upon the home of Dr. Unthank has come to our attention. We would suggest that the Branch do what it can towards an investigation of the matter and let us know its present status."[37]

After the Unthanks' windows were smashed a second time, the Portland Branch did step in to help the family keep its residence.[38] Virgil Keene, Edgar Williams, the Reverend Caston, and President Clarence Ivey were named to a "special committee" that met with Police Chief Leon Jenkins to "demand protection for the Unthanks." According to the *Advocate*, the men "were assured" that a prowl car would drive by the home every hour; if requested, a patrolman also would be sent to watch the premises if the Unthanks left for the evening.[39] Cannady wrote in an editorial that the vandalism was "in keeping with the cowardice and veiled threats and hints intimated by representatives of the intolerant neighborhood during several conferences with the Unthanks." She also condemned the neighbors who failed to intervene; their tacit approval of the vandalism was as bad as if they had thrown the rocks themselves. But, in her opinion, the plan "to frighten the Unthanks" into moving "out of their home willingly" was not going to work. "Negroes who have the courage to go to war and face the enemies' guns in battle certainly are not afraid to live in and protect their homes in 'Christian' America," she wrote. Cannady pointed out that the city should "feel ashamed of the action of the white people in this case and ... do something to prevent being further disgraced. It is most alarming to note the utter intolerance and colossal ignorance on the part of some people who would like to be considered superior," she added, alluding to the Klan's belief in white supremacy.[40]

But the stress finally proved too much for the family. Otto Rutherford said simply, "They harassed the hell out of that man and finally he moved."[41] Years after the incidents, Kathryn Bogle recalled that Dr. Unthank called her and asked her what he should do. She advised him, "'Take care of your family, and then you can be a physician.' And so, he did that; he moved from that house. But, in a sense, he was driven out ... by the people who just objected to their presence, purely because of their color."[42]

William H. Greene, managing editor of the *Southern Oregon Spokesman*, also protested the presence of black people in his community. The weekly had been in existence just three months when, on May 24, 1924, Greene wrote a front-page article titled, "Let's Keep Grants Pass A White Man's Town." It had always been "a white man's town," he argued, and there was "no reason under the shining sun why it shouldn't continue to be a white man's town."[43] He was upset because a local company, the Pine Box Factory, had been purchased recently by an Alabama firm and the new supervisor had brought three black servants with him.[44] "As soon as one nigger is allowed to stay in these parts, this community ceases to be a white man's country, and in as much as it doesn't take very long for a family of niggers to increase into a 'buck town' of large population, the coming of one nigger is the beginning of future trouble," he wrote. He also worried about the effect on employment: "If there are any jobs to hand out in this country, the white man or white woman are ones to get the jobs—this thing of bringing niggers in here to take jobs as chauffeurs, or maids or laborers or in fact any job that may be open here is an infringement on the rights of the white people who have taken pride in this their ideal community." Greene urged "the white people" of Grants Pass to "rise in protest" or suffer the consequences: "Foreigners and niggers will lower the standard of our community morals, as has been done in those mongrelized communities where the color line is not drawn."[45]

Cannady apparently was alerted to the controversy by Charles Hough, an attorney in Grants Pass who sent her copies of the *Spokesman*.[46] She reprinted Greene's article on the *Advocate*'s front page under a banner headline: "GRANTS PASS A WHITE MAN'S TOWN."[47] But two columns of the editorial page were devoted to countering passages in his articles. She apologized "to the intelligent public for giving the matter so much ... valuable space," but she felt it was her "duty to reply." She found the task challenging, however. Greene may have been "educated in the orthodox meaning of the term education," but he had "missed the real purpose of education." So she began with a history lesson. "History informs us (let us suggest that history would help you, too) that at one time in the past Red men inhabited those parts. So therefore," she wrote, "it could not always have been a 'white man's town.'" Cannady then offered the "learned editor" a brief summary of slavery before noting that it was "incumbent upon the white people to treat the 'Negro' whom he forced here, not only with courtesy and respect but with sympathetic tolerance and Love!" Finally, she emphasized that "nothing but God himself can stay the onward march of the progress of the 'Negro' race to success and a place of honor in the affairs of this, its country. ... The Negro is here, and it looks as though he is here for good," she added, "and we advise our learned contemporary to take a different attitude towards his black brother, who is not a 'foreigner' but an American citizen, 100 per cent." With this, Cannady called attention to the Ku Klux Klan and its criterion for membership, and made an oblique reference to the group's attacks on black men in southern Oregon just two years earlier. She concluded the lengthy editorial on a note of forgiveness: With "malice towards none but with a heart full of pity and love, we ask our Father who art in Heaven this day to lead that poor, misguided editor of the *Spokesman* into the sunlight of His love."[48]

In response, Greene verbally attacked the *Advocate* and its "associate negress editor," whom he called a "malicious 'she wizard,'" for attempting to convince "the weak kneed sentimentalist to look upon [him] with scorn because [he had] the audacity to uphold white supremacy." As long as the "leaders of the black race publish newspapers wherein they carry propaganda such as, 'they have rights who dare to maintain them,' the danger cloud will hang over this country." Further, he observed: "If the black race in America today really want peace and the constructive help of the white race, they will use their periodicals to educate their own kind to do what is best for the world in general, rather than to stir up strife over issues they do not like and cannot understand." Although he stopped short of calling her statements lies, he told readers he felt it was his own duty to engage in an "editorial battle" with the *Advocate* because he wanted "readers to know the whole truth, to know the worst and provide for it." In addition, he told his subscribers, "The answer the 'Advocate' makes to this editor's statements about keeping Grants Pass a white man's town are anything but sane and fair. The statement 'that nothing but God himself can stay the onward march of the negro' … is a challenge that will some day be met, and of course with disastrous results for the black race in America." Greene declared he was "ready and willing" to assume "his share of the responsibility" to "keep the white man supreme."[49] Locally, that included offering $5—about $63 today—toward a "fund to buy these black citizens tickets for Alabama, Tennessee … or any place below the Mason-Dixon line."[50]

Two short paragraphs on the editorial page of the June 21st issue of the *Advocate* kept the heated discussion before readers. She pointed out that Greene had "made a futile attempt" to reply to her comments about "his previous editorial about Grants Pass being a white man's town." In fact, he had "failed utterly in two whole columns to present evidence sufficient to support his charges against the Race." She also criticized Greene for picking "out certain words and sentences, segregating them from other sentences, thereby causing them to lose their true meaning and intent."[51] Cannady's decision to use the word "segregating" probably was no accident. The rich metaphor speaks to the power of words written on signs that kept people out of restaurants, bathrooms, and other public places. It conjures images of a group of people separated from society, causing them to "lose their true meaning" and identity. And it points to the fluidity of language in that individuals can take words and passages out of context in order to shore up a weak argument or present an inaccurate version of history.

Cannady's efforts to defend Oregon's black community, and the race generally, were praised in the *California Eagle*. An editorial applauded the "thorough and scientific scalping" she had "administered to the cracker editor" in Grants Pass, and urged people to read the series because it was "a real contribution of worth and merit in defense of freedom and a major offensive against petty prejudice and cowardice."[52] Cannady continued the "scalping" in another long article in the June 28th issue of the *Advocate*. She tackled several themes, including lynching, rape, interracial relations, and emigration; Greene had suggested the latter as a way to rid America of individuals who "force [their] presence upon a race of people who do not want" them. Then she alluded again to the Klan's stronghold in southern Oregon: "If the editor of the *Spokesman* … is so clean and pure, and if the organization which he seems to represent is so noble and good, let us ask him why it is necessary for its members to wear 'diapers' over their faces and do their work at night? If what the organization preaches and practices is right, why not uncover your faces and come out into the open?"[53] During their editorial exchange, Greene neither admitted nor denied his own membership in the KKK. But his racist rhetoric was consistent with Klan doctrine. Greene made his feelings clear in one front-page article that virtually paraphrased the organization's oath: "The *Spokesman* has stood for law and order, the sanctity of the home and the chastity of womanhood."[54] Greene vowed to continue to "champion the white race and white supremacy" until he died or was forced out of business, as he believed "some of his enemies [were] trying to do."[55]

Cannady and other members of the Portland Branch finally had enough of Greene's epithets. Letters protesting articles "in which he slanders, ridicules and attempts to intimidate colored people" were sent to Governor Walter Pierce and Attorney General Isaac H. Van Winkle.[56] Pierce told Branch members he had authorized an investigation into "the situation in Grants Pass" and had asked officials to take necessary action "for the protection of the citizens in that community." Further, he assured the Branch that he would "give personal attention to this matter" during a planned trip to the city.[57] Van Winkle noted that he was "pledged to the enforcement of all of the laws, without reference to race, color or previous condition," but stopped short of informing Branch members what, if anything, he planned to do on their behalf.[58] Sadly, this matter soon was overshadowed by the news of Timothy Pettis' murder in Marshfield. But the Branch's role in the protest, even if nominal, still was a topic of conversation four years later. Dr. Caston, pastor of Mount Olivet Baptist Church and the Branch's delegate to the nineteenthth annual conference, reported to attendees how it had stepped in when white people in Grants Pass "objected" to the "presence" of "several colored people" there.[59]

Cannady had the last words in the editorial debate with Greene. She used the final article in the series to call his attention to news briefs she had read in the *Morning Oregonian* and a white newspaper in California. They proved that it was possible to read about crimes committed by white men—"the dominant race men"—in daily newspapers. The offenses were "regrettable" and she took "no pleasure in printing them," she wrote. "We simply do so for the benefit of these braggadocios who are forever belittling and berating the Colored man, who, after all, learned his vices from the white man in this country." Cannady also pointed out the differences in story placement. News items about crimes committed by white men could be discovered "from time to time," provided the reader hunted "carefully and long in obscure places in the paper." But if the accused had been black men, she observed, "these same newspapers no doubt would have scare headed them" to call attention to the men's race as well as their alleged crimes.[60]

When Cannady raised this issue of misrepresentation in newspapers, she entered into a conversation that had started a century earlier in New York City. John Russwurm and Samuel Cornish, publishers of the nation's first black paper, wrote in 1827, "Our vices and our degradation are ever arrayed against us, but our virtues are passed by unnoticed."[61] Other black editors and publishers also castigated the white press for exacerbating feelings of inferiority in the community. As a South Carolina editor lamented: "One who reads only discouraging news in the opposite race papers concerning him and his is led to believe, argue and act in support of his belief that 'this is a white man's country and a Negro has no right that a white man is bound to respect.'"[62] Cannady used the idea of "scareheads"—large or bold headlines above stories—to point out that "most of the daily papers" exaggerated news about "Colored peoples' alleged crimes." But articles about "creditable" accomplishments were not given similar placement in the daily white press, she argued; such news usually was "tucked away in some corner among the stock quotations, and obituary notices." Cannady observed that these discrepancies had "been the direct cause of many racial clashes in the past" and would "continue to produce race friction and race hate" until "influential papers and individuals (white friends) adopt[ed] a different policy."[63]

She also worried that racial identification might affect a person's right to a fair trial. When the *Oregon Daily Journal* printed a story about a "Portland negro" who had been arrested for brandishing a knife, she wrote: "Since it was the man and not his nationality who did the threatening, and since by emphasizing the nationality of a criminal undue prejudice is invited to the people of that nationality, ... it would do greater good" to omit such prejudicial details.[64] She suggested her own version of the story, which described the events and the sentencing, but omitted any mention of race. Often, though, racism slipped into newspapers in more subtle ways.

The use of dialect when writing about Negroes was commonplace in the white press. It had long been used in "drama, fiction and poetry [as] a way of pointing to the difference between blacks and whites; the form and function of black speech as it was represented was to indicate black inferiority." Dialect, which included improper grammar, malapropisms, and the use of "dats" and "dems," became "a short-hand for perpetuating myths and prejudices about black people."[65] Cannady addressed the use of dialect in an editorial published in December 1924:

> In reporting crimes committed by colored people, except in a few cases, the daily papers not only make the nationality of the criminal plain, especially when those of our race are concerned, by calling them "negroes" and "negresses," but they make it appear that the

> most intelligent man or woman, with few exceptions, uses ridiculous English. A case in point: Last week, in reporting the case of a colored man who was tried for selling liquor, the press supposedly quoting this man used "dis," "dat," "suh," "ah," and other terms. We happen to know the man in question and have heard him talk upon more than one occasion. He uses perfect English and has a very quiet and pleasing manner. ... It would seem that there is so much good to write about colored people that reporters would seek it as a new field of endeavor.[66]

Cannady was particularly critical of the *Portland Telegram*, which she felt was "proving to be one of the worst enemies of [the] race by sowing seeds of race prejudice in the Northwest. Seldom does it make a respectable reference to colored people. Our women are called 'negresses' and too often our men are referred to as brutes."[67] A few months later, Cannady informed the city's white editors that "*The Advocate*, along with many people, regards the use of this term ['negress'] as an insult upon injury. Therefore we ask in all fairness that our local papers discontinue the use of the insulting term."[68]

After observing little improvement in the city's white newspapers, Cannady urged people to "refuse to patronize those papers that persist[ed] in this unnecessary and inhuman practice":

> In the name of common decency and human respect, we call upon the daily newspapers to refrain from using those humiliating and insulting terms as "burly black coons," "negress," etc., when making references to colored people. As we see it, there is no good reason or justification for so doing.
>
> Those terms are just as offensive to the colored group as the terms "wop," "dago," "greaser," and the like to other racial groups.[69]

Cannady emphasized this idea in subsequent editorials, often contrasting the *Advocate*'s role as a champion of the black community with the daily press' general disregard for Negroes. But she also was critical of those black individuals who gave "greater support" to "the white man's papers, which call them 'big burly niggers,' 'coons,' 'shines' and other insulting terms," than their own newspapers and periodicals.[70] This misplaced loyalty was just "foolishness," she observed, "for it's a well known fact that no civilized person can ... keep up with the times and with the activities of their people and affairs of their country without [their own] newspaper."[71]

She was not alone in her struggle to convince white editors to be more respectful. In 1930, she reported that the NAACP was contributing "in a quiet but enormously effective way to the racial pride of the Negro" by conducting a nationwide campaign to encourage editors to capitalize "Negro." The fact that "the Negro race alone should have been designated by a small letter can hardly have been the result of accident," she wrote. "It seemed to reflect the conviction of the white man in our early days that the Negro was in some way inferior to other races." But "constitutional amendments and other pronunciations had put a theoretical end" to that notion.[72] Cannady happily observed that the *Times* in Tacoma, Washington, had changed its policy; there had not been "any replies from Portland dailies upon the question," however.[73]

Despite urging people to boycott the city's white newspapers, she evidently continued to read the leading papers herself. Cannady may have felt it imperative to monitor them for racist language or other offensive issues. That proved to be particularly important in the fall of 1929, when she noticed that "negress" had been used several times in articles about Maxine Maxwell and housing discrimination at the University of Oregon. Cannady sent a letter to the editor of the *Morning Oregonian* that she believed represented "the viewpoint of the majority of colored people": the term "is distasteful to colored people and you will henceforth instruct your compositors and reporters to discontinue its use."[74]

Cannady followed Maxwell's situation closely. According to the *Advocate*, the twenty-year-old sophomore had been notified that her application for a room in Susan Campbell Hall, the women's dormitory, was accepted. But when she arrived on campus and administrators "learned that she was colored, she was told ... there were no vacant single rooms left."[75] The *Eugene Guard* reported that a significant increase in enrollment had "led to serious housing difficulties for women," which resulted in a "misunderstanding with the parents of Maxine Maxwell."[76] A University of Oregon official maintained that the "question of color did not arise"; Maxwell's application simply was received after all of the rooms had been assigned to new and returning students, who had preference over older or transfer students.[77]

But Maxwell reiterated that her application had been accepted and all fees paid. She told the reporter: "When I found out that I would not be allowed to live at Susan Campbell I naturally felt that I was being segregated." She added, "My parents are taxpayers and I am a citizen of the United States."[78] Maxwell was advised by the dean of women to move in with fellow Portlander (and Cannady's future sister-in-law) Nellie Franklin, who was majoring in piano and lived twelve blocks from campus.[79] Maxwell's

THE ADVOCATE

An Independent Paper Devoted to the Interests of the People

Vol. [illegible]—No. 4. IN TWO SECTIONS PORTLAND, OREGON, SATURDAY, OCTOBER 5, 1929.

COLOR LINE DRAWN AT UNIVERSITY OF OREGON

JIM CROW RECTOR REFUSED WAITERS SERVICE

GIRL DENIED ROOM IN DORMITORY

Fine Young Women of Our Race "Footballed" About to Satisfy Prejudice.

NEGRO DAILY APPEARS IN N. Y.

NOT ALL WERE NEGROES

WHITE WOMEN WERE SLAVES IN VIRGINIA

DOUGLASS HOME TO BE CLEARED OF DEBT

Start Headquarters Drive for $15,000.00

THEATRE DRAWS COLOR-LINE

LOCAL BUSINESS MAN INSULTED AT THEATRE

MANY KILLED THROUGH STARVATION

A DAILY PAPER FOR THE NEGRO

WHITE MANAGER UPHOLDS ACTION

NEGRO WAITERS BAN MINISTER WHO BANNED NEGROES

Blackshear's Party Refused Service by Waiters in New York

mother, Marie, and father, Salem businessman Charles H. Maxwell, "appealed to Governor [Isaac L.] Patterson for an adjustment of the matter, but [he] stated that he had no authority to do so, and turned it over" to the Board of Higher Education.[80] The *Morning Oregonian* reported the couple was "determined that their daughter ... receive the same advantages as do the daughters of other citizens and taxpayers."[81]

In a subsequent issue of the *Advocate*, Cannady pointed out that the Twin Cities Branch had successfully challenged the University of Minnesota's discriminatory policies. An applicant to the nursing program had been "refused" in order to "spare [her] ... the embarrassment she would meet as a colored student." The Branch prepared for a court battle, but "the university conceded the legal right of all citizens of the state to enjoy all its privileges."[82] The details of the cases in Minnesota and Oregon differed somewhat, Cannady acknowledged, but the rejection in both instances was "*because of color.*" "We like to point to Oregon as a land of freedom, of justice, equality and of good-will. We can no longer do it with this cloud over our heads," she wrote in an editorial. "Won't the Colored citizens, with the assistance of their white friends who stand for justice, equality and fair play, get a decision in the [Maxwell] case? Don't they owe it to other Colored co-eds that elect to go to our state university in the future, to clear the way now?"[83]

As Cannady observed, many clouds darkened Portland's landscape during the summer and fall of 1929. She reported two more incidents occurring within two months of each other, this time at local theaters. James McArthur, "a fine appearing colored citizen," and "his two bright looking and well dressed minor children" were refused admission to a Sunday matinée at the Pantages. By chance, McArthur bumped into Milo King, a "sympathetic" white attorney at a nearby shop; King accompanied the family back to the theater at Broadway and Yamhill "to make a second demand" for tickets. The box-office employee informed King that "she had orders to deny colored people admission even to their own section or 'nigger heaven,' particularly on week-end days." But, if King wished to wait, he could take up the issue with manager John Johnson. McArthur, King, and the children finally met with Johnson in "his private quarters." King reported that the manager was "inclined to argue the matter"; he said he "had a right to refuse or admit white or black and to seat them separate or apart." King "admitted that something of this kind was within the rights of theatre managers for certain purposes," but advised him that "managers had no legal right to deny a citizen admission to a public theatre on account of his color, particularly a man like [McArthur] who served his country in the Spanish-American war." Johnson reportedly authorized his employee "to admit the colored folks"; King was not satisfied, however. "I said think of the injustice and humiliation they have suffered which would entitle an ordinary white man to a judgment for something like $35,000; you should at least present them with complimentary tickets." Johnson had the family "ushered, free of charge, into some of the best seats in the house, where they no doubt enjoyed to full extent not only the colored comedians but all the other features of an excellent Pantages program," King wrote in the *Advocate*.[84]

That was not the first time the Pantages theater—or its manager—had been in the spotlight. Several years earlier, Cannady turned another incident at the theater into an opportunity to defend Portland's black citizens. In February 1925, the *Morning Oregonian* reported that a transient had beaten and tried to rob Johnson, who was on his way to the bank with thousands of dollars in receipts.[85] Sam Bagley, the black janitor, heard the fight and ran to get Johnson's son, who worked at a cigar shop next door.[86] Claude Johnson grabbed his gun and raced to the theater with Bagley and a customer. The men were able to break up the fight and hold the alleged robber until the police arrived. Meanwhile, a cameraman for the *Oregonian* was credited with "a distinct scoop in local news reel circles" when he filmed officers "taking the robber into custody." Footage was scheduled to be shown at Portland's Rivoli Theatre; it also was to be distributed to "leading theaters" throughout the state. The "bold daylight robbery" was the subject of a long article in the *Oregonian*, too, which reported:

> Like theatrical productions, a strain of the humorous had to enter into the affair. The elder Johnson, after the robber had been manacled, demanded to know from Bagley why he had not come to his assistance immediately, instead of running to the street. The janitor answered in the

> typical negro drawl. "Boss, three years ago when them yeggmen blowed our safe, they hog-tied me. I made up my mind then and there to let the police look after robbers. Ah don't care to get acquainted with them kind of folks."[87]

Cannady was not amused by the report or the use of dialect. She wrote in the *Advocate*, "Some day, Mr. Johnson, … there may not be a 'fleet-of-foot negro janitor' to run for your life."[88]

The second Jim Crow incident that occurred in 1929 was reported October 5th—the same day it was announced that color lines had been drawn at the University of Oregon. This time, the Orpheum made headlines when an usher tried to seat local black hotelier William D. Allen and his youngest son, sixteen-year-old Robert, upstairs. They ignored him and took seats downstairs instead. The manager subsequently asked to see them in the lobby, but Allen replied, "I don't care to go out there; and I do not care to be molested. I came to see the show." When the performance ended and the house lights came on, he noticed Chinese and Japanese people seated around him.[89]

Although Cannady observed that the Portland Branch had plenty of "work to keep itself in a job the whole winter through," she also tried to build her community by focusing on a positive reaction to the series of injustices committed that fall.[90] "We must have absolute and sincere co-operation within the group in order that we may demand and receive any worthwhile recognition," she wrote in an editorial. "Do this and we will make greater progress in things of a civic, economic and political nature."[91]

Unity was particularly important in smaller towns, where racist attitudes made it difficult for black Oregonians to advocate for equal rights. Cannady learned in 1925 that black children in the logging town of Vernonia, sixty miles west of Portland, were embroiled in a bitter fight over school integration that involved their parents, townspeople, and managers at the Oregon-American Lumber Company. So she dropped everything and went to the town to help.[92]

Despite a policy forbidding the employment of anyone "other than white Americans" unless absolutely necessary for the "operation of the sawmill and logging camps," the Oregon-American Lumber Company brought in black laborers who had worked for the Central Coal & Coke Company in Missouri.[93] By 1929, O-A had thirty-nine Negroes on its payroll, constituting 8 percent of its workforce.[94] Paul Robinson, editor of the *Vernonia Eagle*, was particularly angry that his town had been forcibly integrated and expressed his displeasure on the front page of his newspaper: "What is the idea, what is the benefit of importing niggers here, when for years it has been a white man's town. ... This town wants no niggers."[95] But the tenor of his articles changed after neighboring newspapers pointed out "problems of discord" in Vernonia. Robinson reprinted articles from the *Rainier Review* as well as the *St. Helens Mist*, which was "heralding to the world that 'Vernonia Has [a] Race Problem,'" before adding, "Few people in Vernonia seem to be overly 'worked-up' or excited over any 'race problem.'"[96] Nevertheless, he wrote that his town "would appreciate ... being a white man's town."[97] Cannady informed the NAACP's Robert Bagnall that she planned to go there to "see the leading white people and place the matter fairly and squarely before them, appealing to their sense of justice and fair play. Then if that does not work, we will have to step in with the law."[98]

She arrived in Vernonia at about 7:30 p.m. on Sunday, September 13th, and was taken immediately to the "'quarters' occupied by the colored people."[99] Cannady later described to her friend Millie Trumbull the disparate accommodations O-A provided its employees: White workers had houses "in a good district with paved streets and sidewalks and with modern conveniences in the homes. For the colored workers, shacks of two and three rooms were built at the bottom of the hills—no streets, no sidewalks and with but one water tap for two and sometimes three houses; with toilets of the old fashioned kind in the back yards."[100] Twenty-six people gathered that night at the home of Eliza and Eddie Collins and Cannady set to work organizing an NAACP branch and installing officers.[101] Then she discussed the school situation with the residents. White parents had argued that since the company had brought the workers from the South, it was obligated to provide a separate facility for the black children.[102] The company agreed, and equipped a one-room school and hired a teacher from Kansas for the four black youths. One employee already had been fired for sending his child to the public school instead; the rest had been threatened with dismissal if they followed suit. The black community was anxious but, as Cannady told Bagnall, "THEY STOOD AS ONE MAN AGAINST SENDING THEIR CHILDREN TO THE JIM CROW SCHOOL." Nevertheless, the new teacher was expected the following day and residents asked for Cannady's help "in case of a crisis." After promising to return, she left at 11:30 p.m., driving the dirt road "around mountains, through deep valleys and dense forests," finally arriving home at 3 a.m.[103]

Cannady returned to Vernonia by train hours later. After meeting with officers of the new NAACP Branch, she sought out O-A's superintendent.[104] "Somehow this distinguished gentleman had heard I was coming to see him and he conveniently took sick and did not come out while I was there," she wrote Bagnall. Instead, she met with the man "under him," whom she called a "rank Southerner." He stepped outside rather than show her to an office, so she "sat down on the steps and motioned him to a seat beside" her. "I wish I could go over our conversation," she told Bagnall. "He tried to drag into the case the whole race problem in all its phases. We talked for two hours, and I feel that he was somewhat a changed man in his views about the race question when I left him."[105]

Her next stop was the public school, where she met with the principal—"a fine young chap who told [her] that although he did not believe in the races intermarrying or mixing, he would treat those colored children like all of the others if they came to school and ... instruct his teachers to do likewise."[106] By then it was 2 p.m. and the train was about to depart. Cannady was "rushed" to the station eight blocks away and as she climbed aboard her car, a black woman "pressed something" into her hand. Cannady told Bagnall that she opened the package as soon as she had taken her seat; it contained $4—about $50 today—the balance needed to secure the Vernonia Branch's charter.[107] "The beautiful spirit of those colored people, the loss of sleep, the strain of race prejudice, the great goodness of God, was too much for me and I sat in my seat and wept like a little child," she wrote.[108]

It seemed as if Cannady had settled the matter and successfully defended the children's right to attend a mixed school "without invoking the law." But a few days later, she received a telegram from the Branch's vice-president asking her to come at once to the town. The company's general manager, Judd Greenman, had called a meeting of "the colored people" to discuss the school situation. She told Bagnall he "came down purposely to bully those people into sending their children to the jim-crow school." Cannady went to Vernonia and acted as intermediary and "attempted to show him the injustice of his procedure." She noted, "I wanted those people to remain there. We had nothing to offer them to do if they were summarily dismissed; I wanted good-will to take the place of that misunderstanding if I could, instead of trying to force the issue." She left without resolving the dispute, but urged the people to "stand pat, not to send their children to the jim-crow school, nor to any school until [she] notified them later."[109]

Back in Portland, she contacted a number of organizations on the citizens' behalf, including the Federal Council of Churches and the Columbia River Loggers Association. Reportedly, the head of the Oregon Industrial Welfare Commission spoke with a representative of the lumber company about pay inequities and liability for damages in the event of wrongful dismissal. He was "very certain" that O-A would abandon the idea of a segregated school and would not fire any workers. Cannady added a postscript to her long report to Robert Bagnall: "The whole thing in a nutshell is an attempt to duplicate the Southern system here. We will not stand for it!"[110] Bagnall told Cannady her efforts deserved "the highest praise," and hoped that her work would "eventuate in the colored children being permitted to enter the mixed schools."[111] He also informed the NAACP's publicity department of her efforts in Vernonia, as well as concurrent work in Longview, Washington.[112] The press release highlighting her activism was distributed to black newspapers across the country; it was reprinted verbatim in the *Charleston Messenger* in South Carolina and probably many other papers too.[113] That release also mentioned her new role as "volunteer organizer in the Pacific Northwest"—the designation that ultimately created so many problems for her with the Portland Branch.[114]

Despite Cannady's extensive documentation of the discrimination in Vernonia, it is unclear what the final outcome was.[115] Robinson's *Eagle* did not report on the controversy; the *St. Helens Mist* portrayed the black community as ungrateful for the company's willingness to provide a school and teacher.[116] The "negro parents, so it is stated, listened to the advice of a negro woman from Portland, and refused to send the children to the school, claiming that under the laws of Oregon, they had the right to attend the public school."[117] The *Mist* reported that the teacher grew tired of waiting for her students to appear and resigned. Cannady told Millie Trumbull that the mill school had been "dismantled and the teacher sent away"; she said the children had gone to public schools "in other districts," but did not elaborate on where they went in isolated Columbia County.[118] The *Mist* interviewed the school superintendent, who conceded, "Under the Oregon law the negroes have a right to attend the public school and so far as I know there is no law which would compel them to attend any other school." The official "admitted that it was a very embarrassing situation for his office, but under the circumstances, ... he thought that the proper solution of the matter would be for the mill company to get rid of their negro employees and by doing so, Vernonia would be rid of the negro population."[119] The mill did let the workers go, but not until it closed in 1957. A history of the Oregon-American Lumber Company notes that its Negro employees, who had been "treated as social outcasts during their entire history at Vernonia, ... were among the first of those to leave" the area in search of new jobs and new opportunities.[120]

Millie Trumbull observed in 1925: "It is not an easy task to preach tolerance when in this 'land of the free and the home of the brave,' our black men and women are sacrificed to the hate and cruelty of the white race; it is not easy to preach love and kindliness under the weary pettinesses of social ostracism which we white people do not hesitate to practice against our black neighbors." Trumbull, a white subscriber who called the *Advocate* a "torchbearer for [its] people," may have had some awareness of the daily challenges facing Oregon's black community.[121] But most white people were oblivious to the inequities surrounding them. "Once in a while some big hearted individual sends us a clipping" about an "individual of our racial group who has forced his way up to public notice," Cannady wrote in the *Advocate*.[122] Often, a note attached to the article pointed "out that Negroes had the same opportunities as white people." Cannady observed that success stories were the "exception and NOT the rule."[123]

To underscore this, she detailed a list of twelve grievances, including discrimination in residential areas, places of entertainment, and restaurants; job discrimination; and the fact that the so-called Black Laws still were on the "statute books." Cannady also reminded people that no business colleges would "admit a colored girl or boy," a reference to the Behnke-Walker Business College. At the end of the impassioned column, Cannady challenged all the "good friends of [the] race" to get to "work RIGHT HERE in our own city and state to help the under dog to acquire" all the things that may seem inconsequential "to those who already enjoy them," but mean a lot "to those from whom they are withheld." Cannady did not mean tangible items; she wanted "the newspapers of Oregon" to proclaim: "The colored people in this state are treated justly and fairly in every respect; they have equal opportunities with every other class of citizen; they are employed in whatever capacities they are fitted. In Oregon, we take no note of the color of a man's skin, knowing that the Almighty must have known His business when He fashioned us of different colors, it is his character and worth that count here." If white people still would not concede that inequities and race antipathy existed in the state, Cannady had a suggestion: Just "paint your face black and try it yourself. Then you'll understand what we mean when we say colored people are not treated on equality with other racial groups in Oregon."[124]

For nearly a quarter of a century, Cannady fought "uncompromisingly, courageously and ceaselessly" for Oregon's black citizens.[125] That fight entailed publicizing acts of discrimination, editorializing against racism, and dropping her editorial duties to help children attend a public school with their white peers. Agitation was important, but the press also played a critical role in ensuring that issues were documented and a history of the civil rights movement was preserved. As H. Claude Hudson—Cannady's friend in Los Angeles and an *Advocate* subscriber—observed on the occasion of the newspaper's twenty-fifth anniversary: "It is hard to estimate or appraise the good done by this paper during its existence.

Without the Negro press we could not have made the progress we boast of and our future development will be in proportion to our appreciation of our press."[126]

CHAPTER TEN
In the Interest of the Race

Have many battles here to fight but somehow come out on top. I try to keep my hand in His and "dare every peril, save to disobey."

— Beatrice Cannady to Walter White, March 10, 1925,
NAACP Portland Branch files

In the middle of February 1919, W. E. B. Du Bois convened a Pan-African Congress in Paris. The location and timing were no accident: the Versailles Peace Conference was under way at nearby locations and Du Bois hoped to use his meeting to draw attention to the "connection between the fate of Afro-Americans and other oppressed races living under the colonial rule of white Europeans."[1] Subsequent Congresses in 1921 and 1923 continued to bring together representatives from the French West Indies, Haiti, Liberia, France, Nigeria, Jamaica, the United States, and other countries to discuss "relations of the black and white races ... to the end that greater harmony may ensue."[2]

The Fourth Pan-African Congress was scheduled to be held in New York City in August 1927. Many people, including Cannady, "expected" that the gathering there would "be the most important ever held," and she pledged the *Advocate*'s "support" and extended "the use of its columns free of charge."[3] Then came the exciting announcement that she was one of fifty American women chosen to "act as hostesses" at the Congress.[4] The news sent ripples of excitement through Portland's black community.

In the months leading up to her departure, white and black friends held a series of interracial "silver teas" to honor Cannady and raise money to help "underwrite the Congress."[5] Alice Handsaker hosted a tea for one hundred people in March.[6] Shirley McCanns sang "Negro melodies"; Millie Trumbull talked about Langston Hughes; Gwendolyn Hooker read some of James Weldon Johnson's poems; and teacher Blanche Thurston shared information about Countee Cullen's "life and works." Several guests also gave "brief addresses" during the afternoon tea, including Reed College mathematics professor Frank L. Griffin, the Reverend E. C. Dyer, and Cannady, the guest of honor.[7]

More than a hundred guests also dropped by Elise Reynolds' home on Roselawn Avenue in mid-April for a program featuring talks by Trumbull, poet Ken Nakazawa, author of *The Weaver of the Frost*, and many others

representing organizations ranging from the Woman's Christian Temperance Union to the Portland Board of Education. McCanns and Clara Bell, a white woman, helped Reynolds with the pink-themed "affair."[8] The teas were covered in the white press, which made note of Cannady's selection as Oregon's representative by the sponsoring organization, the Circle for Peace and Foreign Relations, the "fund-raising arm" of the Pan-African Congress.[9] Its president was Addie Hunton, "a legend among feminists and civil rights leaders," who had stayed with the Cannadys the previous fall during a speaking tour of the West Coast.[10] Other members of the executive committee included Nina G. Du Bois, the *Crisis* editor's first wife, and Minnie Pickens, who was married to NAACP Field Secretary William Pickens.[11]

Six weeks before the Congress, Cannady and the other hostesses were informed that "the outlook for the attendance of delegates from foreign countries" was "very great."[12] The final update appeared in the *Advocate* fifteen days before the opening session on August 21st. Among other things, the article mentioned the activities of six hostesses—including Cannady—who had been "working very hard to arouse the interest of the United States in the conference and to make the Fourth Pan-African Congress a financial possibility."[13] Cannady contributed $75—more than

$900 today—a sum collected at the interracial teas that was said to be the "second largest amount paid in to the Congress by any of the Hostesses."[14]

Meanwhile, local department stores reportedly were vying "with each other to outfit her for her journey." Cannady told the *Chicago Defender* that her entire wardrobe had been donated "with the compliments of Portland."[15] Meier & Frank or other merchants may have given her clothes for her New York trip, but Cannady also made much of her apparel, including a beautiful embroidered Spanish shawl that was exhibited in the "show windows" of a store at 6th and Morrison in 1926. Cannady was offered $250 for the drape—more than $3,000 today—but refused to sell.[16] The wrap wasn't solely for display, though; Cannady brought it with her to the Fourth Pan-African Congress.[17]

A farewell tea was held in late July at Cannady's home in the "Roland Hayes Garden," named after the tenor she had helped promote to Portland audiences. A "large group ... gathered" for speeches and entertainment in the yard, which "was very lovely with gay Japanese umbrellas and ... baskets of white and yellow flowers suspended from the trees."[18] The next few days probably were spent taking care of loose ends at the newspaper, packing her suitcase, and saying goodbye to her family, for she expected to be gone at least four weeks.[19]

Finally, some six months after learning of her appointment, Cannady boarded a train bound for Washington on Saturday, August 6th.[20] She allotted two weeks for her trip north and then east so she could do some sightseeing before the Congress convened. Cannady also had agreed to a number of speaking engagements along the way. In fact, barely twenty-four hours after leaving Portland she "filled the pulpit" of two churches in Tacoma, Washington, and spoke about interracial friendships before "a large group of women representing three races" at clubwoman Nettie J. Asberry's home.[21] Cannady later wrote, "We shall never forget a little woman of the white race who with tears staining her cheeks, pleaded with the colored women to co-operate with them for better inter-racial relationships."[22] It was a fitting start to Cannady's journey.

The following morning, August 8th, she took the early train to Seattle and caught the steamer *Kathleen* to Vancouver, British Columbia. She went sightseeing in Victoria, spent the evening with some individuals who took her on a "short drive through interesting streets," and "addressed a small group" at a church. Her train was not scheduled to depart until 7:45 p.m. on Tuesday, August 9th, so she browsed a bookstore for volumes on "Negro Life and History," toured "the famous" Stanley Park—dedicated in 1889, the year Cannady was born—and had lunch "on the roof garden" of Spencer's Department Store.[23] Finally, it was time to board Canadian Pacific Railway and begin the "wonderful trip over the Canadian Rockies" and on to points east: Alberta, Saskatchewan, North Dakota, Minnesota, Illinois.[24]

The train pulled into Chicago four days later. Cannady was excited to be back in the city she had enjoyed while a student at the University of Chicago, and looked forward to several busy days of sightseeing and visiting with friends old and new. She was met at the station by her "very dear friend" Marie Preston. The women had their "choice of several conveyances," Cannady wrote in the second installment of her series about her trip East, but they decided to take an elevated train "since Lindy wasn't there to meet [them] in his 'Spirit of St. Louis.'"[25] Had they waited a bit longer, they might have seen Lindbergh flying overhead: he was due to arrive that day from Grand Rapids, Michigan, as part of his nationwide tour to promote aviation.[26]

Cannady barely had time to get settled at a friend's home before Earl Dickerson, an attorney who would become known as "the Dean of Chicago's Black Lawyers," arrived to take her sightseeing in his "smart, grey Lincoln sedan."[27] They stopped at Douglas National Bank on South State Street; when it opened in January 1922, noted the *New York Times*, it was the first bank "to be chartered for negroes."[28] Cannady wrote how pleased she was that President Anthony Overton "took the time to greet [them] in his office." She and Dickerson also toured the Victory Life Insurance Co., which had offices in the bank building. Overton served as president of that company, too; Cannady reminded readers he had just been awarded the prestigious Spingarn Medal by the NAACP "because of his success in a long business career."[29]

From there, Cannady and Dickerson went to the Binga State Bank, whose grand opening on January 3, 1921, had been hailed as "a History-Making Event among the Colored People Residing in Chicago."[30] Cannady "had the pleasure of meeting" its founder, Jesse Binga, who was widely celebrated as "the ideal American hero, an example of Horatio Alger success."[31] Next, Cannady and Dickerson toured the Overton Hygienic Manufacturing Company, another of Anthony Overton's ventures.[32] The company became known for its High Brown Face Powder, a product advertised in the *Advocate* and one that Cannady sold.[33] She concluded her tour of the city with a stop at Dickerson's law offices on Dearborn Street. Cannady told readers he was a graduate of the University of Chicago "law department"; in fact, he was the first black man to graduate from the University of Chicago Law School.[34]

Cannady left Chicago at 11:45 p.m. on the Michigan Central, bound for Detroit.[35] When she arrived she met with former Portlanders George and Allie Benjamin, learned about the city's business section, toured the YMCA, and more.[36] But perhaps most interesting about this layover was her two-hour-long conversation with Ossian Sweet, the Detroit physician who was at the center of a racially charged incident in 1925.[37] That summer, Sweet purchased a home in an all-white neighborhood for $18,500—the equivalent of about $226,000 today—and he and his wife, Gladys, and toddler, Iva, moved in on September 8th. Aware that there might be trouble, the doctor armed himself and asked friends and relatives to help him keep vigil for the first few days. A white crowd gathered outside his home; a *Detroit News* reporter who later testified for the defense said five hundred people eventually mobbed the street and pelted the house with rocks. The next night, a white neighbor was killed and another was shot in the leg. All eleven people in the home were arrested and charged with murder.[38] Cannady reminded readers that the NAACP had come to their defense and hired Clarence Darrow, who had recently participated in one of the most famous trials of the century—*State v. John Scopes*, better known as "The Monkey Trial."[39] Ultimately, all charges were dropped and Ossian Sweet moved back into his home. But it was not the joyful event he expected. His daughter died of tuberculosis in 1926; she was two. His wife died soon after, also of TB.[40] "He appears to be greatly embittered as a result of his terrible experience," Cannady wrote, "but denied that he holds any hatred against anyone for his ordeal." However, she observed that he was "far from being well or hearty."[41] Her comments were prophetic: Sweet would die by his own hand in 1944, "after years of ill health and depression."[42]

From Detroit Cannady traveled to Niagara Falls and Buffalo, where she visited the husband and daughter of the late civil rights advocate Mary B. Talbert. Then she continued to Boston for some sightseeing. Cannady took photos of the usual "places of interest"—Harvard, Bunker Hill Monument, Old South Church, Henry Wadsworth Longfellow's home, and the Paul Revere House. She also visited sites that were particularly meaningful to her: Roland Hayes' home in Brookline, a suburb of Boston, and the monument to Crispus Attucks, a mulatto man who was killed in what became known as the Boston Massacre.[43]

Cannady finally arrived in New York City just after dawn on August 21st. Despite the early hour, Addie Hunton and Viola Brantley-Williams met her at the station. Both women offered her accommodations, but she decided to stay with Brantley-Williams, perhaps in deference to Hunton's busy schedule during the Congress. With their destination settled, the women took a taxi to the "very heart of Harlem." Cannady was awestruck: "On the long ride from the station we had been stretching our eyes and neck all out of proportion trying to see where the tall buildings ended in the sky." She settled into her room but was too excited to rest. "It did not seem possible that we were really in Harlem, that part of Manhattan Island which houses more than 200,000 colored people," she wrote. She marveled at "the wide streets and avenues" and, even though it was only 6 a.m., she observed how 135th Street was "humming with the voices of" people on their way to work or just returning from an "evening's entertainment."[44]

The Congress convened that afternoon in nearby St. Mark's Methodist Episcopal Church and featured talks by William Pickens and W. E. B. Du Bois.[45] The hostesses were introduced, and Cannady was recognized as having "come from the most distant point in this country."[46] The next three days were filled with lectures and discussions; Cannady also had an opportunity to visit the New York Public Library's Division of Negro Literature, History and Prints. Again, she was awestruck: "When we entered the room which houses the collection, we were so thrilled at seeing so many books on the life and history of Negroes that we must have acted like a child with its first pair of new shoes. It also made us realize just how little and insignificant our own little collection of more than a hundred volumes was."[47] Another high point occurred when a message from Oregon Governor Isaac Patterson was selected from among the dozens of letters and telegrams received and shared with attendees.[48] She noted that his greetings "were received with applause."[49] She, too, was applauded after speaking at the closing session—the best-attended meeting of the day, according to the *New York Amsterdam News*.[50] The paper covered Cannady's discussion of "inter-racial fellowship," and reported her success "in getting Negro books and magazines in many" white homes "and Negro history" in Portland schools.[51]

Finally, it was announced that she was one of five people—along with Du Bois and Hunton—appointed to organize the Fifth Pan-African Congress planned for December 1929 in Tunisia.[52] "Never were we so surprised as when chosen as a member of this important committee," Cannady wrote when she returned home.[53] She may have been taken aback by this news, but the appointment was a good indication of her status by the late 1920s. Nationally circulated newspapers such as the *Chicago Defender* were writing about her and her civil rights efforts in Oregon. NAACP officials continually expressed their delight with her work, and press releases detailing her activism were sent to black editors across the country. Had she been closer to the East Coast and its intellectual, cultural, and political nexus—rather than in the remote Northwest—Cannady may well have become a national leader in the fight for equal rights and liberties.

Following the conference, Cannady spent a week in New York City to sightsee and visit friends, including Minnie and William Pickens and George Haynes.[54] She visited a "famous cabaret on Seventh Avenue"—probably a club called Small's Paradise that featured dancing waiters—and observed that "there was a grand intermingling of races" even though it was a "Negro cabaret."[55] She went to popular tourist destinations—Greenwich Village, Central Park, and Broadway—and lesser-known attractions such as the Irvington-on-Hudson mansion of Madam C. J. Walker, an entrepreneur who was one of the first black millionaires.[56] Cannady also reported touring the offices of the *Crisis*, the *Messenger*, and the *New York Amsterdam News*.[57]

Cannady decided to take a southerly train route home so she could visit family in Texas. She left Washington, D.C., at 9:30 p.m. and by morning had crossed into South Carolina. She wrote that she dressed in her "best looking traveling togs" and spent time "dolling up" and polishing her fingernails in order to look her best when she went to the dining car for breakfast. The waiters smiled at her, but the steward "scrutinized [her] closely and did not advance to meet" her. Cannady proceeded to a vacant table and "was about to draw [her] own chair" when the steward laid his hand on it and told her she could not be served with the other travelers. She remembered that "an innocent colored woman" had been lynched in South Carolina the previous year, so she "made no further inquiries." Cannady returned to her car and tried to "swallow a big lump" in her throat. The Pullman porter, a "fine chap" who had been to college, subsequently visited with her. He told her to ignore their behavior—"they are just prejudiced and that's all there is to" it—and advised her to order breakfast from him. Cannady said she would just wait until they pulled into the next station, but that was out of the question, too, due to Jim Crow laws. Then she recalled Langston Hughes' poem, "I, Too," about a man who is sent to eat in the kitchen when company arrives:

> . . .
>
> But I laugh,
> And eat well,
> And grow strong.

Tomorrow,
I'll be at the table
When company comes.
Nobody'll dare
Say to me,
"Eat in the kitchen,"
Then.

...

With this in mind, Cannady did order her meal, "but the big lump kept coming up and [she] could not eat a bite. When the waiter called for [the] tray [she] paid the check and with an extra quarter for him, [she] thanked him kindly for his services."[58]

Cannady turned her thoughts toward New Orleans. She had planned to spend several days getting reacquainted with the city, but the sticky summer heat spurred her on to Crowley—midway between Baton Rouge and Lake Charles—and a visit with her brother and sister-in-law.[59] She was delighted to also see her sister, Mabel Beverley, and her children there; they had been visiting for two weeks. During a "sightseeing and shopping trip," Cannady bumped into a woman who had worked as a clerk at Olds, Wortman & King in Portland. "At the close of our pleasant chat," wrote Cannady, "we remarked that the world isn't so big after all." She continued on to Houston with the Beverleys and spent time with the family there. Before leaving that city, Cannady had a chance to see *Advocate* subscriber Ella Ryan, whose husband was principal of Jack Yates High School.[60]

Her next stop was Littig. Cannady had not been home for ten years, so when the train reached Elgin—about five miles east—she "raised [her] window high" and began "watching for old landmarks" such as the "swimming hole" on her family's farm. The station had been moved a few blocks away; no longer was it in front of her uncle Edward's store and post office. So she left her "weighty luggage" at the depot and walked down the track to greet him and begin "five glorious days" at the farm.[61] But Cannady did not have much time to rest; she was soon "pressed into service" to speak at the Rosenwald School in Elgin. The school—one of more than five thousand built in Southern states as part of an educational initiative by Booker T. Washington and Sears, Roebuck and Co. President Julius Rosenwald—also was an important gathering place for Negroes in the area.[62] Principal John Madison "issued a call ... for all to come to witness a mock trial and to hear one of their former citizens ... speak." Cannady wrote that "young and old,—men, women, boys and girls" packed the auditorium. At the end of her address, she helped organize an NAACP

Cannady's brother John, whom she visited in Crowley.

branch; she already had organized one in Littig. "This was highly pleasing to us as to them, as well as to the National Office," Cannady wrote.[63]

Her long trip was nearing an end. Although she continued to visit with family and friends wherever she stopped, it was time to get back to work. Perhaps mindful that she would soon be asked to share details of the Fourth Pan-African Congress with Portlanders, Cannady "gave a brief report" on the meeting to a "large group of club women" in Dallas. She spent the remaining time talking about "the need of world peace and some ways to bring it about."[64] Following the gathering in her cousin Lula Lightner's rose garden, Cannady headed home to the Pacific Northwest.[65]

Cannady returned from her extended trip East on Saturday, September 17th, six weeks after boarding her first train.[66] Energized by the Congress, the countless talks she had given during her long trip, and visits with publishers and activists including the *Chicago Defender*'s Robert Abbott, W. E. B. Du Bois, and the *Guardian*'s William Monroe Trotter, she was eager to talk about her experiences. The *Advocate* reported that she was "greatly in demand" following her long absence and her calendar filled quickly with speaking engagements at local churches, Reed College, and other venues. For example, she discussed "The Negro's Contribution to American Culture" with "a large audience" at Unity Presbyterian Church in east Portland. Following that talk, Cannady noted that "she was immediately requested to assist some high school students with their reports on Negro activities."[67]

Meanwhile, Cannady was mulling over ways to make the most of her experience at the Pan-African Congress. She went to Alice Handsaker's home in early October for a special meeting of the Fellowship for Better Inter-racial Relations, a group she had founded to try "to iron out some of the misunderstandings between the races."[68] It was during the afternoon tea that Cannady "outlined" her ambitious plans for "reproducing the main features of the Pan-African Congress."[69] Cannady told attendees she envisioned a "unique educational meeting" for "a general discussion of Negro progress." The free, two-day event at Central Library would feature her report on the recent Congress, as well as music, exhibits, lectures, and poetry. She had just over six weeks to pull together the event, planned for November 18th and 19th.[70]

Cannady started lining up speakers for the Miniature Pan-African Congress. Norman F. Coleman, president of Reed College, agreed to give an address on "The Imperative Need of Inter-Racial Co-operation in Solving World Problems."[71] Superintendent Charles A. Rice wrote that he would "be very glad to accept [her] invitation and to bring greetings to the 'Congress' from the Portland Public Schools."[72] The Reverend John F. Moreland, pastor of First AME Zion Church, was scheduled to discuss "The American Negro's Case." Bahá'í leader George Orr Latimer planned to explore "The Pride of Prejudice." Nettie Asberry was writing an address titled, "Federated Club Work and World Peace."[73] Etta Graham, visiting from Liberia, was asked to talk about the education and customs of people there, and the editor of Portland's *Catholic Sentinel* began preparing a related talk on "Changing Africa."[74] In all, more than thirty individuals were invited to participate by preparing new addresses, reading works by Negro poets, performing "spirituals and other music by Negro composers," discussing "internationally known Negroes," or by reading reports given at the Congress in New York.[75]

Plans were coming together remarkably well, so Cannady turned her attention to promoting the event in the *Advocate*. A front-page advertisement invited everyone who was "interested in Negro life and activities"; teachers and "students of Negro history" were "especially requested to attend this educational treat" featuring "outstanding speakers" and an exhibit of "books, magazines, newspapers and pictures of, on, by and about Negroes."[76]

She may also have contacted editors at the local newspapers, because the event garnered a surprising amount of coverage. This exposure brought Negroes from Portland's margins to the forefront and helped raise white editors' awareness of other people and issues in Portland. The *Portland Telegram* announced the upcoming conference and named the speakers—white as well as black—who were scheduled to talk.[77] The *Oregon Daily Journal* reported that the "two-day Inter-Racial Educational meeting" had opened with an invocation by the Reverend James N. Pendleton and a "report by Mrs. Cannady on the congress." She was quoted as saying, "The congress particularly desires that relations of black and white races in various countries be considered to the end that greater harmony may ensue."[78] The *Journal* devoted even more space to the second day's activities, probably because the paper's associate editor, Marshall N. Dana, delivered the keynote address.[79] But the article also listed other individuals on the day's program, including Millie Trumbull, Dr. Elbert Booker and his wife, Maude, Phil Reynolds, and Dr. Coleman, who gave the closing address at 7:45 p.m.

A spontaneous gathering at Central Library the following day demonstrated how powerful the conference was. "Every speaker just opened his heart and showed what was in it," one attendee wrote. By the end, Cannady wept "out of gratitude to her friends who had made the Congress possible."[80] But they also were appreciative "of her untiring efforts in assembling the exhibits, of her genius which conceived the organization of the Congress and of the wide scope of work covered by the programs."[81] A few days later, on Thanksgiving, a *Journal* editorial praised Cannady and the Miniature Pan-African Congress for "contribut[ing] to the good will of the ... season" and observed:

> The fact that in this city, time and again, people without regard to color are drawn together for common study of racial and social problems and that the invitation comes from public spirited colored people gives Portland a stronger position in the greater challenge of the Pacific.
>
> The colors ... must be harmonized before the era of the Pacific can succeed. The races must learn to live together in human brotherhood, common aspiration and peace. There must be understanding and gratitude. The miniature Pan-African conference in Portland might be the preliminary of a Pan-Pacific gathering dedicated to

> the discovery that under the skin all men are brothers. Why not on another Thanks-giving have a conference as Portland's observance of America's most distinctive day?[82]

The *Portland Telegram* stated that the "interesting and creditable exhibit showed something of what the negro is accomplishing in the way of self development and as contribution to the world's work." Reiterating Cannady's belief in the importance of education, the editorial noted: "It is only as the white man learns to know his brothers who are veiled in darker skins, to appreciate what they are doing and what they strive to do, that prejudice will die and tolerance and understanding will take its place. Such conferences as this ... thus serve both races, educating the one and encouraging the other."[83]

Cannady never disclosed attendance figures, but she considered the event a "tremendous success" and noted that "an unusually large audience was present for the closing program" featuring Reed College's president. Nettie Asberry, president of the Washington State Federation of Colored Women's Clubs, was praised for "her lively discussions, her music and her exquisite address," all of which contributed to the positive outcome. Cannady also acknowledged J. K. Gill & Co. and the public library for loaning books and magazines on the "life and literature of the Negro race" and Meier & Frank for supplying flags of the nations represented at the Congress. Grant High School students who created maps and charts "depicting Negro progress" were recognized, too. Resolutions adopted at the closing session recommended that their "exhibit be circulated" to Portland schools so all children could "have access to the valuable information contained therein."[84] And Cannady, inspired by attendees' interest in the literature, began printing "In the Library" in the *Advocate*. The occasional column listed books about "Negroes and Negro Life" in the public library's collection.[85]

The conference attracted national attention. *Legislative Counsellor*, the "official organ" of the Woman's Legislative Council of Washington, carried a brief description of the "epoch making conference" and observed, "The entire program only emphasized the wonderful progress made by American Negroes in a period little over half a century."[86] The National Association of Colored Women called the event "the most outstanding gathering of the kind ever featured in this section."[87] And the February 1928 issue of the *Crisis* featured a large photograph of the literature that was displayed—which included that journal and the *Advocate*—and a brief description of the two-day event.[88] Editor Du Bois commented on Cannady's efforts to educate and inform Portland's citizens. "I am very glad that you are bringing the problems of Africa before the people of the far West," he wrote.[89] Addie Hunton, president of the group that sponsored the New York Congress, also noted: "Your faithful attendance and keen interest at every session of the Congress are in themselves guarantee of an interesting and true recounting of that tremendous and far-reaching event. However, we also know your ability to transmit the spirit of the Congress and to render most valuable help in extending that spirit to all friends of righteousness."[90] That spirit translated into additional resolutions to try to build Portland's black community.

Attendees pointed out the "noticeable lack of printed matter concerning the life of the Negro in the school libraries in Portland" and requested that the board of education add the *Journal of Negro History*, the *Crisis*, the *Messenger*, *Opportunity*, and the *Advocate*—all of which were "devoted to matters concerning the Negro in the United States."[91] This resolution was in keeping with historian Carter G. Woodson's suggestions for "bring[ing] the accomplishments of Negro life to the attention ... of white folk [as well as] to the Negro race itself."[92] Among other things, the publisher of the *Journal of Negro History* encouraged people to talk to their "board of education [about] the adoption of Negro history textbooks."[93] Cannady felt very strongly about this issue, too. In one editorial she argued that school textbooks were to blame for "destroy[ing] racial confidence" because they omitted Negroes' contributions to literature, art, history, and other facets of life.[94] Making this information available enhanced race pride and validated black students' identity; white students benefited as well, because knowledge of "the history and development of the Negro race" improved interracial relations.[95] It also enabled students to dispel misinformation. During a class discussion of Paul Laurence Dunbar, a student described him as white. "There was a small Negro girl in the class who immediately called the teacher's attention to the inaccurate statement and proceeded to give the full history of the poet from his birth to his death," Cannady wrote. "Now *there* was a dissemination of useful information which could not have been given unless that young Negro student had been prepared for just such an emergency."[96]

Cannady continued to ride the wave of success engendered by the Congress. She traveled to Los Angeles for the NAACP conference the following year, and in 1929 she was nominated for the Harmon Foundation's race-relations award. But she seemed to be in a pensive mood that year. She had turned forty in January and may have felt the need to reflect on the significance of her career. Her favorite son, George, celebrated his sixteenth birthday in

May—a happy milestone but one that also heralds changes in a mother and son's relationship.[97] Whether these issues weighed on her mind is unclear, but in June she wrote a long editorial that recounted the development of interracial relations in Portland. "By thoughtful, careful, prayerful and constant cultivation, over a period of many years, there has developed a beautiful spirit of friendship, fellowship, and good will between the colored and white people in Portland," she wrote. She called this "treasure ... the greatest asset any community can have." But Cannady recognized that her work was not yet done. As long as prejudice, discrimination, and race antipathy lingered, this spirit of cooperation could easily be destroyed. She urged her readers to beware: "Let us, colored and white, who have our homes, our children, all of our interests, both material and spiritual, inextricably involved here, guard, carefully, this attainment of interracial friendship and fellowship; let us hold tenaciously to what we already have attained in this way, and build, multiply and expand this bond; let us solicit the support of those who are interested in building for peace."[98] Her optimism soon would come crashing down, along with the stock market.

January 1930 started well enough: Portland's black residents were getting ready to welcome their new doctor, DeNorval Unthank, and his family. But articles about the discrimination they faced quickly pushed the celebratory news off the *Advocate*'s front page. Cannady spent the rest of the year addressing other important issues affecting the community. In March, she asked, "We wonder what the local branch of the [NAACP] is doing to check the wave of discrimination and segregation sweeping our city and state."[99] Two months later, she began advising readers to boycott businesses that would not employ Negroes.[100] Cannady reported in July that a prominent black clubwoman had been refused service at a downtown restaurant.[101] An editorial she wrote about lynching was included in the NAACP's weekly press release in October and distributed throughout the country.[102] At the end of the year, she reported that "several colored men" had applied for jobs with the U.S. Post Office, but none had been employed yet.[103] And in the midst of the worsening situation in Portland, Cannady's own life was in turmoil: she and Edward ended their eighteen-year marriage in June, her brother, Jack, died the same month, and her beloved father and a nephew died in December.[104]

Cannady immersed herself in her work and focused on the effects the Depression was having on her community. She went to the Oregon towns of Pendleton, Astoria, and Salem on business, and spoke to a number of groups about race relations, including the Men's Brotherhood of Central Methodist Church and the First Friends Church.[105] She also began

Beatrice with Yancy Franklin.

spending time socially with her assistant, Yancy Franklin. The couple married, quietly, on July 18, 1931.[106] Throughout the summer and fall of 1931, Cannady—who also went by Franklin and Cannady-Franklin at that time—appears to have kept a lighter-than-normal schedule. This was partly due to the Depression—the editor scaled back her publishing operation to save money—and she may have taken some time off to adjust to her new relationship.

But she did weigh in on the growing controversy in the black community surrounding the radio comedy *Amos 'n' Andy*, heard locally over KGW. *Pittsburgh Courier* editor Robert L. Vann spearheaded the movement to ban the program and the NAACP soon joined in the protest.[107] Cannady, however, observed that more pressing issues were affecting Negroes, including unemployment, lynching, and the ongoing legal fight involving the nine Scottsboro Boys, who had been wrongly convicted of rape. "It is our honest opinion that editor Vann and the Association could put their time to better account," she wrote. A better option, if people did "not care to listen" to the program, was to "tune in on something else or sign off entirely." Cannady also reminded listeners they could make their opinions known by boycotting the sponsor, Pepsodent, and using "Overton's Hygienic toothpaste instead."[108] At least one other journalist agreed with her views: "We rant and foam at insignificant matters when it is so patent that serious things confront us," W. J. Wheaton wrote from San Francisco.

He felt it would be much better to use the power of the press to try to improve the economy. "Then there is the injustice of racial segregation and political ostracism, and oh, ever so many other things more necessary to racial progress than the elimination of 'Amos 'n' Andy,'" he wrote.[109]

Early in 1932, after weathering two particularly difficult years in Portland, Cannady wrote a poignant editorial about "Race Prejudice in Oregon":

> It seems that the people, not content with the trouble brought about by the economic depression, insist on the cultivation of race prejudice. And as the colored race is the target, it is made to suffer more in addition to all its other troubles.
>
> It seems that away out here in Oregon—God's country—there should not be any such thing as race antipathy. But there is, and lots of it. Nearly every colored person who has sought to buy a home has had to fight in the courts and out of them in order to occupy them; there are many public places of accommodation, resort and amusement which draw color lines in different ways.
>
> Why all this meanness? The colored people in Oregon for the most part are good law abiding citizens ... They go to school, to church and contribute freely of their time, talents and money toward civic betterment and still they must suffer the injustice and unreasonableness of race prejudice. What is the matter with the white ministers in their pulpits? Why don't they speak out and influence their own race to do right? What is all this talk about religion and going to heaven? To some of us who live behind the veil, it appears more and more to be nothing but the "bunk," if you please.
>
> As citizens, colored people deserve all the rights and privileges and the protection as any other citizen has.[110]

The charge that religious leaders should be doing more to promote brotherhood was nothing new; Cannady had addressed that issue in other editorials through the years.[111] But this was one of the few times she alluded to the bleakness and invisibility of a life spent "behind the veil," the stark metaphor used by W. E. B. Du Bois in his book, *The Souls of Black Folks.* Although Cannady was more privileged than many Negroes—female or male—during the 1910s and 1920s, she still endured the pain of Jim Crowism on numerous occasions.

After twenty years of working to improve interracial relations in Portland, Cannady may have felt she was running out of options to address inequities. She decided on a bold plan: on April 2, 1932, Cannady announced her candidacy for state representative from Multnomah

County's fifth district.[112] It was time to agitate full time from the capitol's oak-paneled House Chambers.

"For the first [time] in Oregon politics an American Negro is running for State representative," exclaimed Myrtle Campbell, a white woman who wrote occasionally for the *Advocate*. Black Oregonians finally would have a voice in the legislature—even if a lone one—and a successful bid for office just might pave the way for other candidates. "The Negroes of Oregon are rallying to [Cannady's] support," Campbell observed, "because they have confidence in her and know that she has their welfare at heart."[113] One Portlander who was "grateful for the many favors" Cannady had done for him offered to help with her campaign and assured her, "You can count on me and all my relations to vote for you."[114] People living elsewhere were disappointed they could not vote for a race woman whom they held in high esteem.[115]

With the slogan "A new, high-standard legislation adequate to meet the requirements of present-day development," her platform was general enough to satisfy most white voters, though perhaps too vague for some of her district's black constituents. She pledged to "support legislation" to develop "Oregon's natural resources and industries" and put the "unemployed" to work in those areas; she also promised to champion working women and improve the "conditions under which they labor[ed]." Overall, she told voters she would "support all honest, sane legislation" that would "improve the economic and social welfare of" Oregonians.[116] She may have had in mind the new civil rights bill that the Portland Branch planned to introduce when the State Legislature convened on January 9, 1933—Cannady's forty-fourth birthday.[117] She would have enjoyed nothing more than to spend the day discussing equal rights with a room full of white legislators.

News of her candidacy spread quickly among black journalists. Wheaton wrote a glowing recommendation for the *Advocate*:

> Her course has been constructive and for group advancement. As publisher, she has edited one of the best weekly journals on the Pacific coast .... As a lawyer, she not only has the distinction of being the first woman of her race to practice her profession on the coast, but stands among the best. It has been her constant endeavor to bring about a better understanding between the different racial groups .... How she has succeeded is shown by the constant demand for her as a speaker before the various educational institutions where her knowledge of

> Negro history has served to place a different complexion of thought and a more tolerant attitude toward the Negro.

Wheaton concluded the testimonial by noting that Cannady "would represent faithfully the interests of ALL the people" in her district; this may have been an attempt to reach out to some of the *Advocate*'s white readers.[118] Wheaton also wrote an article about the "brilliant journalist" for his own paper, the *San Francisco Spokesman*. "The civic work of the little lady has elicited unbounded praise from the citizens of Portland," he wrote. And her "radio addresses," which had taught white people "more about the Negro ... than ever before," had "been highly commended especially by such powerful and opinion molding journals as the *Oregonian*."[119]

Two weeks later, Wheaton wrote again about Cannady's campaign, noting that voters had an opportunity to send to the capitol someone who was "qualified in every respect." He pointed out that she "thinks clearly, acts wisely, and above all, has courage. There is no question as to her fitness. THERE SHOULD BE NONE TO HER ELECTION."[120] Wheaton's endorsement was accompanied by the first of many advertisements that would run in the *Advocate* prior to election day: "CAST YOUR VOTE AT THE PRIMARY FOR MRS. BEATRICE CANNADY-FRANKLIN."[121] Clifford C. Mitchell, whose columns were carried in at least sixty black papers across the country, also described Cannady's many accomplishments and summarized her platform.[122] Wheaton then commented on Mitchell's "splendid tribute to [her] worth and civic work," further evidence of the scope of the exchange network and its important role in keeping an imagined community of readers informed.[123]

With the primary less than six weeks away, Cannady continued to urge *Advocate* readers to turn out for the election. "Every Citizen Vote In Primaries FRIDAY MAY 20, 1932," commanded one four-column headline.[124] An editorial reminded "all good citizens" that they needed to re-register if they had moved recently; this would allow them "to do their duty on May 20th."[125] Responsibility and obligation were the topics of another editorial published shortly before the primary. "Times are too critical now for people to be the least negligent in their civic duties," she warned. Voters ought to "show some concern for whoever aspires to govern" and the "best way to do that," according to Cannady, was to vote on election day.[126] Of course, she also continued to remind readers to cast their ballot for her, the Republican candidate for state representative from the fifth district.[127]

But trouble was brewing again in the Portland Branch. Members of an advisory committee were working to compile a "political endorsement ticket" for the coming election.[128] They planned to release it at the monthly mass meeting, which was just five days before the primary. DeNorval Unthank, the Branch's vice president, became so upset over the behind-the-scenes wrangling that he typed a two-page, single-spaced letter to Roy Wilkins, the NAACP's assistant secretary. "Many of this group have personal grievances against Mrs. Franklin that they are unable to drop in order to get the greater perspective of the distinction that a Negro representative will bring to Oregon," he wrote about the decision to omit her name from the ticket. He feared that failing to endorse her could have disastrous consequences: "It is embarrassing to the better thinking Negroes of this city to feel that the only Negro group that purports to put out a political platform does not endorse Mrs. Cannady-Franklin. We know positively that this is not the opinion of the majority of Negroes here." Further, he noted: "We feel that her chances for success in this campaign rest greatly with unity of action on the part of our own group here." Unthank implored Wilkins to intervene and use the "power" of his office to stop "the distribution of this ticket."[129] Wilkins sent Branch President Clarence Ivey a telegram on the day of the mass meeting. He reminded Ivey in no uncertain terms that branches had "no authority ... to formally endorse candidates or parties or factions." Political involvement was limited to studying candidates' records "with regard to the Negro" and making that "information known to the voters."[130] Even though Unthank and Wilkins managed to avert the public disavowal of her campaign, the incident must have deeply hurt Cannady.

Support from black voters was important but, as Clifford Mitchell correctly observed, there were "not enough colored votes in all of Oregon, and particularly not in the 5th district," for Cannady to "wage her campaign on racial appeal" alone.[131] She needed the support of white voters if she were to have any chance of advancing to the general election in November. Unthank noted that "many of the white groups [already had] endorsed her and her candidacy" as a result of her "standing in the community."[132] One "American native born white" man who was grateful to Cannady for helping him and his family when he was "out of work, out of funds, out of food," wrote: "I hope you are successful for I know that you will be an honest and efficient legislator if given the opportunity."[133] An optimistic Myrtle Campbell believed "the white race" knew Cannady to be "fair and conscientious ... in her dealings with them," and so would "welcome her presence in the State Capitol to help solve the problems of 'Old Oregon.'"[134] Even a white competitor, Ralph Hoeber, wrote, "Should we both be nominated and elected, I know that we would take pleasure in working together for everything that means improvement of civic life and against all forces of evil, whether in the form of economic selfishness or racial prejudice."[135] Despite Hoeber's gesture, Cannady could not afford to become complacent with forty-eight other individuals hoping to be among the thirteen to advance to the general election.

So she informed *Advocate* readers that she would appreciate invitations to speak, since "personal conversation" was "one of the best methods of advertising."[136] Her calendar quickly filled with appointments to address the Business and Industrial Girls Club, the League of Women Voters, and other white and black groups.[137] Cannady also had several opportunities while campaigning to puncture some pervasive myths and stereotypes. She spoke to a group of white clubwomen gathered at a southeastern Portland home about "The Negro and Crime," telling the women: "While the Negro is not an angel, he is by no means as bad as he is painted by cold statistics." To prove her point, she related a story about a town that reportedly had half of its black population in jail. Ultimately, it was revealed that two Negroes lived in the town.[138] Cannady cited additional examples to illustrate that numbers can be misleading, and urged her listeners not to believe everything they read in newspapers.

Despite positive feedback from groups, letters of support from readers, and recommendations by colleagues, *Oregon Voter* did not show enthusiasm for Cannady's candidacy. Days before the primary, the public-affairs journal described the candidates:

> Of the 49 candidates, 42 have had no previous experience as members of the legislature. They include 26 lawyers, nine business men, two farmers, … a physician, two school-teachers, one labor editor and one colored editor. The majority are excellent material; a few have had sufficient experience in public life to qualify them exceptionally for legislative efficiency; several are citizens of unusual qualification.[139]

Then the journal observed: "Beatrice Cannady-Franklin is a brilliant leader of the Afro-American community and editor of its principal weekly paper. A crusader for her race. Of advanced social views. We do not believe she would be a stabilizing influence if elected."[140] Exactly what the journal meant by the last comment is unclear. Perhaps the editors felt that having a woman—or a black woman—in the capitol would be disruptive. Maybe they believed she would be too forceful in floor debates. Or maybe the sticking point was her "advanced social views," possibly a euphemism for her stance on civil rights.

Lacking support from both *Oregon Voter* and the *Oregonian*, Cannady turned to the people and asked them to reflect on her long career in Portland.[141] "If my work in the interest of mankind for the past 18 years or more is not sufficient to inform you as to my qualifications and as to my sincerity, nothing I can say now will convince you," she wrote in the *Advocate* on the eve of the primary.[142] Ultimately, 7,668 voters did feel she was the right person for the demanding job.[143] The final count placed her forty-second out of forty-nine candidates; considering that there were just 1,243 Negroes of voting age living in Portland as of 1930, the results are impressive and proof of her standing in Portland.[144] Ralph Hoeber, who told Cannady how much he would enjoy collaborating with her in Salem, also lost the election. In fact, he received seventeen fewer votes than she did.[145]

Cannady's campaign places her squarely among the generation of black leaders who felt political activism was the only successful path to equality. Many of those individuals also were publishers who viewed their activism as a logical extension of their journalism. In the Pacific Northwest, she joined two colleagues who turned to politics to effect reform: John H. Ryan, who was elected to the Washington State Legislature three times in the early 1900s, and Horace Roscoe Cayton, who used his *Seattle Republican* and *Cayton's Weekly* "as major weapons" in the fight for equal rights. Cayton was as committed to his community as Cannady was to hers; among other things, he helped found the Seattle NAACP Branch.[146]

Cannady may have had many reasons for running for office. Surely chief among them was her desire to continue to agitate for civil rights and liberties for Portland's sixteen hundred black citizens. And perhaps, in her wildest dreams, she saw a career in local politics leading to a job in the nation's capital. After all, it had worked for Oscar De Priest, the three-term congressman from Illinois who had begun his political career as a member of the Cook County Board of Commissioners.[147] It is possible, too, that Cannady wanted to move to Salem to be closer to her son George, who was a popular freshman at Willamette University. In early May 1932, he attended a lecture on "Progressive Education" held in the House Chambers. He wrote his mother afterward, "I think you'll like the seat I have picked out [for] you in the House of Representatives."[148]

Cannady did not write much about her defeat. A front-page article thanked her "friends and well wishers" for their "exhibition of faith in [her] ability and worth as a public servant." She also was pleased that she had been "treated with the utmost courtesy and respect by [her] fellow campaigners as well as the voters."[149] But if Cannady did not discuss the loss, her friends did. Ralph Clyde, a white city commissioner and *Advocate* columnist, observed, "Very few candidates, in their initial plunge into the stormy sea of politics, ever get such a heavy vote at the start. You are to be congratulated, and you made many friends in conducting a clean and dignified campaign."[150] Lewis B. Stewart, pastor of the AME Church in Anaconda, Montana, wrote, "You have achieved the most glorious defeat in Oregon's history. Accept my honest-to-goodness congratulations and entreaty to continue the work you have so nobly begun."[151] Wheaton also called Cannady's initial "bid for the legislature ... a victory in defeat. ... We claim that her defeat was a victory because she has shown that ability and courage will overcome the handicap of prejudice in whatever guise it be."[152] Cannady pledged to run again, which pleased supporters such as Wheaton, who already was predicting her success in the next biennial election.[153] But it was not to be. Cannady apparently abandoned any other thoughts of a career in politics, and by 1938 had decided to leave Portland for Southern California and a life out of the limelight.

CONCLUSION
Public Citizen

Mrs. E. D. Cannady ... is an out-standing character in the City of Portland and an ambassador of good will between the racial groups. Too much credit cannot be given her for the "trail blazing" and pioneer work she has done in this regard. Inter-racial good will in the city today is a living tribute to her indefatigable efforts and service. One need only inquire of the leading citizenry of the city for confirmation of these truths.

— Daniel G. Hill to the Harmon Award Commission,
August 30, 1929, Cannady Scrapbook

Portlanders were happy to shed the city's rough-and-tumble façade in 1905 and replace it with images of "prosperity and progress."[1] That year, more than 1.5 million visitors attended the Lewis and Clark Exposition and saw a city that was set to tame its landscape with irrigation projects, tourism, and logging.[2] Vice-president Charles Fairbanks, who had traveled across the country to "participate in the formal opening" of the exposition, "marveled at the prodigious possibilities for the commercial development of the Pacific Coast in the near future."[3]

Portland's white population nearly tripled in thirteen years, jumping from about ninety thousand in 1900 to 266,000 in 1913.[4] The number of Negroes increased as well, from 775 to 1,045. Edward Cannady settled in the city during this period, as did the Rutherford families, McCants Stewart, John Logan, and other individuals who were drawn to the Northwest for job opportunities. People put down roots, had children, opened businesses, and formed a community built on common goals, religion, and culture. Beatrice Morrow arrived just in time to witness the exciting changes happening in the city, including the right of women to vote, the grand opening of the Benson and Multnomah hotels, and Lincoln High School's move to its new building on Southwest Park Avenue.

But black Portlanders also discovered that color lines divided the city. In March 1919, members of the Portland Realty Board voted not to "sell property in white residence districts ... to colored people or orientals ... because of the depreciation in property values [that] follows an influx of colored or oriental population." It was strictly a business decision, they said, "and not because of any prejudice against members of these races."[5] Just three weeks earlier, Beatrice Cannady had appeared in Salem before the Committee on Health and Public Morals to argue for a bill "establishing equal rights in places of public accommodation, resort or amusement."[6] Bill No. 344 was sent "back to the house without recommendation," but then, as the *Oregon Daily Journal* reported: "After having narrowly missed sudden death by the unceremonious indefinite postponement route at the hands of members of the house ..., the negro equality bill was sufficiently resurrected ... to provide an hour and a half of excitement, mixed with a considerable amount of levity, before being finally killed by a vote of 31 to 24, with four members absent."[7] Representative Thompson said she voted against it because she was a "Southern Democrat and still harbor[ed] the prejudices of the south toward the colored race."[8]

Cannady faced an uphill battle to try to convert people like Thompson—and those who were prejudiced simply because they "had never been exposed to Negroes"—"to a saner consideration of interracial relations."[9] And continual legal setbacks made it that much more difficult to effect reform. Senate Bill No. 228, introduced during her campaign for state representative in 1932, would have guaranteed "to all persons full enjoyment of civil rights in public places."[10] But it, too, was defeated. It would take twenty more years of work by activists such as Otto Rutherford and his wife, Verdell Burdine Rutherford, to secure passage of such legislation. The couple joined longtime Portlanders Marie Smith and Edgar Williams—contemporaries of Cannady's—to watch Governor Paul L. Patterson sign the Oregon Public Accommodations Act into law in 1953.[11]

Cannady's critics might point to Oregon's long history of racism and argue that her advocacy was for naught. But Sam Gill, the white man who shared his recollections of Frederick Douglass at one of Cannady's

Cannady with Reuben Taylor, her third husband.

interracial teas, accurately assessed her career: "No doubt a feeling comes to you some times as to whether the result of your work is going to be worth the effort, but rest assured that you are doing an efficient work, though the evidence of effects may be long delayed in appearing."[12] Every lecture she delivered to high school and college students, every talk she gave to white congregations and missionary groups, every interracial tea she hosted, every editorial she wrote, every broadcast she did—all of these forms of outreach contributed to the dialog about race relations and equal rights that she fostered during her twenty-five-year career in Oregon.

Her thoughtful messages about the need for contact between the races and the importance of getting to know one another in order to value similarities and differences inspired at least a few white Portlanders to join her cause. Cannady shared a story about a "well-known social worker"—possibly her friend Millie Trumbull—who had "been compelled, after having had many associations with Negroes, to reject the prejudices she had normally acquired as a child and a young woman."[13] Cannady's goal was to develop allies, people who became aware of inequities and how they affected someone's life and then took action to try to create change.

But, after devoting twenty-five years of her life to the struggle for equal rights and liberties in Oregon, Cannady apparently was ready to turn over the fight to the next generation of activists: Kathryn Bogle, Otto and Verdell Rutherford, DeNorval Unthank, and others. She also may have wanted to be closer to family who had settled in Southern California; the dissolution of her marriage to Yancy Jerome Franklin in about 1937 may have factored into her decision to leave Oregon, too.[14] Cannady spent the next four decades in the Los Angeles area, away from the limelight. She eventually married her third husband, Reuben Taylor, and worked for a time with her son Ivan in his real estate business.

Beatrice Morrow Cannady-Taylor died August 19, 1974. She was eighty-five. In keeping with her commitment to Bahá'ísm, members of the Faith officiated at her funeral four days later; H. Claude Hudson, whom she had met at Wiley University decades earlier, served as an honorary pallbearer.[15] The simple memorial program features a striking photograph of the activist when she was in her eighties; markedly absent, however, are the biographical details that would have memorialized permanently her long career as a journalist, editor, civil rights leader, and public intellectual. But her story already had been told in the pages of the *Advocate*.

ACKNOWLEDGMENTS

Soon after I "discovered" Beatrice Cannady in 2002, I read a short article about her and Seattle activist Susie Revels Cayton by Quintard Taylor, a professor of history at the University of Washington. I contacted him to inquire whether he thought a book-length project would be viable. He told me in an e-mail message that he considered Cannady to be "an important and woefully understudied woman in Pacific Northwest history." Professor Taylor confirmed what I already suspected: Cannady was a remarkable woman who advocated continually for her community. I began researching her and her civil rights campaign in Oregon; I had no idea at the time that I would devote seven years of *my* life to learning about *hers*.

Then, in 2005, I had the good fortune to meet Mary Elizabeth Braun, acquisitions editor for Oregon State University Press, on a flight to Boise, Idaho. In between sessions at the 58th Annual Pacific Northwest History Conference, we shared a dinner and talked about Cannady. Mary, too, recognized how important Cannady's career was to the state, the region, and the nation, and encouraged me to keep the Press in mind when I completed the manuscript. I am happy that I did, because I could not have asked for a stronger supporter of my research.

Grants from a number of sources helped to make this book possible. I would like to thank the Oregon Historical Society for its Donald J. Sterling, Jr., Research Fellowship; the University of Oregon Center on Diversity and Community for a Graduate Research Award; the University of Oregon Graduate School for a Research Award; and the University of Oregon School of Journalism and Communication for several scholarships and travel grants. And I would be remiss if I did not thank Janice Dilg for "loaning" me her house while I was in Portland working at the society's research library.

I also appreciate the feedback I received from numerous individuals who read drafts of this book or journal articles. They include: Marianne Keddington-Lang, Stephen Ponder, Elizabeth Reis, H. Leslie Steeves, Quintard Taylor, and reviewers for Oregon State University Press, *American Journalism*, *Oregon Historical Quarterly*, and *Pacific Northwest Quarterly*.

Barbara Redwine, Beatrice Cannady's great-niece, found me through the "other" imagined community—the Internet. She has been most generous with her time and I am very grateful for the personal papers and photographs she shared with me.

Finally, many, many thanks go to James Mangun and Shawn Mangun, who now know as much about Beatrice as I do.

CREDITS

Photos on the cover, half-title, and pages 6, 10, 32, 63, 98, 111, 177, 183, and 193 are courtesy of Barbara J. Redwine.

The following photos have been reprinted with permission from the Oregon Historical Society: page 1 (orHi 63845); page 49 (OrHi 81811); page 191 (OrHi 51169).

The photo on page 170 has been reprinted courtesy of the *Oregonian.*

Previous versions of some chapters have appeared in *American Journalism*, *Oregon Historical Quarterly*, and *Pacific Northwest Quarterly.* Portions of Chapter 8 were published in *Voices from Within the Veil: African Americans and the Experience of Democracy*; they have been reprinted with permission from Cambridge Scholars Publishing. See the bibliography for further details.

NOTES

Introduction

1. Reuben Taylor was born December 17, 1900, and died June 23, 1972. He served in World War II. Barbara Redwine, phone call to the author, February 1, 2006; e-mails to the author, February 2, 2006, and November 30, 2009. Redwine is Cannady's great-niece, the granddaughter of Beatrice's brother Almus.

2. "Collecting Library of Negro Literature for Use of White and Colored Students of Race Relations," CS, 84, and, generally, 84-91.

3. Brief, and sometimes inaccurate, information about Cannady and/or TA can be found in the following sources (see the Bibliography for details): Anderson, *Black Pioneers of the Northwest*; Bosco-Milligan Foundation; City of Portland Bureau of Planning; Dodds and Alzner; Hill, Jr.; Fulton; Hogg; Long; MacColl; McLagan; Oregon Lung Association; Pride and Wilson; Smith, Jr.; Taylor, Jr., "Susie Revels Cayton, Beatrice Morrow Cannady, and the Campaign for Social Justice in the Pacific Northwest"; Walden.

4. Richardson, xv.

5. Kroeger, xvii.

6. Ibid., xvii.

7. Bosco-Milligan Foundation, 38.

8. Clifford L. Miller, "'I Dress to Vamp the Judge' So Says Mrs. E. D. Cannady, an Attorney of Portland, Oregon, Who Came Here As a Delegate To the Pan-African Congress," *TNYAN*, August 27, 1927, 3; reprinted in *TA* as "Mrs. Cannady Talks To *Amsterdam News*; Oregon Is the Best State in the Union, Says Mrs. E. D. Cannady, of Portland, Who Is in the East As a Delegate to the Pan-African Congress," September 10, 1927, 1.

9. According to the Oregon Regional Union List of Serials and WorldCat, the *Beaver State Herald* became the *Mt. Scott Herald*, which became *TA* on May 2, 1923. However, *TA* was founded under that name in September 1903 and when the *Mt. Scott Herald* ceased publishing, the Cannadys apparently took over its advertiser and subscriber lists. "The *Mount Scott Herald* Discontinues Publication," *Mt. Scott Herald*, April 27, 1923, 1; "*Advocate* Takes Over *Mt. Scott Herald* with This Issue," *TA*, May 2, 1923, 1; "The *Mt. Scott Herald*," *TA*, May 2, 1923, 4. Also, the last number filmed was dated December 2, 1933, so people have assumed that was the final issue. She may have continued the paper until at least 1936; she left Portland for Los Angeles by the end of 1938. So, even though records indicate *TA* is available from 1906 to 1933, extant runs are limited to May 1923 until December 1933

Cannady saved *TA* from 1913 until about 1935; the collection passed to her son, Ivan, upon her death in 1974. The following year, a librarian at the Oregon Historical Society began negotiating with Ivan to borrow the papers. For whatever reason, the transaction was not completed before the librarian retired in the fall of 1976. A letter written by the society's chief librarian late in 1977 noted that the University of Oregon had seven reels of film, covering the years from 1906 until December 1933, so Ivan's collection was no longer considered important. He died in December 1987; remaining copies of *TA* may have been thrown away then. Redwine, February 1, 2006; Louis Flannery to Martha Anderson, December 15, 1977, Mss 2854, OBHP.

10. Nadine Jelsing, e-mail message to author, January 10, 2007.

11. Moynihan et al., 3.

12. Although it is not clear exactly when Cannady left Portland, her death certificate lists thirty-eight years of residence in California, which corroborates her reported 1936 departure from Oregon. Mss 2854 OBHP. However, she was elected to the Spiritual

Assembly of the Bahá'ís of Portland on April 21, 1936. "Roll of Local Spiritual Assemblies, The United States and Canada, 1936-1937," NBA. She also appears on membership lists for the Portland Bahá'í Community for January 1937 and January 1938. NBA.

Chapter One

1. Smyrl. According to Redwine, the owner's name was Christopher Hamilton McGinnis. In 1851, he moved his family to Bastrop County, Texas, and began farming in Travis County. He also owned a cotton plantation. Littig stands today where the plantation was located. Redwine, e-mail messages to author, August 22, 2007; February 8, 2008. McGinnis appears in the *1880 Census* for Travis County, but he is not listed in any slaveowner records.

2. Smyrl. He is identified as A. B. Littig. It is possible he was Augustus Littig, who appears in the *1870 Census*, Harris County, Texas. Littig has been called "one of the oldest black communities in the state," yet the Austin History Center considers it an "underdocumented [area] of interest." Smyrl; Riles, 66. The Center has only one vertical file consisting of thirty-six pages of documents.

3. Redwine, August 22, 2007; February 8, 2008. Jackson Morrow appears in the 1910 Census. He was eighty-two and a widower. His birthplace, as well as his parents', was listed as unknown. Living with him were his daughter, Matilda, forty-four, her husband, David Bradley, forty-six, and his granddaughter, Willie, eighteen. *Thirteenth Census*, Travis County.

Jackson and Lucy had at least eight sons—Albert [or Price Albert], Charles, Edward, George, Jessie, Sam, Wesley, Willie—and three daughters, Josephine, Matilda, and Pauline. Redwine, February 8, 2008; "Death Removes Pioneer Texan; George Morrow Passes at 76," *TA*, December 20, 1930, 1.

Edward, who was born in 1860, became a merchant and served as Littig's postmaster for forty years. He married a woman named Mary Jane in 1884; she lived to be at least 102 and was affectionately known as "Aunt Mary" by friends and family. The couple did well in Littig, despite the vagaries of the region. By 1930, they valued their home at $8,000, or more than $102,000 today. *Thirteenth Census*, *Fifteenth Census*, Travis County; "Death Removes Pioneer"; "The Associate Editor Tells of Her Trip East," *TA*, February 18, 1928, 2; "We Celebrate Our Elders," AF L3170, AHC; The Inflation Calculator. They had at least two children: Sam, who became a mortician in Ft. Worth, Texas, and Lula Lightner, who lived in Dallas. Sam does not appear in online census records for Tarrant County for 1920. Lula Lightner is listed in the 1910 Census. She had been married for six years to C. S. Lightner, who worked as a laborer in a drugstore. He and his parents also were born in Texas. *Thirteenth Census*, Dallas County.

Sam, a farmer, was married to Jennie. The couple had five children, three of whom survived. According to the 1910 Census, Sam and Jennie were fifty-nine and had been married for thirty-seven years. They were sharing their home with daughters Ruth, eighteen, and Lizzie, thirty-three, a widow with two young children: Thelma, three, and Quentin, one. *Thirteenth Census*, Travis County. Sam died in 1918. Redwine, February 8, 2008. Jennie appears again in the 1930 Census; she was living alone. *Fifteenth Census*, Travis County.

Charley was a farmer, too. By 1880, the twenty-four-year-old was married to Anna [Annie?], twenty, and they had an infant named William. Tonya, Tena, Cassie, Mattie, Doughtey, and Jessie were born between 1881 and 1897. *1880 Census*, *Twelfth Census*, Travis County. Charley died in 1905. Redwine, February 8, 2008.

4. Kathryn Hall Bogle, "Family Album Northwest," *PO*, October 16, 1980, 7. The spelling of "Morrowtown" was corrected. Bogle wrote a five-part series about Cannady that ran in *PO* from October 9 through October 30, 1980.

5. A copy of the Map of Littig can be found in AF L3170, AHC. By 1890, Travis County, which included Littig, had a Negro population of 10,090; in 1900, Littig had 168 residents. By 1907, the Littig common school district had three one-teacher schools for 185 black students and a one-teacher school for thirty-three white students. But the community began to decline during the 1930s; by 1990 its population was just thirty-seven. Historical Census Browser; Smyrl.

6. *Thirteenth Census*, Travis County; "Death Removes Pioneer Texan."

7. "Death Removes Pioneer Texan." Mary Carter died in 1921 or 1922. Morrow married Mary Bradshaw, a schoolteacher from Columbus, Tennessee, in 1923. He died at his home on December 15, 1930. Morrow was survived by his second wife; by his brothers, Edward and Price Albert, a minister in St. Paul; three sisters, Matilda Bradley of Portland, Dr. Pauline Washington of Kansas City, Kansas, and Josephine Campbell of Littig; two sons, Dr. H. J. J. Morrow of Crowley, Louisiana, and Almus H. Morrow of Berkeley, California; five daughters, Mabel Beverley of Houston, Olive Neal of Los Angeles, Bula Oliver of Austin, Texas, Cora L. Jamison and Beatrice Cannady of Portland; and eleven grandchildren: Mary Jane, Lucy Ann, and Betty Jean Morrow of Berkeley; Orchid Oliver of Austin; James Edwin, Jr., and George Morrow Stamps of Chicago; Rosamond Jones, Mary Francis, and John Beverley of Houston; and George and Ivan Cannady of Portland.

8. *Thirteenth Census*, Travis County.

9. Ibid. Census records typically reflect information for individuals living in the residence when the enumerator visited. So, grown children, such as Beatrice's siblings, often were not included. Beatrice's age does not jibe with her year of birth. Winnifred, whom Beatrice called Olive, married Elvin Vernon Neal on August 1, 1923, in Chicago. She was a teacher; he was a graduate of Meharry School of Dentistry, which was founded under the auspices of the Freedman's Aid Society of the Methodist Episcopal Church. "Wedding Announced," *TA*, August 2, 1924, 4; "About Meharry." The enumerator wrote Buelah, but Beatrice consistently spelled her sister's name as Bula, which has been used here. See, for example, "Miss Bula Morrow-Oliver visits in Portland," *TA*, July 30, 1932, 1. Another sibling may not have been listed in the 1910 Census; Cannady wrote in 1930 that her "baby brother, Jack Morrow, [had] passed in Pittsburgh" and was going to be buried in Littig. "Local Briefs," *TA*, June 28, 1930, 3.

10. Ibid.

11. Millie R. Trumbull, "A Modern Joan of Arc," *TA*, Illustrated Feature Section, September 28, 1929, 2. Punctuation added. According to Cannady, the special insert was carried in some three hundred and fifty newspapers. Even if that number were inflated, thousands of readers across the country would have seen the interview. *TA*, March 23, 1929, 1. Robert Bagnall wrote Cannady: "I received some while ago an article regarding you and your life entitled 'A Modern Joan of Arc.' It is a splendid treatise of your activity and I enjoyed reading it very much." Robert W. Bagnall to Beatrice Cannady, September 11, 1926, NAACP PB. This letter must have been dated incorrectly since the feature came out on September 28, 1929, but no other clues were found to help with verification.

12. John, thirty-four, and Anna Morrow, thirty-two, appear in the 1910 Census. Her parents were born in Florida. The couple had been married nine years. *Thirteenth Census*, Calcasieu Parish. The couple also appears in the *Fourteenth Census*, Jefferson Davis Parish. They had a daughter named Gloria. *TA*, August 29, 1931, 3.

13. Lucy married "a distinguished minister and medical physician" from Liberia. The couple lived there for "many years" while "he conducted a hospital." She returned to the United States—Monrovia, California—for health reasons, but died there in September 1923. See "Dies in California," *TA*, September 29, 1923, 2. The college is now known as

Huston-Tillotson University. Lucy also apparently taught at a "colored school" in Littig for a time. AF L3170, AHC.

14. "Pretty School Ma'am Visits Portland," *TA*, August 6, 1932, 1. The long article also noted that Bula lived in Portland for two years—probably 1920 to 1922—before returning to Texas to finish her degree.

15. Program, Candidates for Degree of Bachelor of Laws, Class of 1922, CS, 59; "Goes To California," *TA*, January 2, 1932, 3. Almus, thirty-six, and his wife, Lillian, thirty-three, appear in the 1920 Census. She was born in Colorado; her father was born in Canada, her mother in Michigan. She was described as a maid in a theater. *Thirteenth Census*, MC.

16. Trumbull; Mather, 59. Through the years, Cannady listed different dates of birth, including 1891 and 1890, but Redwine said she was born in 1889. Redwine, February 1, 2006.

17. "History," Jane Addams Hull House Association; "History of Kodak Cameras."

18. "Biographical Notes on A. Philip Randolph, 1889-1979."

19. Hoffer.

20. Kroeger; "Jefferson Davis Is Dead," *TNYT*, December 6, 1889, 1. Nellie Bly was the pen name of Elizabeth Cochran.

21. "Our History: Aunt Jemima's Historical Timeline."

22. Hoig.

23. Trumbull.

24. "IN Harmony: Sheet Music from Indiana."

25. Trumbull. Punctuation added.

26. Timothy Thomas Fortune, considered to be the "most outstanding and versatile of Negro journalists," died in June 1928 after a brief illness. "Dean of Negro Editors Passes Suddenly," *TA*, June 16, 1928, 1.

27. For more about Wells-Barnett, who was called "Joan of the race" and compared to Joan of Arc, her newspaper, and her bid for a senate seat in Illinois, see her autobiography, or Schechter.

28. See, for example, "Lincoln and Douglas [*sic*]," *TA*, February 13, 1926, 4; "Douglass the Great Emancipator," *TA*, February 12, 1927, 1.

29. Brown, "Carter G. Woodson."

30. Du Bois, "The Talented Tenth," 33.

31. "Carter Woodson," *TA*, February 28, 1931, 2; Woodson, "Negro History Week," April 1926.

32. According to one source, Cannady attended New Orleans University from 1905 to 1906. She told Trumbull she went to New Orleans College. Mather, 59; Trumbull. It is possible that she attended Southern University at New Orleans, an institution for Negroes founded in 1880. "The History of Southern University." Wiley originally was known as a university, but changed its name to Wiley College in 1929. "History of Wiley College."

33. Wiley College Registrar Vanessa Valentine, e-mail message to author, June 12, 2006.

34. "Mission Statement." The award-winning debate team was depicted in the 2007 film, *The Great Debaters*, starring Denzel Washington and Forrest Whitaker. For more about the institution, see Thomas Jesse Jones, *Negro Education: A Study of the Private and Higher Schools for Colored People in the United States*, Bulletin 1916, no. 39, vol. II, 581-83, accessible at Google Books.

35. Trumbull. For reminiscences about Cannady's time at Wiley, see, for example, "Young Dentist Foe of Race Proscription," *TA*, July 28, 1928, 1.

36. "History of Wiley College." Wiley alumnus Emmett J. Scott, who was secretary to Tuskegee Institute President Booker T. Washington and special assistant to the secretary of war during World War I, encouraged Wiley President Matthew Dogan to apply for a

grant from the Carnegie Foundation for the library. When the library relocated to another building in 1968, the Carnegie Library was remodeled for administrative use. It is one of just twelve Carnegie buildings remaining in Texas. "Willis J. King Administration Building." For more about Dogan, see, for example, "History of Wiley College"; Prather and Lee.

37. The illustrated book, published in 1908 by Doubleday, Page & Company, is accessible at Google Books.

38. Ovington, *The Walls Came Tumbling Down*, 108. For more about the founding of *TC*, see 107-8.

39. See, for example, "The 'Wild Cat,'" *TA*, April 2, 1927, 1.

40. Trumbull.

41. M. W. Dogan to Mrs. E. D. Cannady, March 3, 1917, copy in AC.

42. Ibid.

43. M. W. Dogan to Beatrice Morrow-Cannady, September 15, 1917, copy in AC. A capitalization error was corrected.

44. M. W. Dogan to Beatrice Cannady, October 24, 1919, copy in AC; The Inflation Calculator.

45. M. W. Dogan to Beatrice Morrow-Cannady, December 24, 1912, copy in AC.

46. Ibid. Punctuation added, and a typographical error was corrected.

47. Ibid.; The Inflation Calculator.

48. Lansing, 67, 68. Also see Ritz, 5-7.

49. W. M. Ladd to First National Bank, December 4, 1912, copy in AC.

50. John Copeland to W. M. Ladd, December 10, 1912, copy in AC.

51. M. W. Dogan to Beatrice Morrow-Cannady, January 10, 1913, copy in AC. The amount of Ladd's donation was not mentioned.

52. Dogan to Cannady.

53. Trumbull.

54. She said she taught at Gilbert College in Baldwin, but may have meant Gilbert Academy and Agricultural College. Mather, 59; Johnson, "The education of black New Orleans."

55. Trumbull; Mather, 59. Nelda Brown, with the Logan County Genealogical Society, checked the Logan County High School yearbook for 1909, as well as city directories for 1909, 1910, and 1911. She found no listings for Beatrice Morrow. Nelda Brown, e-mail messages to author, August 24 and 26, 2007. In 1910, the capital shifted from Guthrie, which had held the honor since Oklahoma's statehood three years earlier, to its neighbor to the north, Oklahoma City. "History of Guthrie."

56. Trumbull.

57. Ibid.; Mather, 59; D. A. Clippinger, *The Head Voice and Other Problems: Practical Talks on Singing* (Boston: Oliver Ditson Company, 1917), vi. Cannady said she studied at Kimball Hall at the University of Chicago, where Clippinger taught, during the summers of 1908 and 1909. Clippinger wrote numerous articles and books about singing and voice culture. For brief biographical information, see *Putnam's Monthly: A Magazine of Literature, Art and Life* (October 1907-March 1908): 768; *International Who's Who in Music and Musical Gazetteer: A Contemporary Biographical Dictionary and a Record of the World's Musical Activity*, ed. César Saerchinger (New York: Current Literature Publishing Company, 1918), 122.

58. Harris Arts Center and Roland Hayes Museum.

59. Nomination Blank, William E. Harmon Awards for Distinguished Achievement Among Negroes 1929, HFI. Also see Trumbull.

60. Miller; "Portland Hotel's Patrons Miss Old Familiar Faces; Negro Dining Room Staff Replaced By White Waitresses; Hat Man for More Than 30 Years Replaced By

Another," *MO*, April 20, 1931, 5. For more about the Portland Hotel, see Nicoll, 298-335.

61. Mather, 59. The entry also notes that Cannady was in the "money broker business" in Portland between 1904 and 1912. His birthplace and date of birth correspond with information in the *Fourteenth Census*, MC. But, his World War I Draft Registration Card—signed September 12, 1918—lists his age as forty and date of birth as November 27, 1879. The numbers do not jibe. The card is accessible at Ancestry.com.

62. Censuses for 1870, 1880, and 1890 were checked.

63. "Editor Impressed with Portland," *TA*, June 16, 1928, 2.

64. Ibid. See, for example, *The Appeal*, August 9, 1902, 2. Issues published in 1901 and 1902 were checked randomly to see whether Cannady was listed in the masthead or given a byline. He does not appear in online census records for Minnesota for 1890 or 1900.

65. Broussard, "McCants Stewart," 160. He worked for the *Twin-City American* and its successor, the *Afro-American Advance*.

66. "Portland Hotel's Patrons."

67. Ibid. Cannady's obituary also notes that he "gained a wide reputation for his memory when he served in the hat-check room of the Portland hotel and could handle as many as 300 hats, returning each to its rightful owner, without resorting to the use of hat checks." "Edward Cannady," *TO*, July 30, 1941, sec. 1, 8.

68. Miller.

69. The couple were married on June 27, 1912, and divorced eighteen years later, on June 11, 1930. See "Divorce Decree Published," *TA*, June 28, 1930, 1; "Mrs. Cannady Divorced," *TA*, June 21, 1930, 1.

70. Miller.

71. In 1910, Portland had a population of 207,214, including 1,045 Negro residents. *Thirteenth Census of the United States: 1910*, Table 19, 95.

72. "1912 Women's Suffrage Proclamation Transcription." Black men were granted the right to vote when the Fifteenth Amendment was ratified in 1870. However, voting rights remained problematic in many states until the 1960s.

73. "History of the Benson Hotel"; "Multnomah Hotel."

74. "About Reed: Mission and History." When Lincoln High School relocated again in 1952, the classical revival-style building became Portland State University's first classroom building. "Profile: Visit Lincoln Hall." Also see "About Lincoln."

75. "Mrs. Cannady Lectures," *ODJ*, June 4, 1930, 2; reprinted under the same headline in *TA*, June 7, 1930, 1.

76. "Woman Journalist Urges Radio Listeners to Rise Above Petty Race Hates," *The Philadelphia Tribune*, March 12, 1927, 1; reprinted as "Whites Entreated to Rise above Racial & Religious Prejudices," *TA*, March 12, 1927, 1. This statement, however, originated with Carter G. Woodson, who started Negro History Week. See Woodson, April 1926, 240.

77. Kathryn Bogle, who attended high school in Portland in the 1920s, recalled that "about the only reference" to Negroes in the "regular textbooks" was slavery and emancipation. Bogle, "An American Negro Speaks of Color."

78. It is unclear exactly when Cannady took over the editorial duties. In 1913, Edward Cannady sent a letter to the new mayor asking him to consider offering employment to some of the city's "loyal colored citizens." He is listed on the stationery as editor, manager, and notary public, and J. Will Jones is listed as associate editor and manager. E. D. Cannady to H. R. Albee, June 7, 1913, A2000-003, SPA.

79. "Started with Ten Men—Several Now Dead, Others Moved To Distant Cities—One of Original Still Remains—Hardships of First Efforts Recalled," *TA*, September 1, 1923,

1. John C. Logan appears in the 1900 Census. He and his parents were born in South Carolina. His wife, Clara, was born in California; her father was born in Virginia. They had been married eight years and had three children, all born in Oregon. Also living with them was Clara's mother, Anna Jackson, who was described as a housekeeper. She was born in California. *Twelfth Census*, MC. By 1910, the couple had another daughter. Logan was described as a custodian for the custom house; Clara worked as a hairdresser. *Thirteenth Census*, MC. For a photo of John Logan, see *TA*, September 1, 1923, 5.

Ballard does not appear in online census records for Oregon for any available years. A man named Charles Ballard is listed in *Polk's City Directory 1904*; his occupation was editor. But, *TA* consistently referred to him as A. Ballard.

Howard Sproull was continually misidentified as Howard Sproules (and some secondary sources perpetuate this error). He appears in the 1910 Census. He was forty-three then, single, and working as a janitor in an office building. He and his parents were born in Georgia. *Thirteenth Census*, MC. By 1920, he was living in Seattle, where he worked as a deckhand on a steamboat. His age was still listed as forty-three. *Fourteenth Census*, King County, Washington.

None of the following men—William Bolds, who reportedly moved to Los Angeles; the Reverend Moore, who "died many years ago"; or Edward Ward, who moved to Chicago—appear in online census records for Oregon, California, or Illinois for any available years.

The final individual may have been Robert B. Perry. If so, he first appears in the *Census of 1880*. According to *TA*, Perry was deceased by 1923.

80. "Started With Ten Men."

81. "Our Twentieth Anniversary," *TA*, September 1, 1923, 4.

82. "Announcing the 26th Anniversary of *The Advocate* This Week," *TA*, September 14, 1929, 1. When *TA* turned twenty-two, he wrote: "The present standing of *The Advocate*, we attribute not alone to the editor, but the lion's share of the credit rightly belongs to the associate editor and manager." "*The Advocate* Observes 22nd Birthday," *TA*, August 29, 1925, 1.

83. "Birthday of *Advocate*; Twenty-seven Years Old 8th; Cannady Remains Longest with the Publication," *TA*, November 8, 1930, 1. She noted that she had been "intimately connected with the paper" for seventeen years.

84. Streitmatter, *Raising Her Voice*, 3.

85. Smith, "Some Female Writers of the Negro Race," 4-6.

86. "The Associate Editor Tells of Her Trip East," *TA*, October 1, 1927, 3.

87. Ibid. *TCD* claimed a circulation of about two hundred and eighty thousand in 1920. Washburn, 112. Another source notes that circulation peaked at two hundred and thirty thousand in 1915. After World War I, the number of subscribers dropped to one hundred and eighty thousand. Wolseley, 54.

88. "The Associate Editor Tells."

89. Bragg. Also see, for example, Streitmatter, "Delilah Beasley," 61-75.

90. Beasley wrote a short piece about Cannady's visit. Delilah L. Beasley, "Activities Among Negroes," *OT*, May 16, 1926, A13.

91. "Let All Rejoice With Miss Beasley," *OT*, December 18, 1920, 1.

92. Delilah L. Beasley to [Beatrice] Cannady, May 18, 1926, copy in AC.

93. "Twenty-eight Years Old," *TA*, October 3, 1931, 2.

94. Du Bois also made a tour of "the great Northwest" in 1913 and may have interacted with the Cannadys. "The Great Northwest," *TC*, September 1913, 237-40.

95. "Editor to Visit City," *TA*, June 16, 1923, 1; "Editor Bass Visits Portland," *TA*, June 23, 1923, 1.

96. "Bethel A.M.E. Church," *TA*, September 1, 1923, 4; "Editor Bass." Also see "Bethel" for a detailed description of the "beautiful and finely furnished church."

97. "Seventy and Still Young," *TA*, January 17, 1931, 2; "History of *The Call*."

98. "Seventy and Still Young." Cannady also revealed her feelings about the club movement: "As we talked with [Franklin] and enjoyed the glory of her infectious smile, we wondered how it could be done 'running a newspaper,' but the secret leaked out when she announced that she was 'not a club woman—have never belonged to one.'"

99. It is not clear which papers he published. Cannady referred to *Ryan's Weekly* and the *Tacoma Weekly*. Another source indicates that he published the *Weekly*, a short-lived paper in Tacoma, before starting *The Forum*, which the Ryans published from 1903 to 1918. Lowe; Fuller, 29-30, 51-53. However, none of these papers is listed in Danky. *TA* informed readers in 1927 that Ella Ryan, "one of the brightest and most progressive business women ever known in the northwest," had died in Portland while visiting her daughter, Ethel Reese, and her family. *TA*, May 21, 1927, 2. Reese does not appear in online census records for MC for 1920.

100. Lowe. Ella operated a beauty salon; John "became a prominent local businessman."

101. Lowe.

102. "Newspaper Man Visits," *TA*, August 11, 1923, 1; *TA*, January 19, 1924, 1. He was returning for the start of the new legislative session; Ryan had just been elected for a second two-year term in the House of Representatives. In all, he was elected "three times by three different political parties—Farm Labor, Republican, and Democratic—from majority white districts." Lowe; *TA*, March 29, 1924, 4; "Editor Ryan Elected," *TA*, November 8, 1930, 2; "Historical House of Representatives Class Photos."

103. *TA*, September 20, 1924, 4; "Newspaper Man." In 1926, *TA* reported: "John H. Ryan publisher of the *Tacoma Weekly* has filed suit against three of the Tacoma daily papers for $50,000 because these papers referred to him as the Negro Editor." "Called a Negro; Sues for $50,000," *TA*, July 31, 1926, 1.

104. "A Brilliant Young Man," *TA*, May 26, 1928, 2. Little has been written about Newman and his long career, but for one source see Leipold.

105. "A Brilliant Young Man." Punctuation added.

106. Newman founded the paper in 1934 to meet "the news and information needs of African Americans" in the Minneapolis/St. Paul area. "About Us," *Minnesota Spokesman-Recorder*.

107. "*Timely Digest*," *TA*, March 14, 1931, 2; "A New Magazine," *TA*, February 7, 1931, 1. Also see "'Timely Digest' Editor," *TA*, July 4, 1931, 2.

108. "*Timely Digest*"; *TA*, February 21, 1931, 3. Robeson had performed in Portland. See the following in *TA*: "Paul Robeson," February 7, 1931, 2; "Why Robeson Sings Spirituals," February 21, 1931, 2.

109. *TA*, July 4, 1931, 2.

110. Cecil E. Newman, "Personalisms," *TD*, August 1931, 9 (the article was on page 24, but it was printed as page 9); reprinted in *TA*, September 12, 1931, 2.

111. One fall, for example, Isadore and Margaret Maney and their two young children made the trip to Portland from Northern California. Cannady reported the family spent a "goodly part of the night ... in the library of Negro literature." *TA*, October 14, 1933, 3.

112. Toward the end of her career, Cannady gave her collection to family members and schools. Redwine, February 1, 2006. The Cannadys' address was changed from 520 East 26th Street North when street information was streamlined.

113. The complete title is: *William Lloyd Garrison on Non-Resistance, Together with a Personal Sketch by His Daughter, Fanny Garrison Villard, and a Tribute to Leo Tolstoi.*

114. Nicoll.

115. She reported the book was "gratefully and thankfully received." "Negro History," *TA*, April 2, 1927, 1.

116. Locke, 100-101. He added: "Now that a general enlightenment has actually been brought about, the situation is ripe for interpretation."

117. "*The Negro in Our History*," *TA*, February 2, 1924, 1. For a review of the fourth edition, see "Negro History." Cannady was invited to attend the annual meeting of the Association for the Study of Negro Life and History in St. Louis at the end of October 1928. "Association for Study of Negro Life and History to Hold Meeting," *TA*, October 6, 1928, 2. For a time, she published Woodson's columns. See, for example, the following in *TA*: "Negro History Study Seeks Assistance," February 6, 1932, 4; "Blessings of the Depression," February 27, 1932, 4; "Lack of Cooperation Among Negroes," March 5, 1932, 4; "Prophets and Profits of Segregation," July 2, 1932, 4.

118. "Carter Woodson," *TA*, October 19, 1929, 2. A spelling error was corrected. Cannady's Esperanto club became a subscriber in 1931. Rosalie Bird, "In the Realm of Society," *TA*, March 14 1931, 2.

119. The Inflation Calculator; *TA*, February 2, 1924, 4. Cannady promoted the journal again in 1931; see "Carter Woodson," *TA*, February 28, 1931, 2.

120. "To Broadcast During Negro History Week," *TA*, January 26, 1929, 1.

121. *TA*, April 20, 1929, 1. The full title is: *From Negro To Caucasian: Or, How the Ethiopian Is Changing His Skin; a Concise Presentation of the Manner in Which Many Negroes in America ... Have Abandoned Their ... Affiliation with Negroes.*

122. "The Associate Editor Tells of Her Trip East," *TA*, September 24, 1927, 2. She did not include book titles, but wrote that one was ninety-three years old.

123. *TA*, January 5, 1929, 2. Book titles were not included. Webb, who worked as a packer for a shipping company, appears in the 1920 Census. He and his parents were born in Illinois. *Fourteenth Census*, Cook County. He visited Portland in 1924 and stayed with the Cannadys. "Chicagoan Visits Portland," *TA*, July 5, 1924, 1; "Mr. Webb Returns To Chicago," *TA*, July 12, 1924, 1. When Cannady was in Chicago in 1927, he treated her to breakfast at the Vincennes Hotel, gave her a tour of "the famous Dennison's paper house on East Randolph Street," and took her to dinner. "The Associate Editor Tells," October 1, 1927.

124. *TA*, September 1, 1923, 7. Webb's photograph accompanied the caption.

125. See Clifford Mitchell, "Book Review," *TA*, September 12, 1931, 4; Clifford Mitchell, "Book Review," *TA*, October 3, 1931, 4. The complete titles were: *From Captivity to Fame or, The Life of George Washington Carver*, and *School Acres, an Adventure in Rural Education*. For additional reviews, see, for example, the following in *TA*: February 6, 1932, 4; March 5, 1932, 4; November 19, 1932, 3; January 28, 1933, 3.

126. Clifford Mitchell, "Book Review," *TA*, October 31, 1931, 4.

127. Anne M. Mulheron, quoted in "Public Library Gets New Book," *TA*, December 20, 1924, 1.

128. Scott, 1. Capitalization altered. The book is accessible at Google Books. For a review, see, for example, *The Journal of Negro History* 4, no. 4 (October 1919): 466-67.

129. "Books in the Public Library on the Colored Race," *TA*, October 17, 1925, 1. The play—and Gilpin's role—proved to be controversial, however. For more about this see, for example, "Charles Gilpin."

130. Constance Ewing, quoted in "Books." Ewing, head of the order department, told Cannady she had made "a note of the other books for future orders." She appears in the *Fourteenth Census*, MC.

131. "Books."

132. Lewis B. [Stewart] to Beatrice [Cannady], July 26, 1927, copy in AC; "Mrs. Cannady Honored," *TA*, May 12, 1927, 1. The room was called the "Beatrice Morrow Reading Room," and his motto reportedly was "A Beatrice Morrow in Every Community I Pastor." Stewart is listed in the 1930 Butte, Montana, *City Directory*.

133. "Negro History," *TA*, January 30, 1932, 2; *TA*, February 6, 1932, 2.

134. "A New Book," *TA*, October 8, 1927, 2. The book, by Kathryn M. Johnson, who had earlier coauthored a volume with Addie W. Hunton about their work with the American Expeditionary Forces in Europe, contained "a splendid likeness ... of the intrepid abolitionist" and a brief description "of the heroism and accomplishments of a man whose feet wore the fetters of American slavery."

135. "Portraits of Douglass for Negro Library," *TA*, April 23, 1932, 3. The artist, Sarah F. Eddy, was described as well known, but a Google search produced no results. For more about Park, a longtime reader in Palo Alto, see, for example, Winter. Park's papers are housed at the Department of Special Collections and University Archives at Stanford University.

136. "'Way Down South Where the Blues Began,'" *TA*, July 30, 1932, 2.

137. Maud Cuney Hare to Mrs. Cannady, December 29, 1920, copy in AC. She wrote *Negro Musicians and Their Music*, which "remains a respected reference work on African American music." "Maud Cuney Hare Papers, 1843-1936." Hare might have sent *The Message of the Trees*, a collection of poetry published in 1918; or, knowing that Cannady was from Texas, she may have forwarded the biography she wrote about her father, Norris Wright Cuney, an esteemed politician who died in Galveston the year Cannady was born. *The Message of the Trees: An Anthology of Leaves and Branches* is accessible at Google Books; *Norris Wright Cuney: A Tribune of the Black People*. For more about him, see Hales.

138. Fall told Cannady she had sent her a copy of her new book; given the date of the letter, it likely was *Your Mother and Mine*. She also noted: "We, my good publisher, and I are going to use some of the good things you said of me before, on the jacket of the next edition." Nellie M. Fall to Beatrice Cannady, December 7, 1922, copy in AC.

139. *TA*, January 19, 1924, 4.

140. "Secretary of Inter-Racial Commission of Federal Council of Churches Praises Local Woman's Inter-racial Work," *TA*, December 3, 1927, 3.

141. *TA*, June 4, 1932, 3. Also see "Hughes Writes Scottsboro Play," *TA*, September 12, 1931, 1; "Poet Asks Justice for Alabama Boys," *TA*, November 7, 1931, 1.

142. For more about their case, which prompted "one of the most significant legal fights of the twentieth century," see, for example, the *American Experience* documentary, *Scottsboro: An American Tragedy*, and the companion Web site. Also see the following in *TA*: "Charged with Raping White Prostitutes on Freight Train," April 18, 1931, 1; "Legal Lynching," April 18, 1931, 2; "Cases of Nine to Be Appeal'd," April 25, 1931, 1; "The Scottsboro Disgrace," May 2, 1931, 2; "Which Shall it Be?" May 16, 1931, 2; "Colored Ministers Lead" and "The Devil Has His Good Points; Why Not I.L.D.?" May 23, 1931, 2; "Justice in Alabama," June 6, 1931, 2; "A Puzzle," June 13, 1931, 2; "Richard Moore Coming" and "Mass Meeting in Scottsboro Death Case," July 4, 1931, 1; "And Still They Disagree," July 4, 1931, 2; "Plight of Boys Arouses Group," July 11, 1931, 1; "Conflicting Activities," July 11, 1931, 2; "Many Killed in Races' Mix-up," July 18, 1931, 1; "Parliament in Fight for Boys," August 29, 1931, 1; "Darrow Paid Retainer Fee," October 3, 1931, 1; "Clarence Darrow," October 3, 1931, 2; "Darrow and Hays Refuse I.L.D. Proposal," January 9, 1932, 1; "Supreme Court Upholds Death for 7 Boys," March 26, 1932, 1; "N.A.A.C.P. Offer to Aid Defense" and "To Appeal To U.S. Supreme Tribunal," April 2, 1932, 1; "Alabama Lynch Verdict," April 2, 1932, 2;

"U.S. Supreme Court Under Heavy Guard" and "U.S. Court to Grant Hearing," June 4, 1932, 1; "Innocent Boys Await Fate," October 22, 1932, 1; "The Scottsboro Decision," November 19, 1932, 2; "Scottsboro," March 11, 1933, 2; "Shall They Die?" and "Change of Venue Granted in Scottsboro Case" and "Bates Woman Missing," March 18, 1933, 1; "The Scottsboro Boys," March 18, 1933, 2; "Scottsboro," April 1, 1933, 2; "Victory Life Is Saved!" April 8, 1933, 1; "Scottsboro!" April 29, 1933, 2.

143. *Constitution of the State of Oregon*. Voters were asked: "Do you vote for Slavery in Oregon? Yes or No." The answer was a resounding "no"—7,725 to 2,645. Then they were asked to decide: "Do you vote for free Negroes in Oregon? Yes or No." Again, the answer was no by a vote of 8,640 to 1,081. *Constitution*; Richard, "Unwelcome Settlers," 32. For more about slavery in Oregon, the so-called Black Laws, and other issues involving Negroes, see, for example: Berwanger; Carey; Coray; Hill, "The Negro as a Political and Social Issue in the Oregon Country"; Johannsen; Katz; Lockley, "Documentary"; Middleton; Minto; Oliver; Richard, "Unwelcome Settlers"; Schneider, "The 'Black Laws' of Oregon"; Williams.

144. "All Hail! The State of Oregon," *OWT*, November 14, 1857, 2.

145. *Constitution*.

146. Richard, "Unwelcome Settlers," 31.

147. *Constitution*.

148. "A Disgraceful Provision," *TNA*, September 29, 1900, 4.

149. See the following in *TA*: "Legislature Passes 'Black Law Bill,'" February 21, 1925, 4; "Ask Repeal of the State 'Black Laws,'" August 28, 1926, 1; "Free Negroes and Mulattoes," August 28, 1926, 2; "Isn't It Awful?" November 6, 1926, 4; "Oregon to Wipe Out Obselete [*sic*] Laws," February 12, 1927, 1; "The Special Election," May 21, 1927, 2; "Colored Peoples [*sic*] Suffrage," June 4, 1927, 2; "Repeal Black Laws," June 25, 1927, 2. Also see: "Bar for 3 Measures," *MO*, November 4, 1916, 4; "Negro Suffrage," *OV*, November 4, 1916, 9; *MO*, November 6, 1916, 10; "Negro Suffrage," *OV*, December 16, 1916, 11; "Repeal of Free Negro Ban," *OV*, July 31, 1926, 30-31; "Repeal the Negro Clause," *AD-H*, September 29, 1926, 4; "Measures Discussion No. 3," *CG-T*, October 6, 1926, 2; "Ballot Measures—Article No. 2," *TEG*, October 8, 1926, 4; "An Invalid Provision," *TBB*, October 20, 1926, 4; "Measures to Be Voted On," *GO*, October 26, 1926, 1; "White, Black and Gray," *TBB*, October 27, 1926, 4; "What the Measures Mean," *OV*, April 16, 1927, 7.

150. "Oregon Election History."

151. Savage, 199.

152. Taylor, "Slaves and Free Men," 160. Also see Spicer.

153. According to the *1860 Census*, sixty-one native and "foreign-born" mulattoes lived in eight of Oregon's nineteen counties. The population ranged from two in Multnomah County to twenty-eight in Jackson County. In addition, 128 aggregate free colored persons lived in fourteen counties. Historical Census Browser. For more information about Western migration, see, for example, Coray.

154. Taylor, 169. For information about community life in Oregon, Washington, and Montana, see, for example, Taylor, "The Emergence of Black Communities in the Pacific Northwest." For a study of women's experiences, see, for example, de Graaf.

155. For more about black migration, see, for example, Toll, "Black Families and Migration to a Multiracial Society." For census information, see *Population of the United States in 1860*, 403; *Twelfth Census of the United States: 1900*, Table 23, 637.

156. Stewart wrote Adolphus D. Griffin, editor of *TNA*, asking for information about the Black laws. Griffin responded via the newspaper that the law was still on the books, though he was optimistic it would be repealed in the next biennial election because "the people of the state have just begun to realize how outrageous such a law is." "The Oregon

Black Law," *TNA*, October 27, 1900, 4. Griffin may have regretted his encouraging reply, especially after Stewart helped Cannady launch the competing *Advocate* in 1903. For more about Griffin and *TNA*, see Mangun "Editor A.D. Griffin."

157. Broussard, "McCants Stewart," 161. Stewart has been recognized as the first black man to practice law in Oregon after he passed the Bar in 1903. But according to *TNA*, a man named Charles A. Lucas had "passed an exceedingly creditable examination for admission to the bar" two years earlier. See the following in *TNA*: "City News," October 12, 1901, 5; two notices under "City News," October 19, 1901, 5. He advertised his services in *TNA*; see October 26, 1901, 5.

158. "May Revoke Ticket; Theaters Have That Right, Says Judge Frazer," *MO*, May 19, 1905, 14; Broussard, "McCants Stewart," 169; The Inflation Calculator. Taylor does not appear in online census records for Oregon for any available years. Manager Martin Cohn appears in the *Thirteenth Census*, MC. His occupation was listed as president of People's Amusement.

159. "Some of the Joys of Being Colored in Portland," *TA*, December 8, 1928, 3. The theater at Grand and East Morrison was one of the "most ornate" in Portland, with carved dragons on either side of the lobby staircase and replicas of elephant heads decorating the interior walls. For photos, see "Portland Theaters." For information about theater discrimination in other states, see, for example, *TA*, May 28, 1927, 2. Arthur Cox, a longtime resident, noted years later that discrimination at theaters was "just one of the indignities that blacks suffered in Oregon." Mss 2854, OBHP.

160. Rutherford, SR 270; "Window Signs and Race Relations," CS, 64.

161. Rutherford.

162. Committee, Colored Taxpayers League to Mayor Lane, February 2, 1909, A2000-003, SPA. For more about Merrill, see Lansing, 226, 249. Merrill appears in the *Twelfth*, *Thirteenth*, and *Fourteenth Censuses*, MC.

163. Committee to Mayor Lane. Other members were Lewis H. Dawley, S. St. Clair, and F. D. [Fred?] Thomas. Dawley, a white man, appears in the *Thirteenth Census*, MC.

164. Committee to Mayor Lane.

165. Police report, Sgt. E. W. Cole to Captain Bailey, February 4, 1909, A2000-003, SPA. Henry does not appear in online census records for MC for 1900 or 1910.

166. Police report, C. Gritzmacher to Mayor Lane, February 5, 1909, A2000-003, SPA. Gritzmacher immigrated to the U.S. in 1859, the year Oregon achieved statehood. He appears in the *1880 Census*, *Fourteenth Census*, MC.

167. Gritzmacher to Lane.

168. *TA*, July 8, 1933, 2.

169. *TA*, July 15, 1933, 2. Pugh, identified as J. C. Pugh in *TA*, does not appear in online census records for Oregon for any available years, but he is listed in *Polk's Portland City Directory 1931*. The café may have been owned by Carl Heller, whose occupation was listed as a restaurant cook in the *Fourteenth Census*, MC.

170. "Constitution of Portland Branch of National Association for the Advancement of Colored People," January 27, 1914, NAACP PB. According to one report, 165 people were founding members. "Portland, Oregon: 1914-1954," NAACP PB.

171. "Portland, Oregon." Also see Executive Committee, Portland Branch to Hon. H. R. Albee, December 31, 1914, A2000-003, SPA.

172. Executive Committee to Albee. Punctuation added. The restaurant was at the corner of Broadway and Glisan, the same description given for Heller's Café years later.

173. Lansing, 297-98. Albee appears in the *Thirteenth Census*, MC.

174. "The N.A.A.C.P.," *TA*, June 2, 1923, 4. Also see, for example, "N.A.A.C.P. Victories," *TA*, April 30, 1927, 2.

175. "It's a Shame!" *TA*, May 2, 1925, 4. For other editorials promoting duty to the organization, see, for example, the following in *TA*: "The N.A.A.C.P. and Its Relation To the Colored Race," November 13, 1926, 2; "The N.A.A.C.P.," August 25, 1928, 2; "N.A.A.C.P. Drive," October 25, 1930, 2. For editorials and articles about the Branch and its membership drives, see, for example, the following in *TA*: "Branch to Hold Big Membership Drive," August 25, 1928, 1; "N.A.A.C.P. Workers Are Lining Up," September 1, 1928, 4; "Success of Drive Over-Reaching Anticipations," September 29, 1928, 2. Also see "500 New Members Object of Drive By Colored Crusaders," *ODJ*, September 18, 1928, 15; "Campaign Nears End," *MO*, September 21, 1928, 18.

176. "Associate Editor of *The Advocate* Speaks in Longview, Wash.," *TA*, September 12, 1925, 1; Mrs. E. D. Cannady to Robert W. Bagnall, September 10, 1925, NAACP PB. By one account, she "persuaded" some of Longview's "leading white citizens ... to open the public schools to colored children in accordance with the laws of the State of Washington." "N.A.A.C.P. Organizer Gets Schooling for Negro Children in Northwest," News Release, September 25, 1925, NAACP PB; [Robert W. Bagnall] to Mrs. E. D. Cannady, September 22, 1925, NAACP PB. Also see Mrs. E. D. Cannady to Mr. Bagnall, September 15, 1925, NAACP PB. She subsequently told him that she was unsure who "accomplished the feat": "I only know that when I went there there still was no definite policy about the children going to the public schools other than they were not going to be admitted in them." But "now that it is all settled, every one wants the honor." Mrs. Cannady to Robert W. Bagnall, September 28, 1925, NAACP PB.

177. Cannady to Bagnall, September 10, 1925. She included a list of the members with this letter. Also see Beatrice Cannady to Robert Bagnall, October 31, 1925, NAACP PB.

178. Robert Bagnall to Mrs. Cannady, November 6, 1925, NAACP PB.

179. "Officers, Portland, Ore., Branch 1923-1928," NAACP PB.

180. "Associate Editor Appointed on Speakers' Bureau," *TA*, August 1, 1925, 4.

181. "Mrs. Cannaday's [*sic*] Reply," July 27, 1925, in the report "Officers, Portland, Ore."

182. [Robert W. Bagnall] to J. A. Ewing, September 17, 1925, NAACP PB.

183. See, for example, Mrs. E. D. Cannady to Robert Bagnall, September 19, 1925, NAACP PB. At various times she also called herself the Northwest Director of Branches. See, for example, "Mrs. Addie Hunton Charms Splendid Audience," *TA*, September 18, 1926, 1.

184. Lee C. Anderson, untitled report, [November 8, 1926], NAACP PB. Anderson appears in the 1920 Census. He was born in Ohio; his parents were born in Kentucky. He worked as a railroad porter. His wife, Nora, and her father were born in Oklahoma; her mother was born in Missouri. Their children were born in Oregon. *Fourteenth Census*, MC.

185. A. Louise Williams and Helen Logan to the Editor of *The Advocate*, November 10, 1926, NAACP PB. Also see Mrs. E. D. Cannady to Robert W. Bagnall, November 24, 1926, NAACP PB. Logan's parents were Clara and John, the *Advocate* co-founder. She married Huron Melker of St. Paul, Minnesota, in September 1930. *TA*, September 20, 1930, 2. Louise Williams does not appear in online census records for Oregon for any available years.

186. "Colored People Loyal," *MO*, July 19 [?], 1918; copy in CS, 61. The original has not been located. She was described as "head" of NACWC's "department of public posters and prints." Her sister-in-law, Lillian Morrow, chaired the Ways and Means Committee, Oregon Federation of Negro Women's Clubs, in 1920. Katherine Gray to Beatrice H. Cannady, February 19, 1920, copy in AC.

187. [Beatrice Cannady] to Mrs. Garner Grayson, February 19, 1920, copy in AC. Talbert spoke to Lincoln High School students about "The Negro's Right to World Democracy"

as well as to Reed College students and "several other organizations of both white and colored." Cannady was "shocked beyond expression" when she learned of Talbert's sudden death in 1923. "Mary B. Talbert Dies at Her Home," *TA*, October 20, 1923, 1.

188. Asberry contributed "splendid articles" about music to *TA*. "Prominent Club Woman Returns from An Extended Trip," *TA*, September 27, 1924, 1. Typesetting errors in the headline were corrected. Also see "Prominent Race Woman Is Honored," *TA*, November 24, 1923, 1. Her column ran sometime prior to May 2, 1923, the first available issue for *TA*. Asberry may also have been a subscriber; she sent the Cannadys a letter in September 1923 congratulating them on the paper's twentieth anniversary. "Writer Congratulates *The Advocate*," *TA*, September 8, 1923, 4. She taught piano for decades, shared information about Negro history with children in her neighborhood, protested against *The Birth of a Nation*, and more. For information about Asberry, see, for example, Broussard, "Nettie Craig Asberry." The Nettie J. Asberry Papers are housed at the Special Collections Division, University of Washington.

In 1926, *TA* reported on the ninth annual meeting of the Oregon Federation of Colored Women's Clubs; Cannady was not listed as a presenter. "Federation of Colored Women Hold Annual Session," *TA*, October 30, 1926, 1. For more articles about the Oregon or Northwest clubs, see, for example, the following in *TA*: "Federation Holds One Day [*sic*] Annual Session," June 27, 1931, 1; "Northwest Federation Meets," July 18, 1931, 1; "Prominent Club Woman Coming," August 1, 1931, 1; "Noted Woman Coming," August 1, 1931, 2; "National President of Colored Women Delivers Pracital [*sic*] Talk," August 15, 1931, 1; "Retiring President Soynds [*sic*] Unity Note," June 10, 1933, 1.

189. "Constitution of Portland Branch."

190. One source claims the *Portland Times*, with James Merriman as editor and William McLamore as assistant editor, published from 1913 until 1923. Bosco-Milligan Foundation, 36-38. McLagan notes that the *Times* lasted five years, from 1918 to 1923. McLagan, 112. An *Advocate* article appears to corroborate these dates: "The *Portland Times* which was born in August five years ago … is dead." "The *Portland Times* Sleeps," *TA*, August 25, 1923, 4. According to the 1910 Census, Merriman and his mother were born in Alabama; his father was born in South Carolina. He was described as mulatto and a lodger. By 1920, he was described as black; his father's birthplace was listed as Alabama. He had married Barbara. She and her parents were born in Kentucky. *Thirteenth Census*, *Fourteenth Census*, MC. McLamore appears in the 1910 Census. He and his parents were born in Indiana. He was described as mulatto, a lodger, and a hotel waiter. *Thirteenth Census*, MC.

191. M. W. Dogan to Beatrice Cannady, October 24, 1919, copy in AC.

192. "Slander Suit Dropped; *Portland Times* Agrees to Apologize To Mrs. Cannady," *MO*, January 13, 1920, 11; "Libel Suit Against *Times* Is Dropped; Apology Is Made," *TPT*, January 13, 1920, 8. Only one issue of the *Times* as been located; also missing is *TA* from this period.

193. Lee C. Anderson, "The Portland Branch of the N.A.A.C.P.," November 8, 1926, NAACP PB. The vote was thirty-three to thirty. Also see Cannady to Bagnall, November 24, 1926.

194. Executive Committee to James Weldon Johnson, November 18, 1926, NAACP PB.

195. [James Weldon Johnson] to the Executive Committee, December 16, 1926, NAACP PB.

196. Ibid.

197. Executive Committee to James Weldon Johnson, January 6, 1927, NAACP PB.

198. [James Weldon Johnson] to J. A. Ewing, January 19, 1927, NAACP PB.

199. "Meeting of the Board of the Portland Branch," July 10, 1928, NAACP PB.

200. Western branches were established as follows: Tacoma, Washington, 1912; Northern California, June 1913; Seattle, Washington, November 1913; Portland, September 1914; and Los Angeles, December 1914. "Portland, Oregon, 1914-1954." Cannady looked forward to Ovington's visit, and in fact wrote that Portland was "honored with the presence of Miss Mary White Ovington." "Miss Ovington," *TA*, July 14, 1928, 2.

201. Ovington, *The Walls Came Tumbling Down*, 3, 4, 7.

202. That winter, Ovington helped organize a dinner for Washington, whose book, *Up From Slavery*, was being serialized in *The Outlook*. She and other members of the Social Reform Club listened to him talk about the situation in the South as well as the plight of their "dark neighbor living around the corner." Ovington, 11-12.

203. In keeping with the gendered language of the day, she was identified as chairman on letterhead.

204. Mary White Ovington, typed notes describing Portland Branch visit in July 1928, NAACP PB. Authorship was verified by reports in *TA* and NAACP documents. She incorrectly noted June 8th as the beginning of her Portland visit; she meant to type July 8th. Also see "Founder of N.A.A.C.P. Visits Local Branch," *TA*, July 14, 1928, 1.

205. Mrs. E. D. Cannady to Robert W. Bagnall, November 9, 1926, NAACP PB; Ovington, notes. Handsaker appears in the *Fourteenth Census*, MC. Her husband, John, was a "prominent minister and chairman of the Near East Relief Work for the state" whose activities were covered often in *TA*. See, for example: "Prominent Minister to Speak," October 13, 1923, 1; "Near East Worker Speaks at Zion," October 20, 1923, 1; "Near East Relief Thanks Helpers," February 19, 1927, 4; "Orphan sponsored by *The Advocate*," February 19, 1927, 1. The Handsakers graduated from the University of Oregon in about 1903. *TA*, June 16, 1928, 4. Cannady threw a surprise birthday party for Alice in 1926. "Inter-racial Dinner Honors Local Woman," *TA*, November 20, 1926, 1. Other activities were included in the newspaper, too. For example, Handsaker spoke about "A Great Woman" during a Mother's Day service at Bethel AME Church. "Bethel Church Notes," *TA*, July 26, 1930, 2.

206. Ovington. The woman was described as "Mrs [*sic*] Harris, a Jewess."

207. Ibid. A typographical error was corrected.

208. Ibid. Also see L. A. Ashford to Miss Ovington, July 16, 1928, NAACP PB.

209. Cannady to Bagnall, November 24, 1926. Jesse Ewing appears in the 1920 Census. He was described as mulatto and a homeowner. He and his parents were born in Missouri. His wife, Jennie, also was described as mulatto. She and her parents were born in Texas. Her widowed sister, Emma Roberts, lived with them. She was described as mulatto and a caterer for private families. *Fourteenth Census*, MC.

210. Gaines, 130.

211. Ovington, notes; Anderson, "The Portland Branch of the N.A.A.C.P."

212. Ovington. Cannady often commented in *TA* about the Branch's progress, or lack thereof. In 1923, for example, Cannady wrote that the Branch experienced a "rebirth" after an extended period of inactivity. Missouri Congressman Leonidas Dyer, who was in Portland to give a talk, presided and new officers were elected. "Local Branch Is Born for Fifth Time," *TA*, May 19, 1923, 4.

213. Ovington. A typographical error was corrected.

214. Ibid.

215. [Robert W. Bagnall] to Mrs. E. D. Cannady, August 1, 1930, NAACP PB. She reported that he lost his position with the NAACP in 1933 due to its "sharply reduced

income owing to the industrial world crisis." "Forced to Reduce Staff," *TA*, January 7, 1933, 1.

216. Lee C. Anderson to Mary White Ovington, October 20, 1928, NAACP PB.

217. Ibid. Punctuation, typographical, and grammar errors were corrected.

218. Gaines, 129.

219. Beatrice Cannady, "Negro Womanhood As a Power in the Development of the Race and the Nation," copy in AC.

220. "Race Line Is Attacked; Negro Woman Sues for Right to Swim with Whites," *MO*, September 1, 1916, 6.

221. "A Man Who Stands for Justice and Equality," *TA*, May 3, 1924, 4. Cannady wrote that Moulton had worked "sans pay" for Portland's "colored voters" for some twelve years. He appears in the *Thirteenth Census*, MC.

222. "Race Line Is Upheld; Swimming Dates for Colored Persons Held Legal," *MO*, November 1, 1916, 11. The judge, identified only by his last name, likely was Oregon native Henry McGinn, who appears in the *Fourteenth Census*, MC. The buildings housing Shattuck became part of Portland State University in 1969. "Shattuck Hall."

223. Hare to Cannady. Emphasis in the original. She gave a concert in Portland in December 1920; Hare thanked Cannady for the review she wrote for *TA*.

224. Hermann G. Paulo [?] to Mrs. E. D. Cannady, January 2, 1928, copy in AC.

225. Stewart to Cannady. The woman, Nell Holsclaw [?], was from Spokane.

226. See, for example, Daniel G. Hill to the Harmon Award Commission, August 30, 1929, CS, 27.

227. Eleanor T. Colwell to the Harmon Award Committee, August 28, 1929, CS, 26.

228. Executive Committee to Johnson, November 18, 1926.

229. *The California Eagle*, for instance, reported on editor Joseph Bass' "notable address" to a religious group. "Notable Address Delivered at the Ministerial Alliance By Editor Bass of *The California Eagle*," *TCE*, January 30, 1915, 1.

230. "Meeting of the Board."

231. Gaines, 2.

232. Wormser.

233. "Striving for Her Race," *ODJ*, August 29, 1929, 12.

234. Saidie Orr Dunbar to the Harmon Award Committee, August 5, 1929, CS, 10. Among other things, Dunbar chaired the Department of Public Welfare of the General Federation of Women's Clubs and the Oregon State Advisory Committee on Child Care, Health, and Welfare. She appears in the *Thirteenth Census*, MC.

235. Robert W. Bagnall to E. C. Farnham, August 19, 1929, CS, 19.

236. Gaines, 3.

237. Ibid., 2.

238. "Sound the Trumpets: For the First Time, More Than Four Million African Americans Now Hold a Four-Year College Degree," *The Journal of Blacks in Higher Education* (Winter 2007/2008): 16.

239. M. W. Dogan to Beatrice Cannady, October 1919, copy in AC. Typographical errors were corrected.

240. Hare to Cannady.

241. Northwestern College of Law merged with Lewis & Clark College in southwestern Portland in 1965. "About Lewis & Clark College." Also see "First Colored Woman Lawyer in Northwest," *ODJ*, June 5, 1922, 6; "Social Progress," *TC*, November 1921, 37.

242. This text appears on a postcard of the ballroom. See "Multnomah Hotel."

243. Program, Candidates for Degree of Bachelor of Laws, Class of 1922, CS, 59.

244. *By the Waters of Minnetonka* was composed by Thurlow Lieurance, former dean of the Wichita State University School of Music in Kansas. Thurlow Lieurance Memorial Music Library. She wrote that the second song was *To You*. Searches have revealed a few possibilities: *Over the Hills To You* (1921); *Every Road Leads Me Back To You* (1920); *I've Taken A Liking To You* (1907).

245. "Defeat John Hunt Hendrickson," *TA*, October 30, 1926, 1. Hendrickson was a candidate for judge of the district court, department no. 3, Multnomah County. Cannady asked readers, "Colored voters, how would you like to be tried before such a man as he? Do you think he is capable of looking beyond the color of a man's skin?" She urged them to "keep him off the bench by voting" for his opponent. She sent him a "marked copy" of the article to ensure that he saw her views on his candidacy. Hendrickson replied that he was "not at all concerned with the voting end of it, because it is quite probable that all Republican county candidates will come thru with a substantial majority, and further because if I am not elected I can continue to make a satisfactory living out of the practice of the law." J. Hunt Hendrickson to Mrs. E. D. Cannady, October 30, 1926, copy of the first page in AC. He defeated his opponent, Charles Zarzan, by a vote of 48,137 to 15,155. Dave Wendell, reference archivist, Multnomah County Archives, e-mail message to author, November 19, 2009.

246. Trumbull.

247. In 1925, George W. Carry successfully handled the appeal in *Tipton v. State*, a case involving a black man who had been convicted of assault with a deadly weapon. *Tipton v. State*, 1925 OK CR 190, 30 Okl. Cr. 56, 235, p. 259. Another source lists a George W. Carry as principal of Faver High School in Guthrie, Oklahoma; it is unclear whether these are the same men. See Jones. Carry does not appear in online census records for Logan County, Oklahoma, for 1920. The syllabus of the case can be found online at FindLaw for Legal Professionals.

248. George W. Carry to Mrs. B. M. Canady [*sic*], April 22, 1921, copy in AC. Spelling errors were corrected. Carry told her he was forwarding her diploma to her, but she graduated in May 1922 so the date may be incorrect. It is also unclear why he had her diploma; it may have been related to her teaching there, rather than her law degree.

249. Mrs. E. D. Cannady to Robert W. Bagnall, April 13, 1926, NAACP PB. For additional discussion of her court cases, see, for example, the following in *TA*: "Officer Beats Prisoner," September 7, 1929, 1; July 19, 1930, 3; July 30, 1932, 1. On the Harmon award nomination form, she is listed as having practiced law from 1922 to 1929. Nomination Blank. For a personal account of Cannady's disposition of a case, see Otto Rutherford, SR 270. Cannady served as executrix for a number of estates. See, for example, "Notice To Creditors," *TA*, June 23, 1923, 4; *TA*, June 7, 1924, 4.

250. "Why Important News Left Out," *TA*, December 10, 1927, 4; *TA*, December 10, 1927, 4. Trimble does not appear in online census records for Oregon for any available years.

251. December 10, 1927.

252. "Trimble Freed," *TA*, December 17, 1927, 1. A note of appreciation was published on page 2.

253. "First Colored Woman Lawyer." Also see "Social Progress."

254. Lawrence Dinneen to Beatrice Cannady, June 5, 1922, copy in AC. Dinneen overstated her accomplishment; McCants Stewart had been admitted to the Oregon State Bar in 1903. Dinneen appears in the *Fourteenth Census*, MC.

255. She took the examination in 1922, 1923, 1927, 1929, and 1930. Meeting of the Board of Governors of the Oregon State Bar, December 21, 1935. Also see Dodds and Alzner, 54-56.

256. Meeting of the Board of Governors. She was told that if she persisted, the matter would "be presented to the District Attorney for institution of criminal proceedings."

257. About Cannady's status, see, for example, Renee Lee, "She was state's ambassador in resolving racial problems," *TR-G*, February 27, 1994, C1; "First female black lawyer," *SJ*, January 20, 1994, D1; Susan Hobart, "Eight picked as winners of 'notable woman' honors," *TO*, April 19, 1982, C2. For information about Deiz, see Collins, "A Life of Firsts."

258. Bonnie Bogle, "Cannady Family Troubles Reach Divorce Court," *TE*, June 5, 1930, 3. Also see "Yancy Franklin Charged with Assault" on the same page. Bogle, a "pupil" of Pearl Mitchell's, offered piano instruction for beginners. See, for example, the advertisement in *TA*, November 8, 1924, 4. Bogle was Kathryn Bogle's mother-in-law.

259. "Divorce Decree Published," *TA*, June 28, 1930, 1; "A View of Bayocean." Child support was $37.50 per child, but Edward was required only to pay $37.50 in cash. The balance was "credited each month" based on "the rental value of the home, to-wit, $37.50." He also was supposed to pay $44.63 toward the mortgage. Beatrice reportedly held property in her own name, but it was not listed in the decree. It is unclear whether Edward considered repurchasing *TA* when Beatrice decided to leave Oregon.

260. Redwine, February 1, 2006.

261. The couple obtained their marriage license in Cowlitz County, Washington, and were married in Multnomah County—probably Portland. They married under the names Hulon B. Cannady and Jerome Franklin, apparently to maintain their privacy. Redwine, February 2, 2006.

262. *TA*, October 17, 1931, 3. Punctuation altered to combine sentences.

263. Ibid.

264. Redwine.

265. *TA*, February 13, 1932, 3. According to the 1920 Census, Alfred Franklin, Jr., and his parents were born in Tennessee. Cora Franklin and her parents were born in Missouri. *Fourteenth Census*, MC. For more about Alfred, see "He's 72," *TA*, March 14, 1931, 2.

266. The children were Alfreda, Nellie, Yancy, Catherine, Stanfield, and Cora. Alfreda was born in Indiana, but all the other children, who ranged in age from five to thirteen, were born in Washington. Also living with the family was Cora Franklin's widowed mother, Rebecca Yancy. *Fourteenth Census*. The couple also appear in the *Thirteenth Census*, Clark County, Washington. Alfred's brothers, Henry and Isaac, who lived in Kansas City, Missouri, visited Portland in 1930. "Missourian Visits *Advocate* Office," *TA*, September 20, 1930, 1; "Local Briefs," *TA*, June 28, 1930, 3. Cora graduated from Commerce High School in May 1933. Rosalie Holmes, "Social Doings," *TA*, June 10, 1933, 3.

267. D. G. Hill, Jr., "The Art of Printing," *TA*, November 9, 1929, 1. A typographical error slipped into this sentence (!); it was corrected.

268. Hill.

269. See, for example, *TA*, June 21, 1930, 2.

270. *TA*, November 1, 1930, 3.

271. Redwine.

272. "Edward Cannady." He died July 26, 1941. The obituary lists his date of birth as 1867, making him seventy-three years old. As noted earlier, however, other sources list 1877. No cause of death was listed.

273. "Fifth Cycle Prize Won; George Cannady Holder of Many Fete Awards," *MO*, June 16, 1923, 9; reprinted, with additional information, as "Wins First Prize in Floral

Parade; Master George Edward Cannady Captures Blue Ribbon for Fifth Time in Annual Rose Festival Parade," *TA*, June 23, 1923, 1. For articles about some of his parties, see, for example, "Birthday Dinner Enjoyed," *TA*, May 2, 1923, 4; *TA*, May 11, 1929, 1.

274. *ODJ*, June 15, 1923, 9; reprinted in *TA*, June 23, 1923, 1; "Receives Thanks from Management and Invitation To Luncheon," *TA*, June 23, 1923, 1.

275. "Wins First Prize"; The Inflation Calculator.

276. "Spirit Lake (Washington)."

277. "Visit To Spirit Lake Camp," *TA*, July 28, 1928, 4. For more about integrating the camp, see "Mrs. Cannady Uses Daily Press to Reach the People with Her Great Truths," CS, 178-79.

278. "Visit To Spirit Lake"; *TA*, August 13, 1927, 3; "Colored Boy Elected Governor," *TA*, July 6, 1929, 1.

279. "George Cannady Tells More of Camp Life," *TA*, August 16, 1930, 1.

280. "George Cannady," 3.

281. "Portland Youth Is Honored in National Prize Essay Event," *ODJ*, July 14, 1930, 13; "Biographical Note." Dunbar was married to the poet Paul Laurence Dunbar. She was a teacher, writer, publisher, and activist. For more about her, see, for example, Hull.

282. "Ethel L. Payne Biographical Data Sheet."

283. "Ethel Payne, 79, Dies; Was a Correspondent," *TNYT*, June 1, 1991, 34.

284. For information about Harrison and the *Chronicle*, see Johnson, "Black Immigrants in the United States."

285. *TA*, June 13, 1931, 3.

286. See, for example, the following in *TA*: May 4, 1929, 1; "Local Briefs," May 24, 1930, 4; Geneva Ivey, October 18, 1930, 2. Ivey was the daughter of Mr. and Mrs. Harry Ivey. They do not appear in online census records for MC for 1910, but may have been related to Clarence Ivey. In August 1930, Geneva's nine-year-old brother, Curtis Eugene Ivey, drowned in the Willamette River. "Body Recovered After Five Days in Water," *TA*, September 6, 1930, 1; "The Passing of Little Curtis Ivey," *TA*, September 6, 1930, 2.

287. "15 Grant Gridmen Awarded Letters," *TPN*, December 24, 1930, 4; reprinted under the same headline in *TA*, January 3, 1931, 1.

288. "15 Grant Gridmen."

289. "Mrs. Cannady Uses Daily Press," CS, 178.

290. *TA*, February 2, 1929, 2. George spoke at Central Presbyterian Church in the Laurelhurst neighborhood and the Russelville church. Cannady did not provide any other details about the latter venue.

291. "All Classes Sit Together at Dinner," *TA*, November 22, 1930, 1. The guest of honor was Keith Ransom-Kehler, "the brilliant traveler-lecturer-teacher" who was on a speaking tour of the West Coast "in the interest of the Bahá'í movement."

292. *TA*, October 17, 1931, 2.

293. *TA*, April 8, 1933, 1. Another news item reported that he was asked to "deliver a 30-minute address on the progress of the Negro race before the Young People's meeting at the Rose City Park Community Methodist church" and would "deliver an address before the Northeast YMCA [about] some phase of Negro life and history." *TA*, February 15, 1930, 1. For more engagements, see, for example, the following in *TA*: March 1, 1930, 1; March 5, 1932, 3.

294. "Blue Key Names Geo. Cannady," *TA*, October 28, 1933, 2; "Scholarship Goes To Portland Boy for Study in East," *TSO*, August 18, 1935, sec. 1, 13; *TA*, April 29, 1933, 4; "Prominent PGM Members." The honor fraternity is now known as Blue Key Honor Society. "What Is Blue Key Honor Society"; "A Brief History of Blue Key Honor Society."

295. *TA*, September 10, 1932, 2; *TA*, June 17, 1933, 4. Also see Rosalie Bird-Holmes, "In the Realm of Society," *TA*, October 3, 1931, 2.

296. "Cannady and Grannis Show Much Football Knowledge; 'Smiling' George Excellent Student," *WC*, October 23, 1931, 4; reprinted in *TA*, October 31, 1931, 3. During his sophomore year, George served as sports editor of the paper. *TA*, May 28, 1932, 3; *TA*, September 10, 1932.

297. *TA*, November 19, 1932, 4.

298. "Scholarship Goes To Portland Boy."

299. Redwine has described him as "a Los Angeles District attorney," "an assistant district attorney for Los Angeles," and the "second Negro Deputy United States District Attorney." According to a photo caption that may have appeared in the *Los Angeles Sentinel* in 1948, "George E. Cannady this week became the second Negro Deputy United States District Attorney. The first, Ivan J. Johnson, was appointed to the post 15 years ago by the late Republican Senator Samuel Shortridge. Cannady is well known in local civic circles. … His appointment was endorsed by Republican Senator Samuel Shortridge and Congresswoman Helen Gahagan Douglas. Shown congratulating Cannady is United States District Attorney James F. Carter, as *Sentinel* Publisher Leon H. Washington Jr. … looks on." Redwine, e-mail messages to author, January 8, 2004, June 29, 2004, February 2, 2006, November 30, 2009. He is not mentioned in a history of the L.A. County District Attorney's Office. See Parrish. Douglas challenged "prevailing racial attitudes" and was the "first white Representative with African Americans on her staff." She may have endorsed Cannady while still in office, but she lost a reelection bid in 1951 to her Republican opponent, Richard M. Nixon. "Women in Congress: Helen Gahagan Douglas, Representative, 1945-1951, Democrat from California," http://womenincongress.house.gov/member-profiles/profile.html?intID=61.

300. Redwine, e-mail message to author, July 13, 2004.

301. Memorial program for George Edward Cannady, CS, n.p.

302. Memorial program for Ivan Caldwell Cannady, copy in AC. For information about Browning and the Harmony Kings, see, for example, Brooks.

303. "Some June Graduates," *TA*, June 16, 1928, 1. A few of Ivan's birthday parties were described in *TA*. See "Has Birthday Dinner," October 13, 1923, 4.

304. Rosalie Bird-Holmes, "In the Realm of Society," *TA*, June 19, 1932, 3.

305. Ibid.

306. *TA*, June 6, 1925, 1; *TA*, September 12, 1925, 1.

307. "Heifetz Plays at Auditorium," *TA*, February 2, 1924, 4. Ivan was taking violin lessons at that time.

308. *TA*, February 25, 1928, 1.

309. *TA*, June 27, 1931, 2.

310. *TA*, June 21, 1930, 4; *TA*, July 4, 1931, 3.

311. *TA*, September 24, 1932, 1.

312. Ivan Cannady, "Rev. Lee Roy Kinard," *TA*, November 19, 1932, 4. Also see Ivan Cannady, "Why Education for the Negro Youth of Today?" *TA*, March 18, 1933, 2.

313. Redwine, November 30, 2009; Memorial program. It is unclear whether he belonged to the National Urban League, the Los Angeles Urban League, or both organizations.

314. Hobart; Bob Neely and Clair Sagiv to Mr. Cannady, April 28, 1982, copy in AC.

315. Hobart; "Beatrice M. Cannady Blazes Legal Trail in Oregon," *Los Angeles Sentinel*, April 14, 1983, C4 [the dinner was in 1982, so this date is likely incorrect].

316. Memorial program.

317. "Nominated for Award in Race Relations," *TA*, September 7, 1929, 1.

318. "The Harlem Renaissance and the Flowering of Creativity." Also see "Fund Will Reward Negro Achievement," *TNYT*, December 21, 1925, 8.

319. E. C. Farnham to George E. Haynes, August 29, 1929, HFI. Also see "Name Mrs. Cannady For Harmon Award," *ODJ*, August 28, 1929, 9. Farnham does not appear in online census records for Oregon for any available years.

320. For more about Moton, see, for example, "Clarion Call Sounded By Tuskegee Head," *TA*, July 7, 1928, 1.

321. Levi T. Pennington to the Harmon Award Committee, August 8, 1929, CS, 6.

322. Franklin T. Griffith to E. C. Farnham, July 31, 1929, CS, 14.

323. F. M. Haight to Harmon Award Committee, August 20, 1929, CS, 15. Punctuation altered.

324. George L. Baker to the Harmon Award Committee, August 8, 1929, HFI.

325. W. R. Lovell to the Harmon Foundation Awards, August 27, 1929, CS, 16. For all of the letters of endorsement, see CS, 6-17, 20-27, and HFI.

326. "Nominated for Award"; "Dr. Moton Receives $1,000 Harmon Award," *TNYT*, January 6, 1930, 20; The Inflation Calculator.

327. "To Loose [*sic*] Their Jobs," *TA*, January 11, 1930, 1.

Chapter Two

1. A typographical error was corrected.

2. Phil and Elise Reynolds appear in the 1920 Census. Phil worked as a porter. He was born in Florida; his parents were born in Georgia. Elise and her father were born in Missouri; her mother was born in Kentucky. They had a son, Jack. *Fourteenth Census*, MC. They also had a daughter; *TA*, August 28, 1926, 1.

3. *TA*, February 19, 1927, 4. No other details were provided about the restaurant and it was not found in *Polk's Portland City Directory*.

4. *TA*, April 16, 1927, 4. According to the 1920 Census, James and his parents were born in Virginia. At that time, he was working as a porter with the Pullman Co. Martha, a music student, was born in Pennsylvania. Her father was born in Massachusetts; her mother was born in North Carolina. *Fourteenth Census*, MC. For more about the couple, see *TA*, September 25, 1926, 1; *TA*, July 18, 1931, 1.

5. "The Church and Race Relations," *TA*, November 27, 1926, 2; *NYA*, December 18, 1926, 6. The editorial observed, in part: "The church cannot escape responsibility for a large share in the prevailing unfortunate situation in regard to general race relations. Instead of seizing upon the points of unity, as she should have done, she has often helped all the other discrimination among the races."

6. "New Yorker Lauds *The Advocate*," *TA*, January 15, 1927, 4. Also see "Reads *Advocate* with a Deal of Pride," *TA*, February 25, 1928, 4. The 1920 Census lists one George Durham; it is possible he was the *Advocate* subscriber. *Fourteenth Census*, New York County.

7. I draw on Alexis de Tocqueville's idea of an imagined community of readers, and expand on Benedict Anderson's concept of nation as "an imagined political community"—imagined because people understand intuitively, and perhaps existentially, that even though they may never have reason to encounter their "fellow-members," they are similarly living and working and thus "connected" to one another. And nations can be "imagined as a *community*," notes Anderson, because "regardless of the actual inequality and exploitation that may prevail in each, the nation is always conceived as a deep, horizontal comradeship." While this utopian ideal may be true, it is important to remember that this "comradeship" often operates on parallel planes: one white, one "other." In the U.S., Negroes were forced to create their own extended community-within-the-nation since they were excluded from society as a whole. For

many marginalized individuals, Cannady among them, the concept of "nation"—and, by extension, citizenship—assumed even greater importance as the struggle for membership in the community spilled into the twentieth century. Further, Anderson argues that the advent of newspapers was important because they "provided the technical means for 're-presenting' the *kind* of imagined community that is the nation." Because newspapers typically are timely, their immediate "obsolescence ... creates [an] extraordinary mass ceremony: the almost precisely simultaneous consumption ('imagining') of the newspaper-as-fiction." Although the ceremony "is performed in silent privacy," an imagined community is instantly created through the ritual of consuming product and subject matter. Each reader "is well aware that the ceremony he [*sic*] performs is being replicated by thousands ... of others of whose existence he is confident, yet of whose identity he has not the slightest notion." Anderson suggests that when readers do have occasion to see friends and strangers reading the same newspaper, it is comforting because they are "reassured that the imagined world is visibly rooted in everyday life."

However, a different picture emerges when his description of newspapers—and the corresponding readership community that is created—is considered in terms of the black press. Because these newspapers were published weekly, rather than daily, news tended to be issue- rather than event-oriented. Obsolescence was less important because lynching statistics, NAACP activities, reports of Jim Crow laws, and other items often were printed in lieu of local news. That is not to say that local issues were unimportant to Negroes; those could be read in the white press. But relevant items could be found only in the black press, making the imagined community even more meaningful to readers. In addition, the ritual of reading their own newspaper did more than simply reassure them they were not alone. The press confirmed their existence in a society that shunned them and gave them hope by "re-presenting" a far different version of an "imagined community that is the nation"—one in which all citizens are treated equally. See Anderson, *Imagined Communities*, 6-7, 25, 33, 35-36, and de Tocqueville, 119-21.

8. Oregon had a total population of 783,389 in 1920. By 1930, that figure would rise by nearly two hundred thousand, but fewer than one hundred Negroes had moved to the state in the decade between censuses. *Fourteenth Census of the United States: 1920*, Table 13, 47; *Fifteenth Census of the United States: 1930*, Table 1, 609.

9. *Fourteenth Census*, Table 13, 47. According to the 1920 Census, just 1,556 Negroes lived in Portland.

10. Inez Mayberry, Mss 2854, OBHP.

11. Otto Rutherford, Mss 2854, OBHP.

12. Lee C. Anderson, "To the Officers and Members of The National Association for the Advancement of Colored People," June 21, 1925, NAACP PB.

13. "A. Ballard Writes," *TA*, February 21, 1925, 1. He and his wife were acknowledged often for being longtime readers and supporters of the paper. See the following in *TA*: February 5, 1927, 2; January 26, 1929, 2; February 1, 1930, 1; February 7, 1931, 1; August 20, 1932, 1; February 25, 1933, 3. The individual may have been Allen Ballard. *Fourteenth Census*, Norfolk County.

14. See, for example, *TA*, April 11, 1925, 1.

15. "Prominent Southerners Are Charmed with Northwest," *TA*, September 6, 1930, 1; "Southern Educator, Wife Visit West," *TA*, August 16, 1930, 1.

16. Prather and Lee; Kleiner. Today, an elementary school on Solo Street in north Houston bears his name.

17. The couple appear in the *Thirteenth* and *Fourteenth Censuses*, District of Columbia. One scholar notes that Waldron parlayed "his base at the thriving" Bethel Baptist Institutional Church in Jacksonville, Florida, into "a leadership role in antisegregation efforts." Ortiz,

120. For a photo of, and information about, the church, see McCarthy, 49-50. Waldron founded the Afro-American Benefit Association in 1901 and served as president from 1905 until 1908. It was renamed the Afro-American Life Insurance Company in 1925. The institution also created the Afro-American Thrift and Saving System to help people accumulate money. The company finally closed its doors in 1990. *1901-1941, Fortieth Anniversary, Afro-American Life Insurance Co., Jacksonville, Florida* (Jacksonville, Fla.: Afro-American Life Insurance, Co., 1941 [?]), 1, 3, 4, 7; accessible at http://fulltext.fcla.edu/cgi/t/text/pageviewer-idx?sid=7803efdac4d9586fbadcde1b24d6ef54&idno=NF00000033&c=fhp&cc=fhp&view=image&seq=1. For an editorial about the importance of life insurance companies, see "Insurance Companies," *TA*, June 21, 1924, 4. In 1935, the company purchased shorefront property about forty-five miles north of Jacksonville so Negroes would have a place for recreation as well as homeownership. More land was purchased later, bringing the total to 216 acres. In 1941, the community of American Beach, which had a street named after Waldron, was described "as the largest, most promising and profitable ocean-bordered summer resort of homes, cottages, electrically lighted streets, telephone service and adequate water supply in the southland." *1901-1941, Fortieth Anniversary*, 13; McCarthy, 182-84; "History of American Beach."

18. For more about his involvement, see "Niagara Movement."

19. The Call was published February 12, 1909, the centenary of Abraham Lincoln's birth. Ovington, *The Walls Came Tumbling Down*, 103-104; Ovington, "How NAACP Began." Waldron was credited, too, with helping William Monroe Trotter, publisher of *The Guardian*, launch the Negro-American Political League. For more about the NAPL, see, for example, Schneider, *Boston Confronts Jim Crow*, 115-21.

20. "Noted Churchman and Social Worker Visits Here," *TA*, September 18, 1926, 1.

21. "Local and Foreign News Briefs," *TA*, September 18, 1926, 1. *MO* was checked from September 14th through 16th; no articles were found.

22. "Noted Churchman." A grammatical error was corrected.

23. Ibid. For more about the Japanese and Chinese in Oregon, see, for example, Azuma; Johnson, "Anti-Japanese Legislation in Oregon."

24. *TA*, November 20, 1926, 1.

25. Cohen was born a free man of color in New Orleans in 1850. He may have attended St. Louis Catholic School until he was about nine, when both parents died and he was forced to drop out. Cohen reportedly spent the next several years working in the "cigar-making trade" and at a saloon; he also attended Straight College, which merged with New Orleans University in 1930 to form Dillard University. Ingham and Feldman, 145-46; "About Dillard: Dillard Heritage." Following the Civil War, he became the "protégé" of P. B. S. Pinchback, a freeborn man who—among other things—was a delegate to the convention that established Louisiana's Constitution of 1868. Ingham and Feldman, 145-46.

26. *TA*, October 26, 1929, 1. Cohen appears in census records for the first time in 1910; he is listed as registrar for the U.S. Land Office in New Orleans, a position to which he was appointed by President William McKinley and subsequently reappointed by President Theodore Roosevelt. *Thirteenth Census*, Orleans Parish; Ingham and Feldman, 145, 146.

27. Ingham and Feldman, 146.

28. "Negro Gets $5,000 Office," *TNYT*, November 5, 1922, 3; The Inflation Calculator. This appointment by President Warren G. Harding was fraught with controversy. See, for example, the following in *TNYT*: "Senate Sends Back Butler Nomination," December 5, 1922, 5; "Harding Names Negro for New Orleans Post," November 23, 1922, 1; "2,000 Nominations Made By Coolidge," December 11, 1923, 6. Cohen sought Cannady's help with his confirmation. He told her that Oregon Senator Charles McNary had voted

against him and noted, "I dont [*sic*] know whether either of these gentlemen [McNary or Senator Robert N. Stanfield] are solicitous about the colored vote for their reelection but if they are I am sure a movement by the colored voters of Oregon in my behalf will have the desired effect." Cohen also contacted James Merriman, William Allen, Eugene Minor, and Cannady's brother, Almus, and suggested that she "talk the matter over with them" if she felt it "advisable" to do so. Walter L. Cohen to Mrs. E. D. Canady [*sic*], June 18, 1923, copy in AC. Despite Cohen's efforts, his nomination was rejected once more before the Senate finally voted to confirm him by one vote. See, for example, the following in *TNYT*: "Senate Again Rejects Nomination of Negro," February 19, 1924, 2; "Cohen Case Reopened," February 28, 1924, 33; "Cohen Confirmed for Southern Post," March 18, 1924, 12; "Suit to Oust Negro Controller of Customs Denies Legal Adoption of 14th Amendment," October 6, 1924, 1; "Suit to Oust Cohen Filed at New Orleans," October 7, 1924, 25; "Stone to Defend Cohen," October 15, 1924, 39. Ingham and Feldman discuss this controversy, as well as others that plagued Cohen during his career. They note: "Because this was typical of the sort of vilification white southerners heaped upon any blacks who had the temerity to try to remain involved in politics, it is difficult to know if there was much substance to the various charges." Ingham and Feldman, 148. See the following in *TNYT*: "Negro Official Held in Alleged Rum Plot," August 28, 1925, 15; "Cohen Says He Is Innocent," August 29, 1925, 6; "Coolidge to Get Report on Cohen," August 30, 1925, 27; "Bootleg Clean-Up in New Orleans," September 13, 1925, E1.

29. "Walter Cohen," *TA*, January 10, 1931, 2. Typographical errors in the first quote and a spelling error in the second were corrected. Also see "Walter L. Cohen, Negro Leader, Dead," *TNYT*, December 30, 1930, 21.

30. Ball, 295. McPherson's alias came from a popular white baseball player-turned-evangelist named William "Billy" Ashley Sunday. "Billy Sunday Remembered."

31. "Southern Baptist Minister Notes *Advocate* Improvement," *TA*, December 12, 1931, 2. McPherson does not appear in online census records for Orleans Parish for 1910, 1920, or 1930.

32. "Rev. James G. M'Pherson; Negro Was Model for 'De Lawd' in 'The Green Pastures,'" *TNYT*, April 10, 1936, 24. Several of his sermons are featured on the compact disc *Preachers and Congregations*, vol. 1: 1927-1938.

33. David Graham was president of Monrovia College and Industrial Training School.

34. "Send Gretings [*sic*] to Friends," *TA*, March 12, 1927, 1. The couple, identified as Dr. and Mrs. D. A. Graham in *TA*, appear in the 1920 Census. David, a minister, was born in Indiana, where his mother was also born; his father was born in Tennessee. Etta was born in Missouri, as was her mother. Her father was born in Kentucky. *Fourteenth Census*, King County, Washington. Etta Graham returned to Portland a few months later for a visit. *TA*, September 24, 1927, 4.

35. *TA*, September 16, 1933, 1; The Inflation Calculator. Also see *TA*, March 15, 1930, 1. The Jones family does not appear in online census records for MC for 1920, or Los Angeles County for 1930. Another individual who prized the paper was Isaac B. Vessel, who worked as a railroad waiter. He wrote from San Francisco that he read it "every Monday and in that way [kept] in touch with his old friends" in Portland. *TA*, March 15, 1930, 2. Vessel and his parents were born in Louisiana. *Fourteenth Census*, San Francisco County. Other subscribers who felt they could not do without *TA* included Joel A. Cage, who moved about seventy miles south to Albany, where he opened a "shoe shining parlor." "Mr. Gage [*sic*] Moves to Albany," *TA*, September 15, 1923, 1; "Former Portlander Visits Here," *TA*, February 2, 1924, 1. He renewed his subscription again during his visit. Cage, identified as J. A. Cage (and Gage) in *TA*, appears in the 1910 Census; it is unclear

whether his name was John or Joel. He was born in Tennessee and worked as a train porter; his parents were born in Georgia. His wife, Virlinda [?], and her father were born in Kentucky. Her mother was born in Virginia. They had three sons. *Thirteenth Census*, MC. Other individuals who relocated in Oregon and continued to subscribe to the newspaper included Mary Garner, who moved to Bend in 1931, and restaurateur John Mitchell, who moved to Corvallis with his wife Pearl, a music teacher. "At Bend," *TA*, December 19, 1931, 3; *TA*, July 12, 1930, 3. According to the 1920 Census, John and his parents were born in Georgia. He was described as mulatto and a restaurant proprietor. Pearl, also mulatto, was born in California. Her parents were born in the "United States." They operated a boarding house and had a married couple and three single men living with them. *Fourteenth Census*, MC.

36. *TA*, June 20, 1931, 3. Hall does not appear in online census records for Wayne County, Michigan, for 1930. The man had been a "regular subscriber" since visiting the city with his son during the summer of 1928. Cannady reminded readers that Hall's mother lived in Portland, thus creating a point of conversation the next time peominneapolisple saw her. Census records for 1920 reveal a likely individual: Ella Hall was born in Oregon and is described as a lodger who did housework for a family. Her father was born in Indiana; her mother was born in New Mexico. *Fourteenth Census*, MC.

37. "Writes from Down South," *TA*, January 23, 1932, 3; "Young Missourian Graduates," *TA*, June 10, 1933, 2. London Montgomery McGhee was from Cleveland, Ohio, and lived in Portland until 1931. *TA*, May 9, 1931, 2.

38. "Mrs. Gulliford Writes from Dawson," *TA*, July 7, 1923, 1. Alaska did not become a state until January 3, 1959. Gulliford does not appear in online census records for Alaska or Oregon for 1920. Another subscriber, Jennie Meredith (misspelled Meredity in a later reference), received *TA* at her home in Cordova, Alaska, where she was reported at various times to be "engaged in the laundry business" or working as "bookkeeper in her uncle's business." See "We Hear from Alaska," *TA*, October 13, 1923, 1; "Alaska Maid Visits," *TA*, February 12, 1927, 1; *TA*, June 27, 1931, 3. For more about life in Cordova, see "News from Alaska," *TA*, December 22, 1923, 4. Meredith does not appear in online census records for Alaska for 1920. In 1932, Mrs. Roscoe McKnight asked to have *TA* sent to her in Cordova. "From Alaska," *TA*, January 9, 1932, 4.

39. This phenomenon probably was not unique to the Northwest paper. In fact, George Durham may have had the *New York Age* forwarded to him while he was in Boston.

40. *TA*, January 23, 1926, 1. His name was spelled with one "l," which was likely a typographical error. Williams does not appear in online census records for MC, Oregon, for 1920.

41. *TA*, August 29, 1931, 2. Also see "Pollyann," *TA*, March 14, 1931, 2; Rosalie Bird, "In the Realm of Society," *TA*, May 16, 1931, 2. Reed does not appear in online census records for MC for 1920.

42. Robert H. Gilmore, "Congratulates 'The Advocate,'" *TA*, September 8, 1928, 1.

43. Bell System advertisement, *TA*, August 24, 1929, 4. Another advertisement promoted telephones as a way to bridge distance. *TA*, July 23, 1932, 2. Still others instructed people how to place calls. See, for example, *TA*, November 8, 1930, 3. One study about the adoption of telephones and automobiles notes that in 1900 "there were fewer than two [telephones] for each 100 Americans"; further, only one car was "registered per 1,000 Americans." Fischer and Carroll, 1154; also see Fischer. In February 1932, the Pacific Telephone and Telegraph Company hosted a weeklong open house so people could see how switchboard operators handled incoming calls and connected callers to people elsewhere in the U.S. "Telephone Company to Hold Open House," *TA*, February 13, 1932, 1.

44. Kessler, 23.

45. Bosco-Milligan Foundation, 36, 38-39. Oregon's white press included the *Morning Oregonian*, *Oregon Daily Journal*, and *Portland Telegram*. To learn about one woman's "constant search" to find "news about black people in the local newspapers," see "Interview: Kathryn Hall Bogle."

46. Cannady was not alone in her efforts to promote uplift. Ever since the first black newspaper was published in 1827, editors have used the press to document and reflect on the political, social, and cultural changes occurring in the United States while simultaneously exposing the racist foundatioon of this country.

47. "Editorial Appearing in First Issue of *The Advocate*, September 5, 1903," reprinted as part of "*The Advocate* is 25 Years Old Today," *TA*, September 1, 1928, 1.

Birth announcements also serve as a reminder that Negroes had difficulty obtaining medical care due to racism. Otto Rutherford, who was born in Portland in 1911, said James Merriman, the sole black physician in the city, "brought" him and "all the kids" around his age "into the world." Rutherford, SR 270. Some births were attended by a Jewish midwife named Jennie Matilsky, who was born in about 1880 in Vilna, the former capital of the Grand Duchy of Lithuania. She and her husband Abraham, a musician who gave lessons in their home and occasionally gave concerts, appear in the Fourteenth Census, MC. She assisted Cannady's sister-in-law, Lillian Morrow, at the homebirth of her first child in October 1923. "Stork Visits the Morrows," *TA*, October 20, 1923, 1. Lillian and Almus celebrated their thirteenth wedding anniversary a few months later. Trixie Breaux, "In the Realm of Society," *TA*, March 29, 1924, 4. For other birth announcements, see, for example, "Hotel Notes," *TA*, July 12, 1924, 1; *TA*, August 9, 1924, 1. Breaux was not found in online census records for Oregon for any available years.

Obituaries also were important. One column about the differences between the white and black press observed that only "the Negro newspaper ... tells the public [when] a worthy citizen has passed." "White and Colored Papers," *TA*, February 4, 1928, 2. For obituaries, including some about former slaves, see, for example, the following in *TA*: "Staunch Citizen Passes," November 24, 1923, 1; "Pioneer Buried Wednesday," May 24, 1924, 4; "Pioneer Citizens Pass," November 29, 1930, 1; "Mr. Gregory Buried" and "Thos. Davis Dead at 92; Crossed Plains Early," December 20, 1930, 1; "Former Portlander Succumbs in South," March 14, 1931, 1; "Dr. Anderson Passes at 65," July 18, 1931, 1; "Rev. Anderson Passes," July 18, 1931, 2; "Local Woman Succumbs," April 9, 1932, 1; "Death Removes Valuable Citizen," September 24, 1932, 1; "Worthy Citizens Pass," September 24, 1932, 2; "Mrs. Margaret Cain Dies Following Brief Illness," February 25, 1933, 1; "Succumbs Sun.," March 4, 1933, 1; "Medley Dies in Vet Hospital," November 18, 1933, 1.

48. "On Being Late," *TA*, August 1, 1931, 2.

49. "Couple Came To Portland Twenty Seven [*sic*] Years Ago," *TA*, May 14, 1927, 1. Identified as Mr. and Mrs. C. H. Binford in the paper, Edward and Charity Binford were a mulatto couple married for thirty-four years at this time. Edward, described as a common laborer, was born in Alabama; the birthplace of his parents was listed as unknown. Charity and her mother were also born in Alabama; her father was born in Virginia. She was described as a laundress for a private family. *Thirteenth Census*, MC.

50. "Virginian Remembers Happy Time in Portland," *TA*, October 22, 1932, 3. Also see "News Briefs," *TA*, October 1, 1932, 1. A search of online census records for 1920 and 1930 for Pulaski, Floyd, and Montgomery counties produced no likely individuals. Also see "Program of Colored Legionnaires," *TA*, September 10, 1932, 1.

51. Twenty-two individuals were identified by name in one article. "New Subscribers," *TA*, September 13, 1924, 1.

52. Hill, Jr., "The Negro in Oregon," 55.

53. Miller.

54. "Prominent Attorney Likes to Read *The Advocate*," *TA*, March 22, 1930, 1.

55. "New Subscribers," *TA*, August 1, 1925, 1. For brief information about Crumpacker, see "Maurice Edgar Crumpacker" or "Maurice Edgar Crumpacker," *TA*, June 21, 1930, 2. The Boyces' activities often were included in *TA*. See, for example, "Hotel Notes," *TA*, August 25, 1923, 1.

For information about Rand's backing, as well as Cannady's support of his political career, see *TA*, May 26, 1925, 1; "Chief Justice Rand Grateful to Friends," *TA*, June 2, 1928, 1; "Supreme Judge Rand Renews Subscription," *TA*, February 9, 1929, 1; *TA*, September 27, 1930, 1.

For more about Korell, see: "A Brief Letter from Our Congressman," *TA*, January 12, 1929, 1; advertisement, *TA*, October 15, 1927, 2; "Franklin Frederick Korell."

"Governor Wants *The Advocate*," *TA*, February 15, 1930, 1. Norblad succeeded Isaac Patterson and served from 1929 to 1931.

"Leader Has Heart As Well As Brains; Heads Powerful Company for Eighteen Years," *TA*, January 31, 1931, 1. For biographical information, see Lockley, "History of the Columbia River Valley," 429. Portland Railway, Light & Power Co. became PGE.

56. *TA*, January 14, 1928, 3; "*Advocate* Readers in Friendly Rivalry," *TA*, July 14, 1928, 2. Maxville was a logging camp owned by the Bowman-Hicks Lumber Company. McArthur, 543.

57. "*Advocate* Readers."

58. "Prominent Woman Praises *Advocate*," *TA*, April 2, 1927, 1. A grammatical error was corrected.

59. "*The Advocate* in Every White Home in Oregon in 1933," *TA*, February 11, 1933, 1.

60. "Prominent Attorney Congratulates *Advocate*," *TA*, September 16, 1933, 1.

61. See, for example, January 7, 1933, 1; January 21, 1933, 2; January 28, 1933, 3; February 11, 1933, 2.

62. "*The Advocate*."

63. "*Advocate* in Evr'y Home; Urge State-Wide Reading of *Advocate*," *TA*, January 21, 1933, 1; "*The Advocate*." One of the most important new subscribers and advertisers was Benninghoff & Gaddie funeral parlor, which opened on 6th and Market at the end of 1932. "*Advocate* in Evr'y Home"; *TA*, December 3, 1932, 3; *TA*, October 14, 1933, 3. Cannady wrote about her tour of the new facility. "New Funeral Home Opens Doors," *TA*, December 3, 1932, 4. Important, too, was the firm's policy on race relations. H. L. Benninghoff and his partner, Paul E. Gaddie, hired Barbara Hubbard to work as a "lady attendant," and Negroes were welcome to use a room at the parlor for meetings "day or night." "New Funeral Parlor Employs Colored Woman," *TA*, January 7, 1933, 1.

64. Clifford C. Mitchell, "Digesting the News," *TA*, April 8, 1933, 1.

65. "*The Advocate* in Every White Home."

66. See, for example, *TA*, August 3, 1929, 2.

67. For other notices in *TA* about boosters, see, for example: February 2, 1929, 3; "*Advocate*'s Subscription List Enlarged," April 12, 1930, 1. Sherman, a boiler washer for the railroad, lived at 418 Vancouver Avenue. According to the 1920 Census, Sherman Pickett and his parents were born in Alabama. His widowed mother, Matilda Brown, and his niece, Beatrice Ainsbury [?], lived with him. *Fourteenth Census*, MC. Also see *TA*, February 21, 1931, 2.

68. *TA*, August 15, 1931, 3. Six months later, Pickett reported that his nephew in Alabama was taking "great pleasure in reading it each week." *TA*, February 13, 1932, 3.

69. "Ilwaco Man Likes the Old Reliable," *TA*, June 6, 1931, 4. He does not appear in online census records for 1920 for Pacific County, Washington. A few months later he sent Cannady another letter: "Your paper gives me more courage and more joy to look forward to than any paper I ever read. You seem to see more of the bright side of life and not so much of the dark side. Please keep up the good. I will always be with you." "Praises *The Advocate*," *TA*, August 15, 1931, 4.

70. "The Home Paper," *TA*, December 13, 1924, 4.

71. *TA*, December 24, 1927, 4. Two typographical errors were corrected.

72. Advertisement, *TA*, August 25, 1928, 3. Capitalization altered, and punctuation was added. Also see *TA*, September 1, 1928, 2. On the occasion of *TA*'s twentieth anniversary, Cannady observed that the ideal—if overly ambitious—present would be two thousand new subscribers. She asked every reader "to make him or herself a committee of one to bring or send in a new subscriber." "We Want Two Thousand New Subscribers," *TA*, August 25, 1923, 4. Also see "A Substantial Booster," *TA*, September 8, 1923, 1.

73. "Pioneer Citizen First Society Editor of 'The Advocate,'" *TA*, September 8, 1928, 1; "She Has Read Every Issue of *The Advocate*," *TA*, September 15, 1928, 1. Binford's photograph ran with this story. Also see "Subscribers for Twenty-Five Years," *TA*, September 1, 1928, 3; "More 25-Year-Old 'Advocate' Subscribers," *TA*, September 8, 1928, 1.

Daniel Parker of Tacoma, Washington, wrote that he had "seen [the paper] grow from its infancy to its present age" and had "always found its columns filled with the most interesting news." "A 19-Year Subscriber Speaks," *TA*, October 13, 1923, 2. Identified as D. H. Parker in *TA*, he appears in the 1920 Census. Parker, a barber, and his parents were born in Pennsylvania. His wife, Rebecca, was born in Missouri; her parents were born in Kentucky. *Fourteenth Census*, Pierce County.

According to the 1920 Census, Anna Peek was born in Iowa. Her parents were born in the "United States." Her husband, Warren, was born in Georgia. His parents also were born in the "United States." He worked as a waiter at the Portland Hotel. *Fourteenth Census*, MC; *TA*, September 1, 1923, 6.

According to the 1920 Census, Virgil Keene and his parents were born in Missouri. He was described as an expressman for a hauling company. His wife, Dora, was described as mulatto. She and her parents were born in Ohio. Their daughter, Norma, worked as a stenographer for a payroll master. *Fourteenth Census*, MC.

74. See, for example: "Writer Praises *The Advocate*," *TA*, July 11, 1925, 4; "Attention! Subscribers," *TA*, September 7, 1929, 4; "Injured Man Given Farm," *TA*, August 9, 1930, 1. A few readers even paid in advance for a three-year subscription, a testament to their personal wealth as well as their faith in the paper's longevity. See, for example, *TA*, April 21, 1928, 1; *TA*, September 16, 1933, 1.

75. *TA*, October 1, 1932, 3. A grammatical error was corrected. Today, it would cost about fifty cents to mail the renewal notices. The Inflation Calculator.

76. "Bishop Kyles Lauds *The Advocate*," *TA*, September 8, 1923, 4. Identified as L. W. Kyles in *TA*, he was bishop of the church at 4013 West Belle Place. *Year Book of the Churches, 1921-22*, ed. E. O. Watson (Washington, D.C.: Hayworth Publishing House, 1922), 258. He was in Portland in 1931 for the nineteenth annual session of the Oregon-Washington AME conference and may have called on Cannady. "Methodists in Annual Confab," *TA*, October 3, 1931, 1. According to the 1920 Census, Kyles and his parents were born in Virginia. His wife, Luella, and her parents were born in North Carolina. They had six children. *Fourteenth Census*, St. Louis County.

Cannady regularly printed testimonials from subscribers. See, for example, the following in *TA*: "*The Advocate* Given Praise," January 1, 1927, 1; "Likes *The Advocate*," December 14, 1929, 1; "Call *Advocate* Wonderful," January 28, 1933, 2; February 18, 1933, 3; "Writer Praises *The Advocate*," April 1, 1933, 1.

77. "Sends *Advocate* Five Dollars," *TA*, December 13, 1930, 1. According to the 1920 Census, Ella, James, and their parents were born in Texas. She worked as a seamstress. He was principal of Jack Yates High School, the second institution for Negroes in Houston, from the day the school opened in 1926 until his death in 1941. The high school moved to a new location in 1958 and has since been renovated and renamed James D. Ryan Middle School. *Fourteenth Census*, Harris County; "History," Jack Yates High School. The Ryans also contributed to Wiley College. "Negro Philanthropists Give One Thousand Each to Wiley," *TA*, February 14, 1931, 1. Thornton M. Fairchild—president of the Watchtower Mutual Life Insurance Company in Houston, an *Advocate* reader, and a "lifelong" friend of "its editor"—matched the Ryans' donation to Wiley, which had changed its name by then. That would be a gift of more than $14,000 each today. The Inflation Calculator.

78. Willis worked for the paper sometime between 1903 and 1910. According to the 1920 Census, he and his parents were born in North Carolina. His wife, Mary, and her parents were born in Ohio. *Fourteenth Census*, Borough of New York. "Likes *The Advocate*," *TA*, November 3, 1923, 1; "A 25-Year Subscribed Speaks from New York," *TA*, December 22, 1928, 3.

79. "We Hear from Texan," *TA*, September 8, 1923, 1. Also see *TA*, October 3, 1925, 1. According to the 1920 Census, Young, a baker, was born in Texas. His parents were born in Louisiana. His wife, Nettie, was born in Tennessee; her parents were born in Georgia. She was described as a laundress "at home." *Fourteenth Census*, Dallas County. People who heeded her advice to "start the New Year right by paying [their] subscription to *The Advocate*" were recognized, too. See, for example, the following in *TA*: December 29, 1923, 4; "The First to Pay His Subscription in the New Year," January 3, 1925, 1; "Whadja' Know 'bout Mott," January 3, 1931, 1. During the Depression, Cannady encouraged people to include the cost of a one-year subscription to *TA* in their "New Year's budget." *TA*, January 2, 1932, 1. For a creative plea, see "Resolutions," *TA*, January 3, 1931, 2.

80. *TA*, January 3, 1931, 3; The Inflation Calculator.

81. *TA*, August 25, 1923, 4. Clarkston does not appear in online census records for the District of Columbia for 1920. Mrs. W. M. Bannister also was considered "a true race woman" for subscribing soon after relocating to Portland from Houston. *TA*, August 2, 1930, 3. She does not appear in online census records for Harris County, Texas, for 1920.

82. "Reads *Advocate* With a Deal of Pride," *TA*, February 25, 1928, 4. Punctuation added.

83. *TA*, September 19, 1925, 1. Other editorials were more blunt. People who boasted they never read a race paper were "DEAD WEIGHT"; they also were "persons of little or no consequence." "Dead Weight," *TA*, June 2, 1928, 2; *TA*, September 1, 1923, 4. Also see, for example, the following in *TA*: "Race Papers," April 25, 1925, 4; "Live and Let Live," April 25, 1931, 2; "Negro Newspapers," December 24, 1932, 2.

84. "Hudson Straight 8 to Head List of Awards," *TA*, April 18, 1931, 1. Her claim was not quite accurate. *TPT* had spent nearly two months in the fall of 1927 promoting the "$22,000 Automobile & Prize Campaign" to increase circulation; the *VE* sponsored a similar "gigantic subscription campaign" in 1925. *TCE* attempted a subscription contest in November 1915 "for the purpose of placing the greatest Negro journal in the west in thousands more homes and to help ... make this the most modern plant in the entire country owned and conducted wholly by the Race." In *TPT*, see, for example:

October 15, 1927, 18-19; October 26, 1927, 8; November 1, 1927, 13; November 11, 1927, 8. Advertisement, *VE*, August 7, 1925, 4-5. "*The California Eagle*'s Grea [*sic*] Subscription Contest," *TCE*, October 30, 1915, 4.

85. "A New Year," *TA*, January 2, 1932, 2.

86. "Your Paper," *TA*, October 17, 1931, 2. For similar comments on the effect of the Depression on *TA*, see "On Being on Time," *TA*, July 2, 1932, 2.

87. "A New Year."

88. "Announcement," *PT*, May 5, 1931, 1. Cannady observed: "*The Advocate* congratulates the *Daily News* and the *Portland Telegram* upon their recent action in merging the two papers. The action is in keeping with the spirit of the times—the cutting down of overhead, curtailing duplication—yet preserving the best of the two. Their objective is to serve the people of their community in a better way in every respect. More power to the *News-Telegram*—may its life be long and successful!" "Newspaper Merger," *TA*, May 9, 1931, 2.

89. "Announcement," *TA*, June 20, 1931, 1.

90. "Notice to Subscribers," *TA*, August 1, 1931, 2.

91. "Hudson." It is unclear how much she charged for ads, either before or after the contest; insertion rates never were published, but "made known on application." See, for example, *TA*, June 2, 1923, 4.

92. "Hudson," 4.

93. "New Departments," *TA*, March 14, 1931, 2.

94. See, for example, Nancy Lee, "Helpful Hints," *TA*, May 21, 1931, 4.

95. "Keeping Fit," *TA*, March 21, 1931, 4; "Keeping Fit," *TA*, April 4, 1931, 4. Cannady felt very "fortunate ... to secure [Unthank's] services." "Keeping Fit," *TA*, March 14, 1931, 2. These columns joined others that ran semi-regularly in the late 1920s and early 1930s, including "Arrow Tips" by Kits Reid; "Sense and Nonsense" by City Commissioner Ralph C. Clyde; Clifford C. Mitchell's "Digesting the News"; "Verbal Snapshots" by W. J. Wheaton; "Legal Light" by John Jamison; "Denver" Ed Martin's "Sport News"; "Sports Section" by Vernon Baker; "The Motion Picture Situation" by Chester A. Lyon. For more about Clyde's career, see Lansing. Cannady was "proud ... to secure the services of Attorney [and Howard University School of Law alumnus] John H. Jamison to edit [*The Advocate*'s] legal department." "Legal Light," *TA*, February 6, 1932, 2. Cannady occasionally published news about other cities. See, for example, Emma Lue Sayers, "Los Angeles Social Circle," *TA*, October 1, 1927, 2.

96. Advertisement, *TA*, April 18, 1931, 3.

97. "First Votes Published Not Many Very Active; Next Ten Days Offering Real Opportunity for New Entries," *TA*, May 2, 1931, 3; The Inflation Calculator.

98. "Hudson"; The Inflation Calculator. The dealer was Grimm, Schneider and Bacon's—probably Louis Grimm, John Bacon, and Otto Schneider, according to the *Fourteenth Census*, MC.

99. Items ran in *TA* from April 18, 1931, through June 20, 1931.

100. "*Advocate*'s Contest Growing: Our Opportunity Is Here in 'Everybody Wins' Campaign," *TA*, April 25, 1931, 1, 4.

101. "First Votes Published," 1, 3; "Looks Like This New Hudson '8' Will Go for Less Votes than Required for Old 'Piano and Ring' Contest," *TA*, May 2, 1931, 1.

102. "Big Second Vote Period Opens; Tighter Race for Car Is Seen," *TA*, May 30, 1931, 1; "[Candidates] Busy Stacking Up Big Vote Leads; Voting Value Will Be Cut One Week from Wednesday Night," *TA*, May 16, 1931, 1.

103. "Subscriptions Being Deposited in Sealed Ballot Box at No. 312 Macleay Building," *TA*, June 20, 1931, 1. John H. Jamison and DeNorval Unthank served as judges. The final

vote tabulation took hours, Cannady reported, but in the end Alice Marshall won the car; Walter Lovell, pastor of First AME Zion Church, won $100; Irene Patterson, M. L. Brown, and Madeline Gibson won $60, $50, and $40, respectively. "Campaign Ends Thursday Nite; Winners of Grand Capital Prize and Cash Awards Announced," *TA*, June 27, 1931, 1.

104. "Campaign Ends," 1, 4.

105. Advertisement, April 18, 1931; The Inflation Calculator.

106. "*Advocate*'s Contest Growing," 4. For another editorial along this line, see, for example, "Hard Times," *TA*, November 29, 1930, 2.

107. "Physician's Home Stoned; Local Family Victim of Jim-Crow Attack Here Friday," *TA*, April 25, 1931, 1.

108. "Portland Hotel Fires Colored Help in Its Service a Generation," *TA*, April 18, 1931, 1. Also see "Portland Hotel's Patrons"; Henry J. Berkowitz, "Portland Hotel Colored Waiters," *TA*, April 25, 1931, 1. A number of waiters were reinstated later. See *TA*, July 16, 1932, 1; August 20, 1932, 1; September 24, 1932, 3. It is unclear whether Cannady was rehired. *TA* informed readers that he and another man had opened a cigar and boot-black business in downtown Portland. *TA*, October 24, 1931, 2. Previous articles reported friendly relations between owners of the hotel and employees. See, for example, "Hotel Notes," *TA*, August 18, 1928, 2; "Hotel Notes," *TA*, September 1, 1928, 3. Cannady didn't believe that race antipathy was a factor, given Boyce's "fair and just ... attitude towards and dealings with their colored employees as well as their white." "The Portland Hotel," *TA*, April 18, 1931, 2. The Legal Redress Committee of the Portland Branch "interceded on behalf of the waiters who were summarily dismissed from the Portland Hotel." Several meetings were held with management, but the committee was told "that until business conditions improved, they could not return to the use of waiters instead of waitresses." Clarence E. Ivey, "Annual Report of President, the Local Branch of the N.A.A.C.P.," November 15, 1931, NAACP PB.

109. "Pay Up!" *TA*, March 18, 1933, 2. For another notice about sacrifice, see, for example, "To Our Tardy Subscribers," *TA*, July 27, 1929, 2.

110. "Editors and Politics," *TA*, September 27, 1924, 4.

111. This policy accompanied the subscription rates in every issue. Cannady may have had assistance with accounts, but one of her many tasks at the paper was collecting. See "She's Gone," *TA*, August 13, 1927, 1.

112. See, for example, "Announcement Extraordinary," *TA*, October 22, 1927, 1.

113. "*The Advocate*'s Mission," *TA*, December 18, 1926, 2. Punctuation added.

114. *TA*, May 26, 1923, 4. A typographical error was corrected. For more examples of this direct approach, see, for example, the following in *TA*: "Patronize Our Advertisers," May 26, 1923, 4; "Please Pay," June 6, 1925, 4; "Please Pay *The Advocate* What You Owe it So We, Too May Enjoy Xmas," December 19, 1925, 4; "Pay Your Subscription, Please," *TA*, January 22, 1927, 2; December 17, 1927, 2; "Attention Subscribers," August 3, 1929, 1.

115. "Pay Your Subscription," *TA*, June 13, 1925, 4. The collection strategies Cannady used were remarkably similar to those implemented by frontier editors. A scholar who has studied the frontier press writes that this type of request "was usually couched in homey, even humorous language" in an effort "to win over delinquents by friendly persuasion." Halaas, 33. For other humorous appeals, or excuses offered when trying to collect, see, for example, the following in *TA*: "To Our Subscribers," May 1, 1926, 1; "To an *Advocate* Collector," November 7, 1931, 2; "Your Paper," January 30, 1932, 2.

116. "What Is *The Advocate* Worth to You?" *TA*, January 28, 1928, 1. Typographical errors were corrected. For a similar editorial, see *TA*, February 26, 1927, 2.

117. *TA*, August 18, 1923, 4. For notices about dropping individuals, see, for example, the following in *TA*: "Delinquent Subscribers To Be Dropped," October 27, 1923, 1; "To Our Subscribers," June 26, 1926, 4; "To Our Subscribers," March 5, 1927, 1, March 12, 1927, 1.

118. *TA* was published every Saturday, but mailed on Fridays. See "Pardon Us," *TA*, April 10, 1926, 4.

119. "The Newspaper," *TA*, January 18, 1930, 2.

120. "*The Advocate* in Every White Home." Also see "Your Paper."

121. Beatrice Cannady to Walter White, June 16, 1926, NAACP PB. Punctuation added.

122. *TA*, January 31, 1925, 4. The announcement that the *Appeal* had "suspended publication" in August 1924 was particularly troubling, since it left the seven thousand black residents of St. Paul and Minneapolis "without a race paper." Edward Cannady may have worked for this publication; if so, his association with the paper may have inspired this comment: "Mention of the *Appeal* brings back memories of that fearless editor and founder, John Q. Adams, who fought so nobly for many years against discrimination." "Dead, But Not Forgotten," *TA*, August 2, 1924, 4; Historical Census Browser.

Several scholars have noted that financial hardships plagued the early editors, but few have studied "the specific economic, political, and cultural factors that impeded their success"; nor have they considered how the stress of running a newspaper may have affected an editor's ability to focus on reform. Rhodes, "Race, Money, Politics and the Antebellum Black Press," 95. One exception is her biography of Mary Ann Shadd Cary, in which she discusses Cary's struggle to publish the *Provincial Freeman* in Canada due to sexism and financial woes. Rhodes, *Mary Ann Shadd Cary*. Also see Mangun, "Boosting the Black Press' Bottom Line"; Thornbrough, 467-90. These oversights may be due, in part, to the lack of financial records. Cannady, for example, reported that *TA*'s files "for a number of years" were destroyed in a house fire in 1927. "The Editor's Home Catches Fire," *TA*, June 11, 1927, 1. Some years later, other items Cannady had stored at a relative's home—including a number of photographs of the performers she promoted—were destroyed in a fire. Redwine, e-mail message to author, July 15, 2004.

For studies that mention editors' financial difficulties, but focus on the messages contained in the black press, see, for example, Tripp; Pride and Wilson. Even the publishers of *Freedom's Journal*, the nation's first black newspaper, were concerned about the bottom line. John Russwurm and Samuel Cornish asked their "coloured brethren to strengthen [their] hands by" subscribing to the newspaper. Anyone who had not already paid in full was expected to do so by the following week. "To Our Patrons," *FJ*, March 16, 1827, 1; "To Our Subscribers," *FJ*, March 16, 1827, 4.

123. See, for example, advertisements in *TA*: June 8, 1929, 4; July 27, 1929, 3; January 28, 1933, 3; March 5, 1932, 3; February 6, 1932, 4; July 16, 1932, 2; September 24, 1932, 4; June 28, 1930, 3; June 14, 1930, 2. Geisel's creative ads for Flit did not appear in *TA*, but for a number of examples, see "The Advertising Artwork of Dr. Seuss." C. Gee Wo's Chinese Medical Herbs Company, Inc., was at 262-1/2 Alder Street in Portland.

124. Advertisement, Dr. Fred Palmer's Skin Whitener, *TA*, May 24, 1930, 4.

125. Advertisement, Boerner-Fry Co., *TA*, June 14, 1924, 2. In 1899, Prussian immigrant Emil Louis Boerner constructed a multi-story factory building in Iowa City, Iowa, to produce vanilla extract, perfumes, and pharmaceuticals. Boerner helped found the State University of Iowa's pharmacy department and served as its first dean. The building was added to the National Register of Historic Places in 1983. "Walking Tour." The testimonial of such a "prominent" woman as Gresham—who was pictured in the ad—

coupled with the promise to "cheerfully refund" one's money if the product did not give "skin the appearance of being several shades lighter," probably enticed some women to clip the order form at the corner of the ad and send it to the Boerner-Fry Company in Iowa City, Iowa. Gresham also was appointed assistant postmistress of Des Moines, Iowa. U.G. Whitney, *Acts and Joint Resolutions Passed at the Regular Session of the Thirty-Ninth General Assembly of the State of Iowa* (Des Moines, Iowa: The State of Iowa, 1921), x. Cannady also published ads for "Zura Kinkout," a product for straightening nappy hair. See, for example, *TA*, June 14, 1924, 2. For more about beauty and implications for race and gender politics, see Walker.

126. "Passing," *TA*, December 29, 1923, 4. A typographical error was corrected. Also see "Playing White," *TA*, October 20, 1923, 4; "Wash Me White as Snow," *TA*, August 17, 1929, 2.

127. Oak, 112-13. Also, the first black-owned advertising agency was not founded until 1929. Newspaperman Claude Barnett "hoped to change the attitudes of national-brand advertisers, who mostly underestimated the spending power of black consumers and generally did not bother to advertise in African American publications." Walker, 12. Also see Haring.

128. Other longtime white advertisers promoted in the newspaper were Roberts Brothers at 3rd and Morrison and J. P. Finley & Son Morticians at 5th and Montgomery. "Twenty-Two Years' Advertising," *TA*, September 5, 1925, 4. For Roberts Bros. advertisements, see, for example, the following in *TA*: September 1, 1923, 7; June 26, 1926, 4; August 8, 1926, 2; September 18, 1926, 4. For a photograph of the brothers' new store on the corner of 3rd and Morrison, see Douthit, 116. For some institutional history, see "Department Stores." For advertisements for J. P. Finley & Son Morticians, see, for example, the following in *TA*: March 31, 1928, 3; May 31, 1930, 2.

Lipman Wolfe & Co. department store began advertising in 1925. *TA*, November 28, 1925, 4. The ad campaign may have been an outcome of a recent change in management; three months earlier, Cannady observed that Aaron Holtz, the new manager, was "a thorough business man, kind and considerate," with "a host of friends and acquaintances amongst all classes of people here." "Lipman Wolfe & Company," *TA*, August 8, 1925, 4. For the company's ads, see, for example, the following in *TA*: March 27, 1926, 4; December 8, 1928, 3. The store's 1912 building, designed by Portland architect Albert E. Doyle, is now home to the Hotel Monaco Portland. For a brief history, see "History," Hotel Monaco Portland. Doyle also was commissioned to design Central Library, a few blocks northwest of the Park Blocks, and many of the first buildings at Reed College—places Cannady frequented during her career. For more about Doyle and Central Library, see Ritz; Niles.

129. "Popular Clothier Enlarges Store," *TA*, March 15, 1930, 1. A typographical error was corrected. For advertisements in *TA*, see, for example, May 24, 1930, 2; May 31, 1930, 2; January 2, 1932, 2. An owner may have been Winslow Bradford, who worked as an adjustment manager at a department store. *Fourteenth Census*, MC. For an editorial about white merchants demonstrating their "appreciation for the Race's patronage," see "A Merry Christmas To All Our Patrons Is *The Advocate*'s Wish," *TA*, December 22, 1923, 1.

130. Advertisement, Bradford Clothes Shop, *TA*, March 5, 1932, 3; The Inflation Calculator.

131. Advertisement, Eastern Outfitting Co., *TA*, October 20, 1923, 2; The Inflation Calculator. For more advertisements, see, for example, the following in *TA*: June 12, 1926, 4; November 8, 1930, 3.

132. *TA*, March 22, 1930, 2. *TA* gave front-page coverage to Joseph Shemansky, the company's Russian-born owner, when he made plans to build an eight-story retail store in

downtown Portland. "New Building Is Dedicated," *TA*, November 30, 1929, 1; *TA*, March 22, 1930, 1. For information about Portland's Jewish population and brief references to Shemansky, see Toll, "Voluntarism and Modernization in Portland Jewry."

133. "Open House Billed By Meier & Frank," *TSO*, October 2, 1932, 12. The flagship store was designed by Portland architect Albert E. Doyle. Meier & Frank's building was added to the National Register of Historic Places in July 1982. The company was acquired by Federated Department Stores in 2005 and Meier & Frank stores soon bore their new name: Macy's. For more about the store and the Meier family, see, for example, "Meet Me Under the Clock"; Rochlin; "Oregon History: Spread of Settlement."

134. He addressed the Portland Branch in 1930. See "Julius Meier Who Will Be the Principal Speaker at the N.A.A.C.P. Mass Meeting Tomorrow at the Williams Ave. Y.W.C.A.," *TA*, October 18, 1930, 1. Cannady wrote him shortly after the election in 1931 to inquire about a meeting. He replied that he would be in his office at the Portland store and would "be glad to see" her there. Julius L. Meier to Beatrice H. Cannady, March 5, 1931, copy in AC.

135. "Abe Meier Improving in South," *TA*, January 19, 1924, 4.

136. "Abraham Meier Passes," *TA*, March 15, 1930, 2. A typographical error was corrected.

137. See, for example, advertisements in *TA*: September 1, 1923, 10; April 2, 1927, 1; November 15, 1930, 1.

138. See, for example, Mr. and Mrs. Julian G. Henson, Mss 2854, OBHP.

139. For examples of J. C. Penney Co. ads in *TA*, see, for example: April 25, 1925, 4; September 28, 1929, 2; November 8, 1930, 3. For examples of Buick advertisements, see July 2, 1927, 2; July 30, 1927, 4; October 15, 1927, 4.

140. *TA*, May 11, 1929, 2.

141. "About Shell: Our history: The early 20th century."

142. "The Shell Oil Company of California," *TA*, June 11, 1927, 2. Punctuation added.

143. Ibid. For another editorial about the "necessity of patronizing" *TA*'s white advertisers, see, for example, "Our Advertisers," *TA*, August 25, 1923, 4.

144. *TA*, June 21, 1924, 1. See also *TA*, June 7, 1924, 4. Cannady referred to him as E. Richardson, Eurastus, and Erastus Richardson in various articles. He does not appear in online census records for Oregon for any available years. For more about him see: "Confectionery Is Moved," *TA*, August 9, 1930, 1; "E. Richardson, Pioneer Found Dead in Home," *TA*, January 10, 1931, 1; "The Passing of Mr. Richardson," *TA*, January 10, 1931, 2. Richardson was listed as an *Advocate* agent; see March 19, 1927, 2. One reader noted that he looked for *TA* there each week. Cannady was glad that he purchased copies, but noted that the company received only half the cover price, or 2.5 cents. She urged him to take out an annual subscription. "Writer Greatly Appreciates 'The Advocate's' Stand," *TA*, October 20, 1928, 4. For more about the importance of supporting black-owned businesses, see, for example, "Race Patronage," *TA*, July 23, 1927, 2; "Preaching Race Patronage," *TA*, October 29, 1927, 2.

145. Advertisement, *TA*, August 17, 1929, 2. Capitalization was altered. Also see *TA*, December 14, 1929, 1. However, Cannady also criticized business owners who did not advertise. See, for example, the following in *TA*: "Race Papers"; "The All-Revealing Ad," August 27, 1932, 2; June 10, 1933, 1; "Let Him Sink," January 22, 1927, 2.

146. "Technicalities Stop Fine Eating Place; Claim Zoning Ordinance Keeps Maxwell from Operating," *TA*, April 14, 1928, 1. Charles Maxwell and his father were born in Texas; his mother was born in Alabama. He was described as mulatto and a porter at a passenger depot [?]. He and his wife, Marie, had seven children: Merriman, Myrtle, El Ray, LaVada,

Maxine, Chrystalee, and Dolores. *Fourteenth Census*, MC. Chrystalee graduated from Salem High School in June 1928. "Some June Graduates."

Entrepreneurs in other Oregon cities were recognized, too, often in the newspaper's society column. For example, J. F. Stephens and his wife, who had relocated from Texas to the coastal town of Astoria in about 1919, operated the Dixie Lunch. When their restaurant was destroyed in the devastating fire that swept through town on December 8, 1922, they decided to reopen on Exchange Street, "where they were again successful" even though they were "one of the few colored families there." Trixie Breaux, "In the Realm of Society," *TA*, September 22, 1923, 4. The couple does not appear in online census records for Travis or Dallas counties, Texas, for 1910, or Clatsop County, Oregon, for 1920.

The Stephenses' story illustrates *TA*'s role as historian, especially when juxtaposed with institutional memory of the town. In 1978, OBHP researchers asked the Clatsop County Historical Society about the role of black people in the area. "There is no history of black population here," was the succinct reply. May S. Miller to Elizabeth McLagan, June 28, 1978, OBHP. Census records for 1930 show eight Negro residents. *Fifteenth Census of the United States*, Table 11, 618.

147. *TA*, January 17, 1931, 2. An advertisement for the garage listed S. C. Morris as the manager. He does not appear in online census records for MC for 1920. For the advertisement, see *TA*, April 18, 1931, 3. For a cautionary editorial about the pitfalls of entrepreneurship, see, for example, "Entering Business," *TA*, September 13, 1930, 2. Cannady also noted that G. Freeman and Brothers, who operated a "baggage transfer" service at 430 Hoyt Street, "represent[ed] progressive business men of the Race." *TA*, April 5, 1930, 2. For an advertisement, see, for example, *TA*, May 24, 1930, 3. Freeman was not found in online census records for MC.

148. "The Garage Business," *TA*, January 24, 1931, 2. She suggested a service "station or two on Broadway between Union and the [Willamette] river," where "practically all of the Negro activity [was] centered." Cannady urged people to combine their resources to start these stations, which would quickly pay for themselves with patronage and also employ men in need of a job. "Think About It!" *TA*, March 19, 1932, 2. Influencing whites to patronize black-owned businesses was easier said than done, though, according to Marie Smith, who told an interviewer that her husband worked for about a year as a mechanic in a "flourishing" garage. It is unclear whether he worked for U.S.A. Garage, Inc., but she stated flatly that "the pressure of the other [white] automobile people closed the black man's shop." Marie Smith, SR 271, transcript, OBHP. The garage is listed in *Polk's City Directory* 1931 and 1932, but not 1933.

149. Rosalie Bird-Holmes, "In the Realm of Society," *TA*, June 13, 1931, 2; The Inflation Calculator. For more about the club and its owner, see the following in *TA*: "'Little Charley' at Cotton Club," May 30, 1931, 2; "Restaurant Opens Again Under New Management," October 29, 1932, 1; September 16, 1933, 1; "Local News Events," November 18, 1933, 1.

150. E. J. Magruder, "Minister Believes Church Should Advertise," *TA*, June 2, 1923, 4.

151. "Advertising Pays in *The Advocate*," *TA*, June 30, 1923, 1. For advertisements, see for example, *TA*, November 3, 1923, 4; December 8, 1923, 4. Cannady noted the hat was sent from St. Georges; she might have meant St. George's Island, or the town of St. George, now a UNESCO World Heritage site. The Ingersolls do not appear in online census records for MC for any available years, but their daughter, Carrie, was secretary of the Portland Branch.

152. "Rev. Miller Writes from Bermuda," *TA*, February 9, 1924, 1. Also see, "Praises *The Advocate*," *TA*, January 3, 1925, 1. Miller served as pastor of an AME church there before his next posting in Saginaw, Michigan. Miller does not appear in online census records for Oregon for any available years.

153. One article is revealing: "Edward Boyce, one of the owners of this famous hostelry whom the colored people sincerely love, and his estimable wife, have always been fair and just in their attitude towards and dealings with their colored employees .... We recall a rumor of several years ago ... that a certain organization which wore diapers about their heads ... went to the management demanding the discharge of colored help and employment of white in their stead. This request was met with an emphatic stand in favor of retaining their colored help. "The Portland Hotel."

Some years later, *OV* recalled: "Wholesale cancellation of advertising, midnight intimidation by telephone with threats to personal safety of family, and gross slanders of character, were employed against us and against the few publications which denounced the Klan." "One of Only Three," *OV*, April 19, 1947, 21.

154. "Furniture Store Says Race Don't Pay—Patronage Not Wanted," *TA*, August 11, 1923, 1. Gaylor's first name was not mentioned, and he does not appear in online census records for MC.

155. "Furniture Store"; Gaston, 584.

156. "Attention White Advertisers," *TA*, April 11, 1925, 4. Troubling, too, were requests for "the pedigree of a colored man or woman" whom a white person planned to hire. Cannady noted the individuals never offered to pay for her time or trouble. "Do You Need Us?" *TA*, February 16, 1924, 4.

157. *TA*, August 1, 1925, 1.

158. "Our Typesetting Machine," *TA*, August 1, 1925, 4. A typographical error was corrected. Also see, for example, "Merganthaler Linotype Keyboard Layout."

159. For one visitor's reaction, see *TA*, November 28, 1931, 3.

160. "Excuse Us: Do You Owe Us Money?" *TA*, August 8, 1925, 4. For other editorials of a similar nature, see, for example, "A Word To Subscribers," *TA*, December 6, 1930, 2; "Live and Let Live," *TA*, May 2, 1931, 2.

161. "*The Advocate* Observes 22nd Birthday." It is possible that Edward Cannady wrote this editorial.

162. "*Advocate* Installs Typesetting Machine; Equipped for Better Service," *TA*, October 3, 1931, 1.

163. *TA*, October 17, 1931, 1.

164. *TA*, October 24, 1931, 2; "Southern Baptist Minister." Also see "Praises *Advocate*," *TA*, January 23, 1932, 3.

165. "Wheaton Admires High Standards of *Advocate*," *TA*, November 7, 1931, 1. For brief information about Wheaton, his columns, and the Bay Area paper, see Broussard, *Black San Francisco*. Also see "*The Spokesman*," *TA*, January 14, 1933, 2. A William Wheaton, who was a sign writer, appears in the 1920 Census. It is possible he also was a journalist. *Fourteenth Census*, San Francisco County, California.

166. *TA*, October 4, 1930, 2. "Jazz" finish, popular during the 1920s and 1930s, involved using rags or sponges to apply two or three colors of paint on top of each other while still wet.

167. Job printing had been an important source of revenue for the black press since its founding in 1827. See, for example: *The* (New York City) *Rights of All*, May 29, 1829, 2; *TSI*, June 18, 1921, 1.

168. "Make It First," *TA*, June 20, 1931, 2.

169. "We Thank You," *TA*, April 19, 1924, 1.

170. *TA*, March 22, 1924, 1. For another ad for job printing, see, for example, *TA*, August 18, 1928, 2.

171. "Mother's Day Cards," *TA*, May 3, 1924, 1; advertisement, *TA*, October 26, 1929, 1. Also see "Hotel Notes," *TA*, March 22, 1924, 1.

172. "If You Want to Know," *TA*, May 3, 1924, 4. For an advertisement, see, for example, *TA*, May 3, 1924, 4. Overton, whose first name was not mentioned, does not appear in online census records for MC for 1920.

173. *TA*, May 12, 1928, 1. Reed's death was reported the following year. "Pioneer Citizen Passes," *TA*, September 28, 1929, 1. James H. Reed, who lived near Troutdale, was born in Missouri; his parents were born in Kentucky. His wife, Marie, was born in North Carolina and her parents in South Carolina. *Fourteenth Census*, MC. Others who placed orders and subscribed included Chappie H. Grice, a "popular railroad man." *TA*, August 23, 1930, 1. He does not appear in online census records for Oregon for any available years.

174. *TA*, August 22, 1925, 4. Edna Gildon died at her home after a long illness. She was buried in Texas. *TA*, October 17, 1931, 2.

175. Cannady to Bagnall, September 10, 1925; "Associate Editor of *The Advocate* Speaks in Longview, Wash."

176. *TA*, April 6, 1929, 2. Other clients included First National Bank of Portland, the City of Portland, the Elks, a coal dealer and cobbler, and the Old Rose Club. *TA*, April 11, 1931, 4; August 1, 1931, 3. She received another "large job of printing from the county" in 1930. See *TA*, November 1, 1930, 2. For more customers, see, for example, *TA*, August 30, 1930, 1, 2.

177. "Response To Our Appeal Pleasing," *TA*, August 10, 1929, 1.

178. "Parasites," *TA*, May 26, 1923, 4. Also see, for example, *TA*, January 31, 1931, 2. Cannady also used the term "race paper leachers" for people who did not support *TA* but expected its help promoting a "social affair" or celebrating a birth or wedding. "Race Papers."

179. "*Advocate* Knockers," *TA*, December 11, 1926, 4.

180. *TA*, May 30, 1925, 4. Also see: "Do You Believe in Reciprocity? We Do," *TA*, April 19, 1924, 4. For more about choosing white shops over Cannady's company, see, for example, "Fault-Finding," *TA*, October 19, 1929, 2.

181. "A New Year."

182. See, for example, *Postal Laws and Regulations*; Beecher and Wawrukiewicz. For an example of the required statement of ownership, see, for example, *TA*, October 18, 1924, 4; March 31, 1927, 2.

183. See, for example, "Editorial," *The Western Outlook*, March 25, 1922, 2.

184. For more about black newspapers, their anniversaries, special issues, or their demise, see, for example, the following in *TA*: "*The Broad Ax*," January 5, 1924, 4; November 1, 1924, 1; "32nd Anniversary," September 26, 1925, 4; "*The Broad-Ax* [*sic*]," October 3, 1925, 4; "*The Broad Ax*," January 9, 1926, 4; "The *Enterprise*," January 9, 1926, 4; "The *Freeman* Quits," February 20, 1926, 4; "*The Broad-Ax* [*sic*]," November 6, 1926, 4; "The Los Angeles *Eagle*," January 8, 1927, 4; December 3, 1927, 2; "A Daily Paper," July 28, 1928, 2; "Success to You, 'Harlem,'" December 1, 1928, 2; "Two Papers Quit," December 1, 1928, 2; "*The Chicago Defender*," May 24, 1930, 2; "A New Paper," August 1, 1931, 2; "*Crisis* Becomes of Age," October 31, 1931, 2; "The Baltimore *Tribune*," December 19, 1931, 2; "Edits New York Newspaper," February 27, 1932, 1. Also interesting was the notice about *The California News*, a "brand new paper" published in Los Angeles with Mrs. Booker T. Washington, Jr., serving as advertising manager. *TA*, May 31, 1930, 2.

185. "A New Publication," *TA*, June 30, 1923, 4. The paper was published by George W. Kennedy, identified as G. W. Kennedy in *TA*. The editor was identified as P. L. Dorman, but it is likely he was Leander Dorman, a native of Arkansas. City Editor Amelia Ives, identified as Mrs. A. B. Ives in *TA*, was described as a public-school teacher in the 1920 Census. All individuals can be found in the *Fourteenth Census*, Pulaski County, Arkansas.

186. "The *Reflexus* Magazine," *TA*, March 28, 1925, 4. For more about the short-lived publication, see Ingham and Feldman, 11.

187. *TA*, May 2, 1925, 4.

188. "*Seer* Editor Writes *Advocate* for Exchange," *TA*, October 10, 1925, 1.

189. The *Seer* was edited by the general missionary secretary; Matthews served in this role. According to Cannady, he also was the former pastor of Portland's AME Zion Church. "Likes *Advocate*," *TA*, April 2, 1927, 1. Also see C. R. Harris, *Historical Catechism Of The A. M. E. Zion Church*, accessible at http://docsouth.unc.edu/church/harris/harris.html.

190. "Likes *Advocate*." A typographical error was corrected. Cannady noted that he was "writing en route to his office at Washington, D.C."; previous correspondence was from Philadelphia. He was not located in online census records for Philadelphia or Washington, D.C., for 1920.

191. Pride, "Negro Newspapers," 179.

192. "*Western Outlook* 30 Years Old," *TA*, September 22, 1923, 4. John Lincoln Derrick appears in the 1920 Census. He was born in California; his parents were born in South Carolina. His wife, Mabel, and her parents also were born in California. *Fourteenth Census*, Alameda County, California. For more about the newspaper, see Mangun, "*The Western Outlook*, 1894-1928." Also see "32nd Anniversary."

193. "*The Philadelphia Tribune*," *TA*, December 6, 1924, 4.

194. "Fortieth Anniversary," *TA*, August 25, 1923, 4. A grammatical error was corrected. The paper still was going strong two years later, prompting her to observe: "As a fighter against discrimination & segregation, Smith has no equal." "42 Years," *TA*, August 22, 1925, 4.

195. Occasionally, white editors also acknowledged *TA*'s milestones. On its thirtieth anniversary, for example, a local paper observed: "*The Outlook* extends sincere congratulations and best wishes to *The Advocate* on its achievement, appearance and constructive attitude. May it long continue." *GO*, September 15, 1933, 2; reprinted as "*Advocate* Congratulated," *TA*, September 16, 1933, 2.

196. *TWO*, August 28, 1915, 2.

197. Editorial in *TWO*; reprinted as "On Our 20th Anniversary," *TA*, September 22, 1923, 4. The original has not been located. *TWO* observed in 1927: "*The Advocate* of Portland, Ore., has entered on its 25th year and if appearances mean anything our Northwest contemporary is making good. ... *The Western Outlook* felicitates our Northwest co-worker and hopes that the *Advocate* may have many more years to carry on the battle for equal rights." "San Francisco *Outlook* Compliments *The Advocate*," *TA*, September 24, 1927, 4. The original has not been located.

198. "*The Advocate* of Portland, Oregon, Celebrated Its Twentieth Birthday Anniversary Last Week," *TBA*, September 15, 1923, 1; reprinted as "What They Say of Us in Chicago," *TA*, September 29, 1923, 4; *TG*, September 22, 1923, 2; reprinted as "Twenty Years Ago," *TA*, October 6, 1923, 4. Smith also acknowledged *TA*'s twenty-sixth anniversary. *TG*, September 21, 1929, 2; reprinted in *TA*, September 28, 1929, 2. *TBA* was founded in Salt Lake City, Utah, by Julius F. Taylor on August 31, 1895. Taylor shifted operations to Chicago in 1901. Sweeney.

199. "What the Chicago Broadax [*sic*] Says of *The Advocate*," *TA*, September 24, 1927, 4. The original has not been located. Cecil Newman commented on *TA*'s twenty-seventh anniversary. See "Minneapolis Editor Praises *The Advocate*'s Record," *TA*, December 13, 1930, 1.

200. Rutherford, SR 270.

201. *TA*, February 7, 1925, 4. Larger issues occasionally were published, such as the ten-page issue for *TA*'s twentieth anniversary.

202. "Graduates Honored," *TA*, June 14, 1924, 1. Louise R. Lewis was born in Oklahoma. Her father, Joda, was born in Mississippi; her mother, Lillian, was born in Canada. Louise had a brother and a sister. *Fourteenth Census*, MC. Jefferson High School Principal Hopkin Jenkins was a Portland Branch member. Membership Report Blank, September 27, 1928, NAACP PB.

Rutherford's father, Edward, and his brother, William, had moved to Portland from South Carolina in 1897 to work as barbers at the Portland Hotel. Edward also was a co-founder of *TA*. By 1911, the men had purchased property at the corner of Broadway and Flanders, where for many years they operated a haberdashery, ice cream parlor, delicatessen, and five-chair barbershop. Octavia's cousin, Otto, graduated from Jefferson High School in June 1928. "Some June Graduates." Edward and William and their families appear in the *Fourteenth Census*, MC. Also see Rutherford, SR 270; McLagan.

One month after graduating, Allen left for Ohio to attend Oberlin College—probably to study at the Conservatory of Music, which had recently established the "first four-year college degree program in music education." He graduated in June 1928, and then did some postgraduate work in music at the Juilliard School of Music. *TA*, September 6, 1924, 1; "Some June Graduates"; "At A Glance: History"; *TA*, July 27, 1929, 3; "Portland Young Man Returns a Finished Artist," *TA*, July 27, 1929, 1.

Allen returned to Portland for a visit in 1931. He and Nellie, his sister, performed and "thrilled a large audience of colored and white at Bethel church." Allen was teaching piano, organ, and music appreciation at Howard University then. "Allen Recital Success," *TA*, August 15, 1931, 1. Two months later, Nellie Allen's photo was published with the news that she had accepted a position at Bishop College in Marshall, Texas. *TA*, October 31, 1931, 3.

203. "William Duncan Allen." The site includes the transcript of an oral interview done with Allen in Chicago when he was eighty-five. In the interview, he notes that he also wrote the words to the class song, which was chosen unanimously from six other submissions. Also see the site for his recollections about the Golden West Hotel.

Chapter Three

1. "Mrs. E. D. Cannady," *TPT*, March 1, 1919, clipping in CS, 78. The original has not been located. Also see "Colored Tenor Sings Tonight," *TPT*, March 21, 1919, 5.

2. "Presenting Negro Artists As a Means Toward Promoting Better Relations Between Races," CS, 77; "Mrs. Cannady Bringing Two Negro Artists," *OSJ*, April 3, 1927, sec. 4, 4.

3. "Mrs. Cannady Bringing." According to the article, Hayes made his second Portland appearance in 1919. It was "a joint recital" with pianist Lawrence B. Brown. For articles about his career, see, for example, the following in *TNYT*: "As Roland Hayes Sings," November 26, 1922, 102; "Music Notes from Other Centres," March 11, 1923, X6; "Music Notes from Other Centres," March 18, 1923, X6; "English Music Notes," May 6, 1923, X4; "Hayes, Negro Tenor, Delights a Throng," December 2, 1923, S8; "Roland Hayes Sings in O. H. Kahn's Home," January 21, 1924, 17; "Roland Hayes Sings To a Vast Throng," January 28, 1926, 14.

4. "Mrs. Cannady Bringing"; The Inflation Calculator. By 1924, *TNYT* reported that he was on track to earn $100,000—more than $1 million today. "Negro Singer's Struggle To Victory," *TNYT Magazine*, November 23, 1924, SM7.

5. "Mrs. Cannady Bringing"; "A Tenor," *Time*, October 8, 1923, 13. Also see: "Music Notes," *TNYT*, October 29, 1923, 19; "Roland Hayes," *TA*, November 3, 1923, 4; "Art Knows No Color Line," *TA*, September 27, 1924, 4. Hayes was awarded the Spingarn Medal in 1924. "Hayes Wins Gold Medal," *TNYT*, June 29, 1924, E2; "Spingarn Medal To Roland Hayes," *TA*, July 5, 1924, 4; "Roland Hayes Receives Warm Welcome in His

Own Country," *TA*, January 19, 1924, 1. Hayes reflected on his career during an interview conducted when he was eighty; see Woolsey.

6. Advertisement, Elwyn Artist Series season 1924-1925, *TA*, September 20, 1924, 4; "The Elwyn Bureau," *TA*, September 20, 1924, 4.

7. "Hayes Sings at Auditorium Tuesday P.M.," *TA*, March 14, 1925, 1.

8. "Roland Hayes to Appear in City for Recital," *TA*, August 15, 1931, 1.

9. "Hayes Here on Saturday Eve.," *TA*, October 17, 1931, 3.

10. "Hayes' Concert Triumph in Art," *TA*, October 31, 1931, 3. A typographical error was corrected. Also see "Hayes Sings Here Tonight," *TA*, October 24, 1931, 3.

11. "He Sang Straight To Our Hearts," *TA*, October 31, 1931, 2.

12. Rosalie Bird-Holmes, "In the Realm of Society," *TA*, October 31, 1931, 3. Identified as L. L. McGruder in the newspaper, he was born in Missouri. His father was born in Kentucky; his mother in Virginia. He was a lodger in Obie and Schuyler Winston's home and was employed as a U.S. Post Office clerk. *Fourteenth Census*, King County. Cannady arranged for Hayes to meet with a voice student and her teacher. Mildreda Wardell to Mrs. Kennedy [*sic*], March 28, [1929], copy in AC. The student was identified only as Suzanne, but Wardell appears in the *Fourteenth Census*, MC. Perhaps coincidentally, one of her three sons was named Roland. Hayes also purchased some "drawings and paintings" from Thelma Johnson, who graduated from an unidentified Portland high school in 1932. "Graduates," *TA*, January 30, 1932, 3.

13. Bird-Holmes.

14. "Associate Editor Addresses Student Body," *TA*, March 15, 1924, 1; "John Payne, Baritone, Captivates His Audience," *TA*, March 15, 1924, 1.

15. He played in Portland in 1921, and was "on the Orpheum circuit" when he came to Portland in 1923 for several engagements. "J. Rosamond Johnson," *TA*, September 8, 1923, 4.

16. "A Sermon in Jazz," *TA*, September 15, 1923, 1; Trixie Breaux, "In the Realm of Society," *TA*, September 15, 1923, 4. Cannady wrote that he performed at the Heilig as part of the "Orpheum bill." Breaux reported that he was at the Orpheum. For a digitized image of the sheet music for the ballad, see the E. Azalia Hackley Collection.

17. Advertisement, *TA*, April 2, 1927, 4; "Highbrown Highbrow," *Time*, November 11, 1929, 72. This article also discusses *Born To Be*, the autobiography Gordon published that year. For one review of a concert featuring the two men, see "Johnson in Negro 'Spirituals,'" *TNYT*, December 7, 1925, 18.

18. Advertisement; "Mrs. Cannady Bringing."

19. *TA*, April 9, 1927, 4.

20. Mrs. P. S. Davidson to Mrs. Cannady, January 10, 1927, CS, 113. The Davidsons do not appear in online census records for 1920 for Crook County, Oregon.

21. Beatrice Cannady to Mrs. P. S. Davidson, January 14, 1927, CS, 114.

22. The men collaborated on more than two hundred songs. For more about the anthem, see "Present at the Creation."

23. Muna Lee, "Songs from the Heart of the American Negro," *TNYT*, October 18, 1925, BR7. Also see "Books and Authors," *TNYT*, December 20, 1925, BR20. A second volume was released in 1926.

24. Cannady to Davidson.

25. Aileen Davidson to Mrs. Cannady, March 2, 1927, CS, 115. She sent Cannady "a gift of exquisite handkerchiefs" for helping with the "club's study of the Negro." *TA*, March 12, 1927, 1. Also see Mrs. Collins W. Elkins to Beatrice Cannady, CS, 116. Margaret Elkins appears in the *Fourteenth Census*, Crook County, Oregon.

26. Cannady to Davidson.

27. "Prineville Club Reviews 'Green Pastures,'" *TA*, September 27, 1930, 1; J. Brooks

Atkinson, "The Best Play; Pulitzer Prize Matters," *TNYT*, May 18, 1930, X1. The play, by Marc Connelly, received the prize for drama in 1930. Davidson's program may have inspired other clubs in the area to study "The Negro in Music and Literature." In December, Cannady reported that women from La Grande and Union had gathered to study poetry by Countee Cullen and songs inspired by Paul Laurence Dunbar. Amanda Zabel, "head of the English department" at the newly founded Eastern Oregon Normal School—now Eastern Oregon University—"closed the program with her very clever review of Marc Connelly's 'The Green Pastures.'" "Club Women Give Program," *TA*, December 13, 1930, 1; "*Green Pastures*," *TA*, May 2, 1931, 3.

28. It opened on February 26, 1930; advertisement, *The Green Pastures*, *TNYT*, February 21, 1930, 26.

29. *The Green Pastures* (1936). Charles Wesley Hill, the actor who played Gabriel, was killed after a performance when he was struck by a taxi. "Charles Wesley Hill, Leading Actor in 'The Green Pastures,' Hit on Street in Harlem," *TNYT*, December 11, 1930, 23; "'Angel Gabriel' Goes To a Green Pasture," *TNYT*, December 15, 1930, 17.

30. For one review, see J. Brooks Atkinson, "New Negro Drama of Sublime Beauty," *TNYT*, February 27, 1930, 20. He reviewed it again when it entered its second year: "They Are Still Green," *TNYT*, March 1, 1931, X1.

31. "To End Long Run Tonight," *TNYT*, August 29, 1931, 19.

32. "*Green Pastures* Coming," *TA*, April 30, 1932, 1.

33. Ibid. Also see "'The Lawd' to Be on Earth in Portland," "'The Lawd' in Portland," *TA*, May 7, 1932, 1.

34. "*Green Pastures*." The Golden West Hotel had closed by then, leaving only the Medley and private homes for visitors.

35. "'Green Pastures,'" *TA*, May 7, 1932, 2. Cannady was at the KGW studio to welcome the cast and choir. "News Briefs," *TA*, May 7, 1932, 3.

36. "News Briefs"; Rosalie Bird-Holmes, "In the Realm of Society," *TA*, May 14, 1932, 3.

37. Advertisement, *The Green Pastures*, *TA*, May 7, 1932, 3; The Inflation Calculator.

38. *TA*, May 14, 1932, 3.

39. Bird-Holmes. The Spingarn Medal is the NAACP's highest honor. The award was instituted by the organization in 1914 to recognize Negroes for extraordinary accomplishments in their field in the preceding year or over a period of time. "R. B. Harrison Gets Spingarn Medal," *TNYT*, March 23, 1931, 24; "Wins Spingarn Medal," *TNYT*, January 11, 1931, 23. Randol's name was corrected.

40. "Celebrities Visit Portland," *TA*, May 28, 1932, 2. Also see "Langston Hughes in Evening of His Own Readings," *TA*, May 14, 1932, 1. For Cannady's views on poetry, see "Negro Poetry as a Reflection of the Race Movement," CS 95-111.

41. Advertisement, *TA*, May 14, 1932, 3; *TA*, May 28, 1932, 3.

42. Normally, the paper was mailed on Fridays so it is possible she delayed *TA* for a day so she could publish the timely news.

43. "Hughes Proves to Be Delightful," *TA*, May 28, 1932, 3.

44. Rampersad, "Chronology." Gold Coast was the former name of Ghana.

45. "Hughes." See also McLaren, 4; Hughes, 95-98.

46. "Hughes." A typographical error was corrected. Ironically, Cannady identified several of the characteristics that would hinder that rise to fame. His interest in travel, for example, led him to Spain, where he covered the Spanish Civil War for the *Baltimore Afro-American*, and to Cuba; Senator Joseph McCarthy later would accuse him of being a Communist. See, for example, Rampersad, "Hughes's Life and Career"; Milton Bracker, "Books of 40 Authors Banned By U.S. in Overseas Libraries," *TNYT*, June 22, 1953, 1; C. P. Trussell, "Dashiell Hammett Silent at Inquiry," *TNYT*, March 27, 1953, 9. Nevertheless,

Hughes was awarded the NAACP's Spingarn Medal in 1960, and by the time he died of congestive heart failure seven years later, his plays and poems had received critical acclaim as she predicted. "As a chronicler of Negro life in America," noted *TNYT*, "Mr. Hughes was 'telling it like it is' before that phrase became a part of the language." "Langston Hughes Called 'Fighter for Human Dignity,'" *TNYT*, May 24, 1967, 32.

47. "N.A.A.C.P. Branch Will Be Host," *TA*, September 21, 1929, 1. The congressman's name is spelled as DePriest and De Priest in various references. I use the latter, in keeping with the entry in "Black Americans in Congress."

48. "Portlanders Hear Negro Lawmaker," *MO*, September 24, 1929, 22.

49. "Nothing Less than Equality," *TA*, September 28, 1929, 1. But she disagreed with his stance on foreigners. See "The Foreigner," *TA*, September 28, 1929, 2. The Fourteenth Amendment, ratified in 1868, granted citizenship to "all persons born or naturalized in the United States." That included former slaves. The Fifteenth Amendment, ratified in 1870, granted black men the right to vote. It decreed that the "right of citizens of the United States to vote shall not be denied or abridged by the United States or by any state on account of race, color, or previous condition of servitude."

50. *TA*, April 6, 1929, 2. For other editorials along this line, see, for example, the following in *TA*: October 20, 1923, 4; February 2, 1924, 4; August 25, 1928, 2; "Law Enforcement," March 30, 1929, 2; "Hoover and the Negro," July 26, 1930, 2.

51. "Portlanders Hear Negro."

52. "Oscar DePriest [*sic*]," *TA*, September 28, 1929, 2. De Priest continued on to Los Angeles. See "Hundreds Move in Long Parade," *TA*, October 19, 1929, 1. Also see "Burned in Effigy," *TA*, July 5, 1930, 1.

53. "Congressman's Sec. Orders *Advocate*," *TA*, October 12, 1929, 1.

54. Advertisement, *TA*, September 24, 1932, 4; David W. Hazen, "De Priest Predicts Victory for Hoover; Negro Representative Here on Tour for President," *TSO*, October 2, 1932, sec. 1, 14; "Hoover Lauded To Negro," *TSO*, October 2, 1932, sec. 1, 14. Cannady was one of the "distinguished colored citizens" named to a committee to "welcome the honorable gentleman [De Priest]." The others were: Wyatt Williams, Clarence Ivey, Dr. Unthank, Reverend Hill, Bonnie Bogle, Wilbur Mercier, W. H. Holliday, the Reverend W. R. Lovell, and the Reverend J. D. Wilson. "DePriest [*sic*] to Speak in Portland Soon," *TA*, September 24, 1932, 1. Also see "Negro Leader Speaks Tonight," *TA*, October 1, 1932, 1; "DePriest [*sic*] Will Be Here," *TSO*, September 25, 1932, 15. He was taken for a drive on the Columbia River Gorge Highway and treated to lunch at Multnomah Falls Inn. He also spoke at Mount Olivet Baptist Church at 1st and Schuyler, and was taken to breakfast at Frances Turner's café on Williams Avenue. For more about Turner, see "Mrs. Turner Quits Restaurant Business," *TA*, April 15, 1933, 1.

55. "Not Until," *TA*, August 20, 1932, 2.

56. "Democratic Presidential Nominee Visits Here," *TA*, September 24, 1932, 4; "Roosevelt Here to Seek Support," *MO*, September 22, 1932, 1; "U.S. Power Resources Must Be Guarded, Says Roosevelt," *MO*, September 22, 1932, 6. Also see "Negro Servants on Roosevelt Special," *TA*, October 1, 1932, 1. During this period, James W. Ford, the first black candidate for vice-president (on the Communist ticket), spoke in Portland. L. Olson, "Negro Vice-President Candidate to Speak," *TA*, September 10, 1932, 1; "First Negro Candidate for Vice Pres. U.S. Speaks Here," *TA*, September 24, 1932, 4; "Communists Name Foster and Ford," *TNYT*, May 29, 1932, 2.

57. "The Party to Support," *TA*, October 22, 1932, 2. Punctuation altered, and a typographical error was corrected.

58. "Franklin D. Roosevelt Biography." Oregonians cast 213,871 votes for Roosevelt and 136,019 votes for Hoover. "Statistics of the Congressional and Presidential Election of

November 8, 1932," 30.

59. "The Election," *TA*, November 12, 1932, 2; "Franklin D. Roosevelt Biography." Also see the following in *TA*: "Oregon Veers To Democratic State," November 12, 1932, 1; "The Negro Vote," December 3, 1932, 2; "The Inauguration," March 4, 1933, 2; "Race Relations," September 2, 1933, 2. Despite the Democratic Party's success at all levels of government, De Priest managed to hold on to his Republican seat in Congress until 1935. "De Priest, Oscar Stanton"; "DePriest [*sic*] Wins," *TA*, November 12, 1932, 2.

60. "Randolph Will Lecture Here," *TA*, July 9, 1932, 1. *The Messenger*, launched in November 1917, featured editorials, political commentary, poetry, fiction, and more, and sold for fifteen cents a copy. Like other periodicals for Negroes, finances always were a problem and the publishing schedule was erratic. It ceased in 1928.

61. "Randolph Urges Negroes to Unite," *TA*, July 16, 1932, 1, 3. While in Portland, Randolph met with porters and attended a dinner party at Branch President Clarence Ivey's home on Tibbetts Street. Rosalie Bird-Holmes, "In the Realm of Society," *TA*, July 16, 1932, 3; "Named on Republican Committee," *TA*, August 20, 1932, 1. For more about red caps, see Arnesen. Ivey was a porter on a private railroad car. He and his parents were born in Georgia. His wife, Rosa, and her parents also were born in Georgia. She worked as a cook in a private car. The couple was described as mulatto. *Fourteenth Census*, MC.

62. "The Evolution and History of the Union." Punctuation corrected. The Brotherhood of Sleeping Car Porters finally was recognized as a union in 1937, when it became the first to sign a collective bargaining agreement with a major U.S. corporation. "The Evolution and History of the Union: Founding of the Union." Also see "Important Decisions," *TA*, June 14, 1930, 2.

63. "Randolph," 3.

64. "Mr. Randolph," *TA*, July 16, 1932, 2.

65. Itinerary of Mr. Wm. Pickens, duing [*sic*] his visit in Portland Oregon, May 26th, 27th, 28th, 29th, 30th, and 31st, 1926, NAACP PB.

66. William Pickens to Lee C. Anderson, May 18, 1926, NAACP PB. It is unclear which, if any, of the talks were canceled. Anderson informed Pickens that "it would be very embarrassing to" the Branch "to alter the program"; thus, the Branch "expect[ed him] to meet every engagement" as arranged. Lee C. Anderson to William Pickens, May 14, 1926, NAACP PB.

67. Mrs. E. D. Cannady to William Pickens, March 26, 1926, NAACP PB. Program organizers may have contacted her directly for assistance based on a prior working relationship with her and the knowledge that she was active in the NAACP. Some Branch members were critical of her efforts and upset that Pickens planned to stay with the Cannadys—his "dear friends"—rather than at the home of another member. William Pickens to Mr. and Mrs. E. D. Cannady, May 26, 1926, NAACP PB. Her interaction with him was viewed as another attempt to advance her own agenda. J. A. Ewing and Lee C. Anderson to Robert W. Bagnall, June 2, 1926, NAACP PB. But the Branch reportedly had asked Cannady to arrange speaking engagements before "white civic bodies" for Robert W. Bagnall, who visited the previous year, since she was "located in the business district and [had] daily contact [with] them." Mrs. E. D. Cannady to Robert W. Bagnall, April 30, 1925, NAACP PB.

68. "Field Sec. N.A.A.C.P. Holds Mass Meeting," *TA*, May 29, 1926, 1.

69. *TA*, June 5, 1926, 4. A spelling error was corrected.

70. "Wm. Pickens Arrives Here By Airplane," *TA*, March 31, 1928, 1.

71. "Pickens Triumphs!" *TA*, May 24, 1930, 1.

72. Ibid. Also see, "Bethel Church," *TA*, May 24, 1930, 2.

73. "Pickens," 1, 4; Pollyann, "In the Realm of Society," *TA*, May 24, 1930, 2. Also see *TA*, May 17, 1930, 1; "Local Briefs," *TA*, May 24, 1930, 4; "Oregon College Students

Petition for 'Return Address,'" *TA*, May 31, 1930, 1. Cannady noted that he spoke before the Civic Club, but likely meant the City Club.

74. "Local Briefs." Jamison was the assistant pastor of Bethel AME Church. He married Cora Coleman, Cannady's widowed sister, on September 16, 1928. *TA*, September 15, 1928, 2.

75. Pollyann; "The Grotto."

76. Pollyann. The gathering was held at the home of Mr. and Mrs. Charles Bishop. A white man by that name appears in the *Fourteenth Census*, MC. Neither Daniel Hill nor Walter Lovell appears in online census records for Oregon for any available years. Hill quickly assumed a leadership role in Portland. He was invited to preach at white churches and he spoke about "The New World Symphony" at an interracial conference at Pacific College. See, for example, "Rev. Hill to Preach at White Church," *TA*, July 19, 1930, 2; "Inter-racial Program Has Negro Speak'r," *TA*, February 7, 1931, 1; "Inter-racial Conference," *NG*, February 5, 1931, 4; "Inter-racial Conference," *NG*, February 12, 1931, 1. Also see, "Addresses Willamette University Student Body," *TA*, March 25, 1933, 1. A brother, William Allyn Hill, worked for a time on the staff of the *Baltimore Afro-American*. He also was a singer and a poet whose work was published in *Lincoln University Poets*, which included poems by Melvin B. Tolson, coach of the award-winning debate team at Wiley University/Wiley College. For more about Hill, see "Lincoln Univ [*sic*] Singer Wil [*sic*] Be Guest Artist," reprint from the *Baltimore Afro-American* in *TA*, February 7, 1931, 3.

77. "Hill Graduates; Social Science School Holds Convention Meet," *TA*, May 31, 1930, 1; *TA*, May 31, 1930, 2. For a brief history of the UO's School of Applied Social Science, see *Oregana*, http://31yearbook.uoregon.edu/index39.html. Cannady was one of the Portlanders who attended the convocation luncheon for the thirty-four students; she proudly observed that Hill was the "only colored graduate." "Hill Graduates." Also see "Brilliant Reception Honors the Hills," and Rev. and Mrs. Daniel G. Hill, Jr., "A Card of Thanks," *TA*, June 28, 1930, 1. He was awarded a master of arts degree by the UO in 1932. Cannady noted he had previously earned a B.A. from Lincoln University in Pennsylvania and a degree in divinity from the Biff School of Theology in Denver, Colorado. "Local Minister Gets Master's Degree," *TA*, June 19, 1932, 1.

78. "Promises to Be Greatest Headline of the Season," *TA*, May 11, 1929, 1. Hooker does not appear in online census records but her sister, Violet, is listed in the 1910 Census. Their mother, Emily, was English; their father, whose first name is not included in the record, was born in Kentucky. *Thirteenth Census*, MC.

Other performers included James McArthur, Alberta Mayo, Guy Jamison, Arthur Harris, and Bernice Williams. James McArthur and his parents were born in the District of Columbia. He worked as a drill press operator in a machine shop His wife, Mattie, and her parents were born in Missouri. *Fourteenth Census*, MC.

Alberta Mayo lived with her mother and stepfather, Kate and James Henderson. Kate was born in Missouri and worked at home as a dressmaker. James was born in Texas; no occupation was listed. *Fourteenth Census*, MC.

79. "Promises." For other reviews of the film, set in 1870, see, for example, Mordaunt Hall, "The Screen," *TNYT*, February 28, 1929, 22; "The New Pictures," *Time*, March 11, 1929, 34.

80. Barrios, 85. Also see Bradley, 244-46; Berry, 28-30. Born Lincoln Theodore Perry, the actor had a long film career that was alternately celebrated—he was the first black performer to sign a deal with a major studio—and criticized—his career was built on playing stereotypical roles. See, for example, Cripps, *Slow Fade to Black*; Watkins. Fetchit was in Portland in 1931 and became a subscriber. *TA*, June 6, 1931, 2.

81. "Promises"; Cripps, *Slow Fade to Black*, 95. He points out that *Dixie* was important because the main characters "strain against circumstance, grow in self knowledge, and positively alter their group identity." Cripps, 239.

82. "Promises"; Cox, 257. Cannady identified the group as the Billbrew [*sic*] chorus. Cox writes that Bilbrew later directed the radio choir "of a major Los Angeles black church."

83. Cox; *TA*, July 1, 1933, 2. For one man's reflections on working for the Admiral Line, which owned the *H. F. Alexander*, see Fleming, "The Admiral Line." For more about the steamer, "known as the Galloping Ghost of the Pacific Coast for her ability to beat railroad schedules between San Francisco and Seattle by more than three hours," see McKenna, 161. A thirteen-year-old named F. Shaw—Freita?—is listed in the 1910 Census. She and her sister, M. Shaw, were living with their mother, V. Curry, and, probably, their stepfather J. W. Curry. *Thirteenth Census*, MC. He was proprietor of Sunflower Camp in Seaside, Oregon, a place where Negroes could vacation. "Camp Owner Has Ministers' Day at Seaside, Oregon," *TA*, June 28, 1930, 1.

84. McCanns, née Lola Shirley Graham, was born in 1896, in Indianapolis, Indiana. She graduated from Lewis and Clark High School in Spokane, Washington, in 1915, then attended a trade school for a time. She "qualified as an office clerk" before relocating to Seattle, where she worked "part-time at a movie house playing the organ and singing between the changing of the reels." Her biographer writes that she married Shadrach McCants, an Ohio native sixteen years her senior, in 1921. The couple had two sons, Robert and David, before divorcing in Portland nine years later. Graham began calling herself Shirley McCanns at that time. Horne, 47; *Fourteenth Census*, King County, Washington. As noted in Chapter Two, she became W. E. B. DuBois' second wife. The Shirley Graham Du Bois papers are housed at the Arthur and Elizabeth Schlesinger Library on the History of Women in America.

85. Horne, 41-43, 44-46.

86. "To Give Lecture on Negroes' Growth," *TPT*, October 19, 1926, 4.

87. "Colored Women Call on Governor," *TA*, January 22, 1927, 1, 3. For a brief biography of Kozer, see "Oregon Secretaries of State Biographical Sketches."

88. "Mrs. McCanns Speaks To Club," *TA*, April 2, 1927, 1. Also see "Chorus Gives Fine Program," *TA*, May 28, 1927, 1. For an advertisement for a "Glorious Jubilee" by the thirty-member chorus, see *TA*, February 19, 1927, 4.

89. "Mary Garden Praises First Negro Opera; 'Tom-Tom' Is Big Success," *TA*, July 16, 1932, 1. Also see "Music: Cleveland Opera," *Time*, July 11, 1932, 24; Horne, 57-62; Hamalian and Hatch, 231-86.

90. "'Tom-Tom,'" *TA*, July 9, 1932, 2.

91. *TA*, August 15, 1931, 1, 3.

92. "Races: Black, White & Blood," *Time*, August 17, 1931, 10. Also see Raper, 471.

93. Raper, v, 1. For more about the Commission, see Pullen. The group's papers are available on microfilm.

94. For more about the Commission, see, for example, the following in *TA*: "A Higher Appreciation," December 6, 1930, 2; "Study Negro History in South; Foster Better Race Relations," October 31, 1931, 1. At the end of the year, she received in the mail a copy of *Lynchings and What They Mean*, "an exhaustive report" of the Commission's findings. *TA*, December 12, 1931, 2. Findings published in the eighty-page pamphlet were incorporated into *The Tragedy of Lynching*. For more about lynching, see, for example, the following in *TA*: "The Malitia [*sic*] Aids," June 14, 1930, 2; "Lynching" and "A New Year," January 2, 1932, 2; "Tuskegee Releas's Lynching Data for 1931," January 2, 1932, 4; "Boy Killed with Crow-Bar," January 9, 1932, 1; "Negro Lynched in Selma, Ala.," September 2, 1933, 1; "That

Lynching," September 2, 1933, 2; "New Anti-lynch Bill Proposed for Congress," November 18, 1933, 1; "Anti-lynching Law," November 18, 1933, 2.

95. "Community Singing Master of California to Direct Chorus," *TA*, August 15, 1931, 1; Beasley, *The Negro Trail Blazers of California*, 184, 212. Bartlett had organized similar choruses in Spokane, Washington, and Coeur d'Alene, Idaho, before going to Portland on August 8. "Songfests," *TA*, August 29, 1931, 2.

96. Beasley, 212.

97. "Community Singing Master"; "The Negro Spirituelle," *TA*, August 15, 1931, 2.

98. "Directs Chorus," *TA*, September 12, 1931, 1; advertisement, *TA*, September 12, 1931, 1.

99. Joseph Macqueen, "Chorus," *TA*, October 3, 1931, 4. He also observed that organist Nellie Allen had "played three excellent solos" and Gwendolyn Hooker had given "two clever, amusing readings."

100. Advertisement, *TA*, January 2, 1932, 3.

101. "Prof. Bartlet's [*sic*] Pupils to Be Heard in Recital," *TA*, July 9, 1932, 1.

102. "Prof [*sic*] Bartlett Presents His Pupils in Recital," *TA*, July 16, 1932, 1.

103. *TA*, October 17, 1931, 2.

104. "Their Music" and "Bethel Church Notes," *TA*, February 6, 1932, 2.

105. "Bethel Choir to Give Spirituals Presentation," *TA*, July 16, 1932, 1; "Chorus Scores Again Thurs.," *TA*, August 6, 1932, 1; "Really Remarkable," *TA*, August 6, 1932, 2. Two open-air concerts were given; no other articles were discovered in *TA*.

106. Baker to the Harmon Award Committee. Cannady invited Mayor Baker to "welcome Dr. Pickens in behalf of the City" in 1919. He told her he would "be glad to deliver the welcoming address." See Mrs. E. D. Cannady to George L. Baker, June 30, 1919; George L. Baker to Mrs. E. D. Cannady, July 1, 1919; Mrs. E. D. Cannady to George L. Baker, July 22, 1919. All items are in A2000-003, SPA.

Chapter Four

1. A spelling error was corrected.

2. "Boost Your Home Town!" *TA*, September 14, 1929, 2. Punctuation altered. Also see "Help Your City!" *TA*, May 18, 1929, 2.

3. "Knockers," *TA*, December 3, 1927, 2; "Help Your City!"; "Hammer Throwers," *TA*, November 15, 1924, 4. Also see "Gossiping To Visitors," *TA*, December 15, 1928, 2.

4. For example, Frederick Douglass, whom she revered, wrote about these themes in "Our Paper and Its Prospects," *NS*, December 3, 1847, 2.

5. "Boosting for Portland," *TA*, July 14, 1928, 2.

6. "No Broadway Here," *TA*, October 24, 1925, 4.

7. *TA*, May 28, 1932, 3. According to the 1920 Census, Jessie Grayson was born in Iowa. Her father was born in Virginia; her mother in Missouri. Her husband, Garven, worked as a hotel waiter. He and his parents were born in Mississippi. The couple had a daughter, Jennie, fifteen, and a son, Garven, thirteen, both of whom were born in California. *Fourteenth Census*, MC. Jennie graduated from Oregon Agricultural College (Oregon State University) in June 1928. "Some June Graduates." Grayson was an excellent contralto and gave many concerts in addition to singing at teas and other events. See, for example, "Jesse [*sic*] Grayson will appear in Concert Oct. 26th," *TA*, October 17, 1931, 3; "Colored Contralto Sings in Concert, October 26," *TSO*, October 25, 1931, 16; *TA*, March 5, 1932, 3; "Y.W.C.A. Notes," *TA*, April 8, 1933, 1. One source notes that she moved later to Los Angeles and enjoyed a successful acting career. Bosco-Milligan Foundation, 42.

Hayes stayed with the Cannadys for eight days during his Portland performance. "We are having a fine visit together," she wrote the NAACP's Walter White. Mrs. E. D.

Cannady to [Walter] White, March 10, 1925, NAACP PB. Her stationery was imprinted "Mrs. E. D. Cannady, Attorney at Law," again implying that she had passed the Bar examination.

8. Bogle, SR442, tape 2 transcript, OHS.

9. *TA*, September 18, 1926, 1. According to the 1920 Census, Lena Bowers and her parents were born in Tennessee. She worked as a laundress for a private family. Her husband, William, and his parents also were born in Tennessee. He worked as a railroad porter. Living with them was their married daughter and her child. *Fourteenth Census*, MC.

10. *TA*, September 25, 1926, 1.

11. "Tacomans Here on Visit," *TA*, October 13, 1923, 1. Fred Harris does not appear in online census records for Pierce County, Washington, for 1920. For a time he contributed "Tacoma News" to *TA*. See, for example, *TA*, January 19, 1924, 1.

12. "Prominent Missouri Educator and Leader Visits Portland," *TA*, August 16, 1924, 4. For brief information about the school, see Wayman. Today, an elementary school is named for the "renowned educator." Cole Elementary School.

13. Bogle, SR442, tape 4 transcript, OHS.

14. Rutherford, SR270.

15. Cannady announced in 1926 the opening of the "very fine" restaurant and urged readers to see the advertisement and patronize the establishment. *TA*, September 11, 1926, 1; "History: The Chinese in Oregon"; Toll, "The Mature Distribution Center." The couple who owned the restaurant, identified as Mr. and Mrs. Stanley Chin in *TA*, appear in the 1920 Census. Stanley was born in Oregon, Lillian in Washington; their parents were born in China. The Chins' infant daughter, Madeline, was born in Oregon. They were described in the census as owners of a grocery store. *Fourteenth Census*, MC.

16. *TA*, April 9, 1927, 4.

17. Cannady noted her party was "cordially recieved" [*sic*] by Lillian Chin. *TA*, September 25, 1926, 1.

18. Pollyann, "In the Realm of Society," *TA*, July 12, 1930, 2. A single man named William Taylor appears in the 1920 Census; he may have married later. If this is the correct individual, he worked as a janitor at the Concordia Club. *Fourteenth Census*, MC. For other examples of entertaining, see, for example, Trixie Breaux, "In the Realm of Society," *TA*, March 29, 1924, 4.

19. Trixie Breaux, "Mah Jong Party Planned," *TA*, November 3, 1923, 4.

20. *TA*, May 14, 1932, 3. The Lays do not appear in online census records for MC for 1920.

21. "Mrs. Cranshaw Honored," *TA*, September 6, 1924, 1. According to the 1920 Census, Lizzie Weeks was born in Washington, D.C. She was identified as black, even though her father was born in Germany, her mother in Spain. She was described as a probation officer. Her husband, George, was born in Ohio. His parents were born in West Virginia. He worked as a packer of crockery [?]. *Fourteenth Census*, MC. Mrs. R. G. Cranshaw does not appear in online census records for Los Angeles County for 1920.

According to the same census, Cinderella Wisdom was born in Kansas and described as mulatto. Her father was born in the "United States," her mother in Missouri. She worked as a maid in a department store. Her husband, Joseph, and his father were born in Kentucky; his mother was born in Virginia. He was described as mulatto and a janitor for the government. *Fourteenth Census*, MC.

22. "History," The Historic Columbia River Highway. See, for example, Trixie Breaux, "Entertained on Highway," *TA*, October 20, 1923, 4; "Visitors See City's Beauties," *TA*, August 2, 1924, 4; "Society Notes," *TA*, August 9, 1924, 4; *TA*, September 18, 1926, 1.

23. "History"; "Introduction: Welcome to Multnomah Falls."

24. See, for example, "Kansas Matrons Royally Entertained," *TA*, August 9, 1924, 4. The boulevard was named for James Terwilliger, who made the cross-country trek from Illinois to Oregon in 1845. See Gaston; Lansing.

25. "Visitors Delightfully Entertained," *TA*, August 25, 1923, 4.

26. "Hotel Notes," *TA*, October 13, 1923, 1; Breaux, "Entertained on Highway."

27. Several addresses were listed for *TA* over the years. In 1909: 133-1/2 5th Street, Room 5. By 1913: 703-4 Rothchild Building. By 1919: Suite 404, Buchanan Building. By 1924: Suite 312-313, Macleay Building. Committee to Mayor Lane; Cannady to Albee; Cannady to Baker, June 30, 1919; *TA*, October 11, 1924, 4.

28. "Local and Foreign News Briefs," *TA*, September 18, 1926, 1. It is possible the guest was Mary Wilson, who was born in Honolulu, Hawaii. Her parents were born in Portugal. Her husband, August, was born in California. His father was born in England; his mother in Kentucky. He did trucking for a box factory and was described as mulatto. The couple had six children. *Fourteenth Census*, Alameda County, California. The hosts were identified as Mr. and Mrs. Q. C. Logan, but were probably John and Clara.

29. *TA*, September 27, 1930, 2. Duke Diggs and his parents, as well as Estella and her parents, were born in Missouri. He worked for a moving and storage company. *Fourteenth Census*, Cole County.

30. "Visitors in City Call to See Us," *TA*, September 8, 1923, 4. The visitors from Austin, Texas, were "Mesdames" Collins and Larrimore. Census records for Pocatello list a likely individual: Modjeska [?] Robertson. *Fourteenth Census*, Bannock County, Idaho. Margie Danley was from Los Angeles. Laura Diamond and her parents were born in Texas. She did general housework for a living. Her husband, James, and his parents also were born in Texas. He was a hotel porter. *Fourteenth Census*, MC. The other Portlanders, Mrs. Patton and Mrs. Simms, do not appear in online census records for MC for 1920.

31. "Leaves for Sister's Bedside," *TA*, October 27, 1923, 1. Clemens reportedly was from Mound City, Illinois, but she does not appear in online census records for Pulaski County for 1920. Clemens spent several weeks with Ella Smith, who does not appear under her own name in online census records for MC.

32. "Prominent Tex. Medic Tours the Northwest," *TA*, September 7, 1929, 1. John Fridia was born in Texas in August 1865; his wife, Mary, also was born in Texas in June 1871. They were married in 1897. *Twelfth Census*, McLennan County, Texas. Mary was described as a druggist [?] in the *Fourteenth Census*, McLennan County. By 1930, Fridia reported that his home was worth $7,000, or about $90,000 today. *Fifteenth Census*, McLennan County; The Inflation Calculator.

33. "In sickness and in health ...." See this site for the scanned image of an advertisement for his practice that ran in *The Clarion Magazine* May 1, 1929.

34. "Prominent Tex. Medic"; Glasrud, 523.

35. *TA*, August 16, 1930, 3.

36. "Noted Jockey Visits Portland," *TA*, September 27, 1930, 1. Ed Lane and his wife were in Portland again in the fall of 1931. He was described once more as a "well-known jockey." Rosalie Bird-Holmes, "In the Realm of Society," *TA*, October 31, 1931, 3. The spelling of Spreckels was corrected. Also see "100,000 Visitors Expected This Week To 69th State Fair," *TOS*, September 21, 1930, 1. The fair closed one week later. For more information, see "Fair History"; Heine.

37. International News Service, *Press Reference Library, Western Edition, Notables of the West*, vol. II (New York: International News Service, 1915), 300. One of his horses was Morvich, the first California-bred horse to win the Kentucky Derby. "Morvich Wins Kentucky Derby By Two Lengths," *TNYT*, May 14, 1922, 1.

38. “Noted Jockey.”

39. “Rev. J. H. Wilson Here,” *TA*, September 15, 1923, 1. Wilson was en route to a conference in Spokane, Washington.

40. “The Great 1906 San Francisco Earthquake.” Wilson does not appear in online census records for San Francisco or Alameda counties, California, for 1900 or 1910.

41. “History of Bethel A.M.E. Church”; “1906 Earthquake: Fire Fighting.”

42. “History of Bethel.”

43. “Rev. J. H. Wilson.”

44. “Conventions,” *TA*, July 5, 1930, 2.

45. “Welcome!” *TA*, July 12, 1930, 2.

46. “The Convention,” *TA*, August 13, 1932, 2. For more about the need to list rooms and cars with the committees in charge, see “The Convention,” *TA*, August 27, 1932, 2.

47. “The Legion Comes,” *TA*, September 10, 1932, 2.

48. “The Convention,” August 13, 1932. A spelling error was corrected.

49. Advertisements, *TA*, September 10, 1932: Arrow Cleaners, 4; Broadwill Drug Store, 6; Dr. DeNorval Unthank, 4; Elde’s Packard Towing Car Service, 2; United States National Bank, 4. The advertisement for Elde’s business mentioned only his last name, but Norwegian Iver Elde appears in the *Fourteenth Census*, MC.

50. *TA*, September 24, 1932, 3; “History,” Crystal Ballroom. When it was constructed in 1914, “it was said to be unique on the Pacific Coast”; today it may be the only mechanical floor left in the U.S. The attendee from Arizona was Benjamin H. Mills. “The Vet of Many Medals,” *TA*, September 24, 1932, 2. For other activities, see, for example, “Colored Vets Honor Their White Buddies,” *TA*, October 1, 1932, 1.

51. Isaac L. Moore, “Visiting Legionnaire Says Separate Arrangements Vicious,” *TA*, September 17, 1932, 1; “Program of Colored Legionnaires.”

52. Moore. Punctuation altered, and a typographical error was corrected. He listed his address as Minneapolis, but he does not appear in online census records for Hennepin County, Minnesota, for 1920. Also see “Prominent Minnesotan Attends Convention,” *TA*, September 24, 1932, 2. Committee members were Wilbur Mercier, Ervin Flowers, and Leonard Crosswhite. For some information about Mercier, see “Local Chairman Much in Demand,” *TA*, September 10, 1932, 1. Flowers was born in Oregon and worked as a truck driver. He was living with his parents, Allen and Louisa. Living next door were Lloyd and Madaline Flowers—perhaps a brother and sister-in-law. *Fourteenth Census*, MC. Also see “Thanks *Advocate* Staff,” *TA*, September 24, 1932, 2.

53. “Program.” Some homeowners were renting “first-class” rooms for $2 a night.

54. “Segregating Legionnaires,” *TA*, September 17, 1932, 2.

55. “Our Visitors,” *TA*, July 19, 1924, 4.

56. “Newcomers to Make Portland Home,” *TA*, May 3, 1924, 1. Mrs. Robinson was not identified, and the couple does not appear in online census records for Michigan for any available years. For an advertisement for “Mme. M. Robinson Beauty Culturist,” see, for example, *TA*, June 21, 1924, 4.

57. “Texans May Return to Live,” *TA*, July 26, 1924, 4. Mrs. Miller was not identified, and the couple does not appear in online census records for El Paso County, Texas, for 1920. Charles Miller and Henry Myles reportedly became “warm friends” while serving together with the Twenty-fifth U.S. Infantry, one of four regiments that came to be known as the Buffalo Soldiers. See also “Old Supporters,” *TA*, January 23, 1932, 3. Mrs. Myles was not identified, and the couple does not appear in online census records for MC for any available years.

58. “Realty Men Intend to Stop Sales To Negroes, Orientals,” *ODJ*, March 6, 1919, 5. Longtime Portlanders who participated in an oral history project done in the 1980s

recalled the anxiety and humiliation inherent in house hunting. See interviews with the following people: Inez Mayberry; Marie Smith; Mr. and Mrs. J. Henson. Mss 2854, OBHP. Also see Bogle, SR 442, tapes 1 and 2 transcripts, OHS. Also see McElderry.

59. "Owner Will Rent To Colored Tenants," *TA*, March 15, 1930, 1. The spelling of Hoesley's name was corrected and capitalization altered. He does not appear in online census records for any available years, but his death certificate is dated March 18, 1937, Multnomah County. Wendell. Hoesley said "his father ... was well-known on the police force in ... Portland for a quarter of a century [and] had colored friends"; Hoesley "went to school with colored people" and could not understand "why any difference should be made regarding their presence in his district, Albina, where he was born." The Albina neighborhood has had a troubled history of race relations. For more about this, see, for example, the Oregon History Project, http://www.ohs.org/education/oregonhistory/index.cfm.

60. Advertisement, *TA*, May 24, 1930, 2.

61. "Gossiping To Visitors," *TA*, December 15, 1928, 2. A spelling error was corrected.

62. "Editor Impressed with Portland."

63. "Gossiping." *TCE* commented on knocking, too. See, for example, "Less Knocking and More Boost Is What We Need," *TCE*, April 3, 1915, 4.

64. Rutherford, SR 270.

65. *TA*, September 6, 1924, 4.

66. "Portland Is Growing."

67. "Purchase Home," *TA*, November 24, 1923, 3. Cannady misspelled the name as Garnett, but the family appears in the 1920 Census. Roy, Willis, and their parents were born in Texas. The couple had two daughters. *Fourteenth Census*, MC.

68. Almus Morrow is listed as compositor in the March 19, 1927, issue. He may have brokered a deal for his own family: they moved into a "six-room flat at 695 Kearney Street" in 1923. *TA*, November 3, 1923, 1.

69. Advertisement, *TA*, October 13, 1923, 1. Also see October 27, 1923, 1; November 24, 1923, 1; December 8, 1923, 2.

70. "Buys Furnished Home," *TA*, November 10, 1923, 1. A woman with this name appears in the 1910 Census. If the same individual, she was described as mulatto and an officer of the Lincoln Institute in Jefferson Township—specifically a dining-room matron at the state normal school. Schweich and her parents were born in Missouri. *Thirteenth Census*, Cole County, Missouri. However, a person named I. M. Schweich from Wichita, Kansas, signed a petition to ban *The Birth of a Nation* in Portland. J. A. Merriman, Mrs. E. D. Cannady, et al. to the Mayor, et al., July 12, 1915, A2000-003, SPA.

71. *TA*, September 27, 1924, 1.

72. Ibid.; *TA*, September 1, 1923, 8. The Agees do not appear in online census records for MC for any available years.

73. Advertisement, The Elks Sanitary Barber Shop, *TA*, March 22, 1924, 4.

74. "*Advocate* Agents," *TA*, March 19, 1927, 2.

75. "Launch Business New," *TA*, September 7, 1929, 1. A typographical error was corrected. See the advertisements for the Cannady Real Estate Co. in *TA*, September 7, 1929, 4; April 5, 1930, 4. Some years earlier *TA* had observed, "It seems easier for a camel to crawl through the eye of a needle than for a colored family to rent a house in Portland. Why not wake up and buy your homes?" *TA*, November 3, 1923, 4.

76. *TA*, September 1, 1923, 5; "Hotel Notes," *TA*, July 19, 1924, 4. According to the 1920 Census, James Bell and his parents were born in Georgia. His wife, Estella [?], was born in Kansas. Her father was born in Missouri; her mother in Kentucky. She did work in her "own home," but the type of work she did is unreadable. *Fourteenth Census*, MC.

77. "Colored Photographer Sells Out," *TA*, September 20, 1924, 1.

78. September 1, 1923.

79. *TA*, June 7, 1924, 4. Also see *TA*, June 21, 1924, 1.

80. "Colored Photographer." The article did not mention to whom he sold the studio.

81. See, for example, *TA*, August 11, 1923, 1; September 15, 1923, 1.

82. Jiggs, "Portland Bees and Freedman [*sic*] All-star Team to Match Here Sunday," *TA*, August 16, 1924, 1; Jiggs, "Score 4-4, 'Bees' Play Well," *TA*, August 23, 1924, 1; Merriman, Cannady, et al. to Mayor, et al. "Pilot" referred to the team's manager. "For black baseball teams, this was often a player-manager or an owner-manager." Brian Carroll, e-mail message to author, November 13, 2009.

83. "Boost Your Home Town!"

84. "The J. K. Gill Company's Fortieth Anniversary," in *The Publishers' Weekly*, vol. LXXIII, January-June 1908 (February 8, 1908): 814; advertisement, The J. K. Gill Co., *TA*, September 1, 1923, 6.

85. Advertisements, *TA*, September 1, 1923: Portland Railway, Light & Power Co., 3; Lipman Wolfe & Co., 7.

86. "One of Portland's Pretty Modistes," *TA*, September 1, 1923, 7. A photograph accompanied the caption. Isa Vessell and her parents were born in Louisiana. She worked out of her home at 92 North 12th Street doing dressmaking. Her son, Harry, also was born in Louisiana. Living with them were Vessell's brother and three lodgers. *Fourteenth Census*, MC. "Attorney Eugene J. Minor," *TA*, September 1, 1923, 10. A photograph accompanied the caption.

87. "Looking Back Twenty Years," *TA*, September 8, 1923, 4.

88. Bosco-Milligan, 32-33.

89. One source notes that Allen closed the hotel in 1931 due to the Depression. "Tremont House, Old Town/Chinatown, Portland, OR." A caption under a photograph of his daughter, Nellie, reported that he was proprietor of the Medley Hotel. *TA*, October 31, 1931, 3.

90. "The Pullman Porters," *TA*, February 18, 1933, 2. The long editorial discussed inequities in staffing trains and the plight of the porters, who "left good jobs back in their home towns when sent for to come to Portland to work as porters."

91. "Laying of [*sic*] Colored Workers," *TA*, October 28, 1933, 2. In 1930, 85.3 percent of black men in Portland were "gainfully employed." That equates to 948 of 1,112 individuals. In 1920, it was 96 percent. *Negroes in the United States 1920-1932*, Table 20, 300. Another census reported that fifty-nine Negro men (4.9 percent of the total male Negro population of 1,210) were "out of a job, able to work, and looking for a job" in Oregon in 1930. *Fifteenth Census of the United States: 1930, Unemployment*, Table 4, 826.

92. "The Business Woman," *TA*, November 11, 1933, 2. A spelling error was corrected. Apparently, Catherine Byrd was not related to the Byrds living in Portland.

93. "Golden West Hotel Again Opens Doors; Gala Opening Sunday Public Invited," *TA*, November 11, 1933, 1. Also see the advertisement for the "gala opening," *TA*, November 11, 1933, 1. For advertisements welcoming and congratulating Byrd, see *TA*, November 11, 1933, 2. Byrd's daughter, Sylvia Lewis, was completing her studies at a business school in Denver and planned to join the hotel as bookkeeper after graduation. Byrd's oldest son worked as a clerk and elevator operator. Cannady wrote that "other assistants" included a Mr. Ewing from Kansas City, Missouri, Sammie Blanchard—who may have been a Portlander but does not appear in census records for 1920—and a Mr. Duncan. This may have been John A. Duncan, who was originally from Jamaica and worked as a railroad porter. *Fourteenth Census*, MC.

94. "The Business Woman."

95. "Hundreds Attend Grand Opening of Hotel; Business Woman Delivers the Welcome Address," *TA*, November 18, 1933, 3. For more about the accommodations, see *TA*, November 18, 1933, 3.

96. "Golden West Hotel." A spelling error was corrected. Cannady provided few details about Byrd, who may have been in her early 40s. She was "a recent arrival from Denver," but Byrd may have been visiting her daughter there. She does not appear in online census records for Denver County for 1920. Cannady noted that Byrd had lived in Portland "a good many years ago," but Seattle was "her native home." She does not appear in online census records for Oregon or Washington for any available years.

97. "Spirit of Cooperation Shown," *TA*, November 18, 1933, 2. Two weeks later, Cannady printed a list of the out-of-town guests who were staying at the New Golden West. *TA*, December 2, 1933, 1.

98. The last available issue of *TA* is December 2, 1933, so more research needs to be done to tell the complete story of the New Golden West Hotel and the ongoing effect the Depression had on black Portlanders. One source notes that Byrd "managed to keep it open only two years." "Tremont House." The Golden West was in the news again in 1989—the centennial of Cannady's birth—when Kathryn Bogle and others in the black community launched a drive to reclaim the hotel's name and get it listed on the National Register of Historic Places. The Friends of the Golden West were successful on one count: the Broadmoor, as it was then called, was restored to its original name. But the building, now part of Chinatown and owned by Central City Concern, still has not been placed on the historic register. See "Kathryn Hall Bogle"; "Tremont House."

99. "Support Negro Business," *TA*, December 10, 1932, 2. Punctuation added; Cannady, "The Strivings of a Race." For a similar editorial, see "Knocking Negro Business," *TA*, March 4, 1933, 2.

100. "Support Negro Business."

101. "No Depression Here Says Writer," *TA*, April 9, 1932, 1. The Allens first appear in the 1910 Census. Ernest and his parents were born in Kentucky. He worked as a janitor. His wife, Ella, was born in Kansas. Her parents were born in Kentucky. The Allens had been married ten years and had one son. *Thirteenth Census*, Umatilla County, Oregon. Also see *Fourteenth Census*, Umatilla County.

102. "Among Pendleton's Leading Citizens," *TA*, January 3, 1931, 1.

103. See *TA*, March 4, 1933, 3; "Among Pendleton's Leading Citizens."

104. *TA*, February 2, 1929, 2; *TA*, June 6, 1931, 4. Johnson does not appear in online census records for Baltimore County for 1920 or 1930.

105. "Unthanks Arrive Safely," *TA*, July 16, 1932, 1. Also see "Dr. Unthank Called," *TA*, July 2, 1932, 1; "Dr. Unthank's Uncle Dead," *TA*, December 3, 1932, 1; "The Passing of Dr. Unthank," *TA*, December 3, 1932, 2.

106. "Local Business Man Tells of Conditions," *TA*, February 1, 1930, 1. C. M. Prather does not appear in online census records for MC for 1920.

107. "Bird [*sic*] Says Work Poor," *TA*, February 28, 1931, 1. The family's name was spelled Byrd.

108. *TA*, August 20, 1932, 1. Alex Coffey does not appear in online census records for Oregon for any available years. Cannady did not include details about what he did for the city.

109. "Store Restores Discharged Workers; N.A.A.C.P. Wins Recent Victory," *TA*, January 17, 1931, 1. Also see *TA*, January 10, 1931, 2, and Ivey, "Annual Report of President." The employees were not identified in the story. Ivey was elected Branch president at the end of 1930. "Our New President," *TA*, December 20, 1930, 2.

110. "Dr. Coleman to Address Forum," *TA*, March 14, 1931, 1. None of these individuals appears in online census records for MC for 1920. For more about Chuck Williams and Bob Robinson, the first black football players at the University of Oregon, see the following in *TA*: "Colored Men Win Athletic Honors," October 1, 1927, 2; E. M. Flowers, "University Men Speak To Boys Club," March 23, 1929, 2; F. H. Young, "Chuck and Bob Praised," October 27, 1928, 2; "Crack Players on the Webfoot Eleven," October 26, 1929, 3. Also see "The Forgotten Ducks."

111. "1933!" *TA*, January 7, 1933, 2.

112. *TA*, August 6, 1932, 1; "Young Man Buys New Automobile," *TA*, July 26, 1930, 1. Toby Johnson does not appear in online census records for Oregon for any available years.

113. "News Briefs," *TA*, August 6, 1932, 1. J. W. Simms does not appear in online census records for Oregon for 1920.

114. *TA*, April 25, 1931, 3.

115. *TA*, September 10, 1932, 2.

116. "OWR & N Shops Among Last to Cut on Help," *TA*, August 29, 1931, 3.

117. The outlook in Washington was grim. E. H. Holmes, who contributed the semi-regular column, "Spokane Happ'nings," reported that "a large number of race men looking for work [were] passing through" his city in spring 1931. It is possible this was Emmett Holmes, who appears in the *Thirteenth Census*, Spokane County. E. H. Holmes, "Spokane Happ'nings," *TA*, April 18, 1931, 2.

118. *TA*, August 27, 1932, 1. For more about the "transient movement," see, for example, "The New Deal and the Home," *TA*, October 28, 1933, 2. George Williams does not appear in online census records for California for 1920; Jim Bland does not appear in online census records for Oregon for 1920.

119. *TA*, January 28, 1933, 2. George Sanders reportedly was a former Portlander, but he does not appear in online census records for MC for 1900, 1910, or 1920.

120. *TA*, January 14, 1933, 4. George Sampson does not appear in online census records for Mississippi for 1920.

121. *TA*, December 10, 1932, 4. Many black men named Sam Johnson appear in the 1920 Census of Texas.

122. "Our Economic Failure," *TA*, May 31, 1930, 2. Punctuation added. Statewide in 1930, 24,841 white people (20,750 men, 4,091 women, out of the total white population of 937,029) were "out of a job, able to work, and looking for a job." In Multnomah County, 14,506 people (12,193 men, 2,313 women, out of 159,979 "gainful workers") were "out of a job, able to work, and looking for a job." *Fifteenth Census of the United States: 1930, Unemployment*, Table 4, 826; Table 10, 832.

123. For information about the Chicago movement, organized by the *Whip*, see, for example, Smith, "Don't Buy Where You Can't Work Movement (1929-1941)," 236-37. For more about the Memphis boycott, see Wells, 53-55.

124. "Graduation, Then What," *TA*, June 14, 1930, 2. A typographical error was corrected. For another editorial along this line, see, for example, "The Negro's Weakness," *TA*, December 3, 1932, 2.

125. "Restaurant Draws Color-Line," *TA*, July 26, 1930, 1. Cannady reported that it was the Manning restaurant. Pearl Stewart does not appear in online census records for MC for 1920. "Drawing Color Lines," *TA*, July 26, 1930, 2.

126. See, for example, the following in *TA*: June 28, 1930, 3; July 5, 1930, 2; August 16, 1930, 2; May 16, 1931, 1; October 17, 1931, 2; July 16, 1932, 4; September 10, 1932, 1. Du Bois also encouraged readers to boycott white businesses that refused to hire Negroes. See "Buying and Selling," *TC*, November 1931, 393. He began a series about Negro unemployment in the December 1931 issue. See "Negroes and the Relief of

Unemployment," *TC*, December 1931, 414-15. Also see *TA*, October 24, 1931, 2; "Slavery Still in Evidence," *TA*, November 28, 1931, 1.

127. *TA*, January 3, 1931, 2. John Minor does not appear in online census records for MC for 1920.

128. "Jobs," *TA*, March 14, 1931, 2.

129. *TA*, March 21, 1931, 2.

130. "What of the Future?" *TA*, June 27, 1931, 2.

131. For some information about job prospects for both black women and men, see, for example, Emma Hepburn, SR 266, OBHP. Also see "Social Lines," *TA*, April 30, 1927, 2; "Lays off Help," *TA*, June 19, 1932, 3.

132. "News Briefs," *TA*, October 29, 1932, 1. Louise Randolph was born in Alabama. Her father, Benjamin, her mother, Clarice, and their parents also were born in Alabama. He worked as a railroad porter. Living with the family was Clarice's mother, Matilda Johnson. *Fourteenth Census*, MC.

133. "Help Cut Down," *TA*, April 2, 1932, 3; "Baby Born in Bend," *TA*, March 12, 1932, 3. Kate Lewis appears in the 1920 Census. She and her parents were born in Kentucky. Lewis, a divorcée, was working as a maid at a dance hall. She was living with her sister and brother-in-law, Jeanne and Ferdinand Myers, and a boarder named Duke Jackson. *Fourteenth Census*, MC. Mrs. Duke apparently had her daughter, Betty Jean, in Bend, where her mother and grandmother lived. Stanton and Josephine Duke do not appear in online census records for MC for 1920. Cannady subsequently reported that the Dukes had moved to Omaha, Nebraska. *TA*, July 16, 1932, 1. Rutherford said a comfort station was located in downtown Portland at 6th Avenue and Yamhill Street. Rutherford, SR 270.

134. "*Advocate* Establishes Relief Headquart'rs," *TA*, January 28, 1933, 3. Surprisingly, though, employment rates for women increased between 1920 and 1930. In 1920, 39 percent of black women in Portland were gainfully occupied. By 1930, the number was 43.1 percent (383 women out of 888). *Negroes in the United States 1920-1932*, Table 20, 300.

135. "*Advocate* Establishes." A typographical error was corrected.

136. "Zion Church Notes," *TA*, February 25, 1933, 2. Also see "Helping Through Church," *TA*, March 18, 1933, 2.

137. "Davidson's Bakery Company Aids the Unemployed," *TA*, February 11, 1933, 1; *TA*, March 4, 1933, 3. A typographical error was corrected. Davidson's was located at 168 East 22nd; Cannady wrote that *TA* was picking up the bread and delivering it to the church.

138. March 4, 1933, 3; "First A.M.E. Zion Church," *TA*, March 4, 1933, 2. Also see "Patronize 'Em, Folks!" *TA*, February 16, 1929, 2.

139. John P. Davis, "What Price National Recovery," *TC*, December 1933, 271.

140. Mary White Ovington, "The Year of Jubilee," *TC*, January 1934, 7.

141. *TC*, January 1934, 7.

142. "*The Crisis* for 1934," *TC*, December 1933, 269.

Chapter Five

1. James Weldon Johnson to Beatrice Cannady, February 11, 1928, CS, 39; reprinted in *TA*, March 24, 1928, 3.

2. Johnson appreciated her "kind acceptance" of the invitation to speak in L.A. James Weldon Johnson to Mrs. E. D. Cannady, February 25, 1928, copy in AC. The address she planned to give in Chicago, "How to Make the N.A.A.C.P. More Bi-Racial," was read to the audience on June 25, 1926. She reported it "elicited much praise" and that *TC* "anticipate[d] publishing it." *TA*, August 7, 1926, 1. Robert Bagnall said he would "offer" a revised version to the journal because it had "valuable information as to how to best

promote race relations." Robert Bagnall to Beatrice Cannady, October 6, 1926, NAACP PB. Issues of *TC* published between July and December were reviewed, but her speech was not located.

3. I. L. Patterson to James Weldon Johnson, June 22, 1928, copy in AC.

4. "Mrs. E. D. Cannady to Address Colored Peoples' Meeting," *OSJ*, March 4, 1928, sec. 1, 6; *ODJ*, March 10, 1928, 4.

5. *TA*, March 31, 1928, 2. Teacher Hilma Anderson invited her to speak to four history classes at Lincoln High School, but Cannady had to decline the invitation. *TA*, June 16, 1928, 4.

6. "Pleads for Goodwill," *TA*, March 3, 1928, 1; *TA*, April 28, 1928, 2, 4.

7. "Mrs. Cannady Will Speak on the Negro," *OLP*, May 25, 1928, 6; "A Brilliant Young Man." For more about Portland Labor College, see Lembke.

8. Redwine, e-mail message to author, June 29, 2004.

9. "Mrs. Cannady Goes To Convention," *TA*, June 16, 1928, 3.

10. Her address may have been longer than thirteen pages because there are no concluding remarks in the extant copy of the speech. Since she began her address by acknowledging the master of ceremonies, members of the NAACP, and "friends," it is likely that she would have offered a formal conclusion.

11. "N.A.A.C.P. Convention Largest Ever Held; Streets Decorated; Crowd at Station Greets Officials," *TA*, July 21, 1928, 1. A typographical error was corrected. Also see "Conference Delegates Due Today; Negro Race Association Slated to Open Sessions Here Tomorrow," *LAT*, June 26, 1928, part II, 3; "Delegates Arrive for Negro Meet; Mass Meeting Will Open Conference of National Association Here," *LAT*, June 27, 1928, part II, 13.

12. For a copy of the conference program, see CS, 40. Also see "Prominent Men and Women to Address NAACP in Los Angeles," *TCE*, June 22, 1928, 7. For more about Hudson, see "Young Dentist Foe of Race Proscription." He does not appear in online census records for Los Angeles County, California, for any available years. Herbert Hoover ran for president on the Republican ticket in 1928; Al Smith was the Democratic candidate.

For more about the remaining days of the conference, see the following in *LAT*: "Negro Music of All Ages to Be Heard at Shrine," June 28, 1928, part II, 9; "Negro Welfare Topics Debated," June 29, 1928, part II, 3; "Negro-Baby Contests Discussed," June 30, 1928, part II, 9; "Colored Residents to Parade; Thousands Will Take Part in Event Today As Feature of National Conference," July 1, 1928, part II, 7; "Young Lauds Colored Race; Governor Gives Talk at Shrine Auditorium," July 2, 1928, part II, 2; "Colored Group Gives Address," July 4, 1928, part II, 18. During the conference, the *Times* reported that black people who had purchased property in a specific tract of land would "be permitted to hold their property in spite of a clause in their deeds discriminating against colored persons." "Residence Fight Won By Negroes," *LAT*, July 4, 1928, part II, 3. Cannady reprinted the text of the "Address to the American People" that was adopted at the conference. "Address To American People," *TA*, July 21, 1928, 3.

13. "N.A.A.C.P. Host Over-run Huge Philharmonic Auditorium," *TCE*, June 29, 1928, 7.

14. The title varies slightly, depending on the source. The one used here was included in "Mrs. Cannady Goes To Convention." For two slightly different versions, see the program, or CS, 38. For a history of the church, see "About Us," Second Baptist Church.

15. Cannady, "Negro Womanhood As a Power in the Development of the Race and the Nation." She noted later, "According to the *Los Angeles Daily Times*, and comments of those who heard it, her address was among the outstanding ones of the Conference." *TA*, July

14, 1928, 3. Also see "Writer Impressed with Associate Editor's Work," *TA*, July 14, 1928, 1. *LAT* articles cited earlier do not mention her speech. An essay in CS, probably written by her to support her Harmon Award nomination, stated that her speech was "considered a masterpiece." CS, 38. *TCE* may have covered her talk, but the June 29th and July 6th issues are missing.

16. "Advertisers to Hear Mrs. Cannady," *ODJ*, July 31, 1928, 10. She spoke to the Women's Advertising Club at the Benson Hotel; Eleanor Colwell introduced her. Nellie Franklin played some "violin numbers."

17. "Tells of Trip South," *TA*, July 21, 1928, 4. She also attended many "social affairs given in her honor," including an afternoon tea, luncheons, sightseeing trips, a buffet supper, an "ocean bathing party," a picnic and barbecue, a "progressive breakfast," and a dancing party. After returning to Portland, Cannady wrote a long article about the Hefflin Manufacturing Company to share with readers the successful story of its founder, Leon M. Hefflin. "How a Young Negro Succeeded in Business," *TA*, July 21, 1928, 1. He does not appear in online census records for Los Angeles County for 1920 or 1930.

18. [Robert W. Bagnall] to Alice Handsaker, July 6, 1926, NAACP PB.

19. Alice Handsaker to Robert Bagnall, June 30, 1926, NAACP PB.

20. *TA*, June 12, 1926, 1.

21. *TA*, March 28, 1925, 1.

22. *TA*, May 23, 1925, 1; *TA*, May 30, 1925, 1.

23. May 30, 1925.

24. Hilma Anderson to Mrs. Cannady, July 20, 1929, CS, 118-19. Emphasis in the original. Anderson appears in the *Fourteenth Census*, MC.

25. "Interracial Teas," CS, 169.

26. "Inter-racial Good-will," *TA*, December 11, 1926, 2.

27. "News Briefs Local and Foreign," *TA*, April 24, 1926, 1. Cannady misspelled the teacher's last name; it has been corrected based on census records and a signed letter from him to Cannady. E. E. Schwarztrauber to Beatrice Cannady, February 20, 1929, CS, n.p. He appears in the *Fourteenth Census*, MC.

28. "Greatness Should Not Be Measured By Color of Skin," *TA*, April 24, 1926, 2.

29. "Some Reactions of Portland High School Students To the Study of the Negro," *TA*, May 29, 1926, 1. Later, Schwarztrauber sent Cannady "a collection of anonymous 'confessions'" written by students in Hilma Anderson's classes. The pupils had just completed "a study of race problems in America" and were asked to work on their essays at home "with due deliberation." Schwarztrauber felt some of the essays were "quite good" and knew Cannady would want them for her "collection." E. E. Schwarztrauber to Beatrice Cannady, February 20, 1929, CS, n.p.

30. "Hi School Students Study Race Problem; Some Reactions of Portland High School Students To the Study of the Negro," *TA*, April 24, 1926, 1. Cannady also shared them with Robert Bagnall so he could see "their reaction to [her] course on Negro history." Bagnall to Cannady, October 6, 1926.

31. Cannady hoped *Advocate* readers would comment on the compositions. Only one letter was published, however: "Interested in High School Letters," *TA*, May 8, 1926, 1.

32. "Would Educate Him Industrially and Culturally," *TA*, April 24, 1926, 1.

33. "Undecided on the Negro Question," *TA*, April 24, 1926, 2.

34. "Thinks It Is a Good Thing to Teach the Subject," *TA*, April 24, 1926, 2.

35. "A Negro Is Just a Negro," *TA*, May 1, 1926, 4.

36. "Has Eyes Opened," *TA*, May 15, 1926, 2.

37. "Whites Cause Half of Race Problem," *TA*, May 15, 1926, 1.

38. "Understands Clearly Negroes' Need," *TA*, April 24, 1926, 2.

39. "Trivial Prejudice Keeps Negro Down," *TA*, April 24, 1926, 2. Punctuation added. Also see "A Negro Is Just a Negro."

40. *TA*, May 22, 1926, 1.

41. Ibid. A typographical error was corrected.

42. "Some Reactions."

43. Beatrice Cannady to John L. Stewart, November 17, 1926, CS, 50.

44. "Negro History Week," CS, 29.

45. *TA*, January 22, 1927, 3. Cannady gave many more talks to students at Lincoln High School. See, for example, *TA*, January 19, 1929, 2.

46. "Mrs. Cannady Lectures."

47. "Woman Editor, Educator, on *Oregonian* of the Air," *TSO*, September 6, 1931, sec. 4, 4.

48. "Mrs. E. D. Cannady to Address."

49. *ODJ*, March 10, 1928, 4.

50. *TA*, January 18, 1930, 4; "Helps Students; *Advocate* Called Upon for Help from Students," *TA*, April 23, 1932, 1.

51. Hugh B. Fouke, Jr., to Beatrice Cannady, April 26, 1926, CS, 93-94. He does not appear in online census records for Oregon for 1920.

52. See "Collecting Library of Negro Literature," CS, 84-91.

53. Richard Brink to Beatrice Cannady, January 30, 1927, CS, 112-13. Also see "Helps Students."

54. "Helps Students." Harold F. Gosnell's papers are housed at the Harry S. Truman Library and Museum.

55. Hansen, 583, 584. Also see Wolfgang Saxon, "Harold Foote Gosnell, 100, Scholar of American Politics," *TNYT*, January 16, 1997, D25. Gosnell did not cite her or *TA* in his book.

56. "The Pathway of Progress," *TA*, March 28, 1925, 4.

57. "Mrs. E. D. Cannady Guest of University," *WC*, March 10, 1926, 1; reprinted under the same headline in *TA*, April 3, 1926, 1. Also see: "Mrs. Cannady Speaks at Williammette [*sic*] Univ.; Addresses Pi Gamma Mu and F.O.R.," *TA*, March 13, 1926, 1; *TA*, March 6, 1926, 1; Sciva Bright Laughlin to Beatrice Cannady, March 3, 1926, CS, 42. The editor of *WC* took out a one-year membership in the NAACP during Cannady's visit. Cannady to Bagnall, April 13, 1926.

58. "Mrs. Cannady Speaks."

59. Cannady to Bagnall. Also see [Robert W. Bagnall] to Ann Silver, April 21, 1926, NAACP PB.

60. "Mrs. Cannady Speaks." She identified them solely as Dr. and Mrs. Brown.

61. Ibid.

62. "Students Stand for Equal Justice," *TA*, April 17, 1926, 1. According to *TA*, the article was reprinted from the March 17, 1926, issue of *WC*, but it has not been located.

63. Mrs. E. D. Cannady to Mr. [Herbert J.] Seligmann, April 13, 1926, NAACP PB. The spelling of the university's name was corrected. Nothing was found during a cursory review of *TC* from May through July 1926. Seligmann's papers are housed at the Humanities and Social Sciences Library, Manuscripts and Archives Division, New York Public Library.

64. For details about another busy visit, see, for example, Patrick Dahlin to Beatrice Cannady, December 28, 1928, CS, 52; Patrick Dahlin to Beatrice Cannady, January 28, 1929, CS, 53; *TA*, February 16, 1929, 2.

65. "About Reed: Mission and History."

66. *TA*, February 13, 1926, 1. Gill was born in England and immigrated to the United States in the 1850s. But he was still living in Britain when Douglass toured the United Kingdom, giving speeches in Belfast, London, and other cities. Gill may have heard the abolitionist speak in one of those locations. *Fourteenth Census*, MC.

67. Blanche M. Thurston, "Praises Interracial Gathering," *TA*, March 27, 1926, 4. She appears in the *Fourteenth Census*, MC. For more about Cannady's awareness of her public image, see, for example, Miller. A typographical error was corrected.

68. G. Bernard Noble to E. C. Farnham, August 2, 1929, CS, 9; "Manuscript Collections: George Bernard Noble." Cannady continued to visit the school in the 1930s. At the end of March 1930, for example, she addressed a class on contemporary society and was the guest speaker at chapel service. *TA*, March 29, 1930, 2.

69. "Struggle of Negroes Told By Mrs. Cannady; Difficulties Met in Fight for Legal Rights Related By Oregon's Crusader," *RCQ*, December 9, 1931, 1; reprinted under the same headline in *TA*, December 12, 1931, 2; "Editor Speaks Before Club," *TA*, December 5, 1931, 2.

70. "Editor Speaks." A typographical error was corrected.

71. Mrs. E. D. Cannady to George E. Haynes and the Church Women's Committee, October 20, 1927, CS, 175. Haynes nominated her for a seat on the Church Women's Committee on Race Relations, a component of the Federal Council of the Churches of Christ in America. Following her unanimous election to the committee, Haynes asked her to send information about her interracial work. Cannady typed a three-page, single-spaced report describing how the teas started, reactions to them, and their significance to her campaign for better race relations. Haynes, executive secretary of the Department of Race Relations of the Federal Council of Churches, wrote that her "interesting account ... was read in full" and members expressed "deep interest" in her work. George Haynes to Beatrice Cannady, September 6, 1927, CS, 174; "Elect Local Woman To Interracial Committee," *TA*, October 15, 1927, 2; "Secretary of Inter-Racial Commission of Federal Council of Churches Praises Local Woman's Inter-Racial Work."

Haynes graduated from Fisk University and earned an M.A. from Yale University. He was the first Negro to earn a Ph.D. from Columbia University. Haynes taught at Fisk, was appointed special assistant to the U.S. secretary of labor—a position he held from 1918 until 1921—and more. For more information, see, for example, "George Edmund Haynes, 1875-1906"; "George Edmund Haynes, 1880-1960." Haynes had planned a trip to Portland in July 1931, but was forced to cancel it when his son became ill. "Dr. Haynes Cancels Trip West," *TA*, July 4, 1931, 3.

72. "Recital on Front Porch Is Planned," *TPT*, August 5, 1922, CS, 63. The original has not been located. A typographical error was corrected.

73. "Striving for Her Race."

74. Cannady to Haynes, CS, 176. For a brief biographical sketch of Trumbull, see Pogue, 227-28.

75. Miller.

76. Cannady to Haynes, CS, 176.

77. "Negro History Week," CS, 29.

78. Cannady to Haynes, CS, 176. She did not elaborate on the individuals who attended.

79. Cannady to Haynes, CS, 177.

80. Bogle, SR442, tape 3 transcript, OHS. At the same time, many Negroes "were reluctant to let white people come into their homes" because they feared repercussions. Employers, for example, might discover they were "doing well" and retaliate by firing them.

81. "Interracial Teas," CS, 169. Punctuation altered.

82. Cannady to Haynes.

83. "Twelve Races Represented at Afternoon Tea," *ODJ*, May 31, 1926, 2; reprinted under the same headline in *TA*, June 5, 1926, 1; Cannady to Haynes.

84. Cannady to Haynes, CS, 175, 177.

85. *TA*, March 7, 1931, 2; "World-Famed Teacher Welcomed in Portland," *TA*, February 28, 1931, 1. For more about Root's visit, see "Martha Root to Visit in Portland; World Traveler Arrives 23rd," *TA*, February 14, 1931, 1.

86. Garis, 7, 20, 39-42. Root was born August 10, 1872. She also wrote for the *Pittsburg Chronicle Telegraph*, *Pittsburg Press*, *Index of Pittsburg Life*, *Pittsburg Gazette*, and *Pittsburgh Post*. See Garis for detailed information about Root's many trips. Root also visited Portland in 1923 and 1937. She was an expert Esperantist and wrote more than one hundred articles "proclaiming its virtues." "Martha Root to Visit"; Garis, 83.

87. March 7, 1931. Afterward, Cannady presented a bouquet to Root. Her remarks, as well as Root's expression of gratitude, were in Esperanto. Pollyann, "In the Realm of Society," *TA*, March 7, 1931, 2. Cannady printed a series of articles by Root. See, for example, the following in *TA*: "China Today," March 29, 1924, 4; May 10, 1924, 4.

88. "World-Famed Teacher."

89. Ibid.; Pollyann.

90. "Martha Root," *TA*, February 28, 1931, 2. A grammatical error was corrected. Also see "Martha Root," *TA*, February 14, 1931, 2.

91. Miss Swain, "Are Honored at Unusual Reception," *TA*, August 9, 1924, 1; Crawford, 72. According to Crawford, Park, a secretary of the California Equal Suffrage Association, was related to suffragette Lucretia Mott. Mapps, identified as Mrs. John Ernest Mapps in *TA*, appears in the 1920 Census. She was born in Kansas. Her father was born in Missouri; her mother in Louisiana. Her husband, John, worked as a janitor in a bank building. He and his father were born in Texas; his mother was born in Georgia. Living with them were Nellie's father, David Reed, and John's mother, Annie Butler. *Fourteenth Census*, Spokane County, Washington.

92. Swain.

93. Ibid., 4; George Orr Latimer, "Oneness of Humanity Will Bring Peace," *TA*, August 16, 1924, 1. Dunbar served as president of the GFWC from 1938-1941. "OFWC Historical Highlights."

94. Chandler, 276.

95. Ibid.; Hunton and Johnson.

96. Chandler; Ken Nakazawa, "Interracial Tea for Mrs. Hunton Attended By Many Prominent People; Seven or Eight Different Nationalities Represented," *TA*, September 25, 1926, 1.

97. Chandler, 279, 280. According to the 1920 Census, Addie Hunton worked as a secretary for the YWCA. She and her son, William, who was born in Georgia, were lodgers. *Fourteenth Census*, Kings County, New York. Hunton, who stayed with the Cannadys while in Portland, also addressed "the young people" at Rose City Park Methodist Episcopal Church and the congregation of Central Presbyterian Church in the Laurelhurst neighborhood. In addition, she spoke at Reed College's Chapel service, an event that Cannady may have arranged. Cannady treated her friend to an "automobile trip over [the] Columbia River Highway" during her visit. *TA*, September 25, 1926, 1. Also see "Reed College Sends Letter of Appreciation To Mrs. Hunton," *TA*, September 25, 1926, 1. Hunton was "entertained at a delicious course breakfast" by hotelier William D. Allen; she served with his brother in France and was a "dear friend" of a sister-in-law living in Brooklyn. *TA*, September 25, 1926, 1.

98. Nakazawa. Also see "Mrs. Addie Hunton Charms Splendid Audience." For a brief biographical sketch of Trumbull, see Pogue, 227-28.

99. "International Peace Day," in *Report of the Fourth Congress of the Women's International League for Peace and Freedom* (The Women's International League: Washington, D.C., [1924]), n.p., accessible at http://www.archive.org/stream/reportoffourthco24wome/reportoffourthco24wome_djvu.txt. May 18 was selected because it commemorated the anniversary of the first Hague Peace Conference.

100. "Good Will Day Observed Here; Many Nationalities Represented at Gathering at E. D. Cannady Home," *TPT*, May 18, 1926, 6; reprinted under the same headline in *TA*, May 22, 1926, 4. By 1926, the Commission on Race Relations of the Federal Council of Churches was promoting Race Relations Sunday—an observance to draw attention to the need for "friendly goodwill"—to churches across the country as well as in Oregon. See, for example, "Good-Will Day Tomorrow," *TNYT*, May 15, 1926, 18. Also see "To Honor 10th Celebration," *TA*, December 19, 1931, 1; "Race Relation Program Cited," *TA*, November 12, 1932, 1.

101. Hutchinson and Hollinger, 779. Punctuation added to the name of the Faith.

102. "Messages to America by Shoghi Effendi," http://www.ibiblio.org/Bahai/Texts/EN/MA/MA-61.html.

103. "Good Will Day." Violet Hooker also sang, and her sister, Gwendolyn, gave one of the "readings."

104. Ober, 667, 668. Gregory appears in the 1910 Census. He and his parents were born in South Carolina. *Thirteenth Census*, District of Columbia. Cannady later published a series of articles by Gregory. See Louis G. Gregory, "Progress in Racial Amity," *TA*, May 27, 1933, 2; June 3, 1933, 2; June 10, 1933, 2.

105. "Twelve Races Represented." Sell, identified as "Professor Sell of the chair of Sociology," was identified by a listing in "News and Notes," *The American Journal of Sociology* 31, no. 1 (July 1925): 82. George P. Eisman does not appear in online census records for Oregon for any available years. For more about Vail, see Albert R. Vail, "Bahaism: A Study of a Contemporary Movement," *The Harvard Theological Review* 7, no. 3 (July 1914): 339-57. Punctuation altered. Faiths included Jewish, Bahá'í, Roman Catholic, and Protestant.

106. For details about the teas, see the following in *TA*: Rosalie Bird, "In the Realm of Society," April 18, 1931, 2; Rosalie Bird, "In the Realm of Society," August 29, 1931, 2. Finch was in Tokyo on September 1, 1923, when an earthquake measuring 8.3 killed one hundred thousand people and left hundreds of thousands homeless. Garis, 174-75; "The 1923 Tokyo Earthquake." See this site for photos of the damage. Ida Finch does not appear in the 1920 Census for King County, Washington.

107. Pollyann, "In the Realm of Society," *TA*, August 23, 1930, 2.

108. Wilson D. Wallis, "Alexander A. Goldenweiser," *American Anthropologist*, New Series, 43, no. 2, part 1 (April-June 1941): 250, 253. Goldenweiser wrote *Early Civilization: An Introduction to Anthropology*. The Alexander Goldenweiser Papers are housed at Special Collections & Archives, Reed College Library. His wife attended a gathering at Cannady's home honoring Paul Robeson, who was in Portland for a recital. "Paul Robeson," *TA*, February 14, 1932, 1; Pollyann, "In the Realm of Society," *TA*, February 21, 1931, 2.

109. McGinty, 208. John Lovell devoted most of his time to studying and writing about Negro spirituals. His last work, *Black Song: The Forge and the Flame*, was considered "excellent, thorough scholarship" and a "fitting monument to the high professional standards which characterized" his life. McGinty, 209.

110. Pollyann. The other speakers were Allan Rutherford, a "teacher-principal in public schools" in Trenton, New Jersey, and Richard Hill, the Reverend Daniel Hill's brother and a student at Harvard Divinity School. Also see "Prominent Educators Visit in Portland," *TA*, July 18, 1931, 1.

111. *TA*, February 19, 1927, 2.

112. "Negro Poet Honored at Gathering," *OSJ*, February 13, 1927, sec. 1, 11; reprinted in *TA*, February 19, 1927, 1. Also see "Mrs. Maxwell Attends Tea," *TA*, February 12, 1927, 1.

113. "Negro Poet." Adams appears in the 1920 Census. She and her father were born in Minnesota; her mother was born in Ohio. She worked as a stenographer in a law office. Adams and her daughter, Mary, were living with her mother, Josephine Hathaway. *Fourteenth Census*, MC.

114. "Mrs. Maxwell"; "Negro Poet."

115. *TA*, August 15, 1931, 2. Campbell was a member of the Bahá'í community of Portland. See, for example, "Bahá'í Assembly Roll, United States and Canada, 1928-1929," NBA. Grayson "sang a group of songs." Although Asberry did not stay with Cannady this trip, the editor entertained her friend "with a drive about the city and theatre party." "Washington Woman Feted; Mrs [*sic*] Asberry Spends Busy Brief Visit," *TA*, August 15, 1931, 1.

116. Cannady to Haynes, CS, 177.

117. Miller. Until World War I, propaganda had a positive connotation and was seen as an accepted way to promote a new doctrine or system of doctrines, or for proselytizing. *Century Dictionary and Cyclopedia*, vol. VII P-Q (1911), s.v. "propagandist" and "propaganda."

118. "Mrs. Cannady Sees End of Race Trouble," *TCD*, August 20, 1927, 2.

119. "Negro Welfare Aims Discussed; Success of Teas for Black and White Races Told," undated clipping from an unidentified Los Angeles newspaper (possibly the *Los Angeles Times*), circa June 29, 1928, CS, 172.

120. "Writer Impressed with Associate Editor's Work," *TA*, July 14, 1928, 1. Typographical errors were corrected.

121. Millie R. Trumbull, "The Cannady Reception," *TA*, November 21, 1925, 4. The tea was in honor of Joseph Emmanuel Blayechettai and his wife, of Abyssinia, East Africa. He "claimed to be an Ethiopian prince who had ... received an English education"; he "was apparently an extremely popular lecturer on the black Church circuit in the 1920s." Howe, 47. For details about the tea, see Alice M. Handsaker, "Editor and Mrs. Cannady Entertain at Large Tea," *TA*, November 21, 1925, 1. According to the article: "All expressed satisfaction in the meeting together of so many races and nationalities in such fraternal fashion .... Among the guests present were Chinese, Hindus, Irish, Spanish, German, African and Americans, both colored and white."

Chapter Six

1. Fellow, 243, 245; "David Sarnoff: Timeline."

2. Fellow, 247; "To Record Fight Details," *TNYT*, June 10, 1921, 18. Dempsey won. "Dempsey Proves Prowess," *TNYT*, July 3, 1921, 1. "Dempsey Draws Color Line," *TNYT*, July 9, 1921, 13.

3. "To Record Fight"; "Radio Phone to Tell Times Sq. of Fight," *TNYT*, July 1, 1921, 16.

4. "Radio Telephoning," *TNYT*, March 2, 1922, 20. For details about the rapid growth of radio, see, for example, Douglas, 40-54. Radios also made lovely—and newsworthy—gifts. Cannady reported that Juneious Pugh had "presented" his mother and sister "with a beautiful large radio for Christmas." *TA*, December 28, 1929, 2. The spelling of his name was corrected.

5. See Douglas for more about radio music as well as the "symbiotic relationship ... between African American music and radio." Douglas, 94. Such entertaining occurred in other cities, too. Cannady attended a "supper and radio dancing party" hosted by her sister and brother-in-law, Olive and Elvin Neal, and another couple while she was in Los Angeles in 1928 for the NAACP conference. "Tells of Trip South." The Neals do not appear in online census records for 1920 or 1930 for Los Angeles County, but Cannady wrote that

they lived at 1502-1/2 East 23rd Street. For other parties in Portland, see, for example *TA*, January 10, 1931, 2.

6. Rosalie Bird-Holmes, "In the Realm of Society," *TA*, May 14, 1932, 3.

7. Tuskegee President Robert R. Moton gave an address "in a nation-wide hook-up. Local station was KGW. ... Many great things were said in praise of the Negro and the famous school founded by the late Booker T. Washington." Governor Julius L. Meier appointed Cannady to represent Oregon at Tuskegee Institute's anniversary celebration, but without funding, the appointment was nominal. "Editor Chosen," *TA*, April 11, 1931, 1. "Heard Herbert Hoover," *TA*, April 18, 1931, 1. Warren G. Harding had a radio installed in the White House in February 1922; two years later, Calvin Coolidge's address in honor of Washington's birthday was broadcast coast to coast over forty-two stations. "America's Story." For comments about the "educational value of the radio," see "Education Over the Air," *TA*, February 6, 1932, 2.

8. "The Color Line and Ability," *TA*, December 10, 1932, 2. A typographical error was corrected. Although this editorial praised radio for adopting "the policy of the stage in regard to the Negro," it also criticized people for not honoring "the Negro ... in all activities."

9. In 1931, Cannady mentioned that Paul Robeson had been heard over KGW "through a national network." *TA*, March 28, 1931, 3. For a white reader's views on jazz, see Myrtle W. Campbell, "Good Music Versus Jazz," *TA*, February 6, 1932, 2. Douglas points out, "The discourse surrounding jazz was ... a discourse about race, about fears of miscegenation, pollution, and contamination." This climate of fear, exacerbated by the decade's "epidemic of lynchings, spread of the Klan, and new restrictions on immigration," caused many bands and performers such as Bessie Smith to be banned from the air for a time. Douglas, 92, 93. Radio segregation began to change by the 1930s, though, as white "critics [came] to embrace" the new music and white musicians "co-opted, domesticated, and often bastardized black jazz." Douglas, 92, 85.

10. "The Radio Program," *TA*, February 5, 1927, 2. For more about the thirty-member chorus, see, for example, the following in *TA*: Advertisement, February 19, 1927, 4; Millie R. Trumbull, "3,000 Cheer Biggest Concert of Season," February 26, 1927, 1. Bethel AME Church was the religious program featured on the KXL schedule Sundays from 5 p.m. to 6 p.m. See, for example, "Radio News," *TA*, October 12, 1929, 2. The choir also broadcast over the Jubilee Hour on KWJJ. "Bethel Church Notes" and "Their Music," *TA*, February 6, 1932, 2.

11. Davidson to Cannady, March 2, 1927.

12. "The Radio Program." Listeners also sent contributions to Reverend Dyer.

13. "KGW Radio History."

14. "Tuskegee served as the headquarters of National Negro Health Week, and reached thousands of Negroes from 1915 to 1930, when the United States Public Health Service took it over and turned it into a year-round program." "Historical Timeline: National Negro Health Week."

15. "Negro Health Week Comes To a Close; Radio Broadcasts Big Feature in Health Program," *TA*, April 9, 1932, 1.

16. Unthank discussed the "Influence of the Professional on Negro Health"; Lovell was on KTBR to talk about "The Influence of the Negro Church on Negro Health." "Negro Health Week"; "Radio Talks Feature of Health Program," *TA*, March 26, 1932, 3; "Local Group Observes Negro Health Week," *TA*, April 2, 1932, 1. For more about Health Week observances, see, for example, the following in *TA*: "Mt. Oliv't Church," April 11, 1931, 2; "Keeping Fit," April 11, 1931, 4; "Negro Health in 1933," January 14, 1933, 2. Unthank dedicated his "Keeping Fit" column in March 1932 to the upcoming observance. "Keeping

Fit," *TA*, March 5, 1932, 4. For an editorial supporting his efforts, see "Negro Health," *TA*, March 12, 1932, 2. For the 1932 program sent by Tuskegee Institute, see "Health Program Out," *TA*, March 12, 1932, 2. Also see "Keeping Fit," *TA*, March 12, 1932, 4; "Health Program Out," *TA*, March 19, 1932, 2.

17. "KGW Radio History."

18. "To Broadcast Over KEX," *TA*, February 18, 1928, 2. According to this article, she had been on KEX three times in 1927.

19. "Give Radio Program; To Broadcast from KEX," *TA*, April 7, 1928, 3. Hotchkiss was appointed a U.S. Marshal on August 24, 1921. "Historical Summary."

20. *TA*, February 21, 1931, 2. Also see "Editor to Broadcast Over KGW," *TA*, February 14, 1931, 1.

21. "*Oregonian* of Air Presents Variety; Education, Race Distinction, Football on Program," *MO*, September 7, 1931, 7; "Editor Broadcasts," *TA*, October 3, 1931, 4.

22. "*Advocate* Sponsors Negro History Week; Radio Talks Main Feature," *TA*, February 13, 1932, 1; "KOIN Radio from the Heathman Hotel." Several online sources note that KOIN stands for Know Oregon's Independent Newspaper. It is unclear whether the essay was one of the reflection papers Cannady published in *TA* in 1926, or was from a different class. It is also unclear whether she broadcast on KTBR on Saturday, too. Yancy Jerome Franklin discussed "the celebration of Negro week" and "urged radio listeners to read Negro literature"; DeNorval Unthank gave a ten-minute talk on "The Negro Physician."

23. "Radio Program Announcement," *TA*, February 2, 1929, 1. Also see "To Broadcast During Negro History Week."

24. Kessler, 155; "Mrs. Cannady Uses Daily Press to Reach the People with Her Great Truths," CS, 178. In the *Journal* article, she offered background information on Carter G. Woodson and reasons to observe Negro History Week, then discussed the economic, social, cultural, religious, and educational aspects of the lives of black Portlanders. Mrs. E. D. Cannady, "The Strivings of a Race," *ODJ*, February 5, 1929, 10. Also see Mrs. E. D. Cannady, "Negroes in Northwest," *TPT*, February 9, 1929, 24. The latter article cited information from Lockley, "Some Documentary Records of Slavery in Oregon."

She used the *Oregonian* article to discuss "the long and honorable career of American negroes in politics" in order to give readers "an idea" of what men had done—and would do in the future—to build and promote "the welfare of the state and nation." She also called attention to the recent election of Oscar De Priest. Mrs. E. D. Cannady, "Negro Playing Important Part in American Affairs," *TSO*, February 10, 1929, 17.

Cannady called *Advocate* readers' attention "to the liberal space given" her *Journal* article, "the fine position"—page ten—"and also to the fact that the term 'Negro' was used with a capital 'N.' It was no longer treated as an adjective, but as a noun." "The *Daily Journal*," *TA*, February 9, 1929, 1. That was not the case in the other two articles. Cannady undoubtedly capitalized Negro; that it was spelled with an "n" in the *Telegram* and *Oregonian* indicates that her pieces were edited.

25. W. E. Burghardt Du Bois, "Fifty Years Among Black Folks," *TNYT*, December 12, 1909, SMA4. The article discussed homeownership, "spiritual uplift," the importance of black-owned newspapers and periodicals, the cultural contributions of poet Paul Laurence Dunbar and musician J. Rosamond Johnson, and more.

26. "Negro History Week Observed," *TA*, February 9, 1929, 2.

27. "Color Line Drawn: Pupils Leave Rink," *MO*, January 28, 1927, 13; reprinted under the same headline in *TA*, January 29, 1927, 1. Also see "Colored Boy Barred; Class Leaves Rink," *ODJ*, January 28, 1927, 1; reprinted under the same headline in *TA*, February 12, 1927, 1. Rice, identified as C. A. Rice in *MO*, appears in the *Fourteenth Census*, MC. For more about Eisman, see "Mr. Eisman's Record Reviewed," *TA*, October 27, 1928, 1.

28. Frank L. Shull to Hugh E. Dorman, February 2, 1927, quoted in "Schoolboard [*sic*] Member Praises Loyal Pupils," *TA*, February 5, 1927, 1. Dorman may have copied her on the correspondence. Shull appears in the *Fourteenth Census*, MC. Cannady wrote that he was president of the Shull Export Company, "merchandisers of quality flours, with office in the Board of Trade Building." Shull, a county commissioner in 1932, ran for mayor that year but was not elected; he served on the Multnomah County Board of Commissioners from 1931 to 1954. Lansing, 324. Also see "Past Boards of Commissioners."

29. "And a Little Child Shall Lead Them," *TA*, February 12, 1927, 2. A typographical error was corrected.

30. "An Argument for Mixed Schools," *The Philadelphia Tribune*, February 12, 1927, sec. 2, 16, reprinted under the same headline in *TA*, February 26, 1927, 2.

31. "Woman Journalist Urges Radio Listeners to Rise Above Petty Race Hates." The broadcast was publicized by the Pacific Coast News Bureau, an organization established to disseminate "Negro news of national importance" during the 1920s. It was founded by George Perry Johnson, who also was a writer, producer, and distributor for the Lincoln Motion Picture Company. "Abstract."

32. "Whites Entreated to Rise Above Racial and Religious Prejulices [*sic*]," *SR*, March 12, 1927, 1.

33. "Woman Journalist Urges."

34. Mrs. A. E. [Arthur] Mullineaux to Beatrice Cannady, February 10, 1927, CS, 32. Earnie [?] Mullineaux appears in the *Fourteenth Census*, MC.

35. Jean Huntington to KKGW, February 11, 1927, CS, 33.

36. Myra G. McIntire to Beatrice Cannady, February 10, 1927, CS, 31. She appears in the *Fourteenth Census*, MC.

37. "Addresses Club," *TA*, April 16, 1927, 1. The name of the church was misspelled in the story. Cannady revisited the church the following year. See "Gives Many Talks," *TA*, January 28, 1928, 1; Gertrude J. Porter to Beatrice Cannady, January 24, 1928, CS, 57. Cannady frequently discussed the NAACP and its history and mission. See, for example, the following in *TA*: April 30, 1927, 1; March 31, 1928, 2.

38. Cannady to Bagnall, September 28, 1925. She also informed Seligmann of this outreach. Cannady to Seligmann, April 13, 1926.

39. James Weldon Johnson to Mrs. E. D. Cannady, February 25, 1928, copy in AC.

40. *TA*, July 11, 1925, 1. She gave similar talks at First Congregational Church and to the Missionary Society of Moreland Community Church [Moreland Presbyterian?]. *TA*, June 20, 1925, 1; "Associate Editor Addresses Meeting," *TA*, April 10, 1926, 1.

41. "To Fill Pulpits," *TA*, January 26, 1929, 2; *TA*, April 20, 1929, 2. She gave a similar talk on the "Negro's contribution to American civilization" to the Quest Club. "Editor Discusses Negro Achievements," *TA*, May 23, 1931, 1.

42. "Inter-Racial Day Observed at Centenary-Wilbur; The Associate Editor Delivers the Sermon; Mrs. Charles H. Maxwell sings," *TA*, February 14, 1925, 1; "Service is Inter-Racial; Plea for Tolerance Made By Mrs. E. D. Cannady," *MO*, February 9, 1925, 9. The Federal Council of Churches designated a day to promote "better relations between the races." She made a similar plea at the same church during the 1927 observance. Edgar Williams, "Mt. Olivet News," *TA*, February 19, 1927, 1.

43. "Associate Editor and Mrs. Mapps Speak at Newberg, Ore.," *TA*, August 2, 1924, 1; Historical Census Browser. The school was founded by Lotta Hannon, identified as Mrs. David Hannon in *TA*, who was president of the Yamhill County WCTU. She appears in the *Thirteenth Census*, Yamhill County. For information about Cannady's talk to students at the Arleta Daily Vacation Bible School, a summer program run by Alice Handsaker, see

"Associate Editor of *The Advocate* Discusses Race Relations at Bible School," *TA*, July 7, 1923, 1. For another talk to young people, see *TA*, April 30, 1927, 1.

44. "Come To This Unusual Treat," *TA*, October 16, 1926, 1, 4.

45. "Will Give Stereoptican [*sic*] Lecture for Benefit of Church," *TA*, October 9, 1926, 4. Also see *TA*, October 30, 1926, 1.

46. "To Give Lecture on Negroes' Growth," *TPT*, October 19, 1926, 4.

47. "Mrs. Cannady Speaks at Methodist Church," *TA*, December 19, 1925, 1. For the advance notice, see "Mrs. Cannady to Speak," *TA*, December 12, 1925, 1.

48. *TA*, September 1, 1928, 3.

49. "Negro in History," *TA*, February 2, 1929, 1.

50. "Mrs. Cannady Tendered Grand Reception," *California Voice*, May 7, 1926, copy in CS, 63. The original has not been located.

51. "Mrs. Cannady Sees End of Race Trouble."

52. "Gives Many Talks," *TA*, January 28, 1928, 1. Lemon does not appear in online census records for MC for 1920. For details about a talk to the Foreign Missionary Society of Sunnyside Methodist Episcopal Church, see *TA*, February 12, 1927, 1. Cannady discussed "The Negro's Educational Achievements" with the Woman's Association of the Alameda Park Community Church. *TA*, November 10, 1928, 3.

53. "Associate Editor of *The Advocate* Delivers Address," *TA*, March 5, 1927, 3. She gave a similar talk to the white women of Lincoln Methodist Episcopal Church. "Associate Editor and Miss Shaw Give Program to Methodist Women," *TA*, February 21, 1925, 1. Bellingham, identified as Mrs. George Bellingham in the newspaper, appears in the *Fourteenth Census*, MC.

54. *TA*, October 16, 1926, 1. The church's name was corrected. Beeson, identified as Mrs. A. H. Beeson in the paper, appears in the *Fourteenth Census*, MC.

55. "Will Give Stereoptican [*sic*] Lecture." She also was appointed a member of the executive board of the Oregon Council of Religious Education to represent Zion. "Mrs. Cannady on Religious Education Board," *TA*, September 16, 1925, 1.

56. "A Gripping Story of China's Awakening," *TA*, March 29, 1924, 4; Buck, 64. Years later, Cannady wrote that Mrs. Latimer, "a very sincere and enthusiastic Bahá'í," gave her a booklet to read. *The Goal of a New World Order* "proved of such interest," Cannady decided to serialize it in *TA*. See "New World Order," *TA*, January 21 1933, 2. Punctuation added to the name of the Faith. The Latimers, identified in *TA* as Mr. and Mrs. J. W. Latimer, and their son George Orr, appear in the *Fourteenth Census*, MC, Oregon.

57. For more about Latimer and race relations in Portland, see the following in *TA*: Beatrice H. Cannady, "All Classes Sit Together at Dinner," November 22, 1930, 1; "Colored People Guests at Amity Dinner," November 22, 1930, 1; "Racial Amity," November 22, 1930, 2.

58. The local Bahá'í Assembly also hosted a series of world unity dinners, which Cannady attended and wrote about at length in *TA*. See "Great Throng Attend Unity Dinner," June 2, 1928, 1; "World Unity Dinner Draws Big Crowd," June 16, 1928, 1.

59. "Bahá'í Assembly Roll ... 1928-1929."

60. In 1923, for example, she wrote about participating in the Feast of the El Rizwan—she probably meant the final event of the annual Ridván Festival, considered to be the "holiest and most significant" of all the Faith's festivals. It "commemorates the 12 days that Bahá'u'lláh ... camped on the banks of the Tigris River near Baghdad and, while there, proclaimed his mission to a small group of followers." One guest of note was the sister-in-law of the muckraking journalist Ray Stannard Baker, who was visiting from California.

"Feast of the El Rizwan," *TA*, May 2, 1923, 4; "The Festival of Ridván"; "Bahá'ís celebrate 'King of Festivals.'"

61. Louis Gregory, "National Baha'i Convention Reviewed," *TA*, May 29, 1926, 1. She also volunteered to do printing for the Faith, which Roy Wilhelm called "a very wonderful and beautiful thought." "Eighteenth Annual Convention of the Bahá'ís of the United States and Canada, April 29, - May 2, 1926," corrected minutes, 56, NBA.

62. Beatrice Cannady to Horace Holley, November 27, 1926, NBA.

63. Robert W. Bagnall to Beatrice Cannady, May 7, 1926, NAACP PB. Punctuation added to the name of the Faith. Bagnall informed *TC* about her outreach; issues published from June through August 1926 were reviewed but nothing was found. The NAACP also was the topic of Cannady's address to the Portland Bahá'í Assembly at its regular Friday evening meeting in March 1926. *TA*, March 20, 1926, 1.

64. *TA*, October 29, 1927, 2.

65. "The Associate Editor Tells of Her Trip East," *TA*, November 19, 1927, 4. Cannady noted that she first met Wilhelm at the conference in San Francisco. He contributed to the book *In His Presence: Visits To 'Abdú'l-Bahá*.

66. "Speaks on Racial Amity at Meeting in Teaneck," *Bergen Evening Record*, September 2, 1927, sec. 2, 4, copy in CS, 61. The original has not been located. Punctuation added to the name of the Faith.

67. That affiliation was hardly a surprise for followers of the Faith, since Green Acre had been "a focal center for the development of the early Bahá'í community" between 1900 and 1909, and was honored with a visit by 'Abdú'l-Bahá in 1912. "History of Green Acre."

68. "The Associate Editor Tells of Her Trip East," *TA*, October 22, 1927, 4. During her stay, she had lunch with Louis Gregory and his wife, and spent time with Albert Vail, Elizabeth Greenleaf, and Mr. and Mrs. Harlan Ober. She would continue to stress the theme of racial amity in talks to Baháí'ísts. Six years later, in an address to the Portland Assembly, she "gave the Bahai principles of racial amity and urged greater activity on the part of Bahais to hasten more friendship and goodwill between the colored and white races in America." "Editor Speaks Before Bahais," *TA*, July 1, 1933, 1.

69. "Club Formed; To Study Auxiliary Tongue and History of Negro Race," *TA*, August 17, 1929, 1. The club was organized at Rachel Belard's home on Going Street in August 1929; Cannady was elected the group's secretary. Belard appears in the 1920 Census. She and her parents were born in Louisiana. Her husband, Milton, worked as a "shoe-black" in his own establishment. He and his parents also were born in Louisiana. The couple, described as mulatto, had two daughters: Lillian and Louise, both of whom were born in Oregon. *Fourteenth Census*, MC. Lillian ran for "Miss Portland" as part of a membership campaign for the NAACP in 1931; she came in third. See the following in *TA*: "Pretty Girls Vie for Honors in Popularity Contest," April 25, 1931, 1; "Miss Blanchard Takes the Lead in Contest," May 9, 1931, 2; "N.A.A.C.P. Drive," May 16, 1931, 2; "Four Hundred Join N.A.A.C.P.; Julia Mae Blanchard Named 'Miss Portland,'" May 30, 1931, 1. Also in 1931, Rachel and Milton Belard took over The Medley Grille in the Medley Hotel at 484 Interstate Avenue. See "Local News," *TA*, May 2, 1931, 3; advertisement, *TA*, May 30, 1931, 4.

70. "Esperanto Is ...." The language was introduced in 1887 by Polish physician L. L. Zamenhof.

71. Garis, 82.

72. "Club Formed." The women planned to meet every Tuesday morning for breakfast, and then spend forty-five minutes on language instruction and a similar period on history or culture. Members included Henrietta Marshall, Mamie Stanton, Mrs. Frank Adams, and Elnora Deiz (misidentified as Nona in *TA*). Marshall, who lived on Buffalo Street,

later moved to Ogden, Utah, with her husband, who worked for the railroad. See "Mrs. Marshall Writes from Ogden," *TA*, September 12, 1931, 2.

Stanton was elected chair of the courtesy committee and Mrs. Frank Adams was named chair of the entertainment committee. Neither woman appears in online census records for MC for 1920. Both women also were members of the Literary Research Club. *TA*, January 10, 1931, 2.

Elnora Deiz, who appears in the 1920 Census, was chosen to serve as vice-president. She was born in Nebraska. Her father was born in Tennessee; her mother in Missouri. She was married to William, originally from Jamaica. His father was born there; his mother was born in the "United States." He worked as a hotel waiter. They had a baby and lived with her parents, Robert and Mollie Foster. William was sixty-nine, but still worked as a porter in a barbershop. *Fourteenth Census*, MC.

Cora Jamison was elected treasurer and Estelle Gragg was voted chair of the welfare committee. *Advocate* articles about other topics mention a woman named Lula (and Lulu) Gragg. Estelle does not appear in the 1920 Census, but Lulu Gragg does. She and her parents were born in Texas. She worked as a servant for a private family. Her husband, William, and his parents also were born in Texas. He worked as a janitor. *Fourteenth Census*, MC.

73. *TA*, August 24, 1929, 3; "Local Briefs," *TA*, May 24, 1930, 4; Pollyann, "In the Realm of Society," *TA*, May 31, 1930, 2; Pollyann, "In the Realm of Society," *TA*, June 14, 1930, 2; *TA*, October 18, 1930, 2; Pollyann, "In the Realm of Society," *TA*, February 14, 1931, 2. Cannady discussed "Go Down, Death," a poem by James Weldon Johnson that later inspired a movie by the same name, and Hughes' poem "The Negro Speaks of Rivers." On another occasion, Elise Reynolds reviewed poetry by Joseff H. Edwards, an instructor at the Oregon Conservatory of Music in the Brooke Building at the corner of Washington and 7th. Identified as J. H. Edwards in the newspaper, he appears in the *Fourteenth Census*, MC. For some information about the conservatory, see Douthit, 78.

74. Pennington to the Harmon Award Committee.

75. "Mrs. Cannady Tendered Grand Reception."

76. Ralph C. Hoeber, "Compliments Speech," *TA*, May 14, 1932, 1. Cannady spoke at the East Side Commercial Club.

77. For an example of the power of the press to inform, advocate, and change minds, see, for example, "Worth of Our Papers," *TA*, December 29, 1928, 2.

78. Alice M. Handsaker to the Harmon Award Committee, [1929], CS, 24.

Chapter Seven

1. See, for example, advertisements in *LAT*, February 8, 1915, part III, 1; *RDP*, January 1, 1915, 7; and *TMPW*, March 13, 1915, 1671. Also see Grace Kingsley, "Staging 'The Clansman,'" *LAT*, February 7, 1915, part IIIa, 10. The figure is the equivalent of $10.6 million today. The Inflation Calculator. Other accounts place the amount closer to $110,000, still a considerable sum in 1915. See, for example, Lang, 30.

2. Francis Hackett, "Brotherly Love," *TNR*, March 20, 1915, 185; Lang, 30. Also see Louis Sherwin, "The Theatre; 'The Birth of a Nation' at the Liberty," *TGCA*, March 5, 1915, 12.

3. Cripps, "The Reaction of the Negro," 345. Dixon wrote *The Clansman: An Historical Romance of the Ku Klux Klan* and *The Leopard's Spots: A Romance of the White Man's Burden, 1865-1900*. His play, *The Clansman*, incorporated material from the novels. For more about Dixon see, for example, Gillespie and Hall; Cook. Filming lasted until October 31, 1914. Lang, 39.

4. D. W. Griffith in a letter to *Sight & Sound*, quoted in Lang, 3.

5. *The Birth of a Nation* (1988).

6. Niderost, 65.

7. The Klan also was celebrated in advertisements, such as one in *LAT* that featured three large Ks, each bearing a different word: Ku, Klux, Klan. *LAT*, February 7, 1915, part III, 2.

8. Bass, 35.

9. "Great Outdoors Is D. W. Griffith's Stage," *TAC*, November 28, 1915, Magazine Section.

10. "'The Clansman' Motion Picture Masterpiece at Loring Tonight," *RDP*, January 1, 1915, 7. Also see the following in *RDP*: Advertisement, December 29, 1914, 2; "'The Clansman' Is Coming To Loring," December 30, 1914, 5; "'The Clansman' Comes Friday," December 31, 1914, 12.

11. "'The Clansman' Is Wonderful," *RDP*, January 2, 1915, 6. The film's West Coast debut was held at Clune's "Theatre Beautiful" in Los Angeles on February 8, 1915. Advertisement, *LAT*, February 9, 1915, part III, 4. Also see "Clune's Auditorium." But the debut was not without controversy. For more about the legal battles surrounding the film, see, for example, the following in *LAT*: Grace Kingsley, "Film Flams," September 26, 1914, part I, 7; "Despite Council, Clune Will Produce *Clansman*," February 6, 1915, part II, 6; Henry Christeen Warnack, "Trouble Over 'The Clansman,'" February 9, 1915, part II, 6. Also see the following in *TCE*: "In the Civic Walk," January 6, 1915, 1; "Thomas Dickson's [*sic*] Idea of American Liberality," January 30, 1915, 4; "City Council By Unanimous Vote Pass Resolution Which Will Bar the Moving Pictures of the *Clansman* Showing in this City," February 6, 1915, 1; "Was Judge Jackson Just?," "White American's Short-Sightedness," "A Fight for Justice," February 13, 1915, 4; March 13, 1915, 4.

12. Griffin, Dixon, and about seventy-five other guests attended a private screening at a theater at Broadway and 53rd Street shortly before the film opened to the public on March 3, 1915. It was then, as the story goes, that Dixon renamed the film. Cook, 111-12. For more about the film's New York debut, see, for example, the following in *TNYT*: "Written on the Screen," February 14, 1915, X7; advertisement, February 26, 1915, 18; "Written on the Screen," February 28, 1915, X7; advertisement, February 28, 1915, X6. For an ad featuring the Ku Klux Klan, see *TNYT*, February 21, 1915, X7.

13. The board was established in New York City in 1909 in response to growing criticism by local clergy of the "corrupting effect of immoral films on youth." More than that, though, individuals were becoming increasingly concerned about the diffusion of the new medium during a period defined by Prohibition, parades for woman suffrage, jazz clubs, and other issues that challenged "American moral standards and taste." In an effort to dispel concerns and "assert their constitutional freedom of expression," theater owners, led by Marcus Loew, and film distributors, including Edison and Biograph, decided to "organize an advisory committee to evaluate and preview films prior to their public release." That group subsequently became the National Board of Censorship (now called the National Board of Review), which had a censorship committee composed of volunteers from civic and charitable organizations in New York. After reviewing the master film, these individuals voted to approve it, recommend changes, or censure it. Bulletins were then issued weekly to "mayors, chiefs of police, censoring organizations, and voluntary groups throughout the country which had … organized to enforce the decrees of the Board." Feldman, 7, 11, 21. Also see "Films and Births and Censorship," *TS*, April 3, 1915, 4-5; "About the NBR."

14. Mary Childs Nerney to Our Branches and Locals, April 7, 1915, A2000-003, SPA. Punctuation added.

15. Nerney; "Jane Addams Condemns Race Prejudice Film," *TEP*, March 13, 1915, 4;

Hackett. The *Post* article was reprinted in *TCE*; other black newspapers may have reprinted it, too. "Miss Jane Addams Analyzes The 'Clansman,'" *TCE*, March 27, 1915, 1.

16. Nerney.

17. Nerney references Cannady's letter in her own reply. Mary Childs Nerney to Beatrice Cannady, May 18, 1915, A2000-003, SPA.

18. Executive Committee of the Portland Branch of the NAACP to [H. R.] Albee, June 21, 1915, A2000-003, SPA.

19. "Film Is Protested; Negroes Oppose Showing of 'The Birth of a Nation,'" *MO*, July 4, 1915, 3.

20. "Colored Folk Make Protest at Display of Race-Hate Film; 'Birth of Nation' Characterized As Vicious Play By Leader of Association," *OSJ*, July 4, 1915, 8; "Film Is Protested."

21. Hackett. For the synopsis of the "Gus chase," see "The Continuity Script," reprinted in Lang, 118-28.

22. Griffith's use of intertitles—onscreen devices to relate dialogue or convey key points in the story line—enhanced the film's emotional impact. See Hackett, 185. Griffith drew information from President (and Southerner) Woodrow Wilson's five-volume *A History of the American People* to advance the historical narrative, and merged two passages from the final volume to set the stage for the Klan's activities. Wilson, 58, 60; "The Continuity Script," Lang, 94. *History* was criticized by some reviewers. See, for example, Van Tyne, 131-34; "About Woodrow Wilson."

23. Jacobs, *The Rise of the American Film*, 186.

24. "The Continuity Script," 122.

25. "Films and Births and Censorship," 4.

26. "'Birth of a Nation,'" *TEP*, March 4, 1915, 9.

27. "Colored Folk"; "Film Is Protested."

28. The commissioner of public safety was charged with appointing the members and selecting one of them to serve as secretary of the board. Ordinance No. 30154, February 19, 1915, SPA; The Inflation Calculator. It replaced Ordinance No. 28375, January 9, 1914, SPA. Ordinance No. 30154 eventually was repealed and replaced by No. 32571, February 7, 1917, SPA. Also see the following in *MO*: "Censor Act Passes," February 20, 1915, 9; "Movie Men Protest; Proposed Censorship Ordinance to Be Opposed," February 8, 1915, 11; "Public Men Oppose Movie Censorship," August 29, 1915, sec. 1, 11.

29. Ordinance No. 30154.

30. Ibid. Also see Mrs. E. B. Colwell to [Marius B. Marcellus], May 28, 1915, A2000-003, SPA.

31. Ordinance No. 30154.

32. "Afro-Americans Try to Stop Showing of *Clansman* in Los Angeles, but Fail," *TCE*, February 13, 1915, 1.

33. Jordan, 54. For more about Smith, see Stevens and Johnson.

34. "'Birth of a Nation,'" *TB*, April 1, 1916, 4. A typographical error was corrected. Also see Cripps, *Slow Fade to Black*, 63.

35. "Colored Folk."

36. James Withycombe to H. R. Albee, July 8, 1915, A2000-003, SPA. Withycombe references Cannady's communication in his own letter.

37. [H. R. Albee] to James Withycombe, July 9, 1915, A2000-003, SPA.

38. Merriman, Cannady, et. al. to Mayor, et al.

39. A. V. [Angelo V.] Fawcett stated that an ordinance had been passed prohibiting the film from being shown in Tacoma. Newton D. Baker noted in his wire: "Picture has never been authorized for exhibition by the Ohio State Board of Censors and therefore has not

been offered here." And J. L. Davie reported that several scenes, including the Gus chase, had been eliminated before the film played in Oakland. A2000-003, SPA.

40. H. R. Albee to W. B. Brown, August 24, 1915, A2000-003, SPA.

41. Edith Knight Holmes, "'The Birth of a Nation' is Superb," *TSO*, August 29, 1915, sec. 4, 1. The spelling of the Ku Klux Klan was corrected. Another local reviewer was similarly moved by the film. "'Birth of Nation' Film Is Vivid Story of Early Day Events," *ODJ*, August 30, 1915, 6.

42. *MO*, September 6, 1915, 12.

43. "Film Protest Made; Negroes Ask Arrest of Manager of Heilig Show," *MO*, September 1, 1915, 6.

44. "Protest Is Declared Unjust; 'Birth of Nation' Manager Says Historic Facts Portrayed," *MO*, September 1, 1915, 6.

45. The Inflation Calculator.

46. John W. Kelly, "'Birth of Nation' Is Incomparable," *TET*, August 30, 1915, 3. Also see the full-page ad for the film in *TET*, August 28, 1915, 9.

47. "Cheers Greet Film," *MO*, August 30, 1915, 7. An advertisement urged people: "RESERVE YOUR SEATS EARLY." *MO*, August 30, 1915, 2.

48. "Cheers Greet Film." These sorts of artistic touches had been roundly criticized by the Boston Branch of the NAACP in its widely circulated booklet, *Fighting a Vicious Film*. Also see "Negroes Mob Photo Play," *TNYT*, April 18, 1915, 15.

49. Advertisement, *TSO*, September 12, 1915, sec. 4, 5.

50. Advertisement, *TSO*, September 19, 1915, sec. 4, 5. For the first time in Portland, matinée seats were 25 cents. Balcony seats for evening shows were 25 cents; seats on the lower floor were 50 cents.

51. "Feature Film Run Is Record; 'The Birth of a Nation' Makes Strong Impression on Audiences," *TSO*, September 26, 1915, sec. 4, 4.

52. Advertisement, *MO*, March 26, 1918, 6. The film, offered for the "first time at these bargain prices," played for a week beginning March 24th.

53. "Mayor Baker Acts to Suppress Film; 'Birth of a Nation' Results in Many Protests from Colored People," *MO*, March 26, 1918, 13.

54. "Mayor Baker Acts." For a discussion of his alleged membership in the Klan, see MacColl, 167; "Mayor Uses Police for Own Boost," *TPT*, May 12, 1923, 1.

55. "Film Ordinance Hangs in Balance," *MO*, March 27, 1918, 13. $2,000 is the equivalent of about $29,000 today; The Inflation Calculator. Members of the city council were referred to as commissioners.

56. "Play to Continue; Local Efforts to Bar 'Birth of Nation' Fruitless," *MO*, March 28, 1918, 11.

57. Cripps, *Slow Fade to Black*, 52.

58. Guerrero, 14.

59. Telegram, Beatrice Cannady to the NAACP, March 29, 1922, NAACP PB.

60. Telegram, James W. Johnson to Ben W. Olcott, March 30, 1922, NAACP PB.

61. [Walter F. White] to Mrs. E. D. Cannady, March 30, 1922, NAACP PB. There is no documentary evidence that she contacted Ceruti. According to White, Ceruti had managed to ban "it for all times from the state." For some information about this, see *TCE*, February 13, 1915, 8; March 6, 1915, 4.

62. Advertisement, *MO*, April 1, 1922, 8. Originally, there were two scores for *The Birth of a Nation*. One was written to accompany the showing at Clune's in Los Angeles; Griffin helped "create" a second score that was "approved for printing and distribution." Marks, 131-35; Hart, 93.

63. "Moving Picture News," *MO*, April 1, 1922, 12. The original print was 159 minutes

long, but subsequent prints varied in length due to the deletion of scenes, inexpert repairs, and the distributor's carelessness with the negative. Lang, 37. The version at the Blue Mouse was two hours long.

64. Advertisement.

65. "Associate Editor Injured," *TA*, December 22, 1923, 1. The accident occurred at the intersection of East 16th Avenue and Broadway.

66. *TA*, December 29, 1923, 4.

67. See, for example, *TA*, March 22, 1930, 2. For information about other branches, see Cripps, *Slow Fade to Black*, 52-69. Also see "N.A.A.C.P. Stops 'Birth of Nation' in Montclair, New Jersey," *TA*, September 13, 1924, 1.

68. This incident is described in Chapter 8.

69. "French Stop *Birth of a Nation* Film," *TA*, August 25, 1923, 1.

70. "America Could Learn from France a Lesson," *TA*, August 25, 1923, 4.

71. For more information, see, for example, Schneider, "*We Return Fighting*," or Taylor, *In Search of the Racial Frontier.*

72. Cannady closely followed the organization's efforts, often printing updates on the front page and commending the NAACP's work. See, for example, the following in *TA*: "The National Association for the Advancement of Colored People Urge Race People Everywhere to Observe Nov. 11th to Help Free Soldier Prisoners," November 3, 1923, 3; "N.A.A.C.P. Notes," November 10, 1923, 3; "Send Houston Martyrs X-Mas Gifts," December 15, 1923, 1; "War Department Commutes Sentences of Huston [*sic*] Martyrs," April 26, 1924, 1; "War Dept. Says All Houston Martyrs Get Reduced Sentences," May 24, 1924, 1.

73. "America Could Learn."

74. "'Birth of a Nation' Is Again Banned in Paris," *TA*, October 27, 1923, 3.

75. "Nick Childs [*sic*] Says Stop Fighting Segregation," *TA*, February 23, 1924, 4.

76. "'Birth of a Nation,'" *TTP*, January 18, 1924, 1.

77. *TPC*, February 16, 1924, 16; reprinted in *TA* as "Nick Childs [*sic*]."

78. "The 'Birth of a Nation,'" *TA*, March 14, 1931, 2. For other views on the film, see, for example, William Pickens, "'Birth of a Nation' Harmful Picture," *TA*, October 31, 1931, 4.

79. *TA*, February 14, 1931, 2. Punctuation added. There is no evidence that previous protests were successful.

80. See, for example, the following in *TA*: "Southern Whites Protest Showing Film; Don't Want 'B. of Nation,'" February 14, 1931, 1; "Detroit Mayor Stops 'Birth of Nation' Film," February 28, 1931, 1; "Omaha Bars Vicious Film," April 11, 1931, 1; "[Kansas] Censors Object To Picture," December 12, 1931, 3.

81. Minutes, Agenda 2203, City Council Meeting, April 8, 1931, SPA.

82. Carrie L. Ingersoll to Robert W. Bagnall, March 4, 1931, NAACP PB.

83. Minutes. Punctuation added. Ingersoll told Bagnall that Branch members Virgil Keene and the Reverend Caston also went before the council to explain why "the picture should not be shown." That is not reflected in the minutes. Ingersoll to Bagnall.

84. Minutes. Ingersoll reported that Clyde made the motion and members "voted unanimously to prohibit the showing in Portland, much to the gratification of" the Branch. Ingersoll to Bagnall. Also see "Annual Report of President, the Local Branch of the N.A.AC.P.," November 15, 1931.

85. "Commissioner Clyde Speaks," *TA*, January 16, 1932, 1. He spoke to the Branch about "Lincoln Ideals in Every Day Life."

86. "Dr. Coleman to Address Forum."

87. Robert W. Bagnall to Carrie Ingersoll, March 11, 1931, NAACP PB.

88. "The 'Birth of a Nation,'" *TA*, March 14, 1931, 2.

89. "'Birth of Nation' Film Again Unanimously Denied By City," *TA*, April 11, 1931, 1. A typographical error was corrected.

90. "*Birth of Nation* Barred from Portland; Many Groups Protest Exhibit," *TA*, January 2, 1932, 1.

91. "'Birth of a Nation' to Be the Holiday Attraction at the Heilig Theatre," *ODJ*, December 23, 1931, 4; advertisement, *ODJ*, December 23, 1931, 5.

92. "'Birth of a Nation.'"

93. "*Birth of Nation* Barred."

94. "'Birth of a Nation.'"

95. "*Birth of Nation* Barred," 4. Punctuation added, and a typographical error was corrected. Also see Minutes, Agenda 8510, City Council Meeting, December 23, 1931, SPA; "Censors Pass War Film," *MO*, December 24, 1931, sec. 1, 7.

96. "*Birth of Nation* Barred."

97. Ibid.

98. Ibid. Punctuation added. *TA* and *MO* also listed Maxwell as a member of the Board of Motion Picture Censors.

99. Ibid. Also see Minutes, Agenda 8522, City Council Meeting, December 24, 1931, SPA; "Film Permit Request Quashed," *MO*, December 25, 1931, 9. *ODJ*, however, reported the city council had "turned down the promoters who were to give the Portland post of the American Legion 15 per cent of the proceeds." "Council Refuses to O.K. *Birth of Nation*," *ODJ*, December 24, 1931, 3.

100. "That Film Again," *TA*, January 2, 1932, 2.

101. Clarence E. Ivey to Robert W. Bagnall, December 30, 1931, NAACP PB. The clipping was from one of the "daily papers."

102. "'Birth of Nation' Film Stopped by N.A.A.C.P. in Portland, Ore.," January 8, [1932], NAACP PB.

103. "That Film Again." A typographical error was corrected in one of the quotes and punctuation altered in another.

104. "*Birth of Nation* Film Crops Up Here Again; Glover Sues City Council," *TA*, January 16, 1932, 1. Also see "Suit Filed to Present Picture," *ODJ*, January 13, 1932, 11.

105. The lawsuit points to an interesting discrepancy in the contemporaneous accounts. Had the application to show the film been voluntarily withdrawn, as both *TA* and *MO* indicated, there would have been no reason for Glover to file suit.

106. "*Birth of Nation* Film Crops Up," 3. Also see "Injunction Denied in Picture Plea," *ODJ*, January 14, 1932, 6; "Move to Block Censors Fails," *MO*, January 14, 1932, sec. 1, 9.

107. *TA*, November 25, 1933, 4.

108. Cannady likely continued to editorialize against the vicious film, but the final available issue of *TA* is December 2, 1933.

109. Guerrero, 15.

110. In 1929 Baker wrote: "I recall that it was through Mrs. Cannady that my attention, as Mayor of Portland, was called to the 'Birth of a Nation' photoplay which showed here some years ago." Baker to the Harmon Award Committee.

111. "Fair Is Largest Ever Put Over in the County," *TH*, September 15, 1922, 1. For information about the Klan's activities in that city, see Toy, "The Ku Klux Klan in Tillamook, Oregon"; Toll, "Progress and Piety." According to the reference librarian at the Margaret Herrick Library, Academy of Motion Picture Arts and Sciences, "[I]t's generally not possible to determine when and where a film may have been shown after its initial release. This is especially true of a film like 'The Birth of a Nation,' which was distributed on a State Rights basis. It can be difficult to determine what territories it may have been sold to at any given time." Lucia Schultz, e-mail message to author, December 14, 2006.

Chapter Eight

1. Cannady, quoted in the draft of Trumbull's article, "A Modern Joan of Arc." Cannady's comments about the KKK were omitted from the published article. For the draft, with handwritten notes and edits, see CS, n.p.

2. "Leonidas C. Dyer," *TA*, May 19, 1923, 4. Also see "Dyer Creates Sentiment for Bill," *TA*, May 26, 1923, 1. For more about Dyer and his bill, see, for example, Schneider, 210-11, or Howard, 182-84; for more about the race riot, which involved several lynchings, see, for example, Lupton, 185-91.

3. "Negroes Here Hail Victory," *TNYT*, January 27, 1922, 17; "House Passes Bill to Curb Lynching," *TNYT*, January 27, 1922, 17.

4. "Silent Negroes March in Lynching Protest," *TNYT*, June 15, 1922, 3; "Negro Women See Harding," *TNYT*, August 15, 1922, 10.

5. "Filibuster Kills Anti-Lynching Bill," *TNYT*, December 3, 1922, 1. Also see Walter, 436-42.

6. "Congressman Dyer Pleads with Race to Unite for Justice"; "Noted Visitor Speaks at Mt. Olivet"; "Congressman Dyer Presented with Gold Pen," all in *TA*, May 19, 1923, 1. Punctuation added. Also see "Dyer Plans to Push Anti-Lynching Bill," *TNYT*, July 2, 1923, 17; "Dyer Anti Lynch [*sic*] Bill Defeated," *TA*, May 29, 1926, 2. Alarmed over the increase in mob violence in 1930, the NAACP planned to draft its own legislation to try to make lynching a federal crime. See the following in *TA*: "Association Drafts Anti-lynching Measure," September 20, 1930, 1; "Lynching Subject of Two Days' Confab," October 25, 1930, 1.

7. "Olcott Hurls Another Defi; Klan Accepts; Both Make Statements," *ODJ*, May 16, 1922, 1.

8. "Ku Klux Klan Makes Appearance," *THRG*, August 4, 1921, 7; Horowitz, "Social Morality and Personal Revitalization," 366. According to the 1920 Census, four Negroes (three women, one man) lived in Hood River County. Historical Census Browser. It is interesting to note that Edward Cannady was "made an honorary member" of the Hood River Chamber of Commerce three years later. See *TA*, October 23, 1923, 4.

9. "The Broadside of Ridicule," *THRG*, August 11, 1921, 2.

10. "Ku Klux Klan Not Wanted Here," *THRG*, August 11, 1921, 4. The man interviewed for the story was Roy D. Smith, a fruit farmer. He is listed in the *Fourteenth Census*, Hood River County, Oregon.

11. "Klan Returns To Whang Doodle Land," *THRG*, September 29, 1921, 4; The Inflation Calculator.

12. "Ku Klux Klan Stages Monster Spectacle in Receiving Their Charter," *RN-R*, July 17, 1922, 1. Apparently, combustible materials were used to fabricate the shape of a huge cross on the steep hillside. When ignited, the flames could be seen for miles. A typographical error was corrected.

13. "15,000 Klansmen Participate in Night Ceremony," *ODJ*, June 12, 1923, 2.

14. "Klansmen Hold Their Ceremonial in Open Air," *MR*, July 18, 1922, 8. The Klan was still active in Eugene two years later. See, for example, the following in the *MR*: "Klansmen to Parade," June 24, 1924, 3; "Klan to Hold Initiation," June 25, 1924, 8; "Klan Initiation Here Will Bring Thousands," June 27, 1924, 6; parade advertisement, June 27, 1924, 7; "Caravans Here Today," June 28, 1924, 5; "Klan Initiates Men Before Large Crowd," June 29, 1924, 4; "Chief of Police Thanks Citizens of Eugene," July 1, 1924, 5. Also see the parade advertisement, *EDG*, June 27, 1924, 8. For more about the Eugene Klan, see Toy, "Robe and Gown."

15. "Ku Klux Klan Parades City and Initiates," *TOS*, November 11, 1923, 1, 3. Allison delivered a three-hour speech in Klamath Falls the day before he addressed the Salem

crowd. For one discussion of Allison's "fame as an orator," see "Allison Upholds KKK," *TH*, January 4, 1924, 5.

16. See, for example, "The Ku Klux Klan," *MR*, August 7, 1921, 10; Chalmers, 30, 327; Application for Membership in the Invisible Empire Knights of the Ku Klux Klan, Mss 22, KKK.

17. Beatrice Cannady to Robert W. Bagnall, June 21, 1921, NAACP PB.

18. Ibid.

19. Petition from the Portland Branch Committee on Legislation and Legal Redress to Ben W. Olcott, August 18, 1921, NAACP PB. The committee consisted of Cannady, E. W. Agee, and O. S. Thomas. She was elected again to the Legal Redress Committee in June 1923; serving with her were Wyatt Williams and Eugene Minor. "Local Branch Elects Committees," *TA*, June 30, 1923, 1. Oliver S. Thomas appears in the 1920 Census. He and his parents were born in North Carolina. He worked as a hotel waiter, possibly for the Portland Hotel. His wife, Louise, and her parents were born in Florida. She also worked in a hotel, but her occupation is illegible. *Fourteenth Census*, MC. Agee does not appear in online census records for Oregon for any available years.

20. "Negroes Protest Klan," *MO*, August 20, 1921, 9.

21. Ben W. Olcott to Beatrice Cannady, August 20, 1921, NAACP PB. She sent a copy of the petition, Olcott's reply, and possibly the *MO* article to *TC* with the following note: "It may be of interest to the readers of *The Crisis* to know something of what the colored people of the State of Oregon are doing to handicap the efforts of the Ku Klux Klan in getting a foot hold in the state." Beatrice Cannady to W. E. B. Du Bois, August 24, 1921, NAACP PB. *TC* was reviewed from September through December 1921; nothing was located.

22. For a typewritten copy of the telegram [September 22, 1921], see BWOS, vol. 8. Also see "Many Governors Denounce Klan," *TNYW*, September 14, 1921, 1. The *World*, concerned about "the racial prejudices and passions excited by" the Klan, as well as its "secret, oath-bound operations," conducted a nationwide investigation of the Klan over the course of three months. The Pulitzer Prize-winning exposé, which began running September 7, 1921, was initiated by Henry P. Fry, a former Klan kleagle who withdrew from the organization after five months and turned over all of his information to the newspaper. Fry assisted with the investigation and reportedly wrote a number of articles for the paper. His book, *The Modern Ku Klux Klan*, was published the following year. *TCJ* reprinted a chapter a day beginning July 15, 1922. See the advertisement for the series, *TCJ*, July 15, 1922, 6. Cannady observed that Fry had "stepped into the limelight with some interesting scenes from inside the ... Ku Klux Klan." *TA*, June 13, 1925, 4.

23. For a typewritten copy of Olcott's reply [n.d.], see BWOS, vol. 8. His reply was not included in the *NYW* article. However, the paper did print remarks from the governors of Alabama, North Dakota, Kansas, Minnesota, Maine, Utah, Louisiana, Nebraska, West Virginia, and Nevada.

24. The Oregon Klan "joined the movement to require attendance at public schools, to the exclusion of parochial, military, or other private academies," and used its influence to help elect Democrat Walter M. Pierce governor in 1922 and pass an alien land bill as well as "a measure prohibiting the wearing of religious garb in public classrooms." Many scholars have written about these issues and their effect on Oregon. See, for example, LaLande, "Beneath the Hooded Robe," and Horowitz, "Order, Solidarity, and Vigilance." For Cannady's view on the Klan and Catholics, see, for example, "The KKK and the Katholics," *TA*, September 11, 1926, 4. For information about the controversial school bill debate, which was ultimately decided by the United States Supreme Court in 1925, see, for example, Saalfeld; Bryant; Zelman; Holsinger.

25. "The Ku Klux Klan." The issue of newspaper responsibility in bringing the Klan's Oregon activities to light deserves further study. For a brief discussion of the press, see Saalfeld, Chapter 6. The *TCJ* may have been the most outspoken critic of the Klan. See, for example, the following: "Easy Marks," July 25, 1922, 4; "Benefits of Silence," August 3, 1922, 4; "A Revelation," August 5, 1922, 6; "The *Oregonian*'s Discovery," August 12, 1922, 4; "Silence in the Sanctums," August 21, 1922, 4. In southern Oregon, Robert W. Ruhl, editor of *MMT*, may have been the lone voice critical of the KKK. See, for example: "The 'Truth' About the Ku Klux Klan," June 9, 1922, 4; "The Truth Does Prevail," August 4, 1922, 4. Also see Robert W. Ruhl, "Reference To Klan Dodged By 80 Per Cent of Papers, Says Editor," *TPT*, May 1, 1923, 6.

26. "Ten Dollars, Please," *TS-WD*, August 16, 1921 [misprinted as August 13], 2.

27. "Nightshirt Knight Faces Grand Jury," *MO*, August 5, 1921, 14. Also see "Klan Claims 1000 Members in State," *MO*, August 17, 1921, 11; "Old King Kleagle Abandons Oregon," *TSO*, August 28, 1921, 16; "Klan Chief Leaves," *MO*, September 23, 1921, 10.

28. For example, an article in the *Outlook* magazine noted in the first paragraph: "Oregon, politically the most conservative and temperamentally the least romantic State west of the Rocky Mountains, is now under the political control of the Ku Klux Klan." Roberts, 490. The *Outlook* succeeded the *Christian Union* in July 1893 and was "a journal of opinion" with articles, editorials, and departments that addressed topical issues "in the broadest and most dispassionate spirit." Mott, 428.

29. Olcott wrote Sheriff C. E. Terrill for details about the Klan's activities. Terrill replied that he regarded the organization as a "menace to public welfare. Everybody is on their toes looking for something to happen. There have been three outrages committed without justification, yet the Ku Klux Klan claim they had nothing to do with it, yet they do nothing to help the officials catch the guilty parties." Terrill to Ben W. Olcott, May 14, 1922, BWOS, vol. 8. For more about the investigation, see, for example, "Prosecute Night Mobs, Says Olcott," *ODJ*, July 6, 1922, 1; "Move Against Klan in Jackson County Made By Governor," *TOS*, July 7, 1922, 6. For coverage of the recall, see, for example, "Recall of Sheriff Charles E. Terrill Demanded," the *Clarion*, June 23, 1922, 1; "Why a Recall?" *MMT*, June 26, 1922, 4; "Recall Vote Ordered By County Cl'k," *MMT*, July 11, 1922, 1.

30. Arthur Burr had just completed a three-week sentence in the county jail for bootlegging. On the evening of his release, variously reported as March 1, March 13, and March 14, Burr was offered a ride to Medford by two men in an automobile. Instead, they drove into the foothills of the Siskiyou Mountains, near the California border, where a "hooded band of inquisitors" was waiting for them. He reportedly was lifted off the ground and "hanged three times by the neck" as "revolver bullets ... kept his feet doing the double shuffle while they were on the ground." He finally was released and "ordered to leave the community." Burr fled to Modesto, California. He does not appear in online census records for Jackson County, Oregon, for 1920. "Bootblack to Tell How He Was Hanged," *ODJ*, July 26, 1922, 1; "Move against Klan in Jackson County."

Days later, Joseph F. Hale (identified as J. F. Hale in *MMT*) was kidnapped from his home by "several masked Ku Klux men" and driven to an isolated spot known as Table Rock. A "rope was placed around [Hale's] neck and he was threatened with death by hanging unless he dropped a suit ... he had pending against a Medford citizen." Hale was brought back to town unharmed, but his abductors "warned [him] that if he ever uttered a word about the doings of the night and his experience he would be killed." "Local Citizen Victim of Ku Klux Klan," *MMT*, March 18, 1922, 1, 6. Hale appears in the *Fourteenth Census*, Jackson County, Oregon. Also see "Ku Klux K. Denies Hand in Outrage," *MMT*, March 20, 1922, 1.

Henry Johnson, initially described as black, was driving home with three friends when their car broke down near Jacksonville, a former mining town near Medford. Seven men, all wearing "flimsy veils with eyeholes cut out," drove up in two vehicles. The "masked band" ordered two of Johnson's friends to "drive further up the road"; another was "admonished ... to go to work and never be seen with Johnson again." Johnson was taken "a short distance and accused ... of the chicken stealing that had been going on in Jacksonville." When he denied the charges, "his captors shouted for a rope which they put around his neck and pulled taut." He also was accused of bootlegging and associating with white women, charges he "denied ... vehemently." Like Hale, he was finally let go and advised "to speed away." "Third Necktie Party Staged in J'Ville District," *MMT*, April 12, 1922, 8. Johnson does not appear in online census records for 1920 for Jackson or Josephine Counties, Oregon. Several secondary accounts list Johnson as black (McLagan, 139; Saalfeld, 4; "Ku Klux in Jackson," *OV*, August 12, 1922, 12; Toy, "The Ku Klux Klan in Oregon," 72). Race can be inferred from one account of the crime, which referred to his association with white women and included the use of a racial epithet ("Third Necktie Party"). However, race is never mentioned in subsequent reports (see, for example, "Prosecute Night Mobs" and "State to Prosecute Local Outrages," *MMT*, July 6, 1922, 1). If he had been black, all articles would have identified him by race, as was the case for Arthur Burr. Also, newspaper accounts variously list the date of the "outrage" as April 6 ("Move Against Klan in Jackson County") and April 9 ("Grand Jury Invitation Is Issued," *MMT*, July 27, 1922, 1).

31. "Klan Ejects Negro from Roseburg," *RN-R*, April 3, 1922, 1; "Third Necktie Party." Also see "Ku Klux Eject Negro," *MO*, April 3, 1922, 1. Jackson does not appear in online census records for Douglas County, Oregon, for 1920. See the advertisement for Sawyer's lecture and *The Face at Your Window* in *RN-R*, March 30, 1922, 6. Sawyer is listed in the *Fourteenth Census*, MC.

32. "Klan Ejects Negro." Also see the following in *RN-R*: "Klansmen Advertise Coming Lecture," March 30, 1922, 8; "Klan Has Come to Stay Says Sawyers [*sic*]," March 31, 1922, 6; "Capacity Audience at Klan Lecture," April 1, 1922, 1. According to Fry: The "propagation department of the Ku Klux Klan ... uses motion pictures and paid lecturers to spread the germs of Ku Kluxism. There is a picture entitled 'The Face at Your Window' that is being used extensively as an aid to the canvassing Kleagles. The film company arranges with the local Kleagle to have this picture exhibited on a certain day, and each Klansman is requested to bring a friend with him to see it. At the close of the performance the Klansman hands his friend an application blank and through the psychological effect of the picture usually gets the other to join." Henry P. Fry, "Lawlessness, Mob Outrage Follow Klan Organization; Newspapers Silenced By Threat of Boycott When Opposed To Order," *TCJ*, July 18, 1922, 4.

33. Proclamation, May 13, 1922, BWOP.

34. "Midnight Party Held for Negro By Robed Sextet," *ME*, June 3, 1923, 1, 8. Perry Ellis does not appear in online census records for Clackamas County, Oregon, for 1920.

35. "Oregon Stages Near Lynching Party; Perry Ellis, Only Colored Citizen of Oregon City, Victim of Near Lynching By Masked Men in Nearby Country Thought to Be Members of KKK," *TA*, June 9, 1923, 1. The newspaper that published this article was not identified.

36. "'Ku Klux Klan Ain't after Us,'" *TA*, June 23, 1923, 4. Her comments prefaced an article by William Pickens that originally appeared in *TPC*.

37. "Council Votes City Disgraced By Acts of Gang," *ME*, June 9, 1923, 1. The vote was three to two. The *ME* reported that Ellis had "made good his promise" to leave for Tacoma, Washington, despite Sheriff William Wilson's assurances that his departure was unnecessary. "Promise Made To Robed Band Kept By Local Negro," *ME*, June 5,

1923, 1. Identified as W. J. Wilson in *ME*, William Wilson appears in the *Fourteenth Census*, Clackamas County. Pierce succeeded Olcott and served from 1923 to 1927. A number of newspapers around the state commented on the near-lynching as well as the practicality of the resolution. See, for example: *ODJ*, June 11, 1923, 6; *CG-T*, June 12, 1923, 2.

38. "Governor Ready to Aid Officers, Recorder Is Told," *ME*, June 17, 1923, 1. The newspaper was reviewed through July 28th; no additional stories about the resolution or request for assistance were located.

39. "Gov. Pierce to Aid Solve Pettis Murder Mystery," *CBT*, July 15, 1924, 1.

40. Lee C. Anderson to James Weldon Johnson, August 6, 1924, NAACP PB. Thirty Negroes lived in Coos County in 1920. Historical Census Browser.

41. "Think Ku Kluxers Menace Country," *CBT*, November 5, 1923, 6. *TA* reported later that white people objected to having "colored porters" on railroad parlor cars pass through town. "For that reason, the company has put white men on the cars instead and the colored porters who were discharged have been returned to their homes in California." "White Men on the Job," *TA*, October 3, 1925, 4.

42. "Heinous Murder of Negro Shown By Developments," *CBT*, July 14, 1924, 1, 2. Neither Gaston Campbell nor the victim, Timothy Pettis, appear in online census records for Coos County, Oregon, for 1920. It was common for mobs to castrate or otherwise mutilate bodies following a lynching, both to make a statement about the victim's manhood and to obtain a macabre souvenir. The undertaker felt that the "fastened condition of the dead man's underclothing and outer garments was such as to indicate ... he had been the victim of physical mutilation at the hands of someone."

43. "Timothy F. Pettis, Whose Body Was Found in Bay, Victim of Heinous Attack," *TA*, July 19, 1924, 1.

44. "A Brave Man," *TA*, July 19, 1924, 4. Punctuation altered. For more about Campbell or his wife, Omabelle, see, for example, the following in *TA*: November 17, 1923, 4; June 21, 1924, 4; "Goes South on Visit," September 13, 1924, 1.

45. *TA*, July 19, 1924, 4.

46. See, for example, the advertisement in *TA*, December 22, 1923, 4.

47. "Negro Woman Branded; Klan Message Left," *TPT*, October 21, 1921, 1, 2; *Fourteenth Census*, MC.

48. "Gov. Pierce."

49. "No Clue Yet in Murder Case," *CBT*, July 19, 1924, 1.

50. "Run Down Poison Liquor Clew [*sic*] in Pettis Murder," *CBT*, July 17, 1924, 1. Eyewitness accounts of Pettis' disappearance varied widely. See, for example, the following in *CBT*: "Heinous Murder of Negro"; "Sailors Disavow Crime Knowledge," July 25, 1924, 1.

51. Telegram, Lee C. Anderson to the NAACP, July 18, 1924, NAACP PB. Punctuation added.

52. Telegram, James Weldon Johnson to Lee C. Anderson, July 19, 1924, NAACP PB. Punctuation added.

53. Anderson to the NAACP.

54. "Negroes Raise Reward of $100," *CBT*, August 8, 1924, 1; The Inflation Calculator.

55. Anderson to the NAACP.

56. [Walter F. White] to Lee C. Anderson, August 19, 1924, NAACP PB.

57. Anderson, "To the Officers and Members of the [NAACP]."

58. That was not the first time a black man had been murdered in Marshfield. Ten years before Beatrice Cannady moved to Oregon, Alonzo Tucker was lynched for allegedly raping a white woman. See "Fiend Is Lynched," *ODJ*, September 18, 1902, 1; "Mob Pursues Negro," *MO*, September 18, 1902, 4; "Dies at Mob's Hands," *MO*, September 19, 1902,

4; "In Simple Justice," *MO*, September 20, 1902, 6; "The Southern Oregon Lynching," *TNA*, September 20, 1902, 4. Copies of the *Coos Bay News* and the *Coast Mail* have not been located.

59. Following Charles Lindbergh's successful transatlantic flight, he went on a three-month nationwide tour in the Spirit of St. Louis. "Guggenheim Tour."

60. *TA*, January 12, 1924, 4.

61. Rutherford, SR 270, tape 2 transcript, OBHP. The Hensons recalled, "Everybody knew [that] in every town you lived in ... there were groups" of the KKK. Mr. and Mrs. Julian Henson, Mss 2854, OBHP.

62. "'Purifying' the Klan," *OV*, December 8, 1923, 16.

63. Because the Klan was supposed to be a "secret" organization, it is rare to find minutes of klavern meetings and membership rosters. Thus, estimates of "naturalized" members vary depending on the source. Jackson calculates that fifty thousand men and women (as members of the Ladies of the Invisible Empire) were initiated into the Oregon Klan between 1915 and 1944. Jackson, 237. Chalmers estimates that fourteen thousand were naturalized during the Oregon Klan's first year. Chalmers, 88.

64. Other editors, such as Charlotta Spear Bass of *TCE*, were not as fortunate. See, for example, the following in *TCE*: "Chief Mogul of Ku Klux Klan Procures Warrant for Editor and Managing Editor of 'Soaring Eagle,'" May 15, 1925, 1; "Ku Klux Case Set for 18th of June," May 22, 1925, 1; "Ku Klux Complaint Against *Eagle* Editors," June 5, 1925, 1; "Judge Chambers in Notable Decision Finds Defendants in KKK Case Not Guilty," June 26, 1925, 1. Also see Bass' autobiography and Streitmatter, "The Media and Racial Equality."

65. Handsaker to the Harmon Award Committee, CS, 20-21, 23. This incident was not reported in *NG*. Copies of *TA* published from 1920 until May 1923 are missing, so we may never know if the Klan targeted her during that time or if she wrote additional editorials about the organization.

66. Myhra, 80.

67. Delgado, 131.

68. Ibid., 132.

69. See the following in *TADS*: "Negro Slayer Reads Bible As He Waits Death," June 19, 1924, 1; "Slayer of Arizona University Student Dies Today," June 20, 1924, 1; "Wm. Ward Dies on Gallows at Dawn," June 21, 1924, 1.

70. "Lynching of Blacks Causes Slayer to Hate White Race," *TA*, July 12, 1924, 1; "Slayer of Arizona University Student."

71. "Hating the White Race," *TA*, July 12, 1924, 4. A few courageous Oregonians spoke out against the Klan during the 1920s. See, for example: "Methodist Episcopal Church Adopts Resolution Favoring Suppression Ku-Klux-Klan," *RN-R*, August 8, 1921, 1; "Ku Klux Suppression Asked for By People of Neighboring Town," *EDG*, August 8, 1921, 1; "Klan's Suppression Urged," *MR*, August 9, 1921, 6.

Chapter Nine

1. A typographical error was corrected. It is likely that the letter-writer was J. G. Washington, a barber and resident of Tacoma, Washington. He and his parents were born in the "United States." His wife, Atria [?], and her parents were born in Minnesota. *Fourteenth Census*, Pierce County.

2. Frank Jenkins, "Editorials On the Day's News," *RN-R*, May 23, 1930, 1; reprinted in *TA* as "What Some Oregon Editors Think," June 14, 1930, 2. Jenkins appears in the *Fourteenth Census*, MC. Four Negroes lived in Douglas County in 1930. Historical Census Browser.

3. Rutherford, SR 270.

4. Support from readers was meaningful, too. See, for example, *TA*, September 12, 1925, 4.

5. "'Advocate's' Twenty-Fifth Anniversary," *TA*, September 1, 1928, 2. A spelling error was corrected.

6. "Y.W.C.A. Branch Opened," *MO*, October 17, 1921, 20. Capitalization altered.

7. "Right of Negroes to Build Upheld," *MO*, August 30, 1921, 7.

8. Beatrice Cannady to Mr. Grant, September 12, 1921, copy in AC. He appears in the *Fourteenth Census*, MC.

9. "Y.W.C.A. Branch Opened"; "Williams Avenue Y.W.C.A. Notes," *TA*, November 3, 1923, 3.

10. "Branch Y Goes Up," *TA*, February 6, 1926, 1; The Inflation Calculator. For more about the role of the YWCA in Portland, including the Williams Avenue branch, see the articles in *Journal of Women's History* 15, no. 3 (2003). Collins was identified as Mrs. E. S. Collins of 877 Westover Road. These details match information for Mary Collins in the *Fourteenth Census*, MC.

11. "Branch Y." The school, founded in 1900, was described as "the leading institution of its kind in this part of the country" and a source of pride for the city. Douthit, 85.

12. "Business College Bars Christ," *TA*, September 6, 1924, 4. Cannady did not name the church. Elizabeth Summers, the girl who was refused admission, was a graduate of Lincoln High School. She was born in North Carolina. Her father, Peter, and his parents were born in South Carolina. He was described as mulatto and a dealer of second-hand goods. Her mother, Pattie, was born in Tennessee. She was described as a mulatto woman who worked as a "laborer" doing housecleaning. *Fourteenth Census*, MC.

Cannady sought help from the Reverend Clement G. Clarke, the white pastor of the First Congregational Church. He wrote Walker that he shared the women's "sorrow and protest," and added his own "indignation" over the treatment Summers had experienced simply because her "skin was black." He also publicly condemned Walker's "Christian ethics" and named the school during his morning sermon. Clarke to Isaac M. Walker, September 8, 1924; Clement G. Clarke to Mrs. E. D. Cannady, September 23, 1924, copies in AC. Summer was misidentified in his letter as Lucille Triplett; she ended up going "East to school because of the discrimination made in the Behnke-Walker school." Beatrice Cannady to Clement G. Clarke, September 15, 1924, copy in AC. For more about Triplett, see "Portland Maids Enter College," *TA*, September 6, 1924, 4. Years later, Kathryn Bogle complained of the same treatment at the business school. Bogle, "An American Negro Speaks of Color"; "Document."

13. Ovington, notes.

14. "Branch Y." Typographical errors were corrected.

15. "Segregation or Jim-Crowism," *TA*, February 6, 1926, 4. A typographical error was corrected.

16. "A New Subscriber," *TA*, February 6, 1926, 1.

17. "Williams Avenue 'Y,'" *TA*, June 5, 1926, 1.

18. Ovington, notes. Punctuation was added to the first quotation and a typographical error was corrected in the second. Cannady wrote a critical editorial about the decision to change the meeting place. "Local N.A.A.C.P.," *TA*, November 6, 1926, 4. For an article celebrating the *Guardian*'s thirty-second anniversary, see "A Call from New England," *TA*, November 11, 1933, 2.

19. "'Black Belts,'" *TA*, July 12, 1930, 2. A typographical error was corrected.

20. "A Man-Size Feat," *TA*, May 28, 1927, 2. Also see "Portland to Have a Colored Dentist," *TA*, May 28, 1927, 1. She reported that Elbert Booker stood "in bold relief in a class of 86 men," because he was the "only colored member of his class." For a timeline of

the college, see "OHSU: An Historical Chronology." Booker grew up in Seattle. According to the 1910 Census, Elbert (listed as Albert), was living with his parents, James and Ellen. He and his parents were born in Texas. His father worked as a janitor for National Bank. *Thirteenth Census*, King County.

21. "A Man-Size Feat."

22. "Our Opportunity," *TA*, January 25, 1930, 2. A typographical error was corrected in the first quotation. Also see "Dr. Booker Opens Office," *TA*, July 30, 1927, 1. Dr. Booker advertised; see, for example, *TA*, August 17, 1929, 2. He was not the first black dentist to practice in Portland; Dr. Hugh A. Bell had an office with "the latest equipment" at 462 Williams Avenue. "Admitted to Practice Dentistry Here," *TA*, December 6, 1924, 1. By 1931, however, Bell had moved to New York [City?] with his family. Rosalie Bird, "In the Realm of Society," *TA*, May 9, 1931, 2. Various keywords were crosschecked against the *Oregonian*'s index for 1927; no articles about Dr. Booker's quest to find an office were discovered. Cannady missed the "formal opening" of his office because she was in New York City, but Shirley McCanns and Lulu Gragg helped the Bookers greet guests. Among the "distinguished" visitors who stopped by were an *Oregonian* reporter and Mayor Baker, who offered the dentist "hearty congratulations." His greeting was in stark contrast with the article's observation that Booker had had to rely on "patience and perseverance" in order to cross color barriers erected by white businessmen. "Mayor Baker Visits Dr. Booker; Extends Hearty Congratulations," *TA*, August 27, 1927, 1.

23. "Our Opportunity." James Merriman's departure had left Portland temporarily without a physician of color. *TA*, October 26, 1929, 2.

24. "A New Doctor," *TA*, January 25, 1930, 2. Also see, "Portland Has New Doctor," *TA*, January 11, 1930, 1. DeNorval Unthank appears in the 1920 Census. He and his mother were born in Pennsylvania; his father in North Carolina. He was listed as the adopted son of Thomas Unthank, who worked as a physician. *Fourteenth Census*, Jackson County, Missouri.

25. "Race Prejudice Causes Doctor to Seek New Office," *TA*, February 15, 1930, 1. It is unclear why Booker was allowed to return to his former office space after tenants objected to his and Unthank's presence.

26. Unthank may have worked out of his home at 69 East 76th Street North for a time, too. See the following in *TA*: "Local Briefs," September 6, 1930, 3; November 15, 1930, 1; March 7, 1931, 1; "Keeping Fit," April 4, 1931, 4.

27. *TA*, August 29, 1931, 3. Donohue does not appear in online census records for Oregon for any available years. It is unclear why the men decided to practice together. An integrated practice would have been unusual in that era, but not impossible. However, Donohue risked losing white patients because some may have refused to patronize an integrated office.

28. *TA*, April 25, 1931, 3.

29. "Physician's Home Stoned." A typographical error was corrected. Cannady also wrote that a petition had been circulated in an attempt to drive her and her family out of their home. "No Broadway Here." See also: Marie Smith, Mss 2854, OBHP; Kathryn Bogle, SR 442, tape 2 transcript.

30. "Vandals Hit Dwelling of Negro M.D.," *ODJ*, April 24, 1931, 1; "Physician's Home Stoned."

31. "Vandals Hit Dwelling."

32. "Physician's Home Stoned."

33. *TA*, April 25, 1931, 2. Also see "Portland's Mob Spirit," *TA*, April 25, 1931, 2.

34. H. V. Rominger, "Indignant at Vandalism," *ODJ*, April 30, 1931, 8; reprinted as "Indignant at Recent Vandalism," *TA*, May 9, 1931, 2. Rominger had worked as a minister

in Laramie, Wyoming, before moving to Rainier, Oregon, to work as a minister there. He appears in the *Twelfth Census*, Albany County, Wyoming, and the *Thirteenth Census*, Columbia County, Oregon.

35. *TA*, May 9, 1931, 2.

36. Forrest Bailey to the NAACP, May 12, 1931, NAACP PB; Robert Bagnall to Forrest Bailey, May 27, 1931, NAACP PB.

37. Robert Bagnall to Carrie L. Ingersoll, May 27, 1931, NAACP PB.

38. "Vandals Break Windows in Doctor's Home; N.A.A.C.P. Enters Unthank Case," *TA*, July 4, 1931, 1. In an odd turn of events, Thelma Unthank was arrested for "threatening to commit a felony" due to an altercation she had with a neighbor following the second incident of vandalism. She was released on her own recognizance and the trial date was set for July 10th. Cannady, who represented Mrs. Unthank even though she was not a member of the Bar, reported "great interest" in the trial. The charges were dismissed two weeks later. "Vandals Break Windows"; "Charge Dismissed vs. Def. on Friday," *TA*, July 18, 1931, 1.

39. "Vandals Break Windows." Edgar Williams and his parents were born in Texas. He worked as a laborer at a foundry. His wife, Octavia, and her parents also were born in Texas. The couple, described as mulatto, had two daughters, both born in Arizona. *Fourteenth Census*, MC.

40. "Hoodlums Busy Again," *TA*, July 4, 1931, 2. Typographical errors were corrected.

41. Rutherford, SR 270. He undoubtedly was well aware of the doctor's plight, given that his wife, Verdell, was Unthank's secretary for two decades. "Verdell Rutherford." *TA* reported in August 1931 that the Unthanks had "taken" the former home of Henrietta and William Marshall at 464 Buffalo Street and were living there. Thirteen months later, they returned to a former residence in the Montavilla neighborhood for some reason. *TA*, August 15, 1931, 2; *TA*, September 10, 1932, 2.

42. Bogle, SR 442, tape 5 transcript, OHS. Remarkably, the Unthanks did not leave Portland; they weathered the Great Depression and World War II, and lived to see some victories for black Portlanders in the 1950s and 1960s. Dr. Unthank eventually was honored with a number of awards and in 1969 the City of Portland named a four-acre park in east Portland for him in recognition of "his role in bringing down racial barriers." "Past Doctor-Citizen Award Recipients"; "De Norval [*sic*] Unthank Park"; "Self-guided Tour: Downtown, Northeast and Greater Portland." The doctor also was the first African American to be admitted to The City Club of Portland. Lucia, 48, 50-51, 63; "City Club's History." Also see Oz Hopkins, "Dr. Unthank's death saddens city," *OJ*, September 22, 1977, 1. Unthank's son was a "nationally-noted architect, educator and community activist." Farr, 400.

For information about another homeowner who was discriminated against, see, for example, "Sue to Oust Negro Owner; White [People] Do Not Want Colored in District," *TA*, January 16, 1932, 2; Clarence E. Ivey to Robert W. Bagnall, December 30, 1931, NAACP PB; "Jews Support Oregon N.A.A.C.P. in Anti-Segregation Fight," NAACP PB.

43. "Let's Keep Grants Pass a White Man's Town," *SOS*, May 24, 1924, 1. According to the 1920 Census, Josephine County had a total population of 7,655, which included 3,862 native white males; 3,228 native white females, thirty-four Indians/Chinese/Japanese/people of "all other races"; eight Negro women; fourteen Negro men. Historical Census Browser.

44. "Local Box Factory Purchaser Brings Blacks To White City," *SOS*, May 24, 1924, 1.

45. "Let's Keep." A spelling error was corrected. Also see "The White Race," *SOS*, July 3, 1924, 3. Greene reported he had "received quite a number of letters regarding" his editorials; some took him "to task for [his] stand in favor of the white race" while others

supported his views. See, for example, the following in *SOS*: "Let the People Think," May 31, 1924, 3; "God Made Coyotes and Rattlesnakes," June 7, 1924, 1; "Circulation and Success," June 14, 1924, 1.

46. "Grants Pass," *TA*, August 2, 1924, 4.

47. "Grants Pass a White Man's Town," *TA*, June 7, 1924, 1.

48. "Keeping Grants Pass White," *TA*, June 7, 1924, 4.

49. "Negro Publication Demonstrates Mental Depth of Race Today," *SOS*, June 14, 1924, 3. Punctuation was altered, and a spelling error and a typographical error were corrected. It is unclear how Greene learned about *TA* or obtained copies of the Portland newspaper.

50. "Comments, Opinions, Reflections," *SOS*, June 21, 1924, 2; The Inflation Calculator.

51. "Keeping Grants Pass White," *TA*, June 21, 1924, 4.

52. "Good for Mrs. Cannady," *TCE*, June 13, 1924, 8; reprinted under the same headline in *TA*, July 12, 1924, 4.

53. "Associate Editor Answers Charge that Black Men Are Rapists," *TA*, June 28, 1924, 1; "Negro Publication." For more editorials about white supremacy and moral superiority, see, for example, the following in *TA*: "Supremacy Boast," August 22, 1925, 4; "Superiority," January 10, 1925, 4; August 31, 1929, 2.

54. "Dogs Never Bark at a Thing Unless It Shows Some Signs of Constructive Activity," *SOS*, June 7, 1924, 1.

55. "Comments, Opinions, Reflections," *SOS*, July 26, 1924, 2. For an article supportive of the Klan, see "Comments, Opinions, Reflections," *SOS*, July 12, 1924, 2. Weeks later, Greene sold the paper to J. J. Hoogstraat, kleagle of the Medford klavern, and turned to farming "in order to regain his health and build himself up physically." "*Spokesman* Management Changes Hands," *SOS*, August 9, 1924, 1.

56. "Portland Branch N.A.A.C.P.," *TA*, July 19, 1924, 4.

57. Walter M. Pierce to L. C. Anderson, June 26, 1924; reprinted in "Portland Branch." The original correspondence has not been located.

58. I. H. Van Winkle to L. C. Anderson, June 20, 1924; reprinted in "Portland Branch." The original correspondence has not been located.

59. "N.A.A.C.P. Convention Largest Ever Held." Caston resigned his position at the church in 1931, an announcement that "came as a surprise to many members of his congregation." "Reverend J. L. Caston Resigns," *TA*, June 20, 1931, 1.

60. "Attention Editor *Southern Oregon Spokesman*," *TA*, July 26, 1924, 4. The *Oregonian* item, datelined St. Helens, Oregon, was about a man charged with a "statutory crime against his minor daughter." The original article has not been located. The other item, datelined Visalia, California, also involved statutory charges. The newspaper was not identified. Cannady reprinted articles from other black newspapers that addressed the issue of black "criminals" and the white press. See, for example, "Check the White Press (from the *Cleveland Herald*, Sept. 19)," *TA*, October 3, 1925, 4.

61. "To Our Patrons."

62. "One of Our Hopes," *TSI*, July 23, 1921, 2. A spelling error was corrected.

63. "The Daily Papers," *TA*, October 6, 1928, 2.

64. "A Negro and a Knife," *TA*, August 2, 1924, 4. Punctuation altered. The original article was not located, but see, for example, "Negro Gets Thirty Days for Threat," *ODJ*, July 22, 1924, 5.

65. Wideman, 60.

66. "The Daily Press," *TA*, December 20, 1924, 4. Both *TPT* and *ODJ* were reviewed from December 13th through December 20th; the article Cannady referred to was not

located.

67. "*Portland Telegram* Sows Seeds of Race Prejudice," *TA*, March 29, 1924, 4. She also criticized *NG* for using the phrase "darkey choir" when referring to an upcoming concert by a Portland church group. "Uses Obnoxious Term," *TA*, June 19, 1932, 3.

68. "Negress," *TA*, April 4, 1925, 4.

69. "Insulting Terms By Daily Papers," *TA*, February 27, 1926, 4. Punctuation altered.

70. "How Long?" *TA*, August 28, 1926, 4; "Stop My Paper," *TA*, November 8, 1924, 4. Also see "Boycotting the Negro Newspaper," *TA*, January 22, 1927, 2.

71. "Stop My Paper."

72. "The Capital 'N' in Negro," *TA*, April 5, 1930, 2. For another editorial about the media's predilection for "violat[ing] both grammar and commonsense in writing the word Negro with a small 'n,'" see, for example, *TA*, June 5, 1926, 4.

73. "More Editors Adopt Capital 'N,'" *TA*, April 12, 1930, 1.

74. Mrs. E. D. Cannady to the Editor, October 5, 1929; reprinted in "The Term 'Negress,'" *TA*, October 12, 1929, 2. The paper's editorial pages were reviewed from October 5th through October 12th; her correspondence was not located.

75. "Color Line Drawn at University of Oregon," *TA*, October 5, 1929, 1. Also see "University Feels Lack of Housing; Parents of Colored Girl Allege Discrimination Against Race," *EG*, October 1, 1929, 3. A subsequent article described arrangements in the women's dormitory and noted: "Regardless of color, considerable thought is given to making these groupings as harmonious as possible and it is contrary to policy to force the acceptance of any girl by any group unless they want to live with her." "State Board to Act Upon Color Issue," *EG*, October 2, 1929, 12.

76. "University Feels Lack," 1.

77. "Rights Denied Her, Says Negro Co-Ed," *MO*, October 1, 1929, 8. Maxwell was a transfer student from Oregon Agricultural College in Corvallis, where she had studied pharmacy. Cannady, "The Strivings of a Race."

78. "University Feels Lack," 3.

79. "Color Line Drawn"; Cannady, "The Strivings of a Race."

80. "Color Line Drawn." Also see "State Board to Act." For more about the Maxwell family, see, for example, *TA*, September 1, 1923, 6; "Mr. Maxwell in City," *TA*, November 10, 1923, 1. Patterson was elected in 1926 and served from January 10, 1927, until December 21, 1929. He died in office. "Governors of Oregon," *Oregon Blue Book*, http://bluebook.state.or.us/state/elections/elections24.htm.

81. "Rights Denied Her."

82. "Color Bar Removal Gained by N.A.A.C.P.," *TA*, October 19, 1929, 1. No library has been able to supply the *Twin-City Herald* for October 1929.

83. "Why Not Here?" *TA*, October 19, 1929, 2. Emphasis in the original. Maxwell continued to attend the University of Oregon, but eventually the stress overwhelmed her and she dropped out. She may have returned home to Salem to attend Willamette University, but by August 1930 she was headed to Los Angeles "for an indefinite sojourn." See the following in *TA*: August 23, 1930, 2; September 20, 1930, 2; "The Maxwells Move South," March 14, 1931, 3; "Former Salem Girl Applies for Scholastic Credits," August 15, 1931, 1.

84. Milo C. King, "Theatre Refuses Admittance To Negro," *TA*, August 24, 1929, 1, 3. The spelling of McArthur's last name was corrected. Cannady later reported McArthur had been selected to sit on the jury to hear a suit brought against Mayor George L. Baker alleging malfeasance and negligence. *TA*, May 7, 1932, 3; Lansing, 322-23. Attorney Milo King died six months later. "Milo King Passes," *TA*, February 1, 1930, 1. $35,000 is the equivalent of about $440,000 today. The Inflation Calculator. A typographical

error was corrected in the final quotation. The family may have seen *The College Coquette*. Advertisement, Pantages, *TSO*, August 18, 1929, sec. 4, 3.

85. "Theater Robber Is Caught in Act," *MO*, February 25, 1925, 1.

86. Sam Bagley does not appear in online census records for MC for 1920.

87. "Movies of Holdup Taken," *MO*, February 25, 1925, 4; "Theater Robber Is Caught," 4. "Yeggman" is slang for a burglar or safecracker. *The Random House Dictionary of the English Language* (1966); s.v. "yegg."

88. "Pantages Manager," *TA*, March 14, 1925, 4. Punctuation altered.

89. "Theatre Draws Color-Line; Local Business Man Insulted at Theatre," *TA*, October 5, 1929, 1. Robert Allen was seven in 1920, so he would have been about sixteen in 1929. *Fourteenth Census*, MC. They may have seen Bud Harris and Radcliff in *Push 'em Pull 'em*, Davis and Darnell in *Auto Row*, or a vaudeville show. Advertisement, Pantages, *MO*, October 5, 1929, 11. That was not the first time that Allen had been discriminated against. He "brought suit through Attorney McCants Stewart" in 1915 "because the managers of the Star Theater drew the 'color line' on the lower floor of the moving-picture house." The head usher prevented Allen and his wife from "sitting in the parquet." Allen said the "usher grabbed him by the coat and forcibly prevented him from taking the desired seat." He asked for more than $3,000 in damages, which included compensation for the usher's "violence" and the couple's "mortification and chagrin." "Theater Sued By Negro; People's Amusement Company Is Defendant," *MO*, September 17, 1915, 9. Fifty years later, Portlanders still remembered vividly the indignities they endured in the 1920s. Otto Rutherford, for one, recalled that the owner of the Egyptian Theatre at Russell and Union would not permit Negroes to attend shows there. Rutherford, SR 270.

90. "The N.A.A.C.P.," *TA*, October 5, 1929, 2.

91. "What We Advocate," *TA*, October 12, 1929, 2.

92. She reported receiving a letter dated September 8, 1925, from W. C. James, who implored her to come to Vernonia to fight the discrimination. However, he does not appear in online census records for Oregon for 1920, nor is he listed as one of the members of the new NAACP Branch Cannady helped organize in Vernonia, even though she noted 100 percent participation. (Six individuals joined anonymously as a "Friend of the cause"; neither their race nor their occupation was listed.) See Cannady to Bagnall, September 10, 1925; Cannady to Bagnall, September 15, 1925; Application for Charter, Vernonia, Oregon, Branch, September 13, 1925. All items are NAACP PB.

93. Policy quoted in Kamholz et al., 86. For brief details about O-A's black employees, see Fulton, 67.

94. Kamholz et al., 86. Census records for 1930 reflect seventy-two Negroes in Columbia County, where Vernonia is located. In 1920, there were just four Negroes in Columbia County. Historical Census Browser.

95. "No Niggers Wanted," *VE*, June 5, 1925, 1. It is possible that Robinson was a Klansman. Townsfolk welcomed a KKK organizer in October 1922; the following summer the exalted cyclops denied the Klan's involvement in a planned "necktie party." "Good and Interesting Meeting," *VE*, October 6, 1922, 2; "Wrong Propaganda," *VE*, July 13, 1923, 1. For more about the Klan in Vernonia, see Kamholz et al., 85-87. Robinson appears in the *Fourteenth Census*, Washington County, Oregon.

96. "County Papers Go Wild Over Negro Citizens," *VE*, November 6, 1925, 1; "Vernonia Has Race Problem," *TSHM*, October 27, 1925, 1; the *Rainier Review* has not been located. A spelling error was corrected.

97. "County Papers."

98. Cannady to Bagnall, September 10, 1925. A typographical error was corrected.

99. Cannady to Bagnall, September 19, 1925. Also see "Trip to Vernonia an Interesting One," *TA*, October 10, 1925, 1.

100. Trumbull, draft. These comments were deleted from Trumbull's article, "A Modern Joan of Arc." A study of the company notes that "segregated 'Negro, Japanese, Filipino, and Hindu colonies' were constructed right along with the rest of the company's other employee housing." There is no description, though, of what these colonies looked like. Kamholz et al., 86.

101. The Collinses paid $2 to join the NAACP, but they do not appear in online census records for Columbia County, Oregon, for 1920. The Application for Charter lists forty-four names, including Cannady's, and the six anonymous "Friends." NAACP PB.

102. "Vernonia Has Race Problem."

103. Cannady told Bagnall that the company had "sent to Kansas" for a "white teacher, Kansas being the home of the owners of the Mill." Cannady to Bagnall, September 19, 1925.

104. Shedrick Matthews was president; Anita Marks was vice-president; Mary Taylor was secretary; and Mr. Anderson was treasurer. See the Application for Charter. None of these individuals appears in online census records for Columbia County, Oregon, for 1920.

105. Cannady to Bagnall. She did not identify the individual to whom she spoke. A typographical error was corrected.

106. Ibid. The principal was not identified.

107. Cannady to Bagnall; "Honor Roll Branches," *TC*, September 1926, 234-36; The Inflation Calculator. Also see Beatrice Cannady to Robert Bagnall, October 17, 1925, and Robert Bagnall to Beatrice Cannady, October 27, 1925, both of which are in NAACP PB.

108. Cannady to Bagnall, September 19, 1925.

109. Ibid.

110. Ibid.

111. Robert Bagnall to Beatrice Cannady, October 1, 1925, NAACP PB.

112. "N.A.A.C.P. Organizer Gets Schooling for Negro Children in Northwest." Success stories were few and far between, so they were celebrated quickly. Sometimes, though, victories were acknowledged prematurely.

113. "Woman Editor Gets Schooling for Negro Children in Northwest," *Charleston Messenger*, October 3, 1925, clipping in CS, 156. The original has not been located.

114. "N.A.A.C.P. Organizer."

115. An exhaustive study of Oregon-American includes little information about its black workers, and no details about racism they endured. See Kamholz et al. A history of Vernonia mentions residents' fight to educate their children but offers no substantive details. Cannady's name also was misspelled. Fulton, 84.

116. Issues of *VE* were checked from September 11, 1925, through October 2, 1925.

117. "Vernonia Has Race Problem."

118. Trumbull, draft. For a similar account from a contemporary, see J. J. Handsaker to the Harmon Foundation, August 13, 1929, CS, 11-12.

119. Superintendent Anderson, quoted in "Vernonia Has Race Problem." His first name was not mentioned so he could not be located in online census records for Columbia County. A spelling and a typographical error were corrected.

120. Kamholz et al., 329.

121. Millie R. Trumbull, quoted in "*The Advocate* Praised," *TA*, August 29, 1925, 4; "New Subscribers." Typographical errors were corrected.

122. "No Broadway Here." In this instance, she was referring to a letter from Solomon Blumauer, identified as Mr. Blumauer in *TA*. He appears in the *Fourteenth Census*, MC.

123. "No Broadway."

124. Ibid. For another editorial about the white race's responsibility to ensure equal rights for all people, see "Solving the Race Problem," *TA*, August 11, 1923, 4.

125. "Resolutions for 1926," *TA*, January 2, 1926, 1.

126. "Well-Known Dentist Lauds 'The Advocate,'" *TA*, September 22, 1928, 1. Punctuation altered.

Chapter Ten

1. "Du Bois: The Activist Life."

2. "Negro Congress to Meet Here," *TNYT*, August 14, 1921, sec. 7, 20.

3. "Pan-African Congress," *TA*, April 2, 1927, 2.

4. "Negro Poet Honored at Gathering."

5. Ibid. Also see "Mrs. Cannady Sees Opportunity in 'Pan African Congress' for Promotion of Better Race Relations," CS, 66.

6. "A Silver Tea," *TA*, March 5, 1927, 4; "Interracial Tea; Mrs. Handsaker Hostess To Mixed Assembly," *TA*, March 12, 1927, 4.

7. "Interracial Tea." Also see "50 Attend Silver Tea; Program Given for Hostess, Who Will Preside at Congress," *TSO*, April 17, 1927, copy in CS, 171. Griffin retired in 1952 after a forty-one-year career at Reed College. "News and Notices," *The American Mathematical Monthly* 59, no. 7 (August-September 1952), 479.

8. "Silver Tea Is Brilliant," *TA*, April 23, 1927, 1. Also see "Woman Is Feted," *TPN*, April 18, 1927, 8. Ken Nakazawa was the Cannadys' houseguest that weekend. *TA*, April 23, 1927, 1. Lotta Hannon, who invited Cannady to address the Daily Vacation Bible School in Newberg, spoke at the tea. Another speaker was Cynthia Jenkins, identified as Mrs. C. A. Jenkins in *TA*, a widow who was born in Canada. Her father was born in the "United States"; her mother in Pennsylvania. She worked as a professional nurse. According to *TA*, she also was an officer of the First AME Zion Church and a former member of the Board of Management of the Williams Avenue YWCA. *Fourteenth Census*, MC. The Board of Education member was identified as Mrs. G. M. Glines. It is possible she was Myra Glines, George Glines' wife; they appear only in the *Twelfth Census*, MC. Clara Bell appears in the *Fourteenth Census*, MC. McCanns also hosted a "delightful tea" for Cannady in July 1927. "Mrs. McCanns Honors," *TA*, July 9, 1927, 1.

9. "Mrs. Cannady Chosen; Portland Woman to Attend Pan-African Congress," *TSO*, February 6, 1927, sec. 1, 10; "Mrs. Cannady to Attend Convention," *OSJ*, February 6, 1927, 11. Twenty-five women composed the organization, founded by Addie Hunton and others in about 1921. See Chandler, 278.

10. Lewis, 208. Also see "Mrs. Addie Hunton Charms Splendid Audience," *TA*, September 18, 1926, 1.

11. The Executive Committee, Fourth Pan-African Congress, to Mrs. E. D. Cannady, July 9, 1927, copy in AC.

12. The Executive Committee, Fourth Pan-African Congress to [Beatrice Cannady], July 19 [?], 1927, copy in AC. A spelling error was corrected. Also see "N.W. Hostess," *TA*, May 28, 1927, 1. For more about the Congress generally, as well as details about a misunderstanding between Hunton and Du Bois about the program and publicity, see Lewis, 208-11. For a brief summary of the Congress, see Marable, 89-90.

13. "4th Pan-African Congress to Meet in New York City," *TA*, August 6, 1927, 1.

14. "Mrs. Cannady Sees Opportunity"; The Inflation Calculator.

15. "Mrs. Cannady Sees End of Race Trouble."

16. Redwine, June 29, 2004. The shawl was on display at Sherman & Clay Co.; "Mrs. Cannady designed, stamped and embroidered the shawl and tied the fringe on it."

"Exhibits Spanish Shawl," *TA*, October 30, 1926, 1; The Inflation Calculator. A stunning photograph of Cannady draped in the shawl must have been one of her favorites because she supplied it to a newspaper artist who used it as the basis for a pen-and-ink drawing. The day it appeared in *TSO*, Cannady broadcast over KGW on the topic "America Declares a Moratorium." Afterward, she reported that she "was presented the pen drawing of her made by the staff artist." "Woman Editor, Educator, on *Oregonian* of the Air"; "*Advocate* Editor Broadcasts," *TA*, September 12, 1931, 1.

17. Miller, "'I Dress to Vamp the Judge.'"

18. "Mrs. E. D. Cannady to Leave for East Next Saturday," *TA*, August 6, 1927, 1. She wrote that during her trip, she hoped to "visit ... her Alma Mater, Wiley College."

19. For such an extended trip, a steamer or wardrobe trunk would seem more likely. But Cannady wrote later that she "traveled in a suit case and bag." "The Associate Editor Tells of Her Trip East," *TA*, March 10, 1928, 3.

20. "The Associate Editor Tells," September 24, 1927. Cannady wrote that she left August 6th, but the story "Mrs. E. D. Cannady to Leave" places her departure on August 13th. Based on other dates she lists in the recounting of her trip, as well as the ambitious speaking schedule she had on the way to New York, it is likely that she departed on the earlier date. Upon her return to Portland, Cannady detailed her trip in a sixteen-part series that ran in *TA* from September 24, 1927, through March 17, 1928.

21. She spoke at Bethlehem Baptist and AME churches. "The Associate Editor Tells." Also see "Tea Honors Noted Welfare Worker," *TTT*, August 9, 1927, 10.

22. "The Associate Editor Tells."

23. Ibid.; "Welcome To Stanley Park." For more about Spencer's, see "The Importance of Spencer's Department Store."

24. "The Associate Editor Tells."

25. "The Associate Editor Tells," October 1, 1927. Preston was identified as Mrs. L. H. Preston in *TA*. It is likely that Cannady's friend was Marie. She and her parents were born in Mississippi. She worked as a dishwasher at a restaurant. Her husband, Loneia, was born in Illinois. His parents were born in Mississippi. He worked as a laborer at a foundry. *Fourteenth Census*, Cook County.

26. "Guggenheim Tour."

27. "Earl B. Dickerson"; "The Associate Editor Tells." Earl Dickerson appears in the 1920 Census. He and his mother were born in Mississippi; his father in Massachusetts. *Fourteenth Census*, Cook County. Cannady may have stayed with William and Bessie Boyd. In 1920, they were listed as lodgers, but may have purchased their own home by 1927. *Fourteenth Census*, Cook County; "Mrs. Cannady Sees End."

28. "Negroes to Open Bank," *TNYT*, December 7, 1921, 19.

29. "The Associate Editor Tells." Anthony Overton also was recognized for "the crowning achievement of securing the admission of the Victory Life Insurance Company as the first negro [*sic*] organization permitted to do insurance business under the rigid requirements of the State of New York." "Overton Wins Spingarn Medal," *TNYT*, June 4, 1927, 19. Also see "Awarded Spingarn Medal," *TA*, June 18, 1927, 2. Overton appears in the 1920 Census. He and his father were born in Louisiana; his mother in Missouri. A widower, he lived with his son and daughter-in-law. *Fourteenth Census*, Cook County. Overton died in 1946. For one obituary, see "Anthony Overton," *The Journal of Negro History* 32, no. 3 (July 1947): 394-96.

30. "The Opening of Binga State Bank," *TBA*, January 8, 1921, 1.

31. "The Associate Editor Tells"; Osthaus, 39. Jesse Binga appears in the 1910 Census. He was born in Michigan, his mother in New York. His father's birthplace is illegible. *Thirteenth Census*, Cook County.

32. "The Associate Editor Tells." During their visit, the manager was "conducting another mixed group through the laboratories." Overton established the firm specializing in toiletries in Kansas City, Kansas, in 1898, but shifted operations to Chicago in 1911. For more about the company and its founder, see "Anthony Overton."

33. See, for example, advertisement, Overton Hygienic Manufacturing Company, *TA*, October 15, 1927, 2.

34. "Earl B. Dickerson." He would go on to achieve many other "firsts" in his career, but he may be best known for his role in *Hansberry v. Lee*, the U.S. Supreme Court case that successfully challenged restrictive real estate covenants in Hyde Park. The petitioner was the father of Lorraine Hansberry, author of *A Raisin in the Sun*. For more about Dickerson, see Blakely and Shepard.

35. "The Associate Editor Tells."

36. "The Associate Editor Tells of Her Trip East," *TA*, October 8, 1927, 3. The Benjamins appear in the 1920 Census. George was working as a stenographer at a manufacturing plant. By 1927, however, Cannady referred to him as Dr. Benjamin, and wrote that he was secretary of the National Medical Association. He was born in Nebraska; his parents in Virginia. His wife, Allie, and her father were born in Connecticut; her mother in Washington, D.C. [?] The Benjamins had two sons. *Fourteenth Census*, MC.

37. Sweet worked at Dunbar Hospital, the first institution in the city for black patients and doctors. Zacharias.

38. Zacharias; The Inflation Calculator. Also see Turrini; Boyle. Another account notes that Sweet left his daughter, Iva, with his mother-in-law September 8th because he feared for Iva's safety. Linder.

39. "The Associate Editor Tells." Darrow traveled to Portland in October 1930 to debate the issue of Prohibition with Clarence True Wilson, a Methodist Episcopal Church minister and temperance advocate who retired in Oregon in 1937. "Clarence Darrow to Speak; Friend To Negro and Underman," *TA*, October 4, 1930, 1; "Prohibition," *TA*, October 4, 1930, 2. Arthur Garfield Hays, another of Sweet's attorneys and general counsel for the American Civil Liberties Union, also took part in the Scopes trial, the Sacco and Vanzetti case, and the Scottsboro case. He wrote a number of books about these trials, including *Let Freedom Ring* and *City Lawyer: The Autobiography of a Law Practice*. His papers are housed at Princeton University Library. Also see Harris, *Black Rage Confronts the Law*. Cannady and the Portland Branch also assisted Sweet. See, for example, the following in *TA*: "The Case of Doctor Sweet[;] What Will You Do To Help?" October 31, 1925, 4; "Local Branch N.A.A.C.P. Aids the Sweet Defense," November 21, 1925, 1.

40. Zacharias.

41. "The Associate Editor Tells." Also see "Court Holds Dr. Sweet Had Right to Protect Home," *TA*, April 25, 1931, 1.

42. Zacharias.

43. "The Associate Editor Tells of Her Trip East," *TA*, October 15, 1927, 2. On March 5, 1770, five colonists, including sailor Crispus Attucks, were killed by British soldiers. For more about the Boston Massacre, see, for example, the Boston Massacre Historical Society, http://www.bostonmassacre.net/

44. "The Associate Editor Tells of Her Trip East," *TA*, October 29, 1927, 4. Punctuation altered, and typographical errors corrected. She may have overestimated the population. According to the 1920 Census, 109,133 Negroes lived in New York County (Manhattan); Harlem is one neighborhood in Manhattan. Historical Census Browser.

45. For more information about the Congress, see "World Negroes to Open Session," *Christian Science Monitor*, August 20, 1927, 4; "Pan-African Congress Has Many Notables; Dr. W. E. B. Du Bois, Founder of Congress, Greets Delegates," *TA*, August 27, 1927, 1; "The

Associate Editor Tells"; "The Associate Editor Tells of Her Trip East," *TA*, November 5, 1927, 4.

46. Clifford L. Miller, "Pan-African Congress; Meeting of Noted Negroes Held Here for the First Time," *TNYAN*, August 22, 1927, 2.

47. "The Associate Editor Tells," October 29, 1927. Punctuation altered, and a typographical error corrected.

48. Ibid.; "Gov. Patterson Sends Letter," *TA*, December 10, 1927, 2. The original has not been located. For more about the communications received in New York, see Clifford L. Miller, "West Indian-American Negro Problem Cure Is Suggested," *TNYAN*, August 24, 1927, 4.

49. "Oregon Is Honored in Editress' Appointment," *TA*, August 27, 1927, 1.

50. Clifford L. Miller, "Statement Has Bomblike Effect at Congress' Meet," *TNYAN*, August 25, 1927, 7.

51. "The Associate Editor Tells," November 5, 1927; Miller, "Statement Has Bomblike Effect."

52. See "The Pan-African Congresses," *TC*, October 1927, 263-64; "The Associate Editor Tells," October 29, 1927; "Oregon Is Honored"; "Local Woman Is Honored By Negro Leaders," *OSJ*, June 2, 1929, sec. 1, 7. In the fall of 1929, Cannady announced that the Congress had been postponed indefinitely because there were insufficient passengers to charter a ship. *TA*, November 30, 1929, 1. Du Bois blamed the cancellation, in part, on the onset of the Great Depression. The fifth congress finally was held in 1945 in Manchester, England.

53. "The Associate Editor Tells."

54. "The Associate Editor Tells of Her Trip East," *TA*, November 12, 1927, 4.

55. "The Associate Editor Tells," November 5, 1927. Small's Paradise, owned by Ed Small, opened in 1925 and could accommodate fifteen hundred guests and ranked with the Cotton Club as one of the leading establishments in Harlem in the 1920s. Malcolm X reportedly was a waiter there in 1943; Wilt Chamberlain bought the club and changed the name to Big Wilt's Small Paradise in the 1960s. "Small's Paradise"; "Historic Harlem."

56. "The Associate Editor Tells," November 12, 1927. Portlander Zepha Baker, "a popular beauty culturist," attended a three-month-long course at the Madam C. J. Walker College of Beauty Culture in Chicago. "Prominent Hairdresser Goes East to Study," *TA*, October 18, 1930, 1. Also see "Local News," *TA*, March 14, 1931, 3. For an advertisement, see, for example, *TA*, February 7, 1931, 1. Zepha Baker appears in the 1920 Census. She and her father were born in Kansas; her mother in Alabama. Her husband, John, and his parents were born in Kansas. He worked as a waiter. *Fourteenth Census*, MC.

Walker's home was auctioned off after her death. Perhaps remembering her visit three years earlier, Cannady wrote that "the charm of its beauty and luxury will ever remain in the minds of the thousands of race people who availed themselves of the opportunity of visiting it." "The Passing of Villa Le-Wara [*sic*]," *TA*, December 6, 1930, 2. Walker's daughter died suddenly in 1931. "Race's Richest Woman Passes at N.J. Party," *TA*, August 29, 1931, 1; "Mme. A'Leila [*sic*] Walker," *TA*, August 29, 1931, 2. For more about Madam Walker, who lived from 1867 to 1919, see the book by her great-granddaughter, A'Lelia Bundles, who also maintains the official Web site of Madam C. J. Walker.

57. "The Associate Editor Tells."

58. "The Associate Editor Tells of Her Trip East," *TA*, January 7, 1928, 2. She did not discuss her trip from New York City to Washington, D.C., but likely took a train. A typographical error was corrected.

59. "The Associate Editor Tells." Cannady spent time with her brother, John, and his "charming" wife, Anna, whom she had not previously met. Cannady wrote: "Everywhere

we observed the great esteem in which Dr. and Mrs. Morrow are held by both the black and white citizens. Dr. Morrow has a lucrative practice and Mrs. Morrow is a teacher in the public school system." "The Associate Editor Tells of Her Trip East," *TA*, January 14, 1928, 2.

60. "The Associate Editor Tells," January 14, 1928; "The Associate Editor Tells of Her Trip East," *TA*, January 28, 1928, 4. Her brother-in-law John Beverley reportedly was president of Houston College; she may have meant Houston Colored Junior College. The Beverleys do not appear in online census records for 1920 for Harris County, Texas. James Williams Beverley, the couple's four-year-old son, died in December 1930. *TA*, December 20, 1930, 2. Cannady identified the clerk as "Montgomery," and wrote that she had lived in Newberg, Oregon, before moving to Portland to work.

61. "The Associate Editor Tells of Her Trip East," February 18, 1928, 2. Punctuation altered. "The Associate Editor Tells of Her Trip East," *TA*, March 3, 1928, 3.

62. "The Associate Editor Tells," March 3, 1928; "The Associate Editor Tells of Her Trip East," March 10, 1928, 3. When Rosenwald died, Cannady wrote: "In the passing of Julius Rosenwald, the Negro race loses one of its greatest frineds [*sic*] and benefactors. His untiring work and large gifts for Negro education will live down through the ages." "Julius Rosenwald," *TA*, January 9, 1932, 2; also see the news brief on the same page and "Gratitude," *TA*, January 23, 1932, 2. Scarano; "Julius Rosenwald," Sears Archives.

63. "The Associate Editor Tells," March 10, 1928. John Madison appears in the 1920 Census. He and his mother were born in Texas; his father in Tennessee. His wife, Birdie, and her mother were born in Texas. Her father was born in South Carolina. The couple had two children. *Fourteenth Census*, Bastrop County.

64. "The Associate Editor Tells of Her Trip East," *TA*, March 17, 1928, 3.

65. Cannady went to Denver next. Although she promised a column about her stay there and the trip home, she never completed the series about her trip East.

66. "Locals," *TA*, September 24, 1927, 4.

67. "Associate Editor *The Advocate* Greatly in Demand for Addresses," *TA*, October 8, 1927, 4.

68. Cannady to Haynes, CS, 176. Cannady described the group to George Haynes as follows: "Our interracial activities, or movement, have been going on for several years. It is not an organization, yet we are so well organized that in a very brief time, we can assemble together any where from fifty to two hundred and fifty black and white individuals. … We are recognized … as an important institution in the life of our city and state." Alice Handsaker wrote that Cannady "was the originator and the moving spirit" of the group. Handsaker to the Harmon Award Committee.

69. "Pan-African Congress to Be Held Here," *TA*, October 8, 1927, 3. Also see "Delegate Reports on Pan-African Meet in Gotham," *ODJ*, November 10, 1927, 22.

70. "Educators to Meet in Two Days Congress; Speeches, Discussion and Music Fill Day," *TA*, November 12, 1927, 1; Advertisement, *TA*, October 29, 1927, 1.

71. See "Educators to Meet"; Norman F. Coleman to Beatrice Cannady, November 3, 1927, CS, 68. For more about Coleman, see, for example, "Reed College Head Prefers to Instruct," *TA*, January 9, 1932, 1.

72. Chas. A. Rice to Beatrice Cannady, November 2, 1927, CS, 69.

73. "Educators to Meet"; Program of the Miniature Pan-African Congress, *TA*, November 26, 1927, 4.

74. "Educators to Meet." The editor was J. P. O'Hara. He does not appear in online census records for Oregon for any available years.

75. For the entire tentative schedule, see "Educators to Meet."

76. Advertisement. Capitalization altered. The exhibit remained on display at Central Library for some time following the meeting. See "Exhibit Shows Work Done By Colored Race," *TA*, December 3, 1927, 1; reprinted from *ODJ*, November 25, 1927. The original has not been located.

77. "Educators to Hold Portland Conclave," *TPT*, November 17, 1927, 16.

78. "Race Conclave Opens; Greater Harmony Is Aim," *ODJ*, November 18, 1927, 2. Pendleton does not appear in online census records for Oregon for any available years.

79. "Achievements of Noted Negroes Topics of Talks," *OSJ*, November 20, 1927, sec. 1, 6.

80. "Letter Praises Congress," *TA*, December 3, 1927, 1.

81. "Educational Meet a Tremendous Success; Interpretation of Fourth Pan-African Congress Draws Well," *TA*, November 26, 1927, 2.

82. "Their Good Will," *ODJ*, November 24, 1927, 6; reprinted under the same headline in *TA*, November 26, 1927, 2.

83. "The Negro's Progress," *TPT*, November 23, 1927, 6; reprinted under the same headline in *TA*, November 26, 1927, 2. The editorial also drew attention to Du Bois' concept of living behind the veil.

84. "Educational Meet," 1, 2. For more about Coleman's speech, see *TA*, November 26, 1927, 2. For the complete program, see *TA*, November 26, 1927, or CS, 67. For a reader's response to Coleman's talk, as well as a review of the Congress generally, see "Letter Praises Congress."

85. See, for example, *TA*, December 3, 1927, 4.

86. "Interpretation of Fourth Pan-African Congress," *Legislative Counsellor*, November-December 1927, 2; reprinted under the same headline in *TA*, December 24, 1927, 3.

87. "Notes from the Northwest," *National Notes*, January 1928, 15-16. Also see "Congress Lauded," *TA*, February 18, 1928, 1.

88. "Along the Color Line," *TC*, February 1928, 53-54.

89. W. E. B. Du Bois to Beatrice Cannady, October 21, 1927; reprinted in *TA*, December 10, 1927, 2.

90. Addie Hunton to Beatrice Cannady, October 24, 1927; reprinted in *TA*, December 10, 1927, 2. Punctuation added.

91. "Educational Meet." *ODJ* included this resolution in its article, "Exhibit Shows Work Done By Colored Race." It is unclear whether the school board subscribed to these publications as attendees recommended.

92. "Negro in History," *TA*, February 2, 1929, 1.

93. Ibid., 4.

94. "Hang Together Or Separately—Which?" *TA*, August 24, 1929, 2. She also blamed the white press.

95. "Collecting Library of Negro Literature."

96. *TA*, October 28, 1933, 2. Emphasis added, and typographical errors corrected.

97. *TA*, May 11, 1929, 1.

98. "A Community's Greatest Asset," *TA*, June 8, 1929, 2.

99. *TA*, March 22, 1930, 2.

100. "Where Do You Spend Your Money?" *TA*, May 17, 1930, 2.

101. "Restaurant Draws Color-Line."

102. *TA*, October 18, 1930, 2; "N.A.A.C.P. and Lynching," *TA*, September 20, 1930, 2.

103. *TA*, December 20, 1930, 2.

104. Bogle, "Cannady Family Troubles"; "Local Briefs," June 28, 1930; "Death Removes Pioneer Texan"; December 20, 1930.

105. See the following in *TA*: "Race Relations Discussed," February 8, 1930, 1; "*Advocate* Editor Tells of Race Relations," April 12, 1930, 1; June 21, 1930, 1.

106. Redwine, February 1, 2006.

107. See the following in *TA*: "Start Move to Oust *Amos 'n* [*sic*] *Andy*," June 6, 1931, 1; "*Pittsburgh Courier* and N.A.A.C.P. Protest *Amos 'n' Andy* On Air," August 15, 1931, 1; "*Amos 'n' Andy*," August 29, 1931, 2. For a discussion of the show and what it meant to white and black audiences, see, for example, Douglas, 103-10.

108. "*Amos 'n' Andy*," *TA*, August 15, 1931, 2. Cannady referred specifically to that issue's top stories. Spelling and typographical errors were corrected.

109. W. J. Wheaton, "Leading Thinkers and Writers Agree with *Advocat*'s [*sic*] Stand on 'Amos-Andy' Program," *TA*, August 29, 1931, 1.

110. "Race Prejudice in Oregon," *TA*, January 16, 1932, 2. Typographical errors were corrected.

111. Ida Wells-Barnett also expressed her profound disappointment at white ministers' failure to attack the evils of prejudice and discrimination and halt lynching.

112. "Editor Files for State Legislature; For Legislation to Meet Present-Day Need," *TA*, April 2, 1932, 1.

113. Myrtle Campbell, "For the First Time," *TA*, May 7, 1932, 4. For another article by Campbell, see, for example, "Races Fundamentally Same," *TA*, October 17, 1931, 2. Campbell appears in the *Fourteenth Census*, MC. In 1932, Cannady reported "with deep sorrow" that Myrtle's husband, Charles S. Campbell, had died. "He was very fond of the colored race as he traveled a great deal in the South, and had a sympathetic understanding of their hardships and needs. Mr. Campbell was the inspiration for many articles contributed to *The Advocate* by his wife … and the Negro race can feel that they have lost a real friend in his passing." "Mr. Campbell's Passing," *TA*, July 30, 1932, 2.

114. "All Set!" *TA*, May 7, 1932, 1. It is possible that the letter-writer was white.

115. Edw. W. and Leona T. Dickerson, "Wish They Were Here to Vote," *TA*, May 14, 1932, 1. The couple were longtime subscribers in Twin Falls, Idaho. See, for example, "Likes *The Advocate*"; "Support Its Newspapers," *TA*, January 24, 1931, 4.

116. *OV*, April 16, 1932, 25; also see "Editor Files."

117. "N.A.A.C.P. Branch Starts Campaign Drive; To Introduce a Civil Rights Bill," *TA*, April 30, 1932, 1. Also see Ivey, "Annual Report of President."

118. W. J. Wheaton, "Verbal Snapshots," *TA*, April 9, 1932, 1. As noted previously, Cannady apparently never passed the Bar exam. Also see W. J. Wheaton, "Oregon Representative," *TA*, May 7, 1932, 4.

119. W. J. Wheaton, "Verbal Snapshots," *SFS*, April 9, 1932, 1.

120. W. J. Wheaton, "Verbal Snapshots," *TA*, April 23, 1932, 1.

121. *TA*, April 23, 1932, 1. Typographical errors were corrected. For a display advertisement, see *TA*, May 14, 1932, 1.

122. Clifford C. Mitchell, "Digesting the News," *TA*, March 18, 1933, 1; Mitchell, "Digesting the News," *TA*, April 30, 1932, 1. *TA* was the first newspaper to use his column, for which Mitchell remained extremely grateful. Clifford C. Mitchell, "This and That," *TB*, February 26, 1933; reprinted as "Says *Advocate* Started Journalistic Career," *TA*, March 4, 1933, 4. The original has not been located. Also see Clifford C. Mitchell, "Our Women and the Press," *TD*, July 1931, 8-9.

123. W. J. Wheaton, "Verbal Snapshots," *SFS*, May 7, 1932, 8; W. J. Wheaton, "Verbal Snapshots," *TA*, May 7, 1932, 1. Also in this column, he praised Cannady for helping tenor Roland Hayes to "realize his ambitions" and proclaimed: "The voters of Portland will not forget her civic activities."

124. *TA*, April 30, 1932, 2.

125. "Register!" *TA*, April 2, 1932, 2.

126. "Vote," *TA*, May 14, 1932, 2.

127. April 30, 1932.

128. "N.A.A.C.P. Branch Starts Campaign Drive"; DeNorval Unthank to Roy Wilkins, May 11, 1932, NAACP PB.

129. Unthank to Wilkins. Punctuation altered, and a spelling error was corrected in the second quotation.

130. Telegram, Roy Wilkins to C. E. Ivey, May 14, 1932, NAACP PB.

131. Mitchell, April 30, 1932.

132. Unthank to Wilkins. Cannady thanked the Municipal Ownership League, the Woman's Christian Temperance Union, and the Anti-Saloon League "for their endorsements." "*Advocate* Editor Defeated for Legislature; Thanks Voters for Their Loyal Support," *TA*, May 28, 1932, 1.

133. *TA*, May 7, 1932, 1.

134. Campbell.

135. "Compliments Speech." A typographical error was corrected. Hoeber also recalled the "old days" when Cannady sponsored his sister's orchestra. Gertrude Hoeber Peterson went on to teach piano, violin, and voice; she "had a number of talented colored students." He added: "I hope that with your many duties as editor and public citizen, you have not had to, for lack of time, give up your interest in music."

136. "What Can I Do to Help?" *TA*, April 9, 1932, 2.

137. See *TA*, April 23, 1932, 3; April 30, 1932, 3.

138. "*Advocate* Editor Talks to Club Ladies," *TA*, April 2, 1932, 3. She gave a similar talk at a luncheon meeting of the women of Mount Tabor Presbyterian Church, where she was "well received." "*Advocate* Editor to Speak," *TA*, April 30, 1932, 1. Cannady did not name the town.

139. *OV*, May 21, 1932, 28. The other journalist was C. M. Rynerson, editor of the *Oregon Labor Press*. He appears in the *Fourteenth Census*, MC.

140. Ibid., 30.

141. The day before the primary, the *Oregonian* also listed the forty-nine candidates. Cannady was described as "Editress negro paper; negro social and civic worker." "Legislative Race Hard to Predict," *MO*, May 19, 1932, 8.

142. "To *Advocate* Readers," *TA*, May 14, 1932, 2.

143. Republican Primary Election Vote Abstract, May 20, 1932, MCA. Also see "How Portland and Multnomah County Cast Votes," *MO*, May 23, 1932, 4; "Election Totals Given," *MO*, May 26, 1932, 4.

144. Historical Census Browser. Each of the thirteen men who advanced to the general election received between eighteen and twenty-five thousand votes. "How Portland and Multnomah County Cast Votes," *MO*, May 23, 1932, 4; "Election Totals Given," *MO*, May 26, 1932, 4.

145. Hoeber received 7,651 votes. Republican Primary Election Vote Abstract.

146. Diaz, "Horace Roscoe Cayton, 1859-1940"; also see Diaz, *Horace Roscoe Cayton*. Cannady appears to have had minimal contact with Cayton, but in 1930 she thanked him for "honoring" *TA* "with a copy of his splendidly gotten-up year book." "Cayton Year Book," *TA*, January 4, 1930, 2.

147. "Oscar Stanton De Priest (1871-1951)."

148. "Seat Chosen," *TA*, May 7, 1932, 3. He heard a lecture by Dr. Alexander Goldenweiser, who had attended one of his mother's teas in 1930.

149. "*Advocate* Editor Defeated."

150. "Commissioner Clyde Praises Editor's Campaign," *TA*, May 28, 1932, 2.

Clifford Mitchell also offered congratulations. "Clifford Mitchell, *Advocate* Columnist, Congratulates *Advocate* Editor on Showing in Primary Election," *TA*, July 2, 1932, 2.

151. "Writer Says Editor Wins Glorious Defeat," *TA*, May 28, 1932, 3. Capitalization altered. Stewart signed his letter simply "Lewis B.," but authorship was verified by comparing it with the letter he wrote her in 1927.

152. W. J. Wheaton, "Verbal Snapshots," *TA*, July 2, 1932, 4.

153. Wheaton; Alice M. Park, "Writer Says Women Take Defeat Too Seriously," *TA*, June 19, 1932, 1.

Conclusion

1. Abbott; Bosco-Milligan Foundation, 23.

2. Abbott.

3. "Vice President in Portland," *TNYT*, June 1, 1905, 8; "Portland Cheers Fairbanks," *TNYT*, June 3, 1905, 3.

4. In 1900, Portland had a total population of 90,426, including 775 Negroes. See the *Twelfth Census*, Table 23, 637. By 1910, the city had swelled to 207,214, including 1,045 Negro residents. *Thirteenth Census*, Table 19, 95. For the 1913 figure and details about how it was calculated, see *Polk's Portland City Directory 1913*, 18.

5. "Realty Men Intend to Stop Sales To Negroes, Orientals."

6. "Last Equal Rights Bill Reappears; Is Theme of Hearing," *ODJ*, February 18, 1919, 3.

7. Ibid.; A. L. Lindbeck, "Negro Equality Bill Resurrected and Then Slain," *ODJ*, February 21, 1919, 4. Also see "Bill Giving Negroes Equal Rights Loses," *MO*, February 21, 1919, 7.

8. Lindbeck. Mrs. Alex Thompson lived in The Dalles and represented District 29. She does not appear in online census records for Oregon for any available year. "State Government Legislators and Staff, 1919 Regular Session (30th): January 13-February 27," http://arcweb.sos.state.or.us/legislative/histleg/statehood/1919reg.htm#HOUSE.

9. Shelton Hill, Mss 2854, OBHP; "*The Advocate*'s Mission," *TA*, December 18, 1926, 2.

10. "Senators Turn Down Civil Rights Bill; Oregon Solons Deny Rights To Race," *TA*, March 11, 1933, 1; "Text of Civil Rights Bill; How They Voted," *TA*, April 8, 1933, 1.

11. For a photograph of the event, see "Signing Oregon's Civil Rights Bill, 1953."

12. Sam F. Gill, "An Appreciation," *TA*, June 20, 1925, 1.

13. "*Oregonian* of Air Presents Variety." Capitalization altered.

14. According to Redwine, Cannady divorced Franklin before she moved to California. Redwine, February 13, 2006.

15. "In Memoriam," *National Bahá'í Review*, December 1974, 7. Also see the memorial program for Beatrice Cannady Taylor, copy in AC.

BIBLIOGRAPHY

Many sources in the bibliography have been abbreviated in the notes.

Newspapers and Magazines

TA: The (Portland, Oregon) *Advocate*
AD-H: *Albany* (Oregon) *Democrat-Herald*
TADS: The (Tucson) *Arizona Daily Star*
TAC: *Atlanta* (Georgia) *Constitution*
TB: The (Washington, D.C.) *Bee*
TBB: The *Bend* (Oregon) *Bulletin*
TBA: The (Chicago) *Broad Ax*
TCE: The (Los Angeles) *California Eagle*
TCJ: The (Salem, Oregon) *Capital Journal*
TCD: The *Chicago Defender*
CBT: (Marshfield, Oregon) *Coos Bay Times*
CG-T: *Corvallis* (Oregon) *Gazette-Times*
TC: The *Crisis*
DOS: *Daily* (Salem) *Oregon Statesman*, later known as *TOS*: The (Salem) *Oregon Statesman*
TE: The (Seattle) *Enterprise*
EDG: *Eugene* (Oregon) *Daily Guard*, later known as *TEG*: The *Eugene Guard*
TEP: The (New York) *Evening Post*
TET: The (Portland, Oregon) *Evening Telegram*
FJ: (New York City) *Freedom's Journal*
TG: The (Cleveland, Ohio) *Gazette*
TGCA: The (New York) *Globe and Commercial Advertiser*
GO: *Gresham* (Oregon) *Outlook*
THRG: The *Hood River* (Oregon) *Glacier*
LAT: *Los Angeles Times*
MMT: *Medford* (Oregon) *Mail Tribune*
ME: (Oregon City, Oregon) *Morning Enterprise*
MO: *Morning* (Portland) *Oregonian*, later known as *TO*: The (Portland) *Oregonian*
MR: (Eugene, Oregon) *Morning Register*
TMPW: The *Moving Picture World*
TNA: The (Portland, Oregon) *New Age*
TNR: The *New Republic*
NYA: *New York Age*
TNYAN: The *New York Amsterdam News*
TNYT: The *New York Times*
TNYW: The *New York World*
NG: *Newberg* (Oregon) *Graphic*
NS: (Rochester, New York) *North Star*
OT: *Oakland* (California) *Tribune*
ODJ: (Portland) *Oregon Daily Journal*, later known as *OJ*: (Portland) *Oregon Journal*
OLP: (Portland) *Oregon Labor Press*
OSJ: (Portland) *Oregon Sunday Journal*
OV: *Oregon Voter*
TOWT: The (Portland) *Oregon* (Territory) *Weekly Times*
TPC: The *Pittsburgh Courier*
TPN: The *Portland* (Oregon) *News*
PO: *Portland* (Oregon) *Observer*

TPT: The *Portland* (Oregon) *Telegram*
RCQ: *Reed College Quest*
TR-G: The (Eugene, Oregon) *Register-Guard*
RDP: *Riverside* (California) *Daily Press*
RN-R: *Roseburg* (Oregon) *News-Review*
TSHM: The *St. Helens* (Oregon) *Mist*
SFS: *San Francisco Spokesman*
TS-WD: The (Albany, Oregon) *Semi-Weekly Democrat*
TSI: The (Columbia, South Carolina) *Southern Indicator*
SOS: (Grants Pass) *Southern Oregon Spokesman*
SR: (Albuquerque, New Mexico) *Southwest Review*
SJ: (Salem, Oregon) *Statesman Journal*
TSO: The *Sunday* (Portland) *Oregonian*
TS: The *Survey*
TTT: The *Tacoma* (Washington) *Times*
TH: *Tillamook* (Oregon) *Headlight*
TD: *Timely Digest*
TTP: The *Topeka* (Kansas) *Plaindealer*
VE: *Vernonia* (Oregon) *Eagle*
TWO: The *Western Outlook*
WC: *Willamette* (University) *Collegian*

Papers and Special Collections

AC: Author's collection.
AHC: Littig, Travis County. AF L3170. Austin History Center, Austin, Texas.
BWOP: Benjamin Wilson Olcott Papers. Mss 308. Research Library, Oregon Historical Society, Portland.
BWOS: Ben W. Olcott Scrapbook. AX 81. Special Collections and University Archives, University of Oregon, Eugene.
CS: Beatrice Cannady Scrapbook, 1919-1936. Mf 160. Research Library, Oregon Historical Society, Portland.
HFI: William E. Harmon Awards for Distinguished Achievement Among Negroes 1929, Records of Harmon Foundation, Inc., 1913-1967. Mss 51615, Container 59. Manuscript Division, Library of Congress.
KKK: Ku Klux Klan Records. Mss 22. Research Library, Oregon Historical Society, Portland.
NAACP PB: Oregon Black History Project, NAACP Portland Branch files for 1914-1955. Mss 2004-2. Research Library, Oregon Historical Society, Portland.
NBA: Office of the Secretary Records. National Bahá'í Archives, Evanston, Illinois.
OBHP: Oregon Black History Project, Research Notes. Mss 2854. Research Library, Oregon Historical Society, Portland.
Republican Primary Election Vote Abstract, May 20, 1932, Records of the Multnomah County Elections Division, microfilm accession 2008-000759, roll 1. Multnomah County Archives.
SPA: City of Portland, Stanley Parr Archives and Records Center.

Oral Histories

SR 270: Otto Rutherford. Interview by Helen Warbington and Elizabeth McLagan, March 3, 1978. SR 270, transcript. Research Library, Oregon Historical Society, Portland.
SR 442: Kathryn Bogle. Interviews by Rick Harmon, June 26, 1985, July 24, 1985, July 31,

1985. SR 442, transcripts. Research Library, Oregon Historical Society, Portland.

Censuses

HeritageQuest Online has been used to retrieve county-level census data in numerous states. Multnomah County, Oregon, has been abbreviated as MC.

Twelfth Census of the United States: 1900, vol. 1, Population part 1. Washington, D.C.: United States Census Office, 1901.

Twelfth Census of the United States: 1910, Abstract of the Census with Supplement for Oregon. Washington, D.C.: United States Government Printing Office, 1913.

Thirteenth Census of the United States: 1910, Abstract of the Census. Washington, D.C.: United States Government Printing Office, 1913.

Fourteenth Census of the United States: 1920, vol. II, General Report & Analytical Tables. Washington, D.C.: United States Government Printing Office, 1922.

Fifteenth Census of the United States: 1930, Unemployment, vol. I. Washington, D.C.: United States Government Printing Office, 1931.

Fifteenth Census of the United States: 1930, vol. III, part II, Montana-Wyoming. Washington, D.C.: United States Government Printing Office, 1932.

Negroes in the United States: 1920-1932. Washington, D.C.: United States Government Printing Office, 1935.

Population of the United States in 1860; compiled from the original returns of the eighth census. Washington, D.C.: United States Government Printing Office, 1864.

Documents, Reports, and Pamphlets

Boston Branch of the National Association for the Advancement of Colored People. *Fighting a Vicious Film: Protest Against 'The Birth of a Nation.'* Boston: n.p., 1915.

Meeting of the Board of Governors of the Oregon State Bar, December 21, 1935. Oregon State Bar, Salem, Oregon.

Olcott, Ben W. "America Adrift." In *Proceedings of the Fourteenth Conference of Governors of the States of the Union*, held at White Sulphur Springs, West Virginia, December 14-16, 1922 (n.p.).

Polk's Portland City Directory. Portland, Oregon: R. L. Polk, various years.

Postal Laws and Regulations of the United States of America, Edition of 1924. Washington, D.C.: U.S. Government Printing Office, 1924.

Selected Newspaper, Magazine, and Journal Articles

Azuma, Eiichiro. "A History of Oregon's *Issei*, 1880-1952." *Oregon Historical Quarterly* 94, no. 4 (Winter 1993-94): 315-67.

Baker, Houston A., Jr. "Critical Memory and the Black Public Sphere." *Public Culture* 7, no. 1 (Fall 1994): 3-33.

Baldasty, Gerald J., and Mark E. LaPointe. "The Press and the African-American Community: The Role of the Northwest Enterprise in the 1930s." *Pacific Northwest Quarterly* 94, no. 1 (Winter 2002-03): 14-26.

Barrow, Lionel C., Jr. "'Our Own Cause': 'Freedom's Journal' and the Beginnings of the Black Press." *Journalism History* 4, no. 4 (Winter 1977-78): 118-22.

Bogle, Kathryn G. "An American Negro Speaks of Color." *The Sunday Oregonian*, February 14, 1937, sec. 2, 16.

Broussard, Albert S. "McCants Stewart: The Struggles of a Black Attorney in the Urban West." *Oregon Historical Quarterly* 89, no. 2 (Summer 1998): 157-79.

Broussard, Antoinette. "Nettie Craig Asberry: A Pillar of Tacoma's African American Community," *Columbia* 19, no. 3 (Fall 2005): 3-6.

Broussard, Jinx C. "Mary Church Terrell: A Black Woman Journalist and Activist Seeks to

Elevate Her Race." *American Journalism* 19, no. 4 (Fall 2002): 13-35.
Brown, Elsa Barkley. "Negotiating and Transforming the Public Sphere: African American Political Life in the Transition from Slavery to Freedom." *Public Culture* 7, no. 1 (Fall 1994): 107-46.
Brown, Karen F. "The Oklahoma *Eagle:* a study of black press survival." *The Howard Journal of Communications* 1, no. 2 (Summer 1988): 1-11.
Bush, W. Stephen. "'The Birth of a Nation': The D. W. Griffith Feature Film Company Makes Its Debut with a Most Sensational and Spectacular Production, Dealing with the Civil War and the Period of Reconstruction." *Moving Picture World* (March 13, 1915): 1586.
Carey, Charles H. "The Creation of Oregon As a State." *Oregon Historical Quarterly* XXVII, no. 1 (March 1926): 1-40.
Chandler, Susan. "Addie Hunton and the Construction of an African American Female Peace Perspective." *Affilia* 20, no. 3 (Fall 2005): 270-83.
Clarke, Cheryl, et al. "Black Women on Black Women Writers: Conversations and Questions." *Conditions: Nine* 3, no. 3 (Spring 1983): 88-120.
Collins, Patricia Hill. "The Social Construction of Black Feminist Thought." *Signs: Journal of Women in Culture and Society* 14, no. 4 (Summer 1989): 745-73.
———. "Learning from the Outsider Within: The Sociological Significance of Black Feminist Thought." Social Problems 33, no. 6 (October/December 1986): S14-S32.
Coray, Michael S. "Negro and Mulatto in the Pacific West, 1850-1860: Changing Patterns of Black Population Growth." *The Pacific Historian* 29, no. 4 (Winter 1985): 18-27.
Crawford, Madelyn. "California Woman Suffrage: An Anniversary Exhibit." *The Public Historian* 9, no. 4 (Autumn 1987): 70-73.
Cripps, Thomas R. "The Reaction of the Negro to the Motion Picture *Birth of a Nation.*" *The Historian* XXV, no. 3 (May 1963): 344-62.
Cronin, Mary M. "'A Chance to Build For Our Selves': Black Press Boosterism in Oklahoma, 1891-1915." *Journalism History* 26, no. 2 (Summer 2000): 71-80.
Crowell, Evelyn. "Twentieth Century Black Woman in Oregon." *Northwest Journal of African and Black American Studies* 1, no. 1 (Summer 1973): 13-15.
Dagenais, Julie. "Newspaper Language as an Active Agent in the Building of a Frontier Town." *American Speech* XLII, no. 2 (May 1967): 114-21.
de Graaf, Lawrence B. "Race, Sex, and Region: Black Women in the American West, 1850-1920." *Pacific Historical Review* 49, no. 2 (May 1980): 285-313.
"Document: Kathryn Hall Bogle's 'An American Negro Speaks of Color.'" *Oregon Historical Quarterly* 89, no. 1 (Spring 1988): 70-81.
Domke, David. "The Black Press in the 'Nadir' of African Americans." *Journalism History* 20, no. 3-4 (Autumn-Winter 1994): 131-38.
Eisenberg, Bernard. "Only for the Bourgeois? James Weldon Johnson and the NAACP, 1916-1930." *Phylon* 43, no. 2 (1982): 110-24.
Fischer, Claude S., and Glenn R. Carroll. "Telephone and Automobile Diffusion in the United States, 1902-1937." *American Journal of Sociology* 93, no. 5 (March 1988): 1153-78.
Fleming, G. James. "One Hundred and Eight Years of the Negro Press." *Opportunity: A Journal of Negro Life* (March 1935): 75-77.
Fraser, Nancy. "Rethinking the Public Sphere." *Social Text* 25/26 (1990): 56-80.
Fry, Henry P. "Klan Money-Making Scheme for Benefit of Few Insiders; Religious and Racial Hatreds Commercialized for Profit of Grafters." *Capital Journal*, July 19, 1922, 1.
———. "Lawlessness, Mob Outrage Follow Klan Organization; Newspapers Silenced by Threat of Boycott When Opposed to Order." *Capital Journal*, July 18, 1922, 4.
Gordon, Eugene. "The Negro Press." *The Annals of the American Academy of Political and Social*

Science 140 (November 1928): 248-56.

———. "Outstanding Negro Newspapers, 1927." *Opportunity* (December 1927): 358-63.

———. "A Survey of the Negro Press." *Opportunity* (January 1927): 7-11, 32.

———. "Outstanding Negro Newspapers: Reiteration and Detail." *Opportunity* (February 1925): 51-54.

Gregory, Steven. "Race, Identity and Political Activism: The Shifting Contours of the African American Public Sphere." *Public Culture* 7, no. 1 (Fall 1994): 147-64.

Griffith, D. W. "'The Birth of a Nation' Controversy. A Statement by the Producer, D. W. Griffith." *Globe and Commercial Advertiser*, April 9, 1915, 12.

Gross, Bella. "Freedom's Journal and The Rights of All." *Journal of Negro History* 17, no. 3 (July 1932): 241-86.

Hansen, John Mark. "In Memoriam: Harold F. Gosnell." *Political Science and Politics* 30, no. 3 (September 1997): 582-86.

Haring, H. A. "The Negro as Consumer: How to Sell to a Race That Now, for the First Time in Its History, Has Money to Spend." *Advertising & Selling* 3 (September 3, 1930): 20-21, 67-8.

Higginbotham, Evelyn Brooks. "Beyond The Sound of Silence: Afro-American Women in History." *Gender & History* 1, no. 1 (Spring 1989): 50-67.

Hill, D. G. "The Negro As a Political and Social Issue in the Oregon Country." *The Journal of Negro History* 33, no. 2 (April 1948): 130-45.

Hillery, George A., Jr. "Definitions of Community: Areas of Agreement." *Rural Sociology* 20, no. 2 (June 1955): 111-23.

Hogg, Thomas C. "Negroes and Their Institutions in Oregon." *Phylon* 30, no. 3 (Fall 1969): 272-85.

Holsinger, M. Paul. "The Oregon School Bill Controversy, 1922-1925." *Pacific Historical Review*, XXXVII (August 1968): 327-41.

Horowitz, David A. "The 'Cross of Culture': La Grande, Oregon, in the 1920s." *Oregon Historical Quarterly* 93, no. 2 (Summer 1992): 147-67.

———. "Social Morality and Personal Revitalization: Oregon's Ku Klux Klan in the 1920s." *Oregon Historical Quarterly* 90, no. 4 (Winter 1989): 364-84.

Johnson, Daniel P. "Anti-Japanese Legislation in Oregon, 1917-1923." *Oregon Historical Quarterly* 97, no. 2 (Summer 1996): 176-210.

Krieling, Albert. "The Rise of the Black Press in Chicago." *Journalism History* 4, no. 4 (Winter 1977-78): 132-36, 156.

La Brie, Henk III. "Black Newspapers: The Roots Are 150 Years Deep." *Journalism History* 4, no. 4 (Winter 1977-78): 111-13.

LaLande, Jeff. "The 'Jackson County Rebellion': Social Turmoil and Political Insurgence in Southern Oregon During the Great Depression." *Oregon Historical Quarterly* 95, no. 4 (Winter 1994-95): 406-71.

———. "Beneath the Hooded Robe: Newspapermen, Local Politics, and the Ku Klux Klan in Jackson County, Oregon, 1921-1923." *Pacific Northwest Quarterly* 83, no. 2 (April 1992): 42-52.

Lembke, Jerry. "Labor and Education: Portland Labor College, 1921-1929." *Oregon Historical Quarterly* 85 (1984): 117-34.

Link, Arthur S. "The Negro as a Factor in the Campaign of 1912." *The Journal of Negro History* 32, no. 1 (January 1947): 81-99.

Locke, Alain. Review of *The Negro In Our History*, by Carter G. Woodson. *The Journal of Negro History* 12, no. 1 (January 1927): 99-101.

Lockley, Fred. "Documentary: The Case of Robin Holmes vs. Nathaniel Ford." *Oregon Historical Quarterly* 23, no. 1 (March 1922): 111-37.

———. "Some Documentary Records of Slavery in Oregon." *Oregon Historical Quarterly* 17, no. 1 (March 1916): 107-37.

MacMahon, Henry. "The Art of the Movies." *The New York Times*, June 6, 1915, X8.

Mangun, Kimberley. "Editor A.D. Griffin: Envisioning a New Age for Black Oregonians, 1896-1907." *American Journalism* 26, no. 3 (Summer 2009): 79-116.

———. "Boosting the Black Press' Bottom Line: Beatrice Morrow Cannady's Tactics to Promote *The Advocate*, 1923-1933." *American Journalism* 25, no. 3 (Summer 2008): 31-69.

———. "*The* (Oregon) *Advocate*: Boosting the Race and Portland, Too." *American Journalism* 23, no. 1 (Winter 2006): 7-34.

McElderry, Stuart. "Building a West Coast Ghetto; African-American Housing in Portland, 1910-1960." *Pacific Northwest Quarterly* 92, no. 3 (Summer 2001): 137-48.

McGinty, Doris E. Review of *Black Song: The Forge and the Flame*, by John Lovell, Jr. *The Journal of Negro Education* 44, no. 2 (Spring 1975): 208-13.

Minto, John. "Antecedents of the Oregon Pioneers and the Light These Throw on Their Motives." *Oregon Historical Quarterly* 5, no. 1 (March 1904): 38-63.

Myhra, Alison G. "The Hate Speech Conundrum and the Public Schools." *North Dakota Law Review* 68, no. 1 (1992): 71-129.

"Negro History Week Celebration." *The Journal of Negro History* 15, no. 2 (April 1930): 125-33.

Nicoll, G. Douglas. "The Rise and Fall of the Portland Hotel." *Oregon Historical Quarterly* 99, no. 3 (Fall 1998): 298-335.

Niderost, Eric. "*The Birth of a Nation*." *American History* 30, no. 4 (October 2005): 61-67, 78, 80.

Nordin, Kenneth D. "In Search of Black Unity: An Interpretation of the Content and Function of 'Freedom's Journal.'" *Journalism History* 4, no. 4 (Winter 1977-78): 123-28.

Ober, Harlan F. "Louis G. Gregory." *The Bahá'í World: A Biennial International Record* (1950-1954): 666-70.

O'Kelly, Charlotte G. "The Black Press: Conservative or Radical, Reformist or Revolutionary." *Journalism History* 4, no. 4 (Winter 1977-78): 114-16.

Oliver, Egbert S. "Obed Dickinson and the 'Negro Question' in Salem." *Oregon Historical Quarterly* 92, no. 1 (Spring 1991): 4-40.

Osthaus, Carl R. "The Rise and Fall of Jesse Binga, Black Financier." *The Journal of Negro History* 58, no. 1 (January 1973): 39-60.

Park, Robert E. "Urbanization as Measured by Newspaper Circulation." *The American Journal of Sociology* 35, no. 1 (July 1929): 60-79.

Pride, Armistead S. "Negro Newspapers: Yesterday, Today and Tomorrow." *Journalism Quarterly* 28, no. 2 (Spring 1951): 179-88.

Rhodes, Jane. "Race, Money, Politics and the Antebellum Black Press." *Journalism History* 20, no. 3-4 (Autumn-Winter 1994): 95-106.

Richard, K. Keith. "Unwelcome Settlers: Black and Mulatto Oregon Pioneers." *Oregon Historical Quarterly* 84, no. 1 (Spring 1983): 29-48.

———. "Unwelcome Settlers: Black and Mulatto Oregon Pioneers, Part II." *Oregon Historical Quarterly* 84, no. 2 (Summer 1983): 172-205.

Riley, Glenda. "American Daughters: Black Women in the West." *Montana, The Magazine of Western History* 38, no. 2 (Spring 1988): 14-27.

Roberts, Waldo. "The Ku-Kluxing of Oregon." *Outlook*, March 14, 1923, 490-91.

Robinson, Louie. "The Black Press: Voice of Freedom." *Ebony* 30, no. 10 (August 1975): 52-54, 56, 58.

Ross, Felecia G. Jones. "Fragile equality: A Black paper's portrayal of race relations in late 19th century Cleveland." *The Howard Journal of Communications* 6, no. 1-2 (October

1995): 53-68.

Smith, Lucy Wilmot. "Some Female Writers of the Negro Race." *The Journalist*, January 26, 1889, 4-6.

Spicer, Osker. "A trail of many hues; Blacks among first settlers to arrive on Oregon Trail." *The Sunday Oregonian*, March 14, 1993, R25.

Stevens, John D. "The Black Press Looks at 1920's Journalism." *Journalism History* 7, no. 3-4 (Autumn-Winter 1980): 109-13.

Stevens, Summer E., and Owen V. Johnson. "From Black Politics to Black Community: Harry C. Smith and the *Cleveland Gazette*." *Journalism Quarterly* 67, no. 4 (Winter 1990): 1090-102.

Streitmatter, Rodger. "Delilah Beasley: A Black Woman Journalist Who Lifted as She Climbed." *American Journalism* 11, no. 1 (Winter 1994): 61-75.

Taylor, Quintard. "Slaves and Free Men: Blacks in the Oregon Country, 1840-1860." *Oregon Historical Quarterly* 83, no. 2 (Summer 1982): 153-70.

———. "The Emergence of Black Communities in The Pacific Northwest: 1865-1910." *The Journal of Negro History* 64, no. 4 (Autumn 1979): 342-54.

Thornbrough, Emma Lou. "American Negro Newspapers, 1880-1914." *Business History Review* XL, no. 4 (Winter 1966): 467-90.

Toll, William. "Black Families and Migration to a Multiracial Society: Portland, Oregon, 1900-1924." *Journal of American Ethnic History* 17, no. 3 (Spring 1998): 38-70.

———. "Voluntarism and Modernization in Portland Jewry: The B'nai B'rith in the 1920s." *The Western Historical Quarterly* 10, no. 1 (January 1979): 21-38.

———. "Progress and Piety: The Ku Klux Klan and Social Change in Tillamook, Oregon." *Pacific Northwest Quarterly* 69, no. 2 (April 1978): 75-85.

Toy, Eckard Vance, Jr. "The Ku Klux Klan in Tillamook, Oregon." *Pacific Northwest Quarterly* 53, no. 2 (April 1962): 60-64.

Turrini, Joseph. "Sweet Justice." *Michigan History* (July/August 1999): 22-27.

Van Tyne, C. H. Review of *A History of the American People*, by Woodrow Wilson. *Annals of the American Academy of Political and Social Science* 21 (May 1903): 131-34.

Walter, David O. "Legislative Notes and Reviews: Proposals for a Federal Anti-Lynching Law." *The American Political Science Review* 28, no. 3 (June 1934): 436-42.

Williams, George H. "Political History of Oregon from 1853 to 1865." *Oregon Historical Quarterly* 2, no. 1 (March 1901): 1-35.

Woodson, C. G. "The Celebration of Negro History Week, 1927." *The Journal of Negro History* 12, no. 2 (April 1927): 103-109.

———. "Negro History Week." *The Journal of Negro History* 11, no. 2 (April 1926): 238-42.

———. "Negro History Week—The Third Year." *The Journal of Negro History* 13, no. 2 (April 1928): 121-25.

———. "Negro History Week—The Fourth Year." *The Journal of Negro History* 14, no. 2 (April 1929): 109-15.

Woolsey, F. W. "Conversation with ... Roland Hayes." *The Black Perspective in Music* 2, no. 2 (Autumn 1974): 179-85.

Books

Amana, Harry. "African American Media." In *History of the Mass Media in the United States*, ed. Margaret A. Blanchard, 25-30. Chicago: Fitzroy Dearborn Publishers, 1998.

Anderson, Benedict. *Imagined Communities: Reflections on the Origin and Spread of Nationalism*, rev. ed. London: Verso, 1991.

Anderson, James D. *The Education of Blacks in the South, 1860-1935*. Chapel Hill: University of North Carolina Press, 1988.

Anderson, Martha. *Black Pioneers of the Northwest, 1800-1918*. Portland, Oregon: s.n., 1980.

Armitage, Susan H. "The Challenge of Women's History." In *Women in Pacific Northwest History: An Anthology*, ed. Karen J. Blair, 233-45. Seattle: University of Washington Press, 1988.

Arnesen, Eric. *Brotherhoods of Color: Black Railroad Workers and the Struggle for Equality*. Cambridge: Harvard University Press, 2001.

Ball, Edward. *The Sweet Hell Inside: A Family History*. New York: William Morrow, 2001.

Barkley, Mary Starr. *A History of Central Texas*. Austin, Texas: Austin Printing Company, 1970.

Barrios, Richard. *A Song in the Dark: The Birth of the Musical Film*. New York: Oxford University Press, 1995.

Bass, Charlotta A. *Forty Years: Memoirs from the Pages of a Newspaper*. Los Angeles, California: by the author, 1960.

Beasley, Delilah L. *The Negro Trail Blazers of California*. New York: Negro Universities Press, 1969.

Beecher, Henry W., and Anthony S. Wawrukiewicz. *U.S. Domestic Postal Rates, 1872-1999*, rev. 2nd ed. Cama Publishing Co.: Portland, Oregon, 1999.

Berardi, Gayle K., and Thomas W Segady. "The Development of African American Newspapers in the American West, 1880-1914." In *African Americans on the Western Frontier*, eds. Monroe Lee Billington and Roger D. Hardaway, 217-30. Niwot: University Press of Colorado, 1998.

Bernasconi, Robert. "Who Invented the Concept of Race? Kant's Role in the Enlightenment Construction of Race." In *Race*, ed. Robert Bernasconi, 11-36. Malden, Massachusetts: Blackwell Publishers Inc., 2001.

———. "The Invisibility of Racial Minorities in the Public Realm of Appearances." In *Race*, ed. Robert Bernasconi, 284-299. Malden, Massachusetts: Blackwell Publishers Inc., 2001.

Berry, Torriano. *The 50 Most Influential Black Films: A Celebration of African-American Talent, Determination, and Creativity*. New York: Kensington Publishing Corp., 2001.

Berwanger, Eugene H. *The Frontier Against Slavery: Western Anti-Negro Prejudice and the Slavery Extension Controversy*. Urbana: University of Illinois Press, 1967.

Blakely, Robert J., and Marcus Shepard. *Earl B. Dickerson: A Voice for Freedom and Equality*. Evanston, Illinois: Northwestern University Press, 2006.

Boorstin, Daniel J. *The Americans: The National Experience*. London: Phoenix Press, 1965.

Bosco-Milligan Foundation. *Cornerstones of Community: Buildings of Portland's African American History*. Portland, Oregon: The Bosco-Milligan Foundation, 1995.

Boyle, Kevin. *Arc of Justice: A Saga of Race, Civil Rights, and Murder in the Jazz Age*. New York: H. Holt, 2004.

Bradley, Edwin M. *The First Hollywood Musicals: A Critical Filmography of 171 Features, 1927 Through 1932*. Jefferson, North Carolina: McFarland & Company, Inc., 2004.

Brooks, Tim. *Lost Sounds: Blacks and the Birth of the Recording Industry*, 1890-1919. Urbana: University of Illinois Press, 2004.

Broussard, Albert. *African-American Odyssey: The Stewarts, 1853-1963*. Lawrence: University Press of Kansas, 1998.

———. *Black San Francisco: The Struggle for Racial Equality in the West, 1900-1954*. Lawrence: University Press of Kansas, 1993.

Broussard, Jinx Coleman. *Giving a Voice to the Voiceless: Four Pioneering Black Women Journalists*. New York: Routledge, 2004.

Buck, Christopher. *Alain Locke: Faith and Philosophy*. Los Angeles, California: Kalimát Press, 2005.

Bundles, A'Lelia. *On Her Own Ground: The Life and Times of Madam C. J. Walker.* New York: Washington Square Press, 2001.

Chalmers, David M. *Hooded Americanism: The History of the Ku Klux Klan*, 3d ed. Durham, North Carolina: Duke University Press, 1987.

Christian, Barbara. Introduction to *Black Foremothers*, 2d ed., ed. Dorothy Sterling, xxi-xliii. New York: The Feminist Press at the City University of New York, 1988.

City of Portland Bureau of Planning. *History of Portland's African American Community (1805 to the present)*. Portland, Oregon: Portland City Planning Commission, 1993.

Collins, Patricia Hill. *Black Feminist Thought: Knowledge, Consciousness, and the Politics of Empowerment*, 2d ed. New York: Routledge, 2000.

———. "Defining Black Feminist Thought." In *The Second Wave: A Reader in Feminist Theory*, ed. Linda Nicholson, 241-59. New York: Routledge, 1997.

———. "Feminism in the Twentieth Century." In *Black Women in America: An Historical Encyclopedia*, vol. 1, ed. Darlene Clark Hine, 418-25. New York: Carlson Publishing, Inc., 1993.

Conrad, Earl. *Jim Crow America*. New York: Duell, Sloan and Pearce, 1947.

Cook, Raymond Allen. *Fire from the Flint: The Amazing Careers of Thomas Dixon*. Winston-Salem, North Carolina: John F. Blair, 1968.

Cox, Bette Yarbrough. "The Evolution of Black Music in Los Angeles, 1890-1955." In *Seeking El Dorado: African Americans in California*, eds. Lawrence B. de Graaf, Kevin Mulroy, and Quintard Taylor, 249-78. Los Angeles, California: Autry Museum of Western Heritage in association with University of Washington Press, 2001.

Cripps, Thomas. *Slow Fade to Black: The Negro in American Film, 1900-1942*. New York: Oxford University Press, 1977.

Danky, James P., ed. *African-American Newspapers and Periodicals: A National Bibliography.* Cambridge: Harvard University Press, 1998.

Dann, Martin E., ed. *The Black Press, 1827-1890: The Quest for National Identity.* New York: Putnam, 1971.

Delgado, Richard. "Words That Wound: A Tort Action for Racial Insults, Epithets, and Name-Calling." In *Critical Race Theory: The Cutting Edge*, 2d ed., eds. Richard Delgado and Jean Stefancic, 131-40. Philadelphia: Temple University Press, 2000.

Detweiler, Frederick G. *The Negro Press in the United States.* Chicago: The University of Chicago Press, 1922.

Diaz, Ed, ed. *Horace Roscoe Cayton: Selected Writings, vols. 1-2*. Seattle, Washington: Bridgewater-Collins, 2002.

Dodds, Gordon B., ed. *Varieties of Hope: An Anthology of Oregon Prose.* Corvallis: Oregon State University Press, 1993.

———, and Cathy Croghan Alzner. *Serving Justice: A History of the Oregon State Bar, 1890-2000*. Np.: Oregon State Bar, 2004.

Douglas, Susan J. *Listening In: Radio and the American Imagination*. Minneapolis: University of Minnesota Press, 2004.

Douthit, Mary Osborn, ed. *The Souvenir of Western Women*. Portland, Oregon: Anderson & Duniway Company, 1905.

Du Bois, W. E. Burghardt. "The Talented Tenth." In *The Negro Problem: A Series of Articles by Representative American Negroes of To-day*, ed. Booker T. Washington, 30-75. New York: James Pott & Company, 1903.

———. *The Souls of Black Folk*. With introductions by Nathan Hare and Alvin F. Poussaint. New York: New American Library, 1969.

Effrat, Marcia Pelly. "Approaches to Community: Conflicts and Complementarities." In *The Community: Approaches and Applications*, ed. Marcia Pelly Effrat, 1-32. New York: The

Free Press, 1974.
Farr, Libby Dawson. "DeNorval Unthank." In *Architects of Oregon: A Biographical Dictionary of Architects Deceased—19th and 20th Centuries*, ed. Richard Ellison Ritz, 400-401. Portland, Oregon: Lair Hill Publishing, 2002.
Feldman, Charles Matthew. *The National Board of Censorship (Review) of Motion Pictures, 1909-1922*. New York: Arno Press, 1977.
Fellow, Anthony R. *American Media History*, 2d ed. Boston: Wadsworth Publishing, 2010.
Fine, Michelle. "Contextualizing the Study of Social Injustice." In *Advances in Applied Social Psychology*, vol. 3, eds. Michael J. Saks and Leonard Saxe, 103-26. Hillsdale, New Jersey: Lawrence Erlbaum Associates, Inc., 1986.
Finkle, Lee. *Forum for Protest: The Black Press During World War II*. Cranbury, New Jersey: Associated University Presses, Inc., 1975.
Fischer, Claude S. *America Calling: A Social History of the Telephone to 1940*. Berkeley: University of California Press, 1992.
Franklin, John Hope. "Silent Cinema as Historical Mythmaker: *Birth of a Nation*—Propaganda as History." In *Hollywood's America: United States History Through Its Films*, revised ed., eds. Steven Mintz and Randy Roberts, 42-52. St. James, New York: Brandywine Press, 1993.
Fuller, Gary Reese. *Who We Are: An Information History of Tacoma's Black Community Before WWI*. Tacoma, Washington: Tacoma Public Library, 1992.
Fulton, Ann. *Vernonia: A Pocket in the Woods*. Oregon: s.n., 1977.
Gaines, Kevin K. *Uplifting the Race: Black Leadership, Politics, and Culture in the Twentieth Century*. Chapel Hill: University of North Carolina Press, 1996.
Garis, M. R. *Martha Root: Lioness at the Threshold*. Wilmette, Illinois: Bahá'í Publishing Trust, 1983.
Gaston, Joseph. *Portland, Oregon: Its History and Builders in Connection with the Antecedent Explorations, Discoveries and Movements of the Pioneers that Selected the Site for the Great City of the Pacific*, vol. III. Chicago, Illinois: The S. J. Clarke Publishing Co., 1911.
Gates, E. Nathaniel, ed. *Racial Classification and History*. New York: Garland Publishing, Inc., 1997.
Giddings, Paula. *When and Where I Enter: The Impact of Black Women on Race and Sex in America*. New York: Bantam Books, 1984.
Gillespie, Michele K., and Randal L. Hall, eds. *Thomas Dixon Jr. and the Birth of Modern America*. Baton Rouge: Louisiana State University Press, 2006.
Gilmore, Glenda Elizabeth. *Gender and Jim Crow: Women and the Politics of White Supremacy in North Carolina, 1896-1920*. Chapel Hill: The University of North Carolina Press, 1996.
Gish, Lillian, with Ann Pinchot. *The Movies, Mr. Griffith, and Me*. Englewood Cliffs, New Jersey: Prentice-Hall, 1969.
Glasrud, Bruce A. "Harlem Renaissance in the United States: 8—Texas and the Southwest." In *Encyclopedia of the Harlem Renaissance*, vol. 1, A-J, eds. Cary D. Wintz and Paul Finkelman, 521-25. New York: Routledge, 2004.
Grosholz, Emily. "Women, History, and Practical Deliberation." In *Feminist Thought and the Structure of Knowledge*, ed. Mary McCanney Gergen, 173-81. New York: New York University Press, 1988.
Guerrero, Ed. *Framing Blackness: The African American Image in Film*. Philadelphia: Temple University Press, 1993.
Habermas, Jürgen. *The Structural Transformation of the Public Sphere: An Inquiry into a Category of Bourgeois Society*. Trans. Thomas Burger. 1962; Cambridge: MIT Press, 1991.
Halaas, David Fridtjof. *Boom Town Newspapers: Journalism on the Rocky Mountain Mining Frontier, 1859-1881*. Albuquerque: University of New Mexico Press, 1981.

Hales, Douglas. *A Southern Family in White and Black: The Cuneys of Texas*. College Station: Texas A&M University Press, 2003.

Hamalian, Leo, and James V. Hatch, eds. *The Roots of African American Drama: An Anthology of Early Plays, 1858-1938*. Detroit: Wayne State University Press, 1991.

Harris, Paul. *Black Rage Confronts the Law*. New York: New York University Press, 1997.

Hart, James, ed. *The Man Who Invented Hollywood: The Autobiography of D. W. Griffith*. Louisville, Kentucky: Touchstone Publishing Co., 1972.

Hart, Katherine. *Austin & Travis County: A Pictorial History, 1839-1939*. Austin, Texas: The Encino Press, 1975.

Heine, Steven Robert. *Images of America: The Oregon State Fair*. Charleston, South Carolina: Arcadia Publishing, 2007.

Henderson, Robert M. *D. W Griffith: His Life and Work*. New York: Oxford University Press, 1972.

Henry, Susan. "Changing Media History Through Women's History." In *Women in Mass Communication*, ed. Pamela J. Creedon, 341-62. Newbury Park, California: Sage Publications, Inc., 1993.

hooks, bell. *Feminist Theory: From Margin to Center*. 2d ed. Cambridge, Massachusetts: South End Press, 2000.

———. *Talking Back: Thinking Feminist, Thinking Black*. Boston, Massachusetts: South End Press, 1989.

———. *Ain't I a Woman: Black Women and Feminism*. Boston, Massachusetts: South End Press, 1981.

Horne, Gerald. *Race Woman: The Lives of Shirley Graham Du Bois*. New York: New York University Press, 2000.

Horowitz, David A. "Order, Solidarity, and Vigilance: The Ku Klux Klan in La Grande, Oregon." In *The Invisible Empire in the West: Toward a New Historical Appraisal of the Ku Klux Klan of the 1920s*, ed. Shawn Lay, 185-215. Urbana: University of Illinois Press, 1992.

Houston, Marsha. "The Politics of Difference: Race, Class, and Women's Communication." In *Women Making Meaning: New Feminist Directions in Communication*, ed. Lana F. Rakow, 45-59. New York: Routledge, 1992.

Howard, Marilyn K. "Dyer, Leonidas C. (1871-1952)." In *Encyclopedia of American Race Riots*, vol. 1, A-M, eds. Walter Rucker and James Nathaniel Upton, 182-84. Westport, Connecticut: Greenwood Press, 2007.

Howe, Stephen. *Afrocentrism: Mythical Pasts and Imagined Homes*. London: Verso, 1998.

Hughes, Langston. *Autobiography: The Big Sea*. Columbia: University of Missouri Press, 2002.

Hull, Gloria T., ed. *The Works of Alice Dunbar-Nelson*, 3 vols. New York: Oxford University Press, 1988.

Hunton, Addie, and Kathryn Johnson. *Two Colored Women with the American Expeditionary Forces*. Brooklyn, New York: Brooklyn Eagle, 1920.

Huntzicker, William E. "Boosterism: Newspapers Helping to Build Their Communities." In *History of the Mass Media in the United States: An Encyclopedia*, ed. Margaret A. Blanchard, 75-76. Chicago, Illinois: Fitzroy Dearborn, 1998.

Hutchinson, Sandra, and Richard Hollinger, "Women in the North American Bahai Community." In *The Encyclopedia of Women and Religion in North America*, eds. Rosemary Skinner Keller and Rosemary Radford Ruether, 776-86. Bloomington: Indiana University Press, 2006.

Hutton, Frankie. *The Early Black Press in America, 1827 to 1860*. Westport, Connecticut: Greenwood Press, 1993.

Ingham, John N., and Lynne B. Feldman. *African-American Business Leaders: A Biographical Dictionary*. Westport, Connecticut: Greenwood Press, 1994.

Jackson, Kenneth T. *The Ku Klux Klan in the City, 1915-1930*. New York: Oxford University Press, 1967.

Jacobs, Lewis. "D. W. Griffith: *The Birth of a Nation*." In *Focus on The Birth of a Nation*, ed. Fred Silva, 154-68. Englewood Cliffs, New Jersey: Prentice-Hall, Inc., 1971.

———. *The Rise of the American Film: A Critical History*. New York: Teachers College Press, 1967.

Johannsen, Robert W. *Frontier Politics and the Sectional Conflict: The Pacific Northwest on the Eve of the Civil War*. Seattle: University of Washington Press, 1955.

Johansen, Dorothy O. *Empire of the Columbia: A History of the Pacific Northwest*, 2d ed. New York: Harper & Row, Publishers, 1967.

Johnson, Violet M. "Black Immigrants in the United States." In *We Are a People: Narrative and Multiplicity in Constructing Ethnic Identity*, eds. Paul Spickard and W. Jeffrey Burroughs, 57-69. Philadelphia: Temple University Press, 2000.

Jordan, William G. *Black Newspapers & America's War For Democracy, 1914-1920*. Chapel Hill: The University of North Carolina Press, 2001.

Kamholz, Edward J., Jim Blain, and Gregory Kamholz. *The Oregon-American Lumber Company: Ain't No More*. Stanford: Stanford University Press, 2003.

Katz, William Loren. *The Black West*, 3d ed., rev. and expanded. Seattle, Washington: Open Hand Publishing Inc., 1987.

Kerlin, Robert T. *The Voice of the Negro, 1919*. New York: E. P. Dutton Company, 1920. Reprint, New York: Arno Press and *The New York Times*, 1968.

Kessler, Lauren. *The Dissident Press: Alternative Journalism in American History*. Beverly Hills, California: Sage Publications, Inc., 1984.

Kroeger, Brooke. *Nellie Bly: Daredevil, Reporter, Feminist*. New York: Times Books, 1994.

Lang, Robert, ed. *The Birth of a Nation: D. W. Griffith, Director*. New Brunswick, New Jersey: Rutgers University Press, 1994.

Lansing, Jewel. *Portland: People, Politics, and Power, 1851-2001*. Corvallis: Oregon State University Press, 2003.

Leipold, L. E. *Cecil E. Newman, Newspaper Publisher*. Minneapolis, Minnesota: T. S. Denison & Company, Inc., 1969.

Lerner, Gerda, ed. *Black Women in White America: A Documentary History*. New York: Vintage Books, 1972; 1992.

———. *The Majority Finds Its Past: Placing Women in History*. New York: Oxford University Press, 1979.

Lewis, David Levering. *W. E. B. Du Bois: The Fight for Equality and the American Century, 1919-1963*. New York: Henry Holt and Company, 2000.

Lockley, Fred. *History of the Columbia River Valley from The Dalles to the Sea*, vol. 2. Chicago: S. J. Clarke Publishing Co., 1928.

Long, James Andrew. *Marching Forward, Northwest Women's Firsts: 1,444 Role Models*. North Plains, Oregon: Pumpkin Ridge Productions, 2001.

Lucia, Ellis. *The Conscience of a City: Fifty Years of City Club Service in Portland*. Portland, Oregon: The City Club of Portland, 1966.

Lupton, John A. "East St. Louis (Illinois) Riot of 1917." In *Encyclopedia of American Race Riots*, vol. 1, A-M, eds. Walter Rucker and James Nathaniel Upton, 185-91. Westport, Connecticut: Greenwood Press, 2007.

MacColl, E. Kimbark. *The Growth of a City: Power and Politics in Portland, Oregon 1915-1950*. Portland, Oregon: The Georgian Press, 1979.

Mangun, Kimberley. "'The Ku Klux Klan are still scrapping here': African American

Response to the Oregon Klan, 1922-1924." In *Voices from within the Veil: African Americans and the Experience of Democracy*, eds. William H. Alexander, Cassandra L. Newby-Alexander, and Charles H. Ford, 254-85. London: Cambridge Scholars Publishing, 2008.

Marable, Manning. *Black Leadership*. New York: Columbia University Press, 1998.

Marks, Martin Miller. *Music and the Silent Film, Contexts and Case Studies, 1895-1924*. New York: Oxford University Press, 1997.

Marzolf, Marion. *Up from the Footnotes: A History of Women Journalists*. New York: Hastings House, 1977.

Mather, Frank Lincoln, ed. *Who's Who of the Colored Race: A General Biographical Dictionary of Men and Women of African Descent*. Chicago: n.p., 1915.

McArthur, Lewis A. *Oregon Geographic Names*, 6th ed., rev. and enl. Portland: Oregon Historical Society Press, 1992.

McCarthy, Kevin M. *African American Sites in Florida*. Sarasota, Florida: Pineapple Press, Inc., 2007.

McKenna, Robert. *The Dictionary of Nautical Literacy*. Camden, Maine: International Marine/McGraw-Hill, 2003.

McLagan, Elizabeth. *A Peculiar Paradise: History of Blacks in Oregon, 1778-1940*. Portland, Oregon: The Georgian Press Company, 1980.

McLaren, Joseph. "Introduction." In *The Collected Works of Langston Hughes*, vol. 13. Columbia: University of Missouri Press, 2002.

Mecklin, John Moffatt. *The Ku Klux Klan: A Study of the American Mind*. New York: n.p., 1924.

Middleton, Stephen. *The Black Laws in the Old Northwest: A Documentary History*. Westport, Connecticut: Greenwood Press, 1993.

Moore, Shirley Ann Wilson, and Quintard Taylor. "The West of African American Women, 1600-2000." In *African American Women Confront the West: 1600-2000*, eds. Quintard Taylor and Shirley Ann Wilson Moore, 3-21. Norman: University of Oklahoma Press, 2003.

Mott, Frank Luther. *A History of American Magazines, vol. III, 1865-1885*. Cambridge: Harvard University Press, 1938.

Moynihan, Ruth Barnes, Cynthia Russett, and Laurie Crumpacker. General Introduction to *Second to None: A Documentary History of American Women*. vol. 2 (from 1865 to the present), eds. Ruth Barnes Moynihan, Cynthia Russett, and Laurie Crumpacker, 1-8. Lincoln: University of Nebraska Press, 1993.

Mulroy, Kevin. Preface to *Seeking El Dorado: African Americans in California*, eds. Lawrence B. de Graaf, Kevin Mulroy, and Quintard Taylor, ix-xiii. Los Angeles, California: Autry Museum of Western Heritage in association with University of Washington Press, 2001.

Myrdal, Gunnar. *An American Dilemma: The Negro Problem and Modern Democracy*. New York: Harper & Row, 1962.

Niles, Philip. *Beauty of the City: A. E. Doyle, Portland's Architect*. Corvallis: Oregon State University Press, 2008.

Oak, Vishnu V. *The Negro Newspaper*. Yellow Springs, Ohio: Antioch Press, 1948.

O'Leary, Virginia. *Toward Understanding Women*. Monterey, California: Brooks/Cole, 1977.

Oregon Lung Association, Women in the History of Oregon Committee. *Notable Women in the History of Oregon*. Portland, Oregon: Oregon Lung Association, 1983.

Ortiz, Paul. *Emancipation Betrayed: The Hidden History of Black Organizing and White Violence in Florida from Reconstruction to the Bloody Election of 1920*. Berkeley: University of California Press, 2005.

Ovington, Mary White. *The Walls Came Tumbling Down*. New York: Arno Press, Inc., 1969.
Park, Robert E. "The Natural History of the Newspaper." In *The City*, eds. Robert E. Park, Ernest W. Burgess, and Roderick D. McKenzie, 80-98. Chicago: The University of Chicago Press, 1967.
Penn, I. Garland. *The Afro-American Press, and Its Editors*. Springfield, Massachusetts: Willey & Co., 1891. Reprint, New York: Arno Press and the *New York Times*, 1969.
Pieterse, Jan Nederveen. "White Negroes." In *Gender, Race, and Class in Media: A Text-Reader*, 2d ed., eds. Gail Dines and Jean M. Humez, 111-15. Thousand Oaks, California: Sage Publications, Inc., 2003.
Pogue, Anna Holm. "Millie Reid Trumbull." In *With Her Own Wings: Historical Sketches, Reminiscences, and Anecdotes of Pioneer Women*, ed. Helen Krebs Smith, 227-28. Portland, Oregon: Beattie and Company, 1948.
Prather, Patricia Smith, and Bob Lee, eds. *Texas Trailblazer Series* 2. Houston: Texas Trailblazer Preservation Association, 1996.
Pride, Armistead S., and Clint C. Wilson II. *A History of the Black Press*. Washington, D.C.: Howard University Press, 1997.
Rampersad, Arnold. "Chronology." In *The Collected Works of Langston Hughes*, vol. 13, ed. with an introduction by Joseph McLaren, xi-xvi. Columbia: University of Missouri Press, 2002.
Raper, Arthur Franklin. *The Tragedy of Lynching*. New York: Arno Press, 1969.
Rhodes, Jane. *Mary Ann Shadd Cary: The Black Press and Protest in the Nineteenth Century*. Bloomington: Indiana University Press, 1998.
———. "'Falling Through the Cracks': Studying Women of Color in Mass Communication." In *Women in Mass Communication*, 2d ed., ed. Pamela J. Creedon, 24-31. Newbury Park, California: Sage Publications, Inc., 1993.
———. "Mary Ann Shadd Cary and the Legacy of African American Women Journalists." In *Women Making Meaning: New Feminist Directions in Communication*, ed. Lana F. Rakow, 210-24. New York: Routledge, 1992.
Richardson, Marilyn. Preface to *Maria W. Stewart, America's First Black Woman Political Writer*. Bloomington: Indiana University Press, 1987.
Riles, Karen, ed. *African American Bibliography: Sources of Information Relating to African Americans in the Austin History Center of the Austin Public Library*. Austin, Texas: Austin History Center, 2001.
Riley, Glenda. "African American Women in Western History: Past and Prospect." In *African American Women Confront the West: 1600-2000*, eds. Quintard Taylor and Shirley Ann Wilson Moore, 22-27. Norman: University of Oklahoma Press, 2003.
———. "American Daughters: Black Women in the West." In *African Americans on the Western Frontier*, eds. Monroe Lee Billington and Roger D. Hardaway, 160-80. Niwot: University Press of Colorado, 1998.
Ritz, Richard E. *Central Library: Portland's Crown Jewel*. Portland, Oregon: The Library Foundation, Inc., 2000.
Rochlin, Harriet, and Fred Rochlin. *Pioneer Jews: A New Life in the Far West*. Boston, Massachusetts: Houghton Mifflin, 1984.
Royster, Jacqueline Jones. Introduction to *Southern Horrors and Other Writings: The Anti-Lynching Campaign of Ida B. Wells, 1892-1900*, ed. *Jacqueline* Jones Royster, 1-41. Boston, Massachusetts: Bedford/St. Martin's, 1997.
Saalfeld, Lawrence J. *Forces of Prejudice in Oregon, 1920-1925*. Portland, Oregon: University of Portland Press, 1984.
Savage, W. Sherman. *Blacks in the West*. Westport, Connecticut: Greenwood Press, 1976.
Sawyer, Reuben H. *The Truth about the Invisible Empire of the Knights of the Ku Klux Klan*.

Portland, Oregon: n.p., 1922.

Schechter, Patricia A. *Ida B. Wells-Barnett and American Reform, 1880-1930*. Chapel Hill: University of North Carolina Press, 2001.

Schneider, Mark Robert. *"We Return Fighting": The Civil Rights Movement in the Jazz Age*. Boston: Northeastern University Press, 2002.

———. *Boston Confronts Jim Crow, 1890-1920*. Boston: Northeastern University Press, 1997.

Scott, Joan Wallach. "Women's History and the Rewriting of History." In *The Impact of Feminist Research in the Academy*, ed. Christie Farnham, 34-50. Bloomington: Indiana University Press, 1987.

Silva, Fred, ed. *Focus on The Birth of a Nation*. Englewood Cliffs, New Jersey: Prentice-Hall, Inc., 1971.

Simmons, Charles A. *The African American Press: A History of News Coverage During National Crises, with Special Reference to Four Black Newspapers, 1827-1965*. Jefferson, North Carolina: McFarland & Company, Inc., Publishers, 1998.

Sklar, Robert. *Movie-Made America: A Cultural History of American Movies*. New York: Vintage Books, 1976.

Smith, Dorothy V. "The Black Press and the Search for Hope and Equality in Kansas, 1865-1985." In *The Black Press in the Middle West, 1865-1985*, ed. Henry Lewis Suggs, 107-34. Westport, Connecticut: Greenwood Press, 1996.

Smith, J. Clay, Jr. *Emancipation: The Making of the Black Lawyer, 1844-1944*. Philadelphia: University of Pennsylvania Press, 1993.

Smith, Jessie Carney. "Don't Buy Where You Can't Work Movement (1929-1941)." In *Encyclopedia of African American Business*, ed. Jessie Carney Smith, 236-40. Westport, Connecticut: Greenwood Press, 2006.

Startt, James D., and Wm. David Sloan. *Historical Methods in Mass Communication*, rev. ed. Northport, Alabama: Vision Press, 2003.

Sterling, Dorothy. *Black Foremothers*, 2d ed. New York: University of New York, 1988.

Stoneall, Linda. *Country Life, City Life: Five Theories of Community*. New York: Praeger Publishers, 1983.

Streitmatter, Rodger. *Voices of Revolution: The Dissident Press in America*. New York: Columbia University Press, 2001.

———. *Raising Her Voice: African-American Women Journalists Who Changed History*. Lexington: The University Press of Kentucky, 1994.

———. "The Media and Racial Equality." In *The Significance of the Media in American History*, eds. James D. Startt and Wm. David Sloan, 247-65. Northport, Alabama: Vision Press, 1994.

Taylor, Quintard. "Susie Revels Cayton, Beatrice Morrow Cannady, and the Campaign for Social Justice in the Pacific Northwest." In *African American Women Confront the West: 1600-2000*, eds. Quintard Taylor and Shirley Ann Wilson Moore, 189-204. Norman: University of Oklahoma Press, 2003.

———. *In Search of the Racial Frontier: African Americans in the American West, 1528-1990*. New York: W. W. Norton & Company, Inc., 1998.

Tinney, James S. Introduction to *Issues and Trends in Afro-American Journalism*, eds. James S. Tinney and Justine J. Rector, 1-14. Washington, D.C.: University Press of America, Inc., 1980.

Tocqueville, Alexis de. *Democracy in America*, vol. II, the Henry Reeve text as revised by Francis Bowen, further corrected and edited by Phillips Bradley. Alfred A. Knopf, Inc., 1945. Reprint, New York: Vintage Books, 1954.

Toy, Eckard V. "Robe and Gown: The Ku Klux Klan in Eugene, Oregon." In *The Invisible Empire in the West: Toward a New Historical Appraisal of the Ku Klux Klan of the 1920s*, ed.

Shawn Lay, 153-84. Urbana: University of Illinois Press, 1992.

Tripp, Bernell. *Origins of the Black Press: New York, 1827-1847*. Northport, Alabama: Vision Press, 1992.

Vogel, Todd, ed. *The Black Press: New Literary and Historical Essays*. New Brunswick: Rutgers University Press, 2001.

Wade, Richard C. *The Urban Frontier: The Rise of Western Cities, 1790-1830*. Cambridge: Harvard University Press, 1959.

Walden, Janell. "Contributions of Black Women in Media." In *Contributions of Black Women to America, vol. 1, The Arts, Media, Business, Law, Sports*, ed. Marianna W. Davis, 248. Columbia, South Carolina: Kenday Press, Inc., 1982.

Walker, Susannah. *Style & Status: Selling Beauty to African American Women, 1920-1975*. Lexington: University Press of Kentucky, 2007.

Washburn, Patrick S. *The African American Newspaper: Voice of Freedom*. Evanston: Northwestern University Press, 2006.

Watkins, Mel. *Stepin Fetchit: The Life and Times of Lincoln Perry*. New York: Pantheon Books, 2005.

Wells-Barnett, Ida B. *A Crusade for Justice: The Autobiography of Ida B. Wells*, ed. Alfreda M. Duster. Chicago: The University of Chicago Press, 1970.

Wideman, John Edgar. "Charles Chesnutt and the WPA Narratives: The Oral and Literate Roots of Afro-American Literature." In *The Slave's Narrative*, eds. Charles T. Davis and Henry Louis Gates, Jr., 59-78. New York: Oxford University Press, 1995.

Wilson, Woodrow. *A History of the American People*, 10 vols. New York: Harper & Brothers Publishers, 1902.

Winter, Una R., ed. *Alice Park of California, Worker for Woman Suffrage and for Children's Rights*. Upland, California: Susan B. Anthony Memorial Committee of California, 1948.

Wolseley, Roland E. *The Black Press, U.S.A.*, 2d ed. Ames: Iowa State University Press, 1990.

Films and Documentaries

Beatrice Morrow Cannady. Produced and directed by Nadine Jelsing. 29 min. Oregon Public Broadcasting, 2007. DVD.

The Birth of a Nation. Produced and directed by D. W. Griffith. 158 min. United American Video Corp., 1988. Videocassette.

The Green Pastures. Directed by Marc Connelly and William Keighley. 93 min. Warner Bros. Pictures, 1936. DVD.

Unpublished Papers, Theses, and Dissertations

Brownell, Jean. "Negroes in Oregon Before the Civil War." Unpublished paper, Oregon Historical Society, Portland, n.d.

Bryant, Jane W. "The Ku Klux Klan and the Oregon Compulsory School Bill of 1922." M.A. thesis, Reed College, n.d.

Cronin, Mary M. "'The Courage of His Convictions': C. F. Richardson, the *Houston Informer*, and the Fight for Racial Equality in the 1920s." Paper presented at the annual meeting of the Association for Education in Journalism and Mass Communication, Toronto, Canada, August 2004.

Franklin, William Elton. "The Political Career of Peter Hardeman Burnett." Ph.D. diss., Stanford University, 1954.

Hill, Daniel G., Jr. "The Negro in Oregon: A Survey." MA thesis, University of Oregon, 1932.

Hopkins, Oznathylee Alverdo. "Black Life in Oregon, 1899-1907: A Study of the Portland *New Age*." B.A. thesis, Reed College, 1974.

Mangun, Kimberley. "*The Western Outlook*, 1894-1928: A Newspaper 'Devoted to the Interests of the Negro on the Pacific Coast.'" Paper presented at the Association for Education in Journalism and Mass Communication National Conference, Chicago, August 2008.

Schneider, Franz M. "The 'Black Laws' of Oregon." M.S. thesis, University of Santa Clara, 1970.

Strohm, Susan Mary. "Black Community Organization and the Role of the Black press in Resource Mobilization in Los Angeles From 1940 to 1980." Ph.D. diss., University of Minnesota, 1989.

Sweeney, Michael. "A Minority Voice in the Wilderness: Julius F. Taylor and the 'Broad Ax' Of Salt Lake City." Paper presented at the Association for Education in Journalism and Mass Communication National Conference, New Orleans, August 1999.

Toy, Eckard Vance. "The Ku Klux Klan in Oregon; Its Character and Program." MA thesis, University of Oregon, 1959.

Zelman, Donald L. "Oregon's Compulsory Education Bill of 1922." M.A. thesis, University of Oregon, 1964.

Selected Internet Sources

"A Brief History of Blue Key Honor Society." Blue Key Honor Society. http://www.bluekey.org/forms2.html

"A View of Bayocean, Oregon in Tillamook County." Oregon Historic Photograph Collections, Salem Public Library. http://photos.salemhistory.net/cdm4/item_viewer.php?CISOROOT=/max&CISOPTR=3924&CISOBOX=1&REC=20&DMROTATE=90

Abbott, Carl. "Lewis & Clark Exposition." *The Oregon Encyclopedia*. http://www.oregonencyclopedia.org/entry/view/lewis_clark_exposition/

"About Dillard: Dillard Heritage." Dillard University. http://www.dillard.edu/index.php?option=com_content&view=article&id=55&Itemid=63

"About Lewis & Clark College." Lewis & Clark College. http://www.lclark.edu/dept/about/

"About Lincoln." Lincoln High School. http://lincoln.pps.k12.or.us/about

"About Meharry." Meharry Medical College. http://www.mmc.edu/aboutmeharry/index.html

"About Reed: Mission and History." Reed College. http://www.reed.edu/about_reed/history.html

"About Shell: Our history: The early 20th century." Shell. http://www.shell.com/home/content/aboutshell/who_we_are/our_history/early_20th_century/early_20th_century_history_shell_22112006.html

"About the NBR." National Board of Review. http://www.nbrmp.org/about/

"About Us." *Minnesota Spokesman-Recorder*. http://www.spokesman-recorder.com/News/AboutUs.asp?sID=30

"About Us." Second Baptist Church. http://www.sbcla.org/pages.asp?pageid=5778

"About Woodrow Wilson." Woodrow Wilson International Center for Scholars. http://www.wilsoncenter.org/index.cfm?fuseaction=about.woodrow

"Abstract." George P. Johnson Negro Film Collection, 1916-1977. Online Archive of California. http://content.cdlib.org/ark:/13030/tf5s2006kz/

"The Advertising Artwork of Dr. Seuss." Mandeville Special Collections Library, University of California, San Diego. http://orpheus.ucsd.edu/speccoll/dsads/flit/index.shtml

"America's Story." The Library of Congress. http://www.americaslibrary.gov/cgi-bin/page.cgi/jb/jazz/radio_1

"At A Glance: History." Oberlin Conservatory of Music. http://www.oberlin.edu/con/glance.html
"Bahá'ís celebrate 'King of Festivals.'" Bahá'í World News Service. http://news.bahai.org/story/519
"Billy Sunday Remembered." Billy Sunday Online. http://www.billysunday.org
"Biographical Note." Alice Dunbar-Nelson Papers. The University of Delaware Library. http://www.lib.udel.edu/ud/spec/findaids/dunbarne.html
"Biographical Notes on A. Philip Randolph, 1889-1979." A. Philip Randolph Institute. http://www.apri.org/ht/d/sp/i/225/pid/225
"Black Americans in Congress: Oscar Stanton De Priest." http://baic.house.gov/member-profiles/profile.html?intID=28
Bragg, Susan. "Delilah Leonium Beasley." http://www.blackpast.org/?q=aaw/beaseley-delilah-leonium-c-1867-1934
Brown, Korey Bowers. "Carter G. Woodson." The Association for the Study of African-American Life and History. http://www.asalh.org/woodsonbiosketch.html
"Charles Gilpin." Drop Me Off in Harlem: Exploring the Intersections, The Kennedy Center. http://artsedge.kennedy-center.org/exploring/harlem/faces/gilpin_text.html
"City Club's History." The City Club of Portland. http://www.pdxcityclub.org/club-info/history.php
"Clune's Auditorium." Cinema Treasures. http://cinematreasures.org/theater/13960/
Cole Elementary School. http://locations.slps.org/location.asp?RecordID=5B5B5F&Type=newsletter&LocName=Cole%20Elementary%20School
Collins, Cliff. "A Life of Firsts: Mercedes Deiz was a trailblazer by choice." *Oregon State Bar Bulletin*, December 2005. http://www.osbar.org/publications/bulletin/05dec/heritage.html
"Colonization." The African-American Mosaic: A Library of Congress Resource Guide for the Study of Black History & Culture. http://www.loc.gov/exhibits/african/afam002.html
Constitution of the State of Oregon. http://bluebook.state.or.us/state/constitution/orig/const.htm
"David Sarnoff: Timeline." The David Sarnoff Library. http://www.davidsarnoff.org/dsindex.html
"De Norval Unthank Park." City of Portland, Oregon, Portland Parks & Recreation. http://www.portlandonline.com/parks/finder/index.cfm?PropertyID=37&action=ViewPark
"De Priest, Oscar Stanton." Biographical Directory of the United States Congress. http://bioguide.congress.gov/scripts/biodisplay.pl?index=D000263
"Department Stores." PdxHistory.com. http://www.pdxhistory.com/html/department_stores.html
Diaz, Ed. "Horace Roscoe Cayton, 1859-1940." http://www.blackpast.org/?q=aaw/cayton-horace-roscoe-1859-1940.
"Du Bois: The Activist Life." University of Massachusetts Amherst. http://www.library.umass.edu/spcoll/exhibits/dubois/page10.htm
E. Azalia Hackley Collection. The Detroit Public Library. http://www.thehackley.org/gsdl/cgi-bin/library?e=d-000-00---0dplhacsm--00-0-0-0prompt-10---4---Document-dtt--0-1l--1-en-100---20-preferences-three+questions--001-011-0-0utfZz-8-0&a=d&c=dplhacsm&cl=CL3.7.13&d=HASH83cf9665e8d6458b36ab69
"Earl B. Dickerson." The Earl B. Dickerson Chapter of the Black Law Students Association, the University of Chicago. http://blsa.uchicago.edu/edickerson.html

"Esperanto Is ...." Esperanto-USA. http://www.esperanto-usa.org/en/node/3
"Ethel L. Payne Biographical Data Sheet." Washington Press Club Foundation. http://wpcf.org/oralhistory/paynbio.html
"The Evolution and History of the Union: Founding of the Union." A. Philip Randolph Pullman Porter Museum. http://www.aphiliprandolphmuseum.com/evo_history4.html
"Fair History." Oregon State Fair. http://www.oregonstatefair.org/about-the-fair/fair-history
"The Festival of Ridván." http://www.geocities.com/~quddus/feast/fhd0234.html
Fleming, Thomas C. The Free Press. http://www.freepress.org/fleming/flemng31.html
"The Forgotten Ducks." Oregon Documentary Project. http://odp.uoregon.edu/projects/04-05/forgotten/index.html
"Franklin D. Roosevelt Biography." Franklin D. Roosevelt Presidential Library and Museum. http://www.fdrlibrary.marist.edu/fdrbio.html
"Franklin Frederick Korell." Biographical Directory of the United States Congress, 1774-Present. http://bioguide.congress.gov/scripts/biodisplay.pl?index=K000317
"George Edmund Haynes, 1875-1906." *The Tennessee Encyclopedia of History and Culture*. http://tennesseeencyclopedia.net/imagegallery.php?EntryID=H032
"George Edmund Haynes, 1880-1960." National Association of Social Workers Foundation. http://www.naswfoundation.org/pioneers/h/haynes.htm
"The Great 1906 San Francisco Earthquake." U.S. Geological Survey. http://earthquake.usgs.gov/regional/nca/1906/18april/index.php
"The Grotto." The National Sanctuary of Our Sorrowful Mother. http://www.thegrotto.org
"Guggenheim Tour." Charles Lindbergh: An American Aviator. http://www.charleslindbergh.com/history/gugtour.asp
"The Harlem Renaissance and the Flowering of Creativity." The African American Odyssey: A Quest for Full Citizenship, Library of Congress. http://memory.loc.gov/ammem/aaohtml/exhibit/aopart7b.html
Harris Arts Center and Roland Hayes Museum. http://harrisartscenter.com/Events/RolandHayes/tabid/67/Default.aspx
"Historic Harlem." The Big Onion Guide to New York City. http://www.nyupress.org/bigonion/tour03.html
Historical Census Browser, University of Virginia, Geospatial and Statistical Data Center. http://fisher.lib.virginia.edu/collections/stats/histcensus/
"Historical House of Representatives Class Photos." Washington State Legislature. http://www.leg.wa.gov/History/House/houseclassphotos.htm
"Historical Summary." United States Marshal Service. http://www.usmarshals.gov/district/or/general/history.htm
"Historical Timeline: National Negro Health Week." Tuskegee University. http://www.tuskegee.edu/Global/story.asp?S=6349486
"History." Crystal Ballroom, McMenamins. http://www.mcmenamins.com/index.php?loc=2&id=104
"History." Hotel Monaco Portland. http://www.monaco-portland.com/monpmn_history.html
"History." Jack Yates High School: Mission and History. http://poster.4teachers.org/worksheet/view.php?id=121449
"History." Jane Addams Hull House Association. http://www.hullhouse.org/aboutus/history.html
"History of American Beach." Timucuan Ecological and Historic Preserve and Fort

Caroline National Memorial. http://www.nps.gov/timu/historyculture/ambch_history.htm

"History of Bethel A.M.E. Church, San Francisco, CA, 1852-2001." Bethel African Methodist Episcopal Church. http://www.bethelamesf.com/history.htm

"History of Green Acre." Green Acre Bahá'í School, Retreat & Conference Center. http://www.greenacre.org/GreenAcrehistory.aspx

"History of Guthrie." Guthrie, Oklahoma, Chamber of Commerce. http://www.guthrieok.com/history.html

"The History of Jim Crow." http://www.jimcrowhistory.org/home.htm

"History of Kodak Cameras." Kodak. http://www.kodak.com/global/en/consumer/products/techInfo/aa13/aa13.shtml

"The History of Southern University." Southern University System. http://www.sus.edu/about.htm

"History of the Benson Hotel." The Benson. http://www.bensonhotel.com/about/about_history.html

"History of The Call." *The Call*. http://www.kccall.com/article.cfm?articleID=61 (site now discontinued).

"History of Wiley College." Wiley College. http://www.wileyc.edu/history.asp

"History: The Chinese in Oregon." Travel Portland. http://www.travelportland.com/arts_culture/cultural_tours/chinese/history.html

"History." The Historic Columbia River Highway, Oregon Department of Transportation. http://www.oregon.gov/ODOT/HWY/HCRH/history.shtml

Hoffer, Richard. "Fisticuffs John L. Sullivan & Jake Kilrain In The Outlaw Brawl That Started It All," *SI Vault*. http://vault.sportsillustrated.cnn.com/vault/article/magazine/MAG1025687/index.htm

Hoig, Stan. "Land Run of 1889." *Encyclopedia of Oklahoma History & Culture*, Oklahoma Historical Society. http://digital.library.okstate.edu/encyclopedia/entries/L/LA014.html

"The Importance of Spencer's Department Store." Vancouver Historical Society. http://www.vancouver-historical-society.ca/time_capsule.htm

IN Harmony: Sheet Music from Indiana. http://webapp1.dlib.indiana.edu/inharmony/detail.do?action=detail&fullItemID=/lilly/devincent/LL-SDV-236087&queryNumber=1

"In sickness and in health ...," Bridge Street: 1900-1950, Baylor University, Institute for Oral History. http://www.baylor.edu/oral_history/index.php?id=32522

The Inflation Calculator. http://www.westegg.com/inflation/

"Introduction: Welcome to Multnomah Falls." USDA Forest Service. http://www.fs.fed.us/r6/columbia/millennium2/welcome.htm

Johnson, Angela. "The education of black New Orleans—Gilbert Academy: A look back," The Historical Marker Database. http://www.hmdb.org/marker.asp?marker=12678

"Julius Rosenwald." Sears Archives. http://www.searsarchives.com/people/juliusrosenwald.htm

"Kathryn Hall Bogle (1906-2003)." Women City Builders. http://wcb.ws.pdx.edu/?s=bogle

"KGW Radio History." Port of Portland. http://www.radiotowersite.com/rt_kgw_history.asp (site now discontinued).

Kleiner, Diana J. "Fifth Ward, Houston." *The Handbook of Texas*. http://www.tshaonline.org/handbook/online/articles/FF/hpfhk.html

"KOIN Radio from the Heathman Hotel." PdxHistory.com. http://pdxhistory.com/html/koin.html

Linder, Douglas O. "The Sweet Trials: An Account." http://www.law.umkc.edu/faculty/projects/Ftrials/sweet/sweetaccount.HTM

Lowe, Turkiya. "Ella & John Ryan." http://www.blackpast.org/?q=aaw/ryan-ella-john.

"Manuscript Collections: George Bernard Noble." Special Collections and Archives, Reed College. http://library.reed.edu/using/collections/manuscripts.html#noble

"Maud Cuney Hare Papers, 1843-1936." Robert W. Woodruff Library, Atlanta University Center. http://www.auctr.edu/rwwl/Home/tabid/432/Default.aspx

"Maurice Edgar Crumpacker." Biographical Directory of the United States Congress, 1774-Present. http://bioguide.congress.gov/scripts/biodisplay.pl?index=C000959

"Meet Me Under the Clock." Pdx.History.com. http://www.pdxhistory.com/html/meier_frank.html

"Mergenthaler Linotype Keyboard Layout." http://www.rpi.edu/~nebusj/linotype.html

"Mission Statement." Wiley College. http://www.wileyc.edu/mission.asp

"Multnomah Hotel." PdxHistory.com. http://pdxhistory.com/html/multnomahhotel.html

Nat Q. Henderson Elementary School. http://es.houstonisd.org/HendersonES/

"Niagara Movement." W. E. B. Du Bois Library, University of Massachusetts Amherst. http://www.library.umass.edu/spcoll/digital/niagara.htm

"1906 Earthquake: Fire Fighting." National Park Service. http://www.nps.gov/prsf/historyculture/1906-earthquake-fire-fighting.htm

"1912 Women's Suffrage Proclamation Transcription." *Oregon Blue Book*. http://bluebook.state.or.us/state/elections/elections06b.htm

"The 1923 Tokyo Earthquake." Department of Earth & Atmospheric Sciences, St. Louis University Earthquake Center. http://www.eas.slu.edu/Earthquake_Center/1923EQ/

"OFWC Historical Highlights." GFWC/Oregon Federation of Women's Clubs. http://www.gfwc-ofwc.org/History.htm

"OHSU: An Historical Chronology." Oregon Health & Science University. http://www.ohsu.edu/about/history.html

"Oregon History: Spread of Settlement." *Oregon Blue Book*. http://bluebook.state.or.us/cultural/history/history13.htm

"Oregon Secretaries of State Biographical Sketches, 1841-Present." *Oregon Blue Book*. http://bluebook.state.or.us/notable/notsos.htm

"Oscar Stanton De Priest (1871-1951)." Biographical Directory of the United States Congress. http://bioguide.congress.gov/scripts/biodisplay.pl?index=D000263

"Our History: Aunt Jemima's Historical Timeline." Aunt Jemima. http://www.auntjemima.com/aj_history/

Ovington, Mary White. "How NAACP Began." http://www.naacp.org/about/history/howbegan/index.htm

"Past Boards of Commissioners." Multnomah County, Oregon. http://www.co.multnomah.or.us/cc/pastboards.shtml

"Past Doctor-Citizen Award Recipients." Oregon Medical Association. http://www.theoma.org/Page.asp?NavID=110

"Portland Theaters." PdxHistory.com. http://www.pdxhistory.com/html/portland_theaters.html

"Present at the Creation: *Lift Every Voice and Sing*." National Public Radio. http://www.npr.org/programs/morning/features/patc/liftvoice/

"Profile: Visit Lincoln Hall." Portland State University. http://www.pdx.edu/housing/profile/visit-lincoln-hall/

"Prominent PGM Members." Pi Gamma Mu. http://www.pigammamu.org/prominent-members.html

Pullen, Ann Ellis. "Commission on Interracial Cooperation." *The New Georgia Encyclopedia.* http://www.georgiaencyclopedia.org/nge/Article.jsp?id=h-2919
Rampersad, Arnold. "Hughes's Life and Career." *The Oxford Companion to African American Literature.* http://www.english.uiuc.edu/maps/poets/g_l/hughes/life.htm
Rutherford, Charlotte B. "Laws of Exclusion: A foundation of my childhood." *Oregon State Bar Bulletin*, January 2004. http://www.osbar.org/publications/bulletin/04jan/heritage.html
Sarkisian, Nola L. "Progress could spell end to landmark bakery; Lucia Properties to acquire Holland Dutch Bakery in Los Angeles, California." *Los Angeles Business Journal*, August 9, 1999. http://www.labusinessjournal.com
Scarano, Jimmy. "Texas Rosenwald School To Reopen as Museum." National Trust for Historic Preservation, March 21, 2007. http://www.preservationnation.org/magazine/2007/todays-news-2007/texas-rosenwald-school-to.html
"Self-Guided Tour: Downtown, Northeast and Greater Portland." Travel Portland. http://www.travelportland.com/multicultural/tours/african/af_self_tour.html
"Self-Guided Tour: Portland, Oregon." Travel Portland. http://www.travelportland.com/arts_culture/cultural_tours/culture_district/culture_dis_tour.html
"Shattuck Hall." Facilities and Planning, Portland State University. https://www.fap.pdx.edu/floorplans/detail.php?buildingID=34
Shiloh Baptist Church. http://www.shilohbaptist.org
"Signing Oregon's Civil Rights Bill, 1953." The Oregon History Project. http://www.ohs.org/education/oregonhistory/historical_records/dspDocument.cfm?doc_ID=3A81D35B-EF82-BCEB-E518335DD1428E48
"Small's Paradise." New York Party Shuttle Tours. http://www.newyorkpartyshuttle.com/new-york-attractions/smalls-paradise.php
Smyrl, Vivian Elizabeth. "Littig, Texas." *The Handbook of Texas.* http://www.tshaonline.org/handbook/online/articles/LL/hnl33.html
Southern University at New Orleans, Southern University System. http://www.sus.edu/about_sus/default.htm
"Spirit Lake (Washington)." StateMaster.com. http://www.statemaster.com/encyclopedia/Spirit-Lake-(Washington)
"Statistics of the Congressional and Presidential Election of November 8, 1932." http://clerk.house.gov/member_info/electionInfo/1932election.pdf
Thurlow Lieurance Memorial Music Library, Wichita State University. http://library.wichita.edu/music/thurlow_lieurance.htm
Toll, William. "The Mature Distribution Center: The Chinese Community." The Oregon History Project. http://www.ohs.org/education/oregonhistory/narratives/subtopic.cfm?subtopic_ID=198
"Tremont House, Old Town/Chinatown, Portland, OR." Pacific Coast Architecture Database. http://digital.lib.washington.edu/architect/structures/13871/
"Verdell Rutherford." Women's History Month Blog 2007, Diversity Center, City of Portland. http://www.portlandonline.com/omf/index.cfm?a=149251&c=44053
"Walking Tour." Old Capitol Cultural District, Downtown Association of Iowa City. http://icdowntown.com/walkingtour.htm
Wayman, Norbury L. "Grand Prairie Schools." History of St. Louis Neighborhoods. http://stlouis.missouri.org/neighborhoods/history/grand/schools12.htm
"Welcome To Stanley Park." Vancouver Board of Parks and Recreation. http://www.city.vancouver.bc.ca/Parks/parks/stanley/
"What Is Blue Key Honor Society." Blue Key Honor Society. http://www.bluekey.org
"William Duncan Allen." University of Michigan, African American Music Collection.

http://www.umich.edu/~afroammu/standifer/allen.html
"Willis J. King Administration Building." Council of Independent Colleges Historic Campus Architecture Project. http://hcap.artstor.org/cgi-bin/library?a=d&d=p1989
Wormser, Richard. "National Association of Colored Women." The Rise and Fall of Jim Crow. http://www.pbs.org/wnet/jimcrow/stories_org_nacw.html
Zacharias, Patricia. "'I have to die a man or live a coward'—the saga of Dr. Ossian Sweet." *The Detroit News*. http://apps.detnews.com/apps/history/index.php?id=201

Index

Abbott, Robert S., 13, 177
'Abdú'l-Bahá, 105, 118, 262n65, 262n67
abolitionists, 113
Adams, Carrie, 106, 257n113
Adams, Cyrus, 10
Adams, J. Q., 10, 228n122
Adams, Mrs. Frank, 262n72
Addams, Jane, 6, 35, 40, 123, 265n15
Advocate, 161
  advertisements/advertisers in, 48, 50, 52-56, 80-81, 82, 84-85, 172, 223n63, 226n91, 228n125, 229n128, 231n147, 276n22, 285n56
  Advocate Printing Company, 57, 58, 59
  anniversaries of, 12, 13, 46, 47, 56-57, 60-61, 84, 149, 167, 234n195, 234n197, 234n199
  Beatrice Cannady's roles at, 1, 12, 26-27, 50, 51, 202n78, 203n83, 204n98, 227n111
  birth announcements in, 44, 61, 222n47
  book reviews and suggestions in, 15, 16, 180
  circulation/circulation figures of, 42, 44, 46, 54, 83, 230n144
  collection strategies for, 50-51, 227n115
  columnists in, 15, 43, 45, 46, 48, 57, 67, 189, 205n117, 210n188, 226n95, 243n11, 249n117, 256n104, 288n122
  competitors of, 18, 23, 210n190
  delivery problems of, 44
  description of, 1, 2, 3, 27, 61, 80, 84, 161, 167, 234n201
  duty to, 45, 46, 47, 51, 54, 55, 57, 58-59, 159, 233n178
  employees of, 31, 47, 202n78, 225n78
  and exchange network, 50, 59-60, 99, 133, 186
  finances of, 31, 46, 48, 50, 51, 52, 55, 56-58, 149, 183, 228n122
  founders/founding of, 1, 10, 12, 235n202
  as historian, 3, 17, 231n146
  and imagined/real community, 39, 43, 55, 61, 133, 186, 217n7
  and job printing, 50, 57-59, 233n176
  letters from readers/students, 27, 39, 40, 41, 42, 43, 44, 45, 46, 47, 81
  locations of office, 48, 50, 78, 244n27
  mailing rules, 59
  missing issues of, 2, 3, 27, 197n9, 268n108, 274n65
  mission of, 13, 45, 50
  mottos/nicknames/slogans, 45, 46, 89
  Mt. Scott Herald acquired by, 30, 197n9
  as mouthpiece/defender, 4, 17, 39, 47, 51, 59, 148, 149, 159, 162
  obituaries in, 44, 61, 222n47
  press/equipment of, 13, 31, 50, 56-58
  promotes culture, 9, 42, 62-68, 72, 74
  publishing schedule of, 2, 12, 48, 50, 51, 228n118
  subscribers to, 14, 15, 39, 40-47, 49, 58, 77, 79, 80, 82, 87, 97, 151, 167, 205n118, 220n35, 223n51, 240n80, 288n115
  criticism of nonsubscribers, 21
  delinquent subscribers, 48, 50, 57-59, 227n114: criticism of, 51
  subscription drives, 45-49, 224n72
    testimonials, 55, 58
 visitors at office, 13, 14, 56, 78-79
Africa, 68, 108, 115, 169, 181, 237n44
African American press, 12. *See also* Associated Negro Press, black press, Cannady, Beatrice

(articles about in), and names of specific newspapers or editors
African American history, 12. *See also* Negroes, history of
African Methodist Episcopal (AME) Zion Publication House, 60
Afro-American Benefit Association, 40, 219n17
Afro-American Life Insurance Company, 219n17
Agee, Mr. and Mrs. E. W., 83, 270n19
Alaska, 42, 221n38
Albee, Harry Russell, 20-21, 123, 126
Allen, Ella and Ernest, 87, 248n101
Allen, Nellie, 235n202, 242n99, 247n89
Allen, Robert, 280n89
Allen, William Duncan, 61, 85, 220n28, 280n89
Allen, William Duncan, Jr., 61, 235n202, 235n203
Allison, V. K., 140, 269n15
American Civil Liberties Union, 153, 284n39
American Colonization Society, 42
American Expeditionary Forces, 104, 206n134
American Friends Inter-Racial Peace Committee, 34
American Legion, 80-82, 135, 268n99
Amos 'n' Andy, protests against, 183-84
Anaconda, Montana, 16, 27, 190
Anderson, Hilma, 95-96, 251n5, 252n24, 252n29
Anderson, Lee C., 22, 23, 25-26, 40, 70, 71, 209n184, 239n66
Appeal: A National Afro-American Newspaper, 10, 228n122
Arkansas Survey, 59
Armstrong, Louis, 110
Asberry, Nettie J., 23, 106, 120, 171, 178, 180, 210n188, 257n115
Associated Negro Press, 31
Astoria, Oregon, 231n146
Attucks, Crispus, 173, 284n43
"Aunt Jemima," 7
automobiles, 43, 48, 54, 78, 79, 87, 88, 172

Babe Ruth, 145
Bagley, Sam, 162-63
Bagnall, Robert, 21-22, 24, 28, 95, 100, 118, 120, 166, 199n11, 211n215, 239n67
Bahá'í Faith, 13, 24, 27, 35, 95, 103, 104, 105, 106, 113, 118-19, 135, 178, 194, 261n56, 261n58, 261n60, 262n63, 262n68. *See also* Green Acre Bahá'í School, National Spiritual Assembly of the Bahá'í, Portland Bahá'í Assembly
Baker, George L., 1, 37-38 62, 75, 129, 134, 135, 137, 140, 242n106, 266n54, 268n110, 276n22, 279n84
Baker, Ray Stannard, 8
Baker, Vernon, 226n95
Baker, Zepha, 285n56
Baldwin, Louis Fremont, 15, 205n121
Ballard, A., 12, 40, 203n79, 218n13
Baltimore Afro-American, 240n76
Barnett, Claude, 229n127
Bartlett Elmer C., 74-75, 242n95
Bass, Charlotta Spears, 12, 59, 120, 122, 125, 274n64
Bass, Joseph, 13, 59
Beasley, Delilah L., 13, 37, 74, 203n90
Bee, 125
Beeson, Leona, 117, 261n54

Behnke-Walker Business College, 150, 167, 275n11
Belard family, 262n69
Bell, Clara, 170, 282n8
Bell, Estella [?], 246n76
Bell, Hugh A., 276n22
Bell, James S., 20, 84, 85, 126, 246n76, 247n82
Bellingham, Stella, 117, 261n53
Bend High School, 99
Benjamin, Allie and George, 173, 284n36
Benson Hotel, 11, 71, 192
Bertelson, Bart, 127
Bethel African Methodist Episcopal (AME) Church, 13, 64, 67, 71, 74, 79, 116, 204n96, 258n10
Bilbrew, A. C., 72, 241n82
Binford, Charity, 44, 46, 126, 222n49
Binford, Edward, 222n49
Binga, Jesse, 172, 283n31
Binga State Bank, 172
Bird-Holmes, Rosalie, 67
Birth of a Nation, The, 1, 3, 27, 149, 268n111
advertisements for, 128, 131, 264n7, 266n47
audience reactions to, 124, 127, 129
barred from Portland, 134-35
box-office records, 129
cast of, 121, 127, 131
cinematography, 121, 127
in Cleveland, 60, 125, 126, 265n39
cost to make, 121, 128, 263n1
edits to film, 124, 129, 130, 132, 133, 134, 266n63
"Gus chase," 124, 265n21
historical inaccuracies in, 121, 124, 134
intertitles, 124, 265n22
and Ku Klux Klan, 121-22, 124, 127, 128, 131, 136
Los Angeles, opens in, 264n11, 266n62
music in, 127, 131, 266n62
New York City, opens in, 122, 264n12
in Oakland, 126, 266n39
plot of, 121
Portland, opens in, 125, 126
Portland, petition to ban in, 84, 126, 246n70
Portland, returns to, 129, 130, 131, 133, 134, 136, 266n50, 266n52
and Portland City Council, 129-30, 133-34, 136, 268n99
Portland run extended, 128
Birth of a Nation, The, continued
production schedule, 121, 122
protests against
by black editors, 60, 122, 125, 132-33
by Boston NAACP Branch, 131, 136, 266n48
by *California Eagle*, 122, 125, 264n11
by Cannady, 1, 26, 123-37
by Los Angeles NAACP Branch, 131, 137
by Portland NAACP Branch, 123-26, 131, 133, 134-36
renamed, 122, 264n12
reviewer reactions to, 121, 122, 126-27, 129, 131, 266n41

Riverside, opens in, 122
in Tacoma, 126, 265n39
theater decorations, 127, 266n48
in Tillamook, 137
in Topeka, Kansas, 132-33
Black History Month, 3
"Black laws," 18, 207n149, 207n156
black press, 155, 179, 181, 233n184, 263n77
anniversaries, 60-61, 275n18
average lifespan of, 60
duty to, 21, 41, 47, 159, 225n83
editors/journalists, 7, 8, 10, 12, 13, 14, 15, 23, 59, 60, 158, 177
ephemeral nature of, 3
exchange network, 50, 59-60, 99, 133, 186
failures, 12, 52, 210n190
finances/financial difficulties of, 50, 228n122, 232n167, 239n60
founding of, 158
importance of, 12, 21, 43, 51, 57, 159, 167-68
and racial uplift, 222n46
use of for self-promotion, 27
See also Cannady, Beatrice, articles about in black press; names of specific editors and newspapers
black women
in business, 82, 83, 85-86, 95, 175, 238n54
and club movement, 28
and domestic/private, public spheres, 26, 117
employment of, 53, 85-86, 88, 106, 185
gender and civil rights work of, 26, 29, 94
journalists, 7, 12, 13, 28, 34, 37
meet with President Harding, 138
and oppression, 94
recovering histories of, 2, 107
stereotypes of, 64
and suffrage, 11, 192
unpaid labor of, 107
black-owned businesses. *See* Negroes in Portland, businesses
Blake, Eubie, 36
Bland, Jim, 89
Blue Mouse Orchestra and Theatre, 130, 131
Blumauer, Solomon, 281n122
Bly, Nellie, 2, 6, 103, 200n20
Board of Motion Picture Censors, Portland, 123, 124, 125, 126, 127, 129, 133, 134, 135, 136, 265n28, 268n98. *See also* The Birth of a Nation
Boerner, Emil Louis, 228n125
Bogle, Bonnie, 30, 31, 214n258, 238n54
Bogle, Kathryn, 77, 154, 194, 202n77, 222n45, 245n58, 248n98, 275n12
Bolds, William H., 12, 203n79
Booker, Elbert, 25, 36, 71, 72, 152, 179, 275n20, 276n22, 276n25
Booker, Ellen and James, 276n20
Booker, Maude, 71, 73, 179
Booker, Maudie, 72
boosters and boosterism, 15, 46, 47, 80, 82, 84, 87
Boston, Massachusetts, 39, 47, 151, 173, 284n43
Boston Chronicle, 34

Boston Guardian, 34, 151, 177, 275n18
Botts, James and Martha, 39, 217n4
Bowers, Lena, 77, 243n9
Bowers, William, 243n9
boxing, 6, 109
Boyce, Edward, 44, 227n108, 232n153
Boyd, Bessie and William, 283n27
Bradford, Roark H., 66
Bradford, Winslow, 229n129
Bradley family, 198n3
Brantley-Williams, Viola, 173
Brink, Richard, 99
British Columbia, 15, 18, 171
Broad Ax, 61, 234n198
Brown, John, 103
Brown, Lawrence, 64, 235n3
Brown v. Board of Education, 35
Browning, Ivan Harold, 35-36
Buffalo Soldiers, 132, 245n57
Burr, Arthur, 141, 271n30
By the Waters of Minnetonka, 29, 213n244
Byrd, Catherine, 85-86, 248n96, 248n98
Byrd, Dan, 88

Cage, Joel A., 220n35
California, 70, 79-80, 81, 88, 89
    Negroes settling in, 13, 18, 251n12
California Eagle, 13, 14, 59, 94, 156, 225n84, 246n63
California News, 233n184
Campbell, Charles S., 288n113
Campbell, Gaston L., 144, 273n44
Campbell, Myrtle, 106, 185, 187, 257n115, 288n113
Campbell, Omabelle, 273n44
Cannady, Beatrice Hulon Morrow, 1, 98, 170, 183, 191, 193
    ambassador of good will, 27, 28, 38, 95-96, 111, 214n257
Cannady, Beatrice Hulon Morrow, continued
    Amos 'n' Andy, views on, 183
    Bahá'í Faith of, 13, 118, 194, 197n12, 261n56, 261n58, 261n60, 262n61
    speaks at eighteenth annual Bahá'í convention, 13, 118
    beliefs of, 7-8, 25, 28, 117-18
    birth of, 6, 14, 172, 200n16
    Birth of a Nation, protests *The*, 1, 26, 123-36, 268n110
    black elite/intelligentsia, views on, 7-8, 25, 28, 80
    and black actors/musicians, 3, 14, 16-17, 62-67, 242n7
    and black editors/journalists, 3, 13-14, 205n117, 289n146
    and "Black laws," 18, 167, 207n149
    and black poets/authors, 3, 67-68, 237n40
    and black politicians, 3, 41, 68-69, 220n28
    black press, articles about in, 2, 11, 13, 102, 107, 114, 149, 156, 166, 171, 174, 186, 199n11, 260n31
    Cannady, Edward
        courtship with, 4, 10-11
        divorce from, 4, 12, 30-31, 182, 202n69, 214n259
        marriage to, 11, 202n69

car accident, 131, 267n65
childhood of, 5-7, 117-18
civil rights work of, praise for, 17, 27, 37-38, 99, 107, 179-180, 193. *See also* gender and civil rights work; black press, articles about
clothes of, 4, 93, 100-101, 170, 171, 175, 283n16
court cases of in *Advocate*, 30
criticism of, 22-26, 27, 28, 239n67
criticizes federal government, 69, 144
death of, 194, 197n12
discriminated against, 19, 29, 68, 175-76, 276n29
discrimination in Portland, opinions about, 19, 20, 56, 76, 80, 89, 150-51, 158-59
and economic boycott, 89, 148, 182
education of, 5, 7-8, 200n32
and Esperanto. *See* Esperanto
family of, 5, 6
Franklin, Yancy
divorce from, 33, 194, 290n14
marriage to, 31, 183, 214n261
gender and civil rights work of, 26, 29, 94. *See also* spheres, domestic/private and public
and George (son), 4, 33, 181-82, 189
gifts received by, 15-17, 67, 228n122, 236n25
gifts to libraries, 16
graduates from Northwestern College of Law, 29, 112, 213n248
Harmon Award, nominated for, 37-38, 101, 181, 191
health of, 48, 93, 95
home of, 1, 14, 204n112
honored posthumously, 36
houseguests of, 77, 170, 242n7, 282n7
and Ku Klux Klan, 1, 26, 138, 140, 143, 144-45, 146, 147, 269n1, 270n22, 270n24, 274n65
and interracial relations, 1, 3, 11, 16, 28, 51, 95, 99, 182, 192
Cannady, Beatrice Hulon Morrow, continued
and interracial teas, 1, 27, 65, 92, 93, 94-95, 101-107, 120, 169, 171, 193, 254n71, 257n121
lecture/broadcast themes/titles, 11, 26, 93, 94, 95, 97-98, 99, 106-107, 110, 112, 113, 114, 115-117, 171, 178, 260n37, 260n41, 260n42, 261n52, 262n63, 262n68, 283n16, 289n138
legal career/practice of, 19, 29-30, 185, 213n249, 213n255, 214n256, 243n7, 277n38
and Lincoln High School, talks at, 11, 41, 95-98, 138, 251n5, 253n45
as mediator between the races, 28, 45
Miniature Pan-African Congress, organizes, 178-81
and music, 7, 9, 29, 63, 64, 65, 72, 102, 105, 107, 289n135
NAACP
branches, organizes, 21-22, 164, 176-77, 280n92
and nineteenth annual conference, 26, 93-94, 250n2, 251n10, 251n14, 251n15
and officials, 3, 21-22, 24-25, 29, 51, 70-71, 93, 100, 115, 118, 123, 130, 140, 164-66, 169, 203n94, 209n176, 239n67, 250n2, 252n30. *See also* names of specific officials
Portland Branch
roles in, 20, 23, 140
problems with, 7, 22-26, 131, 136, 166, 186-87, 211n212, 239n67
quits organization, 25
and seventeenth annual conference, 93, 250n2

speakers bureau, added to, 22-24, 166
and NACWC, 22-23
and Negro history, 2, 14, 97, 114, 115, 119, 167, 174, 178, 186, 252n30. *See also* Negro History Week, observances in Oregon
and Negro women's obligations, 26, 28, 94
and newspaper boycott, 159-60
and Oregon State Bar, 30
and Pan-African Congress
Fifth, 174, 285n52
Fourth, named hostess of, attends, 169, 170, 174
and parties, 14, 35, 64, 67, 78, 100
"passing," views on, 52-53
personal finances of, 31
personal library of, 2, 14-16, 67, 99, 113, 114, 171, 174, 204n111, 204n112
Portland
arrives in, 3, 11, 18
leaves, 1, 4, 190, 194
Precinct Reporter, writes for, 1
public opinion, attempts to change, 135, 165, 194
public-speaking skills of, 120
radio broadcasts of, 1, 3, 27, 110-114, 186, 193, 259n18, 259n22, 260n31, 283n16. *See also* Portland, radio stations
reading room named in honor of, 16, 206n132
and religion, 117-18. *See also* Bahá'í Faith of
roles at the *Advocate*, 1, 12, 26-27, 50, 51, 202n78 203n83, 204n98, 227n111
sons' role in campaign for race relations, 34
in Southern California, 1, 4, 94-95, 194, 257n5
state representative, campaign for, 1, 22, 184-190, 289n132, 289n141
sues James Merriman, 23
sues Portland Board of Education, 26, 29
talks at churches/to church groups, 3, 72, 93, 115-17, 171, 178, 182, 193, 260n37, 260n40, 260n42, 261n52, 261n53, 283n21, 289n138
talks at Reed College, 11, 64, 73, 101, 178, 254n68
talks at Willamette University, 99-100, 113, 253n64
Taylor, Reuben, marriage to, 1, 194
teaching career of, 9, 201n54, 201n55
trips of, 13, 15, 21, 26, 36, 56, 65, 72, 87, 93-95, 105, 113, 118 , 171-77, 181, 182, 192, 252n17, 258n5, 283n19, 283n20, 285n58, 286n65
University of Chicago, studies at, 9, 10, 172, 201n57
voting, views on, 186
white audiences, reactions to talks of, 27, 30, 95-96, 114-15
white community seeks opinion of, 27
and white officials/politicians, 1, 37, 53, 62, 72-73, 125-26, 129, 137, 140, 149-50, 157, 230n134, 242n106, 258n7, 268n110. *See also* names of specific officials
white people, responds to requests from, 27, 65-66, 114-15, 178, 187
white press
articles about in, 28, 30, 62, 93, 97-98, 105, 116, 118-19, 120, 130, 179, 188, 203n90. *See also* names of specific newspapers
writes for, 87, 113, 259n24
and white students, 14, 98-101
and Wiley University/College, 8-9, 28, 200n35, 283n18
Cannady, Edward Daniel, 4, 18, 191-92, 228n122, 269n8
and *Advocate*, 1, 10, 12, 31, 43, 49, 202n78
Beatrice

courtship with, 4, 10-11
divorce from, 4, 12, 30-31, 182, 202n69, 214n259
marriage to, 11, 202n69
praises work on *Advocate*, 12, 203n82
biographical details, 10-11, 202n61, 202n64
Cannady Real Estate Co., 83-84
and Colored Taxpayers League, 20, 208n163
death of, 33, 214n272
discrimination, protests, 20, 21
dismissed from job, 50, 227n108
personal finances of, 31
NAACP Portland Branch, co-founder of, 20
and Portland Hotel, 10, 11, 202n67
Cannady, George and Caroline Wilkins, 10
Cannady, George Edward, 4, 27, 31, 32, 67, 93, 103, 181-82
and Ivan, 33
articles about in *Advocate*, 33-34
athletic accomplishments of, 32, 34, 35
death/interment of, 35
discriminated against, 19, 36, 113-14
education of, 32, 34, 35, 36, 54, 113, 189, 216n296
and Grand Floral Parade, 33
House of Representatives, chooses mother's seat in, 189
legal career of, 34, 35, 216n299
and parties, 35, 54, 64
at Spirit Lake YMCA Camp, 33
trips with mother, 36
white groups, talks to, 34-35, 215n290, 215n293
Cannady, Ivan Caldwell, 27, 31, 32, 35, 72, 93
accepts award for mother, 36
and *Advocate*, 2, 197n9
articles about/by in *Advocate*, 33-34, 36, 86
career in real estate of, 32, 36, 194
death of, 36
discriminated against, 19
education of, 32, 36
and George, 33, 36
membership in organizations, 36
military service of, 36
and music, 36, 86
and parties, 36, 64
at Spirit Lake YMCA Camp, 33, 36
trips with mother, 36
white groups, talks to, 36
Carlson, Frank E., 105
Carlyle, Richard, 72
Carnegie, Andrew, 8
Carpentier, Georges, 109
Carry, George W., 29, 213n247
Carver, George Washington, 115
From Captivity to Fame, 15, 205n125
Caston, J. L., 153, 157, 267n83, 278n59
Catholic Sentinel, 178
Cayton, Horace Roscoe, 189, 289n146

Cayton's Weekly, 189
Centenary-Wilbur Methodist Episcopal Church, 115
Central Coal & Coke Company, 163
Central Library, Portland, 113, 229n128, 287n76
  Cannady donates books to, 16
  and Miniature Pan-African Congress, 178-79
Central Methodist Church, Men's Brotherhood, 182
Ceruti, E. Burton, 131, 266n61
Charleston Messenger, 166
Chase, W. Calvin, 125
Chicago, Illinois, 12, 15, 39, 43, 60, 77, 89, 99, 105, 123, 151, 172-73, 205n123
Chicago Bee, 13, 60
Chicago Defender, 13, 34, 107, 171, 174, 177, 203n87
Chicago Whip, 148, 249n123
Chiles, Nick, 132-33
Chin family, 77, 104, 243n15
Chin's China Tea Garden, 71, 77, 243n15
Chinese, 52, 105, 146, 219n23
  immigration laws, 41
  population in Josephine County, 277n43
  restaurants, 71, 77
Circle for Peace and Foreign Relations, 104, 170, 282n9
City Club, Portland, 71, 240n73, 277n42
civil rights, 13, 20. *See also* equal rights
Civil War, 15, 40, 121, 129
Clansman, *The*, 122, 123, 127. *See also Birth of a Nation, The*
Clarke, Clement G., 275n12
Clarkston, Emogene, 47
Clemens, Emma, 79, 244n31
Clippinger, David Alva, 9-10, 201n57
Clyde, Ralph, 133-34, 189-90, 226n95, 267n84, 267n85
Coffey, Alex, 88
Cohen, Walter L., 41-42, 47, 219n25, 219n26, 219n28
Cohn, Martin, 208n158
Cole, Richard H., 77, 243n12
Coleman, Norman F., 135, 178, 179, 287n84
Coleman, William T., Jr., 35
Collins, Eddie and Eliza, 164
Collins, Mary, 150-51, 275n10
color line, 17, 192. *See also* Jim Crow
Colored Taxpayers League, 20, 208n163
Columbia River, 11, 24
Columbia River Highway, 41, 78, 79
Colwell, Eleanor, 133, 134, 252n16
comfort stations, 90, 250n133
Commission on Interracial Cooperation, 73, 241n94
Committee on Health and Public Morals, 192
contact, between races, 96, 102, 115, 193
Coolidge, Calvin, 258n7
Cooper, F. D., 45 Coos Bay, Oregon, 143, 273n40
Coos Bay Times, 144-45
Cornish, Samuel, 158, 228n122
Cox, Arthur, 208n159
Cranshaw, Mrs., 78

crime
  allegedly committed by black men, 43, 62, 117, 157-58, 188
  allegedly committed by white men, 157, 278n60
Crisis, 7, 8, 17, 65, 68, 91, 92, 99, 100, 122, 170, 175, 180, 181, 249n126, 270n21
Crosswhite, Leonard, 245n52
Crumpacker, Maurice E., 44, 223n55
Crystal Ballroom, 81, 245n50
Cullen, Countee, 65, 169, 237n27
Cuney, Norris Wright, 206n137
Curry, J. W., 241n83

Daily News, 226n88
Daily Press, 122
Dana, Marshall N., 179
Darrow, Clarence, 173, 284n39
Davidson, Aileen, 65-66, 110, 236n25
Davidson's Bakery Company, 91, 250n137
Davis, Jefferson, 7
De Priest, Oscar, 3, 68-69, 75, 99, 119, 189, 238n47, 238n52, 238n54, 239n59, 259n24
Deiz family, 30, 263n72
Dempsey, Jack, 109
Derrick, John Lincoln, 59, 60, 234n192
Derrick, Mabel, 234n192
Detroit News, 173
dialect, 158-59, 163
Diamond, James and Laura, 244n30
Dickerson, Earl, 172, 283n27, 284n34
Dickerson, Edward W. and Leona T., 288n115
Diggs, Duke and Estella, 79, 244n29
Dinneen, Lawrence, 30, 213n254
discrimination. *See* color line; Jim Crow; Portland and Jim Crow; racial segregation
Dixon, Thomas, Jr., 121, 122, 263n3
Dr. Fred Palmer Skin Whitener Preparations, 52
Dr. Seuss (Theodore Geisel), 52
Dogan, Matthew W., 8-9, 23, 29
Donohue, R. W., 152, 276n27
Dorman, Hugh B., 113-14
Dorman, Leander, 233n185
Douglas National Bank, 172
Douglass, Frederick, 7, 12, 14, 16, 24, 100, 101, 111, 192-93, 206n134, 242n4, 254n66
Doyle, Albert E., 229n128, 230n133
Du Bois, Nina G., 170
Du Bois, Shirley Graham, 42
Du Bois, W. E. B. (William Edgar Burghardt), 3, 7, 12, 14, 112, 120, 122, 177, 249n126
  "Fifty Years Among Black Folks," 113, 259n25
  and NAACP, 40, 93, 94
  The Negro, 14
  and Pan-African Congresses, 169, 174, 282n12, 285n52
  praises Cannady, 180-81
  The Souls of Black Folk, 96, 184
  "Talented Tenth," 7-8, 25
  tours the Pacific Northwest, 203n94
Duke, Josephine, 90, 250n133
Duke, Stanton, 250n133

Dunbar, Paul Laurence, 2, 102, 106, 181, 237n27, 259n25
Birth of Morn, The, 106
Complete Poems of Paul Laurence Dunbar, The, 16
Old Front Gate, The, 106
Who Knows?, 106
Dunbar, Saidie Orr, 28, 104, 105, 212n234, 255n93
Dunbar-Nelson, Alice, 34, 215n281
Duncan, John A., 247n93
Durham, George B., 39, 40, 47, 217n6, 221n39
Dyer, Leonidas C., 21, 100, 120, 138-39, 211n212
Dyer, E. C., 169

Eastern Outfitting Company, 53, 55
Eastman, George, 6
Edwards, Joseff H., 263n73
Egyptian Theatre, 280n89
Eisman, George P., 105, 113-14
Elde, Iver, 81, 245n49
Elgin, Texas, 176
Elkins, Margaret, 236n25
Ellington, Duke, 110
Ellis, Perry, 142-43, 272n37
Ellis Avenue Community Methodist Church, 37
emancipation, 72, 116
Empire State Federation of Women's Clubs, 104
Enterprise, 30
equal rights, 4, 13, 99, 117, 192. *See also* civil rights
Esperanto, 119, 262n70
Esperanto club, 71, 103, 119, 205n118, 262n69, 262n72
Eugene Guard, 160
Evening Post, 123, 124, 265n15
Evening Telegram, 127
Ewing, Jennie, 211n209
Ewing, Jesse A., 22, 25, 105, 211n209

Fairbanks, Charles, 191
Fairchild, Thornton M., 225n77
Fall, Nellie M., 17, 206n138
Farnham, E. C., 37, 136
Federal Council of Churches, 165, 256n100, 260n42
Fellowship for Better Inter-racial Relations, 178, 286n68
Fetchit, Stepin, 72, 240n80
Finch, Ida, 106, 256n106
First African Methodist Episcopal Zion Church, 55, 90-91, 118, 178, 261n55, 282n8
First Christian Church, 36
First Congregational Church, 72
First Friends Church, 182
Flowers family, 245n52
Flowers, Ervin, 126, 245n52
Ford, James W., 238n56
Fortune, T. Thomas, 7, 12, 200n26
Forum, 14, 204n99
France, 131-32, 169
Frank, Emil, 53

Franklin family, immediate and extended, 31, 64, 67, 160, 214n265, 214n266, 252n16
Franklin, Chester, 13
Franklin, Clara Belle, 13, 214n265
Franklin, Yancy Jerome, 31, 33, 111, 183
    divorce from Beatrice Cannady, 33, 194, 290n14
Franklin, Yancy Jerome, continued
    marriage to Beatrice Cannady, 31, 183, 214n261
    radio broadcasts of, 111, 259n22
Fridia, John Walter, 79, 244n32
Fridia, Mary, 244n32
Fry, Henry P., 270n22, 272n32

Gaines, Kevin K., 26, 28
Garner, Mary, 221n35
Garnet, Roy and Willis, 83, 88, 246n67
Garrison, William Lloyd, 14
Gaylor, Mr., 55-56
Gazette, 60, 125
General Federation of Women's Clubs, 104
George Fox University, 71
Gilbert Academy and Agricultural College, 9
Gildon, Edna, 58, 233n174
Gildon, William, 21, 58
Gill, Sam, 100, 192-93, 254n66
Gilpin, Charles, 16, 205n129
Gish, Lillian, 121
Glines, George and Myra, 282n8
Glover, Hunter, 133-34, 136, 268n105
Golden West Hotel, 44, 54, 61, 235n203, 237n34, 247n89. *See also* Allen, William Duncan
Goldenweiser, Alexander, 106, 256n108, 289n148
Gordon, Taylor, 65, 236n17
Gosnell, Harold F., 99, 253n54, 253n55
Gragg, Lulu, 263n72, 276n22
Gragg, William, 263n72
Graham, David, 42, 220n33, 220n34
Graham, Etta, 42, 178, 220n34
Grant, Frank S., 149, 275n8
Grant High School, 103-104, 180
Grants Pass, Oregon, 154-57, 277n43
Grayson, Jennie and Garven [Jr.?], 242n7
Grayson, Jessie Coles, 77, 106, 242n7, 257n115
Grayson, Garven, 77, 242n7
Great Depression, 38, 69, 91, 136, 184
    effect on *Advocate*, 46-49, 50, 51
    effect on black men and women in Portland, 38, 48, 49, 50, 85-86, 87, 88-91, 184
    effect on white men and women in Portland, 50, 89
    effect on white newspapers in Portland, 48
    See also Portland employment statistics
Greater Providence Baptist Church, 42
Green Acre Bahá'í School, 119, 262n67
Green Pastures, The, 42, 66-67, 78, 109-110, 236n27, 237n27, 237n28, 237n29, 237n35
Greene, William H., 154-57, 278n45, 278n49, 278n55
Greenleaf, Elizabeth, 105, 262n68
Greenman, Judd, 165

Gregory, Louis, 27, 105, 118, 256n104, 262n68
Gresham, Elnora, 52, 228n125
Griffin, Adolphus D., 207n15
Griffin, Frank L., 169, 282n7
Griffith, D. W. (David Wark), 27, 121, 122, 127, 128, 136
Griffith, Franklin T., 37, 45, 223n55
Gritzmacher, Charles, 20, 208n166
Grotto, 71
Guerrero, Ed, 136
Gulliford, Dora, 42
Guthrie, Oklahoma, 9, 29, 201n55

H. F. Alexander, 72, 241n83
Hackett, Francis, 123
Haiti, 104, 169
Hale, Joseph F., 141, 271n30
Hall, Ella, 221n36
Hall, R. L., 42
Hamrick, John, 131
Handsaker, Alice, 24-25, 95, 102, 105, 106, 120, 135, 146, 169, 178, 211n205, 261n43, 286n68
Handsaker, John, 104, 105, 211n205
Handy, W. C., 17, 110
Hannon, Lotta, 260n43, 282n8
Hansberry, Lorraine, 284n34
Harding, Warren G., 138, 258n7
Hare, Maud Cuney, 17, 27, 29, 206n137, 212n223
Harlem Renaissance, 28, 37
Harmony Kings, 36
Harper's Ferry, West Virginia, 40
Harris, Arthur, 240n78
Harris, Charles Kassell, 7
Harris, Fred U., 77, 78, 243n11
Harrison, Richard B., 66, 67
Harrison, William Edward, 34
hate speech, 146-47
Hathaway, Josephine, 257n113
Hayes, Roland, 3, 9, 62-64, 75, 77, 171, 173, 235n3, 235n4, 235n5, 236n12, 242n7
Haynes, George E., 17, 175, 254n71
Hays, Arthur Garfield, 284n39
Hearts in Dixie, 72, 241n81
Heathman Hotel, 112
Hefflin, Leon M., 252n17
Heifetz, Jascha, 36
Heilig Theatre, 64, 125, 128, 134
Hello Central, Give Me Heaven, 7
Henderson, James and Kate, 240n78
Henderson, Mamie, 40
Henderson, Nat Q., 40, 218n16
Hendrickson, John Hunt, 29, 213n245
Henry, George, 20
Henson, Mr. and Mrs. Julian, 245n58, 274n61
Hepburn, Emma, 250n131
Hill, Charles Wesley, 237n29

Hill, Daniel G., Jr., 33, 71, 74, 75, 136, 191, 238n54, 240n76, 240n77, 256n110
Hill, Richard, 256n110
Hill, William Allyn, 240n76
Hoeber, Ralph C., 187-88, 189, 289n135, 289n145
Hoesley, William, 82, 246n59
Holliday, W. H., 238n54
Holmes, E. H., 249n117
Holmes, Edith Knight, 126
Holtz, Aaron, 229n128
Hood River, Oregon, 269n8
Hood River Glacier, 139
Hoogstraat, J. J., 278n55
Hooker, Emily, 240n78
Hooker, Gwendolyn, 72, 169, 242n99, 256n103
Hooker, Violet, 240n78, 256n103
Hoover, Herbert, 69, 238n58, 251n12
Hotchkiss, Clarence R., 112, 259n19
Hough, Charles, 154
Houston Informer, 79
Howard University, 15, 32, 35, 105, 106, 235n202
Hudson, H. Claude, 94, 167-68, 194
Hughes, Langston, 3, 67-68, 75, 77, 102, 119, 169, 237n46
 "I, Too," 68, 175-76
 "Negro Speaks of Rivers, The," 68, 114, 263n73
 Scottsboro Limited; Four Poems and a Play in Verse, 17
 Weary Blues, The, 65, 67
Hunter, Nell, 67
Hunton, Addie W., 77-78, 104-105, 170, 173, 174, 181, 206n134, 255n97, 282n9, 282n12

Ingersoll, Carrie, 82, 231n151
Ingersoll, J. W., 82
International Good-Will Day, 105, 256n99
interracial marriage, 14, 165
interracial relations, 16, 28, 50, 62, 82, 95, 100-101, 102, 104, 107, 117, 119, 124, 136, 148, 156, 169, 171, 181, 182, 192
 and children/young adults, 35, 95-97, 99, 101, 114, 115-16, 146, 194
 and religious leaders, 184
Iowa Federation of Colored Women's Clubs, 52
Ives, Amelia, 233n185
Ivey, Clarence, 88, 135, 136, 153, 187, 238n54, 239n61, 248n109
Ivey, Rosa, 239n61

J. C. Penney Co., 54
J. K. Gill & Co., 84, 113, 180
Jackson, Anna, 203n79
Jackson, Sam, 141-42
James, W. C., 280n92
Jamison, Cora Morrow Coleman, 5, 64, 71, 106, 119, 199n7, 240n74, 263n72
Jamison, Elbert, 64, 71, 240n74
Jamison, Guy, 240n78
Jamison, John, 135, 226n95, 226n103
Japanese, 41, 105, 219n23, 277n43
jazz, 110, 258n9
Jefferson High School, 61, 103, 235n202

Jenkins, Cynthia, 282n8
Jenkins, Frank, 274n2
Jenkins, Hopkin, 235n202
Jenkins, Leon, 153
Jennings, John A., 130
Jim Crow, 3, 7, 26, 43, 50, 76, 81, 89, 97, 109, 132, 136, 150-51, 161-64, 175, 182
Johnson, Claude, 162
Johnson, George Perry, 260n31
Johnson, Henry, 141, 272n30
Johnson, J. T., 87
Johnson, J. Rosamond, 64-65, 73, 77, 236n15, 236n22, 236n23, 259n25
Johnson, Jack, 6, 109
Johnson, James Weldon, 3, 23-24, 64, 65, 93, 115, 119, 120, 130, 143, 145, 169, 236n22, 236n23, 250n2, 263n73
Johnson, John, 162-63
Johnson, Kathryn, 104, 206n134
Johnson, Sam, 89
Johnson, Toby, 88
Jones, John L., 42
Journal of Negro History, 15, 181, 205n119
Journalist, 12

Kansas City Call, 13
Kanzler, Jacob, 136
Kaste, John W., 44
Kathleen, 171
Keene, Dora, 46, 224n73
Keene, Norma, 224n73
Keene, Virgil, 46, 136, 153, 224n73, 267n83
Kelly, John W., 127
Kennedy, George W., 233n185
Kilrain, Jake, 6
Kimbrough, D. H., 46, 224n69
Kinard, Lee Roy, 36, 90
King, Milo, 161-62, 280n84
Ko-Verra, 52, 228n125
Kodak camera, 6, 78
Korell, Franklin F., 45
Kozer, Sam, 72
Kroeger, Brooke, 2
Ku Klux Klan, 26, 59, 76, 136, 147, 258n9, 270n22
    in Albany, 141
    and Cannady, 1, 26, 138, 140, 143, 144-45, 146, 147, 269n1, 270n22, 270n24, 274n65
    doctrine of, 139, 140, 154, 155, 157
    editorials about in Oregon newspapers, 141, 271n25
    effect on advertising, 55, 232n153
Ku Klux Klan, continued
    in Eugene, 139, 141, 269n14
    in Grants Pass, 278n55
    in Hood River, 139, 269n10
    initiation ceremonies, 139
    Invisible Empire, 141
    in Jackson County, 141, 271n29
    klaverns, 141, 146

in Marshfield, 143-45
in Medford, 130, 271n30, 278n55
membership of, 146, 155, 274n63
near-lynchings in Oregon, 130, 131, 141-43, 155
in Newberg, 146
in North Bend, 143-44
in Oregon, 1, 3, 17, 130, 137, 140-41, 142, 149, 156, 270n24, 271n28, 274n61, 274n63, 274n71
in Oregon City, 131, 142-43
parades, 130, 139-40
in Portland, 131, 139
"pure Americanism," 55, 131, 140
recruiting films of, 130, 142, 272n31, 272n32
regalia of, 141, 156
in Roseburg, 130, 139, 140, 141-42, 269n12
in Salem, 130, 139-40
in Tillamook, 140, 268n111
in Vernonia, 280n95
Kyles, Luella, 224n76
Kyles, Lywood, 47, 224n76

La Esperanto Matenmango Klubo, 119
Ladd & Tilton Bank, 9
Ladd, William M. and William S., 9
Lane, Ed, 79, 244n36
Lane, Harry, 20
Langston Herald, 7
Latimer, George Orr, 24, 64, 104, 105, 118, 135, 136, 178, 261n56
Latimer, Harriet and James, 118, 261n56
Laurelwood Methodist Episcopal Church, 117
Lawson, Burton K., 20
Lay, Mr. and Mrs., 78
Lee, Effie, 88
Lee, Nancy, 48
Legislative Counsellor, 180
Lemon, Reverend, 117
Lewis, Joda and Lillian, 235n202
Lewis, Kate, 90, 250n133
Lewis, Louise Russell, 61, 235n202
Lewis, Sylvia, 247n93
Lewis & Clark College, 29
Lewis and Clark Exposition, 191
Liberator, 14
Liberia, 42, 169, 178
Library Association of Portland, 16
Lieurance, Thurlow, 213n244
Lightner, C. S., 198n3
Lightner, Lula, 177, 198n3
Lincoln, Abraham, 34, 71, 91, 111
Lincoln High School, 11, 192, 202n74, 275n12
Advocate, subscribes to, 39
Cannady, talks by, 11, 41, 95-98, 138, 251n5, 253n45
Cannady's help, student seeks, 98
De Priest, talk by Oscar, 68-69

Dyer, talk by Leonidas C., 138
student essays, 96-97, 101, 112, 252n29, 252n31, 259n22
Pickens, talk by William, 71
Talbert, talk by Mary, 209n187
Waldron, talk by J. Milton, 41
Lincoln Motion Picture Company, 260n31
Lincoln University Poets, 240n76
Lindbergh, Charles, 146, 172, 274n59
Lipman Wolfe & Co., 85, 88, 229n128
Littig, Texas, 5, 8, 117, 176-77, 198n2, 199n5
Locke, Alain, 118
New Negro, The, 65-66
review of *The Negro In Our History*, 15
Logan, Clara, 79, 203n79
Logan, Helen, 209n185
Logan, John C., 12, 79, 192, 203n79
Longview, Washington, 21-22, 25, 58, 166, 209n176
Los Angeles, California, 77, 78, 84
Cannady speaks to groups in, 95, 252n17
Central Avenue, 151
First African Methodist Episcopal (AME) Church, Los Angeles, 74
and Great Depression, 89
NAACP, 71, 93-94, 107, 157, 211n200
race relations in, 122
real estate restrictions, 251n12
Second Baptist Church, 94
Los Angeles Sentinel, 36
Los Angeles Times, 94
Lovell, John, Jr., 106, 256n109
Lovell, Walter R., 38, 71, 90, 111, 227n103, 238n54, 258n16
lynching, 21, 61, 73, 97, 100, 112, 132, 136, 150, 156, 175, 182, 183, 258n9, 269n6, 273n42, 273n58. *See also* near-lynchings in Oregon
Lyon, Chester A., 226n95

Madison, Birdie, 286n63
Madison, John, 176, 286n63
Magruder, Edward, 55
Maguire, Robert, 30
Malcolm X, 285n55
Mapps, John, 255n91
Mapps, Nellie, 104, 255n91
Marshall, Henrietta, 262n72, 277n41
Marshall, William, 277n41
Marshfield (Coos Bay), Oregon, 143-45, 157, 273n58
Martin, Ed, 226n95
Mason-Dixon Line, 156
Matilsky, Abraham and Jennie, 222n47
Matthews, W. W., 60, 234n189
Maxwell, Charles H., 54, 79, 160-61, 230n146, 279n80
Maxwell family, 230n146
Maxwell, Floyd, 135, 136, 268n98
Maxwell, Marie, 102, 106, 160-61, 230n146
Maxwell, Maxine, 160, 230n146, 279n77, 279n83
Maxwell, Merriman, 79, 230n146

Mayberry, Inez, 245n58
Mayo, Alberta, 240n78
McArthur, James, 161-62, 240n78, 279n84
McArthur, Mattie, 240n78
McCanns, Shirley Graham, 42, 72, 73, 106, 110, 116, 169, 170, 241n84, 276n22, 282n8
McCarthy, Joseph, 237n46
McGhee, London, 42, 221n37
McGinn, Henry, 26, 212n222
McGinnis, Christopher Hamilton, 5, 198n1
McGruder, Levi, 64, 236n12
McIntire, Myra G., 114-15, 260n36
McLamore, William, 210n190
McNary, Charles, 220n28
McPherson, James Gordon, 42, 57, 220n30, 220n31, 220n32
Medford Mail Tribune, 271n25
Medley Hotel, 66, 81, 237n34, 262n69
Meier, Aaron and Abraham, 53
Meier, Julius, 53, 230n134, 258n7
Meier & Frank Co., 53, 55, 113, 171, 180, 230n133
Mercier, Wilbur, 238n54, 245n52
Meredith, Jennie, 221n38
Merrill, Fred T., 20, 208n162
Merriman, James, 20, 23, 52, 55, 126, 210n190, 220n28, 222n47, 276n23
Messenger, 99, 175, 181, 239n59
Miller, Charles, and wife, 82, 245n57
Miller, Clifford, 107
Miller, J. W., 20
Miller, Joseph, 55, 231n152
Mills Brothers, 110
Miniature Pan-African Congress, 178-81
Minnesota Spokesman-Recorder, 14, 204n106
Minor, Eugene J., 20, 85, 220n28, 270n19
Minor, John, 90
Missionary Seer, 60
Mitchell, Clifford C., 187, 288n122
  Advocate, writes about, 45-46
  book reviews by, 15
  Cannady's campaign for state representative, endorses, 186, 289n150
  columns by, 15, 186, 226n95
Mitchell, John and Pearl, 221n35
Moore, Carey F. B., 12, 203n79
Moore, Isaac L., 81
Moreland, John F., 71, 178
Morning Enterprise, 142
Morning Oregonian, 11, 19, 23, 24, 26, 33, 68, 74, 111, 113, 114, 123, 125, 126, 127, 130, 131, 140, 141, 149, 152, 157, 160, 161, 162, 186, 188
Morning Register, 141
Morrow family (immediate and extended), 198n3
  Albert, 5, 199n7
  Almus, 6, 29, 83, 199n7, 200n15, 220n28, 222n47, 246n68
  Anna (wife of John), 199n12, 286n59
  Bula Morrow Oliver, 5, 77, 199n7, 199n9, 200n14
  Carrie, 5
  Cora Morrow Jamison, 5, 64, 119, 199n7. *See also* Jamison, Cora Morrow

Edward, 5, 176, 199n7
Ella, 5
George, 5, 6, 182, 199n7
Georgie, 5
H. J. [John] J., 5, 176, 177, 199n7, 199n12, 286n59
Jack, 182, 199n9
Josephine Morrow Campbell, 199n7
Leroy, 5
Lillian, 6, 126, 200n15, 209n186, 222n47
Lucy (sister of Beatrice), 5, 199n13
Mabel Morrow Beverley, 5, 176, 199n7
Beverley, James Williams, 182, 286n60
Beverley, John, 176, 286n60
Mary Bradshaw Morrow, 199n7
Mary Francis Carter Morrow, 5, 6, 199n7
Matilda Morrow Bradley, 199n7
Pauline Morrow Washington, 199n7
Winnifred [Olive] Morrow Neal, 5, 199n7, 199n9, 257n5
Elvin Vernon Neal, 199n9, 257n5
Morrowtown, 5
motion pictures, 45, 264n13. *See also Birth of a Nation, The*
Moton, Robert R., 37, 38, 258n7
Mott, Eunice, 86
Moulton, Arthur, 26, 212n221
Mount Olivet Baptist Church, 70, 73, 110, 138, 157
Mount Tabor Presbyterian Church, 289n138
Mullineaux, Earnie [?], 260n34
Multnomah County employment statistics, 249n122
Multnomah Falls, 41, 78
Multnomah Hotel, 11, 29, 112, 192
Myers, Ferdinand and Jeanne, 250n133
Myles, Henry, and wife, 82, 245n57

Nakazawa, Ken, 169, 282n8
National Association for the Advancement of Colored People (NAACP), 3
accomplishments of, 21, 173
Advocate's promotion of, 21, 70-71, 209n175
Amos 'n' Andy, protests, 183
anniversary, 91
annual conferences
nineteenth, 26, 71, 107, 157, 250n2
seventeenth, 93, 250n2
Birth of a Nation, protests *The*, 122, 130, 131, 136
branches of, 21, 91, 211n200
campaign to capitalize "Negro," 159-60
Crisis, 7, 8, 17, 65, 68, 91, 92, 99, 100, 122, 170, 175, 180, 181, 249n126, 270n21
Elgin, Texas, Branch, 21, 176-77
founding/founders, 7, 15, 40-41, 219n19
Houston "martyrs," campaign to obtain pardons for, 132, 267n72
Littig, Texas, Branch, 21, 177
Los Angeles Branch, 94
founding/founders, 131, 211n200
and lynching, 21, 138, 269n6
members of, 253n57

need for volunteers, 22, 115
officers, 22, 23, 24, 51, 104, 122, 130, 170, 187
press releases, 135, 166, 182, 281n112
publicity department, 100, 166
Scottsboro Boys, campaign to free, 206n142
Seattle, Washington, Branch, 189, 211n200
speakers bureau, 22
Spingarn Medal, 67, 172, 237n39
Tacoma, Washington, Branch, 14, 23, 77, 211n200
Twin Cities, Minnesota, Branch, 161
Vernonia Branch, 21, 25, 164, 165, 280n92, 281n101, 281n104
See also Portland Branch (NAACP)
National Association of Colored Women, 180
National Association of Colored Women's Clubs (NACWC), 22-23, 204n98, 209n186
National Board of Censorship of Motion Pictures, 122, 124, 264n13
National Broadcasting Company, 110
National Negro Health Week, 110, 258n14
National Urban League, 17, 36
National Spiritual Assembly of the Bahá'ís, 119
near-lynchings in Oregon, 130, 131, 141-43, 155. *See also* lynchings
Negro/Negroes
achievements in music/literature/art/science, 35, 62, 181
and American Legion, 80
and banks/savings institutions, 172, 219n17
capitalization of, 3, 43, 159-160, 259n24, 279n72
and citizenship, 97, 112, 151, 155, 161
Negroes in Oregon, continued
contributions of to "progress of mankind," 11, 181
and education, 13, 28, 97
and Great Depression, 70, 87-91, 183, 185
history of, 2, 15, 16, 34, 92, 97, 107, 119, 167, 174, 186
in Oregon, 3
need to teach, 8, 11, 15, 95-96, 97, 116-17, 181
History Week, 3, 7, 8, 16, 119, 259n24
observances in Oregon, 34, 106, 111, 112, 113
identity of, 28, 68, 146, 156, 158
importance of unity, 28, 76 163
and insurance companies, 172, 219n17, 225n77, 283n29
migration, 3, 207n155
National Anthem, 65
press. *See* black press
"problem," 93, 95, 96, 97, 119, 144, 148
and rape myth, 17, 124, 156
spirituals, 72, 102, 105, 116, 178
and stereotypes, 72, 102, 116, 124, 158, 188
suffrage, male, 202n72
and travel, 43, 77
and voting, 69, 138-39
West
barriers to settling in, 18
experience in, 3
opportunities in, 18, 41, 192
white press, coverage by, 116-17, 157-60, 278n60

Negro-American Political League, 219n19
Negroes in Oregon, 1, 3, 4, 27, 130
  barriers to settling in, 3, 17-18, 146, 154, 163, 184, 207n143
  and citizenship, 151, 155, 160-61, 167, 184
  and community, 18, 207n154
  discriminated against, 26-27, 76, 80, 126, 148, 160-67, 184, 208n159, 273n41
  and education, 160-61, 163-66
  employment of, 73, 141, 154
  equality of, 167
  and Great Depression, 87, 136, 182
  identity of, 18, 146-47, 156
  and Ku Klux Klan, 146, 274n61
  and lynching, 143-45, 273n58
  near-lynchings, 130, 131, 141-43, 155
  population, 18, 39, 145, 148, 207n153, 218n8, 269n8, 273n40, 274n2, 277n43, 280n94
  representation of, 185
  state's history, role in, 3
  stereotypes of, 102
  and voting, 138-39
  white press, coverage by, 43, 62, 87, 116-17, 157-60
Negroes in Portland, 17, 169, 179, 254n80, 259n24
  and Albina neighborhood, 82, 246n59
  black newspapers, importance of, 43, 51, 57, 167-68
Negroes in Portland, continued
  businesses, 18, 20, 31, 44, 53, 54-55, 58, 77, 78, 82, 84, 85-86, 235n202, 238n54, 262n69, 276n22
    and advertising, 229n127, 230n145
    duty to support, 54, 86, 87
    and entrepreneurship, 85, 89, 231n147, 231n148
  and churches, 13, 18, 44, 55, 64. *See also* names of specific churches
  and citizens/citizenship, 21, 151, 162, 184
  and community, 18, 148, 151
  discriminated against, 11, 18-21, 27, 40, 56, 76, 80, 81, 115, 148, 161-63, 167, 192, 222n47, 276n22, 280n89
  duty to boost city, 46, 76, 82, 83, 84, 86
  efforts to settle in, 18
  employment
    of men, 25, 85-86, 148, 162, 182, 247n91, 250n131, 277n39
    of women, 53, 85-86, 88, 148, 185, 250n131, 250n133, 250n134
  and entertaining, 77-78, 109-10
  and Great Depression, 38, 48, 49, 50, 85-86, 88-90, 90-91, 184
  and homeownership, 17, 82-84, 152-54, 246n75
  hosting visitors, importance of, 66, 77, 80
  and hotels, 44, 54, 61, 66, 81, 85-86
  identity of, 43, 156
  isolation of, 39-40, 148
  and Ku Klux Klan, 140, 146
  population, 11, 18, 39, 76, 148, 189, 191, 202n71, 218n9, 290n4
  real estate restrictions on, 18, 82, 149, 151, 152, 167, 184, 192, 245n58, 246n75, 276n29, 277n42
  stereotypes of, 102
  students, 11, 13, 61, 181

unity, importance of, 76, 187
and Westmoreland neighborhood, 152
white press, coverage by, 45, 62, 87, 149-150, 157-60
and Williams Avenue, 55, 81, 82, 88, 149, 151
and voting rights, 11
and YWCA, 44, 73, 81, 149-51, 275n10, 282n8
Nerney, Mary Childs, 122, 123, 124
New Age, 18
New Golden West Hotel, 85-87, 248n98
New Oregon Hotel, 11
New Republic, 123
New York Age, 7, 39
New York Amsterdam News, 2, 11, 44, 102, 107, 174, 175
New York City, 15, 41, 47, 66, 67, 106, 109, 158, 169, 174-75, 284n44, 285n55
New York Public Library, Division of Negro Literature, History and Prints, 174
New York Times, 38, 65, 109, 113, 138, 172
New York World, 140, 270n22, 270n23
Newberg, Oregon, 74, 115, 116, 146, 260n43
Newberg Graphic, 279n67
Newman, Cecil E., 14, 83, 93, 234n199
Niagara Movement, 40
Noble, George Bernard, 101
Norblad, Albin W., 45, 223n55
North Pacific Dental College, 152
Northwestern College of Law, 6, 29, 212n241
Notable Women in the History of Oregon, 36

Oberlin College, 235n202
O'Hara, J. P., 178
Oklahoma, 7, 43, 81
Olcott, Ben W., 1, 3, 130, 140-41, 142, 270n23
Olds, Wortman & King, 88, 176
O'Neill, Eugene, 16
Opportunity, 65, 99, 181
Oregon
attorney general, 157
Bill No. 228, 192
Bill No. 344, 192
Bill of Rights, 17
"Black laws"/exclusionary laws, 17-18, 167, 207n149, 207n156
Board of Higher Education, 161
Constitution, 17-18, 207n143
elections, 17, 18, 21, 207n143, 238n58
employment statistics, 249n122
governors of, 1, 3, 11, 36, 45, 53, 73, 93, 125-26, 140-41, 142, 143-45, 157, 161, 192
history, 3, 17, 155
lynching in, 273n58
Measure 14, 18
mulattos in, 18
Native Americans in, 19-20, 155, 277n43
pioneers, 3, 17
population, 218n8, 277n43
of Negroes, 18, 39, 142, 207n153, 218n8, 277n43

Public Accommodations Act, 192
secretary of state, 72
slavery/involuntary servitude, 17, 207n143
statehood, 9
suffrage, 11
Oregon Agricultural College, 242n7, 279n77
Oregon City, Oregon, 18, 131, 142-43, 272n37, 273n37
Oregon Conservatory of Music, 263n73
Oregon Daily Journal, 14, 24, 30, 33, 62, 87, 93, 97, 98, 105, 111, 112, 114, 123, 125, 134, 152, 153, 158, 179, 192
Oregon Federation of Colored Women's Clubs, 80
Oregon Health & Science University, 152
Oregon Industrial Welfare Commission, 102, 165
Oregon Labor Press, 289n139
Oregon Prison Association, 37
Oregon State Bar, 30
Oregon State Library, 65
Oregon Sunday Journal, 93
Oregon Supreme Court, 19, 44-45
Oregon Territory, 17
Oregon Trail, 18
Oregon Voter, 146, 188, 232n153
Oregon-American Lumber Company, 163-66, 281n100, 281n115
Oregon-Washington Railroad and Navigation Company, 88
Oregon Weekly Times, 17
Oregon Woman Suffrage Proclamation, 11
Oriental Theatre, 19, 208n159
Outlook, 211n202, 271n28
Overton, Anthony, 172, 283n29
Overton Hygienic Manufacturing Company, 172, 183, 284n32
Ovington, Mary White, 24-25, 37, 91, 150, 151, 211n200
and NAACP, 40, 93

Pacific Coast News Bureau, 260n31
Pacific College, 37, 71, 103, 119
Pacific Telephone and Telegraph Company, 43
Pacific University, 35
Pan-African Congress, 119, 169
Fifth, 174, 285n52
Fourth, 65, 169, 170, 174, 178
Pantages Theatre, 161-63
parents' responsibilities, 16
Paris, Texas, 147
Park, Alice, 16, 104, 206n135, 255n91
Parker, Daniel, 46, 77, 78, 224n73
"passing" as white, 52-53
patriarchy, 26, 150
Patterson, Isaac L., 73, 93, 161, 174, 279n80
Patterson, Paul L., 192
Payne, Ethel, 34
Payne, John, 64
Peek, Anna, 46, 224n73
Pendleton, James N., 179
Pennington, Levi T., 37, 119

Perry, Bob, 12, 203n79
Peterson, Gertrude Hoeber, 289n135
Pettis, Timothy, 143-45, 157, 273n42, 273n50
Philadelphia Tribune, 60, 114
Pickens, Minnie, 170, 175
Pickens, William, 22, 24, 70-71, 93, 101, 105, 120, 151, 170, 174, 175, 239n66, 272n36
Pickett, Sherman, 46, 88, 223n67
Pierce, Walter M., 36, 143-45, 157, 270n24, 273n37
Pillsbury, Eva, 45
Pittsburgh Courier, 59, 133, 183
Plessy v. Ferguson, 7
Portland, Oregon
    banks, 9, 81
    businesses, white-owned, 53-56, 223n63, 226n98, 229n128
    Chamber of Commerce, 33, 153
    Chinatown, 77, 248n98
    City Auditorium, 69
    city charter, 20
    City Council, 20, 129-30, 133-34, 136, 149, 266n55
    Civic Auditorium, 67
    elections, 188-89, 213n245, 289n144
    employment statistics, 247n91, 250n134
    interracial relations in, 20, 107, 134, 179-80, 182
    and Jim Crow, 17-20, 26, 29, 80, 89, 161-63, 182, 208n159, 222n47, 280n89
    judges, 26
    Keller Auditorium, 74
    Masonic Temple and Auditorium, 62
    mayors of, 20, 21, 37, 62, 123, 126, 129, 135, 140
    Multnomah Civic Stadium, 74
    Municipal Auditorium, 36
    offensive signs in, 19-20, 80
    office buildings in, 38, 50, 84, 152
    PGE Park, 74
    population of, 202n71, 290n4
        of whites, 39, 191
    progress of, 76, 85
    radio stations, 67, 74, 103, 110, 111, 112, 113, 114, 183, 237n35, 258n7, 258n9, 258n10, 259n18, 259n22
    restaurants, 19-20, 39, 89, 182, 208n169, 208n172
    Rose Festival, 33
    Union Depot, 11, 39, 66, 67, 81, 82, 93
    utilities, 37, 43, 45, 85
Portland Bahá'í Assembly, 35, 103, 113, 118-19, 261n58
Portland Bees, 84
Portland Board of Education, 26, 29, 105, 113, 170, 181
Portland Branch (NAACP)
    and *Advocate*, 21, 209n175
    Bagnall, Robert, criticizes, 22
    Birth of a Nation, protests *The*, 123-26, 134, 267n83
    Cannady, Beatrice, criticizes, 22-26, 27, 186-87, 239n67
    and civil rights bill, 185
    committees of, 20-21, 123, 140, 153, 186-87, 270n19
    and discrimination/segregation, 20-21, 182
    Dyer, talk by Leonidas C., 138, 211n212

and employment issues, 88
founders/founding, 20, 23, 24, 41, 84, 208n170, 211n200
Johnson, James Weldon, criticizes, 24
Marshfield murder investigation, intervenes in, 143-45
meetings of, 22-25, 151, 275n18
officers of, 20, 22, 23, 25, 27, 88, 126, 135, 153, 187, 248n109
petitions, 21, 126, 140
NAACP officers, correspondence with, 22-23, 135, 143, 145
Portland Hotel labor dispute, intervenes in, 227n108
press releases of, 135
Pickens, talks by William, 70, 71, 239n66
Southern Oregon Spokesman, protests comments in, 157
Sweet, Ossian, defense, assists with, 284n39
Unthanks' home, intervenes in attacks on, 153
white members, 22, 24, 26, 102, 235n202
Portland Council of Churches, 37, 136
Portland General Electric Co., 45, 223n55
Portland Hotel, 10, 11, 15, 42, 44, 50, 53, 54, 61, 81, 83, 84, 106, 227n108
Portland Labor College, 93
Portland Metaphysical Library, 103
Portland News, 34, 48
Portland Negro Chorus, 74
Portland Railway, Light & Power Co., 85, 223n55
Portland Realty Board, 192
Portland Telegram, 23, 48, 62, 111, 116, 144, 159, 179, 180, 225n84, 226n88
Portland Times, 23, 52, 55, 210n190
Powell, Luther, 141
Powers, Ira, Sr., 55, 56
Powers Furniture Company, 55-56
Preston, Loneia, 283n25
Preston, Marie, 172, 283n25
Prohibition, 69, 284n39
propaganda, 257n117
public schools, 15, 97, 114, 163-66, 174, 180
Pugh, Juneious, 20, 208n169, 257n4
Pulitzer Prize, 16, 42
Pullman Car porters/conductors, 19, 39, 70, 85, 175, 239n62, 247n90, 273n41

race antipathy/prejudice, 11, 17, 40, 41, 50, 95, 97, 107, 112, 120, 133, 159, 167, 184, 192
race, duty, 21, 47, 76
race riots, 138, 151
racial
epithets, 158-59, 160, 279n67
segregation/discrimination, 13, 17, 20, 50, 56, 61, 82-83, 89, 150, 151, 160
pride, 8, 15, 26, 43, 53, 75, 79, 84, 102, 116-17, 159-60, 181
unity, 76, 163
uplift, 16, 21, 23, 26, 27, 28, 29, 43, 50, 52, 61, 76, 79, 83, 112, 242n4
radio, and color barriers, 109, 110, 258n8, 258n9
Rainier Review, 164
Rand, John M., 45
Randol, George, 67
Randolph, A. Philip, 3, 6, 70, 120, 239n61
Randolph, Benjamin and Clarice, 250n132
Randolph, Louise, 90, 250n132

Ransom-Kehler, Keith, 215n291
Reconstruction, 95, 115, 121, 129, 130
Redd, Charlie, 54, 78
Reed, James H., 58, 233n173
Reed, Marie, 233n173
Reed, Pollyann, 43
Reed College, 11, 64, 70, 71, 73, 100-101, 103, 105, 106, 116, 169, 178, 180, 209n187, 229n128, 254n68
Reflexus, 60
Reid, Kits, 226n95
residential segregation, 151, 153, 160-61, 164, 167. *See also* Negroes in Portland, real estate restrictions on
Reynolds, Elise, 39, 47, 103, 106, 119, 144, 169-70, 217n2, 263n73
Reynolds, Phil, 39, 47, 179, 217n2
Rice, Charles A., 113-14, 178, 260n27
Richardson, Eurastus, 54, 230n144
Richardson, Marilyn, 2
Ringler's Cotillion Hall, 81
Rivoli Theatre, 72, 162
Roberts, Emma, 211n209
Roberts Brothers, 229n128
Robeson, Paul, 14, 110, 204n108, 256n108, 258n9
Robinson, Bill, 67
Robinson, Bob, 249n110
Robinson, Paul, 163-64, 166, 280n95
Robinson, R. T., and wife, 82
Roland Hayes Quartet, 106
Rominger, H. V., 276n34
Roosevelt, Franklin D., 69, 238n58
Roosevelt, Theodore, 11
Root, Martha, 103-104, 106, 118, 119, 255n86, 255n87
Rose City Park Methodist Episcopal Church, 98
Roseburg, Oregon, 148, 274n2
Roseburg News-Review, 139, 141-42, 148
Rosenwald, Julius, 176, 286n62
Rosenwald School, Elgin, Texas, 176
Rosenwald Foundation, 68
Ruhl, Robert W., 271n25
Russwurm, John, 158, 228n122
Rutherford, Allan, 256n110
Rutherford, Edward, 12, 192, 235n202
Rutherford, Octavia, 61
Rutherford, Otto, 154, 194, 213n249, 222n47, 250n133
- *Advocate*, opinion of, 61
- and community, 148
- and discrimination in Portland, 19-20, 77, 280n89
- and economic boycotts, 148
- and homeownership, 83
- Jefferson High School, graduates from, 235n202
- and Ku Klux Klan, 146
- NAACP, involvement in, 19
- and Oregon Public Accommodations Act, 192
- reform, views on, 39-40

Rutherford, Verdell Burdine, 192, 194, 277n41

Rutherford, William, 235n202
Ryan, Ella (Washington), 14, 204n99, 204n100
Ryan, Ella (Texas) and Jack, 47, 176, 225n77
Ryan, John H., 14, 189, 204n99, 204n100, 204n102, 204n103
Ryan Hotel, 10
Rynerson, C. M., 289n139

S. H. Kress & Co., 90
Safeway Stores, Inc., 91
St. Helens Mist, 164, 166
St. Johns Community Church, 115
St. Paul Methodist Church, 5, 117
St. Pierre Ruffin, Josephine, 28
Salem, Oregon, 36, 54, 72-73, 192
Sam Houston State Teachers College, 5
Sampson, George, 89
San Francisco Spokesman, 57, 107, 186
Sanders, George, 89, 249n119
Sarnoff, David, 109
Sawyer, Reuben H., 142, 272n31
School Acres, 15, 205n125
Schwarztrauber, Ernest E., 96, 97, 252n27, 252n29
Schweich, Ida, 83, 246n70
Scott, Emmett J., 200n36
    Scott's Official History of the American Negro in the World War, 16
Scottsboro Boys, 17, 68, 73-74, 183, 206n142, 284n39
Seattle, Washington, 14, 58, 64, 66, 77, 88, 106, 171
Seattle Republican, 189
segregation. *See* Jim Crow; racial segregation
Seligmann, Herbert J., 253n63
Sell, Harry B., 105
Shaw, Freita, 72, 241n83
Shell Oil Company, 54
Shemansky, Joseph, 53, 229n132
Sherman & Clay Co., 283n16
Shiloh Baptist Church, 115
Shull, Frank L., 114, 260n28
Silver, Ann, 100
Simms, J. W., 88
skin-whitening products, 52
slavery, 1, 17, 24, 42, 116, 121, 155
Small's Paradise, 175, 285n55
Smith, Al, 251n12
Smith, Bessie, 258n9
Smith, Harry C., 60, 125, 234n194, 234n198
Smith, Marie, 192, 231n148, 245n58
Smith, Roy D., 269n10
Southern/Southerner, 165, 166, 192
Southern Oregon Spokesman, 154-57
Southwest Review, 114
Spanish-American War, 31, 162
spheres, domestic/private and public, 26, 117
Spreckels, Adolph B., Jr., 79, 244n37
Sproull, Howard, 12, 203n79

Stanfield, Robert M., 62, 220n28
Stanton, Mamie, 262n72
Star Theatre, 19, 280n89
State v. John Scopes, 173, 284n39
Stephens, J. F., and wife, 231n146
Stewart, J. L., 45
Stewart, Lewis B., 16, 27, 190, 206n132
Stewart, Maria W., 2
Stewart, McCants, 10, 12, 18-19, 29, 192, 202n65, 208n157, 213n254, 280n89
Stewart, Pearl, 89
stock market crash, 84, 182
Stowe, Harriet Beecher, 14
suffrage, woman, 11, 16, 104, 113, 192
Sullivan, John L., 6
Summers family, 275n12
Sunday Oregonian, 98, 128, 129
Sunset Theatre, 129
Sweet, Gladys, 173
Sweet, Iva, 173, 284n38
Sweet, Ossian, 173, 284n37, 284n39
swimming, 26, 72

Tacoma Times, 160
Taft, William Howard, 11
Talbert, Mary B., 17, 23, 173, 209n187
Taylor, Julius F., 234n198
Taylor, Oliver, 19
Taylor, Reuben, 1, 193, 197n1
Taylor, William (Mr. and Mrs.), 78, 243n18
telephone, 7, 43, 51, 221n43
Terrill, Charles E., 271n29
Terwilliger Boulevard, 78, 244n24
Texas Freeman, 7
Thomas, Louise and Oliver S., 270n19
Thompson, Mrs. Alex, 192, 290n8
Thurston, Blanche, 100-101, 169, 254n67
Tillotson College, 5, 199n13
Time, 14, 65, 73
Timely Digest, 14
Tipton v. State, 213n247
Tokyo, Japan, 106, 256n106
Tolson, Melvin B., 240n76
Tom-Tom, 73
Topeka Plaindealer, 132
Triangle Film Co., 133
Trimble, Herman, 30
Triplett, Lucille, 275n12
Trotter, William Monroe, 34, 151, 177, 219n19
Trumbull, Millie, 102, 104, 105, 108, 164, 166-67, 169, 179, 193
Tucker, Alonzo, 273n58
Turner, Frances, 238n54
Turner, Wallace, 35
Tuskegee Institute, 7, 37, 98, 110, 258n7, 258n14
24th Infantry, 132

25th Infantry, 245n57
Twin City Herald, 14, 93

Uncle Tom's Cabin, 14
United States Constitution, Amendments to
  Eighteenth, 69
  Fifteenth, 202n72, 238n49
United States Constitution, Amendments to
  Fourteenth, 69, 97, 149, 238n49
  Thirteenth, 149
United States House of Representatives, 21, 138
United States Penitentiary at Leavenworth, 132
United States Senate, 138
United States Supreme Court, 7, 270n24, 284n34
Unity Presbyterian Church, 114, 117, 178, 260n37
University of Arizona, 147
University of Chicago, 10, 99, 172
University of Minnesota, 161
University of Oregon, 15, 71, 88, 106, 120, 160, 249n110, 279n75, 279n83
Unthank, DeNorval, 14, 67, 81, 194, 226n103, 238n54, 276n24, 277n41
  Advocate, writes for the, 48, 226n95, 259n16
  awards, 277n42
  Birth of a Nation, protests *The*, 134
  and City Club, 277n42
  Great Depression, views on, 87-88
  Green Pastures, entertains cast of *The*, 109
  home vandalized, 49-50, 152-54, 182
  medical practice of, 152, 276n25, 276n26
  NAACP Portland Branch's grievance against Cannady, intervenes in, 187
  park named in honor of, 277n42
  radio broadcasts by, 111, 258n16, 259n22
Unthank, Thelma, 67, 81
  altercation with neighbor, 277n38
  Green Pastures, entertains cast of *The*, 109
  home vandalized, 49-50, 152-54, 182
Unthank, Thomas, 276n24

Vail, Albert R., 105, 262n68
Valhalla Cemetery, 35
Van Winkle, Isaac H., 157
Vann, Robert L., 59, 183
veil, living behind, 103, 112, 180, 184
Vernonia, Oregon, 163-66, 280n94, 281n100, 281n103, 281n115
Vernonia Eagle, 163, 166, 225n84
Vessel, Isaac, 220n35
Vessell, Harry, 247n86
Vessell, Isa, 85, 247n86
Victory Life Insurance Co., 172, 283n29
Villard, Henry, 15
Villard, Oswald Garrison, 14, 15, 41
visitors, duty to host, 66, 80

Waco Messenger, 79
Waldron, J. Milton, 40-41, 47, 218n17, 219n19

Waldron, Martha, 40-41, 47
Walker, C. J., 83, 175, 285n56
Walker, Laura, 150
Walker, Isaac, 150, 275n12
Ward, Edward, 12, 203n79
Ward, William R., 147
Wardell, Mildreda, 236n12
Washington, 14, 31, 70, 114, 171
  and *The Birth of a Nation*, 210n188
  and interracial marriage, 14
  legislature, 14, 189
  Negroes in, 18, 88, 249n117
Washington, Atria [?], 274n1
Washington, Booker T., 7, 16, 24, 110, 115, 176
  Up From Slavery, 16, 211n202
Washington, J. A. G., 148, 274n1
Washington High School, 98
Washington State Federation of Colored Women's Clubs, 23, 36, 104, 180
Watchtower Mutual Life Insurance Company, 225n77
Waverly Heights Congregational Church, 105
Webb, Warner, 15, 205n123
Weeks, George, 243n21
Weeks, Lizzie, 78, 243n21
Wells-Barnett (also Wells), Ida, 7, 12, 40, 249n123, 288n111
West, Oswald, 11
Western Outlook, 59, 60, 234n197
Wheaton, W. J., 57, 107, 183-84, 185-86, 190, 226n95, 232n165, 288n123
White, Walter F., 51, 130-31, 145, 169
white supremacy, 146, 154, 155, 157, 278n53. *See also* Ku Klux Klan
white women
  journalists, 2, 6
  recovering histories of, 2, 107
  suffrage of, 11, 104, 192
  unpaid labor of, 107
  womanhood, 139, 157
  Who's Who of the Colored Race, 10
Wiley University/College, 8-9, 16, 23, 28, 94, 194, 200n34, 200n36, 225n77, 240n76
Wilhelm, Roy C., 103, 118, 262n61, 262n65
  In His Presence: Visits To 'Abdú'l-Bahá, 262n65
Wilkins, Roy, 187
Willamette River, 11, 78, 82
Willamette University, 32, 34, 35, 36, 70, 99-100, 113, 253n57, 253n64
William E. Harmon Award for Distinguished Achievement Among Negroes in the field of race relations, 37-38. *See also* Cannady, Beatrice, Harmon Award, nominated for
William Lloyd Garrison on Non-Resistance, 14, 205n113
Williams, Bernice, 240n78
Williams, Chuck, 88, 249n110
Williams, Edgar, 153, 192, 277n39
Williams, George, 89
Williams, James, 20
Williams, James H., 43
Williams, Octavia, 277n39
Williams, Wyatt, 126, 238n54, 270n19
Willis, Frank, 125

Willis, William H., 47, 225n78
Wilson, Alice, 88
Wilson, Clarence True, 284n39
Wilson, J. D., 238n54
Wilson, J. H., 79-80, 245n39
Wilson, James, 44
Wilson, Mary, 78, 244n28
Wilson, August, 244n28
Wilson, William, 272n37
Wilson, Woodrow, 11, 23, 136, 265n22
Wisdom, Cinderella, 78, 243n21
Wisdom, Joseph, 243n21
Withycombe, James, 125-26
Wolf, A. Walter, 127
Woman's Christian Temperance Union, 45, 170, 289n132
Woman's Legislative Council of Washington, 180
women, black. *See* black women
women, white. *See* white women
Women's International League for Peace and Freedom, 104
Woodson, Carter G., 7, 8, 15, 181, 202n76, 205n117, 259n24
Woodstock Methodist Episcopal Church, Cannady talks at, 116
World Conference on Education, 105
world unity dinners, 261n58
World War I, 16, 23, 104, 109, 118

Yancy, Rebecca, 214n266
Yeager, Clarence, 45
Young, Nettie, 225n79
Young, Payton D., 47, 225n79
Young Women's Christian Association (YWCA), 44, 73, 81, 149-51, 275n10, 282n8
youth and race prejudice, 33, 115, 124. *See also* contact between races